INSTITUTIONALIZING STATE RESPONSIBILITY

OXFORD MONOGRAPHS IN INTERNATIONAL LAW

Institutionalizing State Responsibility

Global Security and UN Organs

VINCENT-JOËL PROULX

OXFORD
UNIVERSITY PRESS

OXFORD
UNIVERSITY PRESS

Great Clarendon Street, Oxford, OX2 6DP,
United Kingdom

Oxford University Press is a department of the University of Oxford.
It furthers the University's objective of excellence in research, scholarship,
and education by publishing worldwide. Oxford is a registered trade mark of
Oxford University Press in the UK and in certain other countries

First Edition published in 2016

Published in the United States of America by Oxford University Press
198 Madison Avenue, New York, NY 10016, United States of America

British Library Cataloguing in Publication Data
Data available

Library of Congress Control Number: 2015959805

ISBN 978–0–19–968039–9

A Elsa, ma tendre moitié

Foreword

Institutionalizing State Responsibility: Global Security and UN Organs is the second book to be authored by Dr Vincent-Joël Proulx. In itself, this is an exceptional achievement for such a young scholar and is testament to the commitment and enthusiasm which he brings to his work.

The author's first book, *Transnational Terrorism and State Accountability: A New Theory of Prevention*, was published in 2012 and this new work provides a welcome follow up to it. Where Dr Proulx's earlier book focused on the question of how State responsibility should be conceptualized in respect of transnational terrorism, this new volume addresses how international legal obligations relating to terrorism can be enforced, with sustained focus on what role exists for multilateral institutions in that process.

In particular, the author argues that the United Nations Security Council has a part to play in implementing State responsibility for the violation of international counter-terrorism obligations. Dr Proulx makes the case that the Security Council may be in a position to respond better, under international law, to violations of norms such as those relating to terrorism than States acting individually, actions which may amount to what he describes as 'unchecked unilateralism'. The author accepts that the Security Council may face its own problems in exercising its functions. However, he makes a convincing case that the Council has powers that are apposite to the context of terrorism. While he also notes the possibility of the International Court of Justice and the General Assembly playing a role in relation to implementing obligations relating to terrorism, he observes a number of limitations on what can be expected of these bodies in this field. Nonetheless, this book contains some thought-provoking discussion on the relationship between the three main United Nations organs, and particularly on whether the International Court of Justice can engage in judicial oversight of the Security Council's actions.

Dr Proulx undertakes an extensive review of the practice of the Security Council and highlights that not only has the Council laid down primary norms obliging States to take action with respect to terrorism, but that it has also often engaged in a form of implementation of responsibility for breach of international obligations. The author includes an interesting comparison between the secondary rules of State responsibility as set out in the *Articles on State Responsibility* and what the Council has done in response to various situations. He demonstrates that the Council is a body that at least sometimes takes action that pursues the same function as that of the law of State responsibility. In addition, Proulx makes a creative but compelling argument that there is a functional analogy to be drawn vis-à-vis countermeasures under the law of State responsibility and sanctions employed by the Security Council, arguing that the latter may be viewed as a form of centralized or collective countermeasures. Finally, Dr Proulx addresses the sensitive and topical issue of the use of force in response to terrorism, explaining the link between that question and the law of State responsibility.

Institutionalizing State Responsibility: Global Security and UN Organs helps us to understand how the political and legal aspects of addressing the threats posed by terrorism to the international community can be complementary. Although the author accepts that there may only be certain circumstances in which the Security Council does and should act in a manner that implements State responsibility, he makes a persuasive case for the use of its powers in such a way in appropriate scenarios. Moreover, while the author's focus is on terrorism, he makes it clear throughout the work that his proposals are not limited to it but may also be extended to other international issues. In demonstrating how the Security Council can exercise its powers to implement State responsibility, Proulx's proposals will do much to advance not only the capacity of the Security Council to act in response to global threats, but also international legality as a whole, an outcome that can only be welcomed. One can only hope that the Council Members, in exercising its functions, will always act as an unbiased jury.

This original book, full of interesting ideas and perspectives, is progressive and challenging and is a timely and important addition to the literature. It is sure to appeal to international lawyers, decision-makers, and anyone with an interest in how issues in global security should be addressed on the international plane.

Peter Tomka
Judge and former President of the International Court of Justice
The Hague, December 2015

Series Editors' Preface

Ever since 9/11, international lawyers have debated the question of whether States that are the victims of a private terrorist attack emanating from the territory of another State can use force, either alone or through a coalition, against that State because it harboured or supported the terrorist organization. The question is usually seen in a one dimensional way as one of the use of force in international law. In this innovative study, Dr Proulx looks at the question through the lens of the law on State responsibility. In doing so he examines to what extent the law of State responsibility can justify and/or inform both the Security Council's exercise of its Chapter VII powers and States' invocation of self-defence and other forcible responses to terrorist attacks. He thereby attempts to bridge the gap between what are usually seen as two distinct or self-contained legal regimes: the use of force and State responsibility.

Using international terrorism as his principal case study, Dr Proulx argues more generally for the institutionalization of the implementation of State responsibility in response to global security threats such as terrorism, cyber-terrorism, global warming and ungoverned spaces and territories. UN organs and, in particular, the Security Council can and should play a greater role in implementing international responsibility for States' failure to prevent global security threats. Institutionalizing the implementation of State responsibility is seen as an alternative to unchecked unilateral responses to global security threats, particularly forcible countermeasures.

The merger or conflation of different legal regimes is a matter of considerable complexity and difficulty. Dr Proulx's inventive study exploring the role of State responsibility in informing the use of force is an important contribution to our understanding of regime interaction in international law and a welcome addition to the *Oxford Monographs in International Law* series.

CR, DS, ST

Oxford and Bonn, December 2015

Preface

The role of State responsibility (SR), both as a central institution in international law and as a possible institutionalized implementation tool for legal obligations, is largely underexplored when addressing global security threats. International law and policy experts have engaged in an enriching horizontal dialogue and have propelled to the forefront of academic inquiry the need for further study of the relationship between use of force standards and transnational terrorism. Despite this progress, few advances have been made in extending this discourse to the politically sensitive sphere of SR. From the perspective of counterterrorism, the relationship between recourse to force and SR remains nebulous. This monograph attempts to fill that literary dearth.

More importantly, the connection between United Nations Security Council practice and the creation, interpretation, and application of SR rules remains largely underexplored in global security contexts, especially in the field of counterterrorism. This deficiency must be remedied as such research could advance the intellectual discourse and lead to the formulation of potential deterrence models, especially given the Council's role in maintaining global security. Indeed, starting from the premise that SR can play an important role in the suppression and prevention of certain global security breaches, the question of enforcement remains elusive. It is no secret that responsibility flowing from an internationally wrongful act is typically actuated, and ultimately implemented, through inter-State mechanisms. Aside from self-help remedies and unilateral countermeasures, the question of whether SR for failing to prevent terrorist attacks and other global security violations could be implemented through existing UN organs warrants serious consideration. The present book attempts to address this vital query, whilst tackling other related legal and political questions. All views, errors, and omissions are my own.

Acknowledgements

It would be impossible to acknowledge everyone who provided encouragement, whether direct or indirect, towards the completion of this book. I will nonetheless single out a few individuals whose help and reinforcement have proven indispensable. First of all, I extend my warm gratitude to René Provost for reading previous drafts of some of this book's chapters. He provided feedback of the highest quality, always challenging me to rethink my own conventional wisdom. I am similarly grateful to HE Judge Bruno Simma for providing trenchant but insightful comments on previous iterations of Chapters 3 and 4, and to Simon Chesterman for commenting on my work in this area and for his continued support.

I am profoundly indebted to HE Judge Peter Tomka for contributing the Foreword to this monograph and for his unwavering mentorship over the years. I am honoured to see his name associated with this work and to have the former President of the UN's principal judicial organ setting the tone for the present volume. I feel extremely fortunate to have served in his Chambers, first as his Legal Officer when he was the International Court of Justice's Vice-President, and then as his Special Assistant during his presidency. I am also very grateful for the continuous support and kindness of the other International Court of Justice Members, past and present, especially Judges Sepúlveda-Amor, Keith, Bennouna, Cançado Trindade, Greenwood, Xue, Donoghue, Gaja, and Crawford. The library staff at the Court, especially Corinne Fumé, were all very helpful in accommodating my many requests. I have also been blessed with the benefit of being mentored by a number of inspirational role models over the years, including the Honourable Robert J Sharpe, Stephen Toope, Jaye Ellis, and Frédéric Mégret. I am very fortunate to have joined a vibrant intellectual community at the National University of Singapore's Faculty of Law, and am thankful to have such wonderful colleagues. I wish to acknowledge a few individuals who have made the transition to Singapore particularly pleasant: Robert Beckman, Gary Bell, Juliana Cardinale, Damian Chalmers, Weitseng Chen, Elaine Chew, Sheila Hayre, Arif Jamal, Lin Lin, Mark McBride, James Penner, Nicole Roughan, Andrew Simester, Alan Tan, David Tan, Hsien-Li Tan, and J Christopher Thomas QC. I am very grateful for the research support received through the Singapore Ministry of Education Academic Research Fund Tier 1.

I have no doubt that my thinking on this subject was greatly enhanced during my tenure as Quebec Scholar at the Woodrow Wilson International Center for Scholars. I owe particular thanks to the Canada Institute and the Division of International Security Studies for providing a welcoming intellectual home, and to the staff of the Wilson Center library. I benefited from presenting some of the ideas contained in this book at various conferences and public lectures over the years, including at the University of Amsterdam, Leiden University, the

Asian Society of International Law's 5th Biennial Conference, Fudan University Law School/Deakin Law School, Keele University, McGill University, and the University of Toronto. I also owe a debt of gratitude to Jessica Howley for helpful comments on the manuscript.

It is impossible to acknowledge all my friends for their unwavering support. I am particularly grateful to the following people for challenging me on some of this monograph's premises or for their support: Aaron Dhir, Florence Zaoui, Gérardine Goh, Dominika Švarc, Mario Prost, Jean d'Aspremont, Maurizio Ragazzi, Miriam Cohen, Bart Szewczyk, Patrick Delaney, and Daniel Sheppard. I also extend warm thanks to the OUP team, particularly Nicole Leyland, Emma Endean, Merel Alstein, Anthony Hinton, and John Louth, for their professionalism, kindness, and patience. I express my gratitude to the anonymous reviewers for their helpful comments on the book proposal. I am deeply indebted to my parents, Denise and Pascal, for their unflinching love, support, and tremendous generosity.

Last but not least, I am infinitely grateful to Elsa, my partner in crime, for her love, support, and patience. I thank her sincerely for reminding me of what is important. This work is dedicated to her.

VJP
Singapore
January 2016

Contents

PART II IMPLEMENTING STATE RESPONSIBILITY AFTER 9/11: INSTITUTIONAL PERSPECTIVES

Table of Cases

INTERNATIONAL COURTS AND TRIBUNALS

International Criminal Tribunal for the former Yugoslavia (ICTY)

International Tribunal for the Law of the Sea (ITLOS)

Permanent Court of International Justice (PCIJ)

Special Tribunal for Lebanon

World Trade Organization Dispute Settlement Body (WTO)

NATIONAL COURTS

Canada

USA

Table of Legislation

INTERNATIONAL TREATIES & CONVENTIONS

RESOLUTIONS AND DECISIONS

United Nations General Assembly (UNGA) Resolutions

UNITED NATIONS INTERNATIONAL LAW COMMISSION

Documents and Reports

Special Rapporteurs

Abbreviations

ADF	Allied Democratic Forces
AFDI	Annuaire Français de Droit International
AJIL	American Journal of International Law
AQIM	Al-Qaeda in the Islamic Maghreb
ARSIWA	Articles on Responsibility of States for Internationally Wrongful Acts
ASEAN	Association of Southeast Asian Nations
ASIL	American Society of International Law
BJIL	Berkeley Journal of International Law
BYIL	British Yearbook of International Law
CILJ	Cornell International Law Journal
CJIL	Chicago Journal of International Law
CJTL	Columbia Journal of Transnational Law
CTC	Counter-Terrorism Committee
CTITF	Counter-Terrorism Implementation Task Force
CUP	Cambridge University Press
CWRJIL	Case Western Reserve Journal of International Law
DDOS	Distributed denial of service
DRC	Democratic Republic of Congo
EC	European Commission
ECJ	European Court of Justice
ECtHR	European Court of Human Rights
EJIL	European Journal of International Law
ETA	Euskadi Ta Askatasuna
EU	European Union
FA	Foreign Affairs
FARC	Revolutionary Armed Forces of Colombia
FFWA	Fletcher Forum of World Affairs
FILJ	Fordham International Law Journal
FYIL	Finnish Yearbook of International Law
GA	General Assembly
GJIL	Georgetown Journal of International Law
GRP	Global Responsibility to Protect
GWILR	George Washington International Law Review
GYIL	German Yearbook of International Law
HILJ	Harvard International Law Journal
HJIL	Houston Journal of International Law
HUP	Harvard University Press
IACHR	Inter-American Court of Human Rights
ICISS	International Commission on Intervention and State Sovereignty
ICJ	International Court of Justice
ICLQ	International & Comparative Law Quarterly
ICTY	International Criminal Tribunal for the former Yugoslavia
IHL	International Humanitarian Law

ILC	International Law Commission
ILM	International Legal Materials
IO(s)	International Organization(s)
IOLR	International Organizations Law Review
ISIL	Islamic State of Iraq and the Levant
ITLOS	International Tribunal for the Law of the Sea
IYHR	Israel Yearbook of Human Rights
JCSL	Journal of Conflict and Security Law
JICJ	Journal of International Criminal Justice
JILIR	Journal of International Law and International Relations
JUFIL	Journal on the Use of Force and International Law
LGDJ	Librairie Générale de Droit et de Jurisprudence
LJIL	Leiden Journal of International Law
MJIL	Michigan Journal of International Law
MUJAO	Movement for Unity and Jihad in West Africa
NATO	North Atlantic Treaty Organization
NILR	Netherlands International Law Review
NJIL	Nordic Journal of International Law
NYIL	Netherlands Yearbook of International Law
NYT	New York Times
NYUJILP	New York University Journal of International Law & Politics
OAS	Organization of American States
OSCE	Organization for Security and Co-operation in Europe
OUP	Oxford University Press
PUF	Presses Universitaires de France
PYIL	Polish Yearbook of International Law
R2P	Responsibility to Protect
RBDI	Revue Belge de Droit International
RdC	Recueil des Cours de l'Académie de Droit International de La Haye
RGDIP	Revue Générale de Droit International Public
SC	Security Council
SCT	Studies in Conflict and Terrorism
SFDI	Société Française pour le Droit International
SJIL	Stanford Journal of International Law
STL	Special Tribunal for Lebanon
TWAIL	Third World Approaches to International Law
UK	United Kingdom
UN	United Nations
UNCC	United Nations Compensation Commission
UNCIP	United Nations Commission for India and Pakistan
US	United States of America
VJIL	Virginia Journal of International Law
VJTL	Vanderbilt Journal of Transnational Law
WMDs	Weapons of Mass Destruction
WTO	World Trade Organization
YIEL	Yearbook of International Environmental Law
YILC	Yearbook of the International Law Commission
YJIL	Yale Journal of International Law

Introduction

A. Introductory Remarks

> It is understandable, therefore, that a community such as the international community, in seeking a more structured organization, even if only an incipient 'institutionalization', should have turned in another direction, namely towards a system vesting in international institutions other than States the exclusive responsibility, first, for determining the existence of a breach of an obligation of basic importance to the international community as a whole, and thereafter, for deciding what measures should be taken in response and how they should be implemented. Under the United Nations Charter, those responsibilities are vested in the competent organs of the Organization.[1]
>
> Roberto Ago

More than a decade ago, the United Nations (UN)-mandated High-level Panel on Threats, Challenges and Change emphasized the importance of States in combating contemporary global security threats in its report titled 'A More Secure World'. It declared that 'States [were] still the front-line responders to today's threats. Successful international actions to battle poverty, fight infectious disease, stop transnational crime, rebuild after civil war, reduce terrorism and halt the spread of dangerous materials all require capable, responsible States as partners.'[2] The Panel also concluded that '[i]t follow[ed] that greater effort must be made to enhance the capacity of States to exercise their sovereignty responsibly'.[3] These high-level pronouncements were formulated in the aftermath of the 9/11 attacks, and occurred in tandem with other significant developments, particularly in the counterterrorism field. Unsurprisingly, several issues of legal, political, and sociological relevance

[1] R Ago, 'Eighth Report on State Responsibility' (1979) UN Doc A/CN.4/318 and Add.1–4; II(1) *YILC* 43 [91]–[92].

[2] UNGA 'Report of the High-level Panel on Threats, Challenges and Change: A More Secure World: Our Shared Responsibility' (2 December 2004) UN Doc A/59/565, 18. See also ibid 1, 9. For further discussion of this landmark document and its implications, see I Johnstone, 'Threats, Challenges, and Change: The Secretary-General's High Level Panel: Summary of Remarks' (2005) 99 ASIL Proceedings 61; MO Chibundu, 'Assessing the High-Level Panel Report: Rethinking the Causes and Consequences of Threats to Collective Security' in PG Danchin and H Fischer (eds), *United Nations Reform and the New Collective Security* (CUP 2010) 117–54.

[3] 'A More Secure World' (n 2) 18.

were propelled to the forefront of international legal debate: recurrent and popular themes in the 'war' on terror included investigating potential changes to the parameters of *jus ad bellum*,[4] issues of international jurisdiction over suspected terrorists,[5] constricting the flow of terrorist funding,[6] violations of human rights and due process,[7] and pre-emptive self-defence.[8]

Shortly after 9/11, the UN Security Council (UNSC) issued sweeping and important statements of principle on the prevention of transnational terrorism. They were rhetorically straightforward and imposed categorical duties of prevention on States. For instance, Resolution 1373 emphasized that 'all States shall... [r]efrain from providing any form of support, active or passive, to entities or persons involved in terrorist acts', which the SC paired with other broad-ranging obligations for States to criminalize certain conduct that facilitates terrorism.[9] Undoubtedly, Resolution 1373 confirmed that every State has an obligation to prevent terrorist attacks emanating from its territory and injurious to another State or individuals. However, a crucial query remains: how is this obligation to be implemented? It is now up to scholars, the judiciary, and policymakers to address the enforcement options for this type of obligation, through a multiplicity of legal regimes, including domestic immigration schemes, criminal law, and the law of State responsibility (SR). Even a cursory review of the SC's post-9/11 resolution-making on counterterrorism issues reveals that it is replete with language that suggests enhanced obligations for States, along with increased responsibility in the event of a breach. The SC has also made similar advances in other global

[4] See, eg, M Byers, 'Terrorism, the Use of Force, and International Law After 11 September' (2002) 51 ICLQ 401; JI Charney, 'The Use of Force against Terrorism and International Law' (2001) 95 AJIL 835.

[5] See, eg, CC Joyner, 'International Extradition and Global Terrorism: Bringing International Criminal to Justice' (2003) 25 Loyola LA International and Comparative Law Review 493; V-J Proulx, 'Rethinking the Jurisdiction of the International Criminal Court in the Post-September 11th Era: Should Acts of Terrorism Qualify as Crimes Against Humanity?' (2004) 19 American University International Law Review 1009.

[6] See, eg, ME Engel, 'Donating "Blood Money": Fundraising for International Terrorism by United States and the Government's Efforts to Constrict the Flow' (2004) 12 Cardozo Journal of International and Comparative Law 251; B Zagaris, 'The Merging of the Anti-Money Laundering and Counter-Terrorism Financial Enforcement Regimes After September 11, 2001' (2004) 22 BJIL 123.

[7] See, eg, E Gross, 'The Influence of Terrorist Attacks on Human Rights in the United States: The Aftermath of September 11, 2001' (2002) 28 North Carolina Journal of International Law and Commercial Regulation 1; HH Koh, 'On American Exceptionalism' (2003) 55 Stanford Law Review 1479.

[8] See, eg, MJ Glennon, 'The Fog of Law: Self-Defense, Inherence, and Incoherence in Article 51 of the United Nations Charter' (2002) 25 Harvard Journal of Law and Public Policy 539, 546–9; C Greenwood, 'International Law and the Pre-emptive Use of Force: Afghanistan, Al-Qaida, and Iraq' (2003) 4 San Diego International Law Journal 7.

[9] UNSC Res 1373 (28 September 2001) UN Doc S/RES/1373. Similarly, UNSC Res 1368 (12 September 2001) UN Doc S/RES/1368 [3] declared that 'those responsible for aiding, supporting or harbouring the perpetrators, organizers and sponsors of such acts will be held accountable'. Similar language was reiterated recently by the SC as regards the activities of Islamic State of Iraq and the Levant (ISIL) and the al-Nusra Front in UNSC Res 2249 (20 November 2015) UN Doc S/RES/2249 [4].

security areas, such as piracy and nuclear non-proliferation, thereby emphasizing the nexus between States' international obligations and their potential responsibility for failing to comply with those duties.

Therefore, scholars are increasingly investigating the role that SR repertoire can play in the suppression and prevention of transnational terrorism.[10] After all, it should be recalled that SR is international law's *sacred cow* whilst terrorism remains its *black sheep*.[11] Unsurprisingly, these accounts focus primarily on delivering ontological and structural critiques of that normative scheme, whilst addressing the unilateral implementation of SR by injured States as the principal means of enforcement envisaged by the International Law Commission (ILC) in its Articles on Responsibility of States for Internationally Wrongful Acts (ARSIWA). However, despite these academic advances, little emphasis has been placed on the role of international organizations (IOs) and particularly UN organs, aside from the International Court of Justice (ICJ), in implementing SR law in global security contexts, especially in counterterrorism settings. This is surprising given that those organs, particularly the SC, have been actively engaged in promoting counterterrorism agendas and promulgating broad-reaching obligations of prevention incumbent upon all States. In many ways, the international community is seeking ways to enforce international law whilst taking into account the rise and unprecedented power now wielded by non-State actors.[12]

Indeed, a State's international responsibility for the violation of an international legal norm can result not only from controlling subversive non-State actors but also from the lack of sufficient control over them, or failure to prevent, or negligence, including not complying with legally binding SC resolutions.[13] With these concerns in mind, the present study explores the role that UN organs, particularly the General Assembly (GA), ICJ, and SC can play in implementing SR law in global security contexts, with particular insistence on counterterrorism as its principal case study. Indeed, scholars and policy experts are increasingly turning their minds—both from descriptive and prescriptive standpoints—to the role that UN

[10] See, eg, V-J Proulx, *Transnational Terrorism and State Accountability: A New Theory of Prevention* (Hart 2012); KN Trapp, *State Responsibility for International Terrorism* (OUP 2011); T Becker, *Terrorism and the State: Rethinking the Rules of State Responsibility* (Hart 2006). See also KN Trapp, 'Terrorism and the International Law of State Responsibility' in B Saul (ed.), *Research Handbook on International Law and Terrorism* (Edward Elgar 2014) 39.

[11] The language is borrowed from A Nissel, 'Tal Becker, Terrorism and the State: Rethinking the Rules of State Responsibility (Hart Publishing, 2006)' (2007) 5 JICJ 245, 245 (invoking the term '*bête noire*' to describe terrorism).

[12] See generally R Mandel, *Global Security Upheaval: Armed Nonstate Groups Usurping State Stability Functions* (Stanford Security Studies 2013); K Mulaj (ed.), *Violent Non-State Actors in World Politics* (Columbia University Press 2010). Increasingly, non-State actors are playing an important role in both norm-enforcement and norm-creation. See, eg, E Dannenmaier, 'The Role of Non-State Actors in Climate Compliance' in J Brunnée *et al.* (eds), *Promoting Compliance in an Evolving Climate Regime* (CUP 2012) 149–76; A Peters *et al.* (eds), *Non-State Actors as Standard Setters* (CUP 2009); D Guilfoyle, 'Somali Pirates as Agents of Change in International Law-Making and Organisation' (2012) 1 Cambridge Journal of International and Comparative Law 81.

[13] See J Kranz, 'The Use of Armed Force—New Facts and Trends' (2006) 3 The Polish Quarterly of International Affairs 68, 80.

organs can play in strengthening collective and global security priorities.[14] Whilst this book canvasses the potential contributions of both the ICJ and GA in implementing SR for global security violations, its central claim is that the institutionalization of SR can be pursued through the SC.

Hence, this monograph makes a straightforward argument to the effect that the SC can play some role, sometimes determinant, in implementing SR for global security breaches, particularly in the field of counterterrorism. This central argument suggests that in some instances, the SC's multilateral process—with all its imperfections—can or should be preferred over unchecked unilateralism. Therefore, the prospect of institutionalizing the implementation of SR through UN organs, with particular emphasis on the SC, becomes a welcome alternative to unchecked unilateral reactions to unlawful conduct by injured States. In bolstering these claims, this book canvases and analyses relevant SC practice, along with relevant jurisprudential pronouncements and scholarly opinion. In particular, the study looks at the ways in which the SC has: (i) acted as legislator by promulgating primary international legal obligations, the violation of which is relevant for the purposes of implementing SR; (ii) attributed internationally wrongful conduct to States, thereby holding them responsible and relying upon the central normative operation under SR repertoire;[15] and (iii) imposed legal consequences flowing from its findings of illegality, which are reconcilable with secondary SR norms.

Ultimately, the present study advocates a rapprochement between Chapter VII of the UN Charter and SR repertoire, although it also analyses SC practice falling outside Chapter VII. Building on this central argument, the book then attempts to untangle the thorny relationship between SR repertoire and recourse to force, so as to identify the role of the former scheme in shaping forcible State reactions to unlawful activity, both inside and outside institutional settings. In many ways, therefore, this line of inquiry constitutes the logical continuation of the central contention that institutionalized SR can be pursued through the SC: the prior establishment of SR often acts as a predicate to justify self-defence in response to unlawful activity in extreme cases.[16] Moreover, it is argued that more modest forcible responses to some global security breaches—which undoubtedly amount to the most controversial type of 'countermeasures' under SR repertoire—can be reconciled with some tenets of that normative scheme.

[14] See, eg, MD Niemetz, *Reforming UN Decision-Making Procedures: Promoting a Deliberative System* (Routledge 2015); G Wilson, *The United Nations and Collective Security* (Routledge 2014).

[15] As the principal body vested with the responsibility to maintain global security, the SC has also attributed wrongful acts to terrorist groups. See P-M Dupuy, 'State Sponsors of Terrorism: Issues of International Responsibility' in A Bianchi (ed.), *Enforcing International Law Norms against Terrorism* (Hart 2004) 3, 8.

[16] On the invocation of self-defence against transnational terrorism, as predicated on a prior finding of SR, see AS Weiner, 'The Use of Force and Contemporary Security Threats: Old Medicine for New Ills?' (2006) 59 Stanford Law Review 415, 431–4. See also JM Beard, 'America's New War on Terror: The Case for Self-Defense under International Law' (2002) 25 Harvard Journal of Law & Public Policy 559, 583 (applying similar logic to Afghanistan regarding the 9/11 attacks).

At the outset, it can be queried why global security challenges, some of which are transnational or de-territorialized in nature—terrorism, climate change, environmental degradation, genocide, human rights and IHL violations, cyber-crime, etc—should be tackled through a State-centric legal regime, namely SR repertoire.[17] Otherwise put, do the observations delivered by the High-level Panel on Threats, Challenges and Change still hold true more than a decade later? Even today in its counterterrorism resolutions dealing with Islamic State of Iraq and the Levant (ISIL), for instance, the SC clearly emphasizes the international obligations of States, the violation of which has important implications for the implementation of SR. In dealing with the threats posed by this particular group, the SC has: (i) stressed the importance of active participation and collaboration of all States under the umbrella of a comprehensive counterterrorism approach; (ii) reaffirmed States' fundamental obligations relating to the prevention and suppression of terrorism enshrined in SC Resolution 1373; (iii) reaffirmed States' obligations relating to extradition and prosecution of terrorists, freezing of terrorist assets, counter-radicalization, and border security; and (iv) encouraged States to enhance information-sharing, broader accession to counterterrorism instruments, and implementation of existing obligations.[18] The Council made similar pronouncements concerning terrorism in Lebanon, Iraq, Syria, and Libya whilst emphasizing both the responsibility of States and importance of international law in addressing this specific global security challenge.[19]

The international community is engaged in a balancing act: it is imperative that it strike a delicate balance between upholding State sovereignty and combating terrorism efficiently. Relying on SR repertoire in some circumstances allows it to strike such a balance and strive towards a much needed equilibrium between the principle of non-intervention in the affairs of States, which is sacrosanct under the UN Charter, and the pressing need to stamp out terrorist networks, which is an important global security objective in UN institutional dialogue and beyond. Undoubtedly, States have a vital role to play in reaching this objective: as will be seen, SC practice almost invariably conflates the obligation to prevent terrorism with the duty of all States to refrain from supporting or harbouring terrorists on their soil. However, as many recent incidents have shown, States no longer exert an unparalleled monopoly over recourse to force, as terrorist networks can wield State-like power and influence across a broad range of States and cultures whilst eluding

[17] For instance, some scholars challenge the concept of State-centrism and argue that the State is no longer the central actor on the international plane. See SD Marks, 'State-Centrism, International Law, and the Anxieties of Influence' (2006) 19 LJIL 339, 340. But see JE Alvarez, 'The Return of the State' (2011) 20 Minnesota Journal of International Law 223.

[18] See, eg, UNSC Res 2258 (22 December 2015) UN Doc S/RES/2258; UNSC Res 2253 (17 December 2015) UN Doc S/RES/2253; SC Res 2249 (n 9); UNSC Res 2233 (29 July 2015) UN Doc S/RES/2233; UNSC Res 2199 (12 February 2015) UN Doc S/RES/2199; UNSC Res 2195 (19 December 2014) UN Doc S/RES/2195; UNSC Res 2178 (24 September 2014) UN Doc S/RES/2178; UNSC Res 2170 (15 August 2014) UN Doc S/RES/2170.

[19] See, eg, UNSC Res 2236 (21 August 2015) UN Doc S/RES/2236; UNSC Res 2227 (29 June 2015) UN Doc S/RES/2227; UNSC Res 2214 (27 March 2015) UN Doc S/RES/2214.

legal responsibility.[20] This problem is further compounded, both from a policy and evidentiary standpoint, when preparatory terrorist acts span over several territories. These realities signal that international legal mechanisms should be bolstered with a view to both promoting transnational cooperation on counterterrorism and other global security issues and devising efficient international responsibility schemes.[21]

Contemporaneous events have shown that States do not always exercise much control or influence over private terrorist enterprises taking place on their soil, thereby inheriting a more passive role in the violation of global security duties. However, this by no means absolves them from the application of the SC's categorical pronouncements since 9/11. Moreover, as UN institutional discourse and State practice reveal, States still have an important—sometimes determinant—place and role in the chain of events leading up to the perpetration of transnational terrorist attacks. Consequently, human security and the protection of property remain highly dependent on prevention of transnational harm, and nation-States are often best situated to achieve this objective. Granted, the global security agenda might require rethinking both the role of the State and the State itself, as its involvement and integration into multilevel, regional, or global regulatory governance networks might become increasingly necessary to tackle present-day challenges.[22] Nonetheless, SR repertoire has a role to play in this multiplicity of regimes and actors.

In that regard, this monograph responds to a broader project aimed at enhancing SR and accountability for transnational violence carried out by non-State actors. In so doing, it avoids casting SR as a cure-all or holistic normative scheme, but rather as one of the applicable legal regimes to be harnessed with a view to stamping out terrorist networks and combating other global security violations. A proactive role and concerted efforts by UN organs, particularly the SC, are essential in addressing these contemporary security challenges. Therefore, it must always be kept in mind that the law of SR remains a powerful tool that the SC can incorporate in its decision-making on occasion in fulfilling its core mission of maintaining global security. In many ways, this monograph is about the relationship between UN organs, particularly the SC, and international legal norms, along with the prospects and limits of that dynamic.

B. Overview of Research

Part of this work constitutes an exercise in creative scholarship. There is no doubt that some of its central claims will attract their share of sceptics and detractors, as the monograph embraces a somewhat forward-looking conception of international

[20] See also Becker (n 10) 1.

[21] Needless to say, multilateralism goes hand-in-hand with cooperation on global security issues. See, eg, P Romaniuk, *Multilateral Counter-Terrorism: The Global Politics of Cooperation and Contestation* (Routledge 2010).

[22] See, eg, S Hameiri and L Jones, *Governing Borderless Threats: Non-Traditional Security and the Politics of State Transformation* (CUP 2015). In many ways, this line of argument aligns with the premises advanced in A-M Slaughter, *A New World Order* (Princeton University Press 2004).

responsibility and its implementation. In particular, it unfolds its principal arguments without upholding rigid dichotomies between relevant normative schemes, such as the law of collective security and SR repertoire, or between the respective roles and competences devolved to UN organs by the UN Charter. Its ultimate goal is rather to identify avenues forward, 'outside-the-box' solutions, in order to address pressing global security challenges. The motivation behind this work is more about shedding light on fruitful areas of coordination and interdependence between relevant legal regimes and international institutions than it is about clutching to dogmatic constructions of international law.

That said, it is to be hoped that some of the arguments advanced in the subsequent pages will be seen at least as part *descriptive*, given that there appears to be support in SC practice for pursuing the implementation of SR through UN organs, even though that prospect may be limited. Similarly, relevant institutional and State practice suggests an important nexus between SR repertoire and recourse to force, given that the former often acts as a justification—at least on a *de facto* basis—for the deployment of the latter. Conversely, the reader cannot be faulted for construing other arguments advanced in this monograph as part *prescriptive*, since they require the suspension of rigid constructions of self-contained regimes and other regime dichotomies. Rather, those arguments explore and ultimately exploit opportunity areas situated interstitially between the frontiers of coexisting legal regimes such as SR, the Chapter VII apparatus, and use of force repertoire. It is to be hoped that the idea that SC powers are broad enough—or should evolve—to encompass issues of SR in global security contexts will acquire credence.

Part I frames the discussion to follow by providing background discussion on relevant legal concepts and present-day global security challenges. Chapter 1 explores the interplay between secondary SR rules, with particular emphasis on attribution, and sets the stage for the arguments to follow in Part III by investigating the prospect of injured States responding to unlawful conduct with force. Chapter 2 turns to the impact of contemporaneous events on the development of SR repertoire and *jus ad bellum* before exploring the prospects and limits of SR law in responding to other present-day global security threats such environmental degradation, climate change, cybercrime, etc. This leads to Part II, which unfolds the monograph's central argument that SR law may be implemented by UN organs in certain circumstances in order to respond to global security violations. In that regard, Chapter 3 examines the potential contributions of the GA, ICJ, and SC whilst investigating the interplay between the SC's quasi-judicial powers and the implementation of SR along with other relevant controversies, such as the potential judicial review of SC resolutions and the functional complementary of that organ's functions with that of the ICJ. Chapter 4 delves into the interrelationship between SC action and SR norms, reviewing extensive institutional and State practice to suggest a critical rapprochement between SR law and the Council's more traditional functions, whilst exploring the implications for countermeasures and international relations. Ultimately, Part II reinforces the idea that transnational terrorism constitutes a particularly apt global security candidate for gauging the prospects and limits of institutionalizing SR, thereby making a rapprochement between that normative scheme and SC powers palatable. Finally, Part III turns to more controversial countermeasures in responding to global security breaches, namely forcible reactions adopted by injured States. It assesses whether such courses of action can be reconciled with SR repertoire. Ultimately, Chapters 5 and 6 demonstrate that whilst the prior establishment of SR can serve as a predicate for invoking self-defence in some global security contexts, the concept of 'forcible countermeasure' remains controversial.

PART I

THE ROLE OF STATE RESPONSIBILITY IN THE FACE OF GLOBAL SECURITY THREATS

Underlying Assumptions, Challenges, and Shortcomings

Introduction to Part I

Part I discusses relevant legal concepts and emerging transnational phenomena that pose challenges to global security agendas, with a view to framing subsequent arguments. Whilst Chapter 1 investigates the mechanics of State responsibility (SR) with particular emphasis on the norms codified in the Articles on Responsibility of States for Internationally Wrongful Acts (ARSIWA), the objective is not to provide an exhaustive review of the corpus of secondary SR rules; rather, Chapter 1 critically engages with some of the more problematic aspects of that normative scheme, thereby propelling issues of attribution and recourse to force to the analytical fore which will become even more central in Parts II and III. Indeed, the issue areas flagged in Chapter 1 and the legal challenges they generate will then be reassessed both within and outside institutional settings, namely in the context of both the potential institutionalization of SR through UN organs and the adoption by injured States of forcible response to global security breaches.

Chapter 2 examines various important related questions with a view to framing the arguments to follow without again purporting to provide an exhaustive picture of State or institutional practice or a comprehensive historical overview. Consequently, it sheds light on the evolution of State support of terrorism in order to demonstrate how contemporaneous events have not only (i) enhanced the standing and importance of SR repertoire on the international scene and in the political mainstream, but also (ii) have prompted the analytical merger of that normative scheme and *jus ad bellum* in some instances. The chapter concludes by analysing the potential contributions of SR repertoire in tackling other global security challenges extending beyond the principal case study of terrorism. Ultimately, Part I reinforces the present study's methodological inclination to focus predominantly on transnational terrorism as the 'best global security candidate' for gauging the potential benefits and limits of institutionalizing SR.

1

Crossing the Conceptual Rubicon

Understanding Secondary Norms of State Responsibility

This chapter provides brief introductory observations on relevant fundamental legal questions in order to frame the prescriptive arguments to follow. It thus sheds light on the nature and interplay between secondary SR rules under the aegis of the Articles on Responsibility of States for Internationally Wrongful Acts (ARSIWA), an essential exercise in circumscribing the main field of inquiry effectively. Indeed, Part II of the present book, which explores the potential institutionalization of SR through UN organs, draws heavily on the primary/secondary distinction under SR repertoire. Similarly, when exploring more controversial consequences flowing from States' violations of counterterrorism obligations, Part III delves into this distinction as regards forcible reactions. Therefore, after offering preliminary remarks on extant secondary norm structure, the chapter turns to contemporary perspectives on the prospect of forcibly responding to non-State actors in the light of the International Court of Justice's (ICJ's) seminal *Nicaragua* judgment, with particular emphasis on the mechanism of attribution.

1.1 The Law of State Responsibility: Codification, Attribution, and Secondary Norms

The mechanics of SR, as enshrined in the ARSIWA, may be summarized in straightforward terms.[1] Once a State violates a primary legal obligation, international law sets in motion the application of secondary rules of responsibility which comprise a series of potential legal consequences, including restitution or

[1] There is voluminous scholarship on the mechanics of SR and the content and application of secondary norms. See, eg, LANM Barnhoorn and KC Wellens (eds), *Diversity in Secondary Rules and the Unity of International Law* (Nijhoff 1995); D Alland, *Justice Privée et Ordre Juridique International: Étude Théorique des Contre-mesures en Droit International Public* (Pedone 1994); B Bollecker-Stern, *Le Préjudice dans la Théorie de la Responsabilité Internationale* (Pedone 1973); *Thesaurus Acroasium Vol 20: Responsibility of States* (Institute of Public International Law and International Relations of Thessaloniki 1993); R Provost (ed.), *State Responsibility in International Law* (Ashgate 2002); M Spinedi and B Simma (eds), *United Nations Codification of State Responsibility* (Oceana 1987); D Alland and J Combacau, '"Primary" and "Secondary" Rules in the Law of State Responsibility: Categorizing International Obligations' (1985) 16 NYIL 81.

compensation.[2] This primary/secondary norm distinction has been described as 'the central organizing device' of the ARSIWA by the International Law Commission (ILC) Special Rapporteur who engineered their adoption.[3] Given the principal case study of this monograph, the violation of one relevant primary duty materializes when a State fails to prevent terrorism emanating from its territory, thereby inflicting harm onto the citizens or violating the rights of another State. As seen in Part III, equally important to this book is the query regarding whether forcible responses to terrorism, be they incremental, more ambitious in scope, or tantamount to self-defence, may be encompassed within the scope of secondary norms, either via the institution of a *lex specialis* or as a matter of course.

All simple expositions end there. Described as the 'most ambitious and most difficult topic of the codification work' of the ILC,[4] the ARSIWA are the product of some forty years of work at the ILC and reflect the succession of intellectually divergent and sometimes ideologically driven Special Rapporteurs. Furthermore, this codification project progressively evolved towards creating a political safe space in which the contents of primary obligations (ie substantive international law)—particularly but not exclusively in the field of injuries to aliens—would be eschewed in favour of further developing the rules governing the breaches of those primary norms, and the ensuing consequences.[5] Consequently, several conceptual and practical challenges have cropped up, not least brought on by the once controversial dichotomy between primary and secondary obligations.[6] As René Provost argued, aside from supporting the well-established requirement that 'a breach [of international law] necessarily be sanctioned', the law of SR 'appears unsettled and has generated considerable theoretical debates and practical difficulties'.[7] Whilst the purpose of this chapter is not to address all the theoretical

[2] Articles on the Responsibility of States for Internationally Wrongful Acts, UN Doc A/56/10 (2001); (2001) II(2) *YILC* 26 (and Commentary ibid 31).

[3] JR Crawford, 'The ILC's Articles on Responsibility of States for Internationally Wrongful Acts: A Retrospect' (2002) 96 AJIL 874, 876.

[4] P Malanczuk, *Akehurst's Modern Introduction to International Law* (7th edn, Routledge 1997) 254. See also R Higgins, *Problems & Process: International Law and How We Use It* (OUP 1994) 148 (stressing the inherent difficulty in codification); R Provost, 'Introduction' in Provost (n 1) xii (underscoring the ILC's difficulties in reaching a consensus on the rules to be codified, and emphasizing that 'the diversity of opinions within the Commission mirrors the many real substantial uncertainties which characterize this field of international law').

[5] Consequently, Special Rapporteur Ago decided to shift the focus of the ILC away from the elaboration of substantive norms governing the field of protection of aliens—an exercise originally initiated by Special Rapporteur García-Amador—to the adoption of general and secondary norms of responsibility, formulated at a high level of abstraction. See, eg, Y Matsui, 'The Transformation of the Law of State Responsibility' in *Thesaurus Acroasium* (n 1) 1, 55. Consequently, 'Ago created a politically safe space within which the ILC could work and largely avoid the contentious debates of the day about expropriation and valuation of property.' See D Bodansky and JR Crook, 'Introduction and Overview (Symposium: The ILC's State Responsibility Articles)' (2002) 96 AJIL 773, 780.

[6] Indeed, historically considerable uncertainty regarding the work of the ILC, along with the application of general principles of international liability, has permeated legal scholarship. See, eg, P Allott, 'State Responsibility and the Unmaking of International Law' (1998) 29 HILJ 1, esp 12.

[7] Provost (n 4) xi.

and practical implications of the primary/secondary divide exhaustively, a critical appraisal of the impact of secondary norms on the topic under study is nonetheless useful.

In fact, the challenges to developing effective accountability models in the face of global security threats might be compounded by what some perceive as two features of modern SR, namely the changing of partners and the distinction between primary and secondary obligations. Whilst the second feature is widely accepted and has been consecrated by the ILC in the ARSIWA, the first feature has less purchase in international legal circles. But if accepted as part and parcel of SR, both concepts are interdependent. As soon as a primary obligation is breached, a series of secondary obligations is set in motion and a new legal relationship is formed. It follows that, '*in the expanding field of special legal regimes of international law*, the parties to the primary *are not necessarily the same* as those to the secondary rules. In such cases, there is a *change of partners* and the legal consequences of that change need to be further elucidated.'[8] This transition *might*, therefore, engender a substitution of major actors and/or partners at the primary level, which, whilst involved or directly affected by the events leading to a breach, are shuffled around through the screen of secondary norms. In many ways, this logic underpins the prescriptive arguments advanced in Part II of this book: in some circumstances, once a State violates a global security obligation—by failing to prevent transnational terrorism, for example—the United Nations Security Council (UNSC) can substitute itself for the injured State(s) and implement SR.

This reality is also true of certain types of treaty-based law, such as World Trade Organization (WTO) obligations.[9] Whilst some primary norms are never inherently indivisible, the legal consequences of an internationally wrongful act usually apply between the responsible State and the injured State regarding the particular violated obligation. However, the contracting parties may conventionally set aside these fundamental mechanics and redesignate which injured State(s) can seek out the benefits of the newly formed, secondary relationship under the auspices of SR law. As the ILC underscored,

> [s]tates when creating 'primary' rights and obligations between them may well, at the same time, determine which State or States are to be considered the 'injured' State or States in case of a breach of an obligation imposed by that 'primary' rule, and thereby determine which State or States are entitled to invoke new legal relationships and even which new legal relationships are entailed by such a breach.[10]

It remains unclear, however, how well this doctrine could carry over to the delicate sphere of counterterrorism obligations, for example. Consider a multilateral

[8] E Roucounas, 'Non-State Actors: Areas of International Responsibility in Need of Further Exploration' in M Ragazzi (ed.), *International Responsibility Today: Essays in Memory of Oscar Schachter* (Brill 2005) 391, 399.

[9] See, eg, T Gazzini, 'The Legal Nature of WTO Obligations and the Consequences of Their Violation' (2006) 17 EJIL 723, 729–30.

[10] ILC, 'Report of the International Law Commission on the Work of its 37th Session' (6 May–26 July 1985) UN Doc A/40/10; (1985) 37 II(2) *YILC* 26 [5].

treaty referencing the obligation to prevent terrorism that simultaneously institutes a parallel regime of 'injured' States and operates on the assumptions and distinctions that characterize the doctrine of the changing of partners. One could also envisage a bilateral treaty on counterterrorism setting out certain conditions or standards to trigger the application of SR, but these modalities could simply be equated with treaty stipulations, with the beneficiaries of those provisions ultimately remaining the original contracting parties.

However, should the obligation to prevent terrorism be framed within the scope of either *jus cogens* duties or obligations *erga omnes*, the argument becomes somewhat palatable. If the obligation to prevent terrorism is construed as stemming from some (universal) source other than treaty law (eg general international law), specifically, a case can be made that a responsible State, or an injured State for that matter, may not have initially contracted the original rule it is (or they are) seeking to apply (which may have originated in treaty law). In other words, the primary obligation of prevention may have emerged in a broader setting—for example, as a generally accepted norm amongst the international community—without either State having *specifically* signed up for it. Thus, it can perhaps be said that when the time comes to trigger SR mechanics, the partners at the secondary level of the breach (eg the State that failed to prevent terrorism and the injured State) were not the original partners at the time of the formulation of the relevant primary norm. In fact, it would seem that they were never partners for the purposes of this obligation. It is precisely because of the application of this primary norm that they have now become partners through the application of SR—by way of forced adherence to the violated rule and/or legal osmosis—which empowers one State to reap the benefits of the breached obligation whilst it concomitantly behoves the other State to fulfil its contents. Neither State, however, might have expressly signed up to the norm in question or applied it consistently in the conduct of its own affairs.

Yet, by the very operation of customary international law, coupled with the fact that the State in question did not formally object to the norm, it is bound by the rule. Therefore, the idea of the changing of partners becomes intractable when it is applied to obligations *erga omnes*. However, it may well be resuscitated in the context of the institutionalization of SR: in particular, a changing of partners might indeed occur if and when the SC subrogates itself for the injured State(s), for instance by determining a wrongdoing State's responsibility and imposing consequences upon it. In such a scenario, the second partner in the equation switches from the injured State(s) to a multilateral institution composed of several States (ie one of the UN's political organs). Thus, there is clearly a transformation in the legal relationship, which now exists between the responsible State and the international organization.

For example, if Iran, which has clearly not subscribed to or upheld the obligation to prevent terrorism by sponsoring Hezbollah factions in the past,[11] became

[11] See, eg, V-J Proulx, *Transnational Terrorism and State Accountability: A New Theory of Prevention* (Hart 2012) ch 1, sections C)2–C)4.

the target of the enforcement of that rule through the regime of SR, could that State then be equated with one of the partners involved in the formulation of the primary rule it violated? Alternatively, what if Iran was the target of a terrorist strike emanating from another State and sought to enforce the primary obligation pursuant to SR repertoire: could it then be perceived as having participated in whatever process was prevalent at the primary level of the breach, since it has repeatedly flouted the relevant obligation? First and foremost, this difficult notion of 'changing of partners' appears contingent on the origin and elaboration process of the specific norm in question. Second, a late-game or selective acceptance of the rule by a State may entail that it now assumes a new partnership during the process of applying SR law; a relationship, it should be stressed, that did not exist at the primary level of the breach. However, what still requires clarification in the latter scenario can be summarized as follows: can Iran be 'grandfathered in' as a partner at the primary level of the breach/formulation of the applicable rule by virtue of the sole fact that it adhered to the violated norm at a later stage? Finally, a contrary argument suggests that by accepting to be bound by the relevant norm, even though it was not involved in its initial elaboration, any State therefore associates itself with all other like-minded States; thus, they all become potential partners at the secondary level of a breach of the relevant norm (eg at the stage of applying SR principles) by virtue of their acceptance of the rule (eg partnership at the primary level).

The confusion surrounding the changing of partners, perhaps exacerbated by the pressing need to situate the individual within the international system more effectively, operates on the ARSIWA's logic and poses increasingly difficult challenges to holding States responsible for the acts of non-State actors, as acknowledged in other books[12] and more exhaustive studies.[13] This is relevant given that many determinations of States' responsibility for failing to prevent global security breaches, particularly transnational terrorism, will involve examining the conduct of non-State actors. For comparative purposes, let us recall that one publicist invokes the '*gradual transformation that occurs in the relationship between the ship, the flag State and the port-State control*', underscoring the point that if 'a ship does not meet the internationally agreed standards, *irrespective of her place of registration, her flag State or the citizenship of the owner*, she is retained by the authorities of the port-State and is liable for the violation of these standards'.[14] This clearly reinforces the need to delineate the legal impact of non-State actors on SR mechanics further, whilst this specific example remains 'one more efficient expression of the *genuine link*, which is henceforth required, not only between the

[12] See, eg, Roucounas (n 8) 392, 398–9, 404 (discussing the primary/secondary distinction and exploring its relationship with the changing of partners, whilst also calling for further elucidation of the legal consequences flowing from the new legal relationship engendered by secondary norms).

[13] See SM Villalpando, *L'Émergence de la Communauté Internationale dans la Responsabilité des États* (PUF 2005) 132, 247, 313–14.

[14] Roucounas (n 8) 404. On the relationship between the flagging authority and SR, as seen through a constructivist framework, see JD Ellis, 'Fisheries Conversation in an Anarchical System: A Comparison of Rational Choice and Constructivist Perspectives' (2007) 3 JILIR 1, 36.

ship and her flag State, but also *between the ship and international law*'.[15] Offering one potential avenue to elude the problems associated with the changing of partners, which has generated considerable anguish in some scholarly circles, Part II of this book argues that the SC can sometimes step in and implement SR in global security contexts.

1.2 The ILC's ARSIWA and the Primary/Secondary Divide

Similarly to conceptual and practical impediments in circumscribing relevant primary obligations more effectively, the secondary norms of responsibility are not always clearly delineated. Quite the contrary: significant challenges impair a straightforward (or uniform) interpretation and application of SR rules in many cases. This reality is further compounded when an already too elusive corpus of rules, namely those found in SR repertoire, are extended to politically volatile areas, such as counterterrorism and other global security areas, let alone their consequences implemented through the vehicle of UN organs. This difficulty is most likely to be attributable to the dual reality that 'the international legal system lacks a structured framework' in which to hold States accountable for failing to prevent terrorism,[16] and the law governing the international responsibility of States, coupled with its repertoire of countermeasures, is quintessentially emblematic of the ways in which international law seeks to adapt to the anarchic structure and nature of the global order.[17]

The ensuing argument, therefore, will sometimes align with Robert Keohane's view of this anarchic nature of international relations which will ultimately shape the success of accountability mechanisms—be they inter-State, unilateral, or institutional—through two staples of modern SR repertoire: sovereignty and self-help. This carries with it considerable implications for the notions of cooperation and interdependence that bind actors on the international plane, particularly

[15] Roucounas (n 8) 404. For further discussion of these issues from the perspective of SR law, see JNK Mansell, *Flag State Responsibility: Historical Development and Contemporary Issues* (Springer 2009).

[16] SE Smith, 'International Law: Blaming Big Brother: Holding States Accountable for the Devastation of Terrorism' (2003) 56 Oklahoma Law Review 735, 739.

[17] For a variety of views on the concept of anarchy in the global order and related issues of structure, cooperation, coexistence, power, and coercive measures, see K Waltz, *Theory of International Politics* (McGraw-Hill 1979); K Waltz, 'International Politics Is Not Foreign Policy' (1996) 6 Security Studies 54; I Motoc, 'Controversial Aspects of Democracy in International Law: The Right to Political Participation in Foreign Affairs' in KK Koufa (ed.), *Thesaurus Acroasium Vol 34: State Responsibility and the Individual* (Sakkoulas 2006) 275, 287–8; A-M Slaughter, 'International Law and International Relations Theory: A Prospectus' in E Benvenisti and M Hirsch (eds), *The Impact of International Law on International Cooperation* (CUP 2006) 16, 22; J Mearsheimer, 'The False Promise of International Institutions' (1999) 19 International Security 5, 11–12, 14; RO Keohane, *International Institutions and State Power: Essays in International Relations Theory* (Westview Press 1989); H Bull, *The Anarchical Society: A Study of Order in World Politics* (4th edn, Palgrave Macmillan 2012); A Wendt, 'Anarchy Is What States Make of it: The Social Construction of Power Politics' (1992) 46 IO 392. For an application of these questions in the present book, see Section 4.2.1.

States, not only as directly between them, but also through UN organs. As Keohane underscores, '[t]he anarchic structure of world politics does mean, however, that the achievement of cooperation can depend neither on deference to hierarchical authority nor on centralized enforcement. On the contrary, if cooperation is to emerge, whatever produces it must be consistent with the principles of sovereignty and self-help.'[18] Reflections on SR's (sometimes spectacularly flawed) attempts both to instil a sense of legitimacy in international relations and to implement a structured framework of accountability—in a highly decentralized global order—will lie at the very core of the discussion to follow.

Two conclusions serve as vital building blocks for the further development of potential responsibility models in this volume. First, heeding scholarly and policy calls to engage the SC fully in upholding a global rule of law,[19] the prospect of adapting a generic set of SR norms to this setting will entail a cautious analysis of a distinct yet vital eventuality: that is to say, the possible institutionalization of the implementation of SR. This line of inquiry not only ensures a sense of symmetry in exhausting possible avenues aimed at either (i) bolstering the implementation of SR, or (ii) 'centralizing' its enforcement monopolies within a specific international body in apposite circumstances, such as the SC, but it also might well shed new light on the elaboration of secondary norms. These questions are thoroughly explored in Part II of this book.

Secondly, this project operates on the now obvious premise that additional generalized guidelines and/or standardized rules and principles could be developed and applied to every breach of international law,[20] especially in the field of counterterrorism. Therefore, the re-examination of pertinent secondary rules might assist the international community in redressing this conceptual dearth and lack of specificity in the ARSIWA. Indeed, whilst the concept of State accountability was firmly grounded in international legal consciousness during the ICJ's deliberations in the *Corfu Channel* decision, Judge Alvarez noted in his Separate Opinion that SR law was 'not regulated by any well-established precepts',[21] and thus lacked the horizontal enforcement mechanisms typically found in domestic constitutional and legal orders. However, to maintain this line of argument so many years after the ICJ's ruling and, more precisely, after the adoption of the ARSIWA seems rather tenuous. Whilst it is still true that the international legal system does not comprise a central enforcement mechanism, SR norms have

[18] RO Keohane, 'Reciprocity in International Relations' (1986) 40 IO 1, 1. See also generally B Buzan, *People, States, and Fear: The National Security Problem in International Relations* (University of North Carolina Press 1983) ch 3; RO Keohane, *After Hegemony: Cooperation and Discord in the World Political Economy* (Princeton University Press 1984); Waltz, *Theory* (n 17).

[19] See, eg, S Chesterman, *The UN Security Council and the Rule of Law: The Role of the Security Council in Strengthening a Rules-Based International System: Final Report and Recommendations from the Austrian Initiative, 2004–2008* (Federal Ministry of European and International Affairs 2008).

[20] But see Villalpando (n 13) 140 (highlighting that the ILC's codification strategy could lead to the formulation of general principles of SR, applicable to all internationally wrongful acts, irrespective of the manner in which they arise).

[21] *Corfu Channel Case (UK v Albania)* (Merits) [1949] ICJ Rep 4, 43–4 (Judge Alvarez concurring).

evolved considerably under general international law and have been in large part codified in the ARSIWA. However, what is certain is that the formulation of general principles at a high level of abstraction, such as those resulting from the ILC's codification exercise in the ARSIWA, might lead to idiosyncratic reasoning and inconsistencies in their application, engender 'doctrinal sclerosis', and ultimately dissuade 'creative or critical analysis by imposing a set of basic assumptions'.[22]

1.2.1 The mechanics of the ARSIWA

It should be stressed that both primary and secondary norms are sometimes intertwined, interdependent, or inseparable.[23] Even decades before the adoption of the ARSIWA, it was clear that SR law called for broad reflection on internationally wrongful conduct which inexorably led interlocutors to ponder the modalities of obligations within the confines of that normative scheme.[24] Similarly, learned scholars expounded that in order to apply secondary rules to a given breach, SR mechanics would invariably entail some kind of analysis of the violated primary rule so as to work out the specifics of attribution and related questions.[25] This reality explains the brief overview of the problem of the various shades of State support of terrorism that features in Section 2.2 in the next chapter of this book. In short, devising legal consequences following a State's failure to prevent terrorism invariably entails a context-sensitive, factually driven analysis of the impugned violations, which is achieved by reference to the content of primary counterterrorism obligations (which, in turn, may be expressed as duties to refrain from financing, organizing, or assisting terrorism, obligations to prevent, duties not to harbour or support, obligations to punish or extradite certain individuals, etc).

The very purpose behind the adoption of the ARSIWA was to promulgate key general precepts, applicable to all breaches. Nevertheless, certain scholars level charges against the ARSIWA to the effect that they adapt poorly to all situations, or fail to envisage specific scenarios.[26] Others opine that they provide a sufficient

[22] R Provost (n 4) xx. For similar points, see also I Brownlie, 'The Responsibility of States for the Acts of International Organizations' in Ragazzi (n 8) 360; DD Caron, 'The ILC Articles on State Responsibility: The Paradoxical Relationship between Form and Authority' (2002) 96 AJIL 857; P Reuter, 'Trois Observations sur la Codification de la Responsabilité Internationale des États pour Fait Illicite' in M Virally (ed.), *Le Droit International au Service de la Paix, de la Justice et du Développement: Mélanges Michel Virally* (Pedone 1991) 389, 390.

[23] See, eg, T Treves, 'The International Law Commission's Articles on State Responsibility and the Settlement of Disputes' in Ragazzi (n 8) 227. He further adds that '[t]he consequences of a breach—the main subject of the [ARSIWA]—cannot in most concrete disputes be determined without ascertaining whether there has been a breach, namely without considering the primary rule'. See also generally J Combacau, 'Obligations de Résultat et Obligations de Comportement: Quelques Questions et pas de Réponse' in D Bardonnet *et al.* (eds), *Mélanges Offerts à Paul Reuter: Le Droit International: Unité et Diversité* (Pedone 1981) 181, 192.

[24] See Combacau (n 23) 183.

[25] See, eg, L Condorelli, 'The Imputability to States of Acts of International Terrorism' (1989) 19 IYHR 233, 234.

[26] Consider Brownlie (n 22) 360 (noting the difficulty in applying general principles to the matter at hand and extrapolating this premise to the broader context of international law).

conceptual and legal backdrop, but that some adjustments or evolving interpretations should be taken into account during the further development of the principles enshrined therein.[27] This monograph strives to follow this second line of thinking without, as Dame Rosalyn Higgins cautioned, falling prey to the exercise of transforming the ARSIWA into a veritable 'rag-bag' of topics or expending inordinate effort in defining substantive international obligations which fall outside of the core makeup of SR rules.[28]

Nevertheless, a sometimes nebulous interface between the firmly implanted principle of State accountability and the application of general SR norms, pursuant to the ARSIWA, emerges and poses considerable challenges to the prospect of holding States responsible for failing to prevent terrorism or other global security breaches. As one commentator highlights, '[b]ecause of this haphazard organization, it remains uncertain whether the international community or an individual State can legally hold another sovereign State accountable for sponsoring or supporting terrorist activity. Despite the fact that the system governing terrorism law is disorganized, a significant legal basis nonetheless exists to hold States accountable for terrorist activity.'[29] Moreover, whilst the primary norm elaborated by the ICJ in *Corfu Channel* might appear general or imprecise (eg States must abstain from allowing their territory to be used as a launch pad for harmful activity), Finnemore and Toope nevertheless infer that such a rule—which they cast as falling under the rubric of SR—has generated strong records of compliance and influence.[30]

Whilst the standardized set of secondary rules enshrined in the ARSIWA may be set aside by any *lex specialis* or conventional scheme,[31] one of the principal policy thrusts of this monograph is to steer the reader away from the notion that the 'alternative approach, advanced against the primary/secondary distinction, ***but no longer maintained by scholars***, is that that distinction is artificial and unnecessary, that there is in all cases a single obligation imposed by international law, which carries within itself the definition of the consequences of its breach' (emphasis added).[32] In a narrower sense, reliance on this dichotomy throughout this volume will illustrate that the application of secondary norms flows much more organically from an initial breach of international law than potential detractors would generally concede.

This line of reasoning becomes particularly compelling when coupled with the fact that primary norms—as a result of the ILC's codification on SR—have

[27] See, eg, C Yamada, 'Revisiting the International Law Commission's Draft Articles on State Responsibility' in Ragazzi (n 8) 118.

[28] See Higgins (n 4) 159–65.

[29] Smith (n 16) 739.

[30] M Finnemore and SJ Toope, 'Alternatives to "Legalization": Richer Views of Law and Politics' (2000) 55 IO 743, 747. For the relevant aspect of the decision, see *Corfu Channel Case* (n 21) 22. On the emergence of the obligation of prevention with reference to *Corfu Channel*, see Proulx (n 11) 18–30.

[31] See, eg, H Thirlway, 'Injured and Non-Injured States before the International Court of Justice' in Ragazzi (n 8) 324.

[32] Thirlway (n 31) 323. See also A Cassese, *International Law* (2nd edn, OUP 2005) 244.

arguably seeped into the ARSIWA, most notably in Article 50.[33] In fact, before becoming ILC Special Rapporteur, James Crawford prophetically proclaimed that the 'first principle' underpinning the creation of an appropriate regime for dispute settlement in the realm of secondary obligations resided in circumscribing the scope of reprisals, an exercise simultaneously boiling over to the formulation of primary rules.[34] Additionally, though not without controversy, similar logic could arguably extend to the treatment—and partial alteration—of the rules governing breaches of obligations arising under peremptory norms of international law pursuant to the ARSIWA (which could govern certain global security violations). For instance, hinting at a contentious point of evolution, the jurisprudence of the Inter-American Court of Human Rights underscored that the hierarchy involving *jus cogens* obligations now extends far beyond treaty law. More relevantly, such development occurred in concert with SR law, with that court highlighting that '*ius cogens* is not limited to treaty law. The sphere of *ius cogens* has expanded to encompass general international law, including all legal acts. *Ius cogens* has also emerged in the law of the international responsibility of states and, finally, has had an influence on the basic principles of the international legal order.'[35]

Furthermore, the ARSIWA tack on potentially severe consequences to the violation of such obligations, including the duties of cooperation and assistance between States in order to bring the internationally wrongful act to an end.[36] Whilst this legal development may perhaps not be cast squarely within the sphere of primary international legal norms, it nonetheless significantly affects the application and rationale of those obligations. Ultimately, the scope of the

[33] See, eg, A Nissel, 'The ILC Articles on State Responsibility: Between Self-Help and Solidarity' (2005–6) 38 NYUJILP 355, 361. ARSIWA (n 2) Art 50 provides the following:

1. Countermeasures shall not affect:
   (a) The obligation to refrain from the threat or use of force as embodied in the Charter of the United Nations;
   (b) Obligations for the protection of fundamental human rights;
   (c) Obligations of a humanitarian character prohibiting reprisals;
   (d) Other obligations under peremptory norms of general international law.
2. A State taking countermeasures is not relieved from fulfilling its obligations:
   (a) Under any dispute settlement procedure applicable between it and the responsible State;
   (b) To respect the inviolability of diplomatic or consular agents, premises, archives and documents.

For a similar take on the more recently adopted ILC Articles on the Responsibility of IOs, see generally K Boon, 'Regime Conflicts and the U.N. Security Council: Applying the Law of Responsibility' (2010) 42 GWILR 787, 830. But see MA Drumbl, 'Trail Smelter and the International Law Commission's Work on State Responsibility for Internationally Wrongful Acts and State Liability' in RM Bratspies and RA Miller (eds), *Transboundary Harm in International Law: Lessons from the Trail Smelter Arbitration* (CUP 2006) 98, 99 (contending that the ARSIWA 'do not establish primary obligations that define acceptable or unacceptable standards of conduct').

[34] JR Crawford, 'Counter-Measures as Interim Measures' (1994) 5 EJIL 65, 66.

[35] *Juridical Condition and Rights of the Undocumented Migrants*, Advisory Opinion OC-18, Inter-American Court of Human Rights Series A No 18 (17 September 2003) [99].

[36] This reality will have considerable implications in the context of institutionalized implementation of SR. See Section 4.4.6.

ARSIWA may be more effectively assessed by examining the extent of legal consequences it juxtaposes with breaches of international law—which undoubtedly has varying effects on States' observance of primary norms—as opposed to investigating whether codified SR norms create new (or alter existing) primary international legal obligations. In short, the normative operation at the secondary level of international breaches is not one of primary norm alteration but one of modulation. Put another way, it is submitted that the debate would prove more fruitful by exploring the ways in which secondary norms of responsibility inform and, ultimately, shape the observance of international law. As mentioned, in the field of *jus cogens* obligations the ARSIWA set out particularly severe legal consequences for internationally wrongful acts, which include duties of cooperation and assistance between States to counteract the breach, which may or may not involve the mechanisms of universal jurisdiction. As a corollary, the idea that *jus cogens* obligations may invalidate not only treaty-based undertakings but also SC resolutions and all other legal acts also flows from the ARSIWA.[37] Transposing this rationale to this book, the prospect of incurring international responsibility along with (perhaps severe) legal consequences might, in fact, create incentives for governments to comply with global security obligations rather better than they have done.[38]

However, it is imperative to underscore an alternate viewpoint on the primary/secondary divide permeating SR repertoire. As discussed later, particularly in Part III, the distinction between primary and secondary norms can sometimes hinge on arbitrary considerations, thereby militating in favour of an analytical approach that does not unnecessarily frame potential elucidations of SR in terms of 'primary versus secondary'. A case in point undoubtedly resides in the conceptually loaded notion of 'attribution', which serves as one of the foremost mechanical linchpins of SR at the trans-substantive level.[39] Simply put, attribution constitutes the normative operation that seeks to link the unlawful actions of non-State actors or official State agents to the governing apparatus for the purposes of establishing international responsibility under the ARSIWA, be it through the principles of formal/de facto agency or official State endorsement of an internationally

[37] See, eg, M Ajevski, 'Serious Breaches, the Draft Articles on State Responsibility and Universal Jurisdiction' (2008) 2 European Journal of Legal Studies 12, 36–7.

[38] For a similar, yet more general, line of argument, see K Zemanek, 'Does the Prospect of Incurring Responsibility Improve the Observance of International Law?' in Ragazzi (n 8) 125–34.

[39] Trans-substantive rules are likely to be located in the interstices between primary and secondary norms, without firmly belonging to either category. However, they modulate and ultimately govern the scope and content of primary obligations. See DD Caron, 'The Basis of Responsibility: Attribution and Other Trans-Substantive Rules' in RB Lillich and D Magraw (eds), *The Iran–United States Claims Tribunal: Its Contribution to the Law of State Responsibility* (Transnational Publishers 1998) 109, 128. See also G Gaja, 'Primary and Secondary Rules in the International Law on State Responsibility' (2014) 97 Rivista di Diritto Internazionale 981, 989 (emphasizing that attribution rules come into play to 'define the conditions upon which the primary rule applies'). For critical appraisals of attribution in counterterrorism contexts, see T Becker, *Terrorism and the State: Rethinking the Rules of State Responsibility* (Hart 2006) 236–7; V-J Proulx, 'Babysitting Terrorists: Should States Be Strictly Liable for Failing to Prevent Transborder Attacks?' (2005) 23 BJIL 615; Proulx (n 11).

wrongful act.[40] However, attribution also fulfils a vital role at the primary level and shapes the application of various international obligations in areas as diverse as SR, treaties, the establishment of customary law, diplomatic representation, and, most importantly, self-defence.[41]

As a matter of course, it is therefore not controversial to contemplate the notion of attribution through the prism of primary international legal obligations. In fact, such eventuality has been expressly enshrined in both the WTO Treaty[42] and the Energy Charter Treaty.[43] Thus, under the corresponding legal schemes the primary obligations encompass the acts of sub-federal States and other entities divorced from centralized State governments, thereby disabling the need to revert to default SR rules when allocating blame given the treatment of attribution at the primary level.[44] As explored in Part III, the principle of attribution also finds its foundation in the law governing recourse to force, at least in two ways: (i) on a definitional basis, in order to circumscribe the meaning of proscribed forcible acts under Article 2(4) of the UN Charter or, alternatively, of the notion of 'armed attack' under Article 51 of the same instrument;[45] and (ii) through the application of the concepts of necessity and proportionality insofar as a claim that necessity/ proportionality underpin the exercise of self-defence is only tenable in the event that the initial internationally wrongful act can be attributed to the State being

[40] See ARSIWA (n 2) Arts 4–11. For some feminist critical legal scholars, the classical rule of the non-attribution of private behaviour to States might perpetuate a perhaps undesirable distinction between private and public conduct. In short, '[s]tate responsibility is a legal construct that allocates risk for the consequences of acts deemed wrongful by international law to the artificial entity of the state'. It follows that '[t]he state claims jurisdiction over the totality of functions within its territorial control; it might therefore be appropriate to assert responsibility for all wrongful acts emanating from it'. See C Chinkin, 'A Critique of the Public/Private Dimension' (1999) 10 EJIL 387, 395. On triggering international responsibility through the channels of *ex post facto* endorsement, see *United States Diplomatic and Consular Staff in Tehran (USA v Iran)* (Merits) [1980] ICJ Rep 3, 44–5.

[41] For instance, the relationship between attribution and wrongful acts carried out by individuals, such as armed opposition groups, features prominently in the list of under-explored issues affecting SR repertoire. See L Zegveld, *The Accountability of Armed Opposition Groups in International Law* (CUP 2002) 152–4. On the relationship between SR, self-defence, and attribution issues, see Part III of this book.

[42] See, eg, Agreement on Technical Barriers to Trade (adopted 12 April 1979, entered into force 1 January 1995) 1186 UNTS 276, Art 3. See also generally SM Villalpando, 'Attribution of Conduct to the State: How the Rules of State Responsibility May Be Applied within the WTO Dispute Settlement System' (2002) 5 Journal of International Economic Law 393; V Tomkiewicz (ed.), *Organisation Mondiale du Commerce et Responsabilité* (Pedone 2014); C-E Côté, 'Sécurité Économique et Responsabilité de l'État au Sein de l'Organisation Mondiale du Commerce' in M Rioux (ed.), *Débordement Sécuritaire* (Éditions de l'Institut d'Études Internationales de Montréal 2012) 59–88; RY Simo, 'The Law of International Responsibility: The Case of the WTO as a "*Lex Specialis*" or the Fallacy of a "Self-contained" Regime' (2014) 22 African Journal of International and Comparative Law 184.

[43] See Energy Charter Treaty (adopted 17 December 1994, entered into force 16 April 1998) (1995) 34 ILM 381, Arts 22–23. See also TW Wäelde, 'Energy Charter Treaty-Based Investment Arbitration: Controversial Issues' (2004) 5 Journal of World Investment & Trade 373.

[44] But see Wäelde (n 43) 408–9 (expounding that the principles enshrined in Energy Charter Treaty Arts 22–23 are philosophically congruent with attribution precepts under SR repertoire).

[45] See, eg, A Randelzhofer, 'Use of Force' in B Simma *et al.* (eds), *The Charter of the United Nations: A Commentary* (2nd edn, OUP 2002) 788, 800 fn 30 (also highlighting that the prohibition on recourse to force encompasses forcible acts perpetrated by unofficial, militarily structured groups).

targeted.[46] Granted, it should be stressed that attribution, on the one hand, and proportionality/necessity, on the other, arise at different stages of the legal inquiry. However, within the confines of SC practice, for instance, which will prove central in the analysis pursued in Parts II and III of this book, States routinely elect to debate the virtues of the lawfulness of self-defence in terms of proportionality and necessity.[47]

Yet, whilst the concept of attribution may find various applications in primary normative terrain, this does not simultaneously signal a consistent or uniform construction of that principle across the board.[48] One salient illustration emerges in the institutional practice analysed in Section 4.5.2 of this book, as the SC's application of attribution principles has been anything but straightforward in determining issues of international legal responsibility. Moreover, the semantic content of 'attribution' is subject to various permutations within the discipline and is brandished rather loosely under international law. At times, attribution is equated with some measure of 'factual causality' whilst, within the realm of SR, it becomes interchangeable with a 'strictly normative operation' under the law, ie inheriting an almost mechanical, as opposed to substantive, fate under some lights.[49] Consequently, particular scrutiny should be exercised when attempting to transpose uncritically the notion of 'attribution' from one legal category to another. When casting attribution as a primary norm, some scholars advocate in a radical direction and, quite compellingly, argue that some rules featured in the ARSIWA may not be divorced from the primary corpus of international norms. Such is the contention of Ulf Linderfalk who, basing his theory on an appreciation of international legal language, resists vehemently the overarching separation of primary and secondary rules under SR. Rather, he argues that the norms codified in the ARSIWA belong to the realm of international 'regulative rules' and form part of a primary set of international obligations. Moreover, he subsumes the bases for attributing internationally wrongful acts to States, enshrined in ARSIWA Articles 4-11, within this analysis. He further expounds that these provisions 'lay down conditions for the application of the great majority of primary rules existing in international law: they provide elements of primary regulative rules, rather than secondary ones'.[50]

[46] See, eg, Separate Opinion of Judge Kooijmans, in *Oil Platforms (Iran v USA)* (Merits) [2003] ICJ Rep 161, 263 [54]–[55]. But see Higgins (n 4) 251.

[47] Compare I Brownlie, *International Law and the Use of Force by States* (Clarendon Press 1963) 279; C Gray, *International Law and the Use of Force* (2nd edn, OUP 2004) 124–5.

[48] On the disconnect between attribution in the law of treaties, the law of diplomatic representation, and SR law, see, eg, ILC, 'Report of the International Law Commission on the Work of its 25th Session' (7 May–13 July 1973) UN Doc A/9010/Rev.1; (1973) II *YILC* 188–98. For a similar critique under international criminal law, see T Meron, 'Classification of Armed Conflict in the Former Yugoslavia: Nicaragua Fallout' (1998) 92 AJIL 236.

[49] See A Nollkaemper, 'Attribution of Forcible Acts to States: Connections Between the Law On the Use of Force and the Law of State Responsibility' in N Blokker and N Schrijver (eds), *The Security Council and the Use of Force: Theory and Reality: A Need for Change?* (Nijhoff 2005) 133, 140–1. See also Commentary on Draft Article 3, adopted upon first reading in ILC Report (n 48) 179–84.

[50] U Linderfalk, 'State Responsibility and the Primary-Secondary Rules Terminology: The Role of Language for an Understanding of the International Legal System' (2009) 78 NJIL 53, 62. See also his analysis at 60–2. At 62–3, he applies similar reasoning to ARSIWA (n 2) Arts 20–25, which govern circumstances precluding wrongfulness, although he somewhat tempers the analysis pertaining to those provisions.

Linderfalk's vision is persuasive and may be one of the rationales that has driven the SC's substantive forays into SR repertoire, particularly as regards the 9/11 attacks and other global security incidents discussed in Chapter 4. Indeed, the norms reflected in those ARSIWA prescriptions undoubtedly amount to what could be construed as 'fill-in-the-wrongful-act' guideline provisions. These, in turn, are filled with specific primary content commissioned by the circumstances leading to a State's violation of international law, essentially by failing to prevent specifically proscribed conduct under the relevant primary norm (eg failures to prevent terrorism, human rights abuses, extra-judicial killings, etc). In summary, those prescriptions faithfully follow the template of laying down a rule connecting a wrongful act to a State whilst simultaneously incorporating reference to some foreign, undefined unlawful 'conduct', along with additional criteria that qualify the violation and provide guidance in applying the mechanics regulating the legal breach. At this stage, the ARSIWA are in no way dealing with restitution or reparative arrangements following the establishment of responsibility; the normative operation that ensues is that of actually ascertaining wrongful conduct on part of the State—an exercise carried out with a large degree of reference to the applicable primary norms—as opposed to devising the legal consequences of the violation, a determination belonging solely to the realm of secondary obligations. Otherwise put, if those observations could boil down to simple formulae, they could be expressed along the following lines:

i) the conduct [*insert internationally wrongful act* here] + carried out by any State organ (ie legislative, judicial, or executive) [*qualifier providing authorship criteria for establishing the breach*] = attributable to the State [*responsibility ensues*] (ARSIWA Article 4(1));
ii) the conduct [*insert internationally wrongful act* here] + carried out by an individual or group of persons [*general authorship qualifier indicating the private nature of the actors*] + acting on the instructions of the State [*first disjunctive qualifier providing criteria for establishing the breach*] + acting under the direction of the State [*second disjunctive qualifier providing criteria for establishing the breach*] + under the control of the State [*third disjunctive qualifier providing criteria for establishing the breach*] = attributable to the State [*responsibility ensues*] (ARSIWA Article 8);
iii) the conduct [*insert internationally wrongful act* here] + that is not attributable to the State [*qualifier providing criteria for establishing the breach*] + that is acknowledged or adopted by the State [*qualifier providing substantive guidance as to the mechanics of establishing responsibility*] = converts the hitherto non-attributable act into an act of State [*responsibility attaches on an alternative basis to 'traditional' attribution*] (ARSIWA Article 11); and so on.

Whilst contending that these norms entirely straddle primary terrain, as opposed to being trans-substantive in nature, may not persuade the staunchest detractors, a careful review of the normative makeup of the pertinent rules, as expressed in the formulae above, reveals an interpretive flexibility governing the notion of attribution under the ARSIWA. Nor is it far-fetched to contend that this normative framework strays conceptually from what has traditionally been construed as the exclusive dominion of SR repertoire, namely the application of *secondary* rules of liability (ie legal consequences of a breach and reparation). In many ways, this liberal construction of attribution principles is reflected in the SC's sometimes nebulous applications of attribution explored in Chapter 4. Conversely, it is fair to balance out this line of reasoning by acknowledging that in codifying these provisions, the ILC was not 'legislating', for lack of a better term, nor was it instituting entirely new primary rules. However, by devising a set of norms heavily referencing undefined primary obligations on a 'fill-as-you-go' basis—whilst sharply emphasizing the mechanics of ascertaining international law violations at the primary level—the Commission implemented a regime that will significantly regulate and modulate the application of the primary norms it seeks to enforce. Whilst ARSIWA Articles 4–11 may not categorically attract a 'primary obligation' designation, they do suggest that the perhaps arbitrary conceptual Rubicon dividing both types of obligations can be traversed on occasion, and that both normative categories are, in many respects, interdependent. Furthermore, this scheme warrants a twofold observation. First, the interchangeable dynamic between some norms suggests a flexible margin in reconceptualizing legal rules pertaining to global security; and, secondly, it concomitantly signals that the primary/secondary distinction is by no means an infertile ground for the further elaboration of policy-oriented reforms.

1.2.2 The problems of autoqualification and self-judging

This line of inquiry inevitably diverts the analysis back to a fundamental phenomenon shaping the application of SR principles, namely that of autoqualification by States. In short, it empowers injured States—with varying degrees of input from wrongdoing States—to qualify unilaterally the various aspects of a dispute which entails both self-interpreting and self-judging the initial breach and its legal consequences. The decentralized nature of SR law is characterized by the absence of any mandatory adjudicatory process in its implementation; thus, injured States are left with the option to delve unilaterally into the resulting scheme of countermeasures when enforcing international law, against the backdrop of an anarchic international society. Consequently, injured States will have a large margin of discretion not only in determining if a breach of international law has been perpetrated, but also as to what constitutes 'terrorism' and the failure to prevent it (or the contours of other similar global security breaches), along with the applicable legal consequences flowing from the violation. This central question of autoqualification steers the analysis towards 'Kelsen's proposition that only state parties to a controversy could autoqualify it'.[51]

Given the arguments that will be advanced in Part III of this book, the next logical, perhaps ineluctable, conclusion is that disputing States will retain the ability to ascertain whether there has been an 'armed attack' before invoking the right to self-defence in global security contexts, a proposition that enjoys scholarly support.[52] Speaking to the question of indeterminacy and international law's 'modulated response' to that challenge in the 'context of application and the nature of norms in human rights and humanitarian law', René Provost astutely underscored that there will be a '"dialogue" on international norms between these two or more actors holding possibly divergent views on the nature of the situation'.[53] Here, Provost writes about this 'dialogue' as pertaining to an internal armed conflict, whereby insurgents are afforded a 'measure of functional sovereignty' in order to make a 'valid legal characterization of the conflict', which, in turn, might run against competing qualifications of the conflict formulated by other involved actors.[54]

In a seminal article, Thomas Franck rightly cautioned that various manifestations of autoqualification might bring about undesirable, idiosyncratic, and ultimately destabilizing effects when assigning legal blame:

> [i]n the absence of some universally credible fact-determination procedures, the effort to establish whether a use of force is illegal under Article 2(4) or legal under Article 51 is stymied by contradictory allegations of fact by the parties to the dispute and their allies. It is rather as if the law were to leave to the two drivers in a motor vehicle collision the sole responsibility for apportioning liability, helped only by the unruly crowd gathered around them at the scene of the accident.[55]

Given these challenges to the principles of equality of arms and impartiality endemic to SR repertoire, Part II of this book argues that the SC may step in and implement the legal consequences flowing from global security violations in some circumstances. This proposal aims to identify a viable alternative to unchecked unilateralism by injured States, which is intimately tied to

[51] See R Provost, *International Human Rights and Humanitarian Law* (CUP 2002) 338 fn 2. See also H Kelsen, *Peace Through Law* (Chapel Hill, University of North Carolina Press 1944) 13–4; L Gross, 'States As Organs of International Law and the Problem of Autointerpretation' in G Lipshy (ed.), *Law and Politics in the World Community* (University of California Press 1953) 59, 72–3. See also generally L Gross, 'States as Organs of International Law and the Problem of Autointerpretation' in G Lipshy (ed.), *Selected Essays on International Law and Organization* (Transnational Publishers 1993) 167–97.

[52] See, eg, Alland, *Justice* (n 1) 107–20; Gross, 'States' in Lipshy (n 51) 80–1; Provost (n 51) 338.

[53] Provost (n 51) 338. [54] Provost (n 51) 338.

[55] See TM Franck, 'Who Killed Article 2(4)? Or: Changing Norms Governing the Use of Force by States' (1970) 64 AJIL 809, 817. Compare with O Schachter, 'The Right of States to Use Armed Force' (1984) 82 Michigan Law Review 1620, 1645 (discussing 'hard' cases involving force and underscoring that 'sharp differences of judgment ... rest on conflicting interpretations of the agreed rules, and to a much larger extent, the differences arise from divergent perceptions of facts and motives. Yet underlying the disagreements, there is a considerable area of agreement on the core substantive law').

the exercise of autoqualification, and remove the prospect of those States self-judging both international law violations and the corresponding consequences in the SR implementation process. In 1963, Rosalyn Higgins investigated scenarios in which injured States must be allowed to invoke self-defence on an urgent basis, and she observed that '[t]emporarily, then, a state must be judge in its own cause'.[56] However, she concluded that 'in order that the right shall not be abused, it is essential that it be subjected to international review'; hinting at an important role for the SC in this setting, she added that '[t]his reasoning… becomes even more compelling where there exists an international organization entrusted with the primary responsibility for the maintenance of peace and security'.[57]

Whilst these dimensions of international relations will become evident subsequently, suffice it to say that disputing States' respective qualifications of both 'terrorism' and internationally wrongful acts in the global security context will invariably inform the unilateral deployment of secondary rules of responsibility. A salient example arose in the ICJ's *Nicaragua* judgment. Whilst debate still surrounds the legal nature of the paramilitary activities carried out by the *Contras* rebels, it should be recalled that Nicaragua classified the guerrillas as 'terrorists', thereby propelling the intersection of autoqualification and SR to the fore.[58] In the post-9/11 world, disparate and potentially dire legal and political consequences can result from governments labelling and qualifying certain individuals as 'terrorists', with the notion of 'terrorism' now embodying far more extensive legal content, at least on the domestic plane.[59] These considerations pave the way for the following brief observations on the role of attribution as addressed in *Nicaragua* and often applied across both SR law and self-defence repertoire.

1.3 The Loaded Notion of 'Attribution' and *Nicaragua*'s Legacy: Merging State Responsibility and Use of Force Repertoire

Both the law governing use of force and SR repertoire have developed considerably since 9/11, sometimes in tandem, principally through State and institutional practice. Academic commentary has chronicled this evolution, sometimes critically. One consequence is that there is a growing tendency within legal scholarship to subsume self-defence within SR repertoire, an exercise bordering on what

[56] R Higgins, *The Development of International Law through the Political Organs of the United Nations* (OUP 1963) 205.

[57] Higgins (n 56) 205.

[58] See *Military and Paramilitary Activities in and against Nicaragua (Nicaragua v USA)* (Merits) [1986] ICJ Rep 14, 63–4 [113], 68 [121].

[59] See, eg, S Setty, 'What's in a Name? How Nations Define Terrorism Ten Years after 9/11' (2011) 33 University of Pennsylvania Journal of International Law 1.

some construe as a 'bastardly' conflation of two distinct regimes.[60] This confusion stems in large part from the fact that in its famous *Nicaragua* decision, the ICJ effectively borrowed the central tenets of its inquiry on recourse to force from SR logic, which engendered considerable practical and conceptual uncertainty as to the application of attribution across both these fields.[61] Consequently, an exceedingly pressing question emerged: whether an 'armed attack' carried out by non-State actors (eg transnational terrorism) must be attributable to a State (ie because it failed to prevent it or provided logistical support/sanctuary to the terrorists) before that State can be targeted in self-defence. As a corollary, considerable confusion surrounds the applicable threshold of attribution in cases of State failures to control terrorist units located on their territory adequately.

Since 9/11, three broad strands of legal scholarship have gradually formed on these questions.[62] At one end of the spectrum, commentators seem to maintain that the invocation of self-defence must be predicated on the prior attribution to the targeted State of the terrorist attack, pursuant to SR logic.[63] In summary, the mechanism of attribution thus converts the non-State act into an 'armed attack' by the State. This conversion must be achieved through the onerous test of 'effective control' developed by the ICJ in *Nicaragua* and subsequently confirmed by that Court.[64] Such an exacting standard requires a seemingly inordinate level of State control over the activities of non-State actors, which typically translates into active/direct involvement taking the form of instructions, direction, or control over specific acts. Put another way, *Nicaragua* unequivocally laid down a standard of agency as the dominant paradigm in the field.[65] Obviously, several

[60] J-C Martin, *Les Règles Internationales Relative à la Lutte contre le Terrorisme* (Bruylant 2006) 497.

[61] On the difficulties and challenges associated with deploying attribution mechanics following terrorist attacks carried out by non-State actors, see, eg, KN Trapp, 'The Use of Force Against Terrorists: A Reply to Christian J. Tams' (2009) 20 EJIL 1049.

[62] See, eg, T Ruys, 'Crossing the Thin Blue Line: An Inquiry into Israel's Recourse to Self-Defense Against Hezbollah' (2007) 43 SJIL 265, 274; T Ruys and S Verhoeven, 'Attacks by Private Actors and the Right of Self-Defence' (2005) 10 JCSL 289.

[63] See, eg, G Travalio and J Altenburg, 'State Responsibility for Sponsorship of Terrorist and Insurgent Groups: Terrorism, State Responsibility and the Use of Military Force' (2003) 4 CJIL 97; A Cassese, 'Terrorism Is Also Disrupting Some Crucial Legal Categories of International Law' (2001) 12 EJIL 993, 996–7; I Scobbie, 'Words my Mother Never Taught Me—"In Defense of the International Court"' (2005) 99 AJIL 76. Those who do not consider that the use of defensive force against terrorists is contingent on the prior establishment of SR include Brownlie (n 47) 375; TM Franck, 'Terrorism and the Right of Self-Defense' (2001) 95 AJIL 839, 840; R Wedgwood, 'The ICJ Advisory Opinion on the Israeli Security Fence and the Limits of Self-Defense' (2005) 99 AJIL 52, 58. For a thoughtful discussion of the various arguments for and against the initial position, see Becker (n 39) 158–62.

[64] *Nicaragua v USA* (Merits) (n 58) [115]; *Legal Consequences of the Construction of a Wall* (Advisory Opinion) [2004] ICJ Rep 136, [139]; *Armed Activities on the Territory of the Congo (DRC v Uganda)* (Merits) [2005] ICJ Rep 116, [146]–[160]; *Case Concerning the Application of the Convention on the Prevention and Punishment of the Crime of Genocide (Bosnia and Herzegovina v Serbia and Montenegro)* (Merits) [2007] ICJ Rep 43, [384], [391], [400]–[401].

[65] For both pre- and post-*Nicaragua* scholarly confirmations of agency as the legal basis for triggering SR, see I Brownlie, *System of the Law of Nations: State Responsibility (Part I)* (Clarendon Press 1983) 132–66; Caron (n 39) 109 ff. On the specific question of Osama bin Laden's status as an agent of the State, see J Quigley, 'International Law Violations by the United States in the Middle East as a Factor Behind anti-American Terrorism' (2002) 63 University of Pittsburgh Law Review 815, 826.

commentators construe this agency standard as ill-suited to respond to global security threats, particularly the challenges brought on by terrorism, since the 'effective control' criterion fails to capture adequately the real degrees of State support of or complicity with terrorism, or the polymorphous structural realities of terrorist networks.[66] Others caution against extending this standard to use of force repertoire, concluding that whilst SR law presents criteria that may apply by analogy to use of force, this extension should not be done uncritically given that both normative schemes respond to different rationales. In short, SR governs the legal consequences flowing from international legal breaches whereas the other regime regulates the conditions for the lawful use of force.[67]

At the other end of the spectrum, scholars seemingly advocate the abolishment of attribution, inferring that State involvement has been excised from the purview of the legal calculus, and that the severity of a given non-State attack dictates the level of available responses, including those rooted in self-defence.[68] Alternatively, grounding their thesis on the ICJ's *Corfu Channel* judgment, some publicists depict the potential evolution of international law towards a model of ***automatic attribution***; it would apply in cases where sanctuary States do not adequately control their territory, thereby failing to thwart transnational terrorism and other global security threats. In such instances, as was the case of Lebanon regarding Hezbollah factions operating on its soil in the lead-up to the 2006 conflict between Israel and Hezbollah, the ICJ's decision, coupled with the SC's post-9/11 resolution-making, would all trigger Lebanon's international responsibility.[69] Accordingly, a sanctuary State may be targeted in self-defence, irrespective of whether it has been held internationally responsible for the non-State terrorist attack via the mechanism of attribution.

Finally, advocating a more nuanced approach, other interlocutors flirt with the idea that whilst some degree of attribution might still be required to establish the requisite nexus between a State and non-State terrorism to substantiate resort to self-defence, the resulting applicable standard is not as onerous as that of 'effective control'. Indeed, it may be queried whether the 'effective control' standard for attribution elaborated by the ICJ in *Nicaragua* was perceived, by the

[66] See, eg, Becker (n 39); Proulx (n 11); J Rosenthal, 'Book Annotations' (2006) 39 NYUJILP 141, 147. For a variety of views on this, both before and after *Nicaragua*, see A-M Slaughter and W Burke-White, 'An International Constitutional Moment' (2002) 43 HILJ 1, 20; Condorelli (n 25) 233–46; Y Dinstein, *War, Aggression and Self-Defence* (3rd edn, CUP 2001) 182–3 and 'The International Legal Response to Terrorism' in R Ago (ed.), *International Law at the Time of Its Codification: Essays in Honour of Roberto Ago*, vol 2 (Giuffrè 1987) 139, 140, 142. On the notion of 'complicity' under SR, see HP Aust, *Complicity and the Law of State Responsibility* (CUP 2011).

[67] See, eg, N Tsagourias, 'Non-State Actors in International Institutional Peace and Security: Non-State Actors and the Use of Force' in J d'Aspremont (ed.), *Participants in the International Legal System: Multiple Perspective on Non-State Actors in International Law* (Routledge 2011) 326, 333–4.

[68] See, eg, C Stahn, 'The Right to Self-Defence, Article 51(1/2) of the UN Charter, and International Terrorism' (2003) 27 FFWA 35.

[69] See, eg, S Kirchner, 'Third Party Liability for Hezbollah Attacks against Israel' (2006) 7 German Law Journal 777, 781–2 (also observing that every State is under an obligation *erga omnes* to combat terrorism).

Court itself, as being as exacting as it has been portrayed in the literature and subsequent judicial pronouncements. Granted, the Court invoked a standard of 'effective control' over individuals or non-State actors as the governing criterion for attributing wrongful acts to States.[70] However, it can be argued that such attribution logic did not inform the Court's distinct dismissal of arguments grounded in self-defence. In paragraph 195, the Court did 'not believe that the concept of "armed attack" includes not only acts by armed bands where such acts occur on a significant scale but also assistance to rebels in the form of the provision of weapons or logistical or other support'.[71] One possible construction of this excerpt is to conclude that the Court was further circumscribing the legal test for attribution: in short, such a standard (ie attributing an 'armed attack' to the State) could not be fulfilled had the State merely provided arms or logistical support to the irregulars. By contemplating this passage through the prism of the Court's earlier formulation of 'attribution' in the judgment, one can reasonably infer that the Court was in fact applying that standard to the facts of the case in paragraph 195.[72]

And yet, this conclusion might turn out to be erroneous when examined in tandem with a later passage in the judgment, thereby evincing that the Court was not dealing with attribution in paragraph 195. Its remarks are apposite:

> [e]ven assuming that the supply of arms to the opposition in El Salvador could be treated as imputable to the Government of Nicaragua, to justify invocation of the right of collective self-defence in customary international law, it would have to be equated with an armed attack by Nicaragua on El Salvador. As stated above, the Court is unable to consider that, in customary international law, the provision of arms to the opposition in another State constitutes an armed attack on that State.[73]

Simply put, the Court was underscoring that even in the event that the attribution standard had been satisfied, the wrongful behaviour could not be tantamount to an 'armed attack'. Consequently, when tackling the provision of weaponry in paragraph 195 of the judgment, the ICJ was likely to be distinguishing the question of attribution as a stand-alone and distinct issue from its finding that the provision of weaponry does not amount to an 'armed attack'. Otherwise put, the perception that the Court, at paragraph 195 of its judgment, concluded that the provision of weaponry is insufficient for the purposes of attributing an 'armed attack' to the State might be misguided. One might ponder whether the Court's analytical inquiry would have been more appropriately framed as follows: whether the provision of weaponry could act as a catalyst for attributing responsibility to the State for an actual attack, as opposed to querying whether the act of providing weapons to the rebels could amount to an 'armed attack' and, correspondingly, whether the supply of those arms could in turn be attributed to Nicaragua. Indeed, there

[70] *Nicaragua v USA* (Merits) (n 58) [115].
[71] *Nicaragua v USA* (Merits) (n 58) [195].
[72] See also A Garwood-Gowers, 'Self-Defence against Terrorism in the Post 9-11 World' (2004) 4 Queensland University of Technology Law & Justice Journal 1, 5.
[73] *Nicaragua v USA* (Merits) (n 58) [230].

is no doubt that an *actual* 'armed attack' must be carried out before self-defence repertoire is set into motion. Whilst the ICJ's principal focus should have been on invoking the provision of weaponry as the foremost analytical linchpin for the purposes of attributing responsibility *for the armed attack*, it chose instead, perhaps questionably, to examine whether responsibility *for the provision of arms* could be attributed to the State.[74]

A logical inference could be that the ICJ was not engaging with the question of attribution at all when exploring the legal contours of the concept of 'armed attack'. This conclusion is certainly congruent with the fact that whilst the Court brandished the criterion of 'effective control' as the legal standard governing attribution, no reference to that principle was made by the Court in the context of its discussion on self-defence. Furthermore, it might be queried whether the Court was actually invoking general attribution principles under SR repertoire when examining whether an 'armed attack' had occurred in paragraph 195 of its judgment; in particular, the ICJ was rather seeking inspiration from the General Assembly (GA) resolution on the Definition of Aggression.[75]

As discussed in Part III of this book, it has become generally accepted that in some circumstances, an injured State may target non-State actors and terrorist irregulars inside the territory of another State, in response to a private terrorist strike that was launched from therein. However, the role of SR in this setting remains to be clarified: publicists must determine whether a complete overhaul of the regime of secondary norms, a more modest but still substantial lowering of attribution principles, or the crystallization of a *lex specialis* regarding SR for terrorism has (have) resulted from contemporaneous events. Jutta Brunnée and Stephen Toope captured this uncertainty, whilst leaning towards accepting that relevant secondary SR norms and rules governing recourse to force have been relaxed: '[i]nternational practice seems to have evolved both to allow self-defence against armed attacks by non-state forces, and to loosen the required link between such forces and a state in which armed defence measures are undertaken'.[76]

This evolution in State practice and *opinio juris* unquestionably stems from post-9/11 developments and, consequently, 'aspects of collective response to the September 11 attacks strongly suggest that the threshold for attribution has been lowered substantially'.[77] Some commentators, whether explicitly or by implication, similarly opine that the response targeting Afghanistan has relaxed the relevant legal standards, either through the loosening of use of force principles[78]

[74] On these issues, see also M Brent, 'Responding to Attacks by Non-State Actors: The Attribution Requirement of Self-Defence' (2009) 16 Australian International Law Journal 133, 137–8.

[75] See UNGA Res 3314 (XXIX) (14 December 1974), Annex, Art 3(g).

[76] J Brunnée and SJ Toope, *Legitimacy and Legality in International Law: An Interactional Account* (CUP 2010) 296. See also SR Ratner, '*Jus ad Bellum* and *Jus in Bello* after September 11' (2002) 96 AJIL 905, 908–10; SA Barbour and JA Salzman, '"The Tangled Web": The Right of Self-Defense against Non-State Actors in the *Armed Activities* Case' (2008) 40 NYUJILP 53, 65.

[77] D Jinks, 'State Responsibility for the Acts of Private Armed Groups' (2003) 4 CJIL 83, 89.

[78] See, eg, M Byers, 'Terrorism, the Use of Force, and International Law after 11 September' (2002) 51 ICLQ 401.

or via a contortion of self-defence.[79] Thus, less active forms of support such as toleration, acquiescence, wilful blindness, or the harbouring of terrorists on a State's territory might be sufficient to trigger responsibility as a predicate for the invocation of self-defence.[80] Similarly, a perhaps compatible argument centres on the possible emergence of the 'unwilling or unable' doctrine; that is to say, defensive force could be directed against a State following its failure to prevent transnational terrorism on the basis that it was unwilling or unable to thwart the security threat.[81]

This fairly new canon of scholarship, however, sometimes fails to elucidate several points of importance, chief among them the question whether self-defence is directed against the sanctuary State, on the basis of the prior establishment of its international responsibility, or whether such forcible response solely targets terrorist individuals or entities within that State's territory. In the latter scenario—namely, where an injured State forcibly targets irregulars and non-State actors in another State's territory—there is no doubt that such reaction should conform to the principle of sovereign equality.[82] More broadly, in such instances the role played by the law governing SR in the self-defence calculus is not entirely clear, not to mention that further clarification is needed on whether logistical inability of a State to repress terrorism would be sufficient to fulfil the threshold of attribution, or whether genuine lack of political will (including governmental refusal to divert resources toward counterterrorism structures) constitutes a standard for triggering use of force.[83] Undoubtedly, factual circumstances surrounding State failures to uphold obligations of prevention, be they related to terrorism or other global security threats, will complicate the equation and further obfuscate the

[79] Some scholars argued that the principles of *jus ad bellum* and SR are sufficiently tailored to respond to terrorism, as long as they are viewed in a different light. See, eg, D Brown, 'Use of force against Terrorism after September 11th: State Responsibility, Self-Defense and Other Responses' (2003) 11 Cardozo Journal of International and Comparative Law 1. Other commentators counterargued that the facts surrounding the 2001 military campaign in Afghanistan should not be distorted to 'fit' under the principles of use of force. See Franck (n 63) 840. On the difficulties related to the evidentiary burden in invoking self-defence against terrorism, see JI Charney, 'The Use of Force against Terrorism and International Law' (2001) 95 AJIL 835.

[80] See generally Proulx (n 11). But see JJ Paust, 'Self-Defense Targetings of Non-State Actors and Permissibility of U.S. Drones in Pakistan' (2010) 19 Journal of Transnational Law & Policy 237, 249 fn 32. However, it appears that 'anti-terrorist force' could be directed against the sanctuary State in that scenario. See CJ Tams, 'The Use of Force against Terrorists' (2009) 20 EJIL 359; T Šurlan, 'The Use of Force and Terrorism' (2010) Journal of Criminalistics and Law 51, 59. For a fully fledged discussion, see Part III of this book.

[81] See, eg, DI Ahmed, 'Defending Weak States Against the "Unwilling or Unable" Doctrine of Self-Defense' (2013) 9 JILIR 1; S Regmi, 'Right to Self Defense against International Terrorism' <http://ssrn.com/abstract=2171068> accessed 25 May 2015; A Deeks, '"Unwilling or Unable": Toward a Normative Framework for Extraterritorial Self-Defense' (2012) 52 VJIL 483.

[82] See, eg, HA Noorda, 'The Principle of Sovereign Equality with Respect to Wars with Non-State Actors' (2013) 41 Philosophia 337.

[83] See, eg, L van den Herik and N Schrijver, 'Annex—Leiden Policy Recommendations on Counter-Terrorism and International Law' in L van den Herik and N Schrijver (eds), *Counter-Terrorism Strategies in a Fragmented International Legal Order: Meeting the Challenges* (CUP 2013) 706 paras 42, 49–52.

nexus between SR law and recourse to force.[84] For one thing, it is arguable that lesser forms of State involvement in transnational terrorism falling short of direct support, such as tacit acquiescence, logistical support, mere toleration, or territorial sanctuary, could always be said to facilitate global security threats. Granted, in the *Nicaragua* case the ICJ took the view that the threshold of 'armed attack' would not be fulfilled by mere assistance to guerrillas consisting of provision of weapons or other types of logistical support, absent any other substantial involvement of the sponsoring State in the unlawful activities carried out by non-State actors.[85] However, this stance has been staunchly challenged, even prior to 9/11, in response to the advent of transnational, State-sponsored, or State-condoned terrorism; the principal counterarguments to the ICJ's rationale on this front perhaps hint at the emergence of a *lex specialis*, lying at the intersection of SR and recourse to force, in instances where States harbour or support terrorists on their soil in a manner that falls short of an 'armed attack'.[86]

A State's failure to prevent terrorism emanating from its territory unequivocally violates international legal norms and binding SC resolutions. Moreover, the emergence of a new self-defence legal paradigm under the UN Charter—which remains open to challenge and largely driven by United States (US) foreign policy and practice after 9/11—may have significant implications for the notion of consent. For instance, it has been argued that Pakistan did not consent to US-led counterterrorism activities carried out on its soil, particularly unmanned drone strikes, which would signal a violation of its sovereignty and a contravention of international law.[87] Conversely, a counterargument can be convincingly advanced that if Pakistan is unable to exercise its sovereignty effectively or, at least, in conformity with the cardinal principle of non-intervention in the affairs of third States under the Charter, it has essentially forfeited some of its sovereign prerogatives and could be subject to countermeasures or responses involving self-defence.[88] However, it is equally fair to posit that a State that failed to thwart a global security breach emanating from its territory—terrorist strikes, for example—can perhaps cure this failure, or at least contain any ensuing repercussions, by accepting

[84] Consider the analysis delivered in SR Ratner, 'Self-defence against Terrorists: The Meaning of Armed Attack' in van den Herik and Schrijver (n 83) 334–55.

[85] See *Nicaragua v USA* (Merits) (n 58) [187]–[201].

[86] See, eg, O Schachter, *International Law in Theory and Practice* (Nijhoff 1991) 165. For a contrary view, see B Brun-Otto, 'Self-Defence' in R Bernhardt *et al.* (eds), *Encyclopedia of Public International Law*, vol 4 (Amsterdam, Elsevier 2000) 212. For post-9/11 accounts, see Becker (n 39) (espousing a causation-based model of SR); Proulx (n 11) (advocating a strict liability-infused SR model). See also Part III.

[87] See, eg, the various discussions and posts in KJ Heller, 'Eric Posner Rejects the "Unwilling or Unable" Test!' (9 October 2012) Opinio Juris <http://opiniojuris.org/2012/10/08/eric-posner-rejects-the-unwilling-or-unable-test/> accessed 30 April 2015.

[88] For a similar argument in respect of Lebanon in counterterrorism settings, see Proulx (n 11) 106. For divergent analyses of the notion of 'consent', with particular emphasis on the concept of 'supremacy', see A Deeks, 'Consent to the Use of Force and International Law Supremacy' (2013) 54 HILJ 1; compare with R Mullerson, 'Intervention by Invitation' in L Damrosch and D Scheffer (eds), *Law and Force in the New International Order* (Westview Press 1991) 127; TD Gill, 'Military Intervention at the Invitation of a Government' in TD Gill and D Fleck (eds), *The Handbook of the International Law of Military Operations* (OUP 2010) 229–32.

outside assistance or intervention to repel further threats. Unsurprisingly, in the wake of 9/11 some publicists have argued that States are beholden to an obligation of counterterrorism capacity building and in the absence of such ability have a consequential duty to seek assistance in meeting their primary obligation; moreover, failure to meet this undertaking would subject them to SR.[89] As will be seen in Part III of this book, this scheme of obligations also stems from the post-9/11 security frameworks put into place by the SC.

One example resulted from the situation that arose in Mali in 2012, when terrorists began operating overtly within that State's borders, prompting an urgent request by Malian authorities for external assistance in attempts to repel the terrorist threats percolating within its territory. Consequently, France intervened militarily in Mali from January 2013, targeting several terrorist factions operating within that State. Furthermore, the French troops were backed by a Chadian military contingent, to which other African military personnel were gradually added under the auspices of an SC-sanctioned African force.[90] When taken as a whole, this instance of 'intervention by invitation' was undoubtedly lawful given that, on one hand, the Malian authorities had formulated a legally valid request for such intervention and, on the other, the stated purpose of the campaign was to stamp out a pressing global security threat: terrorism. Furthermore, the SC's decision-making no doubt legitimized the French-led action in Mali, particularly in light of the fact that the UN political organ characterized the subversive factions as 'terrorist groups/organizations'.[91] In fact, three years later, the Council '[w]elcom[ed] the continued action by the French forces, at the request of the Malian authorities, to deter the terrorist threats in the North of Mali'.[92] More importantly, this scenario presented interesting features for present purposes: at the outset, it must be pondered whether Mali attenuated its potential international responsibility—for example, in the event that terrorist factions ultimately launched transnational attacks from Mali into another territory—by accepting outside assistance in thwarting a global security threat it could not control adequately.[93] It is also interesting that the relevant SC resolution is replete with language compatible with SR—particularly oblique references to responsibility to protect (R2P) in respect of Malian authorities and the terrorist threats they faced[94]—which further supports the rapprochement between SR and the action of UN organs, as thoroughly explored in Part II of this book. Similarly, in July

[89] See, eg, N Quénivet, 'You Are the Weakest Link and We Will Help You! The Comprehensive Strategy of the United Nations to Fight Terrorism' (2006) 11 JCSL 371, 390–1; KN Trapp, 'Back to Basics: Necessity, Proportionality, and the Right of Self-Defence against Non-State Terrorist Actors' (2007) 56 ICLQ 141, 147 fn 33.

[90] See UNSC Res 2085 (20 December 2012) UN Doc S/RES/2085.

[91] See, eg, SC Res 2085 (n 90) preamble, [2], [7], [9(b)], [14]. On the legality of this intervention by invitation in the counterterrorism context, see T Christakis and K Bannelier, 'Under the UN Security Council's Watchful Eyes: Military Intervention by Invitation in the Malian Conflict' (2013) 26 LJIL 855.

[92] UNSC Res 2227 (29 June 2015) UN Doc S/RES/2227, preamble.

[93] See, eg, Proulx (n 11) 288.

[94] See, eg, SC Res 2085 (n 90) [9(d)], [17].

2015, Turkey persuaded the US to use its southern airbases in order to launch air-strikes to combat Islamic State of Iraq and the Levant (ISIL) militants along the Syrian border,[95] a decision which could assuage Turkey's potential responsibility and increase its due diligence capital under SR law.

One commentator aptly captures the legal and factual incongruities that may flow from the conflation of SR and use of force repertoire, against the backdrop of polymorphous, transnational, and global security threats: '[i]n the fight against international terrorism the most intrinsic problems of justification of the use of force and State responsibility under international law arise when a State has recourse to forcible measures in the territory of another State without its prior consent'.[96] Thus, academic and political resistance to recent US counterterrorism practice would tend to indicate that there is insufficient State practice and *opinio juris* to support the consecration of the 'unwilling or unable' doctrine in international law. Much of the confusion surrounding this allegedly novel 'doctrine' stems from the fact that 'attribution' remains a normative operation used to trigger both SR and recourse to force repertoire. In many ways, the ICJ's *Nicaragua* decision further perpetuated the conceptual ambiguity surrounding the operation of attribution, particularly in cases of SR for the wrongful use of force.[97]

Whilst compelling arguments support all three strands of scholarship, it has been suggested that '[a]n examination of the decisions of the ICJ, State practice and *opinio juris* will reveal that the most accurate view is that the attribution threshold is now the provision to the attackers of sanctuary and support'.[98] Ultimately, determining both that global security duties have been violated and the modalities governing the engagement of secondary norms remains largely dependent on a factual and context-sensitive analysis of State failures to prevent terrorism and other similarly harmful activities.

1.4 Conclusion: The Evolution of State Practice and *Opinio Juris*

There is rich State and institutional practice, both before and after 9/11, recognizing an injured State's right to pursue terrorists into a neighbouring country, though such reactions have not always been framed unequivocally within SR

[95] See, eg, S Tisdall, 'Syrian Safe Zone: US Relents to Turkish Demands after Border Crisis Grows' *The Guardian* (London, 27 July 2015) <www.theguardian.com/world/2015/jul/27/syrian-safe-zone-us-relents-to-turkish-demands-border-crisis-kurd-uk-military> accessed 12 August 2015; 'US Deal with Turkey over ISIS May Go beyond Simple Use of an Airbase' *The Guardian* (London, 24 July 2015) <www.theguardian.com/world/2015/jul/24/us-deal-turkey-isis-incirlik-airbase-erdogan-obama> accessed 12 August 2015.

[96] J Bóka, 'Forcible Measures against International Terrorism and the Rule of Law' <http://www.uni-miskolc.hu/uni/res/e_publications/pdf/boka.pdf> accessed 2 August 2015.

[97] See, eg, Section 1.3, this chapter.

[98] Brent (n 74) 136. On how the threshold of attribution and control under the ARSIWA might have been lowered, see generally Proulx (n 11).

repertoire (ie countermeasures).[99] Foreshadowing the inquiry unfolded in Part III of this book, Thomas Franck hinted at the inherent compatibility between SR and recourse to force in the year following 9/11. He stated: '[i]t is becoming clear that a victim-state may invoke Article 51 [of the UN Charter] to take *armed countermeasures* in accordance with international law and UN practice against any territory *harboring, supporting or tolerating* activities that culminate in, or are likely to give rise to, insurgent infiltrations or terrorist attack' (emphasis added).[100] Consequently, through the lens of the 'harbouring or supporting' terrorism paradigm, injured States have exercised this right, which remains inextricably linked to SR repertoire because it invariably rests upon prior wrongdoing by the targeted State (ie failures to prevent terrorist strikes, extradite, or punish, suppress terrorist fundraising, etc). Pre-9/11 State practice also supported similar responses, although perhaps not as explicitly as nowadays: Senegal set foot in Guinea-Bissau both in 1992 and 1995 'to strike at safe havens used as bases by opposition forces';[101] 'Tajikistan pursued irregulars into Afghanistan';[102] and the US bombed parts of the Sudan and Afghanistan, following the 1998 attacks on US embassies in Tanzania and Kenya, although this action was initially met with criticism in non-UN fora.[103]

Moreover, by authorizing use of force against the Taliban and Afghanistan after 9/11, the SC might have further reinforced the emergence of a new precedent in SR law (whilst also straddling recourse to force repertoire). Indeed, '[t]he traditionalist position that the right to self-defense under Article 51 of the Charter of the United Nations requires an armed attack by a State has come under increasing challenge in the recent past'.[104] Whilst it now seems acceptable that injured States respond with force against non-State terrorist attacks,[105] the implications of this evolution in State practice for the application of attribution principles (and secondary SR norms, more broadly) remains unclear. It is to be hoped that these implications will come into greater focus in subsequent chapters of this book.

[99] For a survey of relevant practice, see Proulx (n 11) ch 2. At the outset, it is important to emphasize that States often frame their reactions in terms of self-defence even though their conduct might also be compatible with the spirit of countermeasures. Traditionally, however, self-defence was conceived as a regime distinct from SR repertoire, although it has been incorporated into the ILC's codification project as a circumstance precluding wrongfulness. See ARSIWA (n 2) Art 21. These issues will be explored in Part III.

[100] TM Franck, *Recourse to Force: State Action Against Threats and Armed Attacks* (CUP 2002) 67.

[101] Franck (n 100) 65. See also C Gray, *International Law and the Use of Force* (OUP 2000) 103.

[102] Franck (n 100) 64.

[103] See, eg, Franck (n 100) 66.

[104] JT Gathii, 'Irregular Forces and Self-Defense under the UN Charter' in ME O'Connell (ed.), *What Is War? An Investigation in the Wake of 9/11* (Brill 2012) 97 (citing works by Proulx, Jinks, and Ruys and Verhoeven).

[105] See also R Van Steenberghe, 'Self-Defence in Response to Attacks by Non-State Actors in the Light of Recent State Practice: A Step Forward?' (2010) 23 LJIL 183.

2

State Responsibility and Global Security in the Light of Unforeseen Transnational Phenomena

2.1 Introduction

This chapter briefly addresses some of the challenges in applying State responsibility (SR) mechanisms to transnational threats not foreseen at the time the United Nations (UN) Charter was drafted. The world is now faced with exceedingly intractable threats which have cropped up against the backdrop of novel or expanded conceptions of both 'international community' and global security. As prefaced earlier, the principal case study for gauging the potential contributions of institutionalized SR remains transnational terrorism. It is certainly true that present-day terrorism is polymorphous and rarely takes root in bilateral, transborder armed conflict, as was the case with many terrorist excursions in the 1960s, 1970s, and 1980s. Supplanting that model in the 1990s and early 2000s was the cellular structure-orchestrated, large-scale attack type of terrorism which stemmed from the emergence of transnational terrorist networks such as Al-Qaeda. This type of terrorism resulted in several terrorist strikes, including the New York 9/11, London 7/7, Bali, and Madrid attacks. The ensuing 'war' on terror offered considerable media coverage to transnational terrorist networks, thereby enhancing the status of subversive non-State actors on the international scene,[1] a trend that continues today.

However, more recently we have also witnessed a recrudescence of 'lone wolf' and 'home-grown' terrorist plots resulting in attacks, often unsophisticated in nature and directed at soft targets, in Australia, Belgium, Canada, Chad, Denmark, France, Kenya, Lebanon, Malaysia, Mali, Nigeria, Norway, Thailand,

[1] See ME O'Connell, 'Enhancing the Status of Non-State Actors through a Global War on Terror?' (2005) 43 CJTL 435. Even today, some transnational terrorist groups carry out large-scale attacks such as exploding aircrafts. For example, on 31 October 2015 Islamic State of Iraq and the Levant (ISIL) militants destroyed a Russian airliner over the Sinai desert. See, eg, G Topham *et al.*, 'Egypt Plane Crash: Russia Says Jet Was Bombed in Terror Attack' *The Guardian* (London, 17 November 2015). This incident was condemned and ultimately attributed to ISIL by the UN Security Council (SC). See UNSC Res 2249 (20 November 2015) UN Doc S/RES/2249 [1] (also lamenting recent attacks carried out in Sousse, Ankara, Beirut, and Paris). On the role of SR in addressing the conduct of non-State actors, see C Ryngaert, 'State Responsibility and Non-State Actors' in M Noortmann *et al.* (eds), *Non-State Actors in International Law* (Hart 2015) 163.

the United Kingdom, the United States, and elsewhere. These developments have propelled to the fore the need to harness available legal and policy options with a view to preventing such practices, even including bolstering domestic criminal legal regimes.[2] That said, it will become apparent in subsequent sections of this book that SR law and other international legal mechanisms can also play a role in global security strategies. In particular, many other transnational terrorist networks are still very much active in various parts of the globe, including Al-Qaeda, Harakat al-Shabaab al-Mujahideen, and Abu Sayyaf. Such entities often capitalize on territorial solace, weak counterterrorism structures, and governmental toleration. Many terrorist organizations are increasingly gaining access to new and devastating weaponry and making profitable use of virtual social network platforms. In particular, the world has witnessed the creation and horrendous activities of Islamic State of Iraq and the Levant (ISIL) in Iraq, Syria, and Libya, which are increasingly attracting scholarly attention,[3] with some calling into question the potential benefits of counterterrorism strategies in forestalling this particular threat.[4] Moreover, the group's reach and influence are expanding across the globe with, for example, the leaderships of several groups, such as Boko Haram in Nigeria and Abu Sayyaf in Southeast Asia, swearing allegiance to ISIL. ISIL reciprocates by assisting some terrorists groups with their video propaganda activities and funding or supporting others, such as the Libyan group Ansar al-Sharia and Ansar Beit al-Maqdis in the Sinai Peninsula.[5]

This chapter investigates the problematic question of State support of terrorism with some consideration of how a sanctuary State's tacit support, toleration, acquiescence, or logistical support of terrorism, which all contribute to its violation of the obligation to prevent, may affect the deployment of secondary norms

[2] See generally R Spaaij and MS Hamm, 'Key Issues and Research Agendas in Lone Wolf Terrorism' (2015) 38 SCT 167; J McCoy and WA Knight, 'Homegrown Terrorism in Canada: Local Patterns, Global Trends' (2015) 38 SCT 253; H Fenwick, 'Redefining the Role of TPIMs in Combating "Home-Grown" Terrorism within the Widening Counter-Terror Framework' (2015) 1 European Human Rights Law Review 41; M Becker 'Explaining Lone Wolf Target Selection in the United States' (2014) 37 SCT 959; C Appleton, 'Lone Wolf Terrorism in Norway' (2014) The International Journal of Human Rights 127; R Spaaij, *Understanding Lone Wolf Terrorism: Global Patterns, Motivations and Prevention* (Springer 2012); SM Kleinmann, 'Radicalization of Homegrown Sunni Militants in the United States: Comparing Converts and Non-converts' (2012) 35 SCT 278; K Coffey, 'The Lone Wolf–Solo Terrorism and the Challenge of Preventative Prosecution' (2011) 7 FIU Law Review 1; R Spaaij, 'The Enigma of Lone Wolf Terrorism: An Assessment' (2010) 33 SCT 845.

[3] See P Cockburn, *The Jihadis Return: ISIS and the New Sunni Uprising* (OR Books 2014); JA Sekulow *et al.*, *Rise of ISIS: A Threat we Can't Ignore* (Howard Books 2014); V Cheterian, 'ISIS and the Killing Fields of the Middle East' (2015) 57 Global Politics and Strategy 105; D Holbrook, 'Al-Qaeda and the Rise of ISIS' (2015) 57 Global Politics and Strategy 93; I Kfir, 'Social Identity Group and Human (In)Security: The Case of the Islamic State in Iraq and the Levant (ISIL)' (2015) 38 SCT 233; G Stansfield, 'The Islamic State, the Kurdistan Region and the Future of Iraq: Assessing UK Policy Options' (2014) 90 International Affairs 1329.

[4] See, eg, AK Cronin, 'ISIS Is Not a Terrorist Group: Why Counterterrorism Won't Stop the Latest Jihadist Threat' (2015) 2 FA 87.

[5] See, eg, MR Gordon and E Schmitt, 'Coalition Debates Expanding ISIS Fight' *NYT* (New York, 30 April 2015) A11.

under SR repertoire. Given the conclusions in Sections 1.3 and 1.4 in the previous chapter, and to provide a frame for subsequent arguments, particularly in Part III, the chapter then moves on to an exploration of how recent events, particularly the response to 9/11, have effectively merged or conflated certain aspects of SR with use of force repertoire. Stepping away from the principal case study of terrorism, the chapter concludes by analysing briefly the prospects and limits of SR in tackling other global security threats whilst engaging the notions of risk assessment and precautionary approaches.

2.2 The Problem of State Support of Terrorism

The obligation incumbent upon all States to prevent terrorist attacks emanating from their territory can be derived from several international instruments, texts, rules, and principles.[6] In fact, this obligation and its ancillary duties pre-dated 9/11. For example, States have an obligation to prevent the perpetration and financing of terrorism, particularly terrorist hijackings under the Hague Convention of 1971.[7] States also have international legal obligations to prosecute and/or extradite the authors of terrorist acts, pursuant to various multilateral conventions.[8] In fact, scholars have interpreted the provisions of extradition treaties and mutual judicial assistance agreements as fundamental obligations to combat and prevent terrorism for the purposes of triggering SR.[9]

More importantly, through Resolution 1373, the UN Security Council (UNSC) promulgated a general and distinct obligation to prevent transnational terrorism. This autonomous duty, which was described by some in the wake of 9/11 as the new *de minimis* legal basis in global counterterrorism, encompasses both active and passive State support, along with all other types of conceivable assistance to individuals, organizations, or other groups engaged in terrorist activities, ranging from economic to logistical support.[10] The principal polemic as regards

[6] Although other sources also ground this obligation, it can be derived from the *Trail Smelter Case (USA v Canada)* (1941) 3 RIAA 1905; *Corfu Channel (UK v Albania)* (Merits) [1949] ICJ Rep 4, 22. For a pre-UN Charter formulation of this duty, see also C Eagleton, *The Responsibility of States in International Law* (NYU Press 1928) 80. For a fuller discussion, see also V-J Proulx, *Transnational Terrorism and State Accountability: A New Theory of Prevention* (Hart 2012) 18–30.

[7] See, eg, J-M Sorel, 'Some Questions About the Definition of Terrorism and the Fight against Its Financing' (2003) 14 EJIL 365.

[8] See generally DF Vagts, 'Which Courts Should Try Persons Accused of Terrorism?' (2003) 14 EJIL 313.

[9] See, eg, MC Bassiouni, 'International Terrorism' in idem (ed.), *International Terrorism and Political Crimes* (Charles C Thomas 1975) 500–93; WA Kerstetter, 'Practical Problems of Law Enforcement' in AE Evans and JF Murphy (eds), *Legal Aspects of International Terrorism* (Heath 1978) 535–49; JF Murphy, 'Legal Controls and the Deterrence of Terrorism: Performance and Prospects' (1982) 13 Rutgers Law Journal 465, 477. The prescriptions of Resolution 1373 also include a prohibition on providing protection to terrorists. See WP Hoye, 'Fighting Fire with ... Mire? Civil Remedies and the New War on State-Sponsored Terrorism' (2002) 12 Duke Journal of Comparative & International Law 105, 106.

[10] J-C Martin, *Les Règles Internationales Relatives à la Lutte contre le Terrorisme* (Bruylant 2006) 457. Calling into question whether 'control' over non-State actors, which underpins attribution

this duty for SR purposes pertains to its actual content insofar as the facts surrounding a particular breach may or may not justify a response involving force. This is particularly true given the vast range of State passivity, inaction, or 'wilful blindness' vis-à-vis terrorist activities taking root on any given territory.[11] Hence, State toleration of terrorism, particularly the more subtle kinds, will pose considerable challenges to the implementation of SR by UN organs in global security contexts, not least because it is often difficult to attribute the acts of non-State actors to the State from a factual standpoint. As a corollary, this reality may create serious evidentiary impediments to establishing a persuasive case of SR, even in instances where a would-be responsible State could have done more to prevent a given terrorist attack. These ideas were very much alive in a thought-provoking article published in 1989 in which Antonio Cassese identified the 'varying degrees of support or backing which may be given by a State to terrorist groups'.[12]

Amongst possible scenarios, he identified six highly relevant levels of governmental input or involvement in the facilitation of terrorist acts, which in turn may directly affect the establishment and implementation of SR, along with the application of secondary norms of responsibility and/or available remedies. In particular, Cassese explored the possibility of a State: (i) committing terrorist acts through actual State officials (citing the examples of the assassination of Khalil al-Wazir allegedly carried out by Israeli security forces in 1988, and the attack on the Greenpeace ship, *Rainbow Warrior*, by French secret service agents in 1985); (ii) employing, funding, equipping, organizing, controlling, and commanding unofficial agents, mercenaries, or armed bands in the perpetration of terrorist attacks; (iii) supplying financial or military aid to terrorist groups, which remain 'independent' from the official State apparatus; (iv) simply supplying logistical support to terrorist organizations (ie providing training facilities on its territory, which may arguably be analogous to Afghanistan's role in the 9/11 attacks); (v) not providing any sort of 'active' or 'direct' assistance to terrorist organizations (eg aid, arms, etc) but simply allowing them to seek refuge or solace on its territory before and after the perpetration of terrorist attacks against third States; and (vi) not

logic in the ARSIWA, remains an appropriate standard to gauge governmental toleration and/or passive support of terrorists, some ponder whether every State now has a duty to warn other potentially affected States if it 'possesses information about the existence of a terrorist cell on its territory without having sufficient proof for legal action against its members but suspects that the cell is part of a network which targets other States and uses the territory as an operational base'. See K Zemanek, 'Does the Prospect of Incurring Responsibility Improve the Observance of International Law' in M Ragazzi (ed.), *International Responsibility Today: Essays in Memory of Oscar Schachter* (Brill 2005) 125, 131.

11 See also RP Barnidge, Jr, *Non-State Actors and Terrorism: Applying the Law of State Responsibility and the Due Diligence Principle* (TMC Asser Press 2008) 145–6 fn 44; CM Henderson, 'Michael Byers, War Law: International Law and Armed Conflict' (2007) 12 JCSL 150, 152–3. On the notions of 'sponsorship' and 'support' of terrorism, see SC Malzahn, 'State Sponsorship and Support of International Terrorism: Customary Norms of State Responsibility' (2002) 26 Hastings International and Comparative Law Review 83.

12 A Cassese, 'The International Community's "Legal" Responses to Terrorism' (1989) 38 ICLQ 589, 597.

providing any assistance whatsoever (ie direct, indirect, passive, active) to terrorist organizations perpetrating terrorist acts on the high seas or in international airspace against nationals of one or more States.[13] Unsurprisingly, legal scholars have followed suit in the intervening decades by proposing new or updated schematic typologies for State support of terrorism, taking into account contemporaneous developments.[14] As will be seen in subsequent sections of this chapter, however, Cassese's typology holds true today.

The facts surrounding the military campaign in Afghanistan were somewhat novel and complex in character, given that the 9/11 attacks were orchestrated and perpetrated entirely by non-State actors. International law could not endorse a US-led 'war'[15] in Afghanistan solely against bin Laden and high-ranking members of Al-Qaeda because a terrorist organization simply does not constitute a State.[16] Understandably, the US-led response against Afghanistan, along with the broader fight against terrorism, prompted some publicists to query whether such military action could qualify as legitimate self-defence since it was initially difficult to attribute the 9/11 attacks to Afghanistan under classical SR rules.[17] As one commentator observed, '[i]t remains to be seen whether such limited understanding of self-defense would stand the test of time in an age where transnational actors beyond the nation-state, whether terrorist or not, gain ever more factual and legal significance'.[18]

Indeed, modest or passive State involvement in terrorism poses intractable challenges to SR repertoire, be they evidentiary, compensatory, or related to the mechanics of that normative scheme.[19] Moreover, clear-cut cases of direct

[13] Cassese (n 12) 598.

[14] Compare with the respective typologies suggested by the following authors: JA Cohan, 'Formulation of a State's Response to Terrorism and State-sponsored Terrorism' (2002) 14 Pace International Law Review 77, 90–2; Martin (n 10) 457–8; N Lubell, *Extraterritorial Use of Force against Non-State Actors* (OUP 2010) 36–8; Proulx (n 6) 34–50; G Guillaume, 'Terrorisme et Droit International' (1989) 215 RdC 287, 396.

[15] Consider G Battaglini, 'War against Terrorism *Extra Moenia*, Self-Defence and Responsibility: A Pure Juridical Approach' in Ragazzi (n 10) 139.

[16] On this specific question vis-à-vis terrorist organizations, see P-M Dupuy, 'State Sponsors of Terrorism: Issues of International Responsibility' in A Bianchi (ed.), *Enforcing International Law Norms against Terrorism* (Hart 2004) 3, 6–7. Some commentators expounded that the US could not wage war against members of Al-Qaeda. See, eg, JJ Paust, 'War and Enemy Status After 9/11: Attacks on the Laws of War' (2003) 28 YJIL 325, 326 and 'Post-9/11 Overreaction and Fallacies Regarding War and Defense, Guantanamo, the Status of Persons, Treatment, Judicial Review of Detention, and Due Process in Military Commissions' (2004) 79 Notre Dame Law Review 1335, 1344. Incidentally, the validity of the traditional view that only sovereign States can be targeted in self-defence against terrorism is explored in Chapter 6.

[17] See, eg, S Wiessner, 'The Articles on State Responsibility and Contemporary International Law' in KK Koufa (ed.), *Thesaurus Acroasium Vol 34: State Responsibility and the Individual* (Sakkoulas 2006) 246, 260. Compare WH Taft IV and TF Buchwald, 'Agora: Future Implications of the Iraq Conflict: Preemption, Iraq, and International Law' (2003) 97 AJIL 557. See also WM Reisman, 'Assessing Claims to Revise the Laws of War' (2003) 97 AJIL 82.

[18] Wiessner (n 17) 260.

[19] See also Section 1.3. Moreover, certain types of terrorism, particularly cyberterrorism, may further obfuscate evidentiary standards and erect obstacles to the successful establishment of SR in respect of virtual wrongful conduct. See generally M Roscini, 'Evidentiary Issues in International

State involvement in unlawful guerrilla warfare or terrorism—whether waged through agency channels or surrogate paramilitary factions—appear to fit neatly within conventional SR frameworks, at least in theory. Yet, they are not routinely resolved under those schemes. In the prophetic words of Soviet jurist Professor Staroushenko in 1984, 'if a State proclaims terrorism as an instrument of its foreign policy, if the governmental authorities get involved in bringing about the criminal acts following, such activities became terrorist activities of a State'.[20] However, more elusive models, such as those envisioned in scenarios (iii)–(v) above, eschew straightforward application of SR mechanisms and warrant further exploration. Therefore, such conceptually and practically challenging circumstances should always act as a prism through which any reform of SR repertoire, including its potential implementation through UN organs as explored in Part II of this book, should be contemplated.

2.3 The Impact of 9/11: Conflation of Use of Force Repertoire with State Responsibility

As discussed elsewhere,[21] including in Section 1.4 of this book, international law has evolved to recognize an injured State's right to pursue terrorists into a neighbouring country under Article 51 of the UN Charter. The rationale behind this development is as follows: because injured States may now invoke the international responsibility of territorial States via the 'harbouring and supporting' principle (ie for failures to prevent terrorism), this legal scheme carries with it a potential right to adopt measures involving limited force or self-defence against transborder terrorism in the most extreme cases. Indeed, the SC has sometimes approved subsequent use of force by an injured State, judging that the responsible (territorial) State had failed to prevent a terrorist excursion emanating from its territory. Academic commentary has followed suit, with some eminent publicists recognizing the right to use force to counteract violations of international law in such instances. As Professor Franck noted, '[t]his clearly confirms the right of a victim state to treat terrorism as an armed attack and those that facilitate or harbor terrorists as armed attackers against whom, subject to the UN Charter and international law, military force may be used in self-defense'.[22]

Disputes Related to State Responsibility for Cyber Operations' (2015) 50 Texas International Law Journal 233.

[20] International Law Association, 'Report of the Paris Reunion' (1984) 168–9, cited in E McWhinney, *The September 11 Terrorist Attacks and the Invasion of Iraq in Contemporary International Law: Opinions and the Emerging New World Order System* (Nijhoff 2004) 29.

[21] For a review of relevant State and institutional practice, see generally Proulx (n 6) esp ch 2.

[22] TM Franck, *Recourse to Force: State Action Against Threats and Armed Attacks* (CUP 2002) 54. This phenomenon had somewhat been recognized before 9/11. See, eg, MB Baker, 'Terrorism and the Inherent Right of Self-Defense (A Call to Amend Article 51 of the United Nations Charter)' (1987) 10 HJIL 25, 40. See also RJ Beck and AC Arend, '"Don't Tread on Us": International Law and Forcible State Responses to Terrorism' (1994) 12 Wisconsin International Law Journal 153; WA

As will be seen in Part III of this book, the conceptual challenge lies in elucidating to what extent SR law plays a role in facilitating such recourses to force, especially in the more difficult cases where State involvement in terrorism amounts to tacit acquiescence or mere toleration, or is virtually imperceptible, or so indecipherable as to elude the application of classical attribution rules. In fact, the juxtaposition of these two distinct legal regimes[23] was very much at play in the *Armed Activities* case, in which the International Court of Justice (ICJ) concluded that Uganda could not invoke a right to self-defence against the Democratic Republic of Congo (DRC) because it had harboured an armed militia on its territory.[24] This line of inquiry takes us back to a vital query which remains inextricably intertwined with the scheme of countermeasures under SR repertoire: when a State is unable or unwilling to thwart terrorist strikes emanating from its territory, should we expect it to allow extraneous forces on its soil to repel and contain the threat? Surely, the deployment of law enforcement units across that State's border with a view to neutralizing the extremist elements would be permissible in such case,[25] and has been rightly envisaged as a proportionate countermeasure under SR repertoire.[26] However, the more challenging question remains whether a victim-State might be permitted to adopt more ambitious forcible countermeasures in such eventuality, including responses grounded in self-defence.

An affirmative answer to this question on the basis of proportionality and reasonableness, perhaps paired with the proximity of the UN Headquarters to

O'Brien, 'Reprisals, Deterrence and Self-Defense in Counter Terror Operations' (1990) 30 VJIL 421; O Schachter, 'The Extraterritorial Use of Force Against Terrorist Bases' (1989) 11 HJIL 309; O Schachter, 'The Lawful Use of Force by a State against Terrorists in Another Country' in HH Han (ed.), *Terrorism & Political Violence: Limits & Possibilities of Legal Control* (Oceana 1993) 241–66.

[23] But see I Brownlie, *System of the Law of Nations: State Responsibility (Part I)* (Clarendon Press 1983) 375 (stressing that both regimes should not be conflated).

[24] *Armed Activities on the Territory of the Congo (DRC v Uganda)* (Merits) [2005] ICJ Rep 168, 219–21 [131]–[136], 222–3 [146]–[147]. See also TM Franck, 'On Proportionality of Countermeasures in International Law' (2008) 102 AJIL 715, 722 (observing that the majority 'could have replaced the question of attribution with a finding of liability of states for injurious effects emanating from their territory and affecting the rights of neighboring states'). On the treatment of self-defence in that case, see SA Barbour and ZA Salzman, '"The Tangled Web": The Right of Self-Defense against Non-State Actors in the Armed Activities Case' (2008) 40 NYUJILP 53. See also Section 6.2.3 of this book.

[25] Several accounts concede that a State allowing its territory to become a launch pad for terrorism may forfeit its right to sovereignty in various contexts and, correspondingly, is entitled to solicit outside intervention to neutralize the threat. See Baker (n 22) 40; PS Rao, 'International Crimes and State Responsibility' in M Ragazzi (n 10) 68. See also M Byers, 'Letting the Exception Prove the Rule' (2003) 17 Ethics and International Affairs <http://vlex.com/vid/letting-the-exception-prove-rule-53214923> accessed 10 August 2015. It should also be reiterated that 'Security Council resolutions post September 11, asserted a duty on UN member states to deny safe haven to terrorists and to bring them to justice'. See H Duffy, *The 'War on Terror' and the Framework of International Law* (CUP 2005) 493. As a corollary, Resolution 1373 may actually enable States to use defensive force against non-State actors on a theory of 'indirect attribution', should the territorial State be unable to contain or repress the terrorist threat. See Section 4.2.1, this book. On related issues, see RL Johnstone, 'State Responsibility: A Concerto for Court, Council and Committee' (2008) 37 Denver Journal of International Law and Policy 63.

[26] See, eg, Martin (n 10) 493.

the 9/11 attack sites, might have been the driving force behind the approval of US-led military action in Afghanistan. However, the response to 9/11, coupled with the accompanying political rhetoric, further obfuscated the conceptual and practical distinctions underpinning the proper interplay between self-defence and SR in counterterrorism contexts. Whilst the US initially framed its rhetoric within a programme seeking to hold individual terrorists accountable,[27] what was sometimes perceived as a 'secondary goal'[28] cropped up in this counterterrorism campaign and shifted the focal point squarely to holding States accountable for providing assistance or solace to terrorist groups.[29] In summary, whilst it was clear that the US was pursuing both individuals and States responsible for perpetrating or aiding and abetting terrorism, the actual targets of its action in self-defence—and the legal basis for adopting such posture—were not as clear.[30]

Granted, it might sometimes be possible to conclude that the actions of non-State actors amount to the acts of the government itself, as though committed through a prolongation of the State (ie direct SR), thereby fulfilling classical attribution criteria explored in Section 1.3 of this book. This threshold might be more easily traversed where the non-armed wing of a terrorist organization has been subsumed under the State's official governing apparatus (eg Hezbollah in Lebanon).[31] However, the relationship that connected Afghanistan with Al-Qaeda prior to 9/11 arguably fell short in triggering any of the bases for attributing that organization's

[27] See, eg, GW Bush, 'Address Before a Joint Session of the Congress on the United States Response to the Terrorist Attacks of September 11' in 'America's Ordeal: "Our Grief Has Turned to Anger"' *Newsday* (Melville, 21 September 2002) A2; T Blair, 'Why Saddam Is Still a Threat to Britain' *Daily Express* (London, 6 March 2002) 12; J Sullivan, 'Why War Against Terrorism Is Justified' *Financial Gazette* (Harare, 1 November 2001).

[28] See, eg, SE Smith, 'International Law: Blaming Big Brother: Holding States Accountable for the Devastation of Terrorism' (2003) 56 Oklahoma Law Review 735, 736.

[29] See, eg, J Diamond, 'Powell Sets Terms for a New Regime' *Chicago Tribune* (Chicago, 25 October 2011) 6; US National Security Council, *The National Security Strategy of the United States of America* (17 September 2002) <www.state.gov/documents/organization/63562.pdf> accessed 30 April 2015, 6, 13–16; JM Vogelson, 'Multinational Approaches to Eradicating International Terrorism' (2002) 36 International Lawyer 67, 70. But see M Levitt, 'Patterns of Terrorism 2002: Terror, Counterterror, and State Sponsorship' (30 April 2003) Washington Institute for Near East Policy <www.thewashingtoninstitute.org/templateC05.php?CID=1631> accessed 30 May 2015.

[30] This critique keeps in line with post-9/11 scholarly accounts suggesting that we were 'confronting a confusion of international legal norms that threatens to undermine constraints on the use of force in international society'. See J Brunnée and SJ Toope, 'Canada and the Use of Force: Reclaiming Human Security' (2004) 59 International Journal 247, 250 who were particularly vocal about the US merging analytically distinct international legal categories, such as human rights, refugee protection, and threats to peace and security under a single, overriding threat pre-emption model.

[31] See, eg, S Kirchner, 'Third Party Liability for Hezbollah Attacks against Israel' (2006) 7 German Law Journal 777, 780. See also C Bloom, 'The Classification of Hezbollah in Both International and Non-International Armed Conflicts' (2008) 14 Annual Survey of International and Comparative Law 61, 78–82; D Byman, 'Should Hezbollah Be Next?' (2003) 82 FA 54 and 'Hezbollah's Dilemma' (13 April 2005) (author's update) <www.foreignaffairs.com/articles/middle-east/2005-04-13/hezbollahs-dilemma> accessed 30 May 2015; J Slomich, 'The Ta'if Accord: Legalizing the Syrian Occupation of Lebanon' (1998–9) 22 Suffolk Transnational Law Review 619, 633.

wrongful conduct to the State, pursuant to Articles on Responsibility of States for Internationally Wrongful Acts (ARSIWA) Articles 4–11. In short, Afghanistan at best provided logistical support to the terrorist network, without endorsing its excursions or participating in the planning or execution of the 9/11 attacks, a level of involvement far removed from the criteria of control, direction, instructions, and interdependence underpinning the ARSIWA.[32] Whilst difficult to countenance from both legal and factual standpoints in the light of classical attribution precepts, several publicists nonetheless opined—at least implicitly—that a finding of direct SR against Afghanistan for the 9/11 attacks would have probably justified a military campaign against it, thereby conflating use of force and SR repertoires.[33] Going a step further, some authors even argued that the 'law of state responsibility now appear[ed] to include states that are aware of ongoing international terrorism in their territory and who fail to suppress it by refusing to arrest, prosecute, or extradite'; consequently, they observed that 'under this interpretation, acts of self-defense would be justified against not only Al-Qaeda, but the Taliban government of Afghanistan'.[34]

The US rhetoric after 9/11 was eventually substantiated by Congressional authorization to use force against Afghanistan[35] and any State aiding or harbouring terrorists involved in the 9/11 attacks in the following terms:

> [t]he President is authorized to use all necessary and appropriate force against those nations, organizations, or persons he determines planned, authorized, committed, or

[32] This line of argument was fully fleshed out in V-J Proulx, 'Babysitting Terrorists: Should States Be Strictly Liable for Failing to Prevent Transborder Attacks?' (2005) 23 BJIL 615. Moreover, the Taliban maintained that its refusal to extradite bin Laden rested on Muslim customs and did not amount to the adoption or endorsement of Al-Qaeda's cause. See, eg, KN Trapp, *State Responsibility for International Terrorism* (OUP 2011) 54.

[33] See, eg, A-M Slaughter and W Burke-White, 'An International Constitutional Moment' (2002) 43 HILJ 1, 19–21; M Byers, 'Terrorism, the Use of Force, and International Law after 11 September' (2001) 51 ICLQ 401, 405–10; MA Drumbl, 'Victimhood in Our Neighborhood: Terrorist Crime, Taliban Guilt, and the Asymmetries of the International Legal Order' (2002) 81 North Carolina Law Review 1, 34–5; M Sassòli, 'State Responsibility for Violations of International Humanitarian Law' (2002) 84 International Review of the Red Cross 401, 406–9; ME O'Connell, 'Evidence of Terror' (2002) 7 JCSL 19, 28–32. On the 'direct/indirect' responsibility distinction in counterterrorism contexts, see Section 5.2.4.

[34] JP Kelly, 'The International Law of Force and the Fight against Terrorism' (2003) 21 Delaware Lawyer 18, 19.

[35] The US and the international community have never recognized the Taliban as the legitimate government of Afghanistan. See, eg, UNSC Res 1193 (28 August 1998) UN Doc S/RES/1193, 1214 (8 December 1998) UN Doc S/RES/1214, 1267 (15 October 1999) UN Doc S/RES/1267, 1333 (19 December 2000) UN Doc S/RES/1333, 1363 (30 July 2001) UN Doc S/RES/1363. Based on these precedents and international law, it was difficult to justify, on legal grounds, the US-led strikes against Afghanistan. Some resolved this discrepancy by asserting that the Taliban was the de facto government of Afghanistan, irrespective of US or international perception. See, eg, D Brown, 'Use of Force against Terrorism after September 11th: State Responsibility, Self-Defense and Other Responses' (2003) 11 Cardozo Journal of International and Comparative Law 1, 6. Moreover, there is overwhelming evidence that the Taliban wielded de facto control over most of the region. See, eg, GH Aldrich, 'The Taliban, Al Qaeda, and the Determination of Illegal Combatants' (2002) 96 AJIL 891, 891, 893; RA Falk, *The Great Terror War* (Olive Branch Press 2003) 101; M Mofidi and AE Eckert, '"Unlawful Combatants" or "Prisoners of War": The Law and Politics of Labels' (2003) 36 CILJ 59, 81, 83–5.

aided the terrorist attacks that occurred on September 11, 2001, or harbored such organizations or persons, in order to prevent any future acts of international terrorism against the United State by such nations, organizations or persons.[36]

Moreover, as will be seen in Section 5.2.4 of this book, US-led military action in Afghanistan not only gathered significant support from the SC but also from other high-profile international and intergovernmental bodies. Whilst these developments were undoubtedly engendered by exceptional measures taken in light of extraordinary circumstances, they suggest, fifteen years later, an evolution in SR law, which could signal that secondary norms may trigger the application of recourse to force repertoire; more controversially, they hint at the emergence of a *lex specialis* according to which forcible responses—be they incremental or large-scale—might have become an available countermeasure to counteract the most extreme State failures to prevent terrorism.

Furthermore, by granting an authorization to use force against the Taliban and Afghanistan, at least implicitly, the SC seemingly reinforced the emergence of a new precedent in SR law (which happened to also straddle use of force repertoire). It must be queried whether this latter regime might in fact share an intimate—albeit limited—connection with the SR-derived notions of return to legality and cessation. Part III of this book addresses these questions in detail. The foregoing considerations also demonstrated that the law governing the application of SR principles to global security violations is very much in flux and might pose some challenges to the institutionalization of SR, especially through UN organs. Before moving on to more substantive SR implementation proposals in Part II of this book, it is helpful to review other global security challenges that may fall within this book's analytical purview.

2.4 Other Global Security Threats: The Limits of State Responsibility

Whilst transnational terrorism constitutes the principal case study used in this book, SR repertoire may also play a role in addressing other global security challenges. Indeed, the State and institutional practice canvassed in Part II, which investigates the institutionalization of SR through UN organs, pertains to the implementation of that normative scheme in other global security contexts alongside terrorism, including the non-proliferation of weapons of mass destruction (WMDs), international humanitarian law (IHL) violations, human rights abuses, unlawful use of force, etc. The collective security system has considerably expanded since the end of the Cold War and carved out both law enforcement and legislative functions for the SC which seem far removed from its attributions as originally envisaged. Consequently, the Council has been particularly active in

[36] Authorization for Use of Military Force, Public Law No 107–40, 115 Stat 224 (2001).

enforcing human rights and legislating on counterterrorism matters, although the latter exercise is arguably subject to legal, political, and practical limits.[37]

Moreover, the reform-oriented discourse advanced by the High-Level Panel on Threats, Challenges and Change in its report, titled 'A More Secure World: Our Shared Responsibility', carved out a proactive role for the SC in responding to non-military global security threats, including environmental degradation, terrorism, emerging and infectious diseases, nuclear proliferation, civil war, and poverty.[38] For example, the case can arguably be made that climate change constitutes a threat to global security, which might empower the SC to authorize use of force against States whose conduct contributes to this problem, although such interpretation remains controversial.[39] The purpose of this chapter is not to present a comprehensive survey of global security threats that share points of similarity with terrorism but rather to highlight some of the key challenges in institutionalizing the implementation of SR beyond counterterrorism. It is to be hoped that the core analytical focus of this study on terrorism will provide lessons and best practices in tackling other global security breaches. Thus, the remainder of this chapter investigates some of the more problematic aspects of institutionalized implementation in respect of other global security violations. As a corollary, it identifies some of the shortcomings of UN organs in this framework.

2.4.1 Environmental degradation, global warming, and climate change

It must be emphasized that transnational terrorism is akin to the global security threat of climate change, thereby warranting a truly transnational and resolute response.[40] At the very least, the legal struggle against terrorism calls for parallels to be drawn with transboundary pollution. Indeed, some studies addressing the role that SR can play in counterterrorism are replete with analogies extracted from the international environmental field, an exercise that proves helpful when attempting

[37] See, eg, V Gowlland-Debbas, 'The Security Council as Enforcer of Human Rights' in B Fassbender (ed.), *Securing Human Rights?: Achievements and Challenges of the UN Security Council* (OUP 2011) 36–73; LMH Martínez, 'The Legislative Role of the Security Council in its Fight against Terrorism: Legal, Political and Practical Limits' (2008) 57 ICLQ 333.

[38] UNGA 'Report of the High-level Panel on Threats, Challenges and Change: A More Secure World: Our Shared Responsibility' (2 December 2004) UN Doc A/59/565, paras 17–23. See also generally J Wolf, 'Responses to Nonmilitary Threats: Environment, Disease, and Technology' in PG Danchin and H Fischer (eds), *United Nations Reform and the New Collective Security* (CUP 2010) 173–92.

[39] See, eg, C Gray, 'Climate Change and the Law on the Use of Force' in R Rayfuse and SV Scott (eds), *International Law in the Era of Climate Change* (Edward Elgar 2012) 219, 229–35.

[40] In fact, some interlocutors opine that global warming poses a more pressing, and potentially more damaging, challenge to the global order than terrorism. Michael Bloomberg aptly summarized this position: '[t]errorists kill people, weapons of mass destruction have the potential to kill enormous numbers of people. Global warming, long-term, has the potential to kill everybody'. See B Avni, 'Mayor Compares Threat of Global Warming to Terrorism' *The New York Sun* (New York, 12 February 2008) <www.nysun.com/national/mayor-compares-threat-of-global-warming/71103/> accessed 30 May 2015.

to devise effective counterterrorism policies.[41] The International Law Commission (ILC) itself has taken account of environmental challenges in its codification projects, not only in respect of SR for internationally wrongful acts but also in the context of its work on liability for injurious consequences arising out of acts not prohibited by international law.[42] Unsurprisingly, legal scholars are increasingly registering their scholarly and interdisciplinary interests in devising workable prevention and containment models in respect of climate change. In such efforts, several commentators are turning to the benefits that may be derived from international law, generally, and the law governing SR specifically, to counteract climate change and global warming.[43] Similarly, many publicists have merged terrorism and environmental concerns—especially global warming and climate change—into one, integrated legal inquiry.[44] For example, in a widely discussed book, Richard Posner examined apocalyptic catastrophes 'that threaten the survival of the human race', thereby subsuming pandemics, nuclear fallout, terrorism, and irreversible environmental degradation under that rubric.[45]

If we are truly to analogize transnational terrorism to climate change, we must inevitably ponder whether SR repertoire is adequately suited to govern breaches of international law contributing to global warming and, correspondingly extend that rationale to counterterrorism. Certainly, this area of research is in full development, with scholars investigating the benefits that may be derived from SR law in tackling climate change, including under the Climate Change Regime.[46] Whilst SR might appear to be the international legal regime best suited to address some aspects of global warming, its invocation inexorably runs up against the

[41] See, eg, T Becker, *Terrorism and the State: Rethinking the Rules of State Responsibility* (Hart 2006) 57–62; Proulx (n 6) 18–30, 51, 92, 115–16, 138–9, 145–6, 162, 189, 192, 197, 218, 219–20, 224, 232–3, 254, 268, 270, 277–82, 290, 292, 299, 319. But see Becker (n 41) 263 (observing that the fields of 'human rights and environmental law' are to 'be regarded as qualitatively distinct from contemporary cases of terrorism'). On the intersection of SR repertoire and environmental protection, see also RM Bratspies, 'State Responsibility for Human-Induced Environmental Disasters' (2012) 55 GYIL 175.

[42] See, eg, the Draft Articles on prevention of transboundary harm from hazardous activities with commentaries in ILC, 'Report of the International Law Commission on the Work of its 53rd Session' (23 April–10 August 2001) UN Doc A/56/10, 146–70. On the consideration of environmental questions in the elaboration of the ILC's work on SR, see JJ Ruiz, 'Les Considérations Relatives à l'Environnement dans les Travaux de Codification sur la Responsabilité Internationale de l'État' in D Amirante *et al.* (eds), *Pour un Droit Commun de l'Environnement: Mélanges en l'Honneur de Michel Prieur* (Dalloz 2007) 181–205.

[43] See, eg, Rayfuse and Scott (n 39); M Hall, 'State Responsibility for the Adverse Impacts of Climate Change on Individuals: Assessing the Potential for an Interdisciplinary Approach' in SD Farrall *et al.* (eds), *Criminological and Legal Consequences of Climate Change* (Hart 2012) 215–40.

[44] See, eg, S Atapattu, 'Sustainable Development and Terrorism: International Linkages and a Case Study of Sri Lanka' (2006) 30 William & Mary Environmental Law & Policy Review 273; CR Sunstein, 'Irreversible and Catastrophic: Global Warming, Terrorism, and Other Problems' (2005–06) 23 Pace Environmental Law Review 3 and 'On the Divergent American Reactions to Terrorism and Climate Change' (2007) 107 Columbia Law Review 503, 515–6. Others espouse a criminal law-minded approach in tackling transnational pollution. See, eg, R White (ed.), *Transnational Environmental Crime* (Ashgate 2013).

[45] RA Posner, *Catastrophe: Risk and Response* (OUP 2004) 6, 21–91.

[46] See, eg, B Mayer, 'State Responsibility and Climate Change Governance: A Light through the Storm' (2014) 13 Chinese Journal of International Law 539; C Tomuschat, 'Global Warming and

problem of State consent. Hence, 'while state responsibility may theoretically be a more effective instrument to address global warming damages, particularly from the point of view of small developing countries, there is little hope that all states would agree to be bound by a regime of state responsibility.'[47] This concern can be easily transposed, at least upon first glance, to counterterrorism policy: many States, especially those that have weak counterterrorism structures, might not agree to sign on to a treaty embodying the disciplines of SR for failing to prevent transborder terrorism. However, this concern was considerably assuaged by post-9/11 SC resolution-making, which imposed categorical counterterrorism obligations upon *all* States.

It must be recalled that the extant scheme of SR constitutes the bare minimum, a sort of safety net in international relations: recalcitrant States may be hard-pressed to refute the customary character of the 'international breach–attribution–legal consequences' mechanism if they violate their obligation of prevention, be it related to counterterrorism or environmental protection. Furthermore, there is significant academic support for the idea that SR repertoire can be brought to bear upon the responses to global warming.[48] Even in 1991, influential scholarly voices opined that '[i]nternational practice shows that the States have now accepted a general principle that they must answer for environmental harm caused by activities they have carried out or allowed within their own territory or by activities that are under their control.'[49] In the more recent *Pulp Mills Case*, the ICJ echoed these observations and recognized the customary status of the duty to prevent transboundary environmental harm, linking it to States' obligation of due diligence: '[a] State is thus obliged to use all the means at its disposal in order to avoid activities which take place in its territory, or in any area under its jurisdiction, causing significant damage to the environment of another State.'[50]

State Responsibility' in H Hestermey *et al.* (eds), *Law of the Sea in Dialogue* (Springer 2011) 3–9; R Lefeber, 'Climate Change and State Responsibility' in Rayfuse and Scott (n 39) 321–49; RM Fernández Egea, 'State Responsibility for Environmental Harm "Revisited" within the Climate Change Regime' in S Maljean-Dubois and L Rajamani (eds), *Implementation of International Environmental Law* (Nijhoff 2011) 375–417.

[47] P Cullet, 'Liability and Redress for Human-Induced Global Warming: Towards and International Regime' (2007) 43A SJIL 99, 100. In ibid 107, Cuellet also frames the shortcomings of SR in terms of a lack of substantive development at the State level: 'the unwillingness of states to develop the law of state responsibility sufficiently means that it is unlikely to provide an effective tool to compensate for damages'.

[48] See, eg, R Verheyen, *Climate Change Damage and International Law: Prevention Duties and State Responsibility* (Nijhoff 2005) 225–32. For a more nuanced appraisal, see C Voigt, 'State Responsibility for Climate Change Damages' (2008) 77 NJIL 1. For an empirical assessment of both tort law/causal standards of obligations and strict liability regimes for climate change, see DA Weisbach, 'Responsibility for Climate Change, by the Numbers' (2009) <http://ssrn.com/abstract=1324857> accessed 30 May 2015.

[49] R Pisillio-Mazzeschi, 'Forms of International Responsibility for Environmental Harm' in F Francioni and T Scovazzi (eds), *International Responsibility for Environmental Harm* (Graham & Trotman 1991) 15–35.

[50] *Case Concerning Pulp Mills on the River Uruguay (Argentina v Uruguay)* (Merits) [2010] ICJ Rep 38, 55–6 [101] (also citing *Corfu Channel* (n 6) 22; *Legality of the Threat or Use of Nuclear Weapons* (Advisory Opinion) [1996] ICJ Rep 226, 242 [29]).

Despite these advances, considerable obstacles remain to making SR law a truly viable model to address climate change and related challenges. For one thing, climate change poses singular challenges in respect of international regulation. Consequently, careful attention has been paid to available policy options in enhancing the protection of the environment under specific international treaty regimes.[51] Furthermore, the reality on the ground is that many States often choose to exclude the application of SR principles for environmental damage by signing on to particular conventional or liability regimes, presumably to sidestep diplomatic problems stemming from the application of SR and State-to-State adjudication.[52] What is more, despite its centrality in international law, SR repertoire has not been resorted to in dealing with some of the most important environmental disasters of the last century.[53] But even starting from the premise that SR repertoire can play a role in addressing environmental global security threats, there is every indication that the potential implementation of that normative scheme outside inter-State contexts would run against institutional obstacles.

As argued in Part II, the SC can play a role, sometimes determinant, in implementing SR in respect of transnational terrorism. However, it is doubtful whether the rationale underpinning that line of inquiry would carry over seamlessly to environmental protection. As one publicist underscores, 'the Council is ill-prepared for new threats to international peace and security, in particular conflicts arising from environmental disasters, the scarcity of natural resources, including fresh water and grain, or large-scale migrations of people seeking a habitable climate'.[54] That said, the SC made some advances on this front in the past, in particular when it implemented Iraq's SR, declaring that Iraq was 'liable under international law' for 'environmental damage and the depletion of natural resources... as a result of Iraq's unlawful invasion and occupation of Kuwait'.[55] In the same resolution, the Council created the UN Compensation Commission (UNCC) to deal with mass claims arising out of Iraq's international responsibility, including in the environmental field. Indeed, the ILC's Commentary to ARSIWA Article 36 points out that '[c]ompensation claims for pollution costs have been dealt with by UNCC'.[56]

[51] See, eg, BJ Gareau, *From Precaution to Profit: Contemporary Challenges to Environmental Protection in the Montreal Protocol* (Yale University Press 2013).

[52] See, eg, A-C Kiss and D Shelton, *International Environmental Law* (3rd edn, Transnational 2004) 320; HW McGee, Jr, 'Litigating Global Warming: Substantive Law in Search of a Forum' (2005) 16 Fordham Environmental Law Review 371, 391.

[53] See the examples and references invoked in Proulx (n 6) 138.

[54] B Fassbender, 'The Security Council: Progress is Possible but Unlikely' in A Cassese (ed.), *Realizing Utopia: The Future of International Law* (OUP 2012) 52, 58. See also generally CK Penny, 'Greening the Security Council: Climate Change as an Emerging Threat to International Peace and Security' in *International Environmental Agreements: Politics, Law and Economics*, vol 7 (Kluwer 2007) 35–71.

[55] UNSC Res 687 (3 April 1991) UN Doc S/RES/687 [16]. On other aspects of this precedent, see Sections 4.4.3 and 4.5.1 of this book.

[56] Articles on the Responsibility of States for Internationally Wrongful Acts, UN Doc A/56/10 (2001); (2001) II(2) *YILC* 26 (and Commentary ibid 31) p 101 [14]. See also generally CR Payne and PH Sand (eds), *Gulf War Reparations and the UN Compensation Commission: Environmental Liability* (OUP 2011); PH Sand, 'Environmental Damage Claims from the 1991 Gulf War: State

For its part, the ICJ has not dealt with many environmental disputes aside from the *Pulp Mills* case, although it is increasingly seized of disagreements involving environmental issues and the conservation of living resources.[57] However, this UN organ remains significantly fettered by jurisdictional constraints, which are explored in Section 3.1.3.2 of this book. Besides, whilst, for instance, States have contracted conventional obligations to ensure that greenhouse gas emissions emanating from their soil do not engender transboundary harm, some of which are also mirrored in customary international law, there is a disconnect between contracted commitments and actual behaviour on the ground. In summary, States rather subscribe to a general attitude of 'irresponsible treatment of the global commons', which conflicts with their legal undertakings. The road to international litigation in addressing such problems, it is argued, is paved with considerable obstacles; even in the event that international litigation proves successful in tackling State-to-State environmental degradation, this avenue might adversely affect climate change (and other environmental) negotiations and dissuade States to enter into conventional environmental schemes in the first place.[58]

In many ways, SR law is ill-suited to tackle many of the global security threats related to the environment and protection/conservation of living resources. In a critical contribution, Catherine Redgwell astutely points out that SR repertoire constitutes the 'wrong trousers' in addressing violations of international environmental law before unfolding a comprehensive review of major obstacles to that prospect in various environmental sectors.[59] A few of the key obstacles identified warrant mention: the nature of international environmental law and/or the climate change regime, along with intrinsic difficulties in seeking redress under SR repertoire;[60] the existence of alternate avenues to the application of SR principles

Responsibility and Community Interests' in U Fastenrath *et al.* (eds), *From Bilateralism to Community Interest: Essays in Honour of Judge Bruno Simma* (OUP 2011) 1241–61. For further discussion on SC Res 687 (n 55) and related implications for the implementation of SR, see Sections 4.4.3 and 4.5.1, this book.

[57] See, eg, *Aerial Herbicide Spraying (Ecuador v Colombia)* (Removal from List) [2013] ICJ Rep 278 (which was stricken from the ICJ's General List before being heard on the merits, in light of an agreement between the parties); the joined proceedings in *Construction of a Road in Costa Rica along the San Juan River (Nicaragua v Costa Rica)* (Joinder) [2013] ICJ Rep 184 and *Certain Activities Carried Out by Nicaragua in the Border Area (Costa Rica v Nicaragua)* (Joinder) [2013] ICJ Rep 166.

[58] DH Cole, 'The Problem of Shared Irresponsibility in International Climate Law' in A Nollkaemper and D Jacobs (eds), *Distribution of Responsibilities in International Law* (CUP 2015) ch 10. See also generally T Stephens, 'International Environmental Disputes: To Sue or Not to Sue?' in N Klein (ed.), *Litigating International Law Disputes: Weighing the Balance* (CUP 2014) 284–304. As a result, there has been a corresponding increase in domestic litigation, particularly to tackle greenhouse gas emitting operations, to palliate the lack of robust international regulation and enforcement. See generally R Lord *et al.* (eds), *Climate Change Liability: Transnational Law and Practice* (CUP 2012); WCG Burns and HM Osofsky (eds), *Adjudicating Climate Change: State, National and International Approaches* (CUP 2009).

[59] C Redgwell, 'The Wrong Trousers: State Responsibility and International Environmental Law' in P Koutrakos and M Evans (eds), *The International Responsibility of the European Union: European and International Perspectives* (Hart 2013) 257–74 (and authorities cited therein).

[60] See also A Nollkaemper, 'Compliance Control in International Environmental Law: Traversing the Limits of the National Legal Order' (2002) 13 YIEL 165, 186; M Fitzmaurice, 'Responsibility and Climate Change' (2010) 53 GYIL 89, 137. On the difficulty of quantifying environmental

and traditional dispute resolution, such as treaty-based compliance mechanisms;[61] the deficient 'one-size-fits-all' of the ARSIWA; the sometimes unclear or imprecise content of primary international environmental legal obligations; the obstacles in attributing wrongful conduct to States in the environmental field; the challenges in identifying both responsible and injured States, especially when faced with the violation of obligations *erga omnes*; the characterization of harm and identification of the relevant threshold beyond which it becomes an internationally wrongful act;[62] the impossibility of securing restitution, particularly as regards species extinction or global warming, which results in a disconnect between doctrinal endorsement of SR principles and State practice;[63] the multilateral character of regulatory approaches concerning the climate change regime, as opposed to the bilateral character of compensation under SR;[64] the fact that SR repertoire cannot supplant the need for systematic regulatory supervision on both regional and international levels;[65] etc.

One of the most challenging problems in applying SR norms to environmental law violations is both factual and evidentiary and resides in the transnational nature of pollution and climate change. ARSIWA Article 47(1) provides that 'where several States are responsible for the same internationally wrongful act, the responsibility of each State may be invoked in relation to that act'.[66] This provision was presumably adopted specifically to govern situations where an internationally wrongful act spans over several territories and, therefore, engages the responsibility of more than one State.[67] Whilst there are some detractors to the idea that the principle of joint and several liability could be borrowed from the common law and civil law traditions and extended to this setting (ie if a handful of States are not responsible for the 'same wrongful act'),[68] this provision is undoubtedly relevant vis-à-vis both global warming and some instances of transnational terrorism. However, some commentators call into question the

harm for the purposes of compensation under ARSIWA (n 56) Art 36(2), see Proulx (n 6) 217–19. For a comparative study, see J Liu, *Compensating Ecological Damage: Comparative and Economic Observations* (Intersentia 2013).

[61] See also M Fitzmaurice and C Redgwell, 'Environmental Non-Compliance Procedures and International Law' (2000) 31 NYIL 35, 65; A Andrusevych *et al.* (eds), *Case Law of the Aarhus Convention Compliance Committee (2004-11)* (2nd edn, Resource and Analysis Centre Society & the Environment 2011).

[62] See also generally M Bowman and A Boyle (eds), *Environmental Damage in International and Comparative Law: Problems of Definition and Valuation* (OUP 2002); P Wetterstein (ed.), *Harm to the Environment: The Right to Compensation and the Assessment of Damages* (Clarendon Press 1997).

[63] See also A Boyle, 'Remedying Harm to International Common Spaces and Resources: Compensation and Other Approaches' in Wetterstein (n 62) 89. In particular, see also Redgwell (n 59) 267 (critiquing the '"backward-looking" nature of state responsibility with respect to restitution and compensation').

[64] See also Boyle (n 63) 89 (identifying the Iraq–Kuwait scenario as a rare example of exclusive State liability for environmental harm, which was largely implemented through claims submitted in an international forum).

[65] See also P Birnie *et al.*, *International Law and the Environment* (3rd edn, OUP 2009) 237.

[66] ARSIWA (n 56) Art 47(1).

[67] See also Proulx (n 6) 128, 275, 291–2, 299.

[68] See, eg, I Brownlie, *Principles of Public International Law* (6th edn, OUP 2003) 189; Voigt (n 48) 19 (both arguing that there is little State practice and academic support justifying the importation of joint/several liability into international law).

adequacy of this provision 'to address cases of gradual and cumulative pollution arising from numerous sources that are located in different States'; they add that '[t]his kind of pollution happens if natural elements, such as the sea, international rivers or the atmosphere are polluted by land-based sources'.[69] Consequently, they argue that requiring an injured State to establish a causal connection between specific conduct and the resulting environmental damage would be patently unfair, given that 'the contribution of every single source of pollution is extremely difficult to assess'.[70]

Given the manner in which Article 47(1) was drafted, SR law erects relatively few conceptual barriers to making every government involved in the chain of events accountable. Rather, the problem is one of evidence: how can the exact 'wrongful act: ensuing/commensurate responsibility' ratio be precisely ascertained for every single source of harmful activity, be it in the case of the emission of toxic pollutants or the toleration by a State of terrorist activity on its territory leading to transboundary harm? Indeed, leading environmental law publicists have long observed that in the context of compensation under SR, for instance, it is exceedingly difficult to establish a causal nexus between the wrongful act and the harm caused as the 'normal' consequences of that unlawful activity.[71] The answer to these questions will obviously depend on a careful analysis of every case of transnational harm that arises. Furthermore, a delicate balance should be struck between vindicating specific policy objectives underlying global security and international law and justice more generally, and enhancing transnational cooperation on both SR issues and global security efforts.

Therefore, SR principles can play some role in the prevention of global warming and other environmental threats, although a severely limited one. The key point, however, is that it can play *some* role, however small it may be. Surely, analogies can be drawn from global warming in order to identify potential deterrence and prevention models for counterterrorism, yet whilst global warming is—as would-be detractors of invoking SR to fight terrorism might argue—a highly de-territorialized and decentralized phenomenon, compelling arguments nonetheless militate in favour of engaging that normative scheme. Surely, invoking a State-centric legal regime to combat a transnational problem is only part of the equation; the role of States in preventing/failing to prevent global security violations must be assessed on its own merits, alongside the participation

[69] T Scovazzi, 'Some Remarks on International Responsibility in the Field of Environmental Protection' in Ragazzi (n 10) 217–18. This phenomenon also appears to fly in the face of the reasoning extracted from *Corfu Channel*. See, eg, Smith (n 28) 754.

[70] Scovazzi (n 69) 217–18. Moreover, internationally wrongful conduct might engender 'ripple effects' or continuing environmental harm beyond the initial breach. Whilst the extension of that conduct's consequences over time might assist for the quantification of damage, for example, it does not necessarily convert that act into a 'continuing violation'. See ILC Report (n 42) 60 [6]. Similarly, multiple actors, be they States, non-State entities, or individuals, can potentially contribute to the same harmful conduct, which engenders considerable challenges for the purposes of establishing causation. See I Plakokefalos, 'Causation in the Law of State Responsibility and the Problem of Overdetermination: In Search of Clarity' (2015) 26 EJIL 471.

[71] Redgwell (n 59) 266–7; Lefeber (n 46) 341–2.

of actual terrorists, other non-State actors (eg international civil society, the media),[72] informal and implicit networks of governance, etc, in the grander scheme of transnational activity. What is certain is that there is an increasing interest, indeed need, in developing a coherent international legal regime to address transnational pollution and environmental degradation.[73] What is less certain is whether institutional actors—particularly UN organs as explored in Part II of this book—would be sufficiently equipped to oversee effective implementation of SR for environmental breaches; this is especially true given the normative paucity of some primary obligations and the relative uncertainty surrounding applicable legal standards.

Thus, the potential implementation of SR must be pursued in tandem with transnational cooperation and enhanced multilateralism on global security initiatives. One commentator had embodied this impetus in 1989, observing that although 'the principles [of SR] and liability for harm provide a useful starting point for dealing with the issue of global warming… international cooperation will provide a more effective solution'.[74] Ultimately, the interpretation and application of relevant legal norms will be shaped by the ways in which both States and institutional actors internalize the risks posed by transnational pollution, terrorism, and other global security threats. As such, this very notion of 'risk' is analysed briefly in the next section.

2.4.2 Risk assessment and precautionary approaches

Undoubtedly, the prospect of applying SR principles effectively to global security violations constitutes an exercise in risk assessment and management. In the environmental sector and in respect of the global commons, there is renewed interest in international legal questions pertaining to international responsibility, risk, and liability.[75] The international community is imposing a heavier burden of precaution upon States in complying with their counterterrorism obligations; similar advances have been made in other cognate fields such as environmental law. With this in mind, Part II of this book attempts to carve out a role for UN organs in implementing international responsibility models. However, the main policy thrust of any effective institutionalization of SR must be articulated around the vital notion of *prevention*, a concept highly reconcilable with a precautionary approach to the assessment of risk. Therefore, when further exploring the role of SR repertoire in preventing and suppressing global security violations, inspiration

[72] Although not directly on point, consider SJ Toope, 'Public Commitment to International Law: Canadian and British Media Perspectives on the Use of Force' in CPM Waters (ed.), *British and Canadian Perspectives on International Law* (Nijhoff 2006) 13–25.

[73] See, eg, S Vinogradov, 'The Impact of the Deepwater Horizon: The Evolving International Legal Regime for Offshore Accidental Pollution Prevention, Preparedness, and Response' (2013) 44 Ocean Development & International Law: The Journal of Marine Affairs 335.

[74] VP Nanda, 'Global Warming and International Environmental Law: A Preliminary Inquiry' (1989) 30 HILJ 375, 385.

[75] See, eg, J Barboza, *The Environment, Risk and Liability in International Law* (Nijhoff 2010).

could be drawn from the precautionary principle, a concept well developed in the field of international environmental law.

Certain scholars infer that both prevention and precaution operate symbiotically.[76] Similarly, ICJ Judge Mohamed Bennouna emphasized that the obligation of prevention is bolstered by the precautionary principle, which is destined to palliate the scientific uncertainty inherent in certain industrial projects and their impact on the environment or the health of populations.[77] In one global security context, the cost–benefit analysis will hinge, to a large extent, on whether States sufficiently internalize the risk of terrorist activity emanating from their territory to divert and inject funds into counterterrorism policy, so as to avoid international responsibility. In short, a delicate balancing act between compliance/State consent and self-interest/sovereign prerogatives must be struck; that is not to say, however, that by diverting funds to combat terrorism within its territory, a State will *only* be sacrificing sovereignty over compliance with its obligations. Quite to the contrary, a compelling case can be made that compliance with counterterrorism obligations is not only beneficial for States within the immediate geographical radius of the would-be territorial State but also for the international community at large. These mutual interests therefore translate into a shared understanding that combating terrorism can promote political stability and human security on both a regional and global basis.[78] Similar reasoning could extend to other global security challenges.

Aside from extrapolating the benefits of SR law for counterterrorism, it is imperative to recall that any policy ultimately implemented by States will depend on their *perception* of the risks involved. Thus, the costs of actually shifting policy infrastructures and diverting funds to counterterrorism measures in the low or unlikely probability that the risk of a terrorist strike might materialize weighs in the balance when making cost-sensitive policy decisions. Conversely, the prospect of incurring international responsibility—and having to compensate the victim-State for failing to prevent terrorism or some other global security breach—also amounts to a (potentially significant) cost in the analysis, irrespective of the fact that a terrorist risk can seldom be assessed a priori or even quantified with any degree of precision. In a widely discussed book, Cass Sunstein echoed this position regarding terrorism and global warming: '[i]n the context of terrorist threats, it makes sense to adopt a kind of Precautionary Principle against dangers whose probability cannot be assessed but that would be devastating if they materialized. In the context of global warming, the risk of catastrophe, if it cannot be ruled out as insignificant, might similarly justify costly precautions'.[79]

[76] See, eg, N Horbach and P Bekker, 'State Responsibility for Injurious Transboundary Activity in Retrospect' (2003) 50 NILR 327.

[77] M Bennouna, 'Réflexions sur la Régulation Internationale du Risque à Propos du Concept de Prévention' in R Hostiou *et al.* (eds), *Terres du Droit: Mélanges en l'Honneur d'Yves Jégouzo* (Dalloz 2009) 371, 376. See also generally M Bennouna, 'Prevention and International Law' in *Collected Courses of the Xiamen Academy of International Law*, vol 4 (Nijhoff 2013) 157–209.

[78] On the role of SR in stabilizing international relations, see Proulx (n 6) 251–63.

[79] CR Sunstein, *Laws of Fear: Beyond the Precautionary Principle* (CUP 2005) 61. For a critical take on the role of risk in Sunstein's framework, and on the precautionary principle more generally,

Thus, the implementation of obligations of prevention is largely informed by the risks incurred, as perceived by the would-be responsible State, by virtue of available information and knowledge at its disposal. The ICJ's reasoning in the *Bosnian Genocide* case bolsters this proposition, albeit in the context of the obligation to prevent genocide.[80] Indeed, the Court opined that

> a State may be found to have violated its obligation to prevent even though it had no certainty, at the time when it should have acted, but failed to do so, that genocide was about to be committed or was under way; for it to incur responsibility on this basis it is enough that the State was aware, or should normally have been aware, of the serious danger that acts of genocide would be committed.[81]

Conversely, the precautionary principle nonetheless applies in the event that the risk cannot be ascertained or established by virtue of the lacuna of information or knowledge on the impact of the risk-generating activities.[82] Whilst this principle is usually associated with new and relatively unknown fields of activity, there is no reason to preclude transnational terrorism (or other global security threats) from its purview. In summary, it amounts to a politico-moral principle that shifts the burden of justification onto the party wanting to adopt a behaviour that could engender serious or irreversible damage to the public order or the environment, absent any dispositive scientific consensus justifying the proposed measure or behaviour.[83] Whilst scientific uncertainty remains the analytical linchpin under the precautionary principle, the transplantation of that approach to global security contexts is nonetheless particularly apt. For example, weighing the potential policy benefits of the precautionary principle seems logical given that its rationale may be extended, with few conceptual barriers, to the factual uncertainty surrounding the formulation of legal responses to transnational terrorism.

The idea of precaution and its relation to the perception of risk is also mirrored in domestic settings. For instance, attention was drawn to the fact that the costs of insurance against terrorist threats in the context of landowner liability are more acute, precisely because of this perception of risk-to-factual-uncertainty ratio.[84] Similarly, the impact of the precautionary principle can be best illustrated by connecting people's reaction or perception of risk to a 'visualization' or 'imagery' of

see JD Ellis, 'Overexploitation of a Valuable Resource? New Literature on the Precautionary Principle' (2006) 17 EJIL 445.

[80] For a deconstruction of the obligation to prevent genocide in light of that case, see P Gaeta, 'On What Conditions Can a State Be Held Responsible for Genocide?' (2007) 18 EJIL 631.

[81] *Case Concerning the Application of the Convention on the Prevention and Punishment of the Crime of Genocide (Bosnia and Herzegovina v Serbia and Montenegro)* (Merits) [2007] ICJ Rep 43, 223 [432].

[82] See, eg, Bennouna, 'Réflexions' (n 77) 376.

[83] See, eg, C Raffensperger and J Tickner (eds), *Protecting Public Health and the Environment: Implementing The Precautionary Principle* (Island Press 1999).

[84] See, eg, ML Reynolds, 'Landowner Liability for Terrorist Acts' (1996) 47 Case Western Law Review 155, 175. See also TS Renoux and A Roux, 'The Rights of Victims and Liability of the State' in R Higgins and M Flory (eds), *Terrorism and International Law* (Routledge 1997) 251, 252 ('[a]s for the insurance companies, they have for a long time excluded terrorist attacks from their risks covered').

the risk involved.[85] It follows that in the event that the visualization of a negative result is attainable (eg terrorist strike), that image will arouse anxiety about that risk and, correspondingly, propel precautionary considerations to the fore of the decision-making process.[86] A salient example can be extracted from flight insurance scenarios: when asked how much they are willing to disburse for 'terrorism' flight insurance, customers are invariably inclined to pay more than for insurance covering losses resulting from all causes.[87] As Sunstein explains, '[t]he evident explanation for this peculiar result is that the word "terrorism" evokes vivid images of disaster, thus crowding out probability judgments'.[88] When transposed to SR law—itself envisaged as a sort of insurance policy tailored to safeguard common/collective interests (ie protection against terrorism and other global security threats)—the precautionary principle might compel governments to: (i) act and prevent terrorism before an over-imposing threat has materialized or; (ii) act after the fact or in reaction to a completed terrorist attack so as to prevent future excursions (ie similarly to the way in which precaution militates in favour of regulation in the environmental field, even if no scientific consensus convincingly supports the adoption of the measure). This application of the principle seems congruent with the idea of shifting *good* global security incentives to governments advocated throughout this book.

However, the potential contributions of the precautionary principle cannot be overstated. International institutions, individual States, and the international community are all likely to overdramatize—or 'over-visualize' to invoke previous parlance—the perceived risk and, as a result, are prone to overreaction.[89] Otherwise put, the process of devising an effective institutionalized scheme of State accountability for global security violations should gauge the role of other important and competing interests in the equation (eg respecting human rights when instituting measures to suppress terrorism). Invoking the precautionary principle in this setting is also impeded by the fact that virtually all international jurisdictions routinely refuse to classify it as a rule of customary law, be they the ICJ,[90] the World Trade Organization's Dispute Settlement Body,[91] the

[85] The terminology is borrowed from Sunstein (n 79) 40. See also P Slovic *et al.*, 'Violence Risk Assessment and Risk Communication' (2000) 24 Law and Human Behaviour 271.

[86] See, eg, Sunstein (n 79) 40.

[87] See, eg, EJ Johnston *et al.*, 'Framing, Probability Distortions, and Insurance Decisions' (1993) 7 Journal of Risk and Uncertainty 35.

[88] Sunstein (n 79) 40.

[89] See generally JE Mueller, 'Terrorism, Overreaction, and Globalization' in RN Rosecrance and AA Stein (eds), *No More States? Globalization, National Self-Determination, and Terrorism* (Rowman & Littlefield 2006) 47–74.

[90] See Judge Weeramantry's Dissenting Opinion in *Request for an Examination of the Situation in Accordance with Paragraph 63 of the Court's Judgment of 20 December 1974 in the Nuclear Tests (New Zealand v France) Case* (Provisional Measures) [1995] ICJ Rep 288, 342–4; Dissenting Opinion of Judge Palmer in ibid 412; Separate Opinion of Judge Koroma in *Gabčíkovo-Nagymaros Project (Hungary/Slovakia)* (Merits) [1997] ICJ Rep 7, 152.

[91] See, eg, WTO, *European Communities: Measures Concerning Meat and Meat Products (Hormones)—Report of the Appellate Body* (16 January 1998) WT/DS26/AB/R and WT/DS48/AB/R [123]; *European Communities: Measures Affecting the Approval and Marketing of Biotech*

International Tribunal for the Law of the Sea (ITLOS),[92] and various arbitral tribunals.[93] In the *Pulp Mills* case, the ICJ did not address the precautionary principle except to underscore that 'a precautionary approach' might have been 'relevant in the interpretation and application of the provisions' of the contentious instrument between the parties, but did not operate 'as a reversal of the burden of proof'.[94] The Court's silence on this front was pointed out, with varying degrees of admonishment, by some judges writing separately.[95] Furthermore, the normative status of the precautionary principle under international law has been rather divisive in scholarship, with some calling for the acknowledgment of its customary character,[96] and others rejecting it flat out.[97] However, the relevance of precautionary approaches is increasingly prominent in both legal scholarship and international adjudication, as courts and tribunals are called upon to handle

Products—Report of the Panel (29 September 2006) WT/DS291/R, WT/DS292/R, and WT/DS293/R [7.86]—[7.89]; *Australia: Measures Affecting Importation of Salmon (submitted by Canada)—Report of the Panel* (12 June 1998) WT/DS18/R; *Japan: Measures Affecting Agricultural Products—Report of the Panel* (27 October 1998) WT/DS76/R; *Japan: Measures Affecting Agricultural Products—Report of the Appellate Body* (22 February 1999) WT/DS76/AB/R; *India: Quantitative Restrictions on Imports of Agricultural, Textile and Industrial Products—Report of the Panel* (6 April 1999) WT/DS90/R; *Japan: Measures Affecting the Importation of Apples—Report of the Panel* (15 July 2003) WT/DS245/R.

[92] See, eg, *Southern Bluefin Tuna Cases (New Zealand v Japan; Australia v Japan)* (Provisional Measures, Order of 27 August 1999) ITLOS Reports 1999, 75, 77, 79; *The MOX Plant Case (Ireland v UK)* (Provisional Measures, Order of 3 December 2001) ITLOS Reports 2001 [75], [89]. However, the *Bluefin Tuna Cases* have profoundly divided scholarly currents on whether ITLOS in fact applied the precautionary principle in those instances. Some infer that it applied the precautionary principle. See, eg, A Fabra, 'The LOSC and the Implementation of the Precautionary Principle' (1999) 10 YIEL 17. Others opine that the precautionary principle did not seep into the Tribunal's decision-making. See, eg, P Chrestia, 'Chronique de Jurisprudence Internationale' (2000) 104 RGDIP 52; MD Evans, 'The Southern Bluefin Tuna Dispute: Provisional Thinking on Provisional Measures?' (1999) 10 YIEL 14; DM Johnston, 'Fishery Diplomacy and Science and the Judicial Function' (1999) 10 YIEL 35. A third school of thought remains rather vague or contradictory on the subject. See, eg, F Orrego Vicuña, 'From the 1893 Bering Sea Fur-Seals Case to the 1999 Southern Bluefin Tuna Cases: A Century of Efforts at Conservation of the Living Resources on the High Seas' (1999) 10 YIEL 33, 33–4; S Marr, 'The Southern Bluefin Tuna Cases: The Precautionary Approach and Conservation and Management of Fish Resources' (2000) 11 EJIL 816.

[93] See, eg, *Bluefin Tuna Cases (Australia and New Zealand v Japan)* (2000) 23 RIAA 1, 48–9 [72].

[94] *Pulp Mills Case* (n 50) 71 [164].

[95] Consider the Joint Dissenting Opinion of Judges Al-Khasawneh and Simma, the Separate Opinion of Judge Cançado Trindade, and the Dissenting Opinion of Judge ad hoc Vinuesa in the *Pulp Mills Case* (n 50) [23], [62]–[96], [100], respectively.

[96] See, eg, J Cameron and J Abouchar, 'The Status of the Precautionary Principle in International Law' in D Freestone and E Hey (eds), *The Precautionary Principle and International Law: The Challenge of Implementation* (Kluwer 1996) 29, 45; H Hohmann, *Precautionary Legal Duties and Principles of Modern International Environmental Law – The Precautionary Principle: International Environmental Law Between Exploitation and Protection* (Graham & Trotman 1994) 184; A Kiss, 'Émergence de Principes Généraux du Droit International et d'une Politique Internationale de l'Environnement' in I Rens (ed.), *Le Droit International Face à l'Éthique et à la Politique de l'Environnement* (Georg 1996) 30.

[97] See, eg, P Birnie and AE Boyle, *International Law and the Environment* (Clarendon Press 1992) 98; D Bodansky, 'Remarks: New Development in International Environmental Law' (1991) 85 ASIL Proceedings 410; L Boisson de Chazournes *et al.* (eds), *Protection Internationale de l'Environnement* (Pedone 1998) 19; P-M Dupuy, 'Où en est le Droit International de l'Environnement à la Fin du Siècle?' (1997) 101 RGDIP 889; M Fitzmaurice, 'International Environmental Law as a Special Field' (1994) 25 NYIL 220.

science-heavy and factually complex disputes, some of which have a direct connection with global security.[98]

The confusion surrounding the normative status of the precautionary principle is further exacerbated by the uncertainty surrounding its actual contents and contours. In fact, no consensus has been reached on both the substance and scope of this principle. Twenty years ago, Sands rightly underscored that '[t]here [was] no uniform understanding of the meaning of the precautionary principle among States and other members of the international community'.[99] That said, despite the fact that in the 1990s authors cast it as an 'elusive concept'[100] or similarly concluded that it was 'not a term of art',[101] the precautionary principle now comprises a conceptual core that may facilitate its application irrespective of its uncertain legal status. After all, 'terrorism', whilst not universally defined,[102] is understood broadly enough to generate studies, national and international regulation, SC and General Assembly (GA) resolutions, and political and judicial decisions (granted, of course, that unlike the precautionary approach, terrorism is not a legal principle but a method or tactic). Despite the judicial vacuum as to its customary character, the precautionary principle nevertheless underpins the formulation of various national, international, and regional legal policies.[103]

For instance, it has been consecrated as a general and mandatory principle of law under EU structures. Furthermore, it has also been enshrined in several international instruments on environmental matters, most notably in Principle 15 of the Rio Declaration on Environment and Development,[104] the Vienna Convention for the Protection of the Ozone Layer,[105] the 1990 Bergen Ministerial

[98] See generally CE Foster, *Science and the Precautionary Principle in International Courts and Tribunals* (CUP 2013); J D'Aspremont and MM Mbengue, 'Strategies of Engagement with Scientific Fact-Finding in International Adjudication' (2014) 5 Journal of International Dispute Settlement 240; MM Mbengue, *Essai sur une Théorie du Risque en Droit International Public: L'Anticipation du Risque Environnemental et Sanitaire* (Pedone 2009); J Cazala, *Le Principe de Précaution en Droit International* (Anthemis 2006).

[99] P Sands, *Principles of Environmental Law* (Manchester University Press 1995) 212.

[100] L Gundling, 'The Status in International Law of the Precautionary Principle' (1990) 5 International Journal of Estuarine and Coastal Law 25; L Gundling, 'The Status in International Law of the Precautionary Principle' in D Freestone and T Ijilstra (eds), *The North Sea: Perspectives on Regional Environmental Co-operation* (Graham & Trotman 1990) 23–30.

[101] G Handl, 'Environmental Security and Global Change: The Challenge of International Law' (1990) 1 YIEL 3, 23.

[102] For a thoughtful but dated study on the question, see B Saul, *Defining Terrorism in International Law* (OUP 2006).

[103] See, eg, J Chaisse and T Balmelli (eds), *Essays on the Future of the World Trade Organization*, vol 1 (Edis 2008) 382.

[104] Rio Declaration on Environment and Development (adopted 14 June 1992) (1992) 31 ILM 874, Principle 15 reads as follows:

> In order to protect the environment, *the precautionary approach shall be widely applied by States* according to their capabilities. Where there are threats of serious or irreversible damage, lack of full scientific certainty shall not be used as a reason for postponing cost-effective measures to prevent environmental degradation (emphasis added).

[105] The Vienna Convention for the Protection of the Ozone Layer (adopted 22 March 1985, entered into force 22 September 1988) 1513 UNTS 293 and the Montreal Protocol on Substances

Declaration on Sustainable Development,[106] the Convention on the Protection and Use of Transboundary Watercourses and International Lakes,[107] the 1992 Convention on Biological Diversity,[108] and the 1992 UN Framework Convention on Climate Change.[109] Similarly, the Commentary to Article 10(c) of the ILC's Draft Articles on Prevention of Transboundary Harm from Hazardous Activities consecrates the precautionary principle, noting that concerned States take several factors into consideration when adopting preventive measures, including 'the risk of significant harm to the environment and the availability of means of preventing such harm, or minimizing the risk thereof and the possibility or restoring the environment'.[110]

In sum, the precautionary principle can be brought to bear on the future development of SR law in relation to global security challenges, subject to the abovementioned caveats. Whilst the principle needs further elaboration and has yet to attain the status of a binding international obligation,[111] it may nevertheless come to guide the action of UN organs when confronted with global security breaches. The pivotal element thus lies in the fact that the lack of scientific evidence or knowledge should not impede the prospect of adopting certain measures aimed

that Deplete the Ozone Layer (adopted 16 September 1987, entered into force 1 January 1989) 1522 UNTS 3 both allude to 'precautionary measures' in their respective preambles. See also Protocol to the 1979 Convention on Long-Range Transboundary Air Pollution on Further Reduction of Sulphur Emissions (adopted 14 June 1994, entered into force 5 August 1998) (1993) 33 ILM 1540, preamble.

[106] Bergen Ministerial Declaration on Sustainable Development in the ECE Region (adopted 16 May 1990) UN Doc A/CONF.151/PC/10, Annex I, para 7 (stating that its objective of sustainable development must be achieved by adopting measures that are in conformity with the precautionary principle). The document also provides that 'environmental measures must anticipate, prevent and attack the cause of environmental degradation', whilst also incorporating a portion of the wording of Principle 15 (n 104).

[107] Convention on the Protection and Use of Transboundary Watercourses and International Lakes (adopted 17 March 1993, entered into force 6 October 1996) 1936 UNTS 269, Art 2.5(a) provides that members must be guided by '[t]he precautionary principle, by virtue of which action to avoid the potential transboundary impact of the release of hazardous substances shall not be postponed on the ground that scientific research has not fully proved a causal link between those substances, on the one hand, and the potential transboundary impact, on the other hand'.

[108] Convention on Biological Diversity (adopted 5 June 1992, entered into force 29 December 1993) 1760 UNTS 79. However, the preamble of this instrument does not expressly refer to the precautionary principle. For more background on this treaty, see M Bowman and C Redgwell, *International Law and the Conservation of Biological Diversity* (Kluwer 1995).

[109] UN Framework Convention on Climate Change (adopted 9 May 1992, entered into force 21 March 1994) 1771 UNTS 107; see particularly Art 3(3) of that instrument. See also Treaty on European Union (Maastricht Treaty) Art 130R; Bamako Convention on the Ban of the Import Into Africa and the Control of Transboundary Movement and Management of Hazardous Wastes Within Africa (adopted 30 January 1991, entered into force 22 April 1998) 2101 UNTS 177, Art 4(3); Agreement for the Implementation of the Provisions of the United Nations Convention on the Law of the Sea of 10 December 1982 Relating to the Conservation and Management of Straddling Fish Stocks and Highly Migratory Fish Stocks (adopted 4 August 1995, entered into force 11 December 2001) 2167 UNTS 3, Arts 5–6.

[110] ILC Report–53rd Session (n 42) 161–3.

[111] See, eg, L Boisson de Chazournes, 'Precaution in International Law: Reflection on Its Composite Nature' in TM Ndiaye and R Wolfrum (eds), *Law of the Sea, Environmental Law and Settlement of Disputes: Liber Amicorum Judge Thomas A. Mensah* (Nijhoff 2007) 21–34.

at counteracting activities that may engender serious or irreversible effects. When transposed to the specific context of counterterrorism, the notion of an informational lacuna readily translates into the lack of knowledge; knowledge about imminent terrorist attacks, terrorist activity taking place on a State's territory, funding/fundraising of terrorist organizations taking place on that territory, etc. Therefore, it may well be that a precautionary approach also informs the institutionalized implementation of SR by UN organs. In fact, this is one possible rationale behind the SC's implementation of Libya's responsibility in the *Lockerbie* case; by insisting that Libya cease its support of terrorism and attributing the bombings to that State in the face of some factual uncertainty, the Council attempted to prevent further attacks from being carried out (ie by imposing a higher burden of precaution on Libya).[112]

Therefore, the potential contributions of the precautionary principle in the field of global security are numerous, not least at the level of primary international legal norms. Because of its conceptual core identified earlier, this principle could act as a substantive foundation for the further development of customary law.[113] Yet, similarly to many other relevant analogies, the invocation of the precautionary principle in global security contexts might trigger evidentiary challenges (paradoxically, in the case of the precautionary principle, scientific proof/evidence cannot serve as an obstacle when vindicating specific policy objectives, provided its application is ultimately accepted). Given the ICJ's resistance to recognizing the customary status of the precautionary principle, it remains to be seen how it will evolve in the coming years. However, one must register some scepticism about the SC drawing inspiration from that approach, given that this organ appears particularly ill-suited to tackle all present-day, non-military threats. Conversely, for reasons explored earlier, well-calibrated precautionary sensibilities could inform both the formulation of primary legal norms and implementation of SR in other areas, such as counterterrorism and non-proliferation.

2.4.3 Ungoverned spaces and territories

Many global security challenges canvassed in the present volume depend on ungoverned spaces and territories as propitious incubators. Whilst dominant models of transnational terrorism can seldom be dissociated from territorial solace or from some kind of governmental toleration or acquiescence,[114] there is

[112] Various aspects of this precedent are discussed in Sections 3.1.5.1, 3.2.1, 3.2.1.1, 3.2.2, 4.1, 4.4.1, 4.4.5, 4.4.9, 4.5.1, 4.5.2, and 4.6.1.

[113] See, eg, A Pellet, *Recherche sur les Principes Généraux de Droit en Droit International Public* (Thesis, Paris 1974) 428; M Virally, 'Le Rôle des Principes dans le Développement du Droit International' in IUHEI de Genève (ed.), *Recueil d'Études de Droit International en Hommage à Paul Guggenheim* (Tribune 1968) 531, 546; H Kelsen, 'Théorie du Droit International Public' (1953) 84 RdC 182; S Sur, 'Quelques Observations sur les Normes Juridiques Internationales' (1985) 89 RGDIP 901, 906; P Weil, 'Le Droit International en Quête de son Identité—Cours Général de Droit International Public (1992) 237 RdC 9, 148–51.

[114] See, eg, Proulx (n 6) 77–80.

something to be said about taking the territorial component out of the equation when crafting potential legal responses. The growing phenomenon of 'home-grown' terrorists aside,[115] operating within 'ungoverned spaces', or unmonitored areas, constitutes an increasingly attractive option for terrorist networks in preparing and executing their attacks. Recent manifestations of this practice by ISIL and Al-Shabaab have been witnessed in parts of the Middle East and Somalia. Unsurprisingly, '[a]s sovereignty erodes and it becomes harder to control borders, Black Holes, the ungoverned spaces, become breeding grounds for all forms of illicit commodities and provide succor for international terrorism'.[116] Unquestionably, some instances of terrorism move towards a more de-territorialized or decentralized model, thereby seemingly weakening the points of rapprochement with SR repertoire. Many terrorist networks prey on inefficient or wilfully blind governments or seek refuge in sanctuary States endowed with weak or ineffective counterterrorism structures. In such scenarios, when enforcing international law the SC has no choice but to espouse a comprehensive strategy—which it has done when dealing with ISIL and other terrorist networks—in which the duty of States to exercise their sovereignty responsibly is part of a broader counterterrorism mosaic.[117]

This opportunism is further exacerbated in cases of 'failed', ineffective, or government-less States, such as Iraq, Lebanon, Somalia, Sudan, Syria, Yemen, or certain areas of sub-Saharan Africa, a reality that was canvassed thoroughly elsewhere.[118] Consequently, in recent years there has been renewed emphasis in both national and international (pre-emptive and reactive) policy-making on the notion of 'ungoverned spaces'.[119] It must be underscored that '[t]he continuing problem is that ungoverned spaces will be filled by chaos [eg terrorist networks] because frayed, faux, and failed states lack the capacity to monopolize

[115] See, eg, E Rosand, 'The UN-Led Multilateral Institutional Response to Jihadist Terrorism: Is a Global Counterterrorism Body Needed?' (2006) 11 JCSL 399, 401 (discussing the emergence of home-grown terrorism and linking it to both the Madrid and London bombings, along with the assassination of Theo van Gogh). See also Section 2.1.

[116] H Rishikof, 'Long Wars of Political Order—Sovereignty and Choice: The Fourth Amendment and the Modern Trilemma' (2006) 15 Cornell Journal of Law and Public Policy 587, 618. See also JG Dalton, 'The United States National Security Strategy: Yesterday, Today, and Tomorrow' (2005) 52 Naval Law Review 60, 62 (underscoring that '[a]n "arc of instability" stretching from the Western Hemisphere, through Africa and the Middle East, and extending to Asia serves as a "breeding ground" for such activities'). See also L Condorelli, 'The Imputability to States of Acts of International Terrorism' (1989) 19 IYHR 233, 240. As pointed out by JA McCredie, 'The Responsibility of States for Private Acts of International Terrorism' (1985) 1 Temple International and Comparative Law Journal 69, 73, a 'state may be subject to penalties for a failure to exercise jurisdiction if the offense is committed within its borders'.

[117] See Introduction nn 18–19 and accompanying text. The SC has also done so in a variety of other contexts, including in response to terrorist threats in Mali. See, eg, UNSC Res 2227 (29 June 2015) UN Doc S/RES/2227, preamble. On the security risks posed by Al-Shabaab in both Somalia and Yemen, see UNSC Res 2232 (28 July 2015) UN Doc S/RES/2232.

[118] See, eg, Proulx (n 6) 242–8.

[119] See, eg, RM Gates, 'A Balanced Strategy: Reprogramming the Pentagon for a New Age' (2009) 88 FA 28. This is also particularly true in the case of counterinsurgency strategy. See, eg, D Kilcullen, 'Counter-Insurgency *Redux*' (2006) 48 Survival: Global Politics and Strategy 111, 111–12.

power'.[120] Although not directly apropos, a principal concern originally voiced over Kosovo in different circles was that it had the propensity to become a rump Islamist state.[121] Similarly, in the US the African command of the Pentagon was set up because of similar situations, most notably in Somalia and Ethiopia; the policy focus therefore shifted to ungoverned spaces in States that were not formally at war with the US.[122] Therefore, there is increasing policy emphasis on the link between ungoverned spaces and issues of transnational crime and law enforcement, which pose considerable challenges for global security.[123] As will be seen, UN organs will have to grapple with this reality when implementing SR. Suffice it to say that SR principles—particularly attribution standards, at least in their current formulation—prove exceedingly difficult to apply to global security breaches that have tenuous or virtually non-existent territorial connections with any States.[124]

Other de-territorialized security challenges may fall within the purview of institutionalized implementation of SR by UN organs. The problem of international piracy constitutes an example *par excellence* of such practice, which has been acute off the coast of Somalia (particularly in the Gulf of Aden and Arabian Sea), in the Straits of Malacca, in the Gulf of Guinea, and on Falcon Lake on the US–Mexico border.[125] Whilst State-to-State recourses under SR repertoire may be limited in repressing this global security threat, the SC nonetheless has a leading role to play in repressing and preventing this practice.[126] There is no need to exclude the potential application of SR principles by that organ; in fact, as will be seen in Part II of this volume, the broad range of enforcement means available to it might in fact include resort to secondary SR norms to implement the international responsibility of States that fail to comply with counter-piracy obligations. Indeed, States like Somalia must be seen as deploying best efforts—no matter

[120] CH Norchi, 'The Legal Architecture of Nation-Building: An Introduction' (2008) 60 Maine Law Review 281, 290.

[121] See, eg, SP Rosenberg, 'Promoting Equality after Genocide' (2008) 16 Tulane Journal of International and Comparative Law 329, 337 fn 20 and accompanying text; N Cigar, *Genocide in Bosnia: The Policy of 'Ethnic Cleansing'* (Texas A&M University Press 1995) 42–3.

[122] See, eg, B Gellman, 'Secret Unit Expands Rumsfeld's Domain' *Washington Post* (Washington, DC, 23 January 2005) A1.

[123] See, eg, DE Stigall, 'Ungoverned Spaces, Transnational Crime, and the Prohibition on Extraterritorial Enforcement Jurisdiction in International Law' (2013) 3 Notre Dame Journal of International & Comparative Law 1.

[124] See also Proulx (n 6) 305–6 (arguing that in the case of 'failed' or ineffective States, the benefits of SR law 'might have met their match' and the remedy of satisfaction can only play some symbolic role in such instances).

[125] For various views, see, eg, RC Beckman and JA Roach (eds), *Piracy and International Maritime Crimes in ASEAN: Prospects for Cooperation* (Edward Elgar 2012); D Guilfoyle (ed.), *Modern Piracy: Legal Challenges and Responses* (Edward Elgar 2013); C Houry, *La Piraterie Maritime au Regard du Droit International: Incertitudes et Évolutions Contemporaines* (L'Harmattan 2014); R Geiss and A Petrig, *Piracy and Armed Robbery at Sea: The Legal Framework for Counter-Piracy Operations in Somalia and the Gulf of Aden* (OUP 2011). On the role that international law can play in combating piracy, see D Heller-Roazen, *The Enemy of All: Piracy and the Law of Nations* (Zone Books 2009).

[126] See, eg, D Momtaz, 'L'apport du Conseil de Sécurité à la Lutte contre l'Impunité des Pirates Opérant au Large des Côtes de la Somalie' (2010) 15 Annuaire du Droit de la Mer 239.

how limited—in addressing piracy in their geographical vicinity, subject to the eventual invocation of their international responsibility if they fail to do so.[127] Aside from the potential contributions of UN organs, it must be stressed that regional bodies such as the Organization of African Unity, African Union, Arab League, and the Association of Southeast Asian Nations (ASEAN) must play a proactive role in developing counter-piracy and counterterrorism strategies.

Finally, picking up on the thread explored earlier in Section 2.4.1, the increasing practice of space exploration and related activities have brought the relevance of SR frameworks to the fore. Indeed, there is a growing number of States developing outer-space programmes and engaging in space activities, which has implications for global security and remains intertwined with the issue of environmental degradation. As a result of this 'rush to space', many outer-space activities are generating space debris, which in turn can engender significant transboundary damage. Whilst the international legal frameworks and instruments that may be brought to bear on the SR calculus for space activities have been discussed elsewhere,[128] it is also posited that the legal regime governing such activities, and the treatment of space debris specifically, is outdated.[129] Similarly to other de-territorialized global security challenges, the nature of many space activities might obfuscate the straightforward application of SR principles, particularly attribution standards, although those concerns have been partly alleviated by integrating 'objective' and/or 'strict' liability models in certain international instruments.

2.4.4 Cyberterrorism

In terms of de-territorialized security threats, modern technology also provides terrorists and criminals with increased means and methods of inspiring fear and carrying out virtual attacks. This reality had been acknowledged before 9/11.[130] Consequently, there is a growing body of literature dealing with the relationship between cyberterrorism and SR repertoire: at this stage, there appear to be more questions than answers, with interlocutors attempting to circumscribe applicable legal frameworks better than formerly.[131] Unsurprisingly, cyberterrorism and

[127] See, eg, Section 4.6.2 n 465 and accompanying text.

[128] See Proulx (n 6) 232–5, 319–20, and authorities cited therein. See also G Goh, *International Law and Outer Space* (OUP, forthcoming 2016) ch 9.

[129] See, eg, AF Snyman, 'The Environmental Responsibility of States for Space Debris and the Implications for Developing Countries in Africa' (2013) 46 Comparative and International Law Journal of Southern Africa 19.

[130] See, eg, WM Reisman, 'International Legal Responses to International Terrorism' (1999) 22 HJIL 3, 4. On the challenges of cyber-terrorism, generally, see GS McNeal, 'Cyber Embargo: Countering the Internet Jihad' (2007–8) 39 CWRJIL 789.

[131] See, eg, SJ Shackelford, 'From Nuclear War to Net War: Analogizing Cyber Attacks in International Law' (2008) 27 BJIL 191, 214; SJ Shackelford and RB Andres, 'State Responsibility for Cyber Attacks: Competing Standards for a Growing Problem' (2001) 42 GJIL 971. More broadly, publicists and policy experts are also attempting to better define cyber legal frameworks not only as regards SR, but in other international legal fields as well. See N Tsagourias and R Buchan (eds), *Research Handbook on International Law and Cyberspace* (Edward Elgar 2015), and A Antonopoulos, 'State Responsibility in Cyberspace' in ibid 55–71.

cybercrime, more broadly, pose considerable challenges to the application of traditional SR norms, particularly attribution standards.[132] For instance, if an individual or organization sets up a website promoting terrorism under the auspices of an Internet service provider located in a specific State, can that State's responsibility be engaged under the prevailing primary rules of 'harbouring' and 'supporting' terrorist activity? Terrorist networks such as ISIL and Al-Shabaab are increasingly using Internet technology, including social networks, for multiple purposes such as radicalization, recruitment, fundraising, operational planning, training, and public relations. Certainly, failing to prevent such activities, when the State(s) in whose territory they take place have the ability to contain them, might have implications for SR law and signal the violation of different preventive counterterrorism obligations.

As will be seen later,[133] the 'cyber' dimension of transnational subversive activity not only impedes the application of SR norms but also propels the regime interaction between SR law and use of force repertoire (particularly self-defence) to the fore. Consequently, increasing scholarly emphasis is placed on armed conflict in virtual settings[134] and self-defence in response to cyber-attacks.[135] As a corollary, the 'virtual battlefield' and its legal implications have attracted considerable attention, with international legal scholars of all stripes tackling SR issues, be they linked to attribution, countermeasures, due diligence, sovereignty, obligations, or self-defence.[136] Similarly, domestic law scholars have begun to explore

[132] See N Tsagourias, 'Cyber-Attacks, Self-Defence and the Problem of Attribution' (2012) 17 JCSL 229; MN Schmitt and L Vihul, 'Proxy Wars in Cyberspace: The Evolving International Law of Attribution' (2014) Fletcher Security Review 55.

[133] See Section 6.2.4 nn 120–1, authorities cited therein, and accompanying text.

[134] CM Kirsch, 'Science Fiction No More: Cyber Warfare and the United States' (2012) 40 Denver Journal of International Law and Policy 620; JM Beard, 'Law and War in the Virtual Era' (2009) 103 AJIL 1.

[135] M Roscini, *Cyber Operations and the Use of Force in International Law* (OUP 2014); MN Schmitt, 'The Use of Cyber Force and International Law' in M Weller (ed.), *The Oxford Handbook of the Use of Force in International Law* (OUP 2015) 1110–30; MC Waxman, 'Self-defensive Force against Cyber Attacks: Legal, Strategic and Political Dimensions' (2013) 89 International Law Studies 109; C Lotrionte, 'State Sovereignty and Self-Defense in Cyberspace: A Normative Framework for Balancing Legal Rights' (2012) 26 Emory International Law Review 825; JP Kesan and CM Hayes, 'Mitigative Counterstriking: Self-Defense and Deterrence in Cyberspace' (2012) 25 Harvard Journal of Law & Technology 429.

[136] MN Schmitt and CM Pitts, 'Cyber Countermeasures and Effects on Third Parties: The International Legal Regime' (2014) 14 Baltic Yearbook of International Law 1; K Bannelier-Christakis, 'Cyber Diligence: A Low-Intensity Due Diligence Principle for Low-Intensity Cyber Operations?' in ibid 23; ET Jensen, 'State Obligations in Cyber Operations' in ibid 71; AL Kozik, 'The Concept of Sovereignty as a Foundation for Determining the Legality of the Conduct of States in Cyberspace' in ibid 93; N Tsagourias, 'The Law Applicable to Countermeasures against Low-Intensity Cyber Operations' in ibid 105; MN Schmitt, '"Below the Threshold" Cyber Operations: The Countermeasures Response Option and International Law' (2014) 54 VJIL 697; L Grosswald, 'Cyberattack Attribution Matters under Article 51 of the U.N. Charter' (2011) 36 Brooklyn Journal of International Law 1151; MN Schmitt, 'Cyber Activities and the Law of Countermeasures' in K Ziolkowski *et al.* (eds), *Peacetime Regime for State Activities in Cyberspace: International Law, International Relations and Diplomacy* (NATO Cooperative Cyber Defence Centre of Excellence 2013) 659–90; R Geiss and H Lahmann, 'Freedom and Security in Cyberspace: Shifting the Focus Away from Military Responses towards Non-forcible Countermeasures and Collective Threat-prevention' in ibid 621–57

the links between cyberterrorism and SR, specifically, with a view to identifying viable legal regimes to suppress or repress such activity.[137]

A most salient example of cyberterrorism occurred in 2007 when irregulars launched a series of 'distributed denial of service' attacks (DDOS attacks) primarily from Russia on Estonian targets. Among other things, the attacks incapacitated the online portal of Estonia's largest bank, resulting in financial losses exceeding US$1 million in a single day.[138] Whilst previous recorded instances of cyberwar had occurred in the context of international armed conflicts, such as the 2008 conflict between Russia and Georgia over South Ossetia, virtual subversion is taking place in the internal armed conflict in Iraq; online hostilities include computer hacking for intelligence gathering, malware operations to subvert and secure remote control over hostile computer networks, sending booby-trapped email messages, and terrorizing the civilian population through social networks.[139] Given the inadequacy of current legal standards, some advocate the implementation of strict liability models according to which large-scale cyberattacks would be automatically or directly imputed to the State from which the activity was authored.[140] Focusing on the intersection of SR and use of force repertoire, others suggest that any computer attack authored by non-State actors engendering harm akin to that of a military attack should be characterized as an 'armed attack'; thus, '[i]mmediate destruction of life is not a prerequisite'.[141] Whilst this eventuality had been recognized prior to 9/11, the legal discourse pertaining to legal frameworks governing wrongful acts occurring in cyberspace is in

[137] See, eg, OA Hathaway *et al.*, 'The Law of Cyber-Attack' (2012) 100 California Law Review 817, esp 831 (discussing the actions of the 'Kremlin Kids', private hackers who disabled the Georgian Internet during Russia's invasion of South Ossetia, in the context of the intersection of SR and terrorism), 843 (invoking the violation of customary international law by way of clandestine, online State action that violates the norms governing non-intervention), 857–9, 879–80 (examining the scourge of cyber-attacks in the context of countermeasures under SR repertoire). See also generally JT Biller, 'Cyber-Terrorism: Finding a Common Starting Point' (2013) 4 Journal of Law, Technology & the Internet 275.

[138] For an extensive review of this precedent, see Proulx (n 6) 273–5, 297–8 and authorities cited therein (also exploring the challenges in attributing cyber-attacks under SR law). Other relevant incidents occurred in Georgia in 2008 and Iran in 2010.

[139] See D Turns, 'The First Case of Cyberwar in Non-International Armed Conflict? The Matrix in Iraq' (2015) 19 ASIL Insights <http://www.asil.org/insights/volume/19/issue/18/first-case-cyberwar-non-international-armed-conflict-matrix-iraq> accessed 18 August 2015. For another conflict, see also G Boulet, 'Cyber Operations by Private Actors in the Ukraine-Russia Conflict: From Cyber War to Cyber Security' (2015) 19 ASIL Insights <http://www.asil.org/insights/volume/19/issue/1/cyber-operations-private-actors-ukraine-russia-conflict-cyber-war-cyber> accessed 10 August 2015.

[140] See, eg, DE Graham, 'Cyber Threats and the Law of War' (2010) 4 Journal of National Security Law and Policy 87, 92–3, 96. See also generally MJ Sklerov, 'Solving the Dilemma of State Responses to Cyberattacks: A Justification for the Use of Active Defenses against States Who Neglect their Duty to Prevent' (2009) 201 Military Law Review 1, 6–7; J Carr, *Inside Cyber Warfare: Mapping the Cyber Underworld* (2nd edn, O'Reilly 2010) 56.

[141] SR Ratner, 'Self-Defence against Terrorists: The Meaning of Armed Attack' in L van den Herik and N Schrijver (eds), *Counter-Terrorism Strategies in a Fragmented International Legal Order: Meeting the Challenges* (CUP 2013) 334, 352–3.

a state of flux, and relevant State practice is relatively unknown.[142] International policy and legal communities have attempted to fill that void.

In 2013, high-level consultations of policy and legal experts culminated in the *Tallinn Manual*, which sought to articulate the legal frameworks applicable to cyber warfare with particular emphasis on virtual 'armed attacks'.[143] A second edition, *Tallinn 2.0*, is currently being prepared and scheduled to be published in 2016; it will address online activity falling short of the threshold of 'armed attack', with some emphasis on SR principles.[144] However, some publicists rightly lament the *Tallinn Manual*'s extension of the ARSIWA's attribution norms to the cyber realm, which is characterized by 'attribution asymmetry', thereby hardening the narrow approach to attribution and enabling States to use private groups to 'engineer plausible deniability'. A 'virtual control test', they contend, would be better suited to cyberterrorism than classical attribution standards.[145]

Considerable confusion still surrounds applicable legal norms, particularly attribution standards, in virtual settings. For example, seizing relevant Internet Protocol addresses following an online attack can prove unreliable as a basis for attributing virtual wrongful conduct to a 'territorial' State, as online technology is increasingly used by both States and non-State actors to pursue subterfuges, create avatars, control subversive proxies, perpetrate criminal activity, and conceal the origin and authorship of certain acts.[146] Whilst it is possible that UN organs, particularly the SC, will be called upon to handle situations involving cyberterrorism/

[142] Prior to 9/11, the analytical crux focused on the impact of the online attack. See, eg, MN Schmitt, 'Computer Network Attack and the Use of Force in International Law: Thoughts on a Normative Framework' (1999) 37 CJTL 885; TC Wingfield, *The Law of Information Conflict: National Security Law in Cyberspace* (Aegis Research Corporation 2000).

[143] MN Schmitt (ed.), *Tallinn Manual on the International Law Applicable to Cyber Warfare: Prepared by the International Group of Experts at the Invitation of the NATO Cooperative Cyber Defence Centre of Excellence* (CUP 2013). For various views on the *Tallinn Manual*, see D Fleck, 'Searching for International Rules Applicable to Cyber Warfare: A Critical First Assessment of the New Tallinn Manual' (2013) 18 JCSL 331; L Boer, 'Restating the Law "As It Is": On the Tallinn Manual and the Use of Force in Cyberspace' (2013) 5 Amsterdam Law Forum 4; O Kessler, 'Expertise, Uncertainty, and International Law: A Study of the Tallinn Manual on Cyberwarfare' (2013) 26 LJIL 793; WH von Heinegg, 'The Tallinn Manual and International Cyber Security Law' (2012) 15 Yearbook of International Humanitarian Law 19; N Tsagourias, 'The Tallinn Manual on the International Law Applicable to Cyber Warfare: A Commentary on Chapter II—the Use of Force' (2012) 15 Yearbook of International Humanitarian Law 19; C Lecomte, 'Le Manuel de Tallinn au Regard des Principes Posés dans la Jurisprudence de la Cour Internationale de Justice' in SFDI (ed.), *Internet et le Droit International* (Pedone 2014) 309–22. See also generally HH Dinniss, *Cyber Warfare and the Laws of War* (CUP 2012).

[144] For further information, see <https://ccdcoe.org/research.html> accessed 10 August 2015.

[145] See P Margulies, 'Sovereignty and Cyber Attacks: Technology's Challenge to the Law of State Responsibility' (2013) 14 Melbourne Journal of International Law 496. See generally Z Huang, 'The Attribution Rules in ILC's Articles on State Responsibility: A Preliminary Assessment on their Application to Cyber Operations' (2014) Baltic Yearbook of International Law 41.

[146] See, eg, S Brenner, 'At Light Speed: Attribution and Response to Cybercrime/Terrorism/Warfare' (2007) 97 Journal of Criminal Law and Criminology 379, 424. See also generally N Bussolati, 'The Rise of Non-State Actors in Cyberwarfare' in C Finkelstein *et al.* (eds), *Cyber War: Law and Ethics for Virtual Conflicts* (OUP 2015) 102–26.

crime in a global security context, they may lack the benefit of clear legal postulates to govern the implementation of SR for the foreseeable future.

For the time being, UN organs have been pursuing a logical strategy: extending 'terrestrial' legal sensibilities to the 'virtual battlefield', suggesting that virtual internationally wrongful acts are similar to their physical analogues save that they are committed using novel technology, and promulgating broad statements and guidelines on cyberterrorism.[147] Unquestionably, relevant legal standards will have to be revisited and adapted to cyberterrorism to ensure resolute responses to this security challenge. For its part, the SC has adopted resolutions imposing upon States the obligation to criminalize the incitement to terrorism and other related acts, which include online radicalization, fundraising, operational planning, training, and promotion of terrorist enterprises.[148] Therefore, as will be seen in other global security contexts in Part II of this book, it has formulated primary international legal norms; it is only logical that it might eventually be seized of a matter in which it actually has to implement those norms under SR law. Similarly, in Resolution 1963 the Council expressed 'concern at the increased use, in a globalized society, by terrorists of new information and communication technologies, in particular the Internet, for the purposes of the recruitment and incitement as well as for the financing, planning and preparation of their activities'.[149] Furthermore, SC involvement in counterterrorism strategies, aside from those which will be explored in Part II of the present volume, has been active through the Working Group on Countering the Use of the Internet for Terrorist Purposes, which is part of the Counter-Terrorism Implementation Task Force (CTITF).[150]

Finally, the phenomena of cybercrime and cyberterrorism present significant points of similarity with climate change and global warming in that a series of internationally wrongful acts can span over several States and ultimately facilitate the commission of a terrorist act; similarly to transboundary pollution, the exact sources or causes of a given attack—which may be gradual and cumulative—might be difficult to ascertain.[151] Hence, the challenge does not reside at the conceptual level, but rather arises in the factual and evidentiary components of the SR calculus.

[147] See, eg, The United Nations Global Counter-Terrorism Strategy, UNGA Res 60/288 (20 September 2006) UN Doc A/RES/60/288 [12]. See also UNODC, 'The Use of the Internet for Terrorist Purposes' (2012) <https://www.unodc.org/documents/terrorism/Publications/Use_of_Internet_for_Terrorist_Purposes/ebook_use_of_the_internet_for_terrorist_purposes.pdf> accessed 18 August 2015.

[148] See, eg, UNSC Res 1624 (14 September 2005) UN Doc S/RES/1624 (also imposing the obligation on States to deny safe haven to inciters).

[149] UNSC Res 1963 (20 December 2010) UN Doc S/RES1963, preamble. See also UNSC Res 2214 (27 March 2015) UN Doc S/RES/2214.

[150] See, eg, CTITF Working Group Compendium, 'Countering the Use of the Internet for Terrorist Purposes—Legal and Technical Aspects' (2011) <http://www.un.org/en/terrorism/ctitf/pdfs/ctitf_interagency_wg_compendium_legal_technical_aspects_web.pdf> accessed 10 August 2015.

[151] See T Scovazzi (n 69) 217–18. Moreover, shared responsibility mechanisms might be limited in responding to transnational pollution. See Y Tanaka, 'Reflections on Transboundary Air Pollution in the Arctic: Limits of Shared Responsibility' (2014) 83 NJIL 213.

This type of situation challenges the core of the ARSIWA as it is unclear what will constitute the crystallizing moment for the purpose of apportioning liability when several preparatory terrorist acts—be they virtual or physical—span over more than one territory. As seen earlier, ARSIWA Article 47(1) provides one possible solution, at least in theory.[152] As a general rule, it is fair to assume that every State's international responsibility in a chain of failures to prevent, leading to a transnational terrorist attack, might be commensurate with its level of accommodation or support of the harmful activity.[153] Moreover, there appears to be jurisprudential support for assessing each participating State's responsibility independently pursuant to ARSIWA Article 47(1). For instance, in the *Phosphate Lands in Nauru* case the ICJ found that Australia's responsibility could be assessed individually, even though both New Zealand and the UK also administered Nauru whilst it was a trust territory.[154] However, implementing this approach in practice might prove difficult, especially when enforcement of relevant norms is envisaged through UN political organs, which may not dispose of sophisticated or sufficiently exhaustive fact-finding mechanisms.

[152] For the text of the provision, see n 66 and accompanying text. On this provision and its implications in the counterterrorism debate, see Proulx (n 6) 128, 275, 291–3, 298–9.

[153] See, eg, SN Schiedeman, 'Standards of Proof in Forcible Responses to Terrorism' (2000) 50 Syracuse Law Review 249, 261; Smith (n 28) 746.

[154] *Case Concerning Certain Phosphate Lands in Nauru (Nauru v Australia)* (Preliminary Objections) [1992] ICJ Rep 240, 258–9. See also generally JE Noyes and BD Smith, 'State Responsibility and the Principle of Joint and Several Liability' (1988) 13 YJIL 225; A Nollkaemper, 'Issues of Shared Responsibility before the International Court of Justice' in E Rieter and H de Waele (eds), *Evolving Principles of International Law* (Nijhoff 2012) 199–237. On shared responsibility, generally and in relation to terrorists, see KN Trapp, 'Shared Responsibility and Non-State Terrorist Actors' (2015) 62 NILR 141; A Nollkaemper and I Plakokefalos (eds), *Principles of Shared Responsibility in International Law: An Appraisal of the State of the Art* (CUP 2014); A Nollkaemper, 'Concerted Adjudication in Cases of Shared Responsibility' (2014) 46 NYUJILP 809; A Nollkaemper and D Jacobs, 'Shared Responsibility in International Law: A Conceptual Framework' (2013) 34 MJIL 359.

Conclusion to Part I

Ultimately, the picture that emerges is one where it is difficult—both from conceptual and practical standpoints—to apply State responsibility (SR) norms to all global security breaches. The de-territorialized nature of some internationally wrongful acts, their factual complexity, the nature and mechanics of secondary SR norms, and ongoing difficulties in establishing a causal nexus between non-State actors and their territorial State obfuscate the implementation logic of SR. In Part II, arguments will be advanced to the effect that implementation could be pursued through United Nation (UN) organs, particularly the Security Council, as a partial solution to this problem. Given the difficulty of generalizing legal frameworks applicable to global security challenges across the board, especially those that occur on the transnational plane, this book has elected terrorism as its principal case study in order to gauge the potential benefits of institutionalizing SR law. However, it should be reiterated that this limited analytical scope does not entail an exhaustive treatment of terrorism and all relevant State practice, nor does it seek to review all pertinent types of global security breaches. Rather, this study aims to explore the potential implementation of SR by UN organs in global security contexts, along with the role that SR principles can play in informing use of force both within and outside institutional settings.

However, Part II includes analysis of other global security areas in the implementation debate, including non-proliferation of weapons of mass destruction (WMDs), international humanitarian law (IHL) violations, human rights abuses, unlawful use of force, etc. In many ways, the foregoing considerations, including the discussion of precautionary approaches in Section 2.4.2 earlier, serve as a preliminary gloss through which subsequent sections of this study should be contemplated. Given that Part III investigates potential forcible responses to internationally wrongful acts, the analysis operates on the premise that the responsible State's wrongdoing must relate to activity involving unlawful use of force, which considerably limits the scope of eligible global security breaches that may elicit such reactions.

For instance, it might be difficult to maintain that a *lex specialis* exception has cropped up to enable injured States to forcibly target responsible States for their failures to prevent transboundary pollution or transboundary credit card fraud. Conversely, as will be seen in Part III, the same line of argument encounters less resistance in scenarios involving State failures to prevent transnational terrorism. Therefore, it remains the principal case study in investigating whether the institutionalization of SR law can become an attractive policy option, in the hope that this exercise will generate lessons and best practices for other analogous global security violations.

PART II

IMPLEMENTING STATE RESPONSIBILITY AFTER 9/11

Institutional Perspectives

Introduction to Part II

Part II builds upon the conclusions of Part I and delivers the study's principal (and critical) analysis and corresponding policy proposal, namely: strengthening the enforcement and implementation of State responsibility (SR) through institutional channels in counterterrorism contexts. In so doing, one hopes to draw lessons relevant to other global security threats. In particular, Part II delves into the possible implementation of SR through relevant United Nations organs. At the outset, it must be acknowledged that this constitutes a challenging hypothesis given that organization's overall framework, and States' resistance to subjecting their own reputations to the fate of a politically volatile multilateral process. However, amongst institutional actors and other important norm creators, the Security Council (SC) and, decidedly to a lesser extent, the General Assembly (GA) undoubtedly interpret, apply, and develop international legal principles; this has certainly been the case in the field of recourse to force.[1] Part II suggests that similar advances have been made in the field of SR and, as a corollary, in other substantive areas pertaining to global security which may have an impact on the application or implementation of SR.

There is a growing body of literature investigating law-making by international organizations (IOs).[2] For the purposes of SR, this does not pose much of a problem at the conceptual level. As seen in Part II, UN organs, particularly the SC, have been fairly active in promulgating primary norms of international law which are inextricably linked to the implementation of the international responsibility of States. On this front, the SC's contributions have been most notable in the realms of counterterrorism and nuclear non-proliferation. Whilst relevant 'legislative' advances will be canvassed, the real challenge rather resides in determining whether UN organs—especially the SC—can play a role in implementing SR law. Put another way, can that normative scheme be institutionalized?

Whilst principal UN organs, particularly the International Court of Justice (ICJ) and the SC, may appear well-suited to apply and advance that normative

[1] See, eg, P Webb, *International Judicial Integration and Fragmentation* (OUP 2013) 105.

[2] See, eg, JE Alvarez, *International Organizations as Law-makers* (OUP 2005); I Johnstone, 'Law-Making by International Organizations: Perspectives from International Law/International Relations Theory' in JL Dunoff and MA Pollack (eds), *Interdisciplinary Perspectives on International Law and International Relations: The State of Art* (OUP 2013) 266–92; I Johnstone, 'Law-Making through the Operational Activities of International Organizations' (2008) 40 GWILR 87.

scheme, those institutions' incursions into SR repertoire have been rather limited or piecemeal. Furthermore, international judiciaries have often—perhaps overly cautiously—steered clear of the application of SR principles. The ICJ's record is certainly a case in point, as seen in Chapter 3. Indeed, it has often sidestepped SR mechanics in cases where a finding that an internationally wrongful act had been committed could have played a pivotal role in the proceedings. Perhaps more relevantly, the international responsibility of States in specific circumstances, namely that of France and Libya, was established outside international judicial settings in both the *Rainbow Warrior* and *Lockerbie* cases. This certainly suggests that the ICJ is being excluded—perhaps of its own volition in cases where it sidestepped SR mechanics when it could have made a free-standing determination of responsibility—from participating directly in the major growth areas involving the law of SR.[3] As discussed elsewhere, however, the ICJ's analysis of SR principles in the *Bosnian Genocide* case might prove otherwise, as it afforded considerable space to relevant legal norms in its judgment (eg attribution, satisfaction).[4] Whilst it is perhaps unlikely that the ICJ would be inclined to declare that a State has failed to comply with its obligation to prevent terrorism in another scenario, that case evinced the Court's reliance on the rigid formulation of classical agency rules whilst offering little in the way of critical or evolutionary interpretation of those norms.[5]

Despite these reservations, considerable support remains for the possible implementation of SR by IOs. In fact, the International Law Commission (ILC) has, at times, formally contemplated this eventuality. Consequently, the SC seems well-equipped to deal with the determination of SR questions in some situations involving terrorism, and has expressly done so in the *Lockerbie* case. Moreover, the Council disposes of powerful tools, straddling political *and* legal terrain, to exert some influence on the repression of terrorism, a function that has generated some high-level inquiries on the matter.[6] As a corollary, the SC's potential role in applying SR principles may also have some impact, albeit limited, on use of force repertoire and fill some normative void where the application of attribution principles appears intractable. Thus,

[3] In broader terms, compare with the appraisal of the Court's work delivered by a former ICJ President: SR Jennings, 'The International Court of Justice after Fifty Years' (1995) 89 AJIL 493.

[4] See, eg, *Case Concerning the Application of the Convention on the Prevention and Punishment of the Crime of Genocide (Bosnia and Herzegovina v Serbia and Montenegro)* (Merits) [2007] ICJ Rep 43, 140–9, 234–6 [387]–[388], 402–6, 429–31, 438, 463; V-J Proulx, *Transnational Terrorism and State Accountability: A New Theory of Prevention* (Hart 2012) esp ch 1. For a critical take on the Court's silence in that case, see KN Trapp, 'Of Dissonance and Silence; State Responsibility in the *Bosnia Genocide* Case' (2015) 62 NILR 243 (articulating an alternative view of SR and arguing that the Court may have filled existing gaps at the primary normative level by relying on implied obligations).

[5] For a critique of the traditional agency paradigm, see T Becker, *Terrorism and the State: Rethinking the Rules of State Responsibility* (Hart 2006).

[6] See, eg, S Chesterman, *The UN Security Council and the Rule of Law: The Role of the Security Council in Strengthening a Rules-Based International System: Final Report and Recommendations from the Austrian Initiative, 2004–2008* (Federal Ministry of European and International Affairs 2008) 12.

> principles of state responsibility indeed are relevant to a determination of the legality of self-defence, as they can underlie, exist parallel to, and sometimes supplant the criteria contained in the primary rules on self-defence... attempts to disconnect the principles of attribution in the law of state responsibility and the law on the use of force are generally based on weak legal authority and are generally undesirable... the Security Council plays a key role in grey areas where the applicability of principles of attribution is unclear.[7]

Therefore, Part II sets the stage for the analysis to follow in Part III, which explores the role that SR plays in justifying forcible countermeasures and self-defence, both within and outside institutionalized settings. The principal purposes of Part II, however, are to: (i) determine the extent of the role of UN organs in this framework, however limited it may be; and (ii) situate the possible implementation of SR by UN organs within the broader project of devising a scheme of international responsibility better suited to the changing threats of global security. In this regard, transnational terrorism will remain the principal case study when investigating a possible rapprochement between the respective missions of UN organs and SR repertoire.

Part II thus sets out to explore the possible institutionalization of the implementation of SR, with particular emphasis on institutional perspectives within the broader UN framework. Concretely, the study now turns to the UN's contributions in further delineating SR norms for failing to prevent terrorist attacks. Set against the backdrop of a rich legal tapestry, the many relevant *dicta* of the ILC, ICJ, GA, and SC interweave and ultimately inform the development and implementation of SR in global security contexts. Whether some of their more conceptually nebulous interpretations and applications can be disentangled, and clear postulates extracted, remains to be seen. In attempting to elucidate this relationship, Part II proceeds on a two-tiered approach. First, after briefly canvassing possible contributions by other UN organs, it explores the theoretical and practical underpinnings of the SC's contributions to SR implementation and, ultimately, attempts to achieve a rapprochement between the SC's Chapter VII powers and counterterrorism. This analysis is deployed in the hope of identifying available international legal avenues to regulate, or respond to, other global security threats. Secondly, Part II embarks upon a more concrete analysis of this phenomenon as regards transnational terrorism—along with other relevant contributions by UN organs—and finally queries whether any kind of concerted thread, or conclusion, can be drawn from SC practice concerning the SR/terrorism debate.

Chapter 3 examines the prospect of implementing SR through existing UN channels more broadly, with particular insistence on the potential contributions of the ICJ, GA, and SC. Setting the stage for subsequent arguments, the chapter concludes by exploring the prospects and limits of SC powers within the purview of the inquiry at hand, thereby framing the major analytical stakes involved with

[7] A Nollkaemper, 'Attribution of Forcible Acts to States: Connections between the Law on the Use of Force and the Law of State Responsibility' in N Blokker and N Schrijver (eds), *The Security Council and the Use of Force: Theory and Reality—A Need for Change?* (Nijhoff 2005) 133, 139.

specific reference to that organ's 'quasi-judicial' exercise of powers. Brief consideration is also given to important related questions—such as the ICJ's potential judicial review of SC decisions and the issue of *lis pendens* between both organs—the resolution of which is ultimately not essential, although important, for the central arguments advanced in this study.

An initial methodological caveat is warranted, since the analysis in Part II primarily explores the potential contributions of the SC in implementing SR, whilst setting aside regional perspectives, bodies, and mechanisms. Given that the SC has promulgated enhanced and broad-reaching counterterrorism duties and increased States' due diligence obligations after 9/11, as will be seen in Chapter 4,[8] it seems logical to focus almost exclusively on that organ's ability to implement SR. Simply put, this book concerns itself with global security threats and, in many ways, the SC remains the foremost engine of global security. However, this approach should not suggest, in any way, that the work of regional courts and bodies is not important for the advancement of SR repertoire, or that it could not constitute evidence of institutionalized implementation of SR in certain circumstances.

By way of example, it should be recalled that both the Inter-American Court of Human Rights (IACHR) and European Court of Human Rights (ECtHR) have tackled SR issues in their respective dockets.[9] Whilst these regional perspectives will not feature heavily in the analysis, they nonetheless contribute to a multiplicity of legal regimes and frameworks working in harmony, all with a view to strengthening global security. As will be seen in Part II, some of the institutions contributing to this multiplicity of regimes, most notably the SC, have 'legislated' on global security matters. In many ways, therefore, there is synergy between these various institutional actors and, one hopes, harmony between their respective operational frameworks and applicable legal regimes. Consequently, all these mutually reinforcing regimes work complementarily to stamp out the most serious security threats, including transnational terrorism.[10]

The principal focus on the SC's implementation of SR in Part II is also supported by the evolution of international law itself. Rethinking the prospect of implementing SR through institutional channels appears to be compatible with other legal tools used by the SC in its decision-making. For instance, it should be recalled that the Responsibility to Protect (R2P) doctrine was elaborated by the International Commission on Intervention and State Sovereignty (ICISS) in 2001.[11] R2P constitutes a controversial, but arguably, emerging norm of international law according to which States must protect their populations from mass

[8] See also generally Proulx (n 4).

[9] For the IACHR, see, eg, *Velásquez Rodríguez Case*, Inter-Am Ct HR Decisions and Judgments 91 (ser C) No 4 (1988) esp [161]–[185]; *Blake v Guatemala*, Inter-Am Ct HR Decisions and Judgments (ser C) No 36 (1998) esp [67]. For the ECtHR, see, eg, *Papamichalopoulos and Others v Greece*, Eur Ct Hr (ser A) No 260-B (1993) esp [145]; *Loizidou v Turkey* (1996-VI) Eur Ct HR 2216.

[10] See generally KLH Samuel, *The OIC, the UN, and Counter-Terrorism Law-Making: Conflicting or Cooperative Legal Orders?* (Hart 2013).

[11] ICISS, *The Responsibility to Protect: Report of the International Commission on Intervention and State Sovereignty* (International Development Research Centre 2001).

atrocity. Since 2006, the SC has referenced R2P in a series of resolutions and in a variety of contexts, most famously in relation to the situations in Syria and Libya.[12]

For one thing, this practice most likely shows an enhanced focus on international responsibility models grounded in States' control over territory in which unlawful behaviour is taking place, and the corresponding duties to prevent and exercise sovereignty responsibly. It is not far-fetched to infer that similar reasoning could extend to certain global security threats, including transnational terrorism. Indeed, since 9/11 the international legal system has accommodated heightened due diligence obligations, which concomitantly signals a shift in both policy and legal inclinations toward acute prevention.[13] More importantly, this development suggests that the SC can play a role—sometimes determinant—in the implementation of SR.

If the SC can invoke a nascent and controversial legal norm like R2P, surely it should be amenable to incorporate SR principles in its decision-making, when the circumstances warrant it. After all, ontological debates rage on over the normative legitimacy of R2P: its very existence is at stake. By contrast, SR law constitutes a veritable cornerstone of the modern international legal system. It has been the subject of nearly fifty years of discussions, debates, and codification by the ILC, the end-product of which was the ARSIWA, and it has been flagged for possible enshrinement in an international convention by the GA.[14] Its centrality and importance in international law is recognized universally. It seems only logical that it remains available as a conceptual tool to facilitate the SC's primary function of maintaining international peace and security. Furthermore, existing scholarly literature confirms the SC's potential centrality and influence in this debate, at least as regards the institutionalized implementation of SR.[15]

Chapter 4 embarks upon a thorough and methodical examination of the SC's role in counterterrorism and global security contexts, along with its proclivity to apply and interpret secondary SR rules, even if indirectly. The analysis also takes

[12] See, eg, UNSC Res 1674 (28 April 2006) UN Doc S/RES/1674 on the protection of civilians in armed conflict; UNSC Res 1894 (11 November 2009) UN Doc S/RES/1894 on the same subject; UNSC Res 1970 (26 February 2011) UN Doc S/RES 1970 on the situation in Libya; UNSC Res 2117 (26 September 2013) UN Doc S/RES/2117 on small arms and light weapons; UNSC Res 2139 (22 February 2014) UN Doc S/RES/2139 on the situation in Syria; UNSC Res 2150 (16 April 2014) UN Doc S/RES/2150 on threats to international peace and security; UNSC Res 2171 (21 August 2014) UN Doc S/RES/2171 on conflict prevention. On the relationship between R2P, the situations in Libya and Syria, and future implications, see O Stunkel, 'The BRICS and the Future of R2P: Was Syria or Libya the Exception? (2014) 6 GRP 3; BJ Steele and EA Heinze, 'Norms of Intervention, R2P and Libya: Suggestions from Generational Analysis' (2014) 6 GRP 88.

[13] See generally Proulx (n 4). On heightened post-9/11 counterterrorism obligations, see also B Stern, 'La Responsabilité Internationale des États: Perspectives Récentes' in JC Lloréns (ed.), *Cursos Eeuromediterráneos Bancaja de Derecho Internacional*, vol 7 (Tirant lo Blanch 2003) 659, 688–92.

[14] See Section 3.1.4, n 151, and accompanying text.

[15] The SC can also play a role in the enforcement of individual criminal responsibility, a possibility contemplated in many scenarios, not least the situation in Darfur. See, eg, Y Aksar, 'The UN Security Council and the Enforcement of Individual Criminal Responsibility: The Darfur Case' (2006) 14 African Journal of International and Comparative Law (2006).

stock of the SC's formulation of relevant primary norms in those contexts, often equated with a 'legislative' role or function. More importantly, the chapter delves into the interplay between the SC and SR norms by analysing their impact on both Chapter VII powers and resolutions adopted outside that framework. In this regard, this volume chronicles and analyses the extensiveness of SC practice with a view to elucidating this interrelation. Whilst both the process of SC decision-making and the nature of its decisions are difficult to untangle, the chapter operates on the premise that the SC must strike a delicate balance between political and legal *considerations* whilst employing a quasi-judicial *process* or *method* in reaching a decision about international peace and security. This may entail applying SR principles to acts of transnational terrorism. This discussion paves the way for a more comprehensive analysis of the SC's role in actually implementing SR for terrorism. Moreover, the chapter specifically considers the expansion of Chapter VII powers under the UN Charter to include SR, the Council's powers in relation to secondary norms, and the rights of States regarding the implementation of SR notwithstanding SC involvement.

Part II concludes by identifying an overlap of objectives between the *sui generis* mission of counterterrorism and the SC's more traditional 'executive' functions, thereby facilitating the prospect of a rapprochement with SR repertoire. Ultimately, this line of reasoning prompts the conclusion that SR for failing to prevent global security breaches, particularly terrorism, can be implemented by the Council in certain circumstances.

3

Advancing State Responsibility through UN Institutional Mechanisms

This chapter investigates the compatibility between relevant United Nations (UN) organs and State responsibility (SR) law. It does so with a view to determining whether the implementation of this normative scheme can be institutionalized and through which organ this prospect would be most realistic in the global security context. Section 3.1 sets the stage by first canvassing as a general proposition the prospect of institutionalizing the implementation of SR through existing institutional channels. In particular, it considers the major scholarly currents coalescing around, or against, this idea before briefly addressing issues related to fairness. This chapter then frames the role of UN organs in the global security context with reference to transnational terrorism as the primary case study, thus assessing existing institutional mechanisms in implementing SR by looking specifically at structural aspects of the International Court of Justice (ICJ), the General Assembly (GA), and the Security Council (SC). In setting the stage for subsequent arguments in Chapter 4, Section 3.1.5 concludes by exploring the prospects and limits of SC powers within the purview of the present book, namely by reference to the potential institutionalization of SR. The inquiry frames the major analytical stakes involved in this debate with specific reference to the SC's quasi-judicial exercise of powers.

This leads to the conclusion that the SC is best suited in some circumstances to implementing SR in global security contexts, particularly when dealing with counterterrorism issues. By way of conclusion, Section 3.2 briefly addresses three potential obstacles linked to that conclusion, namely: (i) the ICJ's potential judicial review of SC resolutions; (ii) the functional overlap and complementarity between those two organs; and (iii) the potential issue of *lis pendens* in relation to those two organs. Ultimately, this volume concludes that these three would-be problem areas do not erect any insurmountable conceptual barriers to Part II's central arguments. Consequently, a methodical examination of the SC's role in implementing SR is pursued in Chapter 4.

3.1 Assessing Existing Institutional Mechanisms in Implementing State Responsibility

3.1.1 The debate over institutionalized implementation: Scholarly perspectives

Inherent in the debate regarding whether SR can play a role in suppressing and preventing terrorism is the idea of institutionalizing the implementation of that normative scheme. According to textbook legal principles, responsibility flowing from an internationally wrongful act is typically actuated, and ultimately implemented, through inter-State mechanisms. Consequently, this begs the question of whether SR for failing to prevent terrorist attacks could be implemented—even at all—through existing UN mechanisms. Consequently, the relationship between the extant scheme of SR and certain UN organs, especially the SC, must be addressed squarely. It should be noted at the outset that the institutionalization of dispute settlement mechanisms is not synonymous, or even interchangeable, with the separate question of implementing SR in an institutionalized setting.[1] Dispute resolution mechanisms are much more reminiscent of 'jurisdictional' functions which, in turn, signal considerable implications for the interpretation and application of secondary SR rules. By contrast, the more traditionally labelled 'executive' functions of any organ that determines (and perhaps implements) international responsibility imply that it is barred from pursuing similar judicial/jurisdictional inquiries.[2] It is also helpful to recall that international law differs considerably in this respect from municipal law. Ordinarily, in domestic law the 'jurisdictional act' (which determines both the illegality and the culprit) precedes and conditions the implementation of legal responsibility, a task that falls to the executive branch. Conversely, in international law the determination of a wrongful act, coupled with the corresponding implementation of responsibility, are relegated concomitantly to a single legal subject or actor (ie an injured State or international organization (IO) fulfilling an executive function). In the latter scenario, judicial intervention operates an *ex post facto* review of this determination in the context of subsequent dispute settlement proceedings.[3]

More importantly, the application of SR norms has often been linked with the activities of IOs, especially when taking stock of collective interests or interests emblematic of the international community as a whole, which include global security priorities.[4] Consequently, the ensuing scholarly debate has divided sharply

[1] For a multiplicity of views on dispute resolution mechanisms in the field of SR, see 'Symposium: Counter-measures and Dispute Settlement: The Current Debate within the ILC' (1994) 5 EJIL 20–115 (including contributions by Arangio-Ruiz, Vereshchetin, Bennouna, Crawford, Tomuschat, Bowett, Simma, and Condorelli).

[2] See, eg, SM Villalpando, *L'Émergence de la Communauté Internationale dans la Responsabilité des États* (PUF 2005) 421.

[3] For a classical formulation, see, G Scelle, *Droit International Public: Manuel Élémentaire avec les Textes Essentiels* (Domat-Montchrestien 1944) 654.

[4] See, eg, B Graefrath, 'International Crimes and Collective Security' in K Wellens (ed.), *International Law: Theory and Practice: Essays in Honour of Eric Suy* (Nijhoff 1998) 237, 239.

into two respective camps. On the one hand, certain publicists conceptualize the implementation of aggravated community responsibility—that is to say the legal consequences flowing from the perpetration of internationally wrongful acts harming collective interests and usually stemming either from the violation of *jus cogens* norms or obligations *erga omnes*—solely through the lens of institutional mechanisms.[5] On the other hand, detractors of this view acknowledge the existence of an unstructured, somewhat self-regulated system resulting from general international law, a system highly dependent on the notion of self-help and unilateral invocation of SR by aggrieved States.

According to the first view, which has received wide academic support,[6] aggravated community responsibility can only be actuated through institutional channels to improve the coordination of reactions to violations of obligations *erga omnes*. This position carries with it particular significance for counterterrorism, as it has been argued persuasively that the duty to prevent terrorism amounts to an obligation *erga omnes*.[7] Moreover, the International Law Commission's (ILC) work may well lead one to conclude that the progressive affirmation of obligations *erga omnes* in modern international law has paved the way for strong institutional involvement under SR repertoire: namely, an international legal system that enables international institutions to determine the existence of a wrongful act infringing an obligation *erga omnes* and, correspondingly, to devise the legal consequences of such a breach and determine how SR implementation should be envisaged.[8] In turn, this view paves the way for two distinct positions on the possible institutionalization of the implementation of SR.

[5] On obligations *erga omnes*, see the *obiter dictum* in *Barcelona Traction, Light and Power Company, Limited* (Second Phase) [1970] ICJ Rep 3, 32 [33]–[34]. See also *East Timor (Portugal v Australia)* (Jurisdiction) [1995] ICJ Rep 90, 102 [29]; *Legal Consequences of the Construction of a Wall* (Advisory Opinion) [2004] ICJ Rep 136, 199 [157]. For a concise review of obligations *erga omnes*, with particular emphasis on ICJ pronouncements on the issue, see A De Hoogh, *Obligations Erga Omnes and International Crimes: A Theoretical Inquiry into the Implementation and Enforcement of the International Responsibility of States* (Kluwer 1996) 49–56; M Ragazzi, *The Concept of International Obligations 'Erga Omnes'* (Clarendon Press 1997) 7–12. On the question of enforcing such obligations, see CJ Tams, *Enforcing Obligations Erga Omnes in International Law* (CUP 2005).

[6] See, eg, D Alland, 'International Responsibility and Sanctions: Self-Defence and Countermeasures in the ILC Codification of Rules Governing International Responsibility' in M Spinedi and B Simma (eds), *United Nations Codification of State Responsibility* (Oceana 1987) 143, 186–95; JC Lloréns, 'Deberes Jurídicos y Responsabilidad Internacional' in MP Gonzalez (eds), *Hacia un Nuevo Orden Internacional y Europeo: Estudios en Homenaje al Profesor Don Manuel Díez de Velasco* (Tecnos 1993) 147, 158–9. See also ibid 159–63 (arguing that unilateral reactions to breaches remain available to States, regardless of any institutionalized procedure); P-M Dupuy, 'Observations sur la Pratique Récente des "Sanctions de l'Illicite"' (1983) 87 RGDIP 505, 546–8; W Riphagen, 'State Responsibility: New Theories of Obligation in Interstate Relations' in R StJ MacDonald and DM Johnson (eds), *The Structure and Process of International Law: Essays in Legal Philosophy Doctrine and Theory* (Nijhoff 1983) 581, 607.

[7] See, eg, P-M Dupuy, 'State Sponsors of Terrorism: Issues of International Responsibility' in A Bianchi (ed.), *Enforcing International Law Norms against Terrorism* (Hart Publishing 2004) 3, 12.

[8] ILC, 'Report of the International Law Commission on the Work of its 31st Session' (14 May–3 August 1979) UN Doc A/34/10; (1979) II(2) *YILC* 119 (resulting from R Ago, 'Eighth Report on State Responsibility' (1979) UN Doc A/CN.4/318 and Add.1–4; (1979) II(1) *YILC* 43 [91]). On Ago's position, see R Ago, 'Third Report on State Responsibility' (1971) UN Doc A/CN.4/246 and

First, this school of thought acknowledges that existing international procedures and organizations, most notably UN organs, are adequately suited to ensure the implementation of SR. This thinking was pervasive in the commentaries accompanying ILC Article 19 (on international crimes of States)[9] and Article 30 (on countermeasures),[10] both adopted by the ILC during the first reading. It was also the primary driving force behind Special Rapporteur Willem Riphagen's proposed draft articles, which provided for the implementation of the consequences flowing from the commission of international crimes through usual UN procedures on the maintenance of international peace and security.[11] At the time this position was raised within the ILC, the corresponding concern of whether this course of action would actually increase the UN's role in the implementation of SR was simultaneously brought up. More importantly, it was also cautioned that SC involvement in the implementation process might carry with it political impediments, with 'the exercise of the right of veto' being potentially 'incompatible with the requirement of solidarity'.[12] In any event, this line of reasoning signalled that as part of its membership in the international community, any State involved with SR mechanics would be exercising new rights and obligations in the broader context of a concerted community of States.[13] Similarly, several States and commentators rejected the existence of a special regime addressing the consequences of grave violations of *jus cogens* obligations outside the UN framework.

Add. 1–3; (1971) II(1) *YILC* 221, and his remarks in JHH Weiler *et al.* (eds), *International Crimes of State: A Critical Analysis of the ILC's Draft Article 19 on State Responsibility* (De Gruyter 1989) 238–9.

[9] See, eg, Commentary on Art 19, adopted in the first reading: ILC, 'Report of the International Law Commission on the Work of its 28th Session' (3 May–23 July 1976) UN Doc A/31/10; (1976) II(2) *YILC* 102–8 [16], [22]–[29] (with particular emphasis at [18] on 'the fact that the United Nations Charter attaches specific consequences to the breach of certain international obligations'). See also the various positions defended within the ILC: R Ago (1976) I *YILC* 58–9, MK Yasseen (ibid 62–3), and AM Moreno (ibid 70–1). For a brief overview of the positions espoused by various States on this debate, see, eg, M Spinedi, 'International Crimes of States: The Legislative History' in Weiler *et al.* (n 8) 64–5.

[10] Commentary to Art 30, adopted in the first reading: (1979) II(2) *YILC* 121 [21].

[11] See Draft Art 14(3), as proposed in Riphagen, W, 'Sixth Report on the Content, Forms and Degrees of International Responsibility (Part 2 of the Draft Articles); and "Implementation" (mise en oeuvre) of International Responsibility and the Settlement of Disputes (Part 3 of the Draft Articles)' (1985) UN Doc A/CN.4/389; (1985) II(1) *YILC* 21. The relevant portions of the proposed draft article read as follows:

1. An international crime entails all the legal consequences of an internationally wrongful act and, in addition, such rights and obligations as are determined by the applicable rules accepted by the international community as a whole [...]
3. Unless otherwise provided for by an applicable rule of general international law, the exercise of the rights arising under paragraph 1 of the present article and the performance of the obligations arising under paragraphs 1 and 2 of the present article are subject, *mutatis mutandis, to the procedures embodied in the United Nations Charter with respect to the maintenance of international peace and security* (emphasis added).

Much in the same vein, Draft Art 15 stated that an act of aggression triggered all relevant rights and obligations stemming from the UN Charter.

[12] Sixth Report—Riphagen (n 11) 24 [151].

[13] See (1985) II(1) *YILC* 14 [9]; A Gattini, 'A Return Ticket to "Communitarisme", Please' (2002) 13 *EJIL* 1181, 1182. See also generally de Hoogh (n 5) 56–7.

Indeed, they exhibited particular resistance to the notion that countermeasures can be adopted unilaterally by States other than the 'direct' victim of the violation in such instances (ie the 'injured' State).[14]

Secondly, under this first general view it is submitted that the institutionalization of the implementation of SR is clearly desirable inasmuch as it would do away with some of the risks and pitfalls inherent in any State-led unilateral initiatives and reactions.[15] This trend also pervades other important dimensions of international law—it crops up in respect of the institutionalization of mediation between States, for example—and 'rather than by force or threats of force has led to the stability of states and the relations between them'.[16] This second position, however, further implies that the institutionalized implementation of SR fails to find any grounding in international law, as it currently stands, and could only seek steadier footing through the creation of an adequate institutional mechanism (either *ex novo* or by the adaptation of existing mechanisms to the requirements of SR).[17] In that light, we must always keep in mind the possibility of adapting existing UN mechanisms in order to facilitate the implementation of SR for failing to prevent transnational terrorism and, by extension, other global security violations. In many ways, this reasoning animated the proposals formulated by Special Rapporteur Arangio-Ruiz in his quest to subsume UN procedures and organs, along with the creation of a regime of responsibility for international crimes of States under a single framework.[18] Furthermore, different ILC members advanced similar arguments during the Commission's debates surrounding

[14] See, inter alia, certain ILC members in ILC, 'Report of the International Law Commission on the Work of its 52nd Session' (1 May–18 August 2000) UN Doc A/55/10; (2000) II(2) *YILC* 60 [366], or ILC, 'Report of the International Law Commission on the Work of its 53rd Session' (23 April–10 August 2001) UN Doc A/56/10; (2001) II(2) *YILC* 36 [54]; the observations of Mexico in UN Doc A/CN.4/515/Add.1 (3 April 2001) 91–2 and Poland in UN Doc A/CN.4/515/Add.2 (1 May 2001) 94; the observations of Cameroon, Greece, Iran, and Mexico within the Sixth Commission cited in Crawford, J, 'Fourth Report on State Responsibility' (2001) UN Doc A/CN.4/517, 18 [73]; B Simma, 'Does the UN Charter Provide an Adequate Legal Basis for Individual or Collective Responses to Violations of Obligations Erga Omnes?' in J Delbrück (ed.), *The Future of International Law Enforcement: New Scenarios—New Law?* (Duncker & Humblot 1993) 125, 136; SR Carulla, 'El Consejo de seguridad y la defensa de los derechos humanos: Reflexiones a partir del conflicto de Kosovo' (1999) 51 Revista Española de Derecho Internacional 59, 73–4.

[15] On the institutionalization of the implementation of community responsibility through existing UN mechanisms and other institutional vehicles, see P Klein, 'Responsibility for Serious Breaches of Obligations Deriving from Peremptory Norms of International Law and United Nations Law' (2002) 13 EJIL 1241, 1241–55.

[16] R Patton, 'Federal Preemption in an Age of Globalization' (2005) 37 CWRJIL 111, 117. See also PJ Spiro, 'Globalization and the (Foreign Affairs) Constitution' (2002) 63 Ohio State Law Journal 649, 650.

[17] See also Villalpando (n 2) 417.

[18] The theoretical reasoning of the Special Rapporteur was mapped out under the heading 'The Indispensable Role of International Institutions' in Arangio-Ruiz, G, 'Seventh Report on State Responsibility' (1995) UN Doc A/CN.4/469 and Add.1–2; (1995) II(1) *YILC* 25–49 [70]–[138]. See also Arangio-Ruiz, G, 'Fifth Report on State Responsibility' (1993) UN Doc A/CN.4/453/Add.2 and Add.3; (1993) II(1) *YILC* 24–26 [90]–[95]. His project ultimately led him to suggest Draft Art 19 (see ibid 36–7 [139]), which sought to establish an implementation mechanism flowing directly to States, but also simultaneously subject to the intervention of both political (GA or SC) and judicial (ICJ) UN organs.

the first reading.[19] During a different era of the ILC's work, Roberto Ago was also a vocal advocate of the institutionalized implementation of SR under the aegis of international institutions, especially for grave violations of international law. Unsurprisingly, this rationale prompted him to envisage international law gravitating

> towards a system vesting in international institutions other than States the exclusive responsibility, first, for determining the existence of a breach of an obligation of basic importance to the international community as a whole, and thereafter, for deciding what measures should be taken in response and how they should be implemented.[20]

In contrast, according to the second general view, there exists under general international law an aggravated regime of community responsibility hinging on unilateral invocation, along with unilateral adoption of countermeasures, by affected States.[21] Proponents of this view endorse the idea that a breach of an obligation *erga omnes* could be determined, and even acted upon, absent any institutional structure aiming to counteract such breach.[22] This appears to be the rationale underlying the Articles on Responsibility of States for Internationally Wrongful Acts (ARSIWA)[23] which seek to codify customary international law but provide no guidance on the possible institutionalization of the implementation of SR.[24] Moreover, the ARSIWA do not subordinate countermeasures to the prior submission of the underlying dispute to settlement procedures before a tribunal or other entity.[25] Consequently, the relationship between this regime of aggravated

[19] See, eg, ILC, 'Report of the International Law Commission on the Work of its 47th Session' (2 May–21 July 1995) UN Doc A/50/10; (1995) II(2) *YILC* 56–7 [312]–[317]; Commentary to Art 51 adopted in the first reading: ILC, 'Report of the International Law Commission on the Work of its 48th Session' (6 May–26 July 1996) UN Doc A/51/10; (1996) II(2) *YILC* 71 [7]–[13].

[20] Eighth Report—Ago (n 8) 43 [91]–[92]. For an analysis of the ILC's work during this period, see D Alland, 'La Légitime Défense et les Contre-mesures dans la Codification du Droit International de la Responsabilité' (1983) 110 Journal du Droit International 728. For a discussion of Ago's and Arangio-Ruiz's respective proposals, see P-M Dupuy, 'The Deficiencies of the Law of State Responsibility Relating to Breaches of "Obligations Owed to the International Community as a Whole": Suggestions for Avoiding the Obsolescence of Aggravated Responsibility' in A Cassese (ed.), *Realizing Utopia: The Future of International Law* (OUP 2012) 210, 215–21.

[21] The topic of countermeasures is addressed in Section 4.2.

[22] Consider E Wyler, 'From "State Crime" to Responsibility for "Serious Breaches of Obligations under Peremptory Norms of General International Law"' (2002) 13 EJIL 1147, 1151.

[23] Articles on the Responsibility of States for Internationally Wrongful Acts, UN Doc A/56/10 (2001); (2001) II(2) *YILC* 26 (and Commentary ibid 31).

[24] See generally P-M Dupuy, 'A General Stocktaking of the Connections Between the Multilateral Dimension of Obligations and Codification of the Law of Responsibility' (2002) 13 EJIL 1053, 1060 (underscoring that the disappearance of the notion of 'crime' from the ARSIWA had the effect of allowing 'the state's responsibility to be detached from any criminal or penal connotation; over and above getting rid of burdensome symbolism, this terminological innovation may seem *to justify better the absence in the part of the text on implementation of responsibility of any machinery* inspired by the criminal procedures of domestic law'); 1064 ('[t]he "crime" and its substitutes remain a formidable political weapon, which certain states intend to retain mastery of *without undergoing the constraints that any institutionalization of responsibility would risk introducing*') (emphasis added).

[25] On the requirements for the adoption of countermeasures, see Section 4.2.1 of this book. See also C Tomuschat, 'Are Counter-Measures Subject to Prior Recourse to Dispute Settlement Procedures?' (1994) 5 EJIL 77.

responsibility and the activities of IOs, especially those of UN organs, can be analysed through two distinct lenses.

On the one hand, existing institutional mechanisms (especially UN organs, geared towards the maintenance and/or restoration of international peace and security) can be construed as playing a minimal role in the context of international responsibility.[26] In particular, their potential contributions would either be significantly hampered by deficiencies endemic to the UN's nature and makeup (ie ill-suited procedures, inefficiency, or institutional paralysis in the face of grave violations), or simply eschewed because they fall within the ambit of other international law areas.[27] Hence, community responsibility—an area concerned solely with redressing unlawful acts harming collective interests (ie obligations *erga omnes*)[28]—would then flow from general international law and vest, upon individual States, rights and obligations originating from the same source. Interestingly, the conclusion of the ILC's work following the first reading pointed towards this model. In light of indomitable controversies surrounding the attempted establishment of an effective institutional mechanism, the ILC's 1996 Draft Articles ultimately favoured the unilateral implementation of responsibility by injured States.[29]

On the other hand, an alternate viewpoint emphasizes the importance of the reaction of IOs to emergency situations resulting from the commission of serious wrongful acts against the international community as a whole.[30] Thus, although clearly relevant, the general framework of SR would play a marginal role in protecting fundamental community interests.[31] More specifically, this would translate into two possible scenarios: (i) the adoption of unilateral countermeasures would be excluded, or (ii) the adoption of unilateral countermeasures would be subordinated to the primacy of an institutionalized collective action.[32]

This line of reasoning most likely informed Special Rapporteur James Crawford's proposal during the ILC's second reading. Whilst acknowledging the primacy of IOs in dealing with international breaches causing emergency situations vis-à-vis obligations *erga omnes* (with particular emphasis on the UN's pursuit of Chapter

[26] See, eg, Klein (n 15) 1247–50 (discussing this idea in the context of *jus cogens* duties).

[27] See Klein (n 15) 1247–50.

[28] On responsibility for breaches of communitarian norms, see also JR Crawford, *State Responsibility: The General Part* (CUP 2013) 362–94.

[29] See, eg, Commentary to Art 51 in ILC Report 1996 (n 19) 71 [2] (discussing the distinction between 'crimes' and 'exceptionally grave delicts' in this context).

[30] See, eg, V Gowlland-Debbas, 'Security Council Enforcement Action and Issues of State Responsibility' (1994) 43 ICLQ 55, 58, 63.

[31] See, eg, K Wellens, 'The UN Security Council and New Threats to the Peace: Back to the Future' (2003) 8 JCSL 15, 48–53 (and sources cited therein).

[32] See C Chinkin, *Third Parties in International Law* (Clarendon Press 1993) 337; DN Hutchison, 'Solidarity and Breaches of Multilateral Treaties' (1988) 59 BYIL 151, 212–3; L-A Sicilianos, *Les Réactions Décentralisées à L'Illicité: Des Contre-mesures à la Légitime Défense* (LGDJ 1990) 174–5; B Simma, 'From Bilateralism to Community Interest in International Law' (1994) 250 RdC 217, 310–1; I Sinclair's remarks in Weiler *et al.* (n 8) 257. See also L-A Sicilianos, 'Countermeasures in Response to Grave Violations of Obligations Owed to the International Community' in JR Crawford *et al.* (eds), *The Law of International Responsibility* (OUP 2010) 1137–48.

VII objectives), he submitted that secondary SR rules could only play an ancillary, albeit important, role.[33] This conclusion is important for present purposes insofar as large-scale terrorist attacks—an undoubtedly other global security breaches as well—can sometimes generate states of panic and emergency. Following Crawford's lead, should a terrorist strike create a state of social panic or unrest, SR repertoire could operate as a legal supplement to principal humanitarian and crisis management initiatives spearheaded under UN auspices. This is not, however, to suggest that SR law plays the *same* role as those initiatives—or even brings the same efficiency, 'legitimacy', purpose, or implementation model to the table—but rather that it can play *some* role in the grander scheme of things. As will be shown in Chapter 4, holding a State responsible for failing to prevent terrorism might generate international scrutiny and shift power dynamics to ensure accountability and reparation/compensation, whilst mobilizing certain key constituencies in redressing the harm and preventing further terrorist threats originating from the same source.

As was argued, the failure to prevent a terrorist attack may be tantamount to the violation of an obligation *erga omnes*. Such a breach would simultaneously trigger the application of community responsibility (meaning that all members of the international community have a vested interest in counteracting the violation and redressing the harm), along with the involvement of IOs (especially the UN and SC, more precisely). Therefore, SC intervention will often operate in a manner analogous to community responsibility. However, several SC resolutions remain ambiguous on this front: it may be that the violation of international law or the would-be responsible State are not clearly identified, the imposition of certain consequences does not necessarily, or unequivocally, follow from the determination that a wrongful act has been committed, or the imposition of certain measures or sanctions is not expressly linked with the observance of secondary SR norms.[34]

Conversely, it will be shown in Chapter 4 that many of those resolutions can nonetheless be reconciled with the essence of SR precepts; by contrast, other resolutions adopted by the SC will present a more obvious nexus with secondary SR norms. Therefore, one would be hard-pressed to discard the areas of overlap between SC action and the implementation of SR, especially in the field of community responsibility. Indeed, many internationally wrongful acts against the international community as a whole—aggression, genocide, *apartheid*, colonial domination, terrorism, and large-scale human rights or international humanitarian law (IHL) abuses—strike at the very core of the modern conception of international peace and security. As a result, their linchpins, namely the principles

[33] See Crawford, JR, 'Third Report on State Responsibility' (2000) UN Doc A/CN.4/507 and Add. 1–4, 98 [372].

[34] See, eg, Villalpando (n 2) 443. But see JR Crawford, *International Law Commission's Articles on State Responsibility: Introduction, Text and Commentaries* (CUP 2002) 251 (invoking SC resolutions and inferring that '[t]he same obligations are reflected in Security Council and General Assembly resolutions').

of solidarity and cooperation, are equally violated.[35] Consequently, it is rather difficult to envisage the maintenance of international peace and security without upholding international law and, in the event of its violation, without ensuring the SR-mandated return to legality.[36] As discussed in subsequent sections, there are several points of rapprochement between the regime of collective security, which the SC applies and interprets as a matter of course under Chapter VII, and SR law. In some instances, they are mutually reinforcing. It follows that SR repertoire applies to primary obligations pertaining to the collective security regime, as it would in respect of any other primary international legal norms. Whilst both normative schemes remain autonomous and come into play during distinct phases of international law violations, the collective security scheme and its peculiarities may ultimately shape the SC's application of secondary SR norms.[37]

Setting aside institutional perspectives for a moment, the violation of an obligation *erga omnes* under the ARSIWA brings about specific consequences: in particular, third (read: not directly injured) States are entitled to invoke the responsibility of the wrongdoing State. In this regard, ARSIWA Article 48(1)(b) provides that '[a]ny State other than the injured State is entitled to invoke the responsibility of another State in accordance with paragraph 2 if… (b) the obligation breached is owed to the international community as a whole'.[38]

With this in mind, Crawford's original posture becomes particularly relevant in advancing SR repertoire for the failure to prevent terrorism. However, it appears that his view initially rejected the engagement of secondary SR rules when dealing with 'wilfully blind' governments, or the mere 'toleration'/'harbouring' or 'supporting' of terrorist factions,[39] and rather favoured granting organs like the SC extensive powers in dealing with these types of matters. When extrapolated to the context of counterterrorism, Crawford's approach carries distinct resonance,[40] yet

[35] See, eg, Villalpando (n 2) 443.

[36] The concept of return to legality is explored in Sections 4.4.3 and 4.4.4 in connection with specific SC resolutions.

[37] See, eg, M Forteau, *Droit de la Sécurité Collective et Droit de la Responsabilité Internationale de l'État* (Pedone 2006) 370.

[38] ARSIWA (n 23) Art 48(1)(b). On the interaction between that provision and obligations *erga omnes*, see JR Crawford, 'Responsibility for Breaches of Communitarian Norms: An Appraisal of Article 48 of the ILC Articles on Responsibility of States for Wrongful Acts' in U Fastenrath *et al.* (eds), *From Bilateralism to Community Interest: Essays in Honour of Judge Bruno Simma* (OUP 2011) 224; G Gaja, 'States Having an Interest in Compliance with the Obligation Breached' in Crawford *et al.* (n 32) 957–60; Crawford (n 34) 278; L-A Sicilianos, 'The Classification of Obligations and the Multilateral Dimension of the Relations of International Responsibility' (2002) 13 EJIL 1127, 1136–8; M Spinedi, 'From One Codification to Another: Bilateralism and Multilateralism in the Genesis of the Codification of the Law of Treaties and the Law of State Responsibility' (2002) 13 EJIL 1099, 1113–4.

[39] Indeed, the harbouring and supporting of terrorist factions on a State's territory is a widespread practice, which suggests that a law of indirect SR might be better suited to tackle current global security threats. See generally V-J Proulx, *Transnational Terrorism and State Accountability: A New Theory of Prevention* (Hart 2012) esp ch 2.

[40] Third Report—Crawford (n 33) 98 [372] (also citing Report of the Secretary-General pursuant to GA Res 53/35, 'The Fall of Srebrenica' (1999) UN Doc A/54/549; Report of the Independent Inquiry into the Actions of the UN during the 1994 Genocide in Rwanda (15 December 1999) and the Statement of the Secretary-General (16 December 1999) UN Doc S/1999/1257).

these introductory remarks do not completely explain the relationship between the actions of UN organs and SR law.

The customary SR scheme, supplemented by the ARSIWA, suggests that the prevalent implementation model—based on unilateral invocation and implementation of responsibility by individual States, paired with a repertoire of inter-State measures—effectively supplants the prospect of pursuing any sort of (overt) institutionalization of SR implementation, at least for the moment.[41] The involvement of institutional actors in the implementation process remains desirable in some cases, however, especially in the field of community responsibility, but institutional involvement does not constitute a prerequisite for the application of secondary SR norms, or even for the recognition of the existence of those rules or of an internationally wrongful act, for that matter.[42]

Therefore, in light of active participation of UN organs in counterterrorism, the debate over the possible institutionalization of SR generates at least two overarching queries: (i) first, whether the actions of UN organs are governed by SR law (and, as a corollary, whether those organizations can or do play a role in SR implementation or in addressing the consequences of internationally wrongful acts), and (ii) secondly, whether the unilateral implementation of SR by individual States is precluded, tempered, or excluded altogether by the intercession of IOs.

Thus, in framing the broader questions pertaining to the relationship between SR and UN organs, four possible scenarios are readily identifiable.[43] First, the action of an IO may be completely divorced from SR repertoire in that the organization's objectives do not coincide with those of the determination or implementation of the consequences of wrongful acts; as a corollary, its actions would thereby fail to obstruct the ordinary application of secondary SR norms. In such instances, institutional involvement does not affect, nor preclude, the application of SR law as it currently stands. Secondly, the actions of IOs may actually come into conflict with SR repertoire; in that eventuality, the organization in question could determine the consequences of unlawful behaviour or impose sanctions/coercive measures inimical to, or incompatible with, the scheme of secondary SR rules. In such cases, the organization's proposed solution would be likely to supersede the application of the general law of SR, pursuant to the principle of *lex specialis*.[44] Indeed, ARSIWA Article 55 provides that these 'articles do not apply where and to the extent that the conditions for the existence of an internationally wrongful act or the content or implementation

[41] Moreover, the ILC's debates did not present the best locus for venturing upon institutional reforms of IOs. See, eg, Third Report—Crawford (n 33) 98 [372]. On unilateral implementation of SR, see Crawford (n 28) 676–702.

[42] See generally EB Weiss, 'Invoking State Responsibility in the Twenty-First Century' (2002) 96 AJIL 798.

[43] These seek inspiration from the remarks of Villalpando (n 2) 423 in the context of community responsibility. These scenarios can occur individually—in isolation from one another—or in some mixed configuration.

[44] See, eg, B Simma and D Pulkowski, 'Of Planets and the Universe: Self-Contained Regimes in International Law' (2006) 17 EJIL 483, 490 (noting that 'a strong form of *lex specialis* could exclude the application of the general regime of state responsibility altogether, either by explicit provision or by implication, that is, by virtue of a regime's particular structure or its object and purpose').

of the international responsibility of a State are governed by special rules of international law'.[45] Thirdly, an IO's actions could prove totally instrumental in implementing SR, in that the organization would in fact be called upon to apply secondary rules of responsibility, whilst its scope of operation would be regimented concomitantly by the same corpus of norms. Several examples of such SR implementation by the SC are canvassed and analysed in Chapter 4 of this volume. Finally, an IO's actions could turn out to be complementary to the application of general secondary rules of responsibility. Thus, in the event of a breach involving the violation of an obligation *erga omnes* (eg a counterterrorism duty), the IO's repertoire (eg sanctions, lobbying power, regulatory-like influence) might provide additional safeguards or means of protecting community interests, even if the organization's measures fall outside the ambit of typical SR law (ie cannot be squared with an injured State's unilateral SR implementation because they are adopted in an institutional setting). Therefore, somewhat double-coating the protections associated with the application of SR principles would create a scenario in which the organization's action would not hinder the deployment of secondary rules of responsibility. Relevant precedents involving the SC are also canvassed in Chapter 4.

It is apparent from the foregoing that the relationship between the application of SR and the actions of UN organs, especially the SC, needs to be further engaged. The chapter now turns to a brief appraisal of the efficiency of existing UN mechanisms in implementing SR. By way of preface, the very nature of SR implementation first requires a brief review of considerations of fairness.

3.1.2 Fairness in implementation: An overarching concern

Although more relevant to the subsequent discussion on SC implementation, it is important to note that according to Kelsen, the objective of maintaining or restoring peace and international security, as embodied in the enforcement action found at Article 39 of the UN Charter, is not necessarily synonymous with restoring the *law*. Implicit in Kelsen's view was the idea that SC action, possibly the strongest manifestation of pragmatic power in resolving conflicts within the UN, is devoid of any component epitomizing a return to legality. Although thought-provoking, this line of reasoning carries with it serious shortcomings, amongst which is the notion that peace can override law when, in fact, the two are interconnected and should not be dissociated under the UN's mandate. More importantly, it relegates the restoration of applicable law, in this case SR, to a nebulous terrain and as Kelsen argued, consecrates the notion that the underlying philosophy in drafting and applying the Charter rests on 'the predominance of the political over the legal approach'.[46] Unsurprisingly, other eminent publicists espoused Kelsen's viewpoint

[45] ARSIWA (n 23) Art 55.

[46] See H Kelsen, *The Law of the United Nations* (London Institute of World Affairs 1950) 294, 735. See also H Kelsen, 'Collective Security and Collective Self-Defense under the Charter of the United Nations' (1948) 42 AJIL 788; H Lauterpacht, *International Law: A Treatise by Lassa Opphenheim (Vol 2: Disputes, War and Neutrality)* (7th edn, Longmans 1952) 163.

on this front, opining that international peace and security remain the paramount objectives and that SC action shall not be subordinated to any legal principles or processes.[47] That said, this contention is certainly assailable in the context of present-day global security, especially when contrasted against contemporaneous events. Even in the 1950s, other distinguished scholars underscored the importance of ensuring that SC action accord with international legal principles, particularly when it dealt with the adjustment or settlement of disputes.[48]

In any event, this undoubtedly leaves open the question as to what States are actually allowed to do in order to bridge that gap and ensure a return to legality, especially when contrasted with more traditional means of implementing international responsibility. Therefore, the tension between Kelsen's position and self-help remedies and/or countermeasures falls into sharp relief, signalling that States can, at times, become the sole warrantor of the return to legality in the face of unlawful conduct. This dimension of international legal enforcement undoubtedly calls for a closer examination of the relationship between self-help measures and fairness, as disparate and asymmetric power dynamics often pervade international relations between States in the post-breach environment. In an attempt to palliate this discrepancy and respond to detractors of self-help sanctions—whilst joined by Lauterpacht in this line of advocacy—Kelsen argued for the implementation of a third-party, objective decision-maker.[49]

As explored in Section 1.2.2, the fundamental issue of fairness in the application of countermeasures is further compounded by the mechanisms of self-judging and autoqualification, which remain integral facets underpinning the ARSIWA.[50] It is no surprise, therefore, that self-judged and unilaterally applied countermeasures are more readily envisaged by economically powerful States in responding to unlawful activity. In addition, they remain inexorably prone to escalation. In particular, the State that is targeted by countermeasures might, in turn, adopt countermeasures in response to what it perceives as unjust sanctions, thereby creating a vicious circle of diplomatic animosity and further aggravating the dispute.[51] Ultimately, whether seen through the potential institutionalization of SR or through the more traditional prism of inter-State implementation, an effective

[47] See, eg, JF Dulles, *War or Peace* (MacMillan 1950) 194; C Eagleton, 'The Jurisdiction of the Security Council over Disputes' (1946) 4 AJIL 515. See also Kelsen, *The Law* (n 46) 366, 368, 385.

[48] See, eg, E Jiménez de Aréchaga, 'Le Traitement des Différends Internationaux par le Conseil de Sécurité' (1954) 85 RdC 1, 11–12.

[49] See H Kelsen, *The Legal Process and International Order* (Constable & Co 1935) 18; H Lauterpacht, *The Function of Law in the International Community* (Clarendon Press 1933) 424. See also ME O'Connell, 'Controlling Countermeasures' in M Ragazzi (ed.), *International Responsibility Today: Essays in Memory of Oscar Schachter* (Brill 2005) 49, 53 (discussing and contrasting Quincy Wright's conception of self-help with Kelsen's suggestion that an objective third-party decision-maker be instituted to dissipate discrepancies inherent to self-help countermeasures). For a seminal account on fairness in international law, see TM Franck, *Fairness in International Law and Institutions* (Clarendon Press 1995).

[50] For a fuller discussion of countermeasures, see Section 4.2 of this book.

[51] See O'Connell (n 49) 53. On this last point, see also de Hoogh (n 5) 234–41; O Schachter, 'Dispute Settlement and Countermeasures in the International Law Commission' (1994) 88 AJIL 471.

international responsibility regime will have to strive to develop a legal narrative that is sensible to the realities facing the developing world whilst concomitantly affording due consideration to States' sovereign equality.[52] After all, one of the central objectives of this book is to identify helpful alternatives (ie institutionalized implementation of SR) to unchecked unilateralism and uphold this concept of equality.[53] In many ways, therefore, this concern militates in favour of strengthening multilateral frameworks with a view to stamping out global security threats and enhancing accountability models. As one publicist emphasized, 'negotiating international rules in multilateral fora gives weaker states greater influence, and this provides them with an incentive to follow the resulting agreements, leads to quasi-voluntary compliance, and thus lowers the costs of enforcement (pacification)'.[54]

Regardless of one's stance on this debate, it becomes apparent that the prevalent inter-State model of SR implementation should be revisited in light of contemporaneous challenges such as the rise of—and unprecedented power wielded by—non-State actors on the transnational level.[55] In 2013, ICJ President Peter Tomka rightly observed the ever-expanding security picture now inhabited by the international community and called for the adoption of forward-looking solutions in tackling global security threats. The implementation of SR by UN organs (particularly the SC), this work argues, certainly aligns with the essence of his statement, not to mention that such implementation would be deployed alongside a multiplicity of complementary legal regimes and actors.[56] Indeed,

> [n]owadays, there is no question that a broader conception of the maintenance of international peace and security, which may involve several institutional actors and processes—be

[52] Thus, the concerns voiced by Third World Approaches to International Law (TWAIL) scholars must always be borne in mind, especially when contemplating the implementation of SR through institutional channels. See generally A Anghie, *Imperialism, Sovereignty, and the Making of International Law* (CUP 2005); A Anghie, *The Third World and International Order: Law, Politics, and Globalization* (Nijhoff 2003); M Mutua, 'What Is TWAIL?' (2000) 94 ASIL Proceedings 31; DP Fidler, 'Revolt against or from Within the West? TWAIL, the Developing World, and the Future Direction of International Law' (2003) 2 Chinese Journal of International Law 29; 'Special Issue: Situating Third World Approaches to International Law (TWAIL): Inspirations, Challenges and Possibilities: Selected Papers from the Workshop Situating Third World Approaches to International Law (TWAIL)' (2008) 10 International Community Law Review 351–481; M Toufayan *et al.* (eds), *International Law and New Approaches to the Third World: Between Repetition and Renewal* (Société de Législation Comparée 2013).

[53] See generally P-M Dupuy, 'The Place and Role of Unilateralism in Contemporary International Law' (2000) 11 EJIL 19, 23; V Gowlland-Debbas, 'The Limits of Unilateral Enforcement of Community Objectives in the Framework of UN Peace Maintenance' (2000) 11 EJIL 361; P Sands, '"Unilateralism", Values, and International Law' (2000) 11 EJIL 291.

[54] N Krisch, 'International Law in Times of Hegemony: Unequal Power and the Shaping of the International Legal Order' (2005) 16 EJIL 369, 373. See also generally M Bettati, *Le Terrorisme: Les Voies de la Coopération Internationale* (Odile Jacob 2013).

[55] See, eg, K Zemanek, 'Does the Prospect of Incurring Responsibility Improve the Observance of International Law?' in Ragazzi (n 49) 132, 134. See also generally RP Barnidge, Jr, *Non-State Actors and Terrorism: Applying the Law of State Responsibility and the Due Diligence Principle* (TMC Asser Press 2008); K Mulaj (ed.), *Violent Non-State Actors in World Politics* (Columbia University Press 2010).

[56] On the role of SR amidst a multiplicity of complementary regimes, processes, and actors, see Proulx (n 39) 12–13, 124, 148, 227, 261. Whilst this volume focuses primarily on the SC, ICJ, and GA, other important institutional actors can play a vital role in implementing SR. For instance,

they judicial, diplomatic or political—now forms part of the security fabric initially envisaged by the framers of the UN Charter. Consequently, peaceful and creative solutions must be developed to respond to massive humanitarian and human rights violations, boundary disputes, environmental degradation and subversive non-State actors. Undoubtedly, both international law and the Court have a role to play in making the world a safer place.[57]

The consequences of these realities will be further explored, especially in Chapter 4, and should act as a preliminary gloss through which the possible institutionalization of the implementation of SR should be contemplated.

Meanwhile, the potential input of both the ICJ and GA in this debate must be addressed squarely in order to assess how institutional treatment of SR may be brought to bear upon a potential recasting of that normative scheme.

3.1.3 The International Court of Justice

By way of introduction, two important observations are apposite. First, the purpose of this section is not to deliver an exhaustive review of the Court's contributions to SR repertoire. In fact, eminent publicists have explored the Court's forays into that normative scheme, along with the many contributions of its predecessor, the Permanent Court of International Justice.[58] Drawing on a breadth of perspectives and insights, a series of older but thought-provoking accounts similarly tackled the ICJ's treatment of SR norms raised before it whilst also canvassing specific issues relating to this normative scheme.[59] Dame Rosalyn Higgins' contributions are particularly instructive in that regard.[60] However, the purpose of this section

the UN Secretary-General, whose persuasiveness remains contingent on sound legal argument, fits within this multiplicity of processes and actors. See generally I Johnstone, The Role of the UN Secretary-General: The Power of Persuasion Based on Law' (2003) 9 Global Governance 441.

[57] 'Competition and Co-operation between Legal Systems: The Role of Law in Ensuring the Development of Society, the State, and the Economy', Statement by HE Judge Peter Tomka, President of the ICJ, at the Plenary Session of the St Petersburg International Legal Forum (15 May 2013) <www.icj-cij.org/presscom/files/4/17374.pdf> accessed 8 August 2015, 3–4.

[58] See, eg, J Crawford, 'The International Court of Justice and the Law of State Responsibility' in CJ Tams and J Sloan (eds), *The Development of International Law by the International Court of Justice* (OUP 2013) 71–86; S Rosenne, 'Decisions of the International Court of Justice and the New Law of State Responsibility' in Ragazzi (n 49) 298–309; CJ Tams, 'Law-Making in Complex Processes: The World Court and the Modern Law of State Responsibility' in C Chinkin and F Baetens, *Sovereignty, Statehood and State Responsibility: Essays in Honour of James Crawford* (CUP 2015) 287–306; G Cottereau, 'Resort to International Courts in Matters of Responsibility' in Crawford *et al.* (n 32) 1113–26. See also M Evans and P Okowa, 'Approaches to Responsibility in International Courts' in M Evans and P Koutrakos (eds), *The International Responsibility of the European Union: European and International Perspectives* (Hart 2013) 103, 104–8, 112–19.

[59] See, eg, I Brownlie, 'State Responsibility and the International Court of Justice' in M Fitzmaurice and D Sarooshi (eds), *Issues of State Responsibility Before International Juridical Institutions* (Hart 2004) 11–18; M Mendelson, 'State Responsibility for Breach of Interim Protection Orders of the International Court of Justice' in ibid 35–54; MN Shaw, 'The International Court, Responsibility and Remedies' in ibid 19–34; D Shelton, 'Righting Wrongs: Reparations in the Articles on State Responsibility' (2002) 96 AJIL 833, 835–45.

[60] See R Higgins: 'Issues of State Responsibility before the International Court of Justice' in Fitzmaurice and Sarooshi (n 59) 1; *Problems & Process: International Law and How We Use It* (OUP

is also not to discuss exhaustively these academic writings. In fact, later discussion will demonstrate that only a few key ICJ cases directly inform the interplay between SR and counterterrorism. Nevertheless, it remains useful to highlight briefly some of the ICJ's contributions and shortcomings on points of detail, such as attribution of wrongful conduct, in order to ascertain the role and capacity of this institution in implementing SR law.[61]

The ICJ has already taken account of the ARSIWA on several occasions,[62] thereby signalling that it could eventually contribute significantly to the interpretation and implementation of that normative scheme. However, the ICJ has also sidestepped SR mechanics in several decisions, sometimes legitimately avoiding them on jurisdictional grounds, and at others by circumventing the distinct exercise of establishing a finding of responsibility in situations where that normative scheme could have played a central role.[63] On this issue, Higgins formulated an illuminating distinction between 'a finding of illegal conduct' and a 'finding of responsibility', and queried whether both are synonymous. She concluded that

> [t]he answer is yes, and no. Yes, in that findings of illegal conduct and the fashioning of remedies are all, in our modern way of looking at substantive obligations and remedies for breach, 'part of the law of responsibility'. No, in that no separate pleadings, with

1994) 146–68; 'The International Court of Justice: Selected Issues of State Responsibility' in Ragazzi (n 49) 271–86.

[61] For example, for P Weil and D Richemond, 'The Oil Platforms Case before the International Court of Justice: A Non-Case of International Responsibility' in Ragazzi (n 49) 340, the *Oil Platforms Case* remains a salient example of the ICJ's failure to contribute to SR law.

[62] See, eg, *LaGrand (Germany v USA)* (Merits) [2001] ICJ Rep 466, 512–14 [123]–[127] (assurance of non-repetition); *Arrest Warrant of 11 April 2000 (DRC v Belgium)* (Merits) [2002] ICJ Rep 3 [75]–[77] (appropriate remedies: *restitutio in integrum*, assurance of non-repetition); *Avena and Other Mexican Nationals (Mexico v USA)* (Merits) [2004] ICJ Rep 12 [115]–[150] (appropriate remedy as a consequence of the breach of consular obligations: review and reconsideration of the sentences and convictions); *Wall Advisory Opinion* (n 5) [138]–[42], [154]–[60] (elements precluding wrongfulness and serious breaches of obligations under peremptory norms of general international law). See also generally C Yamada, 'Revisiting the International Law Commission's Draft Articles on State Responsibility' in Ragazzi (n 49) 118.

[63] See, eg, *LaGrand Case* (n 62); *Elettronica Sicula S.p.A. (ELSI) (USA v Italy)* (Merits) [1989] ICJ Rep 15; *Military and Paramilitary Activities in and against Nicaragua (Nicaragua v US)* (Jurisdiction and Admissibility) [1984] ICJ Rep 392; *Military and Paramilitary Activities in and against Nicaragua (Nicaragua v USA)* (Merits) [1986] ICJ Rep 14; *Nuclear Tests (Australia v France)* (Merits) [1974] ICJ Rep 253; *Nuclear Tests (New Zealand v France)* (Merits) [1974] ICJ Rep 457; *Oil Platforms (Iran v USA)* (Preliminary Objections) [1996] ICJ Rep 803 (and (Counter-Claim) [1998] ICJ Rep 190; (Merits) [2003] ICJ Rep 161). See also *Legality of Use of Force (Serbia and Montenegro v Belgium)* (Preliminary Objections) [2004] ICJ Rep 279; *Legality of Use of Force (Serbia and Montenegro v Canada)* (Preliminary Objections) [2004] ICJ Rep 429; *Legality of Use of Force (Serbia and Montenegro v France)* (Preliminary Objections) [2004] ICJ Rep 575; *Legality of Use of Force (Serbia and Montenegro v Germany)* (Preliminary Objections) [2004] ICJ Rep 720; *Legality of Use of Force (Serbia and Montenegro v Italy)* (Preliminary Objections) [2004] ICJ Rep 865; *Legality of Use of Force (Serbia and Montenegro v Netherlands)* (Preliminary Objections) [2004] ICJ Rep 1011; *Legality of Use of Force (Serbia and Montenegro v Portugal)* (Preliminary Objections) [2004] ICJ Rep 1160; *Legality of Use of Force (Serbia and Montenegro v UK)* (Preliminary Objections) [2004] ICJ Rep 1307. For scholarly opinions along these lines, see Higgins, 'The International Court' (n 60) 284–5; Weil and Richemond (n 61) 331, 338.

prolonged excursions into the law of responsibility and the work of the International Law Commission, are needed on this issue.[64]

Whilst certain ICJ contributions in the field of SR are highlighted throughout this book, its primary purpose is rather to shed light on some of the Court's structural and systemic aspects that may or may not qualify it as an effective implementer of SR.

Secondly, it should be emphasized that an organ tasked with the judicial settlement of disputes such as the ICJ typically intervenes at a stage subsequent to the invocation of consequences flowing from the commission of internationally wrongful acts. Simply put, the judicial dispute settlement body is then called upon to adjudicate the allegations advanced by the disputing parties over the application or interpretation of secondary SR norms. In short, the Court's involvement can be seen as analogous to that of a 'jurisdictional' body (as opposed to an 'executive' organ), as broadly understood, and operates on the assumption that challenges will be levelled regarding the application of secondary norms between the parties.[65]

By contrast, the SC's implementation of SR, for instance, may come into play at an earlier stage of an emerging dispute, namely immediately after that organ has determined that a given behaviour is tantamount to a wrongful act and correspondingly devises legal consequences flowing from that violation. That said, subsequent sections of this book will reveal that the Council can also implement SR in later stages of a dispute by drawing on its quasi-judicial powers. In many ways, therefore, the creation of a dispute settlement mechanism, perhaps along the lines of what Kelsen and Lauterpacht had envisaged, would solely serve the purpose of ensuring the legality and validity of self-help initiatives by injured States.[66] However, this is certainly not a role that can be ascribed to the ICJ, at least not with its current constitutive instrument, nor does it describe what the Court actually does.

3.1.3.1 Substantive forays into State responsibility and the ICJ as 'legislator'

Whilst the municipal law concept of *stare decisis* is formally absent from international judicial discourse, some confusion still surrounds the actual impact and reach of ICJ decisions on the creation of international law. Pursuant to the ICJ Statute, the Court's decisions are to be regarded as 'subsidiary means' in determining applicable rules of law.[67] Unsurprisingly, this provision has prompted

64 Higgins, 'The International Court' (n 60) 285.

65 See, eg, Villalpando (n 2) 421. On the implementation of SR by judicial process, see Crawford (n 28) 598–643.

66 See, eg, O'Connell (n 49) 53; Villalpando (n 2) 421.

67 Statute of the International Court of Justice (adopted 26 June 1945, entered into force 26 June 1946), 59 Stat 1055, 8 UNTS 993, Art 38(1)(d). For a study on the ICJ's relationship with the judicial function, see G Hernández, *The International Court of Justice and the Judicial Function* (OUP 2014).

several commentators to point to the ICJ's role in evidencing the existence of international legal norms without ascribing a more norm-creating function to it.[68] Conversely, other publicists boldly cross this judicial Rubicon and challenge this traditional posture, suggesting that the Court's authority could be grounded in a more law-determining function.[69]

Perhaps embodying a middle-ground position, Judge Shahabuddeen had clearly foreshadowed the contours of this debate in 1990 by delivering a seemingly accurate interpretation of the ICJ's potential law-making function. He declared, '[i]t is of course an exaggeration to suggest that the Court is a legislator; it is also an exaggeration to assert that it cannot create any law at all'.[70] Yet, by looking for points of rapprochement with municipal law, it is interesting to highlight that Judge Oliver Wendell Holmes had expressed a (perhaps incrementally) more interventionist judicial philosophy in 1917. Indeed, in his Dissenting Opinion he 'recognize[d] without hesitation that judges do and must legislate, but they can do so only interstitially; they are confined from molar to molecule'.[71] Most likely building on this second line of reasoning, one author coined the term 'judgislation' to capture the ICJ's law-making function. According to this publicist, this term adequately encompasses the ICJ's judicial function, namely a process whereby 'judges develop and create law from within the existing law, and/or when judges legislate from within the existing enacted legislation'.[72]

Ultimately, it is probably fair to conclude that the Court will generally not promulgate primary international legal norms, the violation of which typically sets in motion secondary SR norms. When the ICJ appears to be formulating a primary rule of international law it is in reality 'finding' the law; that is to say, it confirms the existence of a norm which is supported by State practice, coupled with the requisite *opinio juris*, that had, up until that point, not been articulated clearly. In this process

[68] See, eg, *Restatement (Third) of Foreign Relations Law of the United States* (American Law Institute, 1987) §§ 102(1), 102 reporters' note 1, 103(2), 103 cmt a; CH Brower, 'Why the FTC Notes of Interpretation Constitute a Partial Amendment of NAFTA Article 1105' (2006) 46 VJIL 347, 357 fn 57; B Wible, '"De-Jeopardizing Justice": Domestic Prosecutions for International Crimes and the Need for Transnational Convergence' (2002) 31 Denver Journal of International Law and Policy 265, 268 fn 16.

[69] See, eg, T Weiler, 'NAFTA Article 1105 and the Principles of International Economic Law' (2003) 42 CJTL 35, 47. See also I Brownlie, *Principles of Public International Law* (6th edn, OUP 2003) 18–23; M Byers, *Custom, Power and the Power of Rules: International Relations and Customary International Law* (CUP 1999) 122 (both highlighting the role of judicial decisions in 'crystallizing' international law). For a domestic construction of this debate, see *Filartiga v Pena-Irala* 577 F Supp 860 (EDNY, 1984) 884 (seemingly placing judicial decisions and State practice on equal footing when identifying the sources of international law).

[70] Cited by Justice RP Sethi in KL Bhatia (ed.), *Judicial Activism and Social Change* (Deep & Deep 1990) 86.

[71] *Southern Pacific Co. v Jensen*, 244 US 205, 221; 37 St Ct 524 (1917). See also F Rigaux, *La Loi des Juges* (Odile Jacob 1997) 247; E Bodenheimer, *Jurisprudence: The Philosophy and the Method of Law* (Harvard University Press 1974) 442. For a commentary on Judge Holmes' invocation of the term 'interstitially', see N MacCormick, *Legal Reasoning and Legal Theory* (Clarendon Press 1978) 122, 187–8.

[72] SRS Bedi, *The Development of Human Rights Law by the Judges of the International Court of Justice* (Hart 2007) 17.

of 'finding' the law, the Court supports its conclusions with different indicators and types of evidence of State practice (eg international conventions and instruments, resolutions adopted by UN organs, domestic legislation and jurisprudence, ILC reports and codification projects, etc), all of which offer varying degrees of reliability; the primary norms under study and the circumstances of each case may also inform this process. In any event, it is unlikely that the ICJ will be called upon by parties to a dispute to promulgate a primary norm of international law. If anything, the facts of a given dispute might enable the Court to confirm that a certain obligation, which was primarily enshrined in bilateral treaties or multilateral conventions, has attained the status of customary international law. For example, since the Court has been increasingly handling environmental disputes, it may have the opportunity, in a future case, to build on the observation it made in the *Pulp Mills* case and further pronounce on the customary character of the obligation to provide an environmental impact assessment under international law.[73] Indeed, such development could have important implications: international legal norms pertaining to environmental impact assessments could contribute to the enforcement of global security obligations stemming from international environmental law by structuring interactions, in order to shape decisions affecting the environment; in turn, this could lead to interest coordination and pave the way for both persuasion and the internalization of relevant norms by States and other actors.[74] However, in the majority of disputes submitted to it with some relevance for SR law, the Court will rather be presented with a *fait accompli*—namely a violation of an established international legal norm—and asked to focus on the application of secondary norms.

In light of the foregoing, a brief word should be mentioned about the interaction between the ICJ and ILC, which has been particularly rich in the field of SR.[75] For one thing, the steady reliance of those bodies on each other's work suggests that the ICJ can be a particularly important vehicle in advancing SR law. Unquestionably, it has done so in several cases. Conversely, some publicists rather view this dynamic as problematic and query whether it has actually impeded the development of that normative scheme.[76] For instance, in the context of both

[73] *Case Concerning Pulp Mills on the River Uruguay (Argentina v Uruguay)* (Merits) [2010] ICJ Rep 38, 60–1 [204] (holding that 'it may now be considered a requirement under general international law to undertake an environmental impact assessment where there is a risk that the proposed industrial activity may have a significant adverse impact in a transboundary context, in particular, on a shared resource').

[74] See N Craik, *The International Law of Environmental Impact Assessment* (CUP 2008).

[75] On the interaction between the ICJ and ILC, see Statement by HE Judge Peter Tomka, President of the ICJ, 64th Session of the ILC (24 July 2012) <www.icj-cij.org/presscom/files/4/17094.pdf> accessed 3 August 2015. See also SM Schwebel, 'The Inter-active Influence of the International Court of Justice and the International Law Commission' in CAA Barea *et al.* (eds), *Liber Amicorum "In Memoriam" of Judge José María Ruda* (Kluwer 2000) 479. On diplomatic protection and human rights, see the following works by K Parlett: 'The ICJ and Diplomatic Protection' in Tams and Sloan, *The Development* (n 58) ch 5; *The Individual in the International Legal System: Continuity and Change in International Law* (CUP 2011).

[76] See, eg, S Sullivan, 'Changing the Premise of International Legal Remedies: The Unfounded Adoption of Assurances and Guarantees of Non-Repetition' (2002–3) 7 UCLA Journal of International Law and FA 265, 300–1; Proulx (n 39) 146 (describing this dynamic as 'incestuous').

the *Gabčíkovo-Nagymaros Project* and *LaGrand* cases, the ILC relied upon ICJ precedents to support its codification efforts whilst the ICJ in turn cited the ILC's Draft Articles on SR to buttress its own reasoning. Unsurprisingly, this practice has been construed as a 'citation carousel' by some scholars.[77] Pursuant to what some call the 'ILC–ICJ feedback loop', it is also common for former ILC members to later join the ranks of the ICJ, where they participate in the judicial construction of the SR norms they helped develop earlier at the ILC.[78] However, the ICJ completely sidestepped SR law in other judgments where that normative scheme and specific provisions of the ARSIWA could have played an important role. This avoidance of the ILC's codified work on SR matters is also mirrored in other decision-making fora, where the codified system of SR and UN law are bypassed at every opportunity. This has certainly been the case in some proceedings involving investor protection in the US, for example.[79]

Because of jurisdictional constraints, the ICJ cannot autonomously and actively play a role in implementing the international responsibility of States, at least not as a matter of course. Obviously, an ideal implementation model of secondary SR norms should be pursued through the channels of formal adjudication. In this light, it seems clear that the ICJ should constitute a particularly apt UN organ for the purposes of this adjudicative task, and a viable forum to engage both with global security issues and SR repertoire. In fact, its jurisprudence unquestionably suggests a rich potential in applying, and perhaps advancing, SR norms. Indeed, it has dealt with a number of disputes involving SR issues and factual complexes relevant to counterterrorism strategies, at least by analogy. For example, the Court was confronted with such litigation in the *Corfu Channel, Tehran Hostages, Military and Paramilitary Activities in and against Nicaragua*, and *Armed Activities* cases.[80]

In the *Corfu Channel* case, the ICJ had to pronounce on Albania's SR after British ships and personnel sustained injuries upon striking exploding mines in Albania's internal waters. Whilst the mines were likely to have been laid by Yugoslavia, 'Albania's responsibility derived from the fact that it knew, or must have known from its border guards, that the mines were there'.[81] Aside from this application of secondary SR norms, the ICJ also delivered an important statement on primary international legal obligations: in essence, it verbalized the norm according to which States should not knowingly allow harmful activity

[77] WM Reisman *et al.*, *International Law in Contemporary Perspective* (2nd edn, Foundation Press 2004) 899–900.

[78] See, eg, DJ Bederman, 'Counterintuiting Countermeasures' (2002) 96 AJIL 817, 819 (invoking the example of the restrictive interpretation of the proportionality requirement for the application of countermeasures in the *Gabčíkovo-Nagymaros Project Case* and ARSIWA (n 23) Art 51).

[79] See generally AT Nissel, 'The Duality of State Responsibility' (2013) 44 Columbia Human Rights Law Review 793.

[80] See *Corfu Channel Case (UK v Albania)* (Merits) [1949] ICJ Rep 4; *United States Diplomatic and Consular Staff in Tehran (USA v Iran)* (Merits) [1980] ICJ Rep 3; *Nicaragua v USA* (Merits) (n 63); *Armed Activities on the Territory of the Congo (DRC v Uganda)* (Merits) [2005] ICJ Rep 116.

[81] Crawford (n 58) 73. In order to reach this conclusion, the ICJ enlisted the assistance of a panel of experts, which went on a site visit to ascertain that the guards who manned the border must have

to emanate from their territory.[82] Unquestionably, this precedent has come to be associated with various obligations of prevention pertaining to global security priorities, including counterterrorism, environmental protection, climate change, cybercrime, and nuclear non-proliferation.[83] As a corollary, this decision clearly has important implications for SR repertoire, both in counterterrorism and other global security contexts; it undeniably buttresses the move towards greater prevention in international law.[84]

In the *Tehran Hostages* case, the ICJ was confronted with highly relevant facts for the purposes of counterterrorism, in particular as regards the application of obligations of prevention incumbent upon States. In short, it had to pronounce on the SR of Iran for failing to prevent the sequestration and ransacking of an American embassy and its consulates in Iran, and the taking of predominantly embassy personnel as hostages by student militants. In its analysis, the ICJ held that the attack and hostage-taking could not be attributed *directly* to Iran, as the student militants could not be equated with agents or organs of that State.[85] The ICJ nonetheless found that Iran's conduct had contravened its international obligations, particularly its duty to protect foreign diplomatic missions and their personnel from attack.[86] The ICJ went on to describe this duty as 'categorical' before holding that Iran had failed to 'take any "appropriate steps" to protect the premises, staff and archives of the United States' mission against attack by the militants, and to take any steps either to prevent this attack or to stop it before it reached its completion'.[87] The implications of this decision for counterterrorism efforts have been discussed elsewhere;[88] for the moment, suffice it to underscore that this jurisprudential development provides great analytical points of comparison for the study of other obligations of prevention pertaining to global security.

known about the unlawful mine-laying. *Corfu Channel Case (UK v Albania)* (Expert Opinion) [1948] ICJ Rep 124.

[82] *Corfu Channel* (Merits) (n 80) 22. See also M García-Mora, *International Responsibility for Hostile Acts of Private Persons against Foreign States* (Nijhoff 1962) 109–12, 130; H Duffy, *The 'War on Terror' and the Framework of International Law* (CUP 2005) 42; J-C Martin, *Les Règles Internationales Relatives à la Lutte contre le Terrorisme* (Bruylant 2006) 454.

[83] For various accounts on this precedent, see RM Bratspies and RA Miller (eds), *Transboundary Harm in International Law: Lessons from the Trail Smelter Arbitration* (CUP 2006) (for the purposes of SR, counterterrorism, and global security, specifically, see MA Drumbl, 'Trail Smelter and the International Law Commission's Work on State Responsibility for Internationally Wrongful Acts and State Liability' in ibid 85–98; C Hoss and P-M Dupuy, 'Trail Smelter and Terrorism: International Mechanisms to Combat Transboundary Harm' in ibid 225–39).

[84] On the obligation to prevent terrorism, with special reference to the *Corfu Channel* decision, see Proulx (n 39) 18–30. On prevention, generally, see M Bennouna, 'Prevention and International Law' in *Collected Courses of the Xiamen Academy of International Law* (Nijhoff 2013) 157–209.

[85] *Tehran Hostages Case* (n 80) [58]. See also D Brown, 'Use of Force against Terrorism after September 11th: State Responsibility, Self-Defense and Other Responses' (2003) 11 Cardozo Journal of International and Comparative Law 1, 10–11.

[86] *Tehran Hostages Case* (n 80) [58].

[87] *Tehran Hostages Case* (n 80) [61]–[62].

[88] See, eg, Proulx (n 39) 24–7, 31, 39, 56, 62, 65, 67, 70–1, 81–2, 85–6, 89, 108, 116, 142, 149, 161–2, 166, 171, 173, 184, 203–4, 303, 318 (including a discussion of the ICJ's treatment of Iran's SR by way of subsequent endorsement or approval of the internationally wrongful act, which now underpins the logic of ARSIWA Art 11).

The ICJ's pronouncements in *Paramilitary Activities in and against Nicaragua* on SR law have been widely discussed elsewhere and have also spawned critical, book-length studies recasting the rules of attribution.[89] As seen in Section 1.3 of this book, the *Nicaragua* decision laid down the 'effective control' standard of attribution in order to impute the acts of non-State entities to the official State apparatus; in the particular circumstances of that case, the ICJ declined to declare that the *Contras* rebels were an extension of the assisting State, despite the fact that US support of their operations had been at times 'preponderant or decisive'.[90] This precedent was undoubtedly the driving force behind ARSIWA Article 8,[91] which was subsequently relied upon by the ICJ in the *Armed Activities* case,[92] and most recently applied in the 2007 *Bosnian Genocide* case.[93]

In this latter—highly criticized—ruling, the ICJ reaffirmed that the concept of 'control' is of paramount importance in ascertaining whether: (i) non-formal State entities can nonetheless be construed as a de facto prolongation of the State through a relationship of 'complete dependence' between the two entities; or (ii) the actions of non-State agents can be attributed to the territorial State by virtue of the 'effective control' test developed by the ICJ in the *Nicaragua* case and now enshrined in ARSIWA Article 8.[94] Whilst the ICJ ultimately found that Serbia was not responsible for perpetrating genocide, it nonetheless found that it had failed to prevent genocide. Despite this finding, which contributed to advancing the *Tehran Hostages* and *Corfu Channel* brand of 'indirect' SR (ie ascertaining legal accountability by way of omission instead of commission), the *Bosnian Genocide* decision was largely seen as a failure in the implementation of SR. Unsurprisingly, eminent publicists staunchly criticized the ICJ's formalistic application of attribution principles which, they argue, was carried out without due regard for evolutionary realities, including the activities of multiple non-State

[89] See, eg, T Becker, *Terrorism and the State: Rethinking the Rules of State Responsibility* (Hart 2006) (taking issue with the 'agency' paradigm derived from this ICJ decision, and advocating a causation-based model); Proulx (n 39) (taking issue with the 'direct responsibility' paradigm derived from the same, and arguing for a strict liability-inspired model).

[90] *Nicaragua v USA* (Merits) (n 63) 62–5 [109]–[15]. See also TM Franck, *Recourse to Force: State Action against Threats and Armed Attacks* (CUP 2002) 60–3.

[91] ARSIWA (n 23) Art 8 provides the following:

> The conduct of a person or group of persons shall be considered an act of a State under international law if the person or group of persons is in fact acting on the instructions of, or under the direction or control of, that State in carrying out the conduct.

[92] *Armed Activities Case* (n 80) 168 [160] (relying on the *Nicaragua* decision and ARSIWA (n 23) Arts 4, 5, 8 to conclude that Uganda did not create or control the Liberation Movement of Congo pursuant to attribution principles).

[93] *Case Concerning the Application of the Convention on the Prevention and Punishment of the Crime of Genocide (Bosnia and Herzegovina v Serbia and Montenegro)* (Merits) [2007] ICJ Rep 43, 142–9.

[94] *Bosnian Genocide Case* (n 93) 140–5. However, these rules are far from coherent or uniformly applied. See particularly ibid 144 [403]–[404] (declining to apply the 'overall control' standard developed in the *Tadić Case* (Judgment) ICTY-94-1-A (15 July 1999) [117], [120], [131]–[132], [137]–[138]). For a critique of the notion of 'control' in the ARSIWA, see Proulx (n 39) 150–5, 165–74.

actors in a multipolar world.[95] Moreover, this precedent suggests that the ICJ may be reticent to implement SR in future, politically volatile cases involving global security issues.

3.1.3.2 Jurisdictional limitations

Despite these substantive advances, the ICJ's jurisdictional limitations must be addressed squarely and acknowledged as a key stumbling block to electing that organ as the foremost implementing agent of SR. Indeed, unlike the SC for instance, the ICJ's main jurisdictional impediments preclude it from unilaterally invoking the consequences flowing from a breach of an international obligation. This jurisdictional feature also constitutes an embodiment of the very essence of the international legal order, which hinges on State consent in order to trigger judicial dispute settlement proceedings. In short, in every dispute submitted to it, the ICJ must satisfy itself that it has jurisdiction to hear the case.[96] There are essentially four ways in which disputing States can confer jurisdiction upon the Court: (i) by making a declaration under Article 36(2) of the ICJ Statute, recognizing that organ's jurisdiction as compulsory, often on condition of reciprocity;[97] (ii) by way of special agreement (termed *compromis* in French) in which both parties to the dispute agree to grant jurisdiction to the ICJ over it;[98] (iii) through the application of a compromissory clause enshrined in a bilateral treaty or multilateral convention granting jurisdiction to the ICJ over the application or interpretation of the relevant instrument;[99] and (iv) by virtue of the doctrine of *forum prorogatum*, a seldom used jurisdictional avenue.[100] Given these inherent institutional impediments, it is probably fair to ponder whether a case involving the violation of counterterrorism duties, for example, would actually be brought to the ICJ and successfully cross the jurisdictional threshold.

[95] See, eg, A Cassese, 'The Nicaragua and *Tadić* Tests Revisited in Light of the ICJ Judgment on Genocide in Bosnia' (2007) 18 EJIL 649; A Cassese, 'On the Use of Criminal Law Notions in Determining State Responsibility for Genocide' (2007) 5 JICJ 875; M Milanović, 'State Responsibility for Genocide: A Follow-Up' (2007) 18 EJIL 669. See also C Tosh, 'Genocide Acquittal Provokes Legal Debate' *Institute for War and Peace Reporting* (4 March 2007) <https://iwpr.net/global-voices/genocide-acquittal-provokes-legal-debate> accessed 4 August 2015.

[96] For a quintessential study on the ICJ's jurisdiction, work, and importance in international law, see S Rosenne, *The Law and Practice of the International Court, 1920–2005* (4th edn, Nijhoff 2006).

[97] ICJ Statute (n 67) Art 36(2). Currently, seventy-two States have Art 36(2) declarations in place recognizing the jurisdiction of the ICJ as compulsory, slightly over a third of the UN's membership: <www.icj-cij.org/jurisdiction/index.php?p1=5&p2=1&p3=3> accessed 20 August 2015.

[98] ICJ Statute (n 67) Arts 36(2) *a contrario*, 40(1); ICJ Rules of Court (adopted 14 April 1978, entered into force 1 July 1978) <www.icj-cij.org/documents/index.php?p1=4&p2=3&p3=0> accessed 18 August 2015, Arts 39, 40(3), 42, 46. Typically, proceedings brought to the Court by way of *compromis* present the distinct advantage of bypassing the preliminary objections phase—be they over jurisdiction, admissibility, or both—as the litigants agree that the ICJ has jurisdiction and the requests they have formulated are admissible.

[99] Currently, there are more than 300 such compromissory clauses in force contained in treaties and conventions. See, eg, 'The Role of the International Court of Justice in World Affairs: Successes and Challenges with Special Reference to OAS Member States and the Pact of Bogotá', Statement by HE Judge Peter Tomka, President of the ICJ, at the OAS (10 April 2014) <www.icj-cij.org/presscom/files/4/18324.pdf> accessed 11 August 2015, 4.

[100] See ICJ Rules (n 98) Art 38(5).

In that regard, some commentators mount a spirited defence of ICJ jurisdiction over potential cases involving the violation of counterterrorism obligations. Kimberley Trapp has been a particularly vocal proponent of this jurisdictional avenue, as an alternative route to the 'traditional' implementation of SR. Whilst she acknowledges that the ICJ's jurisdiction might be difficult to secure under Article 36(2) declarations, she suggests that the Court's counterterrorism docket could nonetheless be increased through the application of compromissory clauses enshrined in multilateral conventions on terrorism.[101] Whilst it is true that judicial adjudication of disputes involving SR and terrorism issues should be the preferred mode of settlement, political pragmatism behoves interlocutors to remain rather cynical about the likelihood of the ICJ handling such disputes.[102] As an alternative to this laudable alternative, the present volume rather advocates the SC's implementation of SR in counterterrorism contexts as a perhaps more realistic prospect.

Given the inherently political nature of claims of accountability pertaining to the violation of counterterrorism duties, the SC appears to be a better forum to implement SR in such scenarios.[103] Indeed, the violation of counterterrorism duties often requires a primarily political solution, which can be a mode of dispute settlement or a means to defuse tensions between disputing States over a host of related questions, including: the surrender, prosecution, or extradition of suspected terrorists; sorting out questions of political and legal accountability for violations of international law; and devising legally sound, but politically motivated, consequences to those violations. These factors, it will be argued, militate in favour of SC involvement: despite its primarily political nature, the SC's process can nonetheless be perceived as a mode of dispute settlement that takes into account relevant legal principles with a view to reaching a politically informed outcome. For instance, commentators observe that the US, UK, and France were 'fully within their rights in bringing before the Security Council the dispute concerning the international responsibility of Libya with a view to obtaining a political solution'.[104] In the absence of compulsory jurisdiction for SR matters under international law, the alternative of unilateral enforcement of international law by injured States brings about its own set of complications, not least the fact that the adoption of unilateral countermeasures is not tantamount to dispute settlement.[105] In that setting, given

[101] See KN Trapp: 'Holding States Responsible for Terrorism before the International Court of Justice' (2012) 3 Journal of International Dispute Settlement 279, 285–95; *State Responsibility for International Terrorism* (OUP 2011) 131–81.

[102] See also Trapp, 'Holding' (n 101) 284.

[103] In fairness, Trapp, *State* (n 101) 178–9, 188–9 acknowledges that the SC can play a role in the implementation of SR, particularly by enforcing ICJ judgments, and that it attributed responsibility to both Libya and Sudan implicitly on two occasions. Moreover, in 'Holding' (n 101) 288 she describes the SC's establishment of Libya's responsibility in the *Lockerbie* incident as 'the most famous example of the "successful" implementation of state responsibility for international terrorism'.

[104] M Bedjaoui, *The New World Order and the Security Council: Testing the Legality of Its Acts* (Nijhoff 1994) 47, 71.

[105] However, unilateral countermeasures may have a 'pacific character'. See D Alland, 'The Definition of Countermeasures' in Crawford *et al.* (n 32) 1130.

that the adoption of countermeasures by an injured State may possibly aggravate the underlying dispute, it could be argued that SC action might be preferable than no institutional involvement at all.

Moreover, even if the ICJ satisfies itself that it does in fact have jurisdiction over a given dispute, this in no way guarantees that it will formally pronounce on the international responsibility of one of the parties; quite to the contrary, a review of the Court's jurisprudence reveals that it is hesitant to attribute wrongful conduct, assign blame, and assess States' legal guilt, at least in unequivocal or categorical terms for the purposes of SR law. When seized of a relevant dispute over which it has jurisdiction, the ICJ will rather often formulate some incarnation of the obligation of reparation when faced with an unlawful situation without predicating its remedy on a 'free-standing' declaration of international responsibility.[106] For instance, when read through a critical lens the 2007 *Bosnian Genocide* decision reveals that the ICJ was very reluctant to declare that Serbia had committed genocide, and hence brand it a violator of international law by reference to *direct* SR. Moreover, the handling of that case presented additional problems related to fact-finding. Determining whether the conduct of the Army of *Republika Srpska* (VRS) could be attributed to the Serbian State, like all matters falling under the rubric of 'attribution', remained contingent on the degree of control exerted by the latter over the former. In attempting to make its case on attribution, Bosnia requested unredacted transcripts of meetings of Yugoslavia's Supreme Defence Council, which it argued would be critical in establishing the requisite level of control. Serbia did not accede to that request on national security grounds and the ICJ refused to compel the production of those documents, despite the fact that they had already been produced in different proceedings before the International Criminal Tribunal for the former Yugoslavia (ICTY). Ultimately, the ICJ concluded that the insufficient evidentiary record before it had failed to establish the requisite level of control. Unsurprisingly, this conclusion generated considerable criticism from Vice-President Al-Khasawneh and various publicists, among others.[107] More importantly for present purposes, it is fair to ponder whether the ICJ would exhibit similar fact-finding reticence in cases involving SR for terrorism or other global security threats. Indeed, in such litigation there is no doubt that States would attempt to shield the production of some evidence behind the veil of national security.

[106] See, eg, *Arrest Warrant Case* (n 62) 31–2 [75]–[76]. Whilst the ICJ's role in the context of advisory proceedings is not to pronounce on the responsibility of a State, but rather to answer the legal question(s) submitted to it by relevant IOs with a view to illuminating their future work, the Court's advisory jurisprudence is nonetheless helpful for present purposes. See, eg, *Wall Advisory Opinion* (n 5) 201–2 [163]. See also Higgins, 'The International Court' (n 60) 284–5; A Nollkaemper, 'Internationally Wrongful Acts in Domestic Courts' (2007) 101 AJIL 760, 768 fn 42.

[107] See Vice-President Al-Khasawneh's Dissenting Opinion in the *Bosnian Genocide Case* (n 93) [35]. See also RJ Goldstone and RJ Hamilton, '*Bosnia v Serbia:* Lessons from the Encounter of the International Court of Justice with the International Criminal Tribunal for the Former Yugoslavia' (2008) 21 LJIL 95, 109–10; A Riddell and B Plant, *Evidence before the International Court of Justice* (British Institute of International and Comparative Law 2009) 216; JE Alvarez, 'Burdens of Proof' (2007) 23(2) ASIL Newsletter 1; D Joyce, 'Fact-Finding and Evidence at the International Court of Justice: Systemic Crisis, Change or More of the Same?' 18 FYIL 283, 298–305.

On the substance of primary norms, there is also strong indication that the ICJ would be reluctant to handle the political 'hot potato' of terrorism beyond what is strictly necessary in any case submitted to it. In addition to sidestepping the application of SR principles in some instances, or at least ascribing a less than central role to it in relevant circumstances, the ICJ has also resisted qualifying internationally wrongful acts as 'terrorism' when the facts arguably lent themselves to such analysis, particularly in the *Tehran Hostages* and *Nicaragua* cases.[108] Interestingly, one publicist suggests that in *Tehran Hostages*, the ICJ eschewed the question whilst in *Nicaragua*, it flirted with the idea of classifying the wrongful acts under the rubric of 'terrorism'.[109] It should be recalled that in the latter case, the Nicaraguan government classified the *Contras* rebels as 'terrorists' and fact-finding missions on the operations and tactics carried out by that group led to testimonial confirmation of that characterization before the ICJ.[110] Whilst it can be argued, as did Gilbert Guillaume, that these cases did not deal with terrorism per se, this characterization is certainly debatable.[111]

Consequently, on two distinct occasions the ICJ: (i) held that the sequestration of US hostages and property by private individuals could be attributed to Iran through the channel of official State endorsement and *ex post facto* ratification; and (ii) lamented US support of Nicaraguan *Contras* by way of indirect SR. Unsurprisingly, some authors suggest that the *Tehran Hostages* scenario aptly symbolized the emergence of State-supported terrorism with a view to using it as a weapon or foreign policy tool.[112] In its 1980 judgment, the ICJ attributed the sequestration and hostage-taking carried out by student militants to Iran by way of official State endorsement, found that it was internationally responsible,[113] and imposed upon it the duties of cessation of the wrongful act and reparation for the damage.[114] At the time the ICJ's judgment was rendered, no international convention in force actually prohibited State support of terrorism; thus, the ICJ could have filled that void, but chose not to do so.[115]

[108] The ICJ also sidestepped this debate in the *Armed Activities Case* (n 80), in which it held that Uganda could not invoke a right to self-defence against the DRC because it had harboured an armed militia on its territory.

[109] J-M Sorel, 'Existe-t'il une Définition Universelle du Terrorisme' in K Bannelier *et al.* (eds), *Le Droit International Face au Terrorisme: Après le 11 Septembre 2001* (Pedone 2003) 35, 44. In fairness, the SC also eschewed labelling the conduct of the Iranian militants as 'terrorism', instead framing its relevant resolutions within the scope of diplomatic and consular immunities and SR. See UNSC Res 457 (4 December 1979) UN Doc S/RES/457; UNSC Res 461 (31 December 1979) UN Doc S/RES/461. See also B Saul, 'Definition of "Terrorism" in the UN Security Council: 1985–2004' (2005) 4 Chinese Journal of International Law 141, 143–4.

[110] *Nicaragua v USA* (Merits) (n 63) 63–4 [113], 68 [121]. See also TD Gill, *Litigation Strategy at the International Court: A Case Study of the Nicaragua v. United States Dispute* (Nijhoff 1989) 193–4 (chronicling the fact-finding mission and testimonies of MJ Glennon and DT Fox).

[111] G Guillaume, 'Terrorisme et Droit International' (1989) 215 RdC 287, 306.

[112] B Hoffman, *La Mécanique Terroriste* (Calmann-Lévy 1999) 230.

[113] *Tehran Hostages Case* (n 80) 44–5 ('the violations of these obligations engage the responsibility of the Islamic Republic of Iran towards the United States of America under international law').

[114] *Tehran Hostages Case* (n 80) items 3–5 of the *dispositif.*

[115] See, eg, H Labayle, 'Droit International et Lutte contre le Terrorisme' (1986) 32 AFDI 105, 126.

In the *Nicaragua* case, the ICJ found that the US provided considerable support to the *Contras* in their perpetration of multiple IHL violations during the armed conflict in Nicaragua. In its judgment on the merits, the ICJ deemed this support unlawful[116] and held that the US had a duty to ensure the cessation of those breaches of international law,[117] and to make reparation for any injury flowing from its internationally wrongful acts.[118] However, it must be stressed that the ICJ's holding on this issue did not expressly stem from the prohibition on providing support to terrorism.[119] Rather, the ICJ cast US support of the *Contras* guerrillas as a breach of the 'obligation under customary international law not to intervene in the affairs of another State'[120] and, additionally, deemed that the field manual on guerrilla warfare circulated to the *Contras* by the US encouraged them to commit acts contrary to IHL. And yet, the ICJ refused to directly attribute the resulting wrongful acts to the US.[121]

These precedents might give pause as to whether the ICJ would be the most propitious forum to implement SR in counterterrorism and global security contexts as a matter of course. Conversely, the ICJ may undertake a complementary function consisting of oversight and review of the implementation of SR by other entities, or ultimately adjudicate disputes arising over the application of secondary rules of responsibility.

As will be discussed, the ICJ's contributions are particularly helpful when addressing the mechanics surrounding the secondary level of international breaches, such as the interpretation of trans-substantive rules (ie attribution), along with the construction of other nebulous legal areas, such as the invocation of responsibility by 'injured' and 'non-injured' States.[122] In light of its apparent impartiality, mission statement, capacity to adjudicate disputes, and its ability to deliver advisory opinions on international legal issues,[123] the ICJ constitutes an attractive forum for upholding legal stability and observance of SR rules, at least upon first glance. In fact, it has done so in other legal areas. Indeed, the Court has enjoyed a solid reputation as one of the world's foremost judicial institutions in developing the law of the sea, particularly the legal framework governing maritime delimitation.[124] Despite cynical predictions in the 1980s—voiced in part by Prosper Weil—that the law of the sea was headed towards a fragmented future,

[116] *Nicaragua v USA* (Merits) (n 63) 146, 148, items 3 and 9 of the *dispositif.*

[117] *Nicaragua v USA* (Merits) (n 63) 149, item 12 of the *dispositif.*

[118] *Nicaragua v USA* (Merits) (n 63) 149, item 13 of the *dispositif.*

[119] See, eg, Martin (n 82) 466.

[120] *Nicaragua v USA* (Merits) (n 63) 146, item 3 of the *dispositif.*

[121] *Nicaragua v USA* (Merits) (n 63) 148, item 9 of the *dispositif.*

[122] On this issue, see H Thirlway, 'Injured and Non-injured States before the International Court of Justice' in Ragazzi (n 49) 311–28. On the invocation of responsibility in various contexts, see, eg, I Scobbie, 'The Invocation of Responsibility for the Breach of "Obligations under Peremptory Norms of General International Law"' (2002) 13 EJIL 1201; J Peirano, 'International Responsibility and Cooperation for Development' in Ragazzi (n 49) 190–4; Weiss (n 42) 798–816.

[123] ICJ Statute (n 67) Arts 65–8.

[124] See, eg, Statement by HE Judge Peter Tomka, President of the ICJ, Sixth Committee of the GA (2 November 2012) <www.icj-cij.org/presscom/files/6/17156.pdf> accessed 19 August 2015.

the ICJ has nonetheless contributed greatly to the stability and predictability of this legal field.[125] In 2010, it cogently distilled complex law of the sea principles and articulated the basic, three-step maritime delimitation methodology in the *Delimitation in the Black Sea* case, which has since been widely endorsed by scholars and other tribunals.[126] There is every indication that the Court's work could have a similar 'stabilizing' impact in the field of SR. In fact, its jurisprudence on this front has remained rather consistent. By way of example, in the 2007 *Bosnian Genocide* case the Court upheld the 'effective control' standard of attribution under customary international law, which it had articulated more than two decades earlier in the *Case concerning Military and Paramilitary Activities in and against Nicaragua*.[127] Unsurprisingly, ARSIWA Article 8 now captures this legal standard, with the accompanying commentary relying heavily on the *Nicaragua* decision.[128]

However, the Court's potential input in interpreting and advancing SR repertoire remains seriously limited in that it may only adjudicate cases in which the wrongdoing State has conceded its jurisdiction over the dispute. Moreover, the Court's judgment is only binding on those States that are parties to the proceedings,[129] thereby signalling that the Court's rulings, and any 'precedential' value that may be ascribed to them, would be significantly hampered. That said, this last observation must be tempered somewhat given that, in practice, ICJ jurisprudence enjoys fairly authoritative value in various legal and policy circles. Hence, whilst the Court's judgments are not formally binding on third States, they are read carefully by international legal scholars, legal advisors to foreign ministers, government lawyers, and practitioners; they feature heavily in the ICJ's own judgments; they are bandied about liberally by counsel and parties appearing before the Court; they are routinely cited and analysed by other international judiciaries and arbitral tribunals,

[125] See, eg, P Tomka, 'The *Guyana/Suriname* Arbitration Award of 2007' (2012) 8 PCA Award Series 1, 16–21. See also P Weil, *The Law of Maritime Delimitation: Reflections* (Grotius 1989); *Perspectives du Droit de la Délimitation Maritime* (Pedone 1988).

[126] *Maritime Delimitation in the Black Sea (Romania v Ukraine)* (Merits) [2009] ICJ Rep 2009 61. In its first case on maritime delimitation, ITLOS relied on this three-step methodology: *Delimitation of the Maritime Boundary between Bangladesh and Myanmar in the Bay of Bengal (Bangladesh/Myanmar)* (Merits, judgment of 15 March 2012) ITLOS Reports 2012 [233]–[240]. Prior to the *Black Sea Delimitation*, the genesis of the equidistance/special circumstances methodology was first articulated in *Continental Shelf (Libyan Arab Jamahiriya/Malta)* (Merits) [1985] ICJ Rep 13, 46 [60]. This approach was also endorsed by other arbitral tribunals. See, eg, *Guyana/Suriname Arbitration* (2008) 47 ILM 166 [342]; *Barbados/Trinidad and Tobago Arbitration* (2008) 27 RIAA 147, 214–15 [242].

[127] *Bosnian Genocide Case* (n 93) 207–11 [398]–[407].

[128] For the text of Art 8, see n 91. See also Crawford (n 28) 141–65, esp 157–8.

[129] ICJ Statute (n 67) Art 59. See also MJ Struett, 'The Transformation of State Sovereign Rights and Responsibilities under the Rome Statute for the International Criminal Court' (2005) 8 Chapman Law Review 179, 189 (observing that Art 59 'proscribes the precedential value for the World Court's decisions'). Furthermore, UN Charter Art 94(1) reads as follows: '[e]ach Member of the United Nations undertakes to comply with the decision of the International Court of Justice in any case to which it is party'. See also Rosenne (n 58) 297. He later adds, at 308, that '[u]nder the new law of responsibility, non-compliance with a judgment on the merits, if established, could be a cause of action'.

including the International Tribunal for the Law of the Sea (ITLOS) and international criminal tribunals; they inform the work and various codification projects of the ILC, including in the field of SR, etc.[130] Therefore, despite its jurisdictional limitations, the pervasive reach and influence of ICJ jurisprudence on SR matters should not be discarded lightly.

3.1.3.3 The Court and obligations erga omnes

The ICJ has also exercised its jurisdiction over disputes involving the implementation of community responsibility. Although community responsibility is a distinct manifestation—or type of enforcement—of traditional SR, it hinges on the same considerations that animate the consequences of any breach of an international obligation. The main distinction, therefore, resides in the fact that community responsibility concerns itself solely with redressing internationally wrongful acts harming collective interests. This approach carries distinct resonance for the present study, as the ideals underpinning counterterrorism strategies (and, by extension, the prevention of other global security risks) often straddle the terrain of collective interests; in fact, they will almost invariably lead us into the realm of obligations *erga omnes*. Furthermore, some publicists increasingly argue that transnational terrorism and other similar global threats subvert collective interests and must, in turn, be met with resolute and collective action by members of the international community. For instance, influential voices within US legal scholarship have maintained that States have a collective 'duty to prevent' humanitarian disasters, along with the harbouring, production, and deployment of weapons of mass destruction (WMDs).[131]

Furthermore, the very fabric and essence of the concept of international community, which hinge to a large extent on the coordination of concerted initiatives in safeguarding collective or common rights and interests, also significantly inform the analysis. In this light, Santiago Villalpando's contribution to the debate becomes particularly insightful in the global security context. Before delving into the intellectual merits of his claims, it is useful to recall that the term 'international community' has generated its share of controversy in legal scholarship.[132]

[130] See, eg, 'Competition and Co-operation' (n 57) 2.

[131] See, eg, L Feinstein and A-M Slaughter, 'A Duty to Prevent' (2004) 83 FA 136. It should be noted, however, that other prominent scholars categorically rejected this approach. For instance, J Brunnée and SJ Toope took issue with it, judging that the duty to prevent unnecessarily merges all justifications for recourse to force into one overriding security threat pre-emption model. See 'Slouching towards New "Just" Wars: International Law and the Use of Force after September 11th' (2004) 51 NILR 363, 387–90; 'The Use of Force: International Law after Iraq' (2004) 53 ICLQ 785, 802–4.

[132] See, eg, C De Visscher, *Theory and Reality in International Law* (rev edn, Princeton University Press 1968) 94; SJ Toope, 'Emerging Patterns of Governance and International Law' in M Byers (ed.), *The Role of Law in International Politics: Essays in International Relations and International Law* (OUP 2000) 91, 103. See also P Allott, *Eunomia: New Order for a New World* (OUP 1990) 3–4, 189–90, 219, 234–5, 239–40, 325–6, 374–5 and 'The True Function of Law in the International Community' (1998) 5 Indiana Journal of Global Legal Studies 391, 411 (discussing and critiquing

For the purposes of SR, suffice it to underscore that the use of the term 'international community' is

> not, however, intended to imply that there is a legal person, the international community. Clearly there is not. But while particular organs or institutions (e.g. the principal organs of the United Nations) may represent community interests, generally or for particular purposes, their failure to act in a given case should not entail that a state in breach of an obligation to the community as a whole cannot be called into account.[133]

In that regard, it should be noted that Villalpando's approach conceptualizes SR in terms of a binary continuum involving individual interests and collective interests at opposite ends, whilst also identifying a common regime of responsibility and a community regime of responsibility. The latter is also subdivided into a common regime (covering all violations of obligations *erga omnes*) and an aggravated regime (applicable to the most serious violations).[134] Villalpando's classification of types of international responsibility is embodied in a bipartite model hingeing solely on the nature—collective versus individual—of the legally protected interests at stake.[135] He further cautions that the seriousness of the international wrongful act in question bears no incidence in determining which regime of responsibility warrants application, as both regimes remain separate, respond to different rules, and serve different purposes and objectives.[136] Pursuant to his framework, both regimes are endowed with their own inherent varying scales of gravity, which in turn inform SR mechanics and ultimately have an impact on the available responses to redress breaches.[137]

For proponents of this view, the modern concept of 'international community' marks a clear departure from ancient communities, which were predominantly spontaneous, limited, and static. The current 'international community' is a rational one and hinges on its members' consciences and cooperation in attaining and safeguarding collective interests. Villalpando concludes that because of its lack of institutional structure, this community cannot be individualized or claim a specific interest.[138] It inexorably follows that all States simultaneously

the concepts of 'international society' and 'international community'). In the same vein, see also J Barberis, 'Nouvelles Questions Concernant la Personnalité Juridique Internationale' (1983) 179 RdC 145, 176–7 (arguing that the international community is not a legal subject); P Cahier, 'Changements et Continuité du Droit International' (1985) 195 RdC 9, 96 (observing that the international community cannot be individualized or express its own will).

[133] See Fourth Report—Crawford (n 14) 11–12. See also ILC, 'Comments and Observations Received by Governments' (2001) UN Doc A/CN.4/515 and Add.1–3, esp 73–7; D Kritsiotis, 'Imagining the International Community' (2002) 13 EJIL 961, 977–8.

[134] Villalpando (n 2) 224, 242, 246–59. On this question and related issues, see also Simma (n 32); S Sahakyan, *Aggravated State Responsibility and Obligations Erga Omnes: The Concept of 'Obligations Erga Omnes' and its Relevance in the Law of State Responsibility* (Lambert Academic Publishing 2010).

[135] Villalpando (n 2) 251. [136] Villalpando (n 2) 252.

[137] See his schema in Villalpando (n 2) 254. See also ibid 98–9.

[138] In many ways, therefore, Villalpando's thesis aligns with various writings of structural realist commentators, some of which are explored in Sections 1.2 and 4.2. Compare also with KN Waltz, *Theory of International Politics* (McGraw-Hill 1979); KN Waltz, 'International Politics Is Not

bear responsibility for safeguarding community interests, an idea that could be analogous to the prescriptions enshrined in SC Resolution 1373, which set broad-reaching counterterrorism obligations. Similar reasoning could extend to the content of Resolution 1540, which likewise lays down onerous nuclear disarmament and non-proliferation duties incumbent upon all States.[139] Collective interests are therefore vindicated via alternate means and through different manifestations of community solidarity.[140] Unsurprisingly, Villalpando's thesis initially starts from a sociological exploration of the concept of 'international community' and ultimately identifies key manifestations of the concept in public international law and, more precisely, in the field of SR.

Whilst steering readers away from the notion that 'international community' derives solely from *de lege ferenda* theoretical constructs, Villalpando's account does not so much deliver an exhaustive review of international responsibility issues but rather elects the realm of SR as a primary intellectual and practical prism through which the idea of 'international community' is investigated.[141] Indeed, his approach is illuminating for present purposes, as the global fight against terrorism (and the prevention of other global security risks) involves an intricate interplay between obligations *erga omnes*, collective enforcement of counterterrorism obligations, and the promotion of collective interests. Needless to say, SR law sometimes has an important role to play in this broader framework.

In sum, this line of argument remains a comprehensive and cogent articulation of the concept of 'international community' in relation to SR repertoire, thereby making this type of discussion particularly welcome—and instructive—in light of other accounts highlighting the vagueness of that term.[142] More importantly, it signals that breaches of specific counterterrorism undertakings might be framed within the realm of obligations owed to the international community as a whole and, as a corollary, attract cooperative responses under the aegis of the SC, for example. Therefore, precedents dealing with the implementation of community responsibility remain

Foreign Policy' (1996) 6 Security Studies 54; A-M Slaughter, 'International Law and International Relations Theory: A Prospectus' in E Benvenisti and M Hirsch (eds), *The Impact of International Law Cooperation* (CUP 2006) 16, 22; J Mearsheimer, 'The False Promise of International Institutions' (1999) 19 International Security 5, 11–12, 14; J Mearsheimer, *The Tragedy of Great Power Politics* (Norton 2001) 30–2; I Motoc, 'Controversial Aspects of Democracy in International Law: The Right to Political Participation in Foreign Affairs' in KK Koufa (ed.), *Thesaurus Acroasium Vol 34: State Responsibility and the Individual* (Sakkoulas 2006) 275, 287–8.

[139] These resolutions are further discussed in Section 4.5.1. For now, suffice it to point out that Resolution 1373 was enacted similarly to legislation, in that it was adopted 'in a general context not directly related to disciplining any individual country or particular non-state actor'. See EJ Cárdenas, 'The United Nations Security Council's Quest for Effectiveness' (2004) 25 MJIL 1341. On Resolution 1540, see DH Joyner, 'The Security Council as a Legal Hegemon' (2012) 43 GJIL 225, 227–38.

[140] Villalpando (n 2) 40–1, 98–9, 296–8.

[141] Villalpando (n 2) 75.

[142] See, eg, E Roucounas, 'Non-State Actors: Areas of International Responsibility in Need of Further Exploration' in Ragazzi (n 49) 399; PS Rao, 'International Crimes and State Responsibility' in ibid 79–80 fn 58. But see Peirano (n 122) 184–5 (noting the revival of a universal international community focused on human rights, and the emergence of a universal community grounded in the advancement of international law through the challenging of State voluntarism and the affirmation of collective values).

quite instructive for understanding SR implications better, and may also implicate the ICJ. For example, the Court has deemed itself competent to handle cases dealing with the consequences of hostage-taking and sequestering of diplomatic personnel in Iran,[143] a prohibited armed attack in international relations,[144] armed activities involving the Democratic Republic of Congo and Uganda,[145] and genocide in two distinct cases.[146] In such instances, the ICJ can potentially be called upon to pronounce on the occurrence of internationally wrongful acts and rule on the resulting consequences of the violations, along with the legality of any (potential) future countermeasures adopted to counteract the unlawful conduct. In this light, the ICJ's role appears almost organic and decidedly compatible with the underlying tenets of SR, especially in the eventuality that two disputing States are deadlocked over the determination of the appropriate breach-to-liability and countermeasure-to-breach ratios. Therefore, SR repertoire provides an environment within which the ICJ may reach political decisions by way of legal/judicial process.

In this light, the judicial settlement of disputes by the ICJ should be encouraged and promoted as one of the ways—albeit limited—in which SR can be implemented in global security contexts. Inexorably, however, the effect of seising the ICJ of a dispute over the application of obligations *erga omnes* will have the effect of 'bilateralizing' that disagreement, although the Court's pronouncements may ultimately carry weight outside the strict confines of the dispute before it. By contrast, the SC might be better suited in some instances to implement SR for those types of obligations and act truly in the collective interest.

3.1.3.4 Conclusion: A legal environment for political decisions

As will be explored in Section 3.1.5 and in the discussion of the *Conditions of Admission of a State to Membership in the UN* Advisory Opinion, it should be stressed that whilst the Court theoretically operates within a legal framework, it nonetheless makes political decisions. This interplay was very much alive in the ICJ's Advisory Opinion on the *Legality of the Threat or Use of Nuclear Weapons*, which required it to make a politically charged decision on the use of nuclear weapons in the absence of an overarching juridical framework.[147] In assessing its

[143] *Tehran Hostages Case* (n 80).

[144] *Nicaragua v USA* (Jurisdiction) (n 63); *Nicaragua v USA* (Merits) (n 63).

[145] *Armed Activities* (n 80).

[146] *Application of the Convention on the Prevention and Punishment of the Crime of Genocide (Bosnia and Herzegovina v Yugoslavia)* (Preliminary Objections) [1996] ICJ Rep 595; *Application of the Convention on the Prevention and Punishment of the Crime of Genocide (Croatia v Serbia)* (Preliminary Objections) [2008] ICJ Rep 412.

[147] The tension between legal and political questions—and between the respective functions of the SC and ICJ—was also raised more recently in the context of advisory proceedings before the ICJ. In fact, it dug divisive lines between the reasoning of the majority and some of the Judges who wrote separately. Compare *Accordance with International Law of the Unilateral Declaration of Independence in Respect of Kosovo* (Advisory Opinion) [2010] ICJ Rep 403; Declaration of Vice-President Tomka in ibid 454–66; Separate Opinion of Judge Keith in ibid 482–90; Dissenting Opinion of Judge Bennouna in ibid 500–14; Dissenting Opinion of Judge Skotnikov in ibid 515–22.

jurisdiction to hand down the Advisory Opinion, the ICJ deemed that the fact that the question before it entailed the consideration of political dimensions—an eventuality pervading the majority of international affairs—failed to eviscerate its content as a 'legal question'.[148] The Court went on to state that

> [w]hatever its political aspects, the Court cannot refuse to admit the legal character of a question which invites it to discharge an essentially judicial task, namely, an assessment of the legality of the possible conduct of States with regard to the obligations imposed upon them by international law.[149]

Undoubtedly, such inference may be readily extended to the ICJ's potential involvement in judicially assessing the SR of a State following its failure to prevent transnational terrorism, for instance. Indeed, the Court's role in that setting would precisely aim to gauge—judicially—the lawfulness of a State's actions under public international law whilst exposing its reasoning to inevitable political considerations. In that regard, SR law would, once again, provide a legal environment within which these considerations could be weighed and ultimately lead to a judicially driven resolution of a political dispute.

Whilst the prospect of implementing SR through the channel of the ICJ might appear promising under some lights, it is unlikely that the Court would be called upon to ascertain the international responsibility of a State for violating counterterrorism obligations on the basis of mutual consent of the parties to a dispute. Similar concerns could be voiced over the potential adjudication of disputes involving other global security breaches. In light of this shortcoming, it is useful to canvass the potential role and contributions of the GA in this setting.

3.1.4 The General Assembly

We may certainly turn to the GA as a viable forum in which both SR rules and counterterrorism issues might be engaged in the dispatch of that organ's business. Undoubtedly, the Assembly has made significant advances in the promotion of counterterrorism strategies, and deployed similar efforts regarding other global security threats. In the counterterrorism context, for instance, shortly after the 9/11 attacks the GA '[u]rgently call[ed] for international cooperation to prevent and eradicate acts of terrorism, and stresse[d] that those responsible for aiding, supporting or harbouring the perpetrators, organizers and sponsors of such acts [would] be held accountable'.[150] In future cases involving the violation of counterterrorism

[148] *Legality of the Threat or Use of Nuclear Weapons* (Advisory Opinion) [1996] ICJ Rep 226, 234. See also *Application for Review of Judgment No. 158 of the United Nations Administrative Tribunal* (Advisory Opinion) [1973] ICJ Rep 166, 172 [14].

[149] *Nuclear Weapons Advisory Opinion* (n 148) 234. See also *Admission of a State to Membership to the United Nations (Charter, Art. 4)* (Advisory Opinion) [1948] ICJ Rep 57, 61–2; *Competence of the General Assembly for the Admission of a State to the United Nations* (Advisory Opinion) [1950] ICJ Rep 4, 6–7; *Certain Expenses of the United Nations (Article 17, paragraph 2, of the Charter)* (Advisory Opinion) [1962] ICJ Rep 151, 155.

[150] UNGA Res 56/1 (12 September 2001) UN Doc A/RES/56/1.

obligations by a State—or breaches pertaining to other threads of the global security fabric—it could well be that the GA's broad-ranging declarations come to play some role in the SR calculus. For instance, an injured State seeking to invoke the SR of another State might feel compelled to make reference to particular GA resolutions in mounting its case. Similarly, the ICJ may also draw from GA resolutions when handing down decisions on SR matters. At a more abstract level, the GA has taken the lead in proposing that the international community move away from the ARSIWA and enshrine SR norms in a multilateral convention.[151] However, some eight or nine years later, there is no indication that this project is politically viable, let alone that a resulting international convention on SR would not disrupt the diffuse, 'soft' authority exerted by the ARSIWA, along with the compromises built into that instrument.[152]

3.1.4.1 Institutional limitations

Although seemingly relevant for bolstering SR implementation in global security contexts, the GA remains fettered by clear institutional limitations. These inbuilt restrictions preclude it from comprising an exclusive and overarching mechanism in applying secondary SR norms. Pursuant to the UN Charter, the GA 'may discuss any questions or any matters within the scope of the present Charter or relating to the powers and functions of any organs provided for in the present Charter' and 'make recommendations to the Members of the United Nations or to the Security Council or to both on any such questions or matters'.[153] Interestingly, the GA's operations have sometimes fallen outside the strict purview of restoring international peace and security, most notably in the fields of human rights, self-determination, and environmental protection, all relevant areas under SR.

[151] UNGA Sixth Committee (62nd Session) 'Draft Resolution—Agenda Item 78: Responsibility of States for Internationally Wrongful Acts' (9 November 2007) UN Doc A/C.6/62/L.20 [4]; UNGA Res 62/61 (8 January 2008) UN Doc A/RES/62/61 [4] (deciding to 'include in the provisional agenda' and to 'further examine, within the framework of a working group of the Sixth Committee, the question of a convention on responsibility of States for internationally wrongful acts or other appropriate action on the basis of the articles'). See also UNGA Sixth Committee (62nd Session) 'Responsibility of States for Internationally Wrongful Acts, Report of the Sixth Committee' (21 November 2007) UN Doc A/62/446 [5]–[7] (confirming that Draft Resolution A/C.6/62/L.20 was adopted by the Sixth Committee without a vote). On the necessity of adopting a convention on SR, see LT Pacht, 'The Case for a Convention on State Responsibility' (2014) 83 NJIL 439; CP Economidès, 'Le Projet de la CDI sur la Responsabilité de l'État pour Fait Internationalement Illicite: Nécessité d'une Convention Internationale (2005) 58 Revue Hellénique de Droit International 77. See also generally JR Crawford and S Olleson, 'The Continuing Debate on a UN Convention on State Responsibility' (2005) 54 ICLQ 959.

[152] See JE Alvarez, *International Organizations as Law-Makers* (OUP 2005) 311–2; DD Caron, 'The ILC Articles on State Responsibility: The Paradoxical Relationship between Form and Authority' (2002) 96 AJIL 857, 858, 862–4, 868–73.

[153] Charter of the UN (adopted 26 June 1945, entered into force 24 October 1945) as amended by UNGA Resolutions 1991 (XVIII) (17 December 1963) (entered into force 31 August 1965) 557 UNTS 143; 2101 (XX) (20 December 1965) (entered into force 12 June 1968) 638 UNTS 308; and 2847 (XXVI) (20 December 1971) (entered into force 24 September 1973) 892 UNTS 119, Art 10.

Moreover, the GA's mandate does not preclude it from intervening in respect of violations of obligations *erga omnes*, especially when the interests at stake turn on a question that is related to the purposes and objectives of the UN.[154] In this light, the GA remains an operational and executive entity—a sort of hybrid institution for the purposes of supporting SR implementation—capable of issuing recommendations in a general sense[155] or on specific matters.[156] Finally, the equal participation of each State in the activities of this organ, characterized by its democratic process in turn quantified and translated into a single vote per member, makes the GA a valuable avenue through which collective interests can be vindicated and SR could potentially be implemented.[157] Absent any clear enforcement mechanisms, the GA can also become a propitious locus in which constituencies of conscience can be built with a view to inducing a wrongdoing State to accept its international responsibility, consider repairing its breach through the payment of compensation or in some other form, and present formal apologies to the injured State(s). Similarly, the GA can provide an apt forum in which to calibrate and discuss any future countermeasures contemplated by the injured State to redress the international law violation.

Amongst other restraints, two considerations significantly restrict the GA's ability to implement SR. First, powers devolved to it considerably limit its scope of action in that it can only issue non-binding resolutions on Member States without the possibility of imposing sanctions to ensure compliance with its directions.[158] As a corollary, it follows that the GA cannot legitimize, or 'make legal', actions undertaken by Member States and otherwise inconsonant with international law. This entails that States are precluded from invoking GA resolutions in attempting to justify violations of primary obligations outside the context of countermeasures, or violations of secondary obligations pertaining to the parameters or conditions governing the adoption of countermeasures. For instance, a State could not justify resorting to the use of force to counteract the violation of an obligation *erga omnes*.[159] Secondly, the GA remains barred from weighing in on any dispute

[154] See, eg, I Scobbie, 'Unchart(er)ed Waters?: Consequences of the Advisory Opinion on the Legal Consequences of the Construction of a Wall in the Occupied Palestinian Territory for the Responsibility of the UN for Palestine' (2005) 16 EJIL 941, 959.

[155] See UN Charter (n 153) Art 11(1) ('The General Assembly may consider the general principles of co-operation in the maintenance of international peace and security').

[156] UN Charter (n 153) Art 11(2) provides:

> The General Assembly may discuss any questions relating to the maintenance of international peace and security brought before it by any Member of the United Nations, or by the Security Council, or by a state which is not a Member of the United Nations ... may make recommendations with regard to any such questions to the state or states concerned or to the Security Council or to both.

[157] See, eg, Fifth Report—Arangio-Ruiz (n 18) [100]; Seventh Report–Arangio-Ruiz (n 18) [91].

[158] See, eg, Fifth Report—Arangio-Ruiz (n 18) [100]–[101]; Seventh Report—Arangio-Ruiz (n 18) [91]–[93]. Not to mention that the GA 'has no competence to make determinations in the area of State responsibility'. See Seventh Report—Arangio-Ruiz (n 18) 21 [93].

[159] See ARSIWA (n 23) Art 51. On this issue, see also de Hoogh (n 5) 241–4; JA Frowein, 'Legal Consequences for International Law Enforcement in Case of Security Council Inaction' in Delbrück (n 14) 118–19.

or situation already under advisement by the SC, unless the latter expressly mandates it to do so. Article 12 of the UN Charter specifies that '[w]hile the Security Council is exercising in respect of any dispute or situation the functions assigned to it in the present Charter, the General Assembly shall not make any recommendation with regard to that dispute or situation unless the Security Council so requests'.[160] It should be recalled, however, that this provision has sometimes been interpreted rather liberally in past and recent UN practice.[161]

Irrespective of how the debates surrounding the roles of both the GA and ICJ in implementing SR are ultimately resolved, however, those resolutions will have little or no impact on the arguments explored in the present monograph.

3.1.4.2 Towards a supportive role

The GA can still take on a supportive role in implementing SR for failing to prevent terrorist attacks or in responding to other global security threats. For instance, it may adopt a resolution establishing that an internationally wrongful act has been committed, enjoining the culprit to fulfil certain international obligations whilst also suggesting the imposition of remedial measures on the responsible State. In such a scenario, the GA might legitimize any subsequent unilateral invocation of SR by an injured State in accordance with the prescriptions enshrined in its resolution. Similarly, the GA might also make reference to international obligations on a more abstract or general level in its resolutions, which may ultimately serve as the basis for establishing the international responsibility of a State for violating international law. For instance, several GA resolutions 'leave no doubt that harboring or supporting terrorist groups violates a state's responsibility under international law'.[162]

Needless to say, the legal persuasiveness and political capital of the injured State's claim would be further reinforced if the GA resolution was adopted by a strong majority. Aside from bolstering the legitimacy of actions taken by any State purporting to invoke SR pursuant to the prescriptions of a GA resolution, that organ would also provide solace to that State in terms of framing its action within the broader framework of the promotion and protection of collective interests.[163]

[160] UN Charter (n 153) Art 12.

[161] See, eg, *Wall Advisory Opinion* (n 5) [27] (noting that 'there has been an increasing tendency over time for the General Assembly and the Security Council to deal in parallel with the same matter concerning the maintenance of international peace and security'); UNGA Res 377 (V) (3 November 1950) (the non-binding 'Uniting for Peace' resolution which enables the GA to consider a matter over which the SC is deadlocked on an emergency basis for the purposes of making recommendations).

[162] G Travalio and J Altenburg, 'Terrorism, State Responsibility, and the Use of Military Force' (2003) 4 CJIL 97, 100. For specific resolutions, see UNGA 'Report of the Special Committee on Principles of International Law Concerning Friendly Relations and Cooperation Among States' UN GAOR 25th Session Supp No 18 UN Doc A/8018 (1970); UNGA Res 3314 (XXIX) (14 December 1974); UNGA Res 40/61 (9 December 1985) UN Doc A/RES/40/61.

[163] See, eg, JA Frowein, 'Reactions by Not Directly Affected States to Breaches of Public International Law' (1994) 248 RdC 347, 383.

In fact, the GA often intercedes in matters involving internationally wrongful acts perpetrated against the international community as a whole.[164] This exercise of its powers would, presumably, also encompass a majority of transnational terrorist attacks, and similarly attach to States' international law violations pertaining to other global security areas.

In addition to wielding some suggestive power—or legalizing effect—over States' actions (ie by supporting a claim of responsibility against the responsible State), GA resolutions may also become influential in judicial or jurisdictional proceedings, such as before the ICJ or in the context of arbitration. In reaching their respective outcomes, both decision-makers may consider the GA's view as holding 'normative value', be it as an indicator of a crystallizing international legal norm or the confirmation of an already existent positive rule.[165] In the *Military and Paramilitary Activities in and against Nicaragua* case, the ICJ clearly ascribed some normative firepower to GA resolutions. The Court expounded that they, along with their reception and the attitudes they generate, can become constitutive of *opinio juris* on the international plane (and, for present purposes, might ostensibly govern some aspects of SR law).[166] Irrespective of the influence of GA resolutions, any actions undertaken by States will have to comport with international law, both at the primary and secondary levels of the norms involved. For example, at the primary level those actions cannot violate the prohibition of the use of force in international relations, pursuant to Article 2(4) of the UN Charter. At the secondary level, those actions should comply with the conditions and guidelines governing the adoption of countermeasures under SR repertoire.

3.1.5 The Security Council

The discussion now turns to the crux of the prescriptive argument: the potential implementation of SR via the SC's channel, which will be fully fleshed out in Chapter 4. Before so doing, this section offers some preliminary remarks on both

[164] See examples in Seventh Report—Arangio-Ruiz (n 18) [79]–[81]; JC Lloréns, 'La Responsabilidad Internacional por Violación Grave de Obligaciones Esenciales por la Salvaguarda de Intereses Fundamentales de la Comunidad Internacional' (1985) 8 Anuario de Derecho Internacional 265, 291–5, 324.

[165] See, eg, *Nuclear Weapons Advisory Opinion* (n 148) 254–5 (underscoring that GA 'resolutions, even if they are not binding, may sometimes have normative value' and that '[t]hey can, in certain circumstances, provide evidence important for establishing the existence of a rule or the emergence of an *opinio juris*'). See also J Castañeda, *Legal Effects of United Nations Resolutions* (Alba Amoia tr, Columbia University Press 1969) 6 ('certain resolutions, whether they have strict legislative character or not, are expressions of law and carry with them obligations in the juridical sense').

[166] *Nicaragua v USA* (Merits) (n 63) 99–100 [188]–[189]. For different views on this possibility, compare O Schachter, 'The Crisis of Legitimation in the United Nations' (1981) 50 Nordisk Tidsskript for International Ret 3, 4–5, 7; C Schreuer, 'Recommendations and the Traditional Sources of International Law' (1977) 20 GYIL 103, 107–9; Dissenting Opinion of Judge Tanaka in *South West Africa* (Second Phase) [1966] ICJ Rep 6, 292; Statement of EA Gross, Agent for the Governments of Ethiopia and Liberia, *South West Africa Cases* ICJ Pleadings (Vol IX) 347; Committee on Formation of Customary (General) International Law, International Law Association, London Conference (2000) <www.ila-hq.org/en/committees/index.cfm/cid/30> accessed 12 August 2015, 55–66; GM Danilenko, *Law-Making in the International Community* (Nijhoff 1993) 88–9.

the prospects and limits of SC involvement in SR implementation and its 'quasi-judicial' role, more broadly.

3.1.5.1 *Prospects and limits*

The SC appears, on its face, to be suited to contribute to the implementation of SR for the failure to prevent terrorism in certain circumstances. This role could presumably also extend to other global security priority areas. Indeed, the UN Charter devolves vast powers to the SC in safeguarding collective interests, thereby aiming to confer upon it the primary responsibility of maintaining and restoring international peace and security.[167] It is no surprise, therefore, that the UN Charter has sometimes been described as the 'constitution of the international legal system'.[168] Whilst operating within the scope of its mandate, the SC thus simultaneously exerts executive and operational powers and can take stock, or act on, fundamental interests concerning the international community as a whole.[169] Moreover, the particular scheme of powers devolved to the SC, which involves recourse to coercive measures, offers a wide range of options in ensuring compliance with international obligations and in implementing SR. For instance, the SC's binding and far-reaching decision-making power, pursuant to Article 25 of the Charter, immediately springs to mind.[170]

A first significant obstacle to the proposition that the SC might exert general competence in implementing SR is attributable to the very structure of the UN. It also hinges, to a large extent, on the tension between restraints imposed on SC action and judicial review of its resolutions, two issues appearing semantically adjacent at first glance but clearly distinct in scope and in practice.[171] As a corollary, an

[167] This language is borrowed from UN Charter (n 153) Art 24(1).

[168] See, eg, B Fassbender, *The United Nations Charter as the Constitution of the International Community* (Nijhoff 2009); 'The United Nations Charter as Constitution of the International Community' (1998) 36 CJTL 531. Other scholars similarly highlight the 'trend towards the constitutionalization of the international legal system', which they attribute primarily to increasing institutionalization and an enhanced focus on individual rights on the international plane. See, eg, V Gowlland-Debbas, 'Security Council Change' (2009-10) 65 International Journal 119, 131; V Gowlland-Debbas and V Pergantis, 'The Rule of Law' in V Chetail (ed.), *Post-Conflict Peace Building: A Lexicon* (OUP 2009) 320–36. On the constitutional effects of the law of international responsibility, see A Nollkaemper, 'Constitutionalization and the Unity of the Law of International Responsibility' (2009) 16 Indiana Journal of Global Legal Studies 535.

[169] See, eg, the ICTY Appeals Chamber's treatment of SC powers in the *Tadić Case* (Decision on the Defence Motion for Interlocutory Appeal on Jurisdiction) ICTY-94-1-AR72 (2 October 1995) [37].

[170] UN Charter (n 153) Art 25. For a judicial application of Art 25 and the binding nature of SC resolutions, see *Legal Consequences for States of the Continued Presence of South Africa in Namibia (South West Africa) Notwithstanding Security Council Resolution 276 (1970)* (Advisory Opinion) [1971] ICJ Rep 16, 54 [114]–[116].

[171] See, eg, K Skubiszewski, 'The International Court of Justice and the Security Council' in V Lowe and M Fitzmaurice (eds), *Fifty Years of the International Court of Justice: Essays in Honour of Sir Robert Jennings* (CUP 1996) 606, 626–7; V Gowlland-Debbas, 'UN Sanctions and International Law: An Overview' in idem (ed.), *United Nations Sanctions and International Law* (Kluwer 2001) 1, 14.

ultra vires SC decision can engender distinct legal consequences outside the context of formal judicial review. Support for this proposition is exemplified through the so-called right of last resort of Member States to evade compliance, in certain cases, with an illegal SC resolution.[172] When engaging in this debate, however, one publicist's cautionary words should be pondered, which signal that 'a violation of the Charter, whilst theoretically possible, is not a serious hypothesis'.[173]

In sum, there exists wide judicial and academic support for the notion that the SC is not above the law (*legibus solutus*).[174] However, although its decisions must observe the objectives and principles laid down in the Charter,[175] along with general international law, there is no corresponding method or formal mechanism to ensure the legality of its decision-making. Framing the inquiry solely within the purview of judicial resolution, it is possible to identify two, albeit imperfect, recourses available to a State targeted by SC-imposed sanctions. First, a State complying with SC sanctions can appear before the ICJ so that the Court may rule on the original sanction-creating resolution, subject to the jurisdictional limitations outlined above. Indeed, this possibility arose in connection with the applications instituting proceedings and the requests for the indication of provisional measures submitted by Libya in the *Lockerbie* cases, although the ICJ never handed down a judgment beyond the preliminary objections phase.[176] Such a

[172] See, eg, M Virally, 'L'ONU devant le Droit' (1972) 99 Journal de Droit International 531; D Ciobanu, *Preliminary Objections Related to the Jurisdiction of the United Nations Political Organs* (Nijhoff 1975) 174. For a contrary opinion, see Q Wright, 'The Strengthening of International Law' (1959) 98 RdC 1, 125; E Osieke, 'The Legal Validity of *Ultra Vires* Decisions of International Organizations' (1983) 77 AJIL 255.

[173] C Dominicé, 'The International Responsibility of the United Nations for Injuries Resulting from Non-Military Enforcement Measures' in Ragazzi (n 49) 366.

[174] See, eg, *Tadić Case* (Interlocutory Appeal on Jurisdiction) (n 169) [28]; N Angelet, 'International Law Limits to the Security Council' in Gowlland-Debbas (n 171) 71–82; M Bothe, 'Les Limites des Pouvoirs du Conseil de Sécurité' in R-J Dupuy (ed.), *The Development of the Role of the Security Council: Peace-Keeping and Peace-Building* (Nijhoff 1993) 67–81; B Conforti, 'Le Pouvoir Discrétionnaire du Conseil de Sécurité en Matière de Constatation d'une Menace contre la Paix, d'une Rupture de la Paix ou d'un Acte d'Agression' in ibid 51–60; M Koskenniemi, 'The Police in the Temple: Order, Justice and the UN—A Dialectical View' (1995) 6 EJIL 325. But see Dulles (n 47) 194–5; AT Saliba, 'Is the Security Council *Legibus Solutus*?: An Analysis of the Legal Restraints of the UNSC' (2012) 20 Journal of International Law and Practice 401.

[175] UN Charter (n 153) Art 24(2). As a corollary, the SC's broad decision-making powers do not, in turn, empower members to comply with *ultra vires* resolutions, or with decisions that are inconsistent with the Charter. See, eg, K Zemanek, 'The Legal Foundations of the International System: General Course on Public International Law' (1997) 266 RdC 9, 96. But see MK Nawaz, 'Law and International Organization—A Perspective on the United Nations' (1977) 17 Indian Journal of International Law 239; E Suy, 'Article 25' in J-P Cot and A Pellet (eds), *La Charte des Nations Unies: Commentaire Article par Article* (2nd edn, Economica 1991) 481.

[176] *Questions of Interpretation and Application of the 1971 Montreal Convention arising from the Aerial Incident at Lockerbie (Libya v UK)* (Provisional Measures) [1992] ICJ Rep 3; *Questions of Interpretation and Application of the 1971 Montreal Convention arising from the Aerial Incident at Lockerbie (Libya v USA)* (Provisional Measures) [1992] ICJ Rep 114. At that stage, the Court discarded the contention that Libya could not benefit from its rights under the Montreal Convention since it was argued that they had been superseded by SC resolutions imposing certain obligation upon Libya. In this regard, the Court insisted upon the fact that its jurisdiction had been established prior to the adoption of those resolutions. See ibid [38], [44]. See also A Paulus, 'Jurisprudence of the International Court of Justice: *Lockerbie* Cases, Preliminary Objections' (1998) 9 EJIL 550; PHF

scenario would not directly subject the SC to the judicial recourse or to formal review, whilst a finding of illegality by the ICJ would probably trigger a power struggle within the UN. Secondly, the aforementioned State could request that the competent organs within its own official governing apparatus submit a request for an advisory opinion from the ICJ. The admissibility of such a request, however, remains doubtful, or at least problematic, whilst the resulting opinion would prove non-binding under the ICJ Statute.[177]

Arguably, such a structure paves the way for potential abuses of power, over-reactions, and political score-settling, all behaviours that, ironically, the institutionalization of SR through UN organs purports to eradicate.[178] By the same token, it is reasonable to infer that the overarching principle of sovereign equality between UN Member States *ipso facto* precludes the SC from deriving unlimited (and unchecked) powers from its mandate.[179] This proposition also finds support in both ICJ and ICTY jurisprudence.[180] Although for some publicists, elucidating the interplay between SC powers and the implementation of SR might remain largely contingent on the resolution of the judicial review question,[181] it is nonetheless immensely helpful to explore the SC's role in implementing this normative scheme. The objective here, therefore, is not to take up a position or resolve the aforementioned debate, a task better left to seasoned international law scholars and policy-makers.[182] In any event, the judicial review question will be revisited in greater detail in Section 3.2.1. However, whilst there is strong

Bekker, 'Questions of Interpretation and Application of the 1971 Montreal Convention Arising from the Aerial Incident at Lockerbie' (1998) 92 AJIL 503.

[177] See G Gaja, 'Réflexions sur le Rôle du Conseil de Sécurité dans le Nouvel Ordre Mondial: À Propos des Rapports entre Maintien de la Paix et Crimes Internationaux des États' (1993) 97 RGDIP 297, 315–17.

[178] See, eg, Gowlland-Debbas (n 30) 73–4; AL Paulus, 'Peace through Justice? The Future of the Crime of Aggression in a Time of Crisis' (2004) 50 Wayne Law Review 1, 20–1; J Trahan, 'Defining "Aggression": Why the Preparatory Commission for the International Criminal Court Has Faced Such a Conundrum' (2002) 24 Loyola LA International and Comparative Law Review 439, 460–1.

[179] See, eg, Simma (n 32) 270; A Constantinides, 'An Overview of Legal Restraints on Security Council Chapter VII Action with a Focus on Post-Conflict Iraq' <www.esil-sedi.eu/sites/default/files/Constantinides_0.PDF> accessed 21 August 2015.

[180] See, eg, *Admission of a State* (n 149) 64 ('[t]he political character of an organ cannot release it from the observance of treaty provisions established by the Charter, when they constitute limitations on its powers or criteria for its judgment'); *Tadić Case* (Interlocutory Appeal on Jurisdiction) (n 169) [28] ('[t]he Security Council is an organ of an international organization, established by a treaty which serves as a constitutional framework for that organization. The Security Council is thus subjected to certain constitutional limitations, however broad its powers under the constitution may be').

[181] See, eg, Bedjaoui (n 104); DW Bowett, 'The Impact of Security Council Decisions on Dispute Settlement Procedures' (1994) 5 EJIL 89 (placing particular emphasis on its correlation with international responsibility); J Dugard, 'Judicial Review of Sanctions' in Gowlland-Debbas (n 171) 83–91. By contrast, this volume argues that the resolution of the judicial review debate is not essential to the elucidation of the question whether the SC can apply SR principles.

[182] See, eg, P-M Dupuy, 'The Constitutional Dimension of the Charter of the United Nations Revisited' (1997) 1 Max Planck Yearbook of UN Law 1, 26–7; V Gowlland-Debbas, 'The Functions of the United Nations Security Council in the International Legal System' in Byers (n 132) 277, 306–11; Graefrath (n 4) 246–8.

scholarly support for the proposition that the ICJ should act as a check on the legality of SC decision-making,[183] it is not likely that the Council would feel compelled to comply with a ruling by the Court purporting to impede or restrict its action.[184] As will be argued in Chapter 4, the SC has interpreted its Chapter VII powers rather broadly, thereby signalling a potential disconnect between, on the one hand, the undesirable scenario of granting it unfettered discretion in the interpretation of its own functions[185] and, on the other, the seemingly prevalent judicial vacuum in reviewing its operations. Hence, it is up to members of the international community to bridge that gap and fill the judicial void: '[i]f the Security Council is not the exclusive interpreter of its own powers (and if there is no competent judicial organ), a residual power to determine the legality of Security Council action rests with the international community and individual member States of the UN'.[186]

Finally, the voting procedure governing the adoption of SC resolutions may be advantageous in implementing SR as regards transnational terrorism and other global security violations, but also simultaneously constitutes an impediment to the development of that normative scheme. On the one hand, the limited membership in the SC might be better equipped to tackle time- and politically sensitive situations involving terrorism and other global security threats in a speedy and efficient manner. Consequently, this approach aligns with the view that concerns for expediency and efficiency underpin the rationale for granting extended responsibility to the SC in maintaining and restoring international peace and security.[187] Moreover, the broader UN community seems somewhat equitably represented through geographical repartition and allotment of seats to non-permanent members. On the other hand, and not surprisingly, the granting of a permanent role within the SC to certain members poses significant challenges to the principle of equal sovereignty. Although this structure was originally intended

[183] See, inter alia, JE Alvarez, 'Judging the Security Council' (1996) 90 AJIL 1; M Bedjaoui, *Nouvel Ordre Mondial et Contrôle de la Légalité des Actes du Conseil de Sécurité* (Bruylant 1994); Bekker (n 176) 503 ff; M Herdegen, 'The "Constitutionalization" of the UN Security System' (1994) 27 VJTL 135; TM Franck, 'The "Powers of Appreciation": Who Is the Ultimate Guardian of UN Legality?' (1992) 86 AJIL 519; J Klabbers, 'Straddling Law and Politics: Judicial Review in International Law' in R StJ McDonald and DM Johnson (eds), *Towards World Constitutionalism: Issues in the Legal Ordering of the World Community* (Nijhoff 2005) 809–35; L Gross, 'The International Court of Justice and the United Nations' (1967) 120 RdC 313, 327.

[184] See G Nolte, 'The Limits of the Security Council's Powers and its Functions in the International Legal System: Some Reflections' in Byers (n 132) 315, 318.

[185] This issue has generated considerable writing and is perfectly summarized by WM Reisman, 'The Constitutional Crisis in the United Nations' (1993) 87 AJIL 83, 92 in the following terms: '[t]he practical questions, then, are: who will review Security Council actions and who will determine the content, if any, of the arguably limiting legal principles'. See also JG Gardam, 'Legal Restraints on Security Council Military Enforcement Action' (1996) 17 MJIL 285, 288–9 fn 11, 296–7.

[186] Nolte (n 184) 318. See also Herdegen (n 183) 158 ff; A Orakhelashvili, 'The Impact of Peremptory Norms on the Interpretation and Application of United Nations Security Council Resolutions' (2005) 16 EJIL 59, 85.

[187] See, eg, E Benvenisti, 'The US and the Use of Force: Double-Edged Hegemony and the Management of Global Emergencies' (2004) 15 EJIL 677, 689–90.

to reflect a post-Second World War reality,[188] some interlocutors still contend that the selection of permanent members accurately reflects the present-day balance between dominant powers. This assertion is certainly open to challenge, both on descriptive and prescriptive grounds.

In particular, whilst attractive when viewing the SC's action *stricto sensu*, namely when the opinions of dominant military powers can help shape efforts in restoring international peace and security, this line of reasoning becomes somewhat untenable when devising a role for the Council in implementing SR for collective interests.[189] Equally alarming is the fact that a veto power is allocated to the permanent members, which essentially subjects SC action to political considerations driving individual States in the pursuit of their own interests. As one publicist rightly observed, '[i]n many important cases the veto rule has prevented effective actions'.[190] Aside from possibly shunning collective interests in some instances, this poses another considerable challenge to the equilibrium that institutionalized implementation of SR would seek to achieve.

This is not to say that political considerations are inherently foreign—or even undesirable—in the institutionalized implementation of SR, but obstacles to its deployment can assuredly originate in the exercise of veto power. Furthermore, the voting process might unnecessarily paralyse SC action in situations involving serious international law violations, whilst also rendering the whole exercise futile in cases involving the commission of an internationally wrongful act by a permanent member or members.[191] However, this observation would obviously extend beyond the purview of SC resolutions pertaining to the peaceful settlement of disputes, pursuant to Chapter VI, under which the parties to the proceedings refrain from voting in accordance with Article 27(3) of the UN Charter.[192] Conversely, from a pragmatic perspective, it is now conventional wisdom that an SC resolution under Chapter VII will generally not be blocked should one of the Permanent Five abstain from voting, provided that nine out of fifteen SC members vote in favour of the resolution. For example, China and the US abstained regarding the referral of the case of Sudan to the International Criminal Court in 2005, whilst China and Russia acted in a similar fashion with respect to military action in Libya in 2011.[193]

Despite these political overtones, disputing States have approached the SC with resounding legal claims to back up their political assertions and accusations. In many ways, several States have participated in the SC's process, which can take on a distinctly SR-inspired flavour when dealing with questions of accountability

[188] See, eg, L Goodrich and A Simons, *The United Nations and the Maintenance of International Peace and Security* (Brookings Institution 1955) 344.

[189] Graefrath (n 4) 252 fn 63; Simma (n 14) 145.

[190] JI Charney, 'Third State Remedies in International Law' (1989) 10 MJIL 57, 93.

[191] See generally DD Caron, 'Governance and Collective Legitimation in the New World Order' (1993) 6 The Hague Year Book of International Law 29.

[192] UN Charter (n 153) Art 27(3).

[193] Compare UNSC Res 1593 (31 March 2005) UN Doc S/RES/1593; UNSC Res 1973 (17 March 2011) UN Doc S/RES/1973.

and legal guilt following the violation of international legal norms. One salient example cropped up during the early days of the Council's work and arose in connection with the disagreement between India and Pakistan over Kashmir; it turned out to be a protracted dispute which persists today and which generated eight SC resolutions between 1948 and 1971.[194] When framing its arguments, each party clearly sought to have the SC pronounce on the other's responsibility whilst hoping that the Council would side with it. For instance, in the original complaint, India accused Pakistan of engaging in 'active aggression'.[195] For its part, Pakistan condemned India's conduct, which it claimed included the unlawful annexation of Kashmir and violence against Muslims, and sought to have the SC ensure that India cease its aggression.[196] In the years that followed, the parties' respective claims were thoroughly chronicled in the UN Commission for India and Pakistan (UNCIP)'s third interim report.

In short, India considered that it exerted valid legal possession over Kashmir by virtue of the instrument of accession, and equated Pakistan's conduct with an invasion of its territory.[197] Conversely, Pakistan viewed Kashmir's accession to India as unlawful given that the Maharaja had already been overthrown when he executed the instrument of accession.[198] Relying on Lord Mountbatten's pronouncement on the matter, Pakistan further claimed that the accession contravened Indian municipal law, which failed to validate a process of 'conditional accession' hingeing on a subsequent plebiscite.[199] Hence, the SC was confronted with allegations of internationally wrongful acts from both sides of the dispute, with each party seeking adjudication by that organ and a clear assignment of legal guilt against the other. India was particularly troubled by the SC's refusal to pronounce on the question of legal responsibility. After all, it should be recalled that India had been particularly vocal on this front, as reported by Sir Owen Dixon in 1950: 'India had advanced not only the contention ... that Pakistan was an aggressor but further the contention that this should be declared'.[200] Indeed, in 1957 Gunnar Jarring reported to the SC that India 'felt aggrieved that the Council had so far not expressed itself on the question of what in their view was aggression committed by Pakistan on India. In their view, it was incumbent on the Council to express itself on this question.'[201]

Ultimately, the SC never pronounced on the issue of legal accountability in the Kashmir dispute, despite the parties' repeated pleas for it to do so. Whilst it is true that the SC did not implement SR in that dispute, this precedent still evinces

[194] On the SC's treatment of this protracted dispute, generally, see BR Farrell, 'The Security Council and Kashmir' (2013) 22 Transnational Law & Contemporary Problems 343.

[195] Letter from the Representative of India Addressed to the SC President (1 January 1948) UN Doc S/628 [11]–[12].

[196] Letter from the Minister of FA of Pakistan Addressed to the Secretary-General: Pakistan's Reply to India's Complaint (15 January 1948) UN Doc S/646 [8]–[10].

[197] UNCIP Third Interim Report (9 December 1949) UN Doc S/1430, 48.

[198] UNCIP Report (n 197) 49.

[199] UNCIP Report (n 197) 49.

[200] Report of Sir Owen Dixon to the SC (15 September 1950) UN Doc S/1791, 7.

[201] Report on the India-Pakistan Question Submitted in Pursuance of the SC Resolution of 21 February 1957 (29 April 1957) UN Doc S/3821, 4.

both a practice and an expectation amongst States that it could do so, manifested quite early on in the SC's existence. In the 1960s and early 1970s, eminent publicists underscored the SC's reticence to implement SR, even suggesting that this reluctance extended beyond the Kashmir dispute and was indicative of a broader, systemic approach in Council decision-making.[202] During that period, Rosalyn Higgins highlighted the fact that whilst the SC's primary mandate was to maintain international peace, that organ was 'not to act as a watchdog to adjudicate on breaches of the Charter or international law by Members'.[203] Oscar Schachter echoed her views, stating that the framers of the UN Charter probably considered that this primary function might be hindered 'if the Council had to decide which side had been guilty of violating its legal obligations'.[204]

In those days, the dominant and pragmatic view was that the SC's pronouncement on the legal guilt or accountability of a given State would not appease the underlying dispute, or bring it closer to a settlement. This position was clear not only in the writings of commentators[205] but also in the SC's own treatment of the Kashmir dispute. In following up on the parties' concerns that the SC had declined to fully adjudicate their respective claims, the UK representative attributed this to an 'impression that a consideration of their merits would not advance the Council any nearer to a solution of the dispute'.[206] As will be seen in Chapter 4, however, the intervening decades have brought about significant changes, along with an ever-expanding concept of international peace and security. As a result, the SC has increasingly used SR repertoire in its decision-making concerning global security matters, thereby imposing measures that could be seen to be analogous to institutional countermeasures. In fact, the SC disposes of vast dispute settlement tools and powers under the Charter which it can put to use even without the consent of the disputing States.[207]

[202] See, eg, R Higgins, 'The Place of International Law in the Settlement of Disputes by the Security Council' (1970) 64 AJIL 1, 17; O Schachter, 'The Quasi-Judicial Role of the Security Council and the General Assembly' (1964) 58 AJIL 960, 961.

[203] Higgins (n 202) 17. She further posited that SC members may not have wanted to contend with the political costs of sitting in judgment of sovereign States. See ibid 3.

[204] Schachter (n 202) 961.

[205] See, eg, Higgins (n 202) 17–18 (observing that in many cases, the SC believes 'settlement is more likely to ensue if one particular party is not branded as having acted illegally', and positing that the determination of legal guilt by that organ might embolden the 'guilty' party to refuse the settlement'). For his part, Schachter perceived the SC's reluctance to assign legal blame as intertwined with the question of its legitimacy. See Schachter (n 202) 961 (observing that 'almost everyone would prefer settlements that did not place in issue the authority of the United Nations—an almost inevitable result of its judgements attributing guilt to a state').

[206] UNSC Verbatim Record (30 March 1951) UN Doc S/PV/539, 13. Whilst Higgins (n 202) 18 acknowledged this reality in the context of the Kashmir dispute, she further cautioned that 'this practice does present grave difficulties to the states concerned'. In particular, their governments would have to convince their municipal constituencies of the utility of pursuing their claims before the SC 'and to heed it, when that body is unwilling publicly to support what they perceive as a legally valid case. And once domestic opinion moves against reference to the United Nations ... then a long-term settlement becomes that much harder to achieve.'

[207] See Alvarez (n 152) 416–24; JG Merrills, *International Dispute Settlement* (3rd edn, CUP 1998) 221–2; B Conforti, *The Law and Practice of the United Nations* (Kluwer 2000) 162–5.

Even those publicists that highlighted the SC's reticence to assign legal blame in the 1960's had nonetheless carved out an important role for international legal principles in Council decision-making. For instance, Higgins insisted that the SC's posture regarding the determination of legal accountability of States did not make it 'essentially a political body'; quite to the contrary, she construed that organ as a political body tasked with carrying out its attributions within the UN Charter's legal framework, which includes settling disputes in accordance with international law.[208] In her view, it followed that UN Member States would advance their contentions before the SC, which would then resort to law in its debates and resolutions without assigning legal responsibility as a matter of course.[209] What is more, the same group of authors acknowledged the difficulty in sidestepping SR law when disputes submitted to the SC bring UN Charter principles into play.[210]

Therefore, the SC's role in applying SR rules in counterterrorism and global security contexts will hinge, to a large extent, on the ways in which its powers are ultimately contemplated and conceptualized. Thus, these concluding remarks lead perfectly into the next section, as careful consideration must be given to the 'quasi-judicial' character of SC action in some circumstances.

3.1.5.2 The Council's 'quasi-judicial' exercise of powers

Any study exploring the potential institutionalization of SR will have to contend with the fact that whatever application of international legal principles the SC engages in will invariably involve concurrent political considerations. Otherwise put, the law of SR provides an environment, or a locus, within which political decisions can be made against a juridical backdrop. As a corollary, this regime is by no means antithetical to the functions habitually carried out by the SC. In short, ascertaining the commission of an internationally wrongful act by a State and devising the ensuing legal consequences remains, in large part, an inherently political endeavour when contemplated through the prism of SC powers. That said, however, this exercise is by no means bereft of legal implications. In fact, such determination often straddles 'quasi-judicial' terrain in that it seeks to facilitate a political decision—that is, assigning blame for failing to prevent terrorism or violating some other international obligation linked to global security.

Yet, this determination is made by the SC whilst also striving to subscribe to legal parameters or criteria—both *objective* (ie the general obligation to provide reparation) and arguably *subjective* (ie attribution)—a process which invariably entails the determination of the rights of the parties involved in a contentious situation, some level of judging (ie either by applying relevant legal norms to the facts at hand or making some juridical finding grounded in a moral appreciation of international law), the legal characterization and qualification of relevant facts and acts, and a legal assessment of appropriate remedies to redress the politically

[208] Higgins (n 202) 1. [209] Higgins (n 202) 1, 3. [210] See Schachter (n 202) 962.

informed evaluation of the internationally wrongful act in question.[211] Several relevant precedents are canvassed and analysed in Chapter 4. Furthermore, in some instances the SC might even carve out a fact-finding role for itself in the exercise of its functions. After all, the Manila Declaration on the Peaceful Settlement of International Disputes calls upon Member States to '[c]onsider making greater use of the fact-finding capacity of the Security Council in accordance with the Charter'.[212] Conversely, it must be recalled that the principle of 'equality of arms', which is stringently applied in proceedings before the ICJ,[213] may be completely absent from some proceedings before the SC. For some, the SC's treatment of the *Lockerbie* incident amounted to one salient illustration of the absence of equality of arms.[214] Similar concerns were voiced against the SC's treatment of Iraq's unlawful invasion of Kuwait, particularly regarding the demarcation of the international border between both States by the Council. Hinting at the fact that the SC holds no hearings, carries out predominantly secret deliberations, does not hear argument from the parties' legal counsels, and fails to comprehensively justify its 'quasi-judicial' findings, Iraq opined that the SC had been improperly 'converted from a political into a judicial body'.[215] However, the fact that the SC's process differs from that of the ICJ's practice does not, in and of itself, strip it of its quasi-judicial character.[216]

[211] But see Seventh Report—Arangio-Ruiz (n 18) 36 [97]; R Provost, *International Human Rights and Humanitarian Law* (CUP 2002) 310. Conversely, see Alvarez (n 152) 416–24 (describing the SC's dispute settlement process as 'adjudicative' in some instances).

[212] Manila Declaration on the Peaceful Settlement of International Disputes, UNGA Res 37/10 (15 November 1982) UN Doc A/RES/37/10, Annex. On the fact-finding role of the Council, see generally Jiménez de Aréchaga (n 48) 40 ff.

[213] In its most recent advisory opinion, the ICJ recalled the importance of the principle of equality in judicial proceedings. In that context, the perceived inequality cropped up in proceedings opposing an IO and one of its officials, though the ICJ ultimately resolved that the principle had been satisfied. See *Judgment No. 2867 of the Administrative Tribunal of the International Labour Organization upon a Complaint Filed against the International Fund for Agricultural Development* (Advisory Opinion) [2012] ICJ Rep 10, 29–31 [44]–[48].

[214] See, eg, M Bennouna, 'L'Embargo dans la Pratique des Nations Unies: Radioscopie d'un Moyen de Pression' in E Yakpo and T Boumedra (eds), *Liber Amicorum Judge Mohamed Bedjaoui* (Kluwer 1999) 555, 562; E de Wet, *The Chapter VII Powers of the United Nations Security Council* (Hart 2004) 348–51. The flipside to this argument is that given that the SC delivers factual and legal determinations, its involvement can become a welcome alternative to treaty-based dispute settlement mechanisms in terrorism matters, offering both expediency and superior legal authority. See NT Ali, 'Between a Rock and a Hard Place: Treaty-based Settlement of Terrorism-related Disputes in the Era of Active United Nations Security Council Involvement' (2013) 6 Erasmus Law Review 79.

[215] UN Doc S/22643 (1991) 2–3 (quoting Iraq). See also BH Weston, 'Security Council Resolution 687 and Persian Gulf Decision Making: Precarious Legitimacy' (1991) 85 AJIL 516. For the exchange of letters between Iraq and the UN Secretary-General on the international border question, see Report of the Secretary-General Regarding Para 3 of SC Res 687 (2 May 1991) UN Doc S/22558, annexes. For an extensive critique of the SC's quasi-judicial determinations on this front, see de Wet (n 214) 352–67. But see O Schachter, 'United Nations Law in the Gulf Conflict' (1991) 85 AJIL 452.

[216] See, eg, Alvarez (n 152) 421. Equally unrealistic are some proposals that when the SC acts in a judicial fashion, subsequent queries should look into whether it acted appropriately as a court. This would include: adopting procedural rules to ensure due process and govern the admissibility/

For some commentators, it is 'important to stress that the determination of the Council is a legal qualification and constitutes an obligation under the Charter',[217] though one would be hard-pressed to argue persuasively that the SC is a judicial organ.[218] However, this reality in no way erects any stumbling blocks for the prospect of implementing SR through the SC. Quite to the contrary, it is common practice for political organs, like the SC for example, to deliver legal determinations as a way to satisfy themselves of their competence to take action under a specific heading related to their powers; in other words, by fulfilling a 'jurisdictional condition'.[219] As will be seen in Chapter 4, the SC's practice is far more pervasive, its relationship with international law rich and complex, and its substantive forays into SR repertoire extending far beyond the mere satisfaction of a jurisdictional condition.

This dichotomous politico-legal dimension inexorably pervades much of international decision-making, especially as regards the activities of the UN's decision-making organs. Indeed, it was very much alive in the ICJ's Advisory Opinion on the *Conditions of Admission of a State to Membership in the United Nations*.[220] In those advisory proceedings, the Court was asked whether UN members could make their votes on the admission of a State to the UN contingent on factors extraneous to Article 4 of the UN Charter, a provision regulating the admission of new States to the organization. In fact, the question put to the ICJ was drafted so as to underscore this push-and-pull between the political and legal spheres, precisely by asking the judicial organ to shed light on whether a Member State was '*juridically* entitled to make its consent to the admission dependent on *conditions not expressly* provided by paragraph I of the said Article' (emphasis added).[221] In sum, the legal conundrum submitted to the ICJ was framed in terms of a conflict of politics versus law. By way of background, Article 4 of the Charter requires that five criteria be met by an applicant State seeking admission to the UN, namely that it (i) have statehood, (ii) be a peace-loving State, (iii) accept the obligations

authentication of evidence, allowing litigants to be heard, precluding interested parties from self-judging their own cases, ensuring equality amongst litigants, and publishing the SC's rationale for reaching its decisions. See, eg, K Harper, 'Does the United Nations Security Council Have the Competence to Act as Court and Legislature?' (1994) 27 NYUJILP 104.

[217] A Tzanakopoulos, *Disobeying the Security Council: Countermeasures against Wrongful Sanctions* (OUP 2011) 63.

[218] See, eg, Schachter (n 202) 960; M Wood, 'The Interpretation of Security Council Resolutions' (1998) 77 Max Planck Yearbook of UN Law 78.

[219] See, eg, P Craig 'EU' in idem and A Tomkins (eds), *The Executive and Public Law* (OUP 2006) 337; Nolte (n 184) 323; Tzanakopoulos (n 217) 64, s 1.II.1 fns 80–2, and accompanying text. In *Tadić Case* (Interlocutory Appeal on Jurisdiction) (n 169) [37], the ICTY Appeals Chamber acknowledged that the SC can exercise a quasi-judicial function when 'effecting determinations or findings'. However, according to some scholars, even if international law governs the SC's competence and determines its functions, that organ 'is not necessarily obliged to apply existing international law'. See K Herndl, 'Reflections on the Role, Functions and Procedures of the Security Council of the United Nations' (1987) 206 RdC 289, 385.

[220] On the relationship between international responsibility and the admission of States to the UN, see TD Grant, 'International Responsibility and the Admission of States to the United Nations' (2009) 30 MJIL 1095.

[221] *Admission of a State* (n 149) 58.

enshrined in the Charter, (iv) have the ability to carry out such undertakings, and v) the willingness to do so.

The Court pointed out that such determination necessarily hinged on the *judgment* of both the GA and SC.[222] More importantly, the ICJ noted that Rule 60 of the Provisional Rules of Procedure of the Security Council expressly prescribed the exercise of the SC's judgment in formulating its recommendation on State membership in the UN.[223] As a corollary, the ICJ rightly underscored that in laying out their reasoning, UN organs could rest their decisions regarding admission on political factors connected to the requirements of admission under the Charter. Hence, the wording of Article 4 provides for some degree of appreciation, which inherently signals that a decision on admission—initially based on the legal exegesis extracted from the Charter—can simultaneously be couched in a political light.[224] Needless to say, this reasoning also extends individually to Member States casting their votes, which can, in the ICJ's view, be predicated on concerns of 'political expediency' falling outside the ambit of Article 4.[225] Thus, the ICJ ultimately held that no conflict existed between the functions of UN political organs and the prescriptions of public international law seemingly entrenched in Article 4.[226]

This conclusion is extremely relevant for the purposes of exploring the potential contributions of SR law in advancing counterterrorism and global security initiatives. In particular, the SC's role in this regard—which has been described by some as 'hybrid'[227]—can possibly straddle both political and judicial terrain when connecting SR rules to the Council's functions. Whilst traditionally perceived as predominantly political in nature, the SC's exercise of powers in this context defies straightforward definition, thereby leading scholars to acknowledge the presence of a distinct, albeit diffuse, adjudicative dimension in its decision-making.[228] Equally important is the notion that whilst SC powers primarily

[222] *Admission of a State* (n 149) 62.

[223] *Admission of a State* (n 149) 63.

[224] In *Admission of a State* (n 149) 63, the Court stated that

> [i]t does not... follow from the exhaustive character of paragraph I of Article 4 that an appreciation is precluded of such circumstances of fact as would enable the existence of the requisite conditions to be verified. Article 4 does not forbid the taking into account of any factor which it is possible reasonably and in good faith to connect with the conditions laid down in that Article. The taking into account of such factors is implied in the very wide and very elastic nature of the prescribed conditions; no relevant political factor—that is to say, none connected with the conditions of admission—is excluded.

[225] *Admission of a State* (n 149) 64.

[226] In *Admission of a State* (n 149) 64, the Court declared that

> [t]o ascertain whether an organ has freedom of choice for its decisions, reference must be made to the terms of its constitution. In this case, the limits of this freedom are fixed by Article 4 and allow for a wide liberty of appreciation. There is therefore no conflict between the functions of the political organs, on the one hand, and the exhaustive character of the prescribed conditions, on the other.

[227] See KR Cronin-Furman, 'The International Court of Justice and the United Nations Security Council: Rethinking a Complicated Relationship' (2006) 106 Columbia Law Review 435, 438–41.

[228] See J Delbrück, 'Functions and Powers: Article 24' in B Simma *et al.* (eds), *The Charter of the United Nations: A Commentary* (2nd edn, OUP 2002) 442, 446 (discussing a philological approach

gravitate towards enforcement logic, confusion nonetheless surrounds the presence of quasi-judicial undertones in the application of its mandate.[229] This ambiguity is undoubtedly exacerbated by the inherent compatibility of the SC's Chapter VI powers—especially Articles 33–8 of the UN Charter (ie those falling under the 'Pacific Settlement of Disputes' rubric)—with what appear to be more traditional judicial functions.

Particularly striking is the wording of Article 37 of the Charter, which provides that:

1. Should the parties to a dispute of the nature referred to in Article 33 fail to settle it by the means indicated in that Article, they shall refer it to the Security Council.
2. If the Security Council deems that the continuance of the dispute is in fact likely to endanger the maintenance of international peace and security, it shall decide whether to take action under Article 36 or to recommend such terms of settlement as it may consider appropriate.[230]

Along similar quasi-judicial lines, Article 38 of the UN Charter also casts SC powers within the ambit of dispute resolution by enabling it to 'make recommendations to the parties with a view to a pacific settlement of the dispute'.[231]

Thus, it is arguably impossible to construe the SC's exercise of powers as purely 'political' or 'judicial' in all circumstances. As will be discussed in Chapter 4, the SC has been called upon to weigh in on SR-related issues in a quasi-judicial fashion, a manifestation of its powers that is easily transposed to counterterrorism and other global security contexts. In fact, it was done expressly vis-à-vis the perpetration of international terrorism—although not unambiguously—in the *Lockerbie* case, as will be discussed in Sections 4.4.2, 4.4.5, 4.5.1, and 4.5.2. Of equally compelling relevance is the SC's treatment of the Iraq–Kuwait conflict in which it determined the boundaries of an international border, demonstrating that its quasi-judicial powers can be exercised quite extensively within the realm of secondary SR rules.[232] There is no doubt that this application of SC powers strikes at the very core of Jost Delbrück's own construction of the debate at hand, which emphasizes that 'binding decisions which are of a judicial nature could be taken in the course of dealing with a case before the SC as, for instance, the adjudication of a contested territory to one of the disputing parties'.[233] With some level of

to interpreting the UN Charter, and concluding that 'unambiguous findings as to the normative and political meaning of Art. 24 cannot be arrived at'); Cronin-Furman (n 227) 438 (highlighting that the SC's decision-making 'frequently seems to include adjudicative powers').

229 See, eg, ND White, *The United Nations and the Maintenance of International Peace and Security* (Manchester University Press 1990) 61 ('[t]he confusion is created because the change of emphasis from policeman to judge did not involve a wholesale revision of the Dumbarton Oaks proposals; instead the judicial provisions were tacked on so that the fundamental role the Council should play in relation to international disputes is unclear').

230 UN Charter (n 153) Art 37.

231 UN Charter (n 153) Art 38. On procedural aspects of the SC's role in handling disputes and the scope of its recommendations regarding methods of dispute settlement or adjustment, as envisaged early in its existence, see Jiménez de Aréchaga (n 48) 23–40, 60–100.

232 See, eg, Alvarez (n 152) 419–20.

233 Delbrück (n 228) 447.

political pragmatism also in mind, however, this controversial precedent cannot escape some sense of potentially stretching the exercise of SC powers to the very limits of its mandate; it should, in turn, prompt interlocutors to query whether the Council's permanent members would accept and implement the prescriptions of such a resolution, had it applied to their own borders. Moreover, this far-reaching exercise of SC functions, albeit at the secondary level of SR, should always be read in tandem with the expansive SC Resolutions 1373 and 1540, which made significant advances at the primary normative level as discussed elsewhere.[234]

Conversely, significant scholarly resistance prevents the construction of SC powers as entirely adjudicative in nature, with particular reluctance to the prospect of contemplating Articles 37 and 38 of the UN Charter through a quasi-judicial prism.[235] Surely, such a posture can find support in the SC's frequent refusal to assign legal blame when dealing with situations involving SR rules, but the same can be said of ICJ practice.[236] Nevertheless, this conventional scheme cannot escape the impression of having, at the very least, been partially promulgated with a view to empowering the SC to make political determinations against a legal backdrop, whilst upholding the maintenance of international peace and security as its foremost concern. The very nature of the disputes dealt with by the SC often involves complex international legal questions and—whilst the Council's invocation and application of international law can sometimes be construed as random or arbitrary—further bolsters the assertion that such provisions must have been 'intended to invest the Council with quasi-judicial powers'.[237] In fact, it would be difficult to discredit entirely the SC's exercise of quasi-judicial powers; rather, its practice points in the other direction and clearly supports the contention that SC decision-making can simultaneously straddle political and judicial spheres.[238]

It is no surprise, therefore, that the SC has been described as a 'quasi-judicial' body, especially given precedents involving the deployment of its dispute settlement

[234] See, eg, Proulx (n 39) esp ch 1, sections B) and E); ch 2, section E); ch 4, section B)5.a); Alvarez (n 152) 195–8; I Johnstone, *The Power of Deliberation: International Law, Politics, and Organizations* (OUP 2011) 93–105 and 'Legislation and Adjudication in the UN Security Council: Bringing Down the Deliberative Deficit' (2008) 102 AJIL 275 (characterizing these resolutions as a form of SC legislation). See also generally M Wood, 'The Security Council as a Law Maker: The Adoption of (Quasi)-Judicial Decisions' in R Wolfrum and V Röben (eds), *Developments of International Law in Treaty Making* (Springer 2005) 233.

[235] See, eg, Schachter (n 202) 960.

[236] See Schachter (n 202) 961; Higgins (n 202) 17.

[237] White (n 229) 61. See also generally Wood (n 234); ND White and M Saul, 'Legal Means of Dispute Settlement in the Field of Collective Security: The Quasi-Judicial Powers of the Security Council' in D French *et al.* (eds), *International Law and Dispute Settlement: New Problems and Techniques* (Hart 2010) 191.

[238] See TJ Kahng, *Law, Politics, and the Security Council* (2nd edn, Nijhoff 1969) 13 ('the Security Council has not only executive power, but also legislative and judicial powers'); V Gowlland-Debbas, 'Commentary' in C Peck and RS Lee (eds), *Increasing the Effectiveness of the International Court of Justice* (Nijhoff 1997) 254, 256 (emphasizing that whilst the Council's role can be primarily cast as political, 'whose determinations under Article 39 are considered to be factual and discretionary and, moreover, it is not bound to follow judicial procedures, it has ... made determinations of law and invoked the responsibility of States with definitive legal effects, as well as extensive legal consequences').

powers.[239] A vocal proponent of this line of argument was Hans Kelsen. Indeed, the intricate, dual role of the SC prompted him to state that both the GA and SC 'in so far as they, too, are competent to settle disputes, are only quasi-judicial organs of the United Nations'.[240] Furthermore, according to Kelsen '[t]his is true even if the interpretation is accepted that recommendations made by the Security Council for the settlement of disputes under Articles 37, 38 or 39 are, as decisions of the Council in accordance with Article 25, binding upon the parties'.[241] Interestingly, Judge Weeramantry endorsed Kelsen's classification of SC powers in his Dissenting Opinion to the oft-discussed *Lockerbie* cases.[242] Therefore, as will be shown in subsequent sections of this volume, SC powers in this context decidedly cannot be construed purely as judicial. More importantly, nor does that perspective underpin the crux of the arguments seeking to reel in the application of SR law within the purview of SC activities in instances involving transnational terrorism or other global security breaches.

Rather, SR law merely provides the opportunity for the SC to pronounce on political matters within a legal framework—albeit in a quasi-judicial fashion—namely by ascertaining unlawful conduct and devising the legal consequences of that behaviour with the furtherance of international peace and security as an organizing principle. In undertaking this mission, the SC's treatment of disputes will involve quasi-judicial findings in some instances. However, this is also the case in the 'traditional' application of SR principles as this international legal area simply cannot be severed from the strident political overtones that pervade it. After all, when an injured State unilaterally applies secondary SR rules outside an institutionalized setting—that is to say, without the intercession of the ICJ or SC—the ensuing process is unquestionably prone to straddle quasi-judicial terrain since it involves self-judging, autoqualification, and unilateral enforcement of legal consequences.[243] In turn, this necessarily entails (i) a unilateral application of international law to the facts at hand, (ii) the determination of the legal rights and positions of the involved parties, and (iii) the legal characterization of certain facts and acts, whilst potentially operating within a politically volatile environment. By contrast, when the SC implements SR, it at least carries out its quasi-adjudicative process in a multilateral framework—however flawed or illegitimate it may appear from some perspectives—which should assuage some of the concerns associated with an injured State's unilateral application of SR norms. After all, Quincy Wright's thoughtful viewpoint rings even truer more than seven decades after it was first elucidated. Indeed, he opined that 'self-help in which the State acts as its own judge and sheriff can hardly be called legal sanctions. They are essentially acts of policy, not law.'[244]

[239] See Schachter (n 202) 961 (opining that even though a quasi-judicial role may not have featured prominently in UN foundational programmes, 'governments have repeatedly called upon the political organs to pass judgments on whether states have observed their obligations').

[240] Kelsen, *The Law* (n 46) 476–7.

[241] Kelsen, *The Law* (n 46) 476–7.

[242] See Dissenting Opinions of Judge Weeramantry in the *Lockerbie Cases* (n 176) 57, 167 respectively.

[243] On unilateral self-judging and autoqualification, see Section 1.2.2.

[244] Q Wright, 'Enforcement of International Law' (1944) 38 ASIL Proceedings 77, 86. See also J Kunz, 'Sanctions in International Law' (1960) 54 AJIL 324.

As explored in Section 3.2 later in this chapter, the SC's dual role is not without some equivocating consequences on the functions of the ICJ.[245] In particular, the framework laying down the scope of SC powers expressly provides for the referral of legal questions to the ICJ, primarily by application of Article 36(3) of the UN Charter. This provision stipulates that '[i]n making recommendations under this Article the Security Council should also take into consideration that legal disputes should as a general rule be referred by the parties to the International Court of Justice in accordance with the provisions of the Statute of the Court'.[246] As seen in Section 3.2.2 later in this chapter, this provision cements the complementary relationship and bonds of collaboration that connect these two bodies. Therefore, the SC can recommend to disputing States that they refer their legal disagreements to the ICJ for adjudication, especially where other avenues of resolution, such as creative solutions (eg joint resource exploitation or management regimes in maritime delimitation cases) or negotiation, have failed. However, the SC has rarely used this referral mechanism. In fact, it only did so in *Corfu Channel*, the ICJ's very first contentious case.[247] In a resolution adopted on 9 April 1947, the Council

> [h]aving considered statements of representatives of the United Kingdom and Albania concerning a dispute between the United Kingdom and Albania arising out of an incident on 22 October 1946 in the Straits of Corfu in which two British ships were damaged by mines, with resulting loss of life and injury to their crews ... recommend[ed] that the United Kingdom and Albanian Governments should immediately refer the dispute to the International Court of Justice in accordance with the provisions of the Statute of the Court.[248]

Similarly, the SC seldom exercises its option to seek extraneous legal guidance in dealing with the disputes of which it is seized. This power derives from Article 29 of the UN Charter, which enables the SC to establish subsidiary organs, and the Provisional Rules of Procedure, which allow it to seek external guidance or assistance.[249] The SC's reluctance to resort to these mechanisms perhaps suggests a tendency towards what could plausibly be construed as quasi-judicial protectionism. In short, on occasion the SC may consider that its powers are sufficient to reconcile

[245] See V Gowlland-Debbas, 'The Relationship between the International Court of Justice and the Security Council in the Light of the Lockerbie Case' (1994) 88 AJIL 643, 655–8 (expanding on the '[a]bsence of a [h]ierarchy between the [t]wo [o]rgans').

[246] UN Charter (n 153) Art 36(3). Consequently, some argue that the Charter suggests clear roles for both relevant organs, namely: the ICJ exercises jurisdiction over legal disputes whilst the SC can deal with dispute settlement solely within the confines of making recommendations. See JW Halderman, *The United Nations and the Rule of Law: Charter Developments Through the Handling of International Disputes and Situations* (Oceana 1966) 65–89.

[247] *Corfu Channel Case* (Merits) (n 80). See original Application instituting proceedings: <www.icj-cij.org/docket/files/1/1499.pdf> accessed 9 August 2015; the text of the Special Agreement of 25 March 1948, drawn up between the parties as a result of the relevant SC resolution, <www.icj-cij.org/docket/files/1/1495.pdf> accessed 9 August 2015.

[248] UNSC Res 22 (9 April 1947) UN Doc S/RES/22.

[249] UN Charter (n 153) Art 29; Provisional Rules of Procedure of the Security Council, UNSC Res 96 (21 December 1982) UN Doc S/RES/96/Rev7, Rule 39.

both the political and legal dimensions of a given dispute involving the application of SR principles. Historically, the SC has rarely relied on the invocation of these formal procedures and even more seldom suggested submission of a dispute to the ICJ (save in the *Corfu Channel* case mentioned earlier). Strikingly, the SC has only once sought an advisory opinion from the ICJ, namely in the *Namibia* case.[250] This apparent quasi-judicial protectionism may very well be motivated by a markedly distinctive settlement method—perhaps even warranting a *sui generis* designation—developed by the SC in dealing with legal issues related to the exercise of its functions. What is more, this distinctive approach, which blends political and legal dimensions in a sometimes arbitrary and random manner, most likely signals an important departure from the practice initially established under the League of Nations.[251]

Ultimately, the foregoing considerations pave the way for the inquiry to follow: the 'quasi-judicial' exercise of SC powers in applying SR rules to transnational terrorism and other global security breaches lies at the very core of what warrants elucidation. Indeed, the line separating political and legal considerations begins to blur in difficult cases, with the SC's delimitation of the Iraq–Kuwait border remaining a quintessential illustration of this conflation and, additionally, of an acutely extensive application of secondary SR norms.[252] When interlocutors are confronted with this specific quasi-judicial manifestation of SC powers, they should necessarily ponder whether the Council's decision-making seeks to apply the international law governing State sovereignty, or rather, is the SC simply deploying its Chapter VII powers with political expediency in mind, an exercise that may be reconciled with the imposition of secondary obligations under SR repertoire? In turn, this line of inquiry generates further distinct queries. In particular, would the ICJ then be bound by the SC's determination of the Iraqi border or, for present purposes, by far-reaching, sovereignty-erosive, and Council-imposed secondary obligations based on a State's SR for failing to prevent terrorism?[253] As a corollary, would such exercise of SC powers be considered *ultra vires* under international law? After all, the SC is no stranger to controversial applications of its functions. Resolution 940 immediately comes to mind, as it marked unprecedented SC involvement in endorsing the use of force for the purposes of restoring democracy, a rationale that could presumably be transposed to extreme cases of egregious transnational terrorism or other global security contexts. In that scenario, the SC unanimously authorized a US-led multinational force to reinstate the lawfully elected President, Jean-Bertrand Aristide, along with the accompanying legitimate State apparatus in Haiti.[254]

[250] See *Namibia Advisory Opinion* (n 170); Kahng (n 238) 5.

[251] See, eg, LM Goodrich, 'Foreword' in Kahng (n 238) vii.

[252] But see the remarks of P Cot in AG de La Pradelle, *La Paix Moderne (1899–1945): De La Haye à San Francisco* (Les Éditions Internationales 1947) 477 (arguing that the Council can maintain or revise international boundaries on the basis of the requirements of international peace and security).

[253] Although not directly on point, consider UNSC Res 248 (24 March 1968) UN Doc S/RES/248.

[254] UNSC Res 940 (31 July 1994) UN Doc S/RES/940. At [9], the SC invoked language compatible with the tenets of SR by '[d]ecid[ing] ... to assist ... the democratic Government of Haiti in fulfilling its responsibilities in connection with ... [the resolution goes on to enumerate specific legal obligations]'.

In attempting to resolve these questions, the present work propels the SC's treatment of, and relationship with, international legal rules to the analytical fore. Prefacing this, it must be stressed that this relationship is anything but straightforward.[255] In that regard, the UN Charter is relatively unhelpful, simply directing the SC to 'act in accordance with the Purposes and Principles of the United Nations'.[256] In her efforts to delineate the scope of this conventional scheme, Higgins astutely contrasted the SC's dispute settlement powers with those of the ICJ as 'operation *within* the law, rather than decision according *to* the law'.[257] Conversely, whilst recurrent arguments have been advanced to the effect that the SC may, in fact, be carrying out its functions outside a legal framework,[258] they mount relatively few conceptual barriers to the hypothesis explored in this book.

The main contention advanced in this book is that SR repertoire offers a locus for the SC to execute its normal political functions, which may or may not be practicable in specific circumstances involving a State's failure to prevent terrorism or some other global security threat. It should therefore be no surprise—and no significant impediment to the exploration of the SC's potential contributions to SR—that this organ's dispute settlement functions are primarily actuated through a political prism. In fact, it is difficult to envisage a category of internationally wrongful acts riper for political considerations—and, at the same time, so legally evocative—than a State's failure to prevent terrorism, for instance. It logically follows that, whilst the SC '[is] bound by the Charter and therefore must apply and interpret it in particular cases, the criteria [it] use[s] are not judicial criteria'.[259] Hence, the guiding mantra should not boil down to 'all judicial or nothing' in exploring the Council's application of SR principles. It should rather take stock of the delicate balance required between political and legal *considerations* the SC weighs whilst employing a quasi-judicial *process* or *method* in reaching a decision about international peace and security. Indeed, this notion is certainly not inimical to counterterrorism objectives, or to other pressing global security challenges, or to the essence of SR law for that matter.

Conversely, a healthy dose of intellectual candour warrants the formulation of an important caveat: exploring the possible institutionalization of the implementation of SR carries with it patent limitations and shortcomings. In particular, the SC's potential applications of SR rules would become ineffective if directed at a non-member of the UN. For example, such would have been the case had

[255] See also Cronin-Furman (n 227) 441.

[256] UN Charter (n 153) Art 24(2).

[257] Higgins (n 202) 16.

[258] See, eg, White (n 229) 69 (observing that international law 'play[s] a residual role in the work of a political body such as the Security Council'); Delbrück (n 228) 447 (suggesting that 'the decision-making procedure of the [SC] is fundamentally different from that of the ICJ' because whilst '[t]he ICJ has to decide exclusively on the basis of international law (Art. 38 of the ICJ Statute)... the SC has to decide primarily according to political criteria').

[259] O Schachter, 'The UN Legal Order: An Overview' in idem and CC Joyner (eds), 1 *United Nations Legal Order* (ASIL 1995) 1, 13.

Switzerland harboured members of a terrorist network on its territory back when it only had observer status within the organization. Also, more persuasive allegations could have perhaps been levelled in light of Palestine's harbouring and support of both Hamas and Hezbollah factions on its territory. Similar logic could ostensibly extend to Western Sahara, a territory in dispute between Morocco and the Polisario Front. Whilst the territorial portions not subject to Moroccan control (ie the 'Free Zone') fall under the direction of the Polisario Front-proclaimed Sahrawi Arab Democratic Republic, the UN nonetheless officially designates Western Sahara as a 'non-self-governing territory'. Regardless of this designation, such States/entities would remain legally obliged to comply with primary counterterrorism obligations and, by implication, would have to observe secondary SR rules in the event of a breach of the primary norms. However, they would eschew the application of the UN Charter, thereby drastically limiting the SC's potential impact in applying international legal rules.

These observations should therefore constitute a preliminary gloss through which the remainder of this book's arguments are to be contemplated; this is particularly so in the light of the intricate interplay between political and legal considerations involved in SR-related situations. These remarks also preface the importance of further exploring the relationship between the SC and the implementation, application, and interpretation of SR rules. Whilst considerable emphasis has been placed thus far on the SC's limited judicial settlement functions, the potential implications of Chapter VII must also be brought into the fold. In its practice, the SC has interpreted the parameters of the powers devolved to it by Chapter VII rather liberally, and has often invoked language and used an approach profoundly compatible with SR repertoire. With this in mind, Chapter 4 will review and analyse a wide range of precedents, both under Chapter VI and Chapter VII of the UN Charter, in order to illustrate the rapprochement between SC powers and SR repertoire. Before so doing, the issue of potential conflicts between SC action and the ICJ's activities must be addressed briefly.

3.2 Potential Conflicts between the ICJ and Security Council

This brief concluding section addresses three potential obstacles that could be invoked vis-à-vis the proposition that the SC might be better situated, in some circumstances, to implement SR in global security contexts. This section solely aims to acknowledge these potential obstacles without addressing them exhaustively, attempting to resolve the underlying debates, or advancing any categorical position.

3.2.1 The judicial review question

It should be emphasized that scholars and policy-makers are increasingly exploring the ideas that the SC is subject to the international rule of law, and that its decisions may (or perhaps should) be subject to oversight.[260] Indeed, there is very little doubt that the SC cannot act in contravention of international legal principles.[261] For one thing, Sir Elihu Lauterpacht recalled in his Separate Opinion to the *Application of the Genocide Convention (Provisional Measures)* case that the SC is not above the law.[262] In recent years, publicists have similarly begun to investigate the exercise of SC powers through the prism of international human rights standards, with many commentators concluding that this normative scheme governs the Council's activities.[263] In global security contexts, the SC itself has demonstrated a willingness to self-correct in order to ensure that the implementation of its existing counterterrorism resolutions remains in accordance with human rights standards. For instance, Resolution 1373—which the SC adopted shortly after 9/11 and in many ways constitutes the cornerstone in modern counterterrorism—failed to mention the safeguarding of human rights standards. Understandably, this approach elicited concern and criticism, including from regional organizations.[264] Scholars similarly took issue with the SC's omission, suggesting that its actions would engender human rights abuses by 'opening the hunting season on terrorism'.[265] However, in subsequent resolutions, the SC emphasized unequivocally the importance of respecting human rights in combating terrorism.[266]

The question of potential judicial review of SC decisions and sanctions by the international judiciary, particularly the ICJ in the *Lockerbie* proceedings, has generated a rich body of literature.[267] Some publicists have been particularly vocal

[260] See generally P Šturma, 'Does the Rule of Law also Apply to the Security Council?: Limiting its Powers by Way of Responsibility and Accountability' (2012) 32 PYIL 301.

[261] See, eg, N Angelet (n 174).

[262] Separate Opinion of Judge ad hoc Lauterpacht in *Case Concerning the Application of the Genocide Convention (Bosnia and Herzegovina v Yugoslavia)* (Provisional Measures) [1993] ICJ Rep 3, 440–1 [102]–[103]. Some commentators explore the potential review of binding SC resolutions from the vantage point of *jus cogens* obligations. See R Kolb, 'Le Contrôle des Résolutions Contraignantes du Conseil de Sécurité des Nations Unies sous l'Angle du Respect du *Jus Cogens*' (2008) 18 Schweizerische Zeitschrift fur Internationales und Europäisches Recht 401.

[263] See, eg, B Fassbender, 'The Role for Human Rights in the Decision-making Process of the Security Council' in idem (ed.), *Securing Human Rights?: Achievements and Challenges of the UN Security Council* (OUP 2011) 74–97; S Zappalà, 'Reviewing Security Council Measures in the Light of International Human Rights Principles' in ibid 172–94.

[264] See, eg, Council of Europe, *Guidelines on Human Rights and the Fight against Terrorism: Adopted by the Committee of Ministers on 11 July 2002 at the 804th Meeting of the Ministers' Deputies* (Council of Europe Publishing 2002), preamble, para (i); Parliamentary Assembly of the Council of Europe Resolution 1271 'Combating Terrorism and Respect for Human Rights' (24 January 2002) <http://assembly.coe.int/nw/xml/XRef/Xref-XML2HTML-en.asp?fileid=16978&lang=en> accessed 19 August 2015; OSCE Charter on Preventing and Combating Terrorism (adopted 7 December 2002) Doc MC(10).JOUR/2 <www.osce.org/odihr/16609> accessed 18 June 2015, para 7.

[265] Duffy (n 82) 351, 359.

[266] See, eg, UNSC Res 1456 (20 January 2003) UN Doc S/RES/1456; UNSC Res 1535 (26 March 2004) UN Doc S/RES/1535 preamble; UNSC Res 1624 (14 September 2005) UN Doc S/RES/1624.

[267] See, eg, Alvarez (n 183); B Fassbender, '*Quis judicabit*? The Security Council, Its Powers and Its Legal Control' (2000) 11 EJIL 219; TD Gill, 'Legal and Some Political Limitations on the Power of the UN Security Council to Exercise Its Enforcement Powers under Chapter VII of the Charter' (1995) 26 NYIL 33; J-M Thouvenin, 'Les Décisions du Conseil de Sécurité en Procès' in J-P Cot (ed.), *Le Procès International: Liber Amicorum Jean-Pierre Cot* (Bruylant 2009)

proponents of judicial review by the ICJ, with this issue sometimes cropping up as inextricably intertwined with the potential recognition of the SC's power to implement SR.[268] Furthermore, the Institute of International Law has mandated a Commission, headed by Rapporteur Rüdiger Wolfrum, to study the question of 'Judicial Control of Security Council Decisions'. The Commission delivered the first version of its *travaux préparatoires* at the 2011 Tokyo Session which generated lively debate and was followed by the presentation of a report at the Tallinn Session.[269] Whilst the potential judicial review of SC action has been alluded to in previous sections, a brief review of the question remains helpful.

3.2.1.1 The International Court of Justice

The question whether the ICJ can review the SC's decisions has engendered considerable anxiety amongst international lawyers.[270] As a matter of principle, nothing precludes the ICJ from reviewing the legality of SC resolutions within the confines of its competence, for instance if two States having recognized its jurisdiction by virtue of Article 36(2) declarations request it to do so.[271] Indeed, in order to avoid the pitfalls of a fragmented international legal system, the ICJ

309–21; J-M Thouvenin, 'Le Juge International Peut-il Contrôler la Légalité des Sanctions Adoptées par le Conseil de Sécurité' (2009) 529 Revue du Marché Commun 373; Gowlland-Debbas, 'UN Sanctions' (n 171) 14–15; M Koskenniemi, 'The Place of Law in Collective Security' (1996) 17 MJIL 455; A Reinisch, 'Should Judges Second-Guess the UN Security Council?' (2009) 6 IOLR 257; K Zemanek, 'Is the Security Council the Sole Judge of Its Own Legality?' in Yakpo and Boumedra (n 214) 629–45; M Plachta, 'The *Lockerbie* Case: The Role of the Security Council in Enforcing the Principle *Aut Dedere Aut Judicare*' (2001) 12 EJIL 125; B Martenczuk, 'The Security Council, the International Court and Judicial Review' (1999) 10 EJIL 517; L Caflisch, 'Is the International Court Entitled to Review Security Council Resolutions Adopted under Chapter VII of the United Nations Charter?' in N Al-Nauimi and R Meese (eds), *International Legal Issues Arising Under the United Nations Decade of International Law* (Nijhoff 1995) 633–62; I Petculescu, 'The Review of the United Nations Security Council Decisions by the International Court of Justice' (2005) 52 NILR 167; S Lamb, 'Legal Limits to United Nations Security Council Powers' in GS Goodwin-Gill and S Talmon (eds), *The Reality of International Law: Essays in Honour of Ian Brownlie* (Clarendon Press 1999) 361–88; Dugard (n 181); K Zemanek, 'Is the Security Council the Sole Judge of its Own Legality? A Re-examination' in A Reinisch and U Kriebaum (eds), *The Law of International Relations: Liber Amicorum Hanspeter Neuhold* (Eleven International Publishing 2007) 483–505; D Richter, 'Judicial Review of Security Council Decision—A Modern Vision of the Administration of Justice?' (2012) 32 PYIL 271.

[268] See generally Bedjaoui (n 104). See also Alvarez (n 183) 1–39; TM Franck, 'The United Nations as Guarantor of International Peace and Security: Past, Present and Future' in C Tomuschat (ed.), *The United Nations at Age Fifty: A Legal Perspective* (Kluwer 1995) 25, 37.

[269] See *Annuaire de l'Institut de Droit International: Vol 75, Session de Tokyo* (Pedone 2013) 43–121.

[270] See, eg, K Roberts, 'Second-Guessing the Security Council: The International Court of Justice and its Powers of Judicial Review' (1995) 7 Pace International Law Review 281; D Akande, 'The International Court of Justice and the Security Council: Is there Room for Judicial Control of Decisions of the Political Organs of the United Nations' (1997) 46 ICLQ 309.

[271] See, eg, M Kohen, 'There Is No Need to Change the Composition of the Security Council: It Is Time for Stressing Accountability' in L Boisson de Chazournes and M Kohen (eds), *International Law and the Quest for its Implementation: Liber Amicorium Vera Gowlland-Debbas* (Brill 2010) 85, 92.

would appear to be the best judicial body to undertake this task.[272] Whilst the ICJ itself first contemplated the idea of judicial review some sixteen years after its inception, it went on to preclude it. In the 1962 *Certain Expenses Advisory Opinion*, the Court underscored that '[i]n the legal systems of States, there is often some procedure for determining the validity of even a legislative or governmental act, but no analogous procedure is to be found in the structure of the United Nations'.[273] It added that '[p]roposals made during the drafting of the Charter to place the ultimate authority to interpret the Charter in the International Court of Justice were not accepted'.[274] In 1971, the ICJ further reinforced this view, quite plainly, by stating that '[u]ndoubtedly, the Court does not possess powers of judicial review or appeal in respect of the decisions taken by the United Nations organs concerned'.[275]

The ICJ's potential judicial review power has most frequently been raised in connection with the *Lockerbie* cases. On 21 January 1992, the SC adopted Resolution 731, which called on Libya to answer fully and effectively to the requests made by the US and UK regarding the surrender of the suspected *Lockerbie* bombers.[276] Alleging violations of the 1971 Montreal Convention for the Suppression of Unlawful Acts against the Safety of Civil Aviation, Libya instituted distinct proceedings before the ICJ against the US and UK. In that setting, Libya contended that the SC resolution was *ultra vires*. Whilst the ICJ rejected Libya's plea for provisional relief, certain judges wrote separately and hinted that judicial review powers may be in the Court's future.[277] However, the respondent States (the US and UK) did not submit a counter-claim pursuant to Article 80 of the Rules of Court[278] in order to raise the question of Libyan responsibility before the ICJ.

Whilst the Court upheld its jurisdiction to hear the extradition cases on the merits, they were stricken from the Court's docket five years after the judgments on Preliminary Objections were rendered, following an amicable resolution between the Parties.[279] Ever since, commentators have waited for the ICJ to deal with the issue of judicial review. It may well be that a relevant case is submitted as a result of both the SC taking on an expanded security mandate and the Court handling various novel legal issues. After all, the interpretation of SC powers is an

[272] See, eg, J Klabbers, 'Book Review: Antonios Tzanakopoulos, Disobeying the Security Council: Countermeasures against Wrongful Sanctions' (2011) 8 IOLR 483, 485.

[273] *Certain Expenses Advisory Opinion* (n 149) 168.

[274] *Certain Expenses Advisory Opinion* (n 149) 168.

[275] *Namibia Advisory Opinion* (n 170) 45. However, some dissenting voices on the bench cautioned against unfettered SC powers, advocating in favour of international legal limits on those powers. See in ibid the Dissenting Opinions of Judge Fitzmaurice, 294 [116]; Judge Gros, 340 [34].

[276] This precedent is discussed in greater detail in ch 4.

[277] In particular, see the Separate Opinion of Judge Shahabuddeen and the Dissenting Opinions of Judges Bedjaoui, Weramantry, and El-Kosheri in the *Lockerbie Cases* (n 176).

[278] ICJ Rules (n 98) Art 80.

[279] Upon mutual notification by the parties, the President of the ICJ ordered that the two disputes be removed from the Court's List on 10 September 2003. See Press Release 2003/29 <www.icj-cij.org/presscom/index.php?pr=168&pt=1&p1=6&p2=1> accessed 1 June 2015.

'evolving process' which remains influenced by the changing needs of collective security and the international community of States.[280]

However, a careful review of the ICJ's own jurisprudence, coupled with the *travaux préparatoires* of the UN Charter, strongly militate against ascribing the role of a constitutional court to the ICJ. In fact, the *Lockerbie* precedent rather suggests that the Court is reticent to second-guess the SC and depart from a resolution adopted under Chapter VII; in that case, Resolution 748, which ordered Libya to 'provide a full and effective response' to the requests formulated by France, the US, and the UK, left the ICJ with 'practically... no choice other than inaction'.[281] What is more, policy considerations also dictate judicial restraint on the part of the ICJ.[282] This observation is exceedingly important in the context of global security, in which the SC may be called upon to endorse the use of force to prevent an immediate humanitarian disaster; promoting a power of judicial review in those scenarios might be detrimental to the collective security scheme envisaged under the UN Charter.[283] Whilst one can certainly speculate as to what the ICJ would do if faced with another *Lockerbie*-type situation, the resolution of this debate, whilst important, is not essential to the central issue explored in Part II of this work: that is, the SC's implementation of SR law in counterterrorism and other global security contexts.

In any event, there is every indication that the ICJ has already engaged in 'incidental review' of SC resolutions, be it in the context of contentious or advisory proceedings over which it exercised jurisdiction.[284] In several cases, the ICJ has, at least implicitly, accepted the validity of SC resolutions before moving on to the legal issues it had to decide. Although it is not called upon explicitly to engage in judicial review of a SC resolution, it must nonetheless first ascertain whether it is valid when the parties task it with determining the legal consequences of that resolution, or when they challenge its validity.[285] However, whilst the ICJ has certainly acknowledged that the SC is not above the law, the Court has yet to explore thoroughly the exact boundaries of SC powers.[286] There is a simple reason to explain this restraint: perhaps it is not its place to do so, or, if it is to pronounce on the extent and limits of SC powers, it might be best for the ICJ to do so in a more politically palatable, abstract fashion, as opposed to flat-out declaring that a given

[280] See generally M Arcari, 'Limits to Security Council Powers under the UN Charter and Issues of Charter Interpretation' (2012) 32 PYIL 239.

[281] Skubiszewski (n 171) 615–22. See also Alvarez (n 152) 561. It has also been suggested that the ICJ refrained from making certain pronouncements on recourse to force given that the SC had made no prior determination on this front. See the Separate Opinions of Judges Elaraby and Simma in the *Armed Activities Case* (n 80) [11], [3] respectively.

[282] See Dugard (n 181) 90.

[283] See, eg, Dissenting Opinion of President Schwebel in *Questions of Interpretation and Application of the 1971 Montreal Convention arising from the Aerial Incident at Lockerbie (Libya v USA)* (Preliminary Objections) [1998] ICJ Rep 115, 164–72. See also M David, 'Passport to Justice: Internationalizing the Political Question Doctrine for Application in the World Court' (1999) 40 HILJ 81, esp fns 174–84.

[284] See, eg, Šturma (n 260) 303; Kohen (n 271) 92–3.

[285] See, eg, Akande (n 270) 331.

[286] See also Roberts (n 270) 304.

resolution is *ultra vires*.[287] After all, 'both Council and Court have roles to play and need to coexist in a state of inevitable and sometimes desirable tension'.[288]

Ultimately, international lawyers may simply have to contend with the fact that there is no judicial organ to review SC decisions. In fact, it appears that this was not the role intended for the ICJ. Consequently, there is much wisdom to the proposition that ICJ powers should not be expanded for it to conduct judicial review where the UN Charter does not delineate such a role for it, either implicitly or expressly.[289] Besides, even if the SC adopted a resolution implementing SR against a State without the possibility of judicial review, this would entail very few departures from the default regime under the ARSIWA, at least in terms of practical result. The only major difference would be that in the case of the SC resolution, SR would be implemented through institutional channels, which may be followed by the adoption of institutional countermeasures. By default under the ARSIWA, SR is typically invoked and enforced unilaterally by the injured State, though it may receive some degree of support from concerned States and/or institutions in vindicating its claims. However, that unilateral implementation, and any subsequent countermeasures flowing from it, is by no means subject to a right of appeal or judicial review. Consequently, a strong case can be made that similar reasoning should extend to SC resolutions implementing SR.

3.2.1.2 Other tribunals

Potential judicial review of the exercise of SC powers was also envisaged by international criminal tribunals and, more recently, revisited by a hybrid international criminal tribunal. In both cases, the tribunals in question were called upon to entertain fundamental challenges to their very existence and, correspondingly, to tackle—heads on, albeit incidentally—the legality of certain SC actions. This eventuality cropped up before the ICTY, in the context of the first proceeding instituted against Dusko Tadić, with the Trial Chamber declining to address these jurisdictional issues in the light of the 'political question doctrine'. However, the Appeals Chamber, under the presidency of Judge Antonio Cassese, espoused contrary reasoning and ventured upon an incidental review of the exercise of SC powers by examining the legality of the establishment of the ICTY. The Appeals Chamber found that the ICTY's creation had been lawful, that the situation in the former Yugoslavia amounted to a 'threat to the peace' pursuant to Article 39 of the UN Charter, and that the institution of the ICTY constituted an appropriate, non-forcible measure according with the ideals underpinning Article 41 of the Charter.[290]

[287] See, eg, Alvarez (n 183) 28–36. [288] Alvarez (n 183) 39.

[289] See, eg, J Wouters and J Odermatt, '*Quis Custodiet Consilium Securitatis?* Reflections on the Lawmaking Powers of the Security Council' Leuven Centre for Global Governance Studies (June 2013) <http://ssrn.com/abstract=2286208> accessed 15 June 2015, 19.

[290] *Tadić Case* (Interlocutory Appeal on Jurisdiction) (n 169) [30], [32]–[40]. See also Dugard (n 181) 87 (characterizing this precedent as 'the best evidence for the proposition that the powers of the Security Council are subject to judicial review').

In the case of *Ayyash and others*, the Trial Chamber of the Special Tribunal for Lebanon (STL) addressed the defence's fundamental challenges, thereby mirroring the foray undertaken by the ICTY Appeals Chamber some seventeen years earlier into the realm of judicial review of SC decisions, even if only by incidental fashion. By contrast, the STL Appeals Chamber declined to tackle those jurisdictional issues, essentially equating them with 'political' questions falling outside the ambit of its review power, and thereby paid homage to the reasoning of the ICTY Trial Chamber.[291] To some publicists, this turn of events was rather retrogressive and signalled those judicial bodies' reluctance (the ICTY Trial Chamber and STL Appeals Chamber) to conduct judicial review of SC decision-making, resulting in 'splintered decisions' between those tribunals' trial and appellate chambers. The staunchest critics levelled the charge that the STL 'Appeal Chamber's refusal to engage in politics, and affirmation that the Security Council is unbound by law, seems to be motivated less by the law than by timidity and fear, thereby putting in doubt the inestimable legacy of Tadić'.[292]

In the European context, particular resistance has been exhibited to the SC acting both as legislator, especially on counterterrorism matters, and as quasi-judicial body in handing down targeted sanctions against individuals suspected of entertaining ties to terrorism.[293] Unsurprisingly, scholars are debating the legitimacy and validity of the exercise of Council powers, with some levelling charges against the perceived lack of due process in its sanctions decision-making.[294] The inevitable collision between SC-mandated counterterrorism measures and human rights standards came into focus in the oft-discussed *Kadi and Al Barakaat* case. In that instance, the European Court of Justice (ECJ) invalidated a regulation adopted by the Council of the EU targeting individuals associated with the Taliban or Al-Qaeda and their assets, pursuant to SC resolutions.[295] Other courts and tribunals,

[291] Compare *Tadić Case* (Decision on Defence Motion on Jurisdiction) ICTY-94-1-T (10 August 1995) and *Tadić Case* (Interlocutory Appeal on Jurisdiction) (n 169) to the following STL decisions: *Ayyash and Others* (Decision on the Defence Challenges to the Jurisdiction and Legality of the Tribunal) STL-11-01/PT/TC (27 July 2012); *Ayyash and Others* (Decision on the Defence Appeals Against the Trial Chamber's Decision on the Defence Challenges to the Jurisdiction and Legality of the Tribunal) STL-11-01/PT/AC/AR90.1 (24 October 2012). For further background analysis prior to the STL decisions, see JE Alvarez, 'Nuremberg Revisited: The *Tadić* Case' (1996) 7 EJIL 245.

[292] See generally JE Alvarez, '*Tadić* Revisited: The *Ayyash* Decisions of the Special Tribunal for Lebanon' (2013) 11 JICJ 291. For another critical outlook on the STL decisions, see M Nikolova and MJ Ventura, 'The Special Tribunal for Lebanon Declines to Review UN Security Council Action: Retreating from "Tadić's" Legacy in the "Ayyash" Jurisdiction and Legality Decisions' (2013) 11 JICJ 615.

[293] See, eg, E Nanopoulos, 'Judicial Review of Measures Implementing Security Council Resolutions: The Relevance of the EU Principle of Loyal Cooperation' (2013) 15 Cambridge Yearbook of European Legal Studies 669. On the SC's counterterrorism sanctions regimes in respect of both States and individuals, see A Charron, *UN Sanctions and Conflict: Responding to Peace and Security Threats* (Routledge 2011) 153–88.

[294] See, eg, D Hovell, *The Power of Process: The Value of Due Process in Security Council Sanctions Decision-Making* (OUP 2016); I Johnstone, 'Legislation and Adjudication in the UN Security Council: Bringing Down the Deliberative Deficit' (2008) 102 AJIL 275; 'Symposium on Responsibility of International Organizations' (2010) 7 IOLR 9.

[295] Joined Cases C-402/05P and C-415/05P *Yassin Abdullah Kadi and Al Barakaat International Foundation v Council and Commission* [2008] ECR I-6341; (2008) 47 ILM 923. For a critical

including national judiciaries, have also engaged in so-called judicial review of SC decision-making.[296]

Therefore, considerable uncertainty remains regarding the possible judicial review of SC decisions by international tribunals, let alone the ICJ. In fact, the principal judicial organ of the UN has itself precluded this possibility in its own jurisprudence, though one can certainly speculate that considerable advances may have occurred had the ICJ dealt with the merits in the *Lockerbie* cases. Conversely, the picture that emerges from the experience of other tribunals presents a more mixed model; one only has to point to the divergent outcomes reached by the Trial and Appeals Chambers of both the ICTY and STL, or of the Court of First Instance and ECJ in the *Kadi* case as evidence of jurisprudential incoherency.[297] There is certainly no *jurisprudence constante* to this effect, especially in an international legal order that has countenanced the proliferation of international tribunals. Perhaps the inconsistent treatment of judicial review of SC decisions amounts to an example of fragmentation.[298] It is submitted, however, that it would be more constructive to sidestep the age-old judicial review debate and focus on the organic bonds of cooperation that exist between UN institutions, especially the ICJ and SC.

3.2.2 Functional overlap and surrounding issues: Towards complementary roles for the Council and ICJ

The *Lockerbie* precedent propelled the need to rethink the relationship between the ICJ and SC to the forefront of scholarly debate over international legal constitutionalism. Indeed, that case was not the first instance in which both organs were seized of essentially the same dispute; this situation arose in the *Aegean Sea Continental Shelf*,[299] *Tehran Hostages*,[300] and *Nicaragua* cases.[301] The principal

take, see F Francioni, 'The Right of Access to Justice to Challenge the Security Council's Targeted Sanctions: After-Thoughts on Kadi' in U Fastenrath *et al.* (n 38) 908–22.

[296] For a survey, see Reinisch, 'Should Judges' (n 267).

[297] See also P Šturma and V Bílková, 'Targeted Anti-Terrorist Sanctions and their Implications for International Law Normative and Institutional Coherency' in A Constantinides and N Zaikos (eds), *The Diversity of International Law* (Brill 2009) 215–37.

[298] For a selection of the rich literature on fragmentation and international law, see: ILC 'Report of the Study Group on Fragmentation of International Law: Difficulties arising from the Diversification and Expansion of International Law—Finalized by Martti Koskenniemi' (2006) UN Doc A/CN.4/L.682; M Koskenniemi and P Leino, 'Fragmentation of International Law? Postmodern Anxieties' (2002) 15 LJIL 553; A Fischer-Lescano and G Teubner, 'Regime-Collisions: The Vain Search for Legal Unity in the Fragmentation of Global Law' (2004) 25 MJIL 999; Simma (n 32) 217; T Treves, 'Conflicts between the International Tribunal for the Law of the Sea and the International Court of Justice' (1999) 31 NYUJILP 809; P Weil, 'Towards Relative Normativity in International Law?' (1983) 77 AJIL 413; G Guillaume, 'L'Unité du Droit International Public Est-elle Aujourd'hui en Danger?' (2003) 55 Revue Internationale de Droit Comparé 23; M Prost, *The Concept of Unity in Public International Law* (Hart 2012).

[299] *Aegean Sea Continental Shelf (Greece v Turkey)* (Interim Protection) [1976] ICJ Rep 3.

[300] *Tehran Hostages Case* (n 80).

[301] *Military and Paramilitary Activities in and against Nicaragua (Nicaragua v USA)* (Provisional Measures) [1984] ICJ Rep 169; *Nicaragua v USA* (Jurisdiction) (n 63).

difference, however, lay in the fact that the same two parties seized both organs in those instances whereas in *Lockerbie* the tension between the SC and ICJ arose precisely because different parties advanced claims before those bodies.[302] Consequently, an inordinate focus on the political versus legal/judicial dichotomy when addressing the relationship between the SC and ICJ could pay a great disservice to the promotion of a more effective international SR system and global security agendas. More importantly, this approach may ultimately obfuscate the fact that there exists a 'functional parallelism' and a 'functional overlap' between the SC and ICJ.[303] As seen earlier, both these organs were invited to pronounce on different aspects of the *Lockerbie* dispute.

The drafters of the UN Charter delineated distinct but interconnected roles for the SC and ICJ in vindicating the ideals enshrined in that instrument. Whilst their respective functions remain complementary in a general sense, this interconnection is particularly acute in matters of global security, which may entail the intercession of both organs at different stages of the same dispute, along with the implementation of SR and pacification of relations between disputing States. Pursuant to Article 24(1) of the Charter, the SC is vested with the primary responsibility of maintaining international peace and security. When the SC exercises quasi-judicial powers, its action is informed by Chapter VI of the Charter although, as seen in Chapter 4, it may also draw on the provisions of Chapter VII. Conversely, Article 92 of the Charter entrusts the ICJ with ensuring the peaceful judicial settlement of disputes between States parties to its Statute, subject to the jurisdictional limitations explored above. By way of overarching framework, Article 1 of the Charter provides that the Court must 'bring about by peaceful means, and in conformity with the principles of justice and international law, adjustment or settlement of international disputes or situations which might lead to a breach of the peace'.[304] This dispute resolution mission aligns with Article 2(2), which obligates States to 'settle their international disputes by peaceful means in such a manner that international peace and security, and justice, are not endangered'.[305] Moreover, Article 33 of the Charter provides a large degree of latitude to States in fashioning dispute settlement modalities, which presumably encompasses a role for both the ICJ and SC in coalescing around the implementation of SR in some cases.

Whilst those organ's respective roles were initially conceived very differently, they nonetheless exhibit points of rapprochement in certain instances, particularly in the global security context, and work in harmony in furthering collective interests.[306] Thus, there is no doubt that the ICJ remains commonly invested

[302] See, eg, Gowlland-Debbas (n 245) 644.

[303] Alvarez (n 183) 3; I Cherneva, 'The UN Security Council in the *Lockerbie* Case' (2012) Centro Studi Strategici Carlo de Cristoforis <www.cestudec.com/act_download.asp?id=138> access 18 August 2015, 22.

[304] UN Charter (n 153).

[305] UN Charter (n 153).

[306] Consider Separate Opinion of Judge Lachs in the *Lockerbie Case (Libya v UK)* (Provisional Measures) (n 176) 27.

alongside the SC in promoting global security, with the Court fulfilling this mission in various ways: by indicating provisional measures to protect parties' rights until the merits of cases are heard; by ruling on allegedly unlawful uses of force; by providing treaty interpretations that may have a significant impact on inter-State relations and the work of IOs; by handling human rights and environmental disputes, which both have a bearing on human health and prosperity; by delivering advisory opinions that may have far-reaching implications on core UN principles and purposes; etc.[307]

Contrary to Article 12, which clearly establishes the SC's precedence over the GA in certain situations,[308] the Charter fails to establish a hierarchy between the ICJ and SC.[309] As a result, the ICJ may secure jurisdiction over a legal dispute submitted to it despite the fact that the SC may already be exercising the functions devolved to it by the Charter in respect of the same disagreement.[310] In the *Tehran Hostages* case, the ICJ spoke to this complementary exercise of powers: 'legal disputes between sovereign States by their very nature are likely to occur in political contexts, and often form only one element in a wider and longstanding political dispute between the States concerned'.[311] Hence, both organs contribute to the peaceful settlement of the dispute, albeit by tackling different aspects, which may involve the implementation of SR in global security contexts. As evinced by the ICJ's *jurisprudence constante*—most notably the *Tehran Hostages* case and the *Wall* and *Kosovo* advisory opinions—the fact that a legal dispute or question submitted to it has political dimensions does not in any way impede the establishment of the Court's jurisdiction, provided that its jurisdictional requirements are met. In other words, the fact that a legal question put to it also has political implications should not enable the ICJ to evade its judicial task.[312]

The SC and ICJ have been called upon to deal with common disputes in several instances, some of which had significant implications for global security. In *Tehran Hostages*, the ICJ underscored that the SC was 'actively seized of the matter' and 'that the Secretary-General was under an express mandate from the Council to use his good offices in the matter when ... the Court decided unanimously that it was competent to entertain the United States' request for an indication

[307] See, eg, Statement by HE Judge Peter Tomka, President of the ICJ, at the SC (28 October 2013) (on file with author).

[308] For the text of this provision see n 160 and accompanying text.

[309] See, eg, P Webb, *International Judicial Integration and Fragmentation* (OUP 2013) 128 (noting that both organs 'exist in a horizontal relationship within the same international system').

[310] Furthermore, an injured State would not be precluded from seizing both organs of the same matter, in which case neither organ would be compelled to bow to the other. See Bedjaoui (n 104) 67; TJH Elsen, *Litispendence between the International Court of Justice and the Security Council* (TMC Asser Instituut 1986) 63, 67.

[311] *Tehran Hostages Case* (n 80) 20 [37]. See also generally A Coleman, 'The International Court of Justice and Highly Political Matters' (2003) 4 Melbourne Journal of International Law 29.

[312] *Tehran Hostages* case (n 80) 20 [37]; *Wall Advisory Opinion* (n 5) 159–62 [51]–[58]; *Kosovo Advisory Opinion* (n 147) 415 [27]. See also *Review of Judgment No. 158 Advisory Opinion* (n 148) 172 [14].

of provisional measures, and proceeded to indicate such measures'.[313] Echoing the foregoing observations, the ICJ highlighted the absence of a clear division of labour between it and the SC, outside the distinct but interconnected functions assigned to each organ by the Charter. Thus, whereas

> Article 12 of the Charter expressly forbids the General Assembly to make any recommendation with regard to a dispute or situation while the Security Council is exercising its functions in respect of that dispute or situation, no such restriction is placed on the functioning of the Court by any provision of either the Charter or the Statute of the Court.[314]

The Court contributes to the pacific settlement of disputes by adjudicating the legal questions submitted to it in such instances: 'It is for the Court, the principal judicial organ of the United Nations, to resolve any legal questions that may be in issue between parties to a dispute; and the resolution of such legal questions by the Court may be an important, and sometimes decisive, factor in promoting the peaceful settlement of the dispute.'[315] Furthermore, the ICJ acknowledged the complementary functions of both organs in the jurisdiction and admissibility phase of the *Case concerning Military and Paramilitary Activities in and against Nicaragua*. Relying on Article 24 of the Charter, the ICJ confirmed that the exercise of its primary judicial role could also help further the maintenance of international peace and security, which is the SC's primary responsibility.

Therefore, it follows that

> [w]hile in Article 12 there is a provision for a clear demarcation of functions between the General Assembly and the Security Council, in respect of any dispute or situation, that the former should not make any recommendation with regard to that dispute or situation unless the Security Council so requires, there is no similar provision anywhere in the Charter with respect to the Security Council and the Court.[316]

In short, the ICJ asserted that it could simultaneously handle a dispute that is also being dealt with by the SC. In such instances, both organs address different aspects of the same dispute but they do so in a complementary manner, with a view to bringing about a peaceful resolution and appeasing tensions between the States involved. The ICJ's conclusion on this front is eloquent: 'the fact that a matter is before the Security Council should not prevent it being dealt with by the Court and that both proceedings could be pursued *pari passu*'.[317] In its own words, the ICJ 'never shied away from a case brought before it merely because it had political implications or because it involved serious elements of the use of force'.[318] It also recalled the distinct but interconnected functions carried out by both organs in the furtherance of common objectives: 'The Council has functions of a political nature assigned to it, whereas the Court exercises purely judicial functions. Both organs

313 *Tehran Hostages Case* (n 80) 21 [40].
314 *Tehran Hostages Case* (n 80) 22 [40].
315 *Tehran Hostages Case* (n 80) 22 [40].
316 *Nicaragua v USA* (Jurisdiction) (n 63) 434–5 [95].
317 *Nicaragua v USA* (Jurisdiction) (n 63) 433 [93].
318 *Nicaragua v USA* (Jurisdiction) (n 63) 435 [96].

can therefore perform their separate but complementary functions with respect to the same events.'[319]

As seen earlier, the ICJ resorted to this reasoning in the *Lockerbie* cases in which both organs were seized of different aspects of the same dispute. The ICJ concluded that its duly established jurisdiction over the extradition dispute could be exercised and maintained in parallel with the SC, which handled the establishment and implementation of SR. In the light of present-day global security threats, it is likely that both organs will once again have to exercise their functions in parallel, so as to further the objectives of the Charter. As regards disputes involving SR norms, the SC will strive to maintain international peace and security through a multilateral political framework, whilst the ICJ will render justice by way of judicial process. In proceedings before both bodies, legal and political considerations will most likely remain integral components of any dispute related to global security violations. Consequently, an organic complementarity between those organs' respective functions emerges under the Charter's framework. In the future, it might prove more constructive to abandon the debate over the legal/political dichotomy, or at least decrease the analytical focus on potential judicial review of SC resolutions, and rather focus on the 'functional co-operation' of both organs in fulfilling Charter objectives.[320] After all, Judge Lachs rightly underscored that 'the dividing line between political and legal disputes is blurred, as law becomes ever more frequently an integral part of international controversies'.[321]

Whilst this book argues that the SC's treatment of disputes may involve important legal questions despite the ICJ being the UN's principal judicial organ, the contrary argument must also be addressed: in sum, the maintenance of international peace and security is not the SC's exclusive dominion, as confirmed by the ICJ on several occasions.[322] The principal problem surrounding this debate seems to be that international legal scholars have endorsed too strict, and/or literal, readings of the division of competencies between the ICJ and SC, along constitutional lines or divisions. However, the reality is that some contemporaneous events were simply not foreseen at the time of drafting the Charter. Thus, the SC will sometimes have to resort, very centrally, to international legal principles in its political decision-making, for instance when determining the international responsibility of a State. As argued in Chapter 4, the SC has expanded its powers very broadly over the last two decades. Conversely, the ICJ will sometimes have to turn its mind, very centrally, to the maintenance of international peace and security in its own judicial decision-making. As a result, it too has extended its 'traditional' role onto SC terrain in recent years. At the provisional measures stage in *Request for Interpretation of the Judgment of 15 June 1962 in the Case concerning the Temple of Preah Vihear (Cambodia v Thailand)*, for instance, the Court imposed a

[319] *Nicaragua v USA* (Jurisdiction) (n 63) 435 [95].

[320] This language is borrowed from Bedjaoui (n 104) 74.

[321] Separate Opinions of Judge Lachs in the *Lockerbie Cases* (Provisional Measures) (n 176) 27, 139 respectively.

[322] See, eg, *Certain Expenses Advisory Opinion* (n 149) 163; *Wall Advisory Opinion* (n 5) [27].

demilitarized zone for the first time in its history, which was called into question in several dissenting opinions.[323]

This example is important for two reasons. In a more immediate sense, it demonstrates the ICJ's potential contributions in furthering global security in real-time settings. Indeed, by adopting a demilitarized zone, the Court prevented the further aggravation of the international dispute prior to hearing the Request for Interpretation on the merits, which it decided in 2013.[324] In a broader sense, this precedent evidenced the organic and complementary roles that both organs can play in resolving international disputes and maintaining international peace and security. The broader conception of international security and threat pre-emption now prevalent in the global order undeniably envisages important roles for both organs, which should also be subject to cooperation and coordination where applicable.

Finally, as already seen, the SC can play a role in strengthening the exercise of the ICJ's judicial function, primarily by reference to Article 36(3) of the UN Charter.[325] However, the SC's contribution extends beyond the mere submission of disputes to the Court for adjudication, as the SC can assume an important function in ensuring compliance with the Court's judgments by the parties after they have been delivered. In this regard, Article 94(2) of the Charter provides that 'if any party to a case fails to perform the obligations incumbent upon it under a judgment rendered by the Court, the other party may have recourse to the Security Council which may, if it deems necessary, make recommendations or decide upon measures to be taken to give effect to the judgment'.[326] However, it should be emphasized that there is generally a high level of compliance with ICJ decisions,[327] so SC involvement in this respect will be exceptional. Nevertheless, this mechanism may come to be used by the SC in the future to ensure the implementation of SR pursuant to an ICJ judgment, thereby offering evidence of the distinct but complementary functions of both organs. Needless to say, this functional complementarity is by no means limited to the interaction between these two organs. As already discussed, the GA and SC must also work in harmony and coordinate their efforts in tackling present-day global security concerns.[328]

3.2.3 *Lis pendens* in the context of global security

In the light of the foregoing considerations, one last line of argument can be disposed of rather summarily. In short, some commentators have raised the

323 (Provisional Measures) [2011] ICJ Rep 537, 552–3 [62], 555 [69]. See in ibid the Dissenting Opinions of Judges Owada, Al-Khasawneh, Xue, Donoghue, and Judge ad hoc Cot.

324 (Request for Interpretation) [2013] ICJ Rep 281.

325 See n 246 and accompanying text.

326 UN Charter (n 153) Art 94(2).

327 See generally A Llamzon, 'Jurisdiction and Compliance in Recent Decision of the International Court of Justice' (2007) 18 EJIL 815.

328 See also ND White, 'The Relationship between the UN Security Council and General Assembly in Matters of International Peace and Security' in M Weller (ed.), *The Oxford Handbook of the Use of Force in International Law* (OUP 2015) 293–313.

possibility that *lis pendens* might arise between the SC and ICJ, particularly in the event that both organs are seized of the same dispute.[329] However, as seen above, both these organs would perform different duties (or, at least, employ different methods in reaching their respective outcomes), even if seized of a common dispute. In the global security context, they may be called upon to play different, but complementary (and compatible), roles in implementing SR. Thus, although perhaps compelling under some lights, the argument that *lis pendens* or genuine litispendence—as traditionally understood—could arise between these organs remains highly dubious.[330] Furthermore, it becomes particularly intractable in the global security context, especially as regards counterterrorism obligations.

For the sake of argument, even if one attempted to envisage litispendence in a dispute arising over a State's failure to prevent terrorism, distinct determinations by the SC and ICJ could coexist when addressing the injured State's claims (provided that both organs were duly seized of the matter). If that State allowed its territory to be used by private terrorist factions to launch terrorist strikes against neighbouring countries, the task of determining the resulting legal issues could be divided between those two organs, albeit within the confines of their respective functions. The SC, through its largely politically driven but also legally informed approach, could deplore the continuing use of that State's territory for the purposes of waging terrorist attacks and rest its assumptions on existing international legal principles (ie through a *renvoi* to primary obligations). Consequently, the SC could order that State to comply with certain legal obligations, either through sanctions or strong language, and ultimately allow the use of self-defence as a countermeasure.[331] This is certainly one viable (albeit extensive) interpretation of the reaction to 9/11 and, more specifically, of US-led military action in Afghanistan. However, in order to make this argument palatable, at least at first glance, one must accept that the reaction to 9/11 was concomitantly framed within SR and recourse to force frameworks.[332]

If the involved parties were to accept its jurisdiction, the ICJ could be called upon to pronounce on the possible SR of the territorial State whose actions (or

[329] On these questions, generally, see Elsen (n 310).

[330] Nevertheless, much has been written on the hypothesis of having two simultaneous pending 'cases' before the ICJ and SC at the intersection of collective security and SR. See, eg, RSJ Macdonald, 'The International Court of Justice and the Security Council of the United Nations' in M Rama-Montaldo *et al.* (eds), *International Law in an Evolving World: Liber Amicorum in Tribute to Professor Eduardo Jiménez de Aréchaga* (Fundación de cultura Universitaria 1994) 457–78; A Pellet, 'Le Glaive et la Balance: Remarques sur le Rôle de la CIJ en Matière de Maintien de la Paix et de la Sécurité Internationales' in Y Dinstein and M Tabory (eds), *International Law at a Time of Perplexity: Essays in Honour of Shabtai Rosenne* (Nijhoff 1989) 545–50; MN Shaw, 'The Security Council and the International Court of Justice: Judicial Drift and Judicial Function' in AS Muller *et al.* (eds), *The International Court of Justice: Its Future Role After Fifty Years* (Nijhoff 1997) 219–59.

[331] For a fully fledged argument framing self-defence as a countermeasure under SR repertoire, see Part III of this volume.

[332] For a concise review of the nebulous and confused relationship between terrorist attacks, use of force, and countermeasures through the lens of the ARSIWA, see Franck (n 90) 53–5; Gowlland-Debbas (n 30) 56.

inaction, as it may be) effectively transformed its territory into a launch pad for terrorism. It is also conceivable that the facts of the case would fail to convincingly establish the requisite link between the terrorist factions and the government (ie under ARSIWA Article 8 and pursuant to the *Nicaragua* and *Genocide* cases). Provided there has been no endorsement of the attacks by the official State apparatus, the ICJ could be compelled to rule that no sufficient nexus between the non-State actors and the State has been demonstrated before it.[333] Conversely, whilst unlikely, the ICJ could expound that the 'effective control' standard has been met and declare that the territorial State is responsible for failing to prevent the attacks, thereby reaching a similar (and compatible) conclusion to that of the SC, at least in terms of legal responsibility. In any event, if the ICJ decided to reject the exception of *lis pendens* and assert jurisdiction over a matter involving SR overtones already pending before the SC, it would implicitly validate the concomitant application of the UN Charter and of SR law to a single fact pattern.[334]

In many ways, therefore, the term 'litispendence' is a misnomer; the problem of parallel suits or procedures in matters involving SR, which could bring about potential impairments to either organ's functions, simply does not arise. Rather, the SC and ICJ employ distinct 'instrumental processes' under the auspices of the legal framework of SR, in order to produce a similar outcome: the return to a 'situation of legality'. In the SC's case, however, the primary and overarching framework governing the adoption of resolutions on global security matters often resides in Chapter VII of the Charter, which remains highly compatible with SR repertoire. Otherwise put, when faced with a common dispute involving global security violations and potential implementation of the wrongdoing State's responsibility, the ICJ relies on 'peaceful settlement procedures', particularly judicial settlement; by contrast, the SC's process is characterized by resort to 'institutional countermeasures'.[335] The ICJ's judicial settlement procedures may come into play (i) early on, in the place of countermeasures, (ii) as a precondition (though not obligatory under international law) for the adoption of countermeasures, or (iii) later on, so that the ICJ may examine the lawfulness of countermeasures taken by the injured State. Conversely, any 'institutional countermeasures' imposed by the SC constitute an enforcement method. It follows that '[t]he Council in reacting to violations of fundamental norms of international law is not acting as an impartial arbitrator or third party, but in lieu and place of the injured States in matters which affect the interest of the international community as a whole'.[336]

[333] The concept of attribution carries with it considerable evidentiary burdens. See, eg, D Shelton, 'Judicial Review of State Action by International Courts' (1989) 12 FILJ 361 (reviewing evidentiary concerns related to omissions). See also generally GA Christenson, 'Attributing Acts of Omission to the State' (1991) 12 MJIL 312; KA Bove, 'Attribution Issues in State Responsibility' (1990) 84 ASIL Proceedings 51. On the difficulties related to the evidentiary burden required in invoking self-defence against terrorist attacks, see JI Charney, 'Use of Force Against Terrorism and International Law' (2001) 95 AJIL 835.

[334] See Forteau (n 37) 324–5.

[335] Gowlland-Debbas (n 30) 73.

[336] Gowlland-Debbas (n 30) 73. See also Gowlland-Debbas (n 182) 308; Gowlland-Debbas (n 53) (positing that electing collectively authorized measures over unilateral measures constitutes an attempt to escape regression to unilateral decisions involving community interests).

3.3 Preliminary Conclusions: The Security Council as Legislator and Implementer

As seen in this chapter, there is considerable support for the implementation of SR by UN organs in global security matters. In the light of structural shortcomings, the role of the GA in enforcing secondary SR norms is essentially reduced to that of sideline supporter. However, this can be an important role, especially in cases where the GA supports a determination of international responsibility made by the SC and ultimately echoes its calls for the wrongdoing State to compensate the injured State. By way of example, as will be seen in Section 4.4.4, the GA bolstered the SC's finding that Israel had violated international law following that State's aerial strikes on nuclear installations located in Iraq. That said, the GA has made considerable advances at the primary normative level, by adopting far-reaching resolutions on global security issues (albeit non-binding). For its part, the ICJ remains a viable forum for implementing SR in global security contexts, although its jurisdiction remains subject to State consent. However, the Court has often sidestepped the application of SR principles in cases where that normative scheme could have played a more important role. It has similarly eluded the concept of terrorism in other cases, particularly *Nicaragua* and *Tehran Hostages*. Despite the spirited defence mounted by some scholars advocating possible ICJ jurisdiction over terrorism cases through the application of compromissory clauses, it is highly doubtful that such disputes would even be submitted to the Court. As a result, the ICJ has never dealt with terrorism and its forays into SR matters extending to global security violations have been tangential, at best.

By contrast, the SC has dealt with terrorism and other global security breaches on various occasions. Furthermore, it has specifically implemented SR for terrorism and other violations of international law related to global security, many instances of which will be discussed in greater detail in Chapter 4. This no doubt offers evidence that international law violations related to terrorism are almost invariably political problems, first and foremost, or are problems with political dimensions that are best addressed through a primarily political prism and institution. In so doing, SR repertoire is only one of the available legal means that may be harnessed with a view to bolstering an acceptable political outcome in dealing with terrorism and other global security threats, via a multilateral political institution. This reality clearly militates in favour of enhanced SC involvement, particularly as regards the implementation of SR; in this regard, SR repertoire provides an environment against which a political decision can be made with due regard for international legal principles, where relevant, without the need to make such reliance explicit. Thus, in some instances, the overlap between SR norms and the exercise of SC powers will be implicit. Further relevant practice is analysed in Chapter 4.

The SC has also made significant incursions into the realm of primary legal norms, particularly in the fields of counterterrorism and nuclear non-proliferation, which directly inform the application of secondary SR rules. Indeed, the SC has adopted far-reaching resolutions and delivered broad-ranging pronouncements imposing categorical obligations on all States, without simultaneously specifying any time or geographical limits for those undertakings. In fact, this new 'legislative' role is part of a broader tendency within the UN, particularly on counterterrorism matters.[337] In many ways, these developments illustrate the powerful role that the SC can play, especially given its unique deliberative process, in advancing international law and, ultimately, in enforcing legal obligations.[338] Thus, it is only logical that attention is increasingly paid to the development of international law—and law-making by IOs, more generally—through their operational activities or decision-making processes, and the impact of normative developments in international law on those operations.[339]

Whilst some equated the SC's post-9/11 resolution-making with a legislative or constitutional revolution in the global order, one would be hard-pressed to deny that this organ has arrogated vast and expansive new powers in dealing with global security challenges. Furthermore, the SC's 'quasi-judicial' exercise of its powers has extended beyond the realm of inter-State relations in order to target individuals, with that organ being particularly active in the context of listing procedures against suspected terrorists. It is not surprising, therefore, that concerns were voiced over (the lack of) potential recourses against SC sanctions in this context, the broader role of the Council as 'legislator' on the international scene, and the potential implications for international human rights.[340] As seen earlier in this chapter, various charges were initially levelled against the SC's expansive exercise of powers in the wake of the *Kadi* saga, with a distinct concern for the safeguarding of fundamental human rights.[341] Therefore, whilst the SC can make significant contributions to both the implementation of SR and global security, more

[337] See W van Genugten, 'The UN: A Law-Maker on the Move' in S Muller and S Zouridis (eds), *Law and Justice: A Strategy Perspective* (Torkel Opsahl Academic Publisher 2012) 281–91; E Rosand, 'The UN Response to the Evolving Threat of Global Terrorism: Institutional Reform, Rivalry, or Renewal?' in PG Danchin and H Fischer (eds), *United Nations and the New Collective Security* (CUP 2010) 250–81; P Klein, 'Le Droit International à l'Épreuve du Terrorisme' (2006) 321 RdC 203, 309–67.

[338] See, eg, I Johnstone, 'The UN Security Council as Legislature' in B Cronin and I Hurd (eds), *The UN Security Council and the Politics of International Authority* (Routledge 2008) 80–104; Johnstone (n 294). For a specific case study on the SC's deliberative track record with respect to counteracting Iran's violations of international law, see J Gordon, 'Crippling Iran: The U.N. Security Council and the Tactic of Deliberative Ambiguity' (2013) 44 GJIL 973.

[339] See, eg, I Johnstone, 'Normative Evolution at the UN: Impact on Operational Activities' in BD Jones *et al.* (eds), *Cooperating for Peace and Security: Evolving Institutions and Arrangements in a Context of Changing U.S. Security Policy* (CUP 2010) 187–214.

[340] See, eg, L Condorelli, 'Le Pouvoir Législatif du Conseil de Sécurité des Nations Unies Vu à la "Loupe Salmon"' in N Angelet *et al.* (eds), *Droit du Pouvoir, Pouvoir du Droit: Mélanges Offerts à Jean Salmon* (Bruylant 2007) 1229–39; G Mébiama, 'Le Pouvoir Normatif du Conseil de Sécurité de l'Organisation des Nations Unies: Entre Nécessité et Légitimité' (2010) 85 Revue Internationale de Droit Africain EDJA 29.

[341] See also L Condorelli, 'Le Conseil de Sécurité, les Sanctions Ciblées et le Respect des Droits de l'Homme' in Boisson de Chazournes and Kohen (n 271) 73–84; J-M Thouvenin and RT Segura, 'Le Conseil de Sécurité des Nations Unies et le Terrorisme: Vers un Organe de Recours contre les Sanctions?' in EDM García Rico *et al.* (eds), *La Seguridad Internacional en el Siglo XXI: Nuevas Perspectivas* (Plaze y Valdés 2011) 19–39.

broadly, it is important not to overstate its potential. For reasons explored in this chapter and beyond, there is every indication that the SC is ill-equipped to act as an international 'terrorism court' across the board.[342] Conversely, strong political misgivings cast doubt over the likelihood of success of the proposal that an international special tribunal for terrorism be instituted, which has been defended by some publicists.[343]

Whilst the SC's promulgation of primary legal norms may appear problematic under some lights, that organ's application of secondary SR norms remains undoubtedly more controversial. This volume now turns to this more challenging aspect of the implementation of SR. As argued in Chapter 4, there is considerable support for equating Chapter VII sanctions with an enforcement mechanism of international law, provided the threat to international peace and security is predicated on a breach of international law.[344] It is not surprising, therefore, that some commentators advocate the merger of more traditional SC functions—that is, the maintenance of international peace and security—with the enforcement of international law.[345] As will be seen, some proponents of this literary canon go a step further and suggest that in specific circumstances, the determination of an international legal breach asserted by the SC should engender definitive legal consequences.[346]

[342] See also H Köchler, *The Security Council as Administrator of Justice?: Reflections on the Antagonistic Relationship between Power and Law* (International Progress Organization 2011) 59–67.

[343] See, eg, B van Ginkel, 'Combating Terrorism: Proposals for Improving the International Legal Framework' in Cassese (n 20) 476–9.

[344] See, eg, J d'Aspremont, 'The Collective Security System and the Enforcement of International Law' in Weller (n 328) 129–56. On the SC's adoption of sanctions, their contents and contours, see Charron (n 293).

[345] See, eg, J Combacau, *Le Pouvoir de Sanction de l'ONU: Étude Théorique de la Coercition Non Militaire* (Pedone 1974) 9–16; L Cavaré, 'Les Sanctions dans le Cadre de l'O.N.U.' (1952) 80 RdC 191, 221; DH Joyner, *International Law and the Proliferation of Weapons of Mass Destruction* (OUP 2009) 178; M Virally, *L'Organisation Mondiale* (Armand Colin 1972) 453; M Roscini, 'The United Nations Security Council and the Enforcement of International Humanitarian Law' (2010) 43 Israel Law Review 334; A Pellet, 'Sanctions' in R Wolfrum (ed.), *Max Planck Encyclopedia of Public International Law* (OUP 2012) <www.mpepil.com/home> accessed 1 June 2014, para 17.

[346] See, eg, Gowlland Debbas (n 30) 74–90; L Damrosch, 'The Permanent Five as Enforcers of Controls on Weapons of Mass Destruction: Building on the Iraq "Precedent"?' (2002) 13 EJIL 305. For critiques of this approach, see G Arangio-Ruiz, 'On the Security Council's 'Law-Making' (2000) 83 Rivista di Diritto Internazionale 609, 633–4; P d'Argent *et al.*, 'Article 39' in J-P Cot *et al.* (eds), *La Charte des Nations Unies: Commentaire Article par Article* (3rd edn, Economica 2005) 1139. On this question, see also generally Forteau (n 37).

4

Institutionalizing the Implementation of State Responsibility in Counterterrorism Contexts

The Interplay between the Security Council and International Legal Norms

4.1 Introduction

As discussed earlier, since the 9/11 attacks international organizations (IOs) have become actively engaged in devising counterterrorism strategies and frameworks. Chapter 3 presented a detailed analysis of the prospect of implementing State responsibility (SR) through existing United Nations (UN) organs in global security contexts, with particular emphasis on the interrelationships between those organs, particularly that existing between the International Court of Justice (ICJ) and UN Security Council (UNSC). Of particular interest are the SC's contributions to counterterrorism policy-making, which are increasingly attracting scholarly and policy attention. Through Resolutions 1368 and 1373, for instance, the SC asserted the right of victim-States to invoke self-defence to counteract terrorism, a posture sometimes construed as enabling States to take unilateral action against terrorist non-State actors.[1]

Indeed, whilst the interplay between use of force and terrorism has attracted some attention in recent years, many academic contributions focus on the possibility of States invoking recourse to force against terrorist networks or individuals located in third States, sometimes offering little in the way of critical insight into the inter-State dynamics that underlie such interventions in the light of SR norms specifically.[2] Consequently, the SC has sometimes approved subsequent use of

[1] See, eg, D Jinks, 'State Responsibility for the Acts of Private Armed Groups' (2003) 4 CJIL 83, 85–6. In response to 9/11, Jinks argued that the SC 'impliedly endorsed, without expressly authorizing, the use of force against Afghanistan'. See also N Rostow, 'Before and After: The Changed UN Response to Terrorism Since September 11th' (2002) 35 CILJ 475. On the SC's role in combating international terrorism, see CA Ward, 'Building Capacity to Combat International Terrorism: The Role of the United Nations Security Council' (2003) 8 JCSL 289.

[2] But for a variety of views, see TM Franck, *Recourse to Force: State Action against Threats and Armed Attacks* (CUP 2002); JN Maogoto, *Battling Terrorism: Legal Perspectives on the Use of Force and the War on Terror* (Ashgate 2005); N Lubell, *Extraterritorial Use of Force against Non-State Actors* (OUP 2010); L Moir, *Reappraising the Resort to Force: International Law, Jus Ad Bellum and*

force by an aggrieved State, judging that the territorial State had failed to prevent a terrorist excursion emanating from its territory; however, confusion persists in both literature and policy circles as to the permissible, legitimate targets of such responses—State structures and infrastructures versus non-State actors or limited State agents—given that no principled or uniform approach has been articulated by the international community in this regard.[3] This particular aspect of the debate constitutes the crux of the analysis in Part III of this book, which attempts to shed light on the role played by SR repertoire in predicating self-defence and other forcible reactions against global security violations, both from unilateral and multilateral perspectives, within and outwith institutionalized settings.

Whilst this shift in institutional discourse might be perceived as widening the scope of permissible self-defence against non-State actors, its impact on State-to-State relations is not as clear when contemplating the implementation of international legal norms outside the use of force scheme. It is debatable whether post-9/11 SC resolutions operated on the premise that sufficient connections were in place between Al-Qaeda and the government of Afghanistan to (a) legally attribute the 9/11 attacks to that State under SR law, and (b) justify the US-led coalition's military intervention in that country. In the wake of 9/11, there is no question that the US-led reaction equally held both non-State and State actors responsible for failing to prevent, aiding or abetting, or even tolerating terrorism.[4] However, whether this stance amounted predominantly to a *political* claim, as opposed to a normative operation purporting to establish a nexus between Afghanistan's repeated failures to prevent and punish terrorism and its international *legal* responsibility, remains unclear.[5]

Consequently, considerable scholarly emphasis has been placed on the SC's role as *legislator*, that is as creator of primary international legal obligations in the field of counterterrorism.[6] In fact, this strand of scholarship has developed in tandem

the War on Terror (Hart 2011); M Williamson, *Terrorism, War and International Law: The Legality of the Use of Force against Afghanistan in 2001* (Ashgate 2009).

[3] For a comprehensive review of relevant practice, see V-J Proulx, *Transnational Terrorism and State Accountability: A New Theory of Prevention* (Hart 2012) esp ch 2.

[4] Consequently, scholars have addressed issues lying at the intersection of SR, international law, and counterterrorism. See, eg, S Malzahn, 'State Sponsorship and Support of International Terrorism: Customary Norms of State Responsibility' (2002) 26 Hastings International and Comparative Law Review 83; T Becker, *Terrorism and the State: Rethinking the Rules of State Responsibility* (Hart 2006); RP Barnidge, Jr., *Non-State Actors and Terrorism: Applying the Law of State Responsibility and the Due Diligence Principle* (TMC Asser Press 2008); KN Trapp, *State Responsibility for International Terrorism* (OUP 2011).

[5] See, eg, H Duffy, *The 'War on Terror' and the Framework of International Law* (CUP 2005) 55.

[6] See, eg, PC Szasz, 'The Security Council Starts Legislating' (2002) 96 AJIL 901; S Talmon, 'The Security Council as World Legislature' (2005) 99 AJIL 175; I Johnstone, *The Power of Deliberation: International Law, Politics and Organizations* (OUP 2011) 93–105; I Johnstone, 'The Security Council as Legislature' in B Cronin and I Hurd (eds), *The UN Security Council and the Politics of International Authority* (Routledge 2008) 80–104; AE Boyle, 'International Lawmaking: Towards a New Role for the Security Council?' in A Cassese (ed.), *Realizing Utopia: The Future of International Law* (OUP 2012) 172–84; Introduction to Part II. Academic studies also explore the role of the Council as global legislator. See, eg, V Popovski and T Fraser (eds), *The*

with other accounts investigating the activities of IOs within an international legislative space, however defined.[7] For instance, there is no question that the SC, in Resolution 1373, promulgated general and far-reaching counterterrorism duties of prevention and punishment incumbent upon all States, a revolutionary exercise of its powers given that such obligations were not limited to any geographical area or specific time frame. Whilst counterterrorism obligations may be grounded in existing international treaties and multilateral conventions—be they tailored towards prevention, criminalization, or cooperation—this book instead rests its principal line of inquiry on post-9/11 SC action. In short, international treaties may be of limited import given that they corral only a certain number of signatory States and, consequently, may only generate a limited radius of influence and/or 'bindingness'. Conversely, SC pronouncements at the level of primary international legal counterterrorism norms have had a far more pervasive effect. In fact, the SC expressly pointed out that the obligations contained in Resolution 1373 are incumbent upon *all* States, irrespective of their ratification of, or non-membership in, particular conventional schemes. Hence, there is very little doubt that the obligation to prevent terrorism, which is now incumbent upon all States, has attained the status of customary international law and has been consecrated in Resolution 1373 as a stand-alone, autonomous legal obligation.[8]

As will become evident in this chapter, SC resolutions over the last fifteen years have invoked language that is profoundly compatible with SR repertoire, with key instruments prompting the international community to combat terrorism by using 'all steps' and 'all means'. When taken as a whole, several SC counterterrorism resolutions articulate a robust legal framework, thereby imposing categorical primary obligations under international law.[9] In this light, this monograph

Security Council as Global Legislator (Routledge 2014). For a broader but compatible argument, see also DH Joyner, 'The Security Council as a Legal Hegemon' (2012) 43 GJIL 225.

[7] See generally JE Alvarez, *International Organizations as Law-makers* (OUP 2005); I Johnstone, 'Law-Making by International Organizations: Perspectives from International Law/International Relations Theory' in JL Dunoff and MA Pollack (eds), *Interdisciplinary Perspectives on International Law and International Relations: The State of Art* (OUP 2013) 266–92; I Johnstone, 'Law-Making through the Operational Activities of International Organizations' (2008) 40 GWILR 87.

[8] See, eg, P-M Dupuy, 'La Communauté Internationale et le Terrorisme' in SFDI (ed.), *Les Nouvelles Menaces contre la Paix et la Sécurité Internationales* (Pedone 2004) 35, 40; J-C Martin, *Les Règles Internationales Relatives à la Lutte contre le Terrorisme* (Bruylant 2006) 457.

[9] See, eg, UNSC Res 1368 (12 September 2001) UN Doc S/RES/1368 [3] (emphatically prompting all States 'to work together urgently to bring to justice the perpetrators, organizers and sponsors of these terrorist attacks and stress[ing] that those responsible for aiding, supporting or harbouring the perpetrators, organizers and sponsors will be held accountable'); UNSC Res 1373 (28 September 2001) UN Doc S/RES/1373 ('all States shall… [r]efrain from providing any form of support, active or passive, to entities or persons involved in terrorists acts… [d]eny safe haven to those who finance, plan, support, or commit terrorist acts, or provide safe havens' and reaffirming 'the need to combat by all means, in accordance with the Charter of the United Nations, threats to international peace and security caused by terrorists acts'); UNSC Res 1378 (14 November 2001) UN Doc S/RES/1378 (condemning 'the Taliban for allowing Afghanistan to be used as a base for the export of terrorism by the Al-Qaida network and other terrorist groups and for providing safe haven to Usama Bin Laden, Al-Qaida and others associated with them'); UNSC Res 1383 (6 December 2001) UN Doc S/RES/1383; UNSC Res 1386 (20 December 2001) UN Doc S/RES/1386. Other UN organs have also been instrumental—at least on a rhetorical level,

advances a straightforward argument to the effect that these 'steps' or 'means', advocated by the SC, could also include the implementation of States' international responsibility—by the Council itself—for failing to comply with its legally binding pronouncements (ie primary counterterrorism obligations). As will be seen in this chapter, this implementation model might actually prove logical and more effective in certain circumstances, not least as a viable enforcement option when the alternative scenario is unchecked unilateralism, which often entails that a State's response to an internationally wrongful act may be subject to overreaction, disproportionate retaliation, or retribution. This book argues that in such circumstances, the SC's intercession at the post-breach level—that is, after a State failed to comply with its counterterrorism obligations, thereby setting in motion secondary SR norms—might in fact assuage those concerns and provide an attractive avenue for the enforcement of international legal obligations. When falling short of this objective because of political impasses or pressures, the melding of SR language and norms with the SC's deliberative function might nonetheless assist in building constituencies of conscience, all with a view to inducing wrongdoing States to modify their behaviour and/or redress past breaches.

That said, Resolution 1373 warrants special consideration as it constituted a particularly striking example of the SC promulgating far-reaching primary international legal obligations. Even today, there is every indication that it still constitutes the 'most important instrument agreed upon since the 9/11 attacks';[10] its scope, contents, and prescriptions against terrorist activities are exceedingly broad and pervasive, running the whole gamut of direct or overt State involvement in terrorism and indirect or covert support of terrorism. It is only fitting that some commentators have called attention to the inherent compatibility between this line of resolution-making and SR repertoire. One author rightly asserted that 'UN resolution 1373 might be seen as approval of an expanded theory of state responsibility attributing the behaviour of non-state terrorists to a state that knowingly "harbors" terrorists and does not take action to prevent further terrorists attacks'.[11] In sum, the SC thereby emphasized that *all* States shall, inter alia: (i) deny safe havens to individuals and groups who finance, plan, support, or commit terrorist acts, or provide safe havens to terrorists; (ii) prevent those who finance, plan, facilitate, or commit terrorist acts from using their respective territories for carrying out those activities against other States or their nationals; and (iii) prevent the movement of terrorists or terrorist groups by implementing

as evidenced by their institutional dialogue—in consecrating far-reaching counterterrorism duties upon all States. See, eg, UNGA Res 56/1 (12 September 2001) UN Doc A/RES/56/1 ('[u]rgently call[ing] for international cooperation to prevent and eradicate acts of terrorism, and stress[ing] that those responsible for aiding, supporting or harbouring the perpetrators, organizers and sponsors of such acts will be held accountable').

[10] PJ van Krieken (ed.), *Terrorism and the International Legal Order: With Special Reference to the UN, the EU and Cross-Border Aspects* (TMC Asser Press 2002) 5.

[11] JP Kelly, 'The International Law of Force and the Fight against Terrorism' (2003) 21 Delaware Lawyer 18, 19.

effective border controls and controls on issuance of identity papers and travel documents, and by adopting mechanisms to prevent counterfeiting, forgery, or fraudulent use of such documents. Similarly, the SC has very plainly imposed the status of criminalization on a range of conduct related to the perpetration or support of international terrorism, thereby further consecrating the far-reaching, revolutionary scope and effects of Resolution 1373.[12] Furthermore, Resolution 1373 and the counterterrorism apparatus it created impose reporting obligations upon States, in particular as regards the specific criminal measures they have implemented to combat terrorism. On the whole, most States have complied with those undertakings assiduously and transparently, despite some cynical scholarly assessments during the first half-decade following the adoption of that resolution.[13]

Indeed, Resolution 1373 constitutes a salient example of the SC delving into the realm of SR, namely at the primary level of international legal norms, by promulgating specific counterterrorism obligations. As a corollary, this type of exercise of the Council's function no doubt forms part of its new 'legislative' role and decidedly serves 'as one of the most striking examples of both the efficiency and the far reaching bearing of "secondary legislation"'.[14] Simply put, this resolution 'imposes binding obligations on states to take extensive counter-terrorist measures', including 'criminalising "terrorism" and support for it, imposing serious penalties,

[12] See, eg, SC Res 1373 (n 9), calling on all States to

> [*c*]*riminalize* the wilful provision or collection, by any means, directly or indirectly, of funds by their nationals or in their territories with the intention that the funds should be used, or in the knowledge that they are to be used, in order to carry out terrorist acts ... [and] ... [e]nsure that any person who participates in the financing, planning, preparation or perpetration of terrorist acts or in supporting terrorist acts is *brought to justice* and ensure that, in addition to any other measures against them, *such terrorist acts are established as serious criminal offences in domestic laws and regulations and that the punishment duly reflects the seriousness of such terrorist acts* (emphasis added).

In addition to criminalizing the perpetration of terrorism as a direct consequence of Resolution 1373, many States have also legislated a range of preparatory and inchoate offences that contribute to terrorism. See generally H Duffy, *The 'War' on Terror and the Framework of International Law* (2nd edn, CUP 2015) 195 ff esp 207–10.

[13] See country reports submitted to the CTC from 2001 to present, pursuant to UNSC Res 1373 (n 9) and 1624 (14 September 2004) UN Doc S/RES/1624, <http://www.un.org/en/sc/ctc/resources/countryreports.html> accessed 10 August 2015. But see the critique in JE Álvarez, 'Hegemonic International Law Revisited' (2003) 97 AJIL 873, 876 (opining that the reporting requirements had produced 'predictably opportunistic' reports from 'reliable human rights violators, purportedly justifying old and new repressive national measures'). See also Alvarez (n 7) 204–13. In any event, this line of critique concerned itself mostly with the actual content of country reports, and the motivations that drove their preparation, as opposed to the level of States' compliance with their obligations under relevant resolutions.

[14] P-M Dupuy, 'The Law after the Destruction of the Towers' (2001) EJIL Discussion Forum, cited in P Kovács, 'Beaucoup de Questions et Peu de Réponses: Autour de l'Imputabilité d'un Acte Terroriste à un État' (2001) 17 Anuario de Derecho Internacional 39, 47–8. See also generally G Arangio-Ruiz, 'On the Security Council's "Law-Making"' (2000) 83 Rivista di Diritto Internazionale 609. On the Council's 'legislative' role, see S Chesterman, *The UN Security Council and the Rule of Law: The Role of the Security Council in Strengthening a Rules-Based International System: Final Report and Recommendations from the Austrian Initiative, 2004–2008* (Federal Ministry of European and International Affairs 2008) 12. See also generally Szasz (n 6).

freezing assets and excluding 'terrorists' from asylum and refugee protection'.[15] Furthermore, the SC and General Assembly (GA) contributed to bolstering counterterrorism frameworks before and after 9/11, with both UN organs operating within their respective spheres of competence and attempting to link counterterrorism efforts to their singular missions and mandates. The GA adopted several resolutions calling for States to ratify counterterrorism treaties and aiming to bolster international cooperation in the fight against terrorism, as well as condemning as criminal all conduct, methods, and practices amounting to terrorism, irrespective of the time or authorship of the offences in question. For its part, the SC had also underscored the nexus between acts of international terrorism and its primary mandate well before 9/11. For instance, in Resolution 579 (1985) it condemned all acts of hostage-taking and kidnapping; it equated international terrorism with a threat to international peace and security in Resolution 731 (1992), also later reiterating this pronouncement in Resolution 1269 (1999). After the 9/11 attacks, the SC adopted a series of resolutions (eg Resolutions 1368, 1373, 1377 (2001), and 1390 (2002)) condemning international terrorism and equating that practice with one of the most serious threats to international peace and security.

Unsurprisingly, there is growing international interest in the topic of SC action in the field of counterterrorism. The scholarly and policy attention paid to the Council's activities was in large part sparked by that organ's extensive development of novel security frameworks after 9/11, which included the creation of the Counter-Terrorism Committee (CTC), reporting requirements for UN members, and the suggestion by the Council of 'fill-in-as-you-go' template legislations for States.[16] A further case in point illustrating the practical and policy effects of SC engagement in counterterrorism issues resides in the Council's handing down of economic sanctions targeting individuals suspected of entertaining links with Al-Qaeda and the Taliban over the last fifteen years.[17] In this era of ever-increasing

[15] Duffy (n 5) 45. On SC Res 1373 and the impact of its measures, see E Rosand, 'The Security Council As "Global Legislator": Ultra Vires or Ultra Innovative' (2005) 28 FILJ 542, 546–51; I Johnstone, 'Legislation and Adjudication in the UN Security Council: Bringing Down the Deliberative Deficit' (2008) 102 AJIL 275; Proulx ((n 3) ch 4, section V.A); M Happold, 'Security Council Resolution 1373 and the Constitution of the United Nations' (2003) 16 LJIL 593. But see Y Dinstein, 'Terrorism as an International Crime' (1989) 19 IYHR 55, 56–7 (emphasizing, prior to 9/11, that the condemnation of terrorism as 'criminal' was hortatory); B Saul, *Defining Terrorism in International Law* (OUP 2006) 204–5.

[16] For the work and mandate of the CTC, see <http://www.un.org/en/sc/ctc/> accessed 20 August 2015. On the legitimacy of the SC's post-9/11 'legislative' forays and the creation of the CTC, see E Rosand, 'Security Council Resolution 1373, the Counter-Terrorism Committee, and the Fight Against Terrorism' (2003) 97 AJIL 333; CH Powell, 'The United Nations Security Council, Terrorism and the Rule of Law' in VV Ramraj *et al.* (eds), *Global Anti-Terrorism Law and Policy* (2nd edn, CUP 2012) 19–43. Another development, which occurred in parallel with other post-9/11 SC initiatives, bears mention: namely, the creation of the Counter-Terrorism Centre. For its activities and resolutions, see <http://www.un.org/en/terrorism/ctitf/resolutions.shtml> accessed 20 August 2015.

[17] See UNSC Res 1267 (15 October 1999) UN Doc S/RES 1267; UNSC Res 1333 (19 December 2000) UN Doc S/RES 1333; UNSC Res 1363 (30 July 2001) UN Doc S/RES/1363; UNSC Res 1388 (15 January 2002) UN Doc S/RES/1388; UNSC Res 1390 (16 January 2002) UN Doc S/RES/1390; UNSC Res 1452 (20 December 2002) UN Doc S/RES/1452; UNSC Res 1455

global governance and multilateral frameworks, it is not surprising that there has also been renewed interest in identifying accountability mechanisms to monitor and sanction the activities of IOs; this area has not only generated academic commentary but has also propelled to the fore the lessons that may be gleaned from SR repertoire in regulating the conduct of IOs.[18] Other scholars espouse an even more radical vision, basing themselves on individual, judicial, and regional challenges to SC action on counterterrorism issues. In short, these publicists expound the view that States and regional organizations, such as the EU, may mount reviews of, or challenges against, Council counterterrorism resolutions; some even frame potential disobedience of the SC's prescriptions within the law of countermeasures.[19]

Despite these advances, very little scholarly emphasis has been placed on the SC's role as an *implementer* of relevant legal norms in counterterrorism contexts, namely at the second stage of the inquiry when it is time to enforce international legal obligations. The absence of discourse on this front thus leaves us with the vital query whether the SC can apply the law of SR, the mechanism invoked to engage States' legal responsibility for failing to comply with international obligations, devise, and implement legal consequences flowing from its findings of illegality. Moreover, existing literature also fails to elucidate the implications of this debate on potential responses to other global security violations.

Hence, there is a dearth of scholarship dealing with the institutionalization of the implementation of SR and, as will be further explored in Part III, on the role of that normative scheme in justifying recourse to force against States harbouring terrorist organizations and networks. In addition, most relevant contributions on the interplay between SR norms and SC powers are dated and exist in book chapter

(17 January 2003) UN Doc S/RES/1455; UNSC Res 1456 (20 January 2003) UN Doc S/RES/1456; UNSC Res 1526 (30 January 2004) UN Doc S/RES/1526; UNSC Res 1617 (29 July 2005) UN Doc S/RES/1617; UNSC Res 1699 (8 August 2006) UN Doc S/RES/1699; UNSC Res 1730 (19 December 2006) UN Doc S/RES/1730; UNSC Res 1732 (21 December 2006) UN Doc S/RES/1732; UNSC Res 1735 (22 December 2006) UN Doc S/RES 1735.

[18] See, eg, V-J Proulx, 'An Uneasy Transition? Linkages between the Law of State Responsibility and the Law Governing the Responsibility of International Organizations' in M Ragazzi (ed.), *The Responsibility of International Organizations: Essays in Memory of Sir Ian Brownlie* (Nijhoff 2013) 109. On the relationship between the SC and the international rule of law, with special emphasis on accountability, see generally S Chesterman: 'UNaccountable?: The United Nations, Emergency Powers, and the Rule of Law' (2009) 42 VJTL 1509 and 'The Security Council and the Rule of Law' (2009) 103 ASIL Proceedings 245.

[19] Compare S Droubi, *Resisting United Nations Security Council Resolutions* (Routledge 2014); A Tzanakopoulos, *Disobeying the Security Council: Countermeasures against Wrongful Sanctions* (OUP 2011); A Reinisch (ed.), *Challenging Acts of International Organizations Before National Courts* (OUP 2010); A Nollkaemper and E de Wet (eds), *Review of the Security Council by Member States* (Intersentia 2003). See also the following works by A Tzanakopoulos: 'L'Invocation de la Théorie des Contre-mesures en tant que Justification de la Désobéissance au Conseil de Sécurité' (2013) 47 RBDI 78; 'The Countermeasure of Disobedience: Implementing the Responsibilty of International Organizations' in Ragazzi (n 18) 361. See also generally N Angelet, 'Protest against Security Council Decisions' in K Wellens (ed.), *International Law: Theory and Practice: Essays in Honour of Eric Suy* (Nijhoff 1998) 277–85.

or article form only,[20] without tackling the present-day, specific, and challenging problems of global security (with particular insistence on transnational terrorism).[21] In fact, this topic has surprisingly attracted very little scholarly attention.

Consequently, the present chapter examines the largely unexplored role of SR law, if any, in catalysing or informing the SC's exercise of its powers. This analysis will in turn set the stage for Part III of this monograph, which delves into the role that SR can play vis-à-vis the deployment of recourse to force/self-defence between States when faced with global security violations related to terrorism, cyberterrorism, climate change, and ungoverned spaces and territories (eg *terra nullius*, uncontrolled enclaves). The principal objective of this volume, it should be recalled, is to shed light on whether the institutionalization of this normative scheme—SR being absolutely central in public international law—can yield interesting policy pay-offs in responding to global security challenges. This approach obviously entails examining the potential institutionalization of the implementation of SR by relevant UN organs—ie the SC, GA, or ICJ—which is the core focus of Part II. However, the inquiry should not stop there: further scholarly investigation is sorely needed to tease out the role of SR as a legal institution that influences and informs State behaviour outside formal institutionalized settings, be it through the exercise of unilateral self-defence, responsibility to protect (R2P), or other modes of collective action. Indeed, post-9/11 SC counterterrorism policies remain inextricably connected with potential recourse to force: the link between that relationship and SR repertoire will be exposed in Part III.

In the interim, the analytical crux of the discussion that follows will focus on the SC's role in implementing SR. As will be seen in subsequent pages, the Council has also ventured into the realm of secondary SR norms on occasion by attributing wrongful conduct to States following their violations of international law and implementing the legal consequences of those breaches, both quintessential normative operations under SR repertoire.[22] Pre- and post-9/11 SC resolutions

[20] One notable, book-length exception is M Forteau, *Droit de la Sécurité Collective et Droit de la Responsabilité Internationale de l'État* (Pedone 2006).

[21] Important—but dated and/or cursory—contributions include: V Gowlland-Debbas, 'Security Council Enforcement Action and Issues of State Responsibility' (1994) 43 ICLQ 55; V Gowlland-Debbas, 'The Limits of Unilateral Enforcement of Community Objectives in the Framework of UN Peace Maintenance' (2000) 11 EJIL 361; V Gowlland-Debbas, 'The Relationship between the International Court of Justice and the Security Council in the Light of the Lockerbie Case' (1994) 88 AJIL 643; V Gowlland-Debbas, 'The Functions of the United Nations Security Council in the International Legal System' in M Byers (ed.), *The Role of Law in International Politics: Essays in International Relations and International Law* (OUP 2000) 269; MP de Brichambaut, 'The Role of the United Nations Security Council in the International Legal System' in ibid 247; A Nollkaemper, 'Attribution of Forcible Acts to States: Connections Between the Law On the Use of Force and the Law of State Responsibility' in N Blokker and N Schrijver (eds), *The Security Council and the Use of Force: Theory and Reality – A Need for Change?* (Nijhoff 2005) 133; G Gaja, 'Comment: The Impact of Security Council Resolutions on State Responsibility' in G Nolte (ed.), *Peace through International Law: The Role of the International Law Commission: A Colloquium at the Occasion of its Sixtieth Anniversary* (Springer 2009) 53–60; R Higgins, 'The Place of International Law in the Settlement of Disputes by the Security Council' (1970) 64 AJIL 1.

[22] See generally M Bennouna, 'L'Embargo dans la Pratique des Nations Unies: Radioscopie d'un Moyen de Pression' in E Yakpo and T Boumedra (eds), *Liber Amicorum Judge Mohamed Bedjaoui* (Kluwer 1999) 555–83.

constituted salient examples of the Council promulgating primary counterterrorism legal obligations, namely through its 'legislative' function. The Afghanistan precedent was an equally persuasive case study illustrating the Council's role in enforcing secondary SR norms, be it through its political, operational, or executive function. At a minimum, the case for the establishment of Afghanistan's international responsibility in respect of the 9/11 attacks can be made on the basis of repeated SC resolutions condemning the use of its territory as a refuge and training ground for Al-Qaeda factions; in aggregate, these resolutions can be construed at least as de facto attribution of internationally wrongful conduct to that State by the Council.[23] Similar reasoning may be extended to the Council's treatment of Libya's and Sudan's responsibility in the *Lockerbie* scenario and following the assassination attempt against President Mubarak in Ethiopia. These incidents, which are discussed later in this chapter, led some scholars to conclude that the SC attributed SR to those States, at least implicitly.[24]

Whilst not always invoking specific SR language, the Council often devises consequences to international law violations that are compatible, if not synonymous, with the remedial scheme underpinning SR repertoire; the Afghanistan case study is no exception, as is the case with several other precedents canvassed in this chapter. The SC's language reveals that even if one resists the idea of the implementation of Chapter VII objectives being analogous to pure SR logic, the latter regime's corpus of norms is often far from removed from the maintenance of international peace and security; quite to the contrary, SR rules increasingly inform, and seep into, the Council's decision-making, under the umbrella of an ever-expanding concept of global security.[25] After all, Article 33 of the UN Charter affords a large degree of latitude to States in fashioning peaceful dispute settlement options, a framework in which the SC can increasingly play an important role, whilst shifting the collective security rationale from reaction to prevention.[26] Surely the law governing the international responsibility of States

[23] For a compatible line of argument, see A Conte, *Security in the 21st Century* (Ashgate 2005) 48–51; P Kovács, 'Beaucoup de Questions et Peu de Réponses autour de l'Imputabilité d'un Acte Terroriste à un État' (2002) 1 Journal of European Integration Studies 20, 26. For a review of relevant SC resolutions, see Proulx (n 3) 24 fn 71, 31 fn 114, 95 fn 228, 97 fn 244, 103 fns 274 and 276, 109 fn 316, 207 fn 236, 223 fn 320, and accompanying text.

[24] See, eg, Trapp (n 4) 188–9.

[25] See, eg, P-M Dupuy, 'Après la Guerre du Golfe' (1991) 95 RGDIP 621; H Dipla, 'Les Résolutions du Conseil de Sécurité Imposant des Mesures Coercitives et leur Mise en Oeuvre: Quelques Réflexions Concernant la Responsabilité des États' in H Ruiz Fabri *et al.* (eds), *L'Effectivité des Organisations Internationales: Mécanismes de Suivi et de Contrôle* (Pedone 2000) 23, 56–7; P-M Dupuy, 'Quelques Remarques sur l'Évolution de la Pratique des Sanctions Décidées par le Conseil de Sécurité des Nations Unies dans le Cadre du Chapitre VII de la Charte' in V Gowlland-Debbas (ed.), *United Nations Sanctions and International Law* (Kluwer 2001) 47–55.

[26] Charter of the UN (adopted 26 June 1945, entered into force 24 October 1945) as amended by UNGA Resolutions 1991 (XVIII) (17 December 1963) (entered into force 31 August 1965) 557 UNTS 143; 2101 (XX) (20 December 1971) (entered into force 12 June 1968) 638 UNTS 308; and 2847 (XXVI) (20 December 1971) (entered into force 24 September 1973) 892 UNTS 119, Art 33 reads as follows:

1. The parties to any dispute, the continuance of which is likely to endanger the maintenance of international peace and security, shall, first of all, seek a solution by

can fit under the rubric of 'peaceful settlement of disputes', even if it is to be implemented through SC channels in some instances.

Therefore, the ensuing analysis engages with various instances in which the SC has—at least on a de facto basis and sometimes relying on language compatible with SR repertoire—attributed wrongful conduct to a State for the purposes of establishing its international responsibility; devised consequences and measures (commonly termed 'sanctions') that could be seen to be analogous with secondary SR norms; etc. As a corollary, this chapter explores the relationship between SC sanctions and international law.[27] More broadly, in many ways the crux of the argument will investigate the relationship between the SC and international law, albeit in a global security context. Whilst some scholarly attention has been paid to this broader question,[28] my intention will be to show that there is far more reliance on international legal norms and principles by the Council in substantiating its decisions—particularly SR law—than might be expected from a (primarily) political organ of its kind. In setting out this objective, I am inspired by Dame Rosalyn Higgins' prophetic words delivered in her seminal doctoral dissertation over a half-century ago. She observed that whilst the SC 'is likely to state that it is basing itself on the law as it conceives it to be, the line between applying law and legislating it becomes thin; certainly a question of developing law becomes involved'.[29]

This chapter attempts to demonstrate that some SC sanctions could be equated with 'countermeasures' under SR repertoire, or could pursue compatible aims with SR in certain circumstances, a prospect that has generated categorical resistance in some circles.[30] This link will also come into greater focus in Part III of the present work, particularly in relation to the ideas of 'forcible countermeasures' and establishing SR as a predicate for the invocation of self-defence in response to global security violations. At the outset, it should be stressed that some commentators

negotiation, enquiry, mediation, conciliation, arbitration, judicial settlement, resort to regional agencies or arrangements, or other peaceful means of their own choice.

2. The Security Council shall, when it deems necessary, call upon the parties to settle their dispute by such means.

On the broader point, see F Orrego Vicuña, 'The Settlement of Disputes and Conflict Resolution in the Context of a Revitalized Role for the United Nations Security Council' in R-J Dupuy (ed.), *The Development of the Role of the Security Council: Peace-Keeping and Peace-Building* (Nijhoff 1993) 41–9.

[27] See also V Gowlland-Debbas, 'UN Sanctions and International Law: An Overview' in ibid (n 25) 5–12.

[28] See, eg, C Eick, 'The UN Security Council and International Law in 2012' (2012) 55 GYIL 537; I Johnstone, 'The Security Council and International Law' in S von Einsiedel *et al.* (eds), *The UN Security Council: From the Cold War to the 21st Century* (2nd edn, Lynne Rienner 2015) 771; SR Ratner, 'The Security Council and International Law' in D Malone (ed.), *The UN Security Council: From the Cold War to the 21st Century* (Lynne Rienner 2004) 592; A Prandler, 'The Security Council and International Law' (1974) 16 Acta Iuridica Acdemiae Scientiarum Hungariae 177.

[29] R Higgins, *The Development of International Law through the Political Organs of the United Nations* (OUP 1963) 5.

[30] See, eg, D Alland, 'The Definition of Countermeasures' in JR Crawford *et al.* (eds), *The Law of International Responsibility* (OUP 2010) 1127, 1135.

persuasively argue that a functional analogy exists between countermeasures and sanctions, whilst others label SC sanctions 'collective countermeasures'.[31] These approaches will ineluctably inform the analysis that follows. More immediately, I will seek to establish that some sanctions adopted by the SC in the global security context could be considered to be specific manifestations of secondary SR rules, such as the obligation of cessation, assurances/guarantees of non-repetition, and satisfaction.[32] Therefore, building on the conclusions presented in Chapter 3, which clearly point to the SC as a potential alternate avenue for implementing SR in the face of global security breaches, the project now turns to the task of elucidating the sophisticated interplay between the Council and SR rules. The thrust of the inquiry will hinge on the exploration of several key aspects of international legal discourse pertaining to SR and international relations, primarily by addressing the following three broad themes.

First, the chapter will canvass the SC's practice and the scope of its powers, more specifically by delving into Chapter VII powers, which enables it to maintain international peace and security and authorize recourse to force, with particular emphasis on Article 39 of the UN Charter.[33] This will also entail gauging relevant scholarly perception and critiques of SC practice, both before and after 9/11. In so doing, my intention will be to circumscribe, to the extent possible, the Council's role in the determination of States' international responsibility and surrounding issues in global security contexts. Whilst the range of global security challenges addressed in Chapter 2 should always be borne in mind, the principal case study of transnational terrorism will remain paramount in testing and calibrating potential enforcement models involving the SC, always with a view to identifying best practices that may be extended to other global security breaches.

Secondly, this chapter critically analyses the interplay between the SC and the implementation of SR, which will invariably entail contemplating the expansion of Chapter VII powers to include that normative scheme. More specifically, this line of inquiry will also include an examination of the Council's powers in relation to secondary SR norms. Conversely, a fair and balanced analysis also warrants that consideration be given to determining the rights of States vis-à-vis the implementation of responsibility, notwithstanding SC involvement.

[31] Compare Tzanakopoulos, *Disobeying* (n 19) 76–9 with L Boisson de Chazournes: 'Economic Countermeasures in an Interdependent World' (1995) 89 ASIL Proceedings 337 and *Les Contre-Mesures dans les Relations Internationales Économiques* (Pedone 1992). See also A Tzanakopoulos, 'Explainer: How Will Sanctions against Russia Work?' (31 July 2014) *The Conversation* <https://theconversation.com/explainer-how-will-sanctions-against-russia-work-29920> accessed 30 May 2015; R Bismuth, 'Odyssé dans le Conundrum des Réactions Décentralisées à l'Illicite' (2014) 141 Journal du Droit international 719.

[32] On these concepts, see JR Crawford, *State Responsibility: The General Part* (CUP 2013) 459–79.

[33] UN Charter (n 26) Art 39 reads as follows:

> The Security Council shall determine the existence of any threat to the peace, breach of the peace, or act of aggression and shall make recommendations, or decide what measures shall be taken in accordance with Articles 41 and 42, to maintain or restore international peace and security.

Thirdly, the chapter will address the interrelationship between the SC and counterterrorism in the global security scheme. The resulting scholarly investigation will seek to identify the extent and boundaries of Council practice with regard specifically to terrorism and SR. Furthermore, it will also attempt—when necessary and as already done in previous chapters in respect of other UN organs—to situate comparative and international policy-making in relation to SC involvement in counterterrorism. Finally, the discussion will ultimately move towards the recognition of an overlap of objectives under the *sui generis* rubric of counterterrorism and the Council's mandate, so as to buttress the rapprochement between this mandate and SR repertoire in the context of global security. Before delving into the principal line of argument, however, a brief and critical review of fundamental concepts and potential obstacles to the monograph's central claim seems apposite.

4.2 The Relationship between the Council and State Responsibility Norms: Countermeasures, Reciprocity, and International Law

Simply put, this chapter's central claim, and its chances of acquiring credence in policy circles, will depend to a large extent on creative analogies and rapprochements between two seemingly insulated regimes: the SC's mandate to maintain or restore international peace and security as governed by the UN Charter, on the one hand, and SR law as regulated by customary international law and codified in part in the Articles on Responsibility of States for Internationally Wrongful Acts (ARSIWA),[34] on the other. Much has already been written on the SC's power to adopt sanctions,[35] which it can direct at States, groups, or individuals. In addition to its powers to establish peacekeeping operations and authorize military action through its resolutions, the SC can also devise diplomatic, economic, military, and sports sanctions in fulfilling its mandate of maintaining and/or restoring international peace and security. In many ways, therefore, this type of enforcement mechanism is perceived as a 'centralized' model, given that the decision-making and operational commands are concentrated within the international community's foremost, multilateral organ responsible for the maintenance of

[34] Articles on the Responsibility of States for Internationally Wrongful Acts, UN Doc A/56/10 (2001); (2001) II(2) *YILC* 26 (and Commentary ibid 31).

[35] See, eg, L Cavaré, 'Les Sanctions dans le Cadre de l'O.N.U.' (1952) 80 RdC 191; G Hakimdavar, *A Strategic Understanding of UN Economic Sanctions: International Relations, Law, and Development* (Routledge 2013); A Charron, *UN Sanctions and Conflict: Responding to Peace and Security Threats* (Routledge 2011); J Farrall and K Rubenstein, *Sanctions, Accountability and Governance in a Globalised World* (CUP 2009); J Farrall, *United Nations Sanctions and the Rule of Law* (CUP 2007); HC von Sponeck, *A Different Kind of War: The UN Sanctions Regime in Iraq* (Berghahn 2006); Gowlland-Debbas (n 25); NJ Schrijver, *The Use of Economic Sanctions by the UN Security Council: An International Law Perspective* (University of Groningen 1993); DL Bethlehem, *The Kuwait Crisis: Sanctions and their Economic Consequences* (Grotius 1991).

international peace and security. Consequently, the Council's decision-making on all sanction matters will remain subject to its multilateral process, which may bring about institutional paralysis or political impasses and challenges given its very nature and makeup.

4.2.1 Inter-State implementation mechanisms: Countermeasures as the classic remedy

By contrast, the law governing the international responsibility of States is animated by an altogether different enforcement logic, at least upon first glance. In codifying SR principles in the ARSIWA, the ILC essentially relegated to inter-State (read: fairly unilateral) devices the tasks of ascertaining breaches of international obligations and devising legal consequences for those violations.[36] As a corollary, as discussed earlier in Section 1.2.2 and will be seen in greater detail in Part III, this codification project inexorably suggests some level of self-judging and autoqualification by injured States, which in turn inform the application of secondary norms of responsibility by those same entities, within the context of often disparate, loosely coordinated, and sometimes asymmetric diplomatic relations. Interestingly, over the last half-century or so, leading neo-liberal and structural realist commentators have called attention to the intersection of international law and politics, in particular by describing the latter field as 'a competition of units in the kind of state of nature that knows no restraints other than those which the changing necessities of the game and the shallow convenience of the players impose'.[37] This realization prompted those scholars to depict the world community as 'anarchic in the sense that it lacks an authoritative government that can enact and enforce rules of behaviour'.[38] Consequently, the argument goes, States are left to rely on 'the means they can generate and the arrangements they can make for themselves'.[39] Thus, inevitably '[c]onflict and war result, since each state is judge in its own cause and can use force to carry out its judgments'.[40] This logic certainly permeates both the law governing the international responsibility of States and the ARSIWA, with the exception that armed reprisals—or the use of force by an injured State to enforce its own 'judgments'—have been expressly proscribed by the international community.[41]

In short, general international law provides that once a primary norm has been violated, that is, an internationally wrongful act is committed—for present purposes, let us assume, by way of example, that State A has supported, armed, and

[36] See also Proulx (n 3) 317 ff.

[37] SH Hoffmann, *The State of War: Essays on the Theory and Practice of International Politics* (Pall Mall Press 1965) vii.

[38] RO Keohane, *After Hegemony: Cooperation and Discord in the World Political Economy* (Princeton University Press 1984) 7.

[39] K Waltz, *Theory of International Politics* (McGraw-Hill 1979) 111.

[40] Keohane (n 38) 7. See also KN Waltz, *Man, the State and War* (Columbia University Press 1959) 159.

[41] See Section 6.2.1.

funded terrorists who launched an attack in the territory of State B—SR repertoire sets in motion the application of secondary rules. As a result, State B can then devise legal consequences vis-à-vis State A (ie apply secondary SR rules) in order to induce the wrongdoing State to comply with its counterterrorism obligations or redress the initial breach. Indeed, ARSIWA Article 28 provides that '[t]he international responsibility of a State which is entailed by an internationally wrongful act in accordance with the provisions of part one [of ARSIWA] involves legal consequences as set out in this part'.[42] Of course, similar reasoning can extend to other global security violations discussed in Chapter 2, particularly in the field of international environmental law, which provides a solid basis for drawing analogies to inform SR law in counterterrorism contexts.[43] At their core, these secondary rules—that is, legal consequences—essentially embody a range of remedial measures which include restitution and compensation for the injury suffered, assurances and guarantees of non-repetition, satisfaction (which may be assimilated to an apology), and so on. The more controversial concept of 'countermeasure' also resides within that corpus of secondary SR norms, although Chapter 1 demonstrated that the rigid conceptual barrier erected by the ILC between primary and secondary norms is not always impenetrable; in fact, it has been argued that it is precisely within Chapter II of the ARSIWA, which governs the adoption of countermeasures, that the Commission has engaged most prominently in 'legislating' primary rules of international law.[44] It should be emphasized that the ICJ, arbitral bodies, and the World Trade Organization (WTO) have all discussed central aspects of the law of countermeasures.[45] Furthermore, the ILC itself has devoted considerable time and energy to the topic.[46]

ARSIWA Article 49(1), which circumscribes the object and limits of countermeasures under SR repertoire, provides that '[a]n injured State may only take countermeasures against a State which is responsible for an internationally wrongful act in order to induce that State to comply with its obligations'.[47] The provision goes on to clarify that '[c]ountermeasures are limited to the non-performance for the time being of international obligations of the State taking the measures towards

[42] ARSIWA (n 34) Art 28.

[43] See generally HB Sverrisson, *Countermeasures, the International Legal System, and Environmental Violations: When Two Wrongs Make a Right for the Environment* (Cambria Press 2008).

[44] See Section 1.2 and authorities cited therein.

[45] See, eg, *Case Concerning the Air Services Agreement of 27 March 1946 (US v France)* (1978) 18 RIAA 416 [83], [90]; *Gabčíkovo-Nagymaros Project (Hungary/Slovakia)* (Merits) [1997] ICJ Rep 7, 55–7 [82]–[87]; WTO, *European Communities: Regime for the Importation, Sale and Distribution of Bananas—Recourse to Arbitration by the European Communities Under Article 22.6 of the DSU—Decision by the Arbitrators* (9 April 1999) WT/DS27/ARB, esp [6.3], [6.16]. For academic discussion, see generally K Doehring, 'The Unilateral Enforcement of International Law by Exercising Reprisals' in R StJ Macdonald (ed.), *Essays in Honor of Wang Tieya* (Nijhoff 1994) 235–42, 235–6; E Zoller, *Peacetime Unilateral Remedies: An Analysis of Countermeasures* (Transnational Publishers 1984); E-U Petersmann, *The GATT/WTO Dispute Settlement System: International Law, International Organizations, and Dispute Settlement* (Kluwer 1997).

[46] See, eg, ILC, 'International Law Commission, Report of the Work of its 52nd Session' (1 May–18 August 2000) UN Doc A/55/10; (2000) II(2) *YILC* 50–64 [290]–[405].

[47] ARSIWA (n 34) Art 49(1).

the responsible State', and that they 'shall, as far as possible, be taken in such a way as to permit the resumption of performance of the obligations in question'.[48] Simply put, under extant international law responsibility flowing from an internationally wrongful act committed by a State is typically actuated, and ultimately implemented, though inter-State mechanisms. This means that a State that has been wronged—or 'injured' to invoke ILC parlance—by a violation of international law committed by another State can unilaterally adopt countermeasures to compel the responsible State to comply with its obligation or repair its initial violation. As mentioned earlier, in practice this type of enforcement takes place in the context of disparate and sometimes asymmetrical diplomatic relations, although it need not be so; indeed, the central argument of this chapter is that the SC's implementation of States' responsibility can be a viable option and an attractive alternative to unchecked, unilateral enforcement of international obligations by States. As a corollary, the injured State seeking to enforce international law against the responsible State possesses a large degree of latitude in devising unilateral countermeasures, in autoqualifying the different aspects of the dispute, and ultimately, in self-judging the violation of international law it suffered and its consequences.[49]

Ironically, countermeasures essentially boil down to the suspension of the performance of an international obligation by one State to induce compliance with an international obligation by another State. A cynical view of the international legal order might cast this mechanism as 'using illegality to fight illegality'; however, the former type of illegality is tolerated within the international legal system.[50] I have written elsewhere that the law of countermeasures epitomizes one of the many ways in which public international law seeks to adapt to the anarchical structure of the international community; by contrast, others invoke far more cautious language, calling that normative scheme 'a law of coexistence'.[51] That said, there is no question that countermeasures constitute a quintessential encapsulation of 'self-help' remedies under international law. Irrespective of the characterization ultimately espoused regarding countermeasures, it is not difficult to envisage countless scenarios in which, for political or practical reasons, enforcement of international obligations by way of countermeasures would simply not yield results. So what happens then? That is the principal query of this chapter: it will be argued that, inherent in the debate of whether SR can play a role in the suppression and prevention of terrorism—and, by extension, in respect of other global security risks—is the idea of institutionalizing the implementation of SR. Put another way, how are international obligations enforced and SR ultimately

[48] ARSIWA (n 34) Art 49(2)(3). See also Commentary ibid 130–1.

[49] On autoqualification and self-judging in SR law, with particular emphasis on counterterrorism and the global security context, see Section 1.2.2. See also Proulx ((n 3) ch 3, section III.A).

[50] See, eg, *Air Services Agreement Case* (n 45) [83] (defining countermeasures as 'contrary to international law but justified by a violation of international law allegedly committed by the State against which they are directed').

[51] Compare Proulx (n 3) 253; P-M Dupuy, 'State Sponsors of Terrorism: Issues of International Responsibility' in A Bianchi (ed.), *Enforcing International Law Norms against Terrorism* (Hart 2004) 3, 15.

implemented when unilateralism is not a viable option? For reasons canvassed earlier,[52] and despite the potential contributions of other UN organs, international/regional courts and bodies to this debate, this work has elected the SC as a vehicle to implement SR in global security contexts; a sort of system of coordination to monitor and ultimately sanction violations of international law.

However, injured States do not dispose of an unfettered margin of discretion in adopting countermeasures in response to violations of international law. Indeed, any countermeasure pursued under SR repertoire is subject to the concept of proportionality, a criterion that has been affirmed in international jurisprudence.[53] What is more, ARSIWA Article 51 clearly codifies this principle and other relevant considerations in the following terms, as a sort of overarching substantive requirement for the adoption of countermeasures: '[c]ountermeasures must be commensurate with the injury suffered, taking into account the gravity of the internationally wrongful act and the rights in question'.[54] Similarly, the ILC Commentary specifies that this provision 'establishes an essential limit on the taking of countermeasures by an injured State... based on considerations of proportionality'; that '[p]roportionality provides a measure of assurance inasmuch as disproportionate countermeasures could give rise to responsibility on the part of the State taking such measures'; and that '[p]roportionality is concerned with the relationship between the internationally wrongful act and the countermeasure'.[55] Indeed, an injured State that adopts disproportionate countermeasures may ultimately trigger its own international responsibility, depending on the circumstances of the particular case. Interestingly, influential scholars have suggested a rapprochement between SR repertoire and UN organs by pointing out that SC action should remain subject to the core tenets of countermeasures norms, particularly the principle of proportionality.[56]

Aside from the requirement of proportionality, the resort to countermeasures is also governed by several procedural conditions, including: the duty of the injured State to call upon the responsible State to fulfil its obligations; the injured State's duty to notify the responsible State of any decision to take countermeasures, which should be accompanied by an offer to negotiate although this obligation does not preclude the injured State's right to devise urgent countermeasures necessary to preserve its rights.[57] Moreover, the ARSIWA provide that countermeasures

[52] See Introduction to Part II; ch 3.

[53] See generally *Gabčíkovo-Nagymaros Project Case* (n 45) [85]; *Air Services Agreement Case* (n 45) [83], [90]. For academic support, see C Antonopoulos, *The Unilateral Use of Force by States in International Law* (Sakkoulas 1997) 319–20; R O'Keefe, 'Proportionality' in Crawford *et al.* (n 30) 1157–68. For a general discussion, see E Cannizzaro, 'The Role of Proportionality in the Law of International Countermeasures' (2001) 12 EJIL 889.

[54] ARSIWA (n 34) Art 51. See also JR Crawford, 'The Relationship between Sanctions and Countermeasures' in Gowlland-Debbas (n 25) 57.

[55] Commentary to ARSIWA (n 34) Art 51 pp 134–5.

[56] See, eg, FL Kirgis, Jr, 'The Security Council's First Fifty Years' (1995) 89 AJIL 506, 517, fn 87; M Bothe, 'Les Limites des Pouvoirs du Conseil de Sécurité' in Dupuy (n 26) 69–70; Gowlland-Debbas, 'Security' (n 21) 91; ME O'Connell, 'Debating the Law of Sanctions' (2002) 13 EJIL 63, 75.

[57] ARSIWA (n 34) Art 52(1)(2).

cannot be resorted to, or must be suspended if already taken, in the event that 'the internationally wrongful act has ceased' and 'the dispute is pending before a court or tribunal which has the authority to make decisions binding on the parties'.[58] Finally, general international law dictates that '[c]ountermeasures shall be terminated as soon as the responsible State has complied with its obligations ... in relation to the internationally wrongful act'.[59]

In counterterrorism contexts, one may invoke a scenario where a State cannot efficiently thwart terrorist excursions emanating from its territory; in actuality, that State may not have effective counterterrorism structures in place, or may have lost control over a portion of its territory where terrorist bases are located, or may engage in tactical self-restraint or acquiescence when failing to repress the threat, or may earnestly attempt to quell the terrorist activities but remain unable to do so effectively. Real examples running the whole gradient from direct State involvement to inaction—that is, from overt State control to passive toleration—can be associated with various States:[60] they include Lebanon's harbouring of armed Hezbollah factions on its territory in contravention of binding SC resolutions; Yemen's failure to control the Abyan, Ma'rib, and Shabwa governorates where extremist elements are present; Pakistan's mixed model of tolerance of terrorism and alliance with the US in the global struggle against terror, resulting in large portions of its territory being occupied by the Taliban, Al-Qaeda members, and other extremist factions; Somalia's failure to control large swathes of its territory where Harakat al-Shabaab al-Mujahideen extremists congregate and carry out preparatory activities; Ecuador's failure to prevent repeated strikes carried out by the Revolutionary Armed Forces of Colombia (FARC) from its territory against Colombian civilians and security forces, and have been thoroughly canvassed through the prism of SR elsewhere.[61]

In cases where a sanctuary State is unable to thwart or repress terrorist groups operating on its territory effectively, and/or refuses to prosecute or extradite the concerned individuals, circumstances may nonetheless (and often) dictate that an all-out military conflict or invasion would amount to a disproportionate countermeasure. Moreover, as discussed in Part III of this book, the ARSIWA prohibit forcible countermeasures although that assertion is open to challenge in the light of contemporaneous State practice, and a strong case can be made for the existence of a *lex specialis* permitting forcible countermeasures in certain circumstances (particularly in counterterrorism contexts and perhaps also in response to other global security violations). In the scenario invoked earlier, the host-State has failed to exercise its sovereignty responsibly; it may even be argued, depending

[58] ARSIWA (n 34) Art 52(3). Art 52(4) further provides that the obligation not to take countermeasures, or to suspend them, enshrined in Art 52(3) 'does not apply if the responsible State fails to implement the dispute settlement procedures in good faith'.

[59] ARSIWA (n 34) Art 53.

[60] On the gradation of State involvement in terrorism, compare the typologies discussed in Section 2.2.

[61] See generally Proulx (n 3).

on the particular facts, that it has become incapacitated, hence unable to actually exercise its sovereignty or, at least, that it is exercising it in a manner that is deeply antipodal to the obligation of non-intervention in the affairs of other Member States under the UN Charter.[62]

In such a scenario, it would be reasonable to deploy a limited amount of police forces, originating from the injured State for example, into the territory of the responsible State, which refuses to prosecute or extradite, in order to capture a terrorist or group of terrorists. Such limited law enforcement incursions may be a viable way to enforce conventional or customary counterterrorism obligations and amount to proportionate countermeasures.[63] After all, the obligation of States to acquire counterterrorism capacity building is part and parcel of the legal and security framework laid down by SC Resolution 1373;[64] in fact, some commentators even posit that in such scenarios, a State that is unable to prevent terrorist threats originating in its territory should accept outside help or, perhaps, seek it out. That State's unwillingness to accept such assistance would concomitantly signal its failure to comply with its counterterrorism obligations and could amount to a violation of international law, pursuant to SR law.[65] Whilst not directly apropos, the situation that arose in Mali in 2013—and the response to it—provided some degree of support for such a construction of proportionate countermeasures.[66] On 10 January 2013, terrorist extremists and armed groups launched attacks in the south of Mali, which the SC strongly condemned. The Council also noted with concern the ongoing activities in the north of Mali and Sahel region of terrorist groups, including Al-Qaeda in the Islamic Maghreb (AQIM), Ansar Eddine, the Movement for Unity and Jihad in West Africa (MUJAO), and Al Mourabitoune.

[62] Interestingly, Hersch Lauterpacht opined that 'the traditional respect for State sovereignty refrained the development of the law of international responsibility, particularly regarding consequences of responsibility'. See AA Cançado Trindade, 'Complementarity between State Responsibility and Individual Responsibility for Grave Violations of Human Rights: The Crime of State Revisited' in M Ragazzi (ed.), *International Responsibility Today: Essays in Memory of Oscar Schachter* (Brill 2005) 253, 261. See also H Lauterpacht, 'Règles Générales du Droit de la Paix' (1937) 62 RdC 95, 339, 349–52. On the nexus between the principle of non-intervention in the affairs of sovereign States and SC action, see N Tsagourias, 'Security Council Legislation, Article 2(7) of the UN Charter, and the Principle of Subsidiarity' (2011) 24 LJIL 539.

[63] See Martin (n 8) 493; Proulx (n 3) 98–9. However, A Cassese, *International Law* (OUP 2001) 305 recalled that 'the victim of aggression must not occupy the aggressor's territory, unless strictly required by the need to hold the aggressor in check and prevent him from continuing the aggression by other means'. For instance, during the 1982 Israel–Lebanon conflict, the three-month and a half invasion of Lebanon by Israel in response to PLO terrorist attacks being launched from Lebanese territory was largely perceived as disproportionate. On the Israel–Lebanon conflict, see V-J Proulx 'Babysitting Terrorists: Should States Be Strictly Liable for Failing to Prevent Transborder Attacks?' (2005) 23 BJIL 615, 632.

[64] See, eg, N Quénivet, 'You Are the Weakest Link and We Will Help You! The Comprehensive Strategy of the United Nations to Fight Terrorism' (2006) 11 JCSL 371, 390–91; Becker (n 4) 144–6.

[65] See, eg, KN Trapp, 'Back to Basics: Necessity, Proportionality, and the Right of Self-Defence against Non-State Terrorist Actors' (2007) 56 ICLQ 141, 147 fn 33; Nollkaemper (n 21) 161.

[66] On the aftermath of terrorist activities in Mali, see R Van Steenberghe, 'Les Interventions Française et Africaine au Mali au Nom de la Lutte Armée contre le Terrorisme' (2014) 118 RGDIP 273.

In attempting to contain such threats, the Malian State sought external assistance from France, an initiative for which the SC commended it in Resolutions 2100 and 2164.[67]

4.2.2 The limits of reciprocity: Moving away from decentralized and unilateral remedies

Setting aside self-help remedies and unilateral countermeasures, this chapter focuses on the question whether SR for failing to prevent terrorist attacks could be implemented by the SC. It advocates this line of thinking on the basis of an unabashed, policy-driven argument: the international community must conceive of alternate methods of implementing SR if it is truly to empower the obligation of prevention and suppress terrorism using, as the SC puts it in Resolution 1373, 'all means, in accordance with the Charter of the United Nations'. This line of argument may be transposable integrally to other global security threats, as seen in Chapter 2. Surely, 'all means' must include one of the most central and fundamental components of public international law, namely SR repertoire, especially in light of the fact that the international rule of law remains the linchpin of the UN Charter.[68] Moreover, for reasons discussed later in this chapter, there is no principled reason to exclude the application of this normative scheme from the SC's mandate, particularly when faced with pressing, and potentially global, security risks. In fact, the SC has expanded its enforcement function to provide dispositive settlements of discrete legal disputes involving questions of extradition, frontier demarcations, and post-invasion SR, in which international legal principles played a determinant role.[69] In those instances, the SC is effectively 'using the law to enforce the law'.[70]

Undoubtedly, many matters involving the application of SR principles are well suited for formal judicial adjudication. Thus, whenever possible, disputing States should submit their disagreements to the jurisdiction of the ICJ for settlement. After all, the Manila Declaration on the Peaceful Settlement of International Disputes underscores that the submission of a dispute to the ICJ by one State should not

[67] In UNSC Res 2100 (25 April 2013) UN Doc S/RES/2100, the Council welcomed

> the swift action by the French forces, at the request of the transitional authorities of Mali, to stop the offensive of terrorist, extremist and armed groups towards the south of Mali and commend[ed] the efforts to restore the territorial integrity of Mali by the Malian Defence and Security Forces, with the support of French forces and the troops of the African-led International Support Mission in Mali (AFISMA).

See also UNSC Res 2164 (25 June 2014) UN Doc S/RES/2164 ('[w]elcoming the continued action by the French forces, at the request of the Malian authorities, to deter the terrorist threat in the North of Mali').

[68] See generally HE Judge Peter Tomka, President of the ICJ, 'The Rule of Law and the Role of the International Court of Justice in World Affairs', Inaugural Hilding Eek Memorial Lecture, Stockholm Centre for International Law and Justice, Stockholm University (2 December 2013) <http://www.icj-cij.org/presscom/files/8/17848.pdf> accessed 30 June 2015.

[69] See generally Alvarez (n 7) 193. [70] Ratner (n 28) 601–2.

be perceived as an 'unfriendly' act by the respondent State.[71] However, as seen in Chapter 3, this prospect is severely limited, both for jurisdictional and political reasons. Since there is no compulsory judicial recourse to implement SR under international law, there is every indication that the *sine qua non* means of enforcement outside the judicial context resides in the concept of reciprocity. At least, this has proven to be a recurrent mantra in classical SR literature.[72] In fact, there is little doubt that the concept of reciprocity underpins much of the rationale and vision underpinning the ARSIWA. One might add that reciprocity—or the fear of incurring international responsibility by States, should they violate international law—might in fact help neutralize asymmetrical power dynamics in the global order and induce governments to comply with their international obligations.

In sum, according to this theory of compliance States observe their obligations because they expect the same behaviour from other States. This encapsulation of the 'do unto others as you would have them do unto you' principle has long been the subject of scholarly discussion, quite extensively in the fields of human rights and international humanitarian law (IHL),[73] but it has also captured the interest of a wide range of experts. Hence, it is not uncommon to see the concept of reciprocity dissected or analysed by international judges,[74] international legal scholars,[75] neo-liberal institutional political scientists,[76] international relations scholars,[77] and philosophers.[78] Furthermore, the notion of reciprocity has been explored in a

[71] Manila Declaration on the Peaceful Settlement of International Disputes, UNGA Res 37/10 (15 November 1982) UN Doc A/RES/37/10, Annex.

[72] On the role of reciprocity and other rationalist elements in SR law in the global counterterrorism context, see Proulx ((n 3) ch 1 section I; ch 4 section V.B; ch 5 section III.A). For a recent book-length account on reciprocity, including an assessment of the relationship between that concept and equality between States, see SN Fard, *Reciprocity in International Law: Its Impact and Function* (Routledge 2016).

[73] On the concept of reciprocity in these fields, see R Provost, *International Human Rights and Humanitarian Law* (CUP 2002) 121–238; 'Reciprocity in Human Rights and Humanitarian Law' (1995) 65 BYIL 383.

[74] On the importance of reciprocity in the application and development of international law, see Separate Opinion of Judge Simma in *Application of the Interim Accord of 13 September 1995 (the former Yugoslav Republic of Macedonia v Greece)* (Merits) [2011] ICJ Rep 644, 699 [10].

[75] J Brunnée and SJ Toope, 'Persuasion and Enforcement: Explaining Compliance with International Law' (2002) 13 FYIL 273, 279 ('[f]or some, reciprocity or reciprocal advantage, quintessentially rationalist concepts, lie at the root of legal obligation'); R Higgins, *Problems & Process: International Law and How We Use It* (OUP 1994) 16 ('consensus comes about because states perceive a reciprocal advantage in cautioning self-restraint'). See also M Koskenniemi, *From Apology to Utopia: The Structure of International Legal Argument* (Lakimiesliiton Kustannus 1989) 74; A Watts, 'The International Rule of Law' (1993) 36 GYIL 15, 41; JS Watson, 'A Realistic Jurisprudence of International Law' (1980) 30 Year Book of World Affairs 265, 283.

[76] Keohane (n 38) 214 (expounding that reciprocity 'seems to be the most effective strategy for maintaining cooperation among egoists').

[77] On the role of reciprocity in international relations see generally RO Keohane, 'Reciprocity in International Relations' (1986) 40 IO 1 and 'Reciprocity in International Relations' in S Chan and C Moore (eds), *Theories of International Relations*, vol 2 (Sage 2006) 228–53; DW Larson, 'The Psychology of Reciprocity in International Relations' (1988) 4 Negotiation Journal: On the Process of Dispute Settlement 281.

[78] Although not directly on point, consider D Hume, F Watkins (ed.), *Theory of Politics* (Nelson 1951) 119.

variety of contexts, often in connection with the global struggle against terrorism, thereby prompting various commentators to emphasize the increasing importance of reciprocity throughout different eras, including by highlighting its role in international relations among allies in the fight against terrorism (eg US–Pakistan);[79] assess its role in the context of the laws of war, with particular insistence on international relations theory;[80] determine its potential impact on the prohibition against torture;[81] ascertain its broader impact within the *jus ad bellum* scheme;[82] critically review its failure in the context of transnational legal process and rights-based discourse;[83] or adopt a more cynical posture vis-à-vis reciprocity by calling into question its application in counterterrorism contexts.[84]

Some international legal scholars pursue the analysis of reciprocity even further, perhaps to its breaking point according to some, by investigating that principle through the prism of the eventual recognition of full equality between States. In that context, they surmise, the notion of reciprocity becomes systematized, which signals 'that reciprocity moves from a bilateral to a systemic level, whereby the state accepts to bear an obligation on the basis of a legitimate expectation that the system will generally ensure the imposition of similar or corresponding obligations on all members of the system'.[85] However, this view must be balanced by the wise words of caution offered by Bruno Simma when analysing the notion of reciprocity though a strictly unilateral lens: '[t]o unilaterally submit the fulfilment of existing international obligations to the requirement of reciprocity is illegal and entails international responsibility'.[86] Granted, 'systematized' reciprocity may work and generate desirable governmental incentives,

[79] See, eg, RO Keohane, 'The Public Delegitimation of Terrorism and Coalition Politics' in K Booth and T Dunne (eds), *Worlds in Collision: Terror and the Future of Global Order* (Palgrave 2002) 141, 143. See also generally DW Larson, 'Exchange and Reciprocity in International Negotiations' (1998) 3 International Negotiation 121, 127; DA Baldwin, *Economic Statecraft* (Princeton University Press 1985) 292–4.

[80] See, eg, KW Abbott, 'International Relations Theory, International Law, and the Regime Governing Atrocities in International Conflicts' (1999) 93 AJIL 361, 369; JL Dunoff and JP Trachtman, 'The Law and Economics of Humanitarian Law Violations in Internal Conflict' (1999) 93 AJIL 394, 403.

[81] See, eg, P Sands, *Lawless World: America and the Making and Breaking of Global Rules* (Penguin 2005) 205.

[82] See, eg, Abbott (n 80) 370; Dunoff and Trachtman (n 80) 403; RA Falk, 'What Future for the UN Charter System of War Prevention?' (2003) 97 AJIL 590, 594.

[83] See, eg, HH Koh, 'Jefferson Memorial Lecture Transnational Legal Process after September 11th' (2004) 22 BJIL 337, 348–9; V-J Proulx, 'If the Hat Fits, Wear It, If the Turban Fits, Run for your Life: Reflections on the Indefinite Detention and Targeted Killing of Suspected Terrorists' (2005) 56 Hastings Law Journal 801, 812, 853, 857, 886; Sands (n 81) 21–2.

[84] On the non-applicability of reciprocity to terrorists, see R Provost, 'Asymmetrical Reciprocity and Compliance with the Laws of War' in B Perrin (ed.), *Modern Warfare: Armed Groups, Private Militaries, Humanitarian Organizations, and the Law* (UBC Press 2012) 17, fn 13; MJ Osiel, *The End of Reciprocity: Terror, Torture, and the Law of War* (CUP 2009). But see S Watts, 'Reciprocity and the Law of War' (2009) 50 HILJ 365, 431.

[85] Provost, *International* (n 73) 122. See also A Paulus, 'Reciprocity Revisited' in U Fastenrath *et al.* (eds), *From Bilateralism to Community Interest: Essays in Honour of Judge Bruno Simma* (OUP 2011) 113, 120–1.

[86] B Simma, 'Reciprocity' in R Wolfrum (ed.), *Max Planck Encyclopedia of Public International Law* (OUP 2008) <http://www.mpepil.com> accessed 30 May 2015, para 13.

enhance the need to observe certain international legal obligations, and ultimately increase both States' compliance and the cost of breach in the context of multilateral frameworks, in which the vast majority of States have a vested interest in upholding the *status quo*. Yet, the persuasiveness of this line of thinking begins to wane when dealing with counterterrorism and other intractable global security threats; resulting scenarios may involve recalcitrant or 'rogue' States;[87] isolated one-time terrorist strikes outside multilateral frameworks; isolationist or inimical stances against particular sanctuary States that have diminished political standing or questionable credibility; and transboundary excursions that may result in diplomatic tempers flaring up and potential emotive responses. In such contexts, unilateral overreaction is a significant risk and the notion of reciprocity may have met its match.

Thus, this sometimes utopian concept of reciprocity is by no means infallible; its compliance pull starts to wane not only in the context of terrorism and other global security threats, particularly when dealing with inefficient or wilfully blind governments and recalcitrant States, but also when the inter-State implementation mechanisms codified by the ILC become inefficient or paralysed. In responding to these challenges, the thrust of my policy argument is that an institutional structure would seek to fill this gap and define standard responses to these situations in appropriate circumstances. In the light of Chapter 3, the SC appears, on its face, best suited for the implementation of SR as the UN Charter devolves vast powers to it in safeguarding collective interests under the organizing principle of international peace and security. There is no doubt that many of the global security challenges canvassed in Chapter 2 fall under that rubric. For one thing, the particular scheme of powers devolved to the SC, which involves recourse to coercive measures under Chapter VII of the UN Charter, potentially offers a wide range of options in ensuring compliance with international obligations and implementing SR. In particular, the constellation of Chapter VII powers enshrined in Articles 39–42 (particularly Articles 41 and 42) enable the Council to, inter alia: (i) determine the existence of a threat to the peace, a breach of the peace, or an act of aggression; (ii) indicate provisional measures of protection to prevent aggravation of a situation or dispute; (iii) indicate non-forcible measures such as the interruption of economic relations and of communication; and (iv) indicate forcible measures by air, sea, or land forces such as demonstrations and blockades.[88]

One must certainly concede that the SC's process is not without its problems and challenges, be they grounded in structural reservations, political misgivings, or broader concerns over legitimacy. A charge closely associated with these concerns and often levelled in the same breath pertains to the actual effectiveness of

[87] On the concept of 'rogue' States, see RS Litwak, *Rogue States and U.S. Foreign Policy: Containment after the Cold War* (Woodrow Wilson Center Press 2000).

[88] Interestingly, H Kelsen, *Principles of International Law* (Rinehart & Company 1952) 46 pointed out that Art 41 measures 'have the technical character of reprisals', a concept that is today equated with countermeasures under SR repertoire.

SC action (or lack thereof), especially since the end of the Cold War.[89] Whilst the topic of UN reform falls outside the scope of this work, it should be acknowledged that some publicists have drawn attention to the legitimacy deficit that has plagued SC activities and shaped the public perception of its work and efficacy. In responding to this challenge, those commentators advocate a range of solutions aimed at enticing institutional behavioural modification and enhancing accountability,[90] yet surely, in some instances the SC's multilateral process—with all its imperfections—can or should be preferred over unchecked unilateralism.

Whilst subjecting the implementation of SR for States' international law violations to the SC's multilateral process might prove a viable avenue in certain circumstances—especially as an alternative to undesirable or disproportionate unilateral responses—one must not lose sight of the broader context in which this UN organ operates. Indeed, the risk in implementing SR through SC action 'would be of replacing one subjectivity (of states) by another (of the SC)', a situation that 'would be only slightly attenuated by the more collective nature of the decision-making processes of the SC, without it being possible for the state concerned to employ any outside review mechanism'.[91] Inevitably, in some instances the Council will remain deadlocked in its deliberations over counterterrorism or other global security breaches. Unsurprisingly, the very nature and makeup of this body will sometimes engender value conflicts and other clashes over culturally driven interpretations of international law, not to mention divisions in decision-making as seen in cases involving imprecise mandates and the exercise of veto power.[92] Setting aside these challenges for the moment, there is nonetheless every indication that SR repertoire can assist the SC in dealing with global security violations and, in some cases, stabilizing situations in which reliance on reciprocity seems futile.

When compared to domestic constitutional systems, it is no doubt fair to characterize the scheme of enforcement that accompanies SR repertoire as *sui generis*, its most salient features being reciprocity and countermeasures.[93] That said, whilst

[89] For a variety of views, see D Hannay, 'Effectiveness and Ineffectiveness of the UN Security Council in the 20 Years Since the Fall of the Berlin Wall: A European Perspective' in J Krause and N Ronzitti (eds), *The EU, the UN and Collective Security: Making Multilateralism Effective* (Routledge 2012) 37–52; J Van Oudenaren, 'Effectiveness and Ineffectiveness of the UN Security Council in the Last 20 Years: A US Perspective' in ibid 53–69; MJ Glennon, 'Why the Security Council Failed' (2003) 82 FA 16.

[90] See, eg, M Kohen, 'There Is No Need to Change the Composition of the Security Council: It Is Time for Stressing Accountability' in L Boisson de Chazournes and M Kohen (eds), *International Law and the Quest for its Implementation: Liber Amicorum Vera Gowlland-Debbas* (Brill 2010) 85–94. For a more critical take, see L Mälksoo, 'Great Powers Then and Now: Security Council Reform and Responses to Threats to Peace and Security' in PG Danchin and H Fischer (eds), *United Nations Reform and the New Collective Security* (CUP 2010) 94–113. See also generally B Fassbender, 'The Security Council: Progress is Possible but Unlikely' in Cassese (n 6) 52–60.

[91] P Klein, 'Responsibility for Serious Breaches of Obligations Deriving from Peremptory Norms of International Law and United Nations Law' (2002) 13 EJIL 1241, 1249.

[92] See, eg, A Reinisch, 'Value Conflicts within the United Nations Security Council' (2013) 14 Austrian Review of International and European Law 41; I Johnstone, 'When the Security Council Is Divided: Imprecise Authorizations, Implied Mandates, and the "Unreasonable Veto"' in M Weller (ed.), *The Oxford Handbook of the Use of Force in International Law* (OUP 2015) 227–50.

[93] See, eg, D Alland, 'International Responsibility and Sanctions: Self-Defence and Countermeasures in the ILC Codification of Rules Governing International Responsibility' in M Spinedi and B Simma (eds), *United Nations Codification of State Responsibility* (Oceana 1987) 143–97.

reciprocity works well in theory, its efficiency may also be challenged by asymmetric power dynamics and *rapports de force* on the international plane, giving way to unchecked unilateralism or defeating the very purpose for which countermeasures exist in the first place. Ultimately, it may well be that an injured State's attempts to enforce international law by way of countermeasures actually backfires, thereby eviscerating its resort to countermeasures of any meaningful effect and disabling its efforts to implement legal obligations. As one publicist underscores, the notion of reciprocity provides States with 'a shared interest in the maintenance of predictable patterns of conduct', but it should be borne in mind that

> [a] State which disrupts this web of reciprocal relations by a countermeasure risks to suffer more injury than the target State, unless it is the dominant power in one of the abovementioned asymmetrical relations which, in the world of today, means almost exclusively the United States, with the European Union and China as potential candidates.[94]

SC involvement in the implementation phase of SR, it is argued, might help neutralize these situations in some cases. Granted, the Council's process poses some obvious challenges but, by the same token, offers some checks and balances that are typically absent in scenarios involving unilateral enforcement by States. Ultimately, the institutionalized implementation of SR, though it can sometimes run up against (perhaps predictable) stumbling blocks, may in fact help build constituencies of conscience within the international community, exert pressure in a multilateral setting, and create incentives for responsible States to comply fully with international law and/or undertake active steps in redressing violations.

4.2.3 Moving beyond the 'political v legal' divide: Resisting overly rigid dichotomies

For reasons that are challenged later in this chapter,[95] a recurrent argument brandished by detractors of the institutionalization of SR is that SC involvement would amount to a political solution, which is (inexplicably) at odds with the nature of SR law. As a corollary, the argument goes, the implementation of SR should thus be pursued through judicial or arbitral channels, dispute settlement by an impartial body being preferred to the SC's multilateral process. At the outset, one would be hard-pressed to disagree with the proposition that judicial settlement of disputes over violations of counterterrorism obligations (or other global security duties) can be one of the best avenues in enforcing international law; however, for reasons canvassed in Part II of this book, this is an ideal solution and, in practice, is far removed from the default scenario. Most importantly, this line of thinking erroneously casts SR repertoire as purely legal, its implementation being correspondingly judicial; among other problematic aspects, this posture ignores the

[94] K Zemanek, 'Does the Prospect of Incurring Responsibility Improve the Observance of International Law' in Ragazzi (n 62) 129.

[95] In particular, see Section 4.5.

very fact that the ILC itself has left the implementation of SR within the hands of injured States, a process invariably characterized by strong political overtones, unilateral enforcement, self-judging, and autoqualification. Indeed, the ILC's finalized text by no means elects judicial settlement of disputes as the default or principal mode of enforcement and SR implementation.

Furthermore, any study of this kind must point to the obvious fact that the implementation of SR will never be devoid of some political dimension(s). In many ways, it sometimes mirrors the SC's own balancing exercise between its primary mission of restoring international peace and security, deliberative process, and consideration of international law when relevant, even if arbitrary or 'strategic'; there is no question that the manner in which it carries out its work lies at the intersection of law and politics.[96] Similarly, SR's primary mission is to trigger consequences for violations of international law, but this process also engages political considerations when relevant, even if arbitrary. The undeniable political character of SR implementation comes into sharp focus when pointing to that normative scheme's decentralized rationale—a rationale quintessentially embodied by the repertoire of countermeasures—prompting some commentators to assimilate the unilateral enforcement of international law with a 'function of power'. It follows that political and economic considerations will first register as incentivizing priorities in inducing States to comply with their legal obligations; considerations of law and justice will only crop up as secondary—and sometimes distant—motivators in shaping and informing State behaviour.[97]

Any attempt to make this chapter's central argument more palatable will hinge, to a large extent, on the relationship between countermeasures and sanctions. Ultimately, this project is concerned with the implementation of SR—that is, enforcement of international law—which requires an assessment of whether decentralized modes of implementation (countermeasures) are compatible with centralized/collective modes of enforcement (sanctions). Therein lies perhaps the most challenging stumbling block to the arguments advanced in this work, a difficulty which must be acknowledged squarely. Thus, it might prove challenging to envisage the SC's implementation of SR if a rigid distinction between sanctions and countermeasures is maintained; in that light, the logic of SR might be difficult to square with the rationale underpinning the Council's primary function, which concerns itself with the maintenance of international peace and security.[98] It is therefore important to acknowledge this challenge to the potential institutionalization of SR and briefly review its main components before proceeding to

[96] See generally D Shraga, 'Politics and Justice: The Role of the Security Council' in A Cassese *et al.* (eds), *The Oxford Companion to International Criminal Justice* (OUP 2009) 168. See also R Deplano, *The Strategic Use of International Law by the United Nations Security Council* (Springer 2015) (arguing that whilst international law plays an important role in shaping the SC's politics, that organ's resolutions fail to contribute significantly to the development of that discipline).

[97] See, eg, Zemanek (n 94) 128; K Zemanek, 'The Unilateral Enforcement of International Obligations' (1987) 47 Zeitschrift für ausländisches öffentliches Recht und Völkerrecht (ZaöRV) 32, 43.

[98] See, eg, MJ Aznar, 'Réponse: La Distinction entre Sanctions et Contre-mesures' (2013) 47 RBDI 109.

unfold the finer points of the central argument which will, it is hoped, convince the reader that this challenge is ill-founded.

When delving into this topic, we must always keep in mind the distinction articulated by the eminent publicist, René-Jean Dupuy, between relational and institutional aspects of the international legal system, which he framed as *droit relationnel* versus *droit institutionnel*.[99] Immediately, this vision of the global legal order appears to erect a conceptual barrier to the prospect of advocating a rapprochement between the logic underpinning SR and the Council's function. When invoking the concept of sanctions pursuant to SC practice, the frame of reference governing the analysis would be that of *droit institutionnel*, which responds to its own specific and internal logic.[100] Conversely, the law of countermeasures under SR repertoire rather falls under the rubric of *droit relationnel* as this type of recourse deals primarily with *private* justice in the sense that it is animated by a relational logic which may—potentially and arguably—not be transposed to the law governing SC action. This line of critique, though familiar in the field of SR, has most recently been levelled against similar attempts to see analogies between the law governing the responsibility of IOs and the framework applicable to UN activities. However, there is presumably no reason why this challenge could not be extended to SR law, at least by analogy. After all, the ARSIWA served as the ILC's principal inspiration when it finalized its text on the responsibility of IOs; hence, scholarly accounts cautioning against confounding countermeasures and sanctions would presumably apply to both normative schemes.[101]

As will be seen in subsequent sections, eminent publicists have long recognized that a SC determination under Article 39 of the UN Charter amounts to a 'judgment in law'; correspondingly, it results in the Council's legal characterization of facts or of a situation, from which legal consequences will flow.[102] Hence, a 'threat to the peace' pursuant to Article 39 constitutes a situation that may trigger SC powers to declare that the situation indeed threatens international peace and institute sanctions.[103] Consequently, the recurrent argument espoused by would-be detractors of this chapter's central thesis is that SC decisions are embedded with political determinations, which happen to engender legal effects.[104] For reasons explored in Chapter 3 and the following,[105] this conception of the SC's role is not at odds with SR repertoire; rather, if the objective is truly to instil life into the SC's broad-ranging pronouncements on primary counterterrorism obligations and other global security threats, the focus should be on the complementarity between both schemes; that is, how they can mutually reinforce or inform each other, as opposed to maintaining overly rigid legal dichotomies.

[99] See, eg, R-J Dupuy, *Le Droit International* (3rd rev edn, PUF 1969) 21.

[100] See, eg, Aznar (n 98) 112.

[101] See, eg, Y Kerbrat, 'Sanctions et Contre-mesures: Risque de Confusion dans les Articles de la CDI sur la Responsabilité des Organisations Internationales' (2013) 46 RBDI 101.

[102] See, eg, M Virally, *L'Organisation Mondiale* (Armand Colin 1972) 452. See also Tzanakopoulos, *Disobeying* (n 19) 63–4.

[103] See, eg, J Combacau, *Le Pouvoir de Sanction de l'O.N.U.: Étude Théorique de la Coercition Non Militaire* (Pedone 1974) 99–100.

[104] See, eg, Aznar (n 98) 112.

[105] See, eg, Section 3.1.5.2.

A second, perhaps more systemic, problem in responding to potential conflicts between the ARSIWA and *le droit institutionnel* (the law of sanctions) stems from a perceived hierarchy between UN law and whatever legal obligations would be set in motion under SR repertoire in any given situation. I would qualify this as a false hierarchy; not because other international legal norms should not be subordinated to the UN Charter, but because this does not pose any problems in many cases involving global security threats. As will be discussed in greater detail later on, with special reference to Article 103 of the UN Charter, counterterrorism and many other global security risks—including the legal and/or political tools to suppress them—share an inherent compatibility with the UN's system of collective security. In case of potential conflicts, however, ARSIWA Article 59 clearly resolves the tension in favour of the UN Charter by emphasizing that '[t]hese articles are without prejudice to the Charter of the United Nations'.[106] The historical debates in the ILC over previous iterations of this provision (formerly Draft Article 39), especially those that occurred in the 1996 session, have been widely discussed.[107] In fact, it has been suggested that these discussions within the Commission prompted the resignation of Special Rapporteur Arangio-Ruiz; contrary to his initial vision, the ILC's finalized text constitutes a fairly clear acknowledgement that SR law remains subordinated to SC decisions in application of Chapter VII.[108] Surprisingly, the instances of institutional practice, which are thoroughly reviewed later in this chapter, invoked by those scholars who might be detractors of this chapter's argument are framed by those same putative critics in SR language, be they the Council's decisions *attributing an internationally wrongful act* to Libya in 1992 and to Sudan in 1996, or the *reparation* scheme imposed upon Iraq in 1991.[109] According to these commentators, these precedents clearly evince the subordination of SR precedents to the UN Charter.[110] The aim of this book is not to quarrel with this proposition, but by the very admission of those authors, their interpretation of the relevant practice suggests that SR can be implemented by the SC. The relevant question, therefore, is not whether a potential conflict will arise between the secondary norms in question and the UN Charter, under some overarching normative hierarchy, but rather whether there is (perhaps inherent) compatibility between SR repertoire and the SC's function, particularly in global security contexts. The answer to this latter query appears to be affirmative.

Nevertheless, some scholars insist that reconciling the (allegedly) strict legal logic of SR with the predominantly political logic of the SC's maintenance of international peace and security constitutes a challenging exercise. In that regard, recurrent arguments include emphasizing that: (i) the purpose of the law

[106] ARSIWA (n 34) Art 59.

[107] See generally MJ Aznar, *Estado y Acción del Consejo de Seguridad de las Naciones Unidas* (Ministerio de Asuntos Exteriores 2000); Forteau (n 20). For further discussion on Special Rapporteur Arangio-Ruiz's efforts to disable the substance of Draft Art 39, see Section 4.4.9.

[108] See, eg, Aznar (n 98) 113.

[109] Aznar (n 98) 113 (invoking several SC Resolutions analysed in greater detail below).

[110] Aznar (n 98) 113. See also Dupuy (n 51); Aznar (n 107).

governing international responsibility is to ensure the return to legality on the international plane, whereas the SC seeks to restore peace, a process in which law is only one component; (ii) the event giving rise to SR is the commission of an internationally wrongful act whereas in the context of collective security, the relevant event is a threat to the peace which may not always constitute an internationally wrongful act; (iii) the process by which international responsibility is set in motion is of a legal nature whereas the SC's determinations are essentially of a political nature; (iv) these two processes are different given that the implementation of international responsibility is rarely institutionalized whereas the collective security scheme is managed and administered within a pre-established and regulated organ; and (v) the law of international responsibility typically engenders reparative effects whereas SC sanctions rather bring about coercive and sometimes punitive effects.[111]

Undoubtedly, the most challenging aspect of reconciling SR repertoire with the SC's function resides in equating centralized/institutional sanctions with decentralized and/or unilateral countermeasures or, at least, in suggesting that they respond to similar logic and typology. In 2001, Professor James Crawford, the former Special Rapporteur who engineered the finalization of the ARSIWA, acknowledged the difficulty in such a rapprochement. He took the view that sanctions were probably not reconcilable with SR rationale, despite the historical debates within the ILC in which such rapprochement had been attempted. Interestingly, his account also revealed that the genesis of countermeasures in the ILC's codification work sought great inspiration from the law of sanctions pursuant to SC practice. Moreover, the former Special Rapporteur stressed the fact that the SC may play a role in monitoring or enhancing proportionality vis-à-vis collective countermeasures that may be adopted under SR repertoire.[112]

Indeed, the main detractors of this monograph's central thesis might insist on the fact that countermeasures pursuant to SR law are to be envisaged exclusively in response to an internationally wrongful act.[113] By contrast, their argument would presumably run as follows: when adopting sanctions the Council often takes action without ascertaining the breach of an international legal obligation.[114] Whilst this is certainly true, it should be recalled that the Council often points to a violation of international law in the context of its adoption of sanctions.[115] Thus,

[111] See, eg, Aznar (n 98) 113. [112] See generally Crawford (n 54) 57–68.

[113] See, eg, ARSIWA (n 34) Art 49(1) and accompanying Commentary ibid 130–1.

[114] See, eg, S Talmon, 'The Constitutive versus the Declaratory Theory of Recognition: *Tertium Non Datur*? (2004) 75 BYIL 101, 156; M Craven, 'Humanitarianism and the Quest for Smarter Sanctions' (2002) 13 EJIL 43, 52. It also follows that the Council's pre-emptive action to forestall a threat to the peace need not be subject to its prior determination that an internationally wrongful act has been committed. See, eg, JA Frowein and N Krisch, 'Introduction' in B Simma *et al.* (eds), *The Charter of the United Nations: A Commentary* (2nd edn, OUP 2002) 701, 705; Tzanakopoulos, *Disobeying* (n 19) 77.

[115] See, eg, Gowlland-Debbas, 'Security' (n 21) 63–8; P-M Dupuy, 'Sécurité Collective et Construction de la Paix dans la Pratique Contemporaine du Conseil de Sécurité' in U Beyerlin *et al.* (eds), *Recht Zwischen Umbruch und Bewahrung: Völkerrecht, Europarecht, Staatsrecht: Festschrift für Rudolf Bernhardt* (Springer 1995) 41, 51.

even if these two concepts are different in nature, SR law and SC determinations and/or sanctions can sometimes pursue the same aims.

A scenario could be envisaged whereby the SC imposes sanctions on a sanctuary State for failing to prevent terrorism or comply with other counterterrorism duties. In that situation, the injured State (ie which suffered harm resulting from the first State's failure) will have secured political legitimacy as a result of the Council's multilateral process, in addition to obtaining the outcome it was seeking: an acknowledgment of wrongdoing and consequences flowing from that conduct, validation by a coalition of States, institutional support for its accusations, etc. One may ponder whether that injured State could then unilaterally take countermeasures against the responsible State under SR repertoire? It probably could do so, although that might engender a 'pile-on' effect. Besides, the prospect of doing so successfully might prove difficult in scenarios involving weak or ineffective States (eg Somalia, Syria, Lebanon) or, in the case of recalcitrant States, when diplomatic engagement or political dialogue seem futile (eg Iran). Thus, in some instances SC action is just another way of attaining the same objectives—perhaps more efficiently and with enhanced political legitimacy or, at least, support—than through unilateral means, that is: (i) a return to legality (provided the recalcitrant State complies with the SC's decision, which is arguably more likely when faced with a multilateral decision rendered by the UN's principal organ responsible for the maintenance of international peace and security than when confronted with a unilateral countermeasure adopted by a disgruntled State); and (ii) some form of reparation (often embodied in SC pronouncements and/or sanctions).

As will be seen in greater detail later, there are certainly institutional precedents militating in favour of this rapprochement. Furthermore, there is also solid scholarly support for treating some aspects of SC practice as concrete applications of SR principles, with special reference to the affinity between sanctions and collective countermeasures.[116] Some commentators increasingly, and convincingly, defend the idea that several instances in which the SC exercised its mandate to maintain international peace and security nonetheless amounted to collective responses to serious breaches of the international legal order, particularly in the fields of counterterrorism and IHL.

Furthermore, the very concept of international peace and security has evolved beyond the traditional collective security paradigm, which rested upon the underlying assumption of a large-scale, collective response to an armed attack; the security fabric has now expanded to include breaches of fundamental norms and entails an enhanced focus on the protection of collective interests.[117] In many ways, this

[116] See, eg, ME O'Connell, *The Power and Purpose of International Law: Insights from the Theory and Practice of Enforcement* (OUP 2008); O'Connell (n 56) 75; Dipla (n 25) 23–57; Gowlland-Debbas (n 27) 5–13; L Picchio Forlati and L-A Sicilianos (eds), *Economic Sanctions in International Law* (Nijhoff 2004); C Leben, 'Les Contre-Mesures Inter-Étatiques et les Réactions à l'Illicite dans la Société Internationale' (1982) 28 AFDI 9.

[117] See generally V Gowlland-Debbas: 'Responsibility and the United Nations Charter' in Crawford *et al.* (n 30) 115–38; 'The Security Council and Issues of Responsibility under International Law' (2011) 353 RdC 185; 'Security Council Change' (2009–10) 65 International Journal 119.

evolution also mirrors recent developments in SR repertoire, which has shifted from a traditionally 'bilateral', 'individualistic', and 'privatistic' conception[118] to a more multilateral system. As a corollary, an ever-increasing margin has developed to accommodate institutionalized reactions to internationally wrongful conduct, of which collective countermeasures form an integral part under SR law. In turn, this reality signals a dual role for the SC in protecting fundamental, collective interests, which undoubtedly include protection from global security threats: that of *legislator* of primary international legal norms, and that of *implementer* of those (and other) rules.[119] Thus, subsequent sections should be read in tandem with Bruno Simma's visionary work, which called attention to the ever-changing nature of the international legal system; a system once solely concerned with purely bilateral transactions and relationships, but now firmly devoted to the protection of fundamental collective interests, and characterized by a multilateral outlook.[120]

This evolution engendered profound implications for fundamental aspects of the international legal order, not least the notion of sovereignty; in short, commentators rightly highlight a 'tectonic shift' in the essence of sovereignty when analysing contemporaneous developments.[121] The R2P doctrine, which is explored in greater detail in Part III, and the schools of thought it spawned similarly suggest an important shift, within international law, from a 'right to intervene' to a 'responsibility to protect'; this evolution can also be cast as a transition from collective security to a responsibility to protect.[122] Therefore, the international community must defend and vindicate its values, particularly when confronted with violations of community norms, an impetus which has considerable significance in the global security context and for the purposes of the present book. In light of these developments, it will be argued that the international community should accommodate this shift by electing a multilateral venue and forum to ensure proportionate and well-calibrated responses to global security

[118] For a critique of the ARSIWA along those lines, see generally R Pisillo-Mazzeschi, 'The Marginal Role of the Individual in the ILC's Articles on State Responsibility' (2004) 15 Italian Yearbook of International Law 39.

[119] See generally V Gowlland-Debbas: 'Security Council Change' (n 117); 'The Security Council and Issues of Responsibility under International Law', Australian Civil–Military Center and the ANU Centre for International Governance and Justice Working Paper No 2.2 <http://regnet.anu.edu.au/sites/default/files/publications/attachments/2015-05/Debbas_2.2_0_0.pdf> accessed 20 August 2015.

[120] See, eg, B Simma: 'From Bilateralism to Community Interest in International Law' (1994) 250 RdC 217 and 'Universality of International Law from the Perspective of a Practitioner' (2009) 20 EJIL 265, 268. See also B Kingsbury and M Donaldson, 'From Bilateralism to Publicness in International Law' in Fastenrath *et al.* (n 85) 79; B Simma and A Paulus, '"The International Community": Facing the Challenge of Globalization' (1998) 9 EJIL 266, 268. See generally A-L Vaurs-Chaumette, 'The International Community as a Whole' in Crawford *et al.* (n 30) 1023–8.

[121] A-M Slaughter, 'Security, Solidarity, and Sovereignty: The Grand Themes of UN Reform' (2005) 99 AJIL 619, 627.

[122] ICISS, *The Responsibility to Protect: Report of the International Commission on Intervention and State Sovereignty* (International Development Research Centre 2001) 11–12. The Commission added at 12 that 'while it [the shift in language] can remove a barrier to effective action, [it] does not, of course, change the substantive issues which have to be addressed'. See also RC Thakur, *The United Nations Peace and Security: From Collective Security to the Responsibility to Protect* (CUP 2006).

violations in appropriate circumstances. The SC's implementation of SR is one way to achieve this objective. In this light, the chapter now turns to more specific aspects of the SC's mandate with a view to supporting the central argument on the institutionalization of SR.

Before so doing, it should be stressed that it would be difficult to resolve persuasively the polemical question whether SC-imposed sanctions can amount to 'centralized' countermeasures under SR law, especially as regards the protection of fundamental collective or community interests. Indeed, this question is divisive and has polarized interlocutors around both sides of the idea that SC action, particularly under Chapter VII, can disable States' ability to adopt countermeasures (be they taken collectively or individually by States other than the injured State(s)). For some authors, limited SC sanctions in a given situation do not foreclose the possibility of States adopting unilateral countermeasures in response to an internationally wrongful act.[123] Other influential scholars take an opposite view, opining that resort to countermeasures remains possible as long as a competent international body has not decided and imposed sanctions.[124] Extending this type of rationale to grave violations of obligations *erga omnes* (which most likely capture some global security breaches), it follows for some commentators that the adoption of collective countermeasures by States not directly injured by the wrongful conduct, pursuant to ARSIWA Article 48, would assume a 'subsidiary character in relation to the powers of the Security Council'.[125] Otherwise put, SC action under Chapter VII precludes the adoption of individual measures that would prove incompatible with the sanctions decided by the Council. As a corollary, States not individually injured by the internationally wrongful act would be barred from adopting collective countermeasures that do not align with the Council's sanctions.[126] In sum, once the SC has triggered the Chapter VII machinery, those States become obedient implementers of SC sanctions; any countermeasure adopted after that point should aim solely to serve that objective.

It should be recalled that this debate raged at the ILC during its work leading up to the adoption of the ARSIWA. Unsurprisingly, this polemic was revived in the context of the Commission's subsequent programme of work on the responsibility of IOs. It not only demonstrates that reasonable people can disagree but also that international legal experts can diverge on whether centralized sanctions can be equated to

[123] See, eg, NJ Calamita, 'Sanctions, Countermeasures, and the Iranian Nuclear Issue' (2009) 42 VJTL 1393, 1418.

[124] See, eg, A Pellet's remarks in (1992) I *YILC* 144 (commenting on G Arangio-Ruiz, 'Fourth Report of on State Responsibility' (1992) UN Doc A/CN.4/444 and Add.1-3; 1992 II(1) *YILC* 1). See also P-E Dupont, 'Countermeasures and Collective Security: The Case of the EU Sanctions against Iran' (2012) 17 JCSL 301.

[125] L-A Sicilianos, 'Countermeasures in Response to Grave Violations of Obligations Owed to the International Community' in Crawford *et al.* (n 30) 1138.

[126] See Sicilianos (n 125) 1142. This view is typically accompanied by a reminder that it accords with ARSIWA (n 34) Art 59, which states that '[t]hese articles are without prejudice to the Charter of the United Nations'.

countermeasures.[127] Indeed, some ILC members concluded that sanctions imposed by the SC under Chapter VII 'could be regarded, in certain situations, as countermeasures in their essence, since they were directed against States that had breached international law and were frequently aimed at stopping internationally wrongful acts'.[128] Conversely, '[a]ccording to several members, such sanctions were subject to a different regime and should therefore remain outside the scope of the topic' and, to buttress this position, 'reference was made to their punitive character and to their main purpose which was the maintenance of international peace and security rather than the enforcement of obligations under international law'.[129] This tension underpinned some of the Commission's preliminary work leading to the adoption of its finalized text, whilst tipping the scale in favour of a more permissible construction of the relevant concepts. For instance, the commentary accompanying Article 30 following the first reading of the Draft Articles espoused a liberal construction of the term 'countermeasure', which would have arguably given credence to the SC's role in implementing SR.[130] However, the Commission ultimately preferred the term 'countermeasure' in the context of SR law, thereby opting to reserve the expression 'sanction' for reactions adopted by IOs.[131] Nevertheless, this careful terminological consideration by the ILC suggests—perhaps even beyond challenge—the existence of a functional analogy between countermeasures and sanctions.[132]

It should also be stressed that the issue of collective countermeasures brings about a particularly challenging set of questions, especially regarding enforcement of international legal obligations in the global security context. Let us assume that a grave violation of fundamental human rights has been perpetrated by a State. Since, at least in theory, all States are entitled to take countermeasures in response to that fundamental breach, the question of proportionality of those reactions, and how exactly it would operate in this setting, remains highly uncertain.[133] In fact,

[127] See, eg, ILC, 'Report of the International Law Commission on the Work of its 60th Session' (5 May–8 August 2008) UN Doc A/63/10, 258 [152] ('[d]ivergent views were expressed on whether sanctions imposed by the United Nations Security Council could be regarded as countermeasures').

[128] ILC Report (n 127) 259 [152].

[129] ILC Report (n 127) 258 [152]. This latter position garnered the support of several ILC members, including the Special Rapporteur. Several States and IOs, particularly the OSCE and EC, coalesced around this viewpoint. For the reaction and comments of States, in particular the approaches defended by Germany and Portugal, see ILC, 'Responsibility of International Organizations: Comments and Observations Received from Governments' (2011) UN Doc A/CN.4/636, 22, 24.

[130] See (1979) II(2) *YILC* 121 [21].

[131] See, eg, (1979) I(1) *YILC* 54–63; (1979) II(2) *YILC* 121; ILC Report (n 127) 259 [153]. See also Leben (n 116) 17; H Lesaffre, 'Circumstances Precluding Wrongfulness in the ILC Articles on State Responsibility' in Crawford *et al.* (n 30) 472.

[132] See, eg, Tzanakopoulos, *Disobeying* (n 19) 76–7. But see Crawford (n 32) 706–10 (demonstrating that the relationship between these concepts is unclear).

[133] On the requirement of proportionality of countermeasures, see Section 4.2.1. On the adoption of countermeasures in response to violations of obligations *erga omnes*, see C Tams, *Enforcing Obligations Erga Omnes in International Law* (CUP 2010); JA Frowein, 'Reactions by Not Directly Affected States to Breaches of Public International Law' (1994) 248 RdC 345, 345ff. More broadly, see C Tams, '*Erga Omnes, Jus Cogens* and their Impact on the Law of Responsibility' in MD Evans and P Koutrakos (eds), *The International Responsibility of the European Union: European and International Perspectives* (Hart 2013) 163–88.

former Special Rapporteur James Crawford alluded to this difficulty in a book chapter published the same year the ARSIWA were adopted.[134] By definition, the scope of collective countermeasures is broader than what is envisaged under the more traditional, bilateral typology associated with countermeasures adopted unilaterally by injured States (or classical recourse to force logic, for that matter). In most circumstances, collective countermeasures and the global security obligations they seek to vindicate will affect stakeholders beyond the State apparatus, such as groups, individuals, and other entities at the sub-State level. Thus, it will be argued that collective countermeasures could be directed, in some instances, against State failures to prevent global security violations as a viable solution to uphold the principle of proportionality. Indeed, the likelihood of disproportionate countermeasures (which may transform into reprisals) is significantly more acute when States address the consequences of internationally wrongful conduct on a bilateral basis. For example, the Israeli–Arab record is replete with disproportionate responses to unlawful behaviour.[135] As a partial solution, it will be argued that SC involvement might be a way to disable some of the inherent problems identified in the proportionality calculus raised by Special Rapporteur Crawford in the context of collective countermeasures. Whilst far from perfect, the SC's political decision-making process might in fact help protect against unchecked retaliation or disproportionate countermeasures.

4.3 Chapter VII Powers

Pursuant to Article 39 of the UN Charter, SC action is predicated on a two-pronged approach: first, on the requisite situation, namely that the Council 'shall determine the existence of any threat to the peace, breach of the peace, or act of aggression'; and second, on its purpose, in that the Council 'shall make recommendations, or decide what measures shall be taken in accordance with Articles 41 and 42, to maintain or restore international peace and security'.[136] SC decision-making powers on SR matters most likely also stem from a textual exegesis falling outside the strict ambit of the UN Charter. For example, one author underscores that the definition of 'aggression' adopted by the GA in 1974 was 'not intended to provide a basis for individual criminal responsibility, but to provide guidance to the Security Council in determining state responsibility'.[137]

Upon first glance, however, the purview of the Charter's text does not seem to allot much margin for the implementation of SR by the Council. With this in mind, it might be tempting to state—by way of blanket postulate—that SC

[134] See Crawford (n 54) 67. See also Crawford (n 32) 703–6.

[135] For a survey of relevant State and institutional practice, see Proulx (n 3) ch 2. See also DW Bowett, 'Reprisals Involving Recourse to Armed Force' (1972) 66 AJIL 1.

[136] UN Charter (n 26) Art 39.

[137] G Schofield, 'The Empty U.S. Chair: United States Nonparticipation in the Negotiations on the Definition of Aggression' (2007) 15 Human Rights Brief 20, 21.

action under Chapter VII usually gravitates towards stabilizing situations where a single, collective interest remains in peril: international peace.[138] The underlying rationale leading to the adoption of this set of provisions was most probably animated by *stricto sensu* logic, thereby conceptualizing the substance of international peace and security as narrowly encompassing a one-dimensional construction of use of force through a primarily inter-State model.[139] It is unsurprising, therefore, that contemporary scholarly advances exploring the intersection of counterterrorism and SR repertoire have resisted the analytical merger of Chapter VII considerations with the normative scheme applicable to the legal consequences flowing from internationally wrongful acts. The typical argument in that vein goes as follows: 'the purpose and limits of Chapter VII measures are driven by a security paradigm, rather than one concerned with questions of legal responsibility' and, consequently, '[t]he Security Council Chapter VII framework is legally and conceptually different from that of state responsibility'.[140] In the same vein, Chapter VII SC action has sometimes been construed as a 'police intervention', or interpreted as aiming to restore international order given the Council's overarching mission of ensuring international peace and security.[141] Most classical constructions of SC powers do not interpret this objective as including a supervisory mechanism or capacity over State behaviour, nor do they 'read in' the implementation of SR within the arsenal of Council powers. In fact, proponents of this view often dissociate both aspects in their own scholarship.[142] Drawing on Article 1(1)

[138] See, eg, P-M Dupuy, 'Observations sur la Pratique Récente des "Sanctions" de l'Illicite' (1983) 87 RGDIP 505, 544.

[139] See, eg, G Gaja, 'Réflexions sur le Rôle du Conseil de Sécurité dans le Nouvel Ordre Mondial: À Propos des Rapports entre Maintien de la Paix et Crimes Internationaux des États' (1993) 97 RGDIP 297, 301; M Koskenniemi, 'The Place of Law in Collective Security' (1996) 17 MJIL 457.

[140] Trapp (n 4) 12. However, Trapp raises the possibility of the SC addressing behaviour concomitantly amounting to (i) a threat to international peace and security, and (ii) a violation of an international obligation. In this regard, she queries whether the SC could 'displace or suspend the regime of state responsibility in respect of the breach including an injured state's right to demand cessation and assurances of non-repetition, or to adopt countermeasures to induce the wrongdoing state to comply with its secondary obligations of cessation and reparation'. She ultimately concludes that 'there is no Security Council practice that has suspended the regime of state responsibility' in such circumstances. Obviously, this conundrum takes on a particular relevance in the context of grave violations of international law. On this debate, compare Gowlland-Debbas, 'Responsibility' (n 117) 115–38; Sicilianos (n 125) 1141–2.

[141] See, eg, Cassese (n 63) 234, 323; JE Alvarez, 'Judging the Security Council' (1996) 90 AJIL 1, 39. For various critiques of the distribution of those police powers within the SC framework, see JE Alvarez, 'Constitutional Interpretation in International Organizations' in J-M Coicaud and V Heiskanen (eds), *The Legitimacy of International Organizations* (UN University Press 2001) 104, 108; B Fassbender, 'Pressure for Security Council Reform' in DM Malone (n 28) 341; UNGA 'Report of the High-level Panel on Threats, Challenges and Change: A More Secure World: Our Shared Responsibility' (2 December 2004) UN Doc A/59/565, 1, 9, 18.

[142] See, eg, G Cohen-Jonathan, 'Article 39' in J-P Cot and A Pellet (eds), *La Charte des Nations Unies: Commentaire Article par Article* (Economica 1985) 648; H Kelsen, *The Law of the United Nations* (London Institute of World Affairs 1950) 293–5, 735–7; H Kelsen, 'Collective Security and Collective Self-Defence Under the Charter of the United Nations' (1948) 42 AJIL 783, 788–9. On the interplay between security considerations and the enforcement of international law, see C Eagleton, 'International Law and the Charter of the United Nations' (1945) 39 AJIL 751.

of the UN Charter, a similar viewpoint could posit that the principles of justice and international law are inextricably linked to the settlement of disputes, in accordance with Chapter VI of the UN Charter, as opposed to the adoption of collective measures aiming to prevent or counteract threats to peace, or repress acts of aggression or other breaches of the peace grounded in Chapter VII. It follows from this reasoning that the application of general international law would then fall outside the ambit of SC powers.[143]

As confirmed by the International Criminal Tribunal for the former Yugoslavia (ICTY) Appeals Chamber, the SC exerts discretionary power in interpreting both prerequisites laid down in Article 39 of the UN Charter,[144] yet this power is not unlimited and the SC's discretion is not unfettered.[145] Furthermore, the Charter does not shed any light on, or provide a definition of, the terms 'threat to the peace', 'breach of the peace', and 'act of aggression',[146] whilst when confronted with a choice of which measure and/or sanction to apply, the Council retains, through a *renvoi* to Articles 41 and 42 of the Charter, an unfettered margin of discretion in making this determination. Consequently, '[t]his conceptual imprecision provides a broad scope of manoeuvre to the Council in assessing whether a situation constitutes a threat to peace, a breach of the peace, or an act of aggression'.[147] Thus, the SC has often pursued a very broad line of reasoning under the aegis of Chapter VII, at least in two relevant ways: (i) first, it has interpreted the idea of 'breach to the peace' in a very liberal fashion, making it more expansive and inclusive of scenarios not only directly linked to the potential initiation of armed hostilities in the context of an international armed conflict, such as instances involving the maintenance of colonial domination, apartheid, grave and massive human rights violations, and terrorism;[148] and ii) secondly, in the spirit of Article 39's open-ended

[143] See, eg, G Abi-Saab, 'De la Sanction en Droit International: Essai de Clarification' in J Makarczyk (ed.), *Theory of International Law at the Threshold of the 21st Century: Essays in Honour of Krzysztof Skubiszewski* (Kluwer 1996) 61, 74; W Czaplinski, 'Concepts of *Jus Cogens* and Obligations *Erga Omnes* in International Law in the Light of Recent Developments' (1997–8) 23 PYIL 87, 96; Gowlland-Debbas, 'The Functions' (n 21) 287.

[144] See *Tadić Case* (Decision on the Defence Motion for Interlocutory Appeal on Jurisdiction) ICTY-94-1-AR72 (2 October 1995) [28]–[31].

[145] See, eg, Bothe (n 56) 69–70; B Conforti, 'Le Pouvoir Discrétionnaire du Conseil de Sécurité en Matière de Constatation d'une Menace contre la Paix, d'une Rupture de la Paix ou d'un Acte d'Agression' in Dupuy (n 26) 51–60.

[146] See also the definition of 'aggression' in UNGA Res 3314 (XXIX) (14 December 1974), Annex, Art 2, confirming the SC's discretionary power on this issue:

> The first use of armed force by a State in contravention of the Charter shall constitute *prima facie* evidence of an act of aggression *although the Security Council may, in conformity with the Charter, conclude that a determination that an act of aggression has been committed* would not be justified in the light of other relevant circumstances, including the fact that the acts concerned or their consequences are not of sufficient gravity (emphasis added).

See also Gaja (n 139) 299–300; P Kooijmans, 'The Enlargement of the Concept "Threat to the Peace"' in Dupuy (n 26) 111.

[147] De Brichambaut (n 21) 270.

[148] See, eg, TM Franck, 'The Security Council and "Threats to the Peace": Some Remarks on Remarkable Recent Developments' in Dupuy (n 26) 83–110; Gaja (n 139) 301–7; Klein (n 91) 1245; Kooijmans (n 146) 111–21.

construction, the SC has imposed sanctions and measures purporting to maintain or restore international peace and security which, admittedly, exceeded the scope and list of enumerated eventualities in Articles 41 and 42 of the UN Charter.

Although these issues are addressed thoroughly in subsequent sections, one preliminary conclusion seems apposite here: the field of counterterrorism does not appear so far removed from the objectives pursued by the SC or from its practical operations. It can surely be included within the gamut of priorities encompassed by Chapter VII as many transnational terrorist attacks will invariably engender some kind of destabilizing effect on international peace and security. In fact, after enumerating ethnic cleansing, genocide, and other gross violations of human rights—and including the right to self-determination and grave breaches of IHL—as forming part of the security fabric, one commentator posits that '[t]he concept of international peace and security has thus acquired a meaning that extends far beyond that of collective security (envisaged as an all-out collective response to armed attack)'.[149]

In attempting to shed light on this evolution, the chapter now turns to a brief study of SC practice whilst bearing three objectives in mind. First, by reviewing select Council incursions into different areas, including SR, the extensiveness of its practice, along with its corresponding pervasiveness and relevance to counterterrorism, comes into sharp relief. Secondly, by understanding these incursions better and how they pertain to SR, more precisely, one will venture upon steadier analytical terrain in drawing preliminary rapprochements and move closer to elucidating the relationship between the Council and SR, whilst placing emphasis on counterterrorism and other global security challenges. Finally, this exercise will provide an opportunity to canvass academic reactions to this practice in order to frame the argument accurately, delve deeper into specific issues and potential restraints on SC contributions to SR, and ultimately take a position on the role of the Council in applying that normative scheme in counterterrorism contexts.

4.4 The Extent of Council Practice

In the broad exercise of its Chapter VII powers, the SC has sometimes rested its own practice on reasoning all too reminiscent of SR considerations. Therefore, it has relied upon its operational function to engage in concrete acts or deeds, namely the issuing of resolutions, whilst also invoking SR-inspired language. In other words, it has somewhat exhibited SR sensibilities both through positive actions and, to use constructivist parlance, via rhetorical processes. Whilst detractors and legal theorists might readily identify flaws in this approach, this argument is (perhaps) appreciated more by pushing the constructivist analogy

[149] Gowlland-Debbas, 'The Functions' (n 21) 289. See also Gowlland-Debbas, 'The Limits' (n 21) 365. For a comprehensive account on the relationship between collective security and SR, generally, see Forteau (n 20) 17 ff. On the same topic, see Gowlland-Debbas, 'The Limits' (n 21) 364–6.

a step further and by likening the SC to a State for the purposes of advancing SR because it is composed of States. In fact, this idea is by no means far-fetched when contemplated through the prism of other SC powers: '[t]he truth is that the Security Council in doing certain things—such as creating criminal courts—has State-like qualities'.[150] With this in mind, certain constructivists collapse both positive State actions and rhetorical commitments under the heading of State practice.[151] Although this line of reasoning is difficult to countenance in the present context, it highlights beautifully the difficulty in striking a balance between State actors and IOs when identifying norm-creating precedents, especially in a volatile field like counterterrorism or in the broader setting of global security. A case in point is the response to 9/11 and will be addressed in more detail in subsequent sections.[152]

Therefore, one could be particularly swayed by the idea that SR law is not only affected by norm-creating precedents, be they spearheaded by IOs and State actors, but can also be shaped by language, especially in high-level settings and fora like that of the SC.[153] Otherwise put, language becomes an integral part of the precedent-setting process, especially in politically sensitive areas like counterterrorism—where primary stakeholders and actors tend to weigh their words carefully—and the language ultimately adopted reflects a profound resolve in embodying, in the most precise terms possible, the principles and philosophy underlying a specific position, decision, or resolution.

Although the roles of both IOs and State actors in implementing SR will require further exploration, these brief remarks act as a preliminary gloss through which subsequent sections should be read whilst also steering the inquiry away from classical notions that positive deeds, not language, are necessarily and always more instrumental in situations involving various players and competing interests. For instance, the communication of clear and compelling messages remains a *sine qua non* criterion in Fuller's theoretical inquiries, a notion that seems hardly reconcilable with setting aside the idea that language may play a prominent role in shaping relations and norms in hostile settings.[154] Nevertheless, picking up on the thread

150 JR Crawford and T Grant, 'International Court of Justice' in TG Weiss and S Daws (eds), *The Oxford Handbook on The United Nations* (OUP 2007) 193, 205.

151 See, eg, F Kratochwil, 'Citizenship: On the Border of Order' in Y Lapid and F Kratochwil (eds), *The Return of Culture and Identity in IR Theory* (Lynne Rienner 1996) 181, 190–4; NG Onuf, 'Constructivism: A User's Manual' in V Kubàlkovà *et al.* (eds), *International Relations in a Constructed World* (ME Sharpe 1998) 58, 59; A Wendt, 'Collective Identity Formation and the International State' (1994) 88 American Political Science Review 384, 390.

152 See also Chapter 2 of this book.

153 On the power of interpretation in shaping the meaning of international legal texts and making law, see I Venzke, *How Interpretation Makes International Law: On Semantic Change and Normative Twists* (OUP 2012).

154 See, eg, LL Fuller, 'Human Interaction and the Law' (1969) 14 American Journal of Jurisprudence 1, 31 (discussing his interactional theory of law but suggesting that enemies bargain better through deeds rather than words). For a reconcilable constructivist approach to this idea, albeit through the lens of intervention, see MJ Finnemore, *The Purpose of Intervention: Changing Beliefs about the Use of Force* (Cornell University Press 2003) 5.

explored earlier, it is probably safe to contend that both language and action converge in a symbiotic rapport and contribute, simultaneously, to shaping international relations in the delicate areas of counterterrorism and global security.[155] Thus, at this stage it is sufficient to emphasize that the SC has sometimes relied upon SR logic in substantiating its political decisions, a notion that has received academic support and prompted some authors to analyse certain facets of Council practice in the light of SR repertoire.[156]

Such practice indeed warrants closer examination and has manifested itself in a variety of ways in at least three distinct manifestations, often compatible with SR logic and repertoire. First, as canvassed in earlier and later sections of this book, the SC has unquestionably engaged in a legislative exercise on counterterrorism issues, particularly when adopting Resolution 1373, thereby promulgating wide-ranging primary legal obligations. The nexus between that resolution-making and SR repertoire is undeniable: the violation of a State's categorical obligation to prevent terrorism would clearly set in motion legal consequences embodied in the secondary international legal norms codified by the ILC. Secondly, in other instances the Council relies on SR mechanics in actually attributing an internationally wrongful act to a State as part of its role of maintaining international peace and security. Relevant scenarios, whereby the Council assigns *legal* blame in addition to fulfilling its primary function, have been discussed earlier and will be explored thoroughly in subsequent sections.[157] Finally, in a more mixed bag, the SC sometimes delivers political statements and imposes specific measures or resolutions that straddle both its primary function of maintaining/restoring international peace and security (and the observance of Charter principles), on the one hand, and SR terrain, on the other. In so doing, the Council effectively mixes or melds distinct legal regimes to reach its outcomes, in particular by reeling in SR logic in its decision-making. The discussion now turns to this third type of scenario.

4.4.1 Protection of collective interests and obligations *erga omnes*

The SC has intervened in situations where internationally wrongful acts had been perpetrated against the international community as a whole. After all, the ILC itself defined the term 'sanctions' fairly broadly, thereby linking such measures to internationally wrongful conduct and potentially subsuming their application under the rubric of SR in the case of serious breaches. In this light, the Commission's definition appears to militate in favour of a rapprochement, or

[155] For thought-provoking accounts on interaction and international law, see the following works by J Brunnée and SJ Toope, *Legitimacy and Legality in International Law: An Interactional Account* (CUP 2010); 'International Law and Constructivism: Elements of an Interactional Theory of International Law' (2000) 39 CJTL 19; 'Interactional International Law' (2001) 3 International Law Forum du Droit International 186.

[156] See, eg, Dupuy, 'Quelques' (n 25) 47–55 (highlighting select aspects); Gaja (n 139) 297–320; Gowlland-Debbas, 'Security' (n 21); Gowlland-Debbas, 'The Functions' (n 21) 288–94; Gowlland-Debbas (n 27) 8–12.

[157] See Sections 4.2; 4.4.5; 4.5.

functional analogy, between sanctions and (collective) countermeasures. For the ILC, sanctions are

> reactive measures applied by virtue of a decision taken by an international organization following a breach of an international obligation having serious consequences for the international community as a whole, and in particular ... certain measures which the United Nations is empowered to adopt, under the system established by the Charter, with a view to the maintenance of international peace and security.[158]

An ILC report also suggested that competent UN organs would have been 'empowered not only to authorize, but even to direct a Member State other than the one directly injured by a particular international offence, or a group of Member States' or, in certain circumstances, 'all Member States, to apply certain sanctions not involving the use of force against a State which ha[d] committed an offence of a specified content and gravity'.[159]

Although the SC has never formally pronounced on a possible 'act of aggression', a scenario expressly recognized in Article 39 of the UN Charter but never defined elsewhere within the same instrument—possibly because the Council dreads invoking such undefined language[160]—it has nonetheless equated 'threats to the peace' with State behaviours amounting to violations of obligations *erga omnes*. As will be seen in the practice discussed later in this chapter, the SC seems more comfortable with labelling internationally wrongful conduct a 'breach of the peace' or 'threat to the peace' than to invoke formally the notion of 'aggression'.[161] Moreover, when it has condemned acts of aggression, it has done so in the context of resolutions not adopted under Chapter VII.[162] As one publicist highlights, SC resolution-making on this front is renowned for 'the plasticity of the circumstances

[158] ILC, 'Report of the International Law Commission on the Work of its 31st Session' (14 May–3 August 1979) UN Doc A/34/10; (1979) II(2) *YILC* 121 [21]. See also France in *Repertoire of the Practice of the Security Council 1959–1963: Chapter XI* <http://www.un.org/en/sc/repertoire/59-63/59-63_11.pdf> accessed 10 August 2015, 267; G Arangio-Ruiz, 'Third Report on State Responsibility' (1991) UN Doc A/CN.4/440 and Add.1; (1991) II(1) *YILC* 10 [15]. Interestingly, Ago considered it possible that the violation of an international obligation by one State would create a new relationship between that State and an IO, namely at the secondary normative level. Consequently, the organization would then be empowered, and perhaps obliged, to 'react against the internationally wrongful conduct by applying sanctions collectively decided upon'. See R Ago, 'Third Report on State Responsibility' (1971) UN Doc A/CN.4/246 and Add 1–3; (1971) II(1) *YILC* 210 [40]. See also UN Legal Counsel in (1972) *UN Juridical Yearbook* 194–5.

[159] R Ago, 'Eighth Report on State Responsibility' (1979) UN Doc A/CN.4/318 and Add.1–4; (1979) II(1) *YILC* 43 [92]; ILC Report–31st Session (n 158) 119 [13].

[160] See P-M Dupuy, 'L'impossible Agression: Les Malouines entre l'O.N.U. et l'O.E.A.' (1982) 28 AFDI 337, 342–3. See also Gowlland-Debbas, 'Security' (n 21) 63.

[161] For instance, the Council strongly condemned Iraq's unlawful invasion of Kuwait but failed to invoke the language of 'aggression' or 'act of aggression'. See UNSC Res 660 (2 August 1990) UN Doc S/RES/660; UNSC Res 661 (6 August 1990) UN Doc S/RES/661; UNSC Res 662 (9 August 1990) UN Doc S/RES/662. Similarly, the Council termed both the attack of North Korea on South Korea and Argentina's invasion of the Falkland Islands a 'breach of the peace'. See UNSC Res 82 (25 June 1950) UN Doc S/1501; UNSC Res 502 (3 April 1982) UN Doc S/RES/502; UNSC Verbatim Record (2 April 1982) UN Doc S/PV/2346.

[162] See, eg, the resolutions canvassed in P Webb, *International Judicial Integration and Fragmentation* (OUP 2013) 127–8.

in which [it is] prepared to assert its primary responsibility for international peace and security'.[163] Ironically, the Council readily invokes the concept of 'terrorism' and adopts far-reaching resolutions on that topic without working from any universally accepted definition of the term, although its indication in Resolution 1566 (2004) that it relies on a working definition of the term partly filled that void. In interpreting this strand of SC resolution-making, certain commentators highlight that resolutions imposing sanctions predicated on a 'threat to peace' are contingent on considerations revolving around the principle of legality, which is a central tenet of SR law. For those scholars, the violation of an international obligation constitutes a *sine qua non*, and determinant, element in the establishment of a 'threat to the peace'.[164] Similarly, one author rightly emphasizes that '[d]eterminations under Article 39 have thus been linked to alleged breaches of international law and imputed to particular legal entities, with the violation becoming a constituent element of the threat to or breach of the peace'.[165] By reading the prior requirement of SR into its decision-making, namely the violation of an obligation leading to the analysis of the concept of legality, the SC thus initiates an important rapprochement with secondary norms, thereby significantly narrowing the gap between its functions and SR implementation.

Amongst the aforementioned violations of obligations *erga omnes*, the Council has intervened in the following cases, inter alia: acts involving aggression or the use of force;[166] the unlawful invasion of a State's territory by another;[167] interferences (both military and non-military) on the territory of another State;[168]

[163] S Chesterman, *Just War or Just Peace? Humanitarian Intervention and International Law* (OUP 2001) 236.

[164] See, eg, Abi-Saab (n 143) 75; Combacau (n 103) 104–6; P Weckel, 'Le Chapitre VII de la Charte et son Application par le Conseil de Sécurité' (1991) 37 AFDI 169.

[165] Gowlland-Debbas, 'The Functions' (n 21) 288. See also ibid 292 (remarking that 'findings of illegality have formed in practice a constituent part of Council determinations' and that 'it is evident that peace could not be restored without putting an end to the violation'). For a contrary view, particularly critical of Gowlland-Debbas' position, see G Nolte, 'The Limits of the Security Council's Powers and its Functions in the International Legal System: Some Reflections' in Byers (n 21) 322–3 ('[i]t is true that the Council has the power to impute responsibility, but again, this is limited to the extent that it is necessary for the exercise of its other powers').

[166] See the following SC resolutions counteracting recourses to force (also sometimes termed 'acts of aggression' by the Council): by Portugal against Zambia (UNSC Res 268 (28 July 1969) UN Doc S/RES/268), Guinea (UNSC Resolutions 275 (22 December 1969) UN Doc S/RES/275, 289 (23 November 1970) UN Doc S/RES 289, and 290 (8 December 1970) UN Doc S/RES/290), or Senegal (UNSC Resolutions 273 (9 December 1969) UN Doc S/RES/273, 294 (15 June 1971) UN Doc S/RES/294, and 321 (23 October 1972) UN Doc S/RES/321); by Southern Rhodesia against neighbouring States (UNSC Resolutions 326 (2 February 1973) UN Doc S/RES 326), 328 (10 March 1973) UN Doc S/RES 328, 403 (14 January 1977) S/RES/403, and 424 (17 March 1978) UN Doc S/RES/424); by South Africa against neighbouring States (UNSC Resolutions 300 (12 October 1971) UN Doc S/RES/300, 418 (4 November 1977) UN Doc S/RES/418, and 466 (11 April 1980) UN Doc S/RES 466).

[167] See, eg, Iraq's invasion of Kuwait: SC Res 660 (n 161); SC Res 661 (n 161); UNSC Res 665 (25 August 1990) UN Doc S/RES/665; UNSC Res 687 (3 April 1991) UN Doc S/RES/687.

[168] See, eg, the interferences by neighbouring States in the territory of Bosnia-Herzegovina (UNSC Resolutions 752 (15 May 1992) UN Doc S/RES/752, 757 (30 May 1992) UN Doc S/RES/757, and 836 (4 June 1993) UN Doc S/RES/836); or the interferences in the territory of the DRC (UNSC Resolutions 1234 (9 April 1999) UN Doc S/RES/1234 and 1304 (16 June 2000) UN Doc S/RES/1304).

the refusal of the peoples' right to self-determination;[169] systematic and massive human rights violations[170] (in particular genocide,[171] racial discrimination,[172] apartheid[173] and ethnic cleansing[174]); contraventions to IHL;[175] and terrorist attacks.[176] By broadening the scope of its decision-making authority to include acts of terrorism, coupled with its reliance on SR principles to underpin some aspects of its reasoning, the Council in many ways signals its potential role in implementing SR. Under this light, a prima facie parallel with the events following 9/11 unquestionably comes full circle.

4.4.2 The cessation of internationally wrongful conduct

An absolutely vital component of the law governing the international responsibility of States resides in the obligations of cessation and non-repetition. In sum, an obligation to cease the wrongful conduct incumbent upon the responsible State and, if required by the circumstances, to provide assurances or guarantees of non-repetition flows from its internationally wrongful act and, by extension, from its

169 See the case of Southern Rhodesia (UNSC Resolutions 232 (16 December 1966) UN Doc S/RES/232 and 253 (29 May 1968) UN Doc S/RES/253).

170 See, inter alia, the following examples: political repression in Southern Rhodesia (SC Res 253 (n 169) and UNSC Res 277 (18 March 1970) UN Doc S/RES/277); massive violence and acts of murder against African peoples in South Africa (SC Res 418 (n 166)); the expulsion and poor treatment of people, and their property, carried out by Iraq in Kuwait (UNSC Res 670 (25 September 1990) UN Doc S/RES/670); the repression of Iraqi civilian populations (UNSC Res 688 (5 April 1991) UN Doc S/RES/688); the repression in Kosovo by Yugoslavian authorities (UNSC Res 1199 (23 September 1998) UN Doc S/RES/1199); the situation in East Timor (UNSC Res 1264 (15 September 1999) UN Doc S/RES 1264).

171 See, eg, the situation in Rwanda (UNSC Resolutions 918 (17 May 1994) UN Doc S/RES/918 and 925 (8 June 1994) UN Doc S/RES 925). It should be noted, however, that in these resolutions the SC did not attribute the perpetration of the genocide to specific persons or entities, including the Rwandan government. Instead, an expert commission and an international criminal tribunal were subsequently instituted by UNSC Resolutions 935 (1 July 1995) UN Doc S/RES/935 and 955 (8 November 1994) UN Doc S/RES/955, respectively, but with the sole purpose of imposing individual criminal responsibility upon guilty individuals.

172 See, inter alia, the following examples: the declaration of independence voiced by a racist minority in Southern Rhodesia (UNSC Res 216 (12 November 1965) UN Doc S/RES/216); the situation in South Africa (SC Res 418 (n 166)).

173 See, eg, the situation in South Africa (SC Res 418 (n 166)).

174 See, eg, the situation in Bosnia-Herzegovina (UNSC Resolutions 757 (n 168), 787 (16 November 1992) UN Doc S/RES/787, and 820 (17 April 1993) UN Doc S/RES/820.

175 See, inter alia, the following examples: Iraq's invasion of Kuwait (UNSC Resolutions 666 (13 September 1990) UN Doc S/RES/666 and 670 (n 170)); the conflict in Bosnia-Herzegovina (UNSC Resolutions 787 (n 174) and 827 (25 May 1993) UN Doc S/RES/827; the situation in Rwanda (SC Res 918 (n 171)); the repression in Kosovo by Yugoslavian authorities (SC Res 1199 (n 170)); the situation in East Timor (SC Res 1264 (n 170)).

176 See, eg, UNSC Res 748 (31 March 1992) UN Doc S/RES/748 (calling upon Libya to cease all forms of terrorism); UNSC Res 1054 (26 April 1996) UN Doc S/RES/1054 (directed against Sudan following the assassination attempt of the Egyptian President in Addis Ababa because it had harboured terrorists on its soil). On the latter resolution, see also Bennouna (n 22) 564. In a subsequent resolution, the SC reiterated its demands and imposed sanctions on Sudanese aircraft. See UNSC Res 1070 (16 August 1996) UN Doc S/RES/1070 [3].

international responsibility. The ILC has captured this fundamental aspect of SR in ARSIWA Article 30, which provides:

> The State responsible for the internationally wrongful act is under an obligation:
> (*a*) to cease that act, if it is continuing;
> (*b*) to offer appropriate assurances and guarantees of non-repetition, if circumstances so require.[177]

Thus, when read in tandem with this provision, it becomes apparent that the decisions and requests issued by the SC in many global security contexts hinge, to a large extent, on logic congruent with SR repertoire.[178] For instance, the Council often calls upon a wrongdoing State to cease a given behaviour that is synonymous with a 'threat to the peace' and concomitantly amounts to the violation of an international obligation incumbent upon said State. In fact, the Commentary to ARSIWA Article 30 also acknowledges this eventuality, pointing out that cessation 'is frequently demanded not only by States but also by the organs of international organizations such as the General Assembly and Security Council in the face of serious breaches of international law'.[179]

Certain examples immediately come to mind and span several decades. For instance, in 1965 the SC expressed grave concern over the situation prevalent in Southern Rhodesia following the unilateral declaration of independence made by the racist minority in that territory. The Council then imposed several obligations on the UK, which was the administering Power of Southern Rhodesia, with a view to achieving the cessation of the internationally wrongful act. In particular, the SC: (i) determined that the administering Power 'should put an end to [the situation] and that its continuance in time constitute[d] a threat to international peace and security'; (ii) called upon the UK 'to quell [the] rebellion of the racist minority'; and further called upon that State 'to take all other appropriate measures which would prove effective in eliminating the authority of the usurpers and in bringing the minority régime in Southern Rhodesia to an immediate end'.[180] In a resolution adopted under Chapter VII three years later, the SC observed that the unlawful situation in Southern Rhodesia had not come to an end and reiterated the obligation of cessation incumbent upon the UK. In this regard, it called

[177] ARSIWA (n 34) Art 30.

[178] See, eg, V Gowlland-Debbas, 'Sanctions Regimes Under Article 41 of the UN Charter' in idem (ed.), *National Implementation of United Nations Sanctions: A Comparative Study* (Nijhoff 2004) 3, 19–20; Bennouna (n 22) 560–64 (discussing SC precedents involving the cessation of internationally wrongful conduct, including in the counterterrorism context). On counterterrorism contexts, see also S Clavier, 'Contrasting Perspectives on Preemptive Strike: The United States, France, and the War on Terror' (2006) 58 Maine Law Review 566, 575.

[179] Commentary to ARSIWA (n 34) Art 30 p 89 [4].

[180] UNSC Res 217 (20 November 1965) UN Doc S/RES/217 [1], [4]–[5]. Interestingly, at [3] the Council also made express reference to international law, thereby '[c]ondemn[ing] the usurpation of power by a racist settler minority' and 'regard[ing] the declaration of independence by it as having no legal validity'.

upon that State to 'take urgently all effective measures to bring to an end the rebellion in Southern Rhodesia'.[181]

As discussed in greater detail in the next Section 4.4.3, SC resolution-making in the aftermath of Iraq's unlawful invasion of Kuwait in the 1990s sought considerable inspiration from SR principles. For the moment, suffice it to point out that the Council's initial reaction to the unlawful invasion incorporated an obligation of cessation which it imposed on Iraq in the hope that it would immediately cease its unlawful conduct. In its initial Resolution 660 adopted on 2 August 1990, the SC condemned the invasion as a breach of international peace and security; in paragraph 2 of that document, it '[d]emand[ed] that Iraq withdraw immediately and unconditionally all its forces to the positions in which they were located on 1 August 1990'.[182] In the next resolution, adopted on 6 August 1990, the Council lamented the fact that Iraq had not complied with the obligation of cessation it had set out in its previous resolution. Acting under Chapter VII, the SC '[d]etermine[d] that Iraq so far ha[d] failed to comply with paragraph 2 of resolution 660 (1990) and ha[d] usurped the authority of the legitimate Government of Kuwait'.[183] Over a year after the unlawful invasion, in April 1991 the SC drew once again on SR repertoire and imposed an obligation of cessation upon Iraq. This time, in Resolution 688 the Council expressed grave concern over the repression of the Iraqi civilian population in many parts of that State, particularly in the Kurdish-populated areas. After condemning this unlawful conduct, the Council '[d]emand[ed] that Iraq, as a contribution to removing the threat to international peace and security in the region, *immediately end* this repression' (emphasis added).[184]

SC resolution-making in the aftermath of the infamous *Lockerbie* incident[185] also became particularly relevant for the objectives underpinning the global security project, particularly counterterrorism strategies. More importantly for present purposes, it incontrovertibly established a nexus between the Council's primary function of maintaining international peace and security and the law governing the international responsibility of States. In the preamble of Resolution 748, the SC stressed that it was '[c]onvinced that the suppression of acts of international terrorism, including those in which States are directly or indirectly involved, is essential for the maintenance of international peace and security'.[186] Then, invoking Article 2(4) of the UN Charter, the Council reaffirmed that 'every State has the duty to refrain from organizing, instigating, assisting or participating in terrorist acts in another State or acquiescing in organized activities within its territory directed towards the commission of such acts, when such acts involved a threat or use of force'.[187] Moving on to formulating specific prescriptions under Chapter VII and drawing from SR repertoire, the Council went on to impose a

181 SC Res 253 (n 169) [2]. 182 SC Res 660 (n 161) [1]–[2].
183 SC Res 661 (n 161) [1]. 184 SC Res 688 (n 170) [2].
185 On the Council's application of attribution principles in that context, see Section 4.5.2.
186 SC Res 748 (n 176). 187 SC Res 748 (n 176).

categorical duty of cessation on Libya regarding terrorist actions and support of terrorist groups. In this regard, it '[d]ecide[d] also that the Libyan Government must commit itself to *cease all forms of terrorist action and all assistance to terrorist groups* and that it must promptly, by concrete actions, demonstrate its renunciation of terrorism' (emphasis added).[188]

In fulfilling its primary function, the SC has also adopted a series of resolutions incorporating obligations of cessation which, unlike in the scenarios canvassed earlier in this chapter, were addressed to both States and non-State entities. When these obligations of cessation cropped up in the context of armed hostilities within the territory of a single State, this in no way absolved the relevant State—or neighbouring States in some instances—from deploying their best efforts to comply with the Council's prescriptions. In such scenarios, the SC often directs the obligation to cease hostilities at all parties concerned. For instance, when confronted with serious human rights and IHL violations in Rwanda, the Council '[d]emand[ed] that all parties to the conflict *immediately cease hostilities*, agree to a cease-fire, and *bring an end* to the mindless violence and carnage engulfing Rwanda' (emphasis added).[189] Similarly, when faced with the repression of civilians in Kosovo and serious human rights and IHL violations, the SC '[d]emand[ed] that all parties, groups and individuals *immediately cease hostilities* and maintain a ceasefire in Kosovo' (emphasis added).[190]

In other circumstances, such as the situations in Bosnia-Herzegovina and the Democratic Republic of Congo discussed immediately below, the Council's prescriptions directed at non-States entities were coupled with specific obligations of cessation incumbent upon States. Therefore, this line of precedents evinces both (i) the Council's willingness to draw from SR logic, specially the concept of cessation of wrongful conduct, when dealing with mixed internationally wrongful conduct authored by States and non-State entities, and (ii) the extensiveness of its practice on this front. The SC borrowed from this line of reasoning when confronted both by the interferences of neighbouring States in Bosnia-Herzegovina in 1992 and by hostilities occurring in that territory. With respect to the hostilities, the Council '[d]emand[ed] that all parties and others concerned in Bosnia and Herzegovina *stop the fighting immediately*' (emphasis added).[191] Moving on to deal with specific aspects of the situation directly linked to SR law, the SC then '[d]emand[ed] that all forms of interference from outside Bosnia and Herzegovina, including by units of the Yugoslav People's Army as well as elements of the Croatian Army, *cease immediately*' and that 'Bosnia and Herzegovina's

[188] SC Res 748 (n 176) [2]. In this regard, it should be recalled that in the preamble of the same resolution, the Council had determined that the failure by Libya 'to demonstrate by concrete actions its renunciation of terrorism ... constitute[d] a threat to international peace and security'. By way of follow-up, UNSC Res 883 (11 November 1993) UN Doc S/RES/883 [1]–[7], [9]–[10] called for Libya to comply with the earlier resolutions and imposed additional aircraft and financial sanctions upon it.

[189] SC Res 918 (n 171) [1].

[190] SC Res 1199 (n 170) [1].

[191] SC Res 752 (n 168) [1].

neighbours take swift action *to end such interference* and respect the territorial integrity of Bosnia and Herzegovina' (emphasis added).[192]

Similarly, the hostile situation that arose in the DRC at the end of the twentieth century elicited strong condemnation from the SC, particularly concerning outside interferences in the territory of that State. In April 1999, the Council began by reaffirming 'the obligation of all States to respect the territorial integrity, political independence and national sovereignty of the DRC and other States in the region, including the obligation to refrain from the threat or use of force'; it then reaffirmed 'the need for all States to *refrain from any interference* in each other's internal affairs, in accordance with the Charter of the United Nations' (emphasis added).[193] After deploring the ongoing hostilities and the presence of foreign forces in the DRC, the SC called upon 'those States *to bring to an end the presence of these uninvited forces* and to take immediate steps to that end' (emphasis added).[194] The Council went on to frame the obligation of cessation broadly, thereby '[d]emand[ing] an *immediate halt* to the hostilities' (emphasis added).[195]

In a subsequent resolution, the Council lamented the continuing hostilities in the DRC and the serious human rights and IHL violations taking place therein, before formulating a series of obligations geared towards the cessation of unlawful behaviour. In particular, acting under Chapter VII, the Council called upon 'all parties *to cease hostilities* throughout the territory of the [DRC]'; it similarly reiterated 'its unreserved condemnation of the fighting between Ugandan and Rwanda forces in Kisangani in violation of the sovereignty and territorial integrity of the [DRC]' and demanded 'that these forces and those allied to them *desist from further fighting*' (emphasis added).[196] In order to induce compliance with its prescriptions related to cessation, the Council further demanded that: (i) 'Ugandan and Rwanda forces as well as forces of the Congolese armed opposition and other armed groups *immediately and completely withdraw* from Kisangani'; (ii) 'Uganda and Rwanda, which ha[d] violated the sovereignty and territorial integrity of the [DRC], *withdraw all their forces* from the territory of the [DRC] without further delay'; and (iii) 'all other foreign military presence and activity, direct and indirect, in the territory of the [DRC] *be brought to an end*' (emphasis added).[197]

Again, these precedents establish a clear link between the Council's primary function and SR repertoire in relevant circumstances. What is more, the SC itself expressly connected the threats to international peace and security that arose in the DRC hostilities with international law. In the preambles of the two aforementioned resolutions, it expressed deep concern for widespread violations of human rights and IHL in the territory of the DRC (which included acts of, and incitement to, ethnic hatred).[198] Going a step further in its directions to the parties

[192] SC Res 752 (n 168) [3]. At [4], the Council further demanded that those military units be either withdrawn, or be subject to the authority of Bosnia and Herzegovina, or be disbanded and disarmed according to specific modalities.

[193] SC Res 1234 (n 168) [1].

[194] SC Res 1234 (n 168) [2].

[195] SC Res 1234 (n 168) [3].

[196] SC Res 1304 (n 168) [1]–[2].

[197] SC Res 1304 (n 168) [3], [4(a)], [4(c)].

[198] SC Res 1234 (n 168) 6th preambular; SC Res 1304 (n 168) 15th preambular.

to the conflict, the Council called upon all parties to 'protect human rights and to respect international humanitarian law' which included express reference to 'the Geneva Conventions of 1949 and the Additional Protocols of 1977, and the Convention on the Prevention and Punishment of the Crime of Genocide of 1948'.[199] Thus, the obligations of cessation imposed by the Council were also unequivocally aimed at redressing violations of international *legal* obligations in addition to restoring international peace and security.

4.4.3 Obligation of reparation and return to legality under Chapter VII

It might come as no surprise to domestic lawyers that SR law has incorporated in its remedial scheme a common feature of many municipal legal orders, namely the idea of reparation. It follows that much like the obligation of cessation canvassed in the previous section, the obligation of reparation is absolutely central to SR repertoire.[200] In fact, it has become trite to say—and SC resolutions examined in subsequent pages further lend credence to this idea—that '[i]t is a principle of international law that the breach of an engagement involves an obligation to make reparation in an adequate form'.[201] With this in mind, the ILC codified the governing principle in Article 31 of its finalized text in the following terms:

1. The responsible State is under an obligation to make full reparation for the injury caused by the internationally wrongful act.
2. Injury includes any damage, whether material or moral, caused by the internationally wrongful act of a State.[202]

In many ways, this provision encapsulates a basic and straightforward juridical idea which finds many analogies in municipal legal orders: a State that is internationally responsible for wrongful conduct must repair its breach. As a corollary, ARSIWA Article 34 spells out that reparation can take on several forms and in any mixed configuration: '[f]ull reparation for the injury caused by the internationally wrongful act shall take the form of restitution, compensation and satisfaction, either singly or in combination, in accordance with the provisions of this chapter'.[203] Interestingly, reparative justice and compensatory redress have been incorporated into the decision-making of both the ICJ and SC, predominantly in the form of compensation or satisfaction. In the global security context, this should come as no

[199] SC Res 1234 (n 168) [6]. See also SC Res 1304 (n 168) [15].

[200] See generally Crawford (n 32) 480–505.

[201] *Case Concerning the Factory at Chorzów (Germany v Poland)* (Jurisdiction) PCIJ Rep Series A No 9, 21. See also *Case Concerning the Factory at Chorzów (Germany v Poland)* (Merits) PCIJ Rep Series A No 17, 29. See also CP Economides, 'La Responsabilité de l'État pour Fait Internationalement Illicite: Les Points Positifs et Négatifs du Projet de la Commission du Droit International' in KK Koufa (ed.), *Thesaurus Acroasium Vol 34: State Responsibility and the Individual* (Sakkoulas 2006) 165, 203–4; C Gray, 'Is There and International Law of Remedies?' (1985–86) 56 BYIL 25, 29; Higgins (n 75) 148.

[202] ARSIWA (n 34) Art 31.

[203] ARSIWA (n 34) Art 34.

surprise as it may simply be impossible in some cases for the internationally responsible State to provide restitution for its breach of international law. In fact, the ILC itself in its Commentary to ARSIWA Article 59 proclaimed that 'the competent organs of the United Nations have often recommended or required that compensation be paid following conduct by a State characterized *as a breach of its international obligations*' (emphasis added).[204]

For its part, whilst the ICJ's forays into the realm of compensation have been rather rare,[205] it is conversely not uncommon for it to reflect the principle of satisfaction in its decision-making by way of declaratory relief. In short, it often declares—be it in the operative part of its judgment or in the reasons for judgment—that the claimant State has received adequate satisfaction by virtue of the Court's declaration that the respondent State has violated international law.[206] The discussion now turns to the treatment of the obligation of reparation by the Council, which features centrally in that body's practice.[207]

At least on one occasion, it imposed an obligation of reparation upon Iraq in the context of its unlawful invasion of Kuwait, thereby mirroring an integral component of SR repertoire in its decision-making. As seen above,[208] many resolutions following Iraq's unlawful invasion of Kuwait set the stage for the invocation of Iraq's international legal responsibility by the Council. These documents were absolutely fundamental because they embodied the very notion of international responsibility, along with the corresponding ideas of reparation and return to legality. By way of example, Resolution 674 clearly established a nexus between international legal obligations and the Council's primary function of maintaining peace and security. In that resolution, it '[r]emind[ed] Iraq that *under international law it is liable* for any loss, damage or injury arising in regard to Kuwait and third States, and their nationals and corporations, as a result of the invasion and *illegal occupation* of Kuwait by Iraq' (emphasis added).[209] The Council then

[204] Commentary to ARSIWA (n 34) Art 59 p 143 [1].

[205] See, eg, *Corfu Channel Case (UK v Albania)* (Compensation) [1949] ICJ Rep 244; *Ahmadou Sadio Diallo (Guinea v DRC)* (Compensation) [2012] ICJ Rep 324. Similarly, after finding that Uganda was 'under obligation to make reparation to the Democratic Republic of the Congo for the injury caused' in the *Armed Activities* case, the Court unanimously decided that 'failing agreement between the Parties, the question of reparation due to the [DRC] shall be settled by the Court, and reserve[d] for this purpose the subsequent procedure in the case'. See *Armed Activities on the Territory of the Congo (DRC v Uganda)* (Merits) [2005] ICJ Rep 116, 281 [345(5)]–[345(6)]. In its Order of 1 July 2015, the ICJ resumed the proceedings in the case and fixed the time limits for the submission of written pleadings on the reparation issue: <http://www.icj-cij.org/docket/files/116/18720.pdf> accessed 24 August 2015.

[206] See, eg, *Corfu Channel (UK v Albania)* (Merits) [1949] ICJ Rep 4, 35–6; *Case Concerning the Application of the Convention on the Prevention and Punishment of the Crime of Genocide (Bosnia and Herzegovina v Serbia and Montenegro)* (Merits) [2007] ICJ Rep 43, 234 [463], 239, [471(9)]; *Pulp Mills on the River Uruguay (Argentina v Uruguay)* (Merits) [2010] ICJ Rep 14, 106 [282(1)]; *FYROM v Greece* (n 74) 693 [169]. For further views on satisfaction and other, more 'creative', reparative outcomes reached by regional courts, see B Simma, 'Peace through Law: The Role of the ILC' in Nolte (n 21) 190–1.

[207] See also Dipla (n 25) 39–41.

[208] See, eg, SC resolutions discussed in nn 182–4 and accompanying text.

[209] UNSC Res 674 (29 October 1990) UN Doc S/RES/674 [8].

situated the operative part of its decision squarely within the remit of secondary SR norms, by '[i]nvit[ing] States to collect relevant information regarding their claims, and those of their nationals and corporations, *for restitution or financial compensation by Iraq*, with a view to such arrangements as may be established *in accordance with international law*' (emphasis added).[210] Similarly, in Resolution 686 the SC demanded that Iraq 'implement its acceptance' of the twelve resolutions that preceded it and, inter alia, that it '[a]ccept in principle its liability under international law for any loss, damage or injury arising in regard to Kuwait and third States and their nationals and corporations, as a result of the invasion and illegal occupation of Kuwait by Iraq'.[211]

In resolution 687 of 3 April 1991, the Council reaffirmed:

> that Iraq, without prejudice to the debts and obligations of Iraq arising prior to 2 August 1990 ... *is liable under international law* for any direct loss, damage, including environmental damage and the depletion of natural resources, or injury to foreign Governments, nationals and corporations, *as a result of Iraq's unlawful invasion and occupation* of Kuwait (emphasis added).[212]

One has to look no further than the Commentary to the ARSIWA for confirmation that SC decision-making in this particular context was not only guided by SR law but was actually facilitated by that normative scheme. In its Commentary to Article 31, which governs the question of reparation,[213] the ILC cites—*expressis verbis*—wording from SC Resolution 687 before underscoring that '[t]his was a resolution adopted with reference to Chapter VII of the Charter of the United Nations, but *it is expressed to reflect Iraq's liability* "under international law ... as a result of its unlawful invasion and occupation of Kuwait"' (emphasis added).[214] Furthermore, leading publicists even suggest that '[i]f lawyers take this language seriously, Resolution 687 seems, by its terms, intended to be cited as an application of general principles of state responsibility that can be applied elsewhere'.[215]

[210] SC Res 674 (n 209) [9].

[211] UNSC Res 686 (2 March 1991) UN Doc S/RES/686 [2(b)].

[212] SC Res 687 (n 167) [16]. Some twenty years later, Germany referred to this groundbreaking resolution in its oral argument before the principal judicial organ of the UN. Its interpretation of the resolution's wording is particularly noteworthy: '[o]nly the Security Council has the power to impose particular ways and means of providing reparation, which it did in a particularly conspicuous manner when, dealing with Iraq's responsibility for the invasion of Kuwait'. See *Jurisdictional Immunities of the State (Germany v Italy: Greece intervening)*, Public Sitting (12 September 2011) <http://www.icj-cij.org/docket/files/143/16677.pdf> accessed 30 May 2015, 23–4. For a comprehensive study on legal aspects, drafting, and implementation history of SC Res 687, see I Johnstone, *Aftermath of the Gulf War: An Assessment of UN Action* (Lynne Rienner 1994).

[213] For the text of that provision, see n 202 and accompanying text.

[214] ILC, 'Report of the International Law Commission on the Work of its 53rd Session' (23 April–10 August 2001) UN Doc A/56/10; (2001) II(2) *YILC* 92 [10] fn 461 and accompanying text.

[215] Alvarez (n 7) 422. See also generally B Saul, 'Definition of "Terrorism" in the UN Security Council: 1985–2004' (2005) 4 Chinese Journal of International Law 141, 143 (pointing out that '[i]n applying legal rules to specific situations over time, [SC] resolutions may have precedential effects in equivalent situations'); P Hulsroj, 'The Legal Function of the Security Council' (2002) 1 Chinese Journal of International Law 59, 69; WM Reisman, 'The Constitutional Crisis in the United Nations' (1993) 87 AJIL 83, 85; Higgins (n 21) 6.

In the same resolution, the Council instituted the United Nations Compensation Commission (UNCC) responsible for managing a fund, also therein created, for the purposes of indemnifying victims of the conflict, again pursuant to SR logic.[216] It was also determined that the UNCC would be 'financed by a percentage of the value of the exports of petroleum and petroleum products from Iraq'.[217] This initiative was no doubt an innovation in the implementation of SR on the part of the SC, which sought considerable inspiration from the US mass tort claims model, both substantively and procedurally.[218] This precedent not only proved the Council's ability to draw from SR repertoire—a conclusion that clearly flows from the text of Resolution 687 and other related resolutions—but also its willingness to set up parallel implementation structures grounded in the same normative scheme. In this particular case, the Council ostensibly proceeded in this fashion to ensure the effective and swift handling of claims against the internationally responsible State. It should be recalled, however, that some authors queried whether the creation of this entity fell outside the ambit of SC powers and was, therefore, *ultra vires*.[219]

Granted, this precedent must be perceived as a particularly broad application of SR principles, given that Iraq was also made liable for damage caused by coalition forces.[220] Nevertheless, the implementation of SR by the Council can prove conceptually beneficial in sidestepping the evidentiary impasses identified elsewhere,[221] especially when it comes to establishing unilaterally a State's

[216] SC Res 687 (n 167) [18]–[19]. Several commentators agree that the SC's action in this case, coupled with the creation of the UNCC, amounted to the implementation of SR. See, eg, JA Frowein, 'Comment: State Responsibility and Peace' in Nolte (n 21) 47–8; Alvarez (n 7) 424–8; Dipla (n 25) 34–5; D Petrović, 'Other Specific Regimes of Responsibility: The UN Compensation Commission' in Crawford *et al.* (n 30) 847–59. On the responsibility of Iraq for environmental damage stemming from its invasion of Kuwait, see CR Payne and PH Sands (eds), *Gulf War Reparations and the UN Compensation Commission: Environmental Liability* (CUP 2011); ch 2 nn 55–6 and accompanying text.

[217] See UNSC Presidential Statement (1992) in *Repertoire of the Practice of the Security Council 1989–1992: Chapter VIII* <http://www.un.org/en/sc/repertoire/89-92/Chapter%208/MIDDLE%20EAST/item%2022_Iraq-Kuwait_.pdf> accessed 24 August 2015, 698 [24].

[218] See, eg, D Shelton, 'Righting Wrongs: Reparations in the Articles on State Responsibility' (2002) 96 AJIL 833, 856; DJ Bederman, 'The United Nations Compensation Commission and the Tradition of International Claims Settlement' (1994) 27 NYUJILP 1, 19; LC Owen, 'Between Iraq and a Hard Place: The U.N. Compensation Commission and Its Treatment of Gulf War Claims' (1998) 31 VJTL 499, 514; G Townsend, 'The Iraq Claims Process: A Progress Report on the United Nations Compensation Commission & U.S. Remedies' (1995) 17 Loyola LA International and Comparative Law Journal 973, 986; K Myers, 'Gulf War Continuing for U.S. Lawyers: Attorneys Battle Iraq in Courtrooms over Billions in Invasion-Related Damages' *National Law Journal* (Washington, DC, 20 June 1994) A1.

[219] See, eg, B Graefrath, 'International Crimes and Collective Security' in Wellens (n 19) 244–5. For more background and divergent views on the efficiency of the UNCC, see, inter alia, G Affaki, 'La Commission d'Indemnisation des Nations Unies: Trois Ans d'Épreuve au Service du Règlement des Différends Internationaux' (1994) 20 Droit et Pratique du Commerce International 471, 516; GA Christenson, 'State Responsibility and the UN Compensation Commission: Compensating Victims of Crimes of State' in RB Lillich (ed.), *The United Nations Compensation Commission* (Transnational 1995) 311, 348–58; P d'Argent, 'Le Fonds et la Commission de Compensation des Nations Unies' (1992) 25 RBDI 485, 499.

[220] On the unprecedented nature of this decision, see *Repertoire of SC Practice* (n 217) 654–5.

[221] See, eg, Proulx (n 3) Part I.

international responsibility or surmounting the exorbitant burden of proof associated with attribution. Consequently, by confirming Iraq's international liability, Resolution 687 absolved claimants 'from the otherwise heavy burden of proving the liability of a sovereign state'.[222] Moreover, it should be recalled that Iraq accepted liability for its internationally wrongful act and, by necessary implication, the Council's pronouncements on its unlawful conduct, which was guided by SR principles. Indeed,

> [o]n 6 April 1991, three days after the adoption of resolution 687 (1991), the Minister for Foreign Affairs of Iraq, in identical letters to the Secretary-General and the President of the Security Council, accepted the terms of the resolution, thereby accepting legal responsibility for damage directly caused to Governments, nationals and corporations by its invasion and occupation of Kuwait.[223]

In subsequent resolutions, the Council reiterated the international responsibility of Iraq whilst emphasizing the link between its decision-making and SR repertoire. For instance, in the preamble of Resolution 778 the Council '[r]ecall[ed] that Iraq, as stated in paragraph 16 of resolution 687 (1991), *is liable* for all direct damages resulting from its invasion and occupation of Kuwait, without prejudice to its debts and obligations arising prior to 2 August 1990' (emphasis added).[224] However, in recent years—namely over two decades after the adoption of its series of unprecedented resolutions—the Council has increasingly welcomed Iraq's willingness to comply with the prescriptions enshrined in those documents. Furthermore, the Council has begun terminating some of the measures it had implemented through those resolutions.[225]

Undoubtedly, the precedents of SC action pertaining to Iraq's unlawful invasion and occupation of Kuwait are certainly the most striking, particularly in terms of establishing a clear nexus between SR norms and the maintenance of international peace and security. However, it is by no means the only example of the Council drawing on SR repertoire to inform its decision-making under the aegis of Chapter VII. For example, as canvassed earlier in the context of Resolution 1304,[226] the SC found that both Uganda and Rwanda had authored various interferences, both military and non-military, on the territory of the DRC. As a result of this unlawful activity, the Council imposed a number of obligations of cessation and, acting under Chapter VII, enlisted support from SR's reparative

[222] M Kazazi, 'An Overview of Evidence before the United Nations Compensation Commission' (1999) 1 International Law Forum du Droit international 219, 221. See also Bederman (n 218) 19 (expounding that SC Res 687 'obviated the need for claimant countries [and claimants] to litigate whether there had been a predicate act implicating Iraq's state responsibility'); JJ Chung, 'The United Nations Compensation Commission and the Balancing of Rights Between Individual Claimants and the Government of Iraq' (2005) 10 UCLA Journal of International Law and FA 141, 155.

[223] *Repertoire of the Practice of the Security Council 1989–1992: Chapter V* <http://www.un.org/en/sc/repertoire/89-92/89-92_05.pdf> accessed 30 May 2015, 169–70.

[224] UNSC Res 778 (2 October 1992) UN Doc S/RES/778.

[225] See, eg, UNSC Res 2107 (27 June 2013) UN Doc S/RES/2107.

[226] See nn 168, 196–9 and accompanying text.

scheme in handing down its decision. In particular, it '[e]xpresse[d] the view that the Governments of Uganda and Rwanda should make reparations for the loss of life and the property damage they ha[d] inflicted on the civilian population in Kisangani, and request[ed] the Secretary-General to submit an assessment of the damage as a basis for such reparations'.[227]

4.4.4 Obligation of reparation and return to legality outside the Chapter VII framework

The Council's posture in the aftermath of Iraq's unlawful invasion of Kuwait marked a departure from previous practice in that it connoted a significant diversification in the imposition of secondary obligations stemming from the violation of primary obligations.[228]Although SR was deemed to be established in the relevant resolutions by virtue of the text alone, those documents nonetheless embodied the disciplines of responsibility and the corresponding ideas of reparation and return to legality.[229] It should be emphasized, however, that the resolutions dealing with Iraq's internationally wrongful conduct were primarily adopted expressly by reference to Chapter VII.

The SC has also drawn from SR repertoire in other types of decisional settings—perhaps even more closely related to its quasi-judicial powers—thereby illustrating the pervasive reach of that normative scheme. Indeed, the Council has previously invoked the SR-inspired obligation of reparation following the commission of an internationally wrongful act by a State, albeit without resting its finding on Chapter VII. One early example arose in Resolution 138, adopted in 1960, which addressed the abduction of Adolf Eichmann by Israel and established a clear nexus between SR law and the Council's primary functions. In the preamble of that resolution, the Council highlighted the 'violation of the sovereignty' of Argentina; in the operative part of the resolution, the Council requested 'the Government of Israel to make *appropriate reparation* in accordance with the Charter of the United Nations *and the rules of international law*' (emphasis added).[230] In fact, one eminent publicist (now ICJ Judge) concluded plainly that this resolution 'assessed the existence of a breach of an obligation under international law and outlined its legal consequences, albeit in general terms'.[231] Several other relevant cases come

[227] SC Res 1304 (n 168) [14]. [228] See, eg, Martin (n 8) 467.

[229] This proposition has received wide support. See Kazazi (n 222) 221; A Gattini, 'The UN Compensation Commission: Old Rules, New Procedures on War Reparations' (2002) 13 EJIL 161, 172; JR Crook, 'The United Nations Compensation Commission: A New Structure to Enforce State Responsibility' (1993) 87 AJIL 144, 147; MF di Rattalma, 'Le Régime de Responsabilité Internationale Institué par le Conseil d'Administration de la Commission de Compensation des Nations Unies' (1997) 101 RGDIP 45; B Stern, 'Un Système Hybride: La Procédure de Règlement Pour la Réparation des Dommages Résultant de L'occupation Illicite du Koweit par l'Irak' (1992) 37 McGill Law Journal 625.

[230] UNSC Res 138 (23 June 1960) UN Doc S/RES/138 [2].

[231] Gaja (n 21) 54. The two concerned States eventually resolved the matter by way of negotiation. See C Rousseau, 'Chronique des Faits Internationaux' (1960) 64 RGDIP 770, 782–3.

to mind and they form a rich body of older precedents that may be brought to bear on future situations involving global security violations. Furthermore, these resolutions also embody the corresponding idea of return to legality, which is a central component of SR repertoire.[232]

For instance, in March 1976 the Council expressed grave concern over South Africa's aggression against Angola, which amounted to a serious violation of the latter's sovereignty and territorial integrity. In the resulting resolution, the SC thus 'condemn[ed] South Africa's aggression against the People's Republic of Angola' and imposed an obligation of cessation upon South Africa, demanding that it 'scrupulously respect the independence, sovereignty and territorial integrity of [Angola]'.[233] Most importantly, the Council then imposed a clear obligation of reparation upon South Africa, pursuant to SR logic. In this regard, its prescription was unequivocal when it '[c]all[ed] upon the Government of South Africa *to meet the just claims of the People's Republic of Angola for a full compensation for the damage and destruction inflicted on its State* and for the restoration of the equipment and materials which its invading forces seized' (emphasis added).[234]

A few years later, the SC was confronted with the perpetration of crimes against civilians in the occupied territories in Israel. In particular, the Council: (i) voiced concerns over Israeli settlements in the occupied territories as a 'flagrant violation of the Geneva Convention relative to the Protection of Civilian Persons in Time of War'; (ii) lamented the recent assassination attempts against the Mayors of Nablus, Ramallah, and Al Bireh; and (iii) registered its profound concern that Jewish settlers in the occupied territories were allowed to bear arms which enabled them to commit crimes against the civilian Arab population.[235] Consequently, in Resolution 471 the Council '[c]ondemn[ed] the assassination attempts', thereby 'call[ing] for the immediate apprehension and prosecution of the perpetrators of these crimes' before expressing 'deep concern that Israel, as the occupying Power, ha[d] failed to provide adequate protection to the civilian population in the occupied territories in conformity with the provisions of the Geneva Convention'.[236] Most importantly for present purposes, the Council then proceeded to call 'upon the Government of Israel to *provide the victims with adequate compensation for the damages suffered* as a result of these crimes' (emphasis added).[237]

Another highly relevant example arose in the aftermath of Israel's aerial assault of nuclear installations in Iraq in 1981, the so-called Operation Opera and/or

[232] In fairness, the objective of return to legality has been associated more explicitly with specific remedial tools found in SR repertoire, particularly countermeasures and self-defence. See, eg, HP Aust, 'Circumstances Precluding Wrongfulness' in A Nollkaemper and I Plakokefalos (eds), *Principles of Shared Responsibility in International Law: An Appraisal of the State of the Art* (CUP 2014) 169, 205. However, some scholars query whether these remedial measures ensure a return to legality in an 'archaic' or 'primitive' manner, namely in a fashion reminiscent of 'old' international law, that is, before the advent of judicial and/or institutionalised dispute settlement methods. See, eg, ibid (also citing B Fassbender, *The United Nations Charter as the Constitution of the International Community* (Nijhoff 2009) 128).

[233] UNSC Res 387 (31 March 1976) UN Doc S/RES/387 [1]–[2].

[234] SC Res 387 (n 233) [4].

[235] UNSC Res 471 (5 June 1980) UN Doc S/RES/471, preamble.

[236] SC Res 471 (n 235) [1]–[2]. [237] SC Res 471 (n 235) [3].

Operation Babylon.[238] In Resolution 487, the Council prefaced the operative part of that document by expressing its deep concern 'about the danger to international peace and security created by the premeditated Israeli air attack on Iraqi nuclear installations' and recalled the obligation of all States to comply with the prescriptions enshrined in Article 2(4) of the UN Charter.[239] The Council then proceeded to characterize Israel's wrongful conduct as a violation of international law—that is, as an internationally wrongful act—by '[s]strongly condemn[ing] the military attack by Israel in clear violation of the Charter of the United nations and the norms of international conduct'.[240] With equally comparable clarity, the Council then imposed an obligation of reparation upon Israel in response to its unlawful behaviour. In this regard, the SC '[c]onsider[ed] that Iraq [was] *entitled to appropriate redress for the destruction it ha[d] suffered*, responsibility for which ha[d] been acknowledged by Israel' (emphasis added).[241]

This precedent lends particularly compelling support to the central thesis of this book: it clearly confirms that SR repertoire can inform the Council's decision-making, always in harmony with its primary mission related to the maintenance and restoration of international peace and security. What is more, it illustrates the Council's inclination—in relevant cases and by interweaving regimes along political/legal lines—to rely on the remedial scheme underpinning SR repertoire so as to ensure compliance with its resolutions. In this case, Resolution 487 was followed up by GA Resolution 36/27, in which that organ expressed 'its deep alarm over the unprecedented Israeli act of aggression on the Iraqi nuclear installations on 7 June 1981, which created a grave threat to international peace and security'.[242]

Unsurprisingly, the Assembly then echoed many of the Council's own findings, not least its strong condemnation of Israel's aerial assault as a 'premeditated and unprecedented act of aggression in violation of the Charter of the United Nations and the norms of international conduct'.[243] More importantly, after recalling the Council's Resolution 487, the GA proceeded to reiterate the obligation of compensation formulated earlier by the Council. Furthermore, the Assembly expressly linked that decision with the international responsibility of Israel for its internationally wrongful act. In this regard, the GA's own words are strikingly indicative of a strong nexus between SR law and the maintenance of global security, as it '[d]emand[ed] that Israel, *in view of its international responsibility for its act of aggression, pay prompt and adequate compensation* for the material damage and loss of life suffered as a result of the said act' (emphasis added).[244]

[238] See DK Shipler, 'Israeli Jets Destroy Iraqi Atomic Reactor; Attack Condemned by U.S. and Arab Nations' *NYT* (New York, 9 June 1981) A1.

[239] UNSC Res 487 (19 June 1981) UN Doc S/RES/487, preamble.

[240] SC Res 487 (n 239) [1].

[241] SC Res 487 (n 239) [6]. For a full background of the dispute before the SC, see *Repertoire of the Practice of the Security Council 1981–1984: Chapter VIII* <http://www.un.org/en/sc/repertoire/81-84/Chapter%208/81-84_08-6-Complaint%20by%20Iraq%20.pdf> accessed 30 May 2015, 202–4.

[242] UNGA Res 36/27 (13 November 1981) UN Doc A/RES/36/27, preamble.

[243] GA Res 36/27 (n 242) [1].

[244] GA Res 36/27 (n 242) [6].

Interestingly, in the last seven years since the time of writing, Iraq has undertaken steps towards obtaining compensation from Israel as a result of Resolution 487. As an injured State under SR law, it is clear that Iraq considers that the SC effectively pronounced on the international responsibility of Israel in that resolution. Certain high-ranking Iraqi officials and politicians have asserted their State's right to seek compensation from Israel by virtue of Resolution 487, with some initially placing the envisaged compensatory figure in the range of billions to take into account both the damage suffered and the lost revenue a completed nuclear reactor would have generated.[245] Other early reports indicated that the Iraqi Parliament's Foreign Affairs Committee had actively discussed the matter with a view to securing billions of dollars in compensation from Israel.[246] Later on, various reports suggested that in 2009, Iraqi Prime Minister Nouri al-Maliki demanded compensation from Israel for the destruction of the nuclear installations, with one Iraqi MP emphasizing that the country's leadership had already 'turned to the UN and the Security Council demanding that Israel pay [Iraq] reparations for damage caused to the reactor'.[247] Other sources similarly suggested that 'Prime Minister Nuri al-Maliki and the Ministry of Foreign Affairs [had] petitioned the United Nations and the U.N. Security Council to demand that Israel pay compensation ... for the 1981 bombing'.[248] In early 2010, one Iraqi MP pointed out that 'Al-Maliki's appeal follow[ed] an answer received from the UN Secretariat by the government of Iraq on November 25, which [said] Iraq ha[d] a right to demand compensation for the damage Israel did to it with the attack on the reactor, through a neutral committee, which [would] assess the extent of the damage'.[249] Whilst considerable uncertainty remains as to the exact status of Iraq's claim against Israel, the particulars of such a claim, and any future steps Iraq is contemplating in this regard, this precedent nonetheless illustrates the pervasive reach of SR. In this scenario, the SC not only acted as invocator and implementer of SR, but its resolution also subsequently informed the enforcement of the responsibility of Israel by the injured State.

Reverting to instances of State and institutional practice supporting this chapter's central argument, it should be stressed that SC condemnation of South Africa's hostile act against Lesotho in 1982 warrants consideration. In that context, the

[245] See, eg, 'Iraq: Israel Should Compensate Osirak Attack' *PressTV* (Tehran, 4 May 2009) <http://edition.presstv.ir/detail/93522.html> accessed 30 May 2015.

[246] See, eg, D Peskin, 'Iraq Wants Israel to Pay for Bombing Reactor' *YNetNews* (Tel Aviv, 5 October 2009) <http://www.ynetnews.com/articles/0,7340,L-3713494,00.html> accessed 30 May 2015.

[247] 'Iraq Wants Israel to Pay for Destroyed Nuclear Reactor' *Israel Today* (Jerusalem, 5 January 2010) <http://www.israeltoday.co.il/NewsItem/tabid/178/nid/20317/Default.aspx?archive=article_title> accessed 30 May 2015.

[248] TB Gedalyahu, 'Iraq: Sue Israel for Billions for 1981 Bombing of Nuclear Site' *Arutz Sheva* (Jerusalem, 6 January 2010) <http://www.israelnationalnews.com/News/News.aspx/135383#.VTuDFZscTVI> accessed 30 May 2015. See also 'Iraq Demanding Compensation for 1981 Israeli Airstrike' *Iran Daily* (Tehran, 6 January 2010) <http://old.iran-daily.com/1388/10/16/MainPaper/3587/Page/1/index.htm#> accessed 30 May 2015.

[249] 'Iraq Pursuing Compensation for Israel Nuke Attack' *The Siasat Daily* (Hyderabad, 6 January 2010) <http://www.siasat.com/news/iraq-pursuing-compensation-israel-nuke-attack-70950/> accessed 30 May 2015.

Council '[s]trongly condemn[ed] the *apartheid* régime of South Africa for its premeditated aggressive act against the Kingdom of Lesotho which constitut[ed] a flagrant violation of the sovereignty and territorial integrity of that country'.[250] In a now familiar stroke of the pen, the Council then proceeded to impose an obligation of reparation upon South Africa, pursuant to SR repertoire. More specifically, it '[d]emand[ed] the payment by South Africa of *full and adequate compensation* to the Kingdom of Lesotho for the damage to life and property resulting from this aggressive act' (emphasis added).[251]

Similarly, the Council levelled charges against Israel following its unlawful intervention in the Tunisian area of Hammam Plage in 1985. In the preamble to Resolution 573, the Council observed that Israel 'claimed responsibility for the attack as soon as it had been carried out'.[252] This precedent lends persuasive credence to the ideas that the SC is animated by international law in certain circumstances and acts as a viable implementer of secondary SR norms in global security contexts. Indeed, in Resolution 573 the Council again established an express nexus between a State's conduct that contravened both the UN Charter and international law, on the one hand, and secondary SR norms, on the other. Otherwise put, the Council clearly couched Israel's violation in *legal* terms in addition to underscoring that it represented a threat to international peace and security, thereby pointing to a rapprochement between its inherent mission and SR law. That link comes into sharp focus when reading the wording of the resolution, in which the Council '[c]ondemn[ed] vigorously the act of armed aggression perpetrated by Israel against Tunisian territory in flagrant violation of the Charter of the United Nations, *international law* and norms of conduct' (emphasis added).[253] To complete the aforementioned rapprochement, the Council then proceeded to draw from secondary SR norms, and '[c]onsider[ed] that Tunisia [had] *the right to appropriate reparations* as a result of the loss of human life and material damage which it ha[d] suffered and for which Israel ha[d] claimed responsibility' (emphasis added).[254]

On the one hand, the above review of relevant practice evidences States' reliance on international legal argument when appearing before the SC. On the other, SC resolutions are equally instructive in demonstrating that organ's willingness to use SR logic in its own decision-making as a way to complement its primary task of maintaining international peace and security. Whilst select precedents have been canvassed earlier, numerous others could also be invoked to support the proposition that the SC sometimes implements SR and devises

[250] UNSC Res 527 (15 December 1982) UN Doc S/RES/527 [1].

[251] SC Res 527 (n 250) [2]. Two years earlier, the Council had also imposed an obligation of reparation upon South Africa for its unlawful conduct in and against Lesotho. See UNSC Res 580 (30 December 1985) UN Doc S/RES/580 [2] (demanding 'the payment by South Africa of *full and adequate compensation* to the Kingdom of Lesotho for the damage and loss of life resulting from this act of aggression' (emphasis added)).

[252] UNSC Res 573 (4 October 1985) UN Doc S/RES/573, preamble.

[253] SC Res 573 (n 252) [1].

[254] SC Res 573 (n 252) [4].

legal consequences, particularly cessation and reparation (often in tandem). For instance, in 1964 the SC deplored the occurrence of violent incidents engendered by the excursion of Vietnamese forces into Cambodian territory. Consequently, the Council '[r]equest[ed] *that just and fair compensation should be offered* to the Royal Government of Cambodia' and imposed an obligation of cessation (emphasis added).[255] Similarly, in 1970 the Council condemned in the strongest terms Portugal's invasion of Guinea and '[d]emand[ed] that *full compensation by the Government of Portugal be paid* to the Republic of Guinea for the extensive damage to life and property caused by the armed attack and invasion'.[256] In 1984, the SC chastised South Africa for its 'renewed, intensified, premeditated and unprovoked bombing' of Angola, along with its continuing occupation of parts of that territory.[257] After imposing an obligation of cessation, the Council '[r]eaffirm[ed] further that Angola [was] entitled to *prompt and adequate compensation* for the damage to life and property consequent upon these acts of aggression and the continuing occupation of parts of its territory by the South African military forces' (emphasis added).[258] In other resolutions, the Council reiterated and imposed further obligations of reparation on South Africa for its acts of aggression in both Angola and Botswana.[259]

Moreover, the SC has promulgated broader decisional guidelines in specific fields, whilst seeking considerable guidance from SR repertoire and general international law. In this regard, its forays into nuclear war prevention and non-proliferation expressly link its potential task of determining adequate compensation for nuclear aggression with international legal norms. This exercise would presumably entail that the Council first determine the international responsibility of the aggressor State by virtue of SR rules and/or ascertain that that State's behaviour was wrongful. Otherwise put, the Council made a direct reference to international legal rules governing the question of compensation for internationally wrongful conduct (in this case, nuclear aggression), which are part and parcel of SR law. The wording of Resolution 984 is eloquent, as the Council

> [e]xpresse[d] its intention to recommend appropriate procedures, in response to any request from a non-nuclear-weapon State party to the Treaty on the Non-Proliferation of

[255] UNSC Res 189 (4 June 1964) UN Doc S/RES/189 [1]–[3].

[256] SC Res 290 (n 166) [3]. In the same provision, the Council 'request[ed] the [UN] Secretary-General to assist the Government of the Republic of Guinea in the assessment of the extent of damage involved'.

[257] UNSC Res 546 (6 January 1984) UN Doc S/RES/546 [1].

[258] SC Res 546 (n 257) [3], [7]. The obligation to repair had been articulated initially by the Council in UNSC Res 545 (20 December 1983) UN Doc S/RES/545 [4]. The Council had also imposed a similar obligation of reparation four years earlier on South Africa following its unlawful activity in and against Angola. See UNSC Res 475 (27 June 1980) UN Doc S/RES/475 [6].

[259] See, eg, UNSC Res 567 (20 June 1985) UN Doc S/RES/567 [4]; UNSC Res 568 (21 June 1985) UN Doc S/RES/568 [5]; UNSC Res 571 (20 September 1985) UN Doc S/RES/571 [6]; UNSC Res 572 (30 September 1985) UN Doc S/RES/572 [4]; UNSC Res 577 (6 December 1985) UN Doc S/RES/577 [7]. Similarly, in 1979 the Council imposed an obligation of reparation on the 'responsible authorities', which were presumably South Africa and Southern Rhodesia, following acts of aggression suffered by Zambia. See UNSC Res 455 (23 November 1979) UN Doc S/RES/455 [5].

Nuclear Weapons that is the victim of such an act of aggression, *regarding compensation under international law* from the aggressor for loss, damage or injury sustained as a result of the aggression (emphasis added).[260]

In many ways, therefore, the SC has itself executed a rapprochement between its core mission and SR repertoire. As seen in this section, it has done so in the operative language of its resolutions dealing with specific global security threats and States' violations of international law. It has also pointed to such rapprochement in its more general resolutions, which lay down universal principles, such as in the case of Resolution 984.

4.4.5 Satisfaction, guarantees, and assurances of non-repetition

Although invariably subject to political considerations, collective action taken under UN auspices embodies the essence of return to legality, an objective either facilitated by reverting back to pre-breach conditions or by effecting practical change. Thus, '[n]evertheless, in their *consequences*, these mechanisms, as sanctions, have an important, law-enforcement function, their objective being to restore legality, which may be achieved either by a return to the *status quo ante* or by instituting change, though in some cases such measures may even appear to acquire a punitive character'.[261] Whilst some might insist that coercive economic sanctions pursue a punitive objective against internationally responsible States,[262] there is some level of consensus to the effect that such measures are devised primarily as a means of ensuring compliance with international law by such States.[263] In fact, most definitional efforts aiming to circumscribe the concept of 'sanctions' actually incorporate the idea of inducing compliance as the central aim of such measures.[264]

260 UNSC Res 984 (11 April 1995) UN Doc S/RES/984 [6].

261 Gowlland-Debbas, 'Security' (n 21) 63.

262 See, eg, Zoller (n 45) 106; ILC Report (n 127) 258 [152]. O Schachter, 'Self-Help and the Iranian Crisis' (1984) 37 Journal of International Affairs 231, 233 also highlighted the punitive character of countermeasures, a proposition that has been rebuked by the ILC in Commentary to ARSIWA (n 34) Art 51 p 135 [7]. For further rejection of this line of argument, see also UNSC Verbatim Record (14 April 1995) Un Doc S/PV/3519, 4 (Honduras), 6 (Nigeria), 12 (France).

263 See, eg, UNSC Verbatim Record (31 July 2006) UN Doc S/PV/5500, 3 (US); UNSC Verbatim Record (22 June 2006) UN Doc S/PV/5474, 12 (Slovakia), 22 (Tanzania), 32–3 (Austria); ibid (Resumption 1), 15 (Iraq), 17 (Venezuela); UNSC Verbatim Record (22 October 2001) UN Doc S/PV/4394, 4 (Germany); UNSC Verbatim Record (20 March 1998) UN Doc S/PV/3864, 18 (Portugal), 29 (France); UNSC Verbatim Record (14 April 1995) UN Doc S/PV/3519, 2 (Italy). See also D Cortright and GA Lopez, 'Reforming Sanctions' in Malone (n 28) 170, 172; A Reinisch, 'Developing Human Rights and Humanitarian Law Accountability of the Security Council for the Imposition on Economic Sanctions' (2001) 95 AJIL 851; ILC Report (n 127) 258–9 [152]. See also V Gowlland-Debbas, *Collective Responses to Illegal Acts in International Law: United Nations Action in the Question of Southern Rhodesia* (Nijhoff 1990) 472–3 (reviewing scholarship by Kelsen, Combacau, Giraud, and Virally and concluding that the purpose of Chapter VII sanctions 'is one of law enforcement and that they are not punitive').

264 See, eg, S/PV/5474 (n 263) 18 (Greece), 24 (France), 28 (Congo); S/PV/3519 (n 263) 2 (Italy), 4 (Honduras), 12 (France). See also J Combacau, 'Sanctions' in R Bernhardt *et al.* (eds), *Encyclopedia of Public International Law*, vol 4 (Elsevier 2000) 311, 312; CC Joyner, 'United Nations Sanctions

This is not to say, however, that the conceptual chasm dividing the law governing the responsibility of States and the SC's imposition of sanctions was always cogently articulated or unambiguously traversed in UN activities. Nor does it bolster the assertion that imposing such collective sanctions is effective or uncontroversial in the grander scheme of things.[265] In that regard, the sanctions imposed by the Council upon Iraq during a period spanning over a decade were particularly instructive and signalled the conflation of SR repertoire with other international legal schemes. In particular, it becomes clear that the sanctions against Iraq primarily served a punitive character, a response that, arguably, could have been articulated more clearly within the ambit of SR principles. This undoubtedly led some publicists to view these measures as a 'disguised form of punishment of a defeated aggressor state', a punitive application of the Council's powers that would have, on this view, benefited more if formulated unequivocally under the law of international responsibility. What is more, the 'Council was unable to explain convincingly which of these different rationales [punishment versus SR] prevailed at a given time, whether their relative importance could change, and how this could influence the Council's preparedness to modify the sanctions regime'.[266]

Nevertheless, several measures and sanctions imposed by the SC could undoubtedly be construed as distinct and particularly binding manifestations of the SR-derived concepts of satisfaction or assurances and/or guarantees of non-repetition.[267] As canvassed earlier,[268] the obligation of cessation—coupled

after Iraq: Looking Back to See Ahead' (2003) 4 Chinese Journal of International Law 329, 331; Tzanakopoulos, *Disobeying* (n 19) 76. Interestingly, some publicists subsume both countermeasures and UN sanctions under the umbrella term 'sanctions', whilst suggesting that 'sanctions' are geared towards deterring and redressing violations of international law. See, eg, F Swindells 'UN Sanctions in Haiti: A Contradiction under Articles 41 and 55 of the UN Charter' (1997) 20 FILJ 1878, 1984–5; Cavaré (n 35) 221. But see K Herndl, 'Reflections on the Role, Functions and Procedures of the Security Council of the United Nations' (1987) 206 RdC 289, 334 (opining that 'Cavaré's view that the purpose of a sanction should be in any event the complete restoration of the state of the law' and 'that sanctions should consequently be directed against anyone who violates international law in general, would seem to go too far').

[265] See generally M Miyagawa, *Do Economic Sanctions Work?* (St Martin's 1992); C Dominicé, 'The International Responsibility of the United Nations for Injuries Resulting from Non-Military Enforcement Measures' in Ragazzi (n 62) 369; DJ Halliday, 'The Impact of the UN Sanctions on the People of Iraq' (1999) 28 Journal of Palestine Studies 29; R Normand, 'A Human Rights Assessment of Sanctions: The Case of Iraq, 1990-1997' in WJM Van Genugten and GA de Groot (eds), *United Nations Sanctions: Effectiveness and Effects, Especially in the Field of Human Rights: A Multi-Disciplinary Approach* (Intersentia 1999) 19, 25.

[266] B Fassbender, 'Uncertain Steps into a Post-Cold War World: The Role and Functioning of the UN Security Council after a Decade of Measures Against Iraq' (2002) 13 EJIL 273, 281–2.

[267] See, eg, Gowlland-Debbas, 'The Functions' (n 21) 293. For a concrete example of this practice by the SC, see the measures imposed in SC Res 687 (n 167) esp [4], in which the Council reaffirmed the necessity of obtaining assurances that Iraq's intentions were peaceful following its illegal invasion and occupation of Kuwait. On these two concepts and related issues, both before and after the adoption of the ARSIWA, see, eg, I Brownlie, *System of the Law of Nations: State Responsibility (Part I)* (Clarendon Press 1983) 208–10; JR Crawford, *International Law Commission's Articles on State Responsibility: Introduction, Text and Commentaries* (CUP 2002) 196–206; B Graefrath, 'Responsibility and Damages Caused: Relationship Between Responsibility and Damages' (1984) 185 RdC 9, 87–91; A Watts, 'The Art of Apology' in Ragazzi (n 62) 107–16.

[268] See Section 4.4.2.

with the need to provide assurances or guarantees of non-repetition in certain circumstances—is part and parcel of SR law and has also seeped into the Council's decision-making on occasion. Similarly, the concept of satisfaction remains very much a central feature of the remedial scheme associated with SR repertoire and is codified in ARSIWA Article 37(1) in the following terms: '[t]he State responsible for an internationally wrongful act is under an obligation to give satisfaction for the injury caused by that act insofar as it cannot be made good by restitution or compensation'.[269] The provision goes on to specify the forms that the remedy of satisfaction can take, which 'may consist in an acknowledgement of the breach, an expression of regret, a formal apology or another appropriate modality' before also subjecting this form of redress to the requirement of proportionality.[270] When read in tandem with these provisions, relevant SC precedents ostensibly draw considerable inspiration from SR law. Notable examples, most stemming from Iraq's unlawful invasion and occupation of Kuwait, include: the devising of procedures for the purposes of demarcating an international boundary;[271] the creation and imposition of a demilitarized area (10 kilometres into Iraq and 5 kilometres into Kuwait);[272] the reaffirmation of the international obligations of a given State;[273] the disarmament and the subjection of a State to weapons inspections;[274] and the implementation of an international security response and presence in Kosovo.[275]

On a related note, whilst the ICJ did not have to pronounce on Libya's international responsibility in the context of the *Lockerbie* cases, the SC was called upon to weigh in on the question of attribution of the impugned terrorist acts to that State.[276] One can, therefore, extract a form of satisfaction—albeit an acutely political application of that mode of reparation in that scenario—from SC Resolutions 731,

[269] ARSIWA (n 34) Art 37(1).

[270] ARSIWA (n 34) Art 37(2). Para 3 of the provision lays down the requirement of proportionality as follows: '[s]atisfaction shall not be out of proportion to the injury and may not take a form humiliating to the responsible State'.

[271] See, eg, the invasion of Kuwait by Iraq in SC Res 687 (n 167).

[272] See, eg, SC Res 687 (n 167) [5]–[6].

[273] SC Res 687 (n 167) [2] (highlighting the inviolability of the border between both States), [7] (dealing with obligations prohibiting the use of certain weapons), [32] (addressing international terrorism). On this last aspect of the resolution, see also Saul (n 215) 147 (stating that '[n]ormatively, the resolution is significant because of its binding character under Chapter VII and because it admits not only State-sponsored terrorism, but also direct State terrorism (by requiring Iraq not to "commit" it)', but concluding that '[i]t is doubtful whether this description adds anything to the legal framework of States' obligations'). On this last point, see also R Higgins, 'The General International Law of Terrorism' in R Higgins and M Flory (eds), *Terrorism and International Law* (Routledge 1997) 13, 20–1.

[274] SC Res 687 (n 167) [7]–[14]. Additional international obligations—ranging from the control of biological and ballistic weapons to nuclear disarmament—were also imposed on Iraq.

[275] See, eg, the situation in Kosovo (UNSC Res 1244 (10 June 1999) UN Doc S/RES/1244).

[276] See, eg, Dissenting Opinions of Judge Bedjaoui in *Questions of Interpretation and Application of the 1971 Montreal Convention arising from the Aerial Incident at Lockerbie (Libya v UK)* (Provisional Measures) [1992] ICJ Rep 3, 37 [10]; *Questions of Interpretation and Application of the 1971 Montreal Convention arising from the Aerial Incident at Lockerbie (Libya v USA)* (Provisional Measures) [1992] ICJ Rep 114, 147 [10].

748, and 883.[277] In fact, by virtue of its own decision-making the Council seemed to provide satisfaction to the US, UK, and France by proclaiming a 'condemnation' of Libya's support of the terrorist bombings of 1988 (Pan Am Flight 103 over Lockerbie) and 1989 (UTA Flight 772 over Chad and Niger). On its face, this application of the concept of satisfaction could reasonably fall within the ambit of the ARSIWA and partially fulfil the requirements of reparation under SR law.[278] Perhaps more compelling was the Council's imposition of obligations of cessation of the internationally wrongful act and assurances/guarantees of non-repetition upon Libya in the same setting, pursuant to the then non-formulated ILC Draft Article 30.[279]

More generally, the transplantation of this principle into modern counterterrorism initiatives would be straightforward: a salient manifestation of this exercise would be the obligation incumbent upon States to cease harbouring and supporting terrorist groups on their territory, as evidenced by the case of Afghanistan both before and after 9/11.[280]

4.4.6 Obligation of non-recognition of third States and the duty to cooperate

Furthermore, the SC has often reaffirmed and imposed, upon third States, an obligation of non-recognition of situations flowing from internationally wrongful acts. Although the ICJ had clearly pronounced approvingly on this issue in the *Namibia Advisory Opinion*,[281] it subsequently refused to acknowledge that an obligation of non-recognition automatically flows from the determination of an internationally wrongful act,[282] thereby seemingly challenging the connection between an international breach and an automatic obligation of non-recognition in the scheme of collective security.[283] Nevertheless, some interlocutors resolve this discrepancy by inferring that no express determination of illegality had been put forth in the resolutions under study in the *East Timor* case.[284] Therefore, it can be said with certainty that there exists an obligation of non-recognition originating from any internationally wrongful act.[285] More importantly, this obligation

277 See, eg, Martin (n 8) 468 fn 76 and accompanying text.

278 See ARSIWA (n 34) Art 37.

279 See SC Res 748 (n 176) [2].

280 See also Dupuy (n 51) 11.

281 See *Legal Consequences for States of the Continued Presence of South Africa in Namibia (South West Africa) Notwithstanding Security Council Resolution 276 (1970)* (Advisory Opinion) [1971] ICJ Rep 16, 54 [117].

282 See *East Timor (Portugal v Australia)* (Jurisdiction) [1995] ICJ Rep 90, 103–4 [31]–[32].

283 See, eg, Forteau (n 20) 198 fn 98 and accompanying text (also citing VH Ascensio, *L'Autorité de la Chose Décidée en Droit International Public* (Thesis, University of Paris X-Nanterre 1997) 410–13, 407–15).

284 See *East Timor Case* (n 282) 198.

285 See J Crawford, 'The General Assembly, The International Court and Self-Determination' in V Lowe *et al.* (eds), *Fifty Years of the International Court of Justice: Essays in Honour of Sir Robert Jennings* (CUP 1996) 585, 605 (noting that this obligation is 'generally held to be automatic and not contingent on action by the political organs of the United Nations'). See also generally G Abi-Saab, 'The Concept of "International Crimes" and its Place in Contemporary International Law' in JHH Weiler *et al.* (eds), *International Crimes of States: A Critical Analysis of the ILC's Draft Article 19 on State Responsibility* (de Gruyter 1989) 141, 141–2; H Lauterpacht, *Recognition in International Law* (CUP 1947).

does not stem from the UN Charter but rather from both SR law and general international law;[286] the secondary rules of international responsibility actually fill the void whenever the Council decides to incorporate SR reasoning within its own logic. Implicit in this proposition is the fact that should the Council determine the existence of a wrongful act (although this might prove to be a nebulous exercise in itself), the obligation of non-recognition would automatically attach to the SC's decision. These premises reinforce the idea that SR is compatible with the broader scheme of the Council's decision-making, and that this normative scheme may on occasion provide a framework for that organ's own action.[287]

In this regard, two cases in point are the unlawful acquisition of a territory resulting from the use of force[288] and the acquiescence to a government perpetrating, or resulting from, a serious violation of international law.[289] In such cases, the SC reaffirms the obligation of *all* States to cooperate with the directly affected injured State and/or other States in order to ensure cessation of the internationally wrongful act.[290] Taken in the aggregate, this set of international obligations has been described as 'an essential legal weapon in the fight against grave breaches of the basic rules of international law',[291]

[286] For an application by the ICJ, see *Legal Consequences of the Construction of a Wall* (Advisory Opinion) [2004] ICJ Rep 136 [163(3)D] ('[a]ll States are under an obligation not to recognize the illegal situation resulting from the construction of the wall and not to render aid or assistance in maintaining the situation created by such construction'). See also C Yamada, 'Revisiting the International Law Commission's Draft Articles on State Responsibility' in Ragazzi (n 62) 118 (linking the Court's formulation of the obligation of non-recognition with ARSIWA Art 41).

[287] Forteau (n 20) 198 elegantly summarizes this line of argument, hypothesizing a scenario where the ICJ would have held that the SC resolutions determined the existence of an internationally wrongful act in the *East Timor* case (n 282).

[288] See, inter alia, the following examples: the Israeli occupation of the Syrian Golan (UNSC Res 497 (17 December 1981) UN Doc S/RES/497 [1]); the invasion of Kuwait by Iraq (SC Res 670 (n 170)); the hostilities in Bosnia-Herzegovina (UNSC Res 819 (13 April 1993) UN Doc S/RES/819 ('reaffirming that any taking or acquisition of territory by the threat or use of force, including through the practice of "ethnic cleansing", is unlawful and unacceptable') and SC Res 836 (n 168)). See also Crawford (n 267) 250 (also listing 'attempted acquisition of sovereignty over territory through the denial of the right of self-determination of peoples'). The ICJ has also unequivocally called upon States not to recognize the denial by a State of the right of self-determination of peoples. See *Namibia Advisory Opinion* (n 281) 56 [126] (holding that 'the termination of the Mandate and the declaration of the illegality of South Africa's presence in Namibia are opposable to all States in the sense of barring *erga omnes* the legality of a situation which is maintained in violation of international law').

[289] See, inter alia, the following examples: the regime imposed by the racist minority in Southern Rhodesia (UNSC Resolutions 216 (n 172), 217 (n 180), and 277 (n 170)); any regime imposed by the occupier in Kuwait (SC 661 (n 161)); the unilateral declaration of any entity in Bosnia-Herzegovina (SC Res 787 (n 174)).

[290] See, inter alia, the following examples: the situation in Southern Rhodesia (SC Res 217 (n 180) (granting the cessation of unlawful activity solely in favour of the UK) and UNSC Res 254 (18 June 1968) UN Doc S/RES/254 (requesting moral and material assistance to be provided to the peoples of Southern Rhodesia in their quest for freedom and independence)); the invasion of Kuwait by Iraq (SC Res 661 (n 161)). This will obviously have a tremendous impact on counterterrorism efforts. See, eg, Gowlland-Debbas, 'The Functions' (n 21) 292 ('Council resolutions have therefore included calls for the cessation of the acts in question, such as withdrawal from occupied territory, an end to violations of human rights or humanitarian law, *or the renunciation of terrorism*') (emphasis added).

[291] C Tomuschat, 'International Crimes by States: An Endangered Species?' in Wellens (n 19) 259.

and clearly mirrors the contents of ARSIWA Article 41. This provision reads as follows:

1. States shall cooperate to bring an end through lawful means any serious breach within the meaning of article 40.
2. No State shall recognize as lawful a situation created by a serious breach within the meaning of article 40, nor render aid or assistance in maintaining that situation.
3. This article is without prejudice to the other consequences referred to in this Part and to such further consequences that a breach to which this Chapter applies may entail under international law.[292]

Although this provision, coupled with ARSIWA Article 40, most probably constitutes the ILC's compromise on the very controversial 'crime of State' debate,[293] it is nonetheless quite illuminating for present purposes. First, it clearly corroborates the theory that SR logic effectively permeates SC decision-making in some instances. Suffice it to borrow from one publicist to declare that '[i]t is clear from the Draft Articles, commentaries and debates that in this optique of State responsibility, UN mechanisms for peace maintenance are encompassed as legal sanctions'.[294] Secondly, this legal scheme might be brought to bear upon a future situation involving State-sponsored or State-condoned terrorist attacks and may perhaps be extended to other global security violations. After all, it must be recalled that the Commentary to ARSIWA Article 41 'laconically'[295] highlights that '[c]ooperation could be organized in the framework of a competent

[292] ARSIWA (n 34) Art 41. For a discussion of this provision, see B Stern, 'A Plea for 'Reconstruction' of International Responsibility Based on the Notion of Legal Injury' in Ragazzi (n 62) 95–6.

[293] For radically divergent views on the criminalization of SR, see DW Bowett, 'Crimes of State and the 1996 Report of the International Law Commission on State Responsibility' (1998) 9 EJIL 163; Weiler *et al.* (n 285); NHB Jørgensen, *The Responsibility of States for International Crimes: State Responsibility for the Commission of Crimes Against International Law* (OUP 2000); S Rosenne, 'State Responsibility and International Crimes: Further Reflections on Article 19 of the Draft Articles on State Responsibility' (1998) 30 NYUJILP 145; Brownlie (n 267) 32–3; Crawford (n 267) 16–20; K Marek, 'Criminalizing State Responsibility' (1978-9) 14 RBDI 460; A Pellet, 'Can a State Commit a Crime? Definitely, Yes!' (1999) 10 EJIL 425; A Pellet, 'The New Draft Articles of the International Law Commission on the Responsibility of States for Internationally Wrongful Acts: A Requiem for State's Crimes?' (2001) 32 NYIL 55; A Pellet, 'The Responsibility of Government Leaders for International Crimes of the State: From the Perspective of International Law' in G Doucet (ed.), *Terrorism, Victims and International Criminal Responsibility* (SOS Attentats 2003) 289–97; R Rosenstock, 'An International Criminal Responsibility of States?' in ILC (ed.), *International Law on the Eve of the Twenty-First Century: Views from the International Law Commission* (UN 1997) 265; B Simma, 'Bilateralism and Community Interest in the Law of State Responsibility' in Y Dinstein and M Tabory (eds), *International Law at a Time of Perplexity: Essays in Honour of Shabtai Rosenne* (Kluwer 1989) 821, 827–8, 835–44; Cançado Trindade (n 62) 253–70.

[294] Gowlland-Debbas, 'Security' (n 21) 58. However, at 61 she goes on to state the following:

> This link which has been made by the International Law Commission between Charter mechanisms for peace maintenance and the regimes of responsibility may appear to be both novel and controversial. For after all, the condition for the application of such mechanisms is not the existence of an internationally wrongful act, and they are not subjected to the conditions said to govern unilateral countermeasures.

[295] The expression is borrowed from Gaja (n 21) 58.

international organization, in particular the United Nations. However, paragraph 1 also envisages the possibility of non-institutionalized cooperation'.[296]

In a broader sense, whilst ARISWA Article 41 and its Commentary are not dispositive on whether cooperation should be institutionalized or not, they do not appear, on their face, to preclude reactions taken by individual States.[297] As former Special Rapporteur James Crawford highlighted, the idea of cooperation is better explained by the fact that 'it is often the only way of providing an effective remedy'.[298] This very suggestion lends further credence to the idea that collective countermeasures under SR—rebranded as 'centralized/institutional countermeasures' or 'sanctions' because they are taken by the SC in the context of institutionalized SR—could become a viable alternative in implementing States' international responsibility for violating global security norms.

4.4.7 Towards stricter sanctions in global security: Counterterrorism and beyond

Finally, the SC has imposed particularly strict sanctions aiming at bringing violations of international law to an end,[299] such as the severance of relations (diplomatic, consular, military) with the wrongful State,[300] along with embargo-type measures.[301] In respect of the Council's imposition of economic (and other)

[296] Commentary to ARSIWA (n 34) Art 41 p 114 [2]. The second scenario, namely non-institutionalized cooperation, is explored in Part III of this book, particularly as regards forcible responses under SR repertoire.

[297] In fact, Commentary to ARSIWA (n 34) Art 41 p 114 solely refers to cooperation amongst States. Judge Kooijmans emphasized this idea in his Separate Opinion in the *Wall Advisory Opinion* (n 286). See also A Gattini, 'A Return Ticket to "Communitarisme", Please' (2002) 13 EJIL 1181, 1186–7.

[298] Crawford (n 267) 249. See also G Gaja, 'Do States Have a Duty to Ensure Compliance with Obligations Erga Omnes by Other States?' in Ragazzi (n 62) 34; NHB Jørgensen, 'The Obligation of Cooperation' in Crawford *et al.* (n 30) 695–701. However, on whether the violation of obligations *erga omnes* brings about substantive obligations for third parties, see Judge Higgins' Separate Opinion in the *Wall Advisory Opinion* (n 286) [37] (suggesting that whilst there are 'certain rights in which, by reason of their importance, "all States have a legal interest in their protection"', this 'has nothing to do with imposing substantive obligations on third parties to a case'). By contrast, others opine that 'the obligation of States to cooperate with each other' has attained *jus cogens* normative status. See, eg, J Peirano, 'International Responsibility and Cooperation for Development' in Ragazzi (n 62) 192–3.

[299] On this issue, see Combacau (n 103) 17–24 (positing that UN sanctions are inherently infused with coercive character with a view to compelling responsible States to put an end to their unlawful behaviour).

[300] See, eg, SC Res 277 (n 170) (purporting to bring an end to racial discrimination in Southern Rhodesia). These types of sanctions should be read in tandem with UN Charter (n 26) Art 41, which reads as follows:

> The Security Council may decide what measures not involving the use of armed force are to be employed to give effect to its decisions, and it may call upon the Members of the United Nations to apply such measures. These may include complete or partial interruption of economic relations and of rail, sea, air, postal, telegraphic, radio, and other means of communication, and the severance of diplomatic relations.

[301] See, inter alia, examples of sanctions against: Southern Rhodesia (UNSC Resolutions 232 (n 169) and 253 (n 169)); South Africa (SC Res 418 (n 166)); Iraq (SC Res 661 (n 161), 665 (n 167), 670 (n 170), and SC Res 687 (n 167)); Yugoslavia (Serbia and Montenegro) (SC Res 757 (n 168), 787

sanctions, the increasingly intractable problem of non-State actors, such as terrorist organizations, comes into sharp relief. Indeed, it might prove difficult to sanction 'abstract entities' linked to terrorism, aside from targeting obvious sources of support and funding, whilst the indiscriminate imposition of sanctions upon sanctuary States could engender devastating effects on their populations.[302] Implicit in this proposition is the need to circumscribe the role of territorial/sanctuary States in counterterrorism (and other global security) strategies further, thereby bolstering the case for a SR-expansive regime premised on *prevention*, as argued elsewhere.[303] Similarly, the imposition of sanctions in counterterrorism contexts may also require that a State wield extraterritorial control over abstract entities, such as terrorist groups, another problematic facet engendered by both the pervasiveness of ever-present transnational phenomena and the advent of the disaggregated State.[304] This requirement of State 'control' over non-State actors, a notion central in the ARSIWA, has been thoroughly and critically addressed in other accounts.[305]

The execution of such measures (ie sanctions in counterterrorism or global security contexts) necessarily entails the breach (or suspension) of international obligations owed to the concerned State, and could rest upon the initial unlawful act on which the Council has ruled in its resolutions.[306] If one accepts this line of argument, SC-imposed sanctions and measures could be potentially construed as 'countermeasures', a veritable staple of modern SR.[307] In other words, the SC would preside over a three-tiered legal process, somewhat redolent of syllogistic reasoning, which would first take into account the existence of an unlawful act and, ultimately, be followed by the establishment of international responsibility (through the normative operation of attribution) and the determination *and* application of available/adequate remedies. Unsurprisingly, there is ample evidence pointing to the fact that the SC already engages in this type of reasoning: '[a]

(n 174), and 820 (n 174)); Libya (SC Res 748 (n 176) and UNSC Res 883 (11 November 1993) UN Doc S/RES/883); Rwanda (SC Res (n 171)).

[302] The language is borrowed from Gowlland-Debbas, 'The Functions' (n 21) 292 (speaking of SC-imposed economic and financial measures and stressing that whilst '[d]irected against abstract entities, these measures also have far-reaching effects on the populations of sanctioned States, despite the problematic Security Council practice of including so-called humanitarian exceptions (exempting, for example, medical supplies and foodstuffs "in humanitarian circumstances")').

[303] See generally Proulx (n 3).

[304] See Gowlland-Debbas, 'The Functions' (n 21) 293 (speaking to the binding nature of SC resolutions and noting that '[t]hey require the exercise of control over the activities of private parties, even extraterritorially, which raises major problems today in view of the non-territorial nature of financial and other transactions').

[305] See, eg, Proulx (n 3) ch 4 and authorities cited therein.

[306] Consider H Xue's remarks in 'The State of State Responsibility' (2002) 96 ASIL Proceedings 168, 175–6.

[307] This argument is very difficult to countenance, without accepting some degree of creative analogy, given that the validation of State-led 'countermeasures' is found under SR repertoire, whilst the adoption of SC measures is supported by Chapter VII of the UN Charter. Thus, this regime compartmentalization constitutes a significant conceptual stumbling block to the line of argument advanced earlier.

number of the Security Council resolutions adopted under Chapter VII contain all the legal elements which are familiar to international lawyers when they deal with the responsibility of States for breaches of international law: the finding of a prior breach, imputability, and the application of legal sanctions'.[308] Whilst this view constitutes a considerable affront to the preferred model of inter-State countermeasures, now firmly enshrined in the ARSIWA, it nonetheless signals innovative but challenging ways to attain the objectives of counteracting unlawful behaviour and ensuring return to legality in global security contexts.

4.4.8 Towards a broader remedial scheme: Forcible countermeasures and beyond

Finally, with a view to invoking 'all necessary means' in implementing its resolutions under UN auspices, the SC has also permitted States to use force. For instance, Council deliberations produced that outcome in the situation pertaining to Iraq's unlawful invasion of Kuwait, in which the SC authorized

> Member States co-operating with the Government of Kuwait, unless Iraq on or before 15 January 1991 fully implement[ed], as set forth in paragraph 1 above, the above-mentioned resolutions, *to use all necessary means* to uphold and implement resolution 660 (1990) and all subsequent relevant resolutions and to restore international peace and security in the area (emphasis added).[309]

This categorical type of language is increasingly present in SC resolutions dealing with counterterrorism, most notably in the oft-cited Resolutions 1368 and 1373 following the 9/11 attacks. Scholars ponder whether such authorizations to use force turn on the notion of collective security, pursuant to Article 42 of the UN Charter or Chapter VII, generally, or if they should instead be framed within the inherent right of collective self-defence, which exceptionally accrues following SC intervention.[310]

From the foregoing considerations, it becomes clear that the SC can, in some circumstances, play a role in implementing SR. The outstanding question remains: to what extent? One inference can be drawn from the Council's extensive practice regarding SR: the Council has the capacity to play an active role in promoting counterterrorism and other priority areas related to global security, based on its tendency to interpret its powers in a liberal fashion. However, the impact

[308] Gowlland-Debbas, 'The Functions' (n 21) 288. See also by idem: 'Security' (n 21) 53; 'The Limits' (n 21) 364; *Collective* (n 263).

[309] UNSC Res 678 (29 November 1990) UN Doc S/RES/678 [2].

[310] See, eg, C Dominicé, 'La Sécurité Collective et la Crise du Golfe' (1991) 2 EJIL 97; C Greenwood, 'New World Order or Old? The Invasion of Kuwait and the Rule of Law' (1992) 55 The Modern Law Review 165; Y Le Bouthillier and M Morin, 'Réflexions sur la Validité des Opérations Enterprises contre l'Iraq en Regard de la Charte des Nations Unies et du Droit Canadien' (1991) 29 Canadian Yearbook of International Law 142; Weckel (n 164) 188–92; BH Weston, 'Security Council Resolution 678 and Persian Gulf Decision Making: Precarious Legitimacy' (1991) 85 AJIL 516.

and influence its resolutions can wield on the development of SR law remains to be ascertained. In the field of collective interests, for instance, several impediments militating against the argument that international liability can effectively be implemented under that organ's auspices can be readily enumerated: unclear designation of the responsible State(s); ambiguous establishment of the violated obligation(s); indirect or equivocal proclamation of ensuing legal consequences; and fuzzy nexus between the imposition of measures and secondary SR norms.[311] One could further posit that SC practice vis-à-vis a host of situations is not always uniform or conclusive in terms of SR implementation, such as instances involving Somalia, where rebels were carrying out IHL violations, Liberia, Haiti, and Sierra Leone.[312] Therefore, additional scholarly and policy discussion is needed on the relationship between secondary rules of international responsibility and SC functions. Moreover, as discussed subsequently, the elucidation of this question will most likely hinge on identifying compatibility areas between the application of Chapter VII objectives and SR mechanics. As a corollary, it will also be useful to shed more light on the relationship between the Council's own decision-making and the application of secondary SR rules.

However, as shown by SC practice canvassed earlier, there are few conceptual or practical impediments to claiming that certain Council resolutions are at least partly predicated on the idea of international responsibility and, in turn, set in motion the principle of return to legality and the deployment of (centralized) countermeasures. The confusion, however, persists in that it remains unclear whether the SC actually relies on SR mechanics in reaching those decisions, or if the determination of the violation of an international obligation flows organically by virtue of its very existence and purpose,[313] namely without the need to invoke secondary norms. Otherwise put, are SC measures independent and, therefore, divorced from the ideology underpinning the concept of 'countermeasure'? It should be recalled that the introductory discussion in Section 4.2 advocated in favour of a negative answer to that query. The elements required to take to an informed view about the relationship between sanctions and countermeasures will come into greater focus when addressing more substantial issues linking SR to SC operations, such as the determination of responsibility and restraints on Council action. In the interim, a brief overview of the scholarly reactions to the SC's extensive practice will prove illuminating in securing building blocks towards better circumscribing that organ's role in applying SR principles.

[311] See SM Villalpando, *L'Émergence de la Communauté Internationale dans la Responsabilité des États* (PUF 2005) 443. But see Crawford (n 267) 251 (invoking SC resolutions and inferring that '[t]he same obligations are reflected in Security Council and General Assembly resolutions').

[312] Villalpando (n 311) 443 fn 1534 (canvassing other precedents involving Libya, Bosnia-Herzegovina and neighbouring States, and Iraq). See also Gowlland-Debbas, 'The Functions' (n 21) 288 fn 38.

[313] Although not dispositive when contrasted with other scholarly accounts, the remarks in Nolte (n 165) 323 are far from encouraging when attempting to reconcile SR with SC powers: he cautions against expanding the Council's treatment of IHL/recourse to force violations as tantamount to permutations of the attribution of liability.

4.4.9 Scholarly reactions and debates

It is apparent from the foregoing that the SC has interpreted its powers in a broad fashion.[314] More importantly, its potential role in implementing SR has generated considerable academic debate, at least on a theoretical and/or principled level. Although the discussion addressing this theme has essentially polarized influential voices within the academy, from these scholarly accounts emerges a clear postulate: there is an inherent compatibility between SR repertoire and SC activities in a wide array of fields. In fact, several commentators have already initiated a rapprochement of classical SR rationale with SC powers and decision-making. Whilst some fine-tuning is still required regarding the specific challenges posed by counterterrorism and other global security priorities, possible avenues to address this difficult question will be considered in due course.

For a first group of authors,[315] the extensive SC practice—along with its broad interpretation of the maintenance of international peace and security and general Chapter VII powers—might be indicative of an ongoing, or completed, shift of Council functions towards more active implementation of international responsibility. According to this school of thought, such power could be derived from the UN Charter or from general international law. Under this structure, SC action would be framed within known international law logic, thereby making the Council's discretionary margin of interpretation contingent on the application of secondary rules of responsibility, and simultaneously coextensive with the notions of assurance of legality and protection of collective interests.[316] Consequently, a proponent of this view would infer that UN Member States could even derogate from otherwise legally enforceable obligations, including flouting human rights treaties (as long as the rights contained therein do not qualify as *jus cogens* undertakings), on the basis of an SC resolution. Such construction would be grounded in the wording of Article 103 of the UN Charter, which provides as follows: '[i]n the event of a conflict between the obligations of the Members of the United Nations under the present Charter and their obligations under any other international agreement, their obligations under the present Charter shall prevail'.[317]

[314] See also TM Franck, *Fairness in International Law and Institutions* (Clarendon Press 1995) 218 ff; M Koskenniemi, 'The Police in the Temple: Order, Justice and the UN—A Dialectical View' (1995) 6 EJIL 325.

[315] See, inter alia, Cannizzaro (n 53) 913–5; B Graefrath and M Mohr, 'Legal Consequences of an Act of Aggression: The Case of the Iraqi Invasion and Occupation of Kuwait' (1992) 43 Austrian Journal of Public and International Law 109 (discussing aggression); B Stern, 'La Responsabilité Internationale Aujourd'hui ... Demain ... ' in A Castagné *et al.* (eds), *Perspectives du Droit International et Européen: Recueil d'Études à la Mémoire de Gilbert Apollis* (Pedone 1992) 75, 94–6; P Tavernier, 'Harmonie et Contradictions dans l'Évolution du Droit de la Responsabilité Internationale' in RB Achour and S Laghmani (eds), *Harmonie et Contradictions en Droit International* (Pedone 1996) 215, 224–6; C Tomuschat, 'Obligations Arising for States Without or Against Their Will' (1993) 241 RdC 195, 368–9. Generally, these authors also agree with the premise that SC powers do not preclude individual States from unilaterally invoking SR against responsible States.

[316] See, eg, Gowlland-Debbas: 'The Functions' (n 21) 304–6; 'UN Sanctions' (n 27) 5–12.

[317] UN Charter (n 26) Art 103. For general discussion on Art 103, see R Kolb, 'L'Article 103 de la Charte des Nations Unies' (2014) 367 RdC 9. For specific analysis of the interplay between the UN

However, should these obligations or treaties acquire a 'special status' (ie *jus cogens*) under international law, SC action would then be correspondingly restrained and that organ could not adopt a resolution that violates the norms in question.[318] This construction further reinforces the propositions that international law does act as a check on SC action, that secondary rules of responsibility are set in motion and govern the legal situation following the Council's determination of a breach, and that the safeguarding of collective interests remains a determinant element for the study at hand.

It should be noted, however, that ILC Draft Article 39, as envisioned in the 1996 first reading, provided the following qualifications: '[t]he legal consequences of an internationally wrongful act of a State set out in the provisions of this part are subject, as appropriate, to the provisions and procedure of the Charter of the United Nations relating to the maintenance of international peace and security'.[319] During his tenure as Special Rapporteur, Gaetano Arangio-Ruiz was a particularly staunch objector to Draft Article 39, judging that it conferred disproportionate discretion to the SC in interpreting the legal consequences of an internationally wrongful act.[320] It is likely that Arangio-Ruiz's posture was informed—perhaps even triggered—by a strong majority within the ICJ in the *Lockerbie* cases, which confirmed the binding nature of SC resolutions irrespective of their congruence with other international legal standards. Arangio-Ruiz's claim, therefore, targeted what he perceived to be an unnecessarily broad '"constitutional" interpretation of the UN Charter of the main UN Charter-based institutions at the expense of a more strict, statutory construction approach favoured by jurists of the positivist school of law'.[321] For this Special Rapporteur, implicit in the argument was the fact that the adoption of Draft Article 39 would seriously compromise the integrity of international law.[322] It would appear that Arangio-Ruiz's lobbying against over-extending the SC's role in determining the consequences of internationally wrongful acts fell on sympathetic ears at the ILC. As such, his suggestion was ultimately embodied in the reformulated, open-ended final Article 59.[323]

Therefore, it is no surprise that a second contingent of scholars discards the rapprochement between SR and SC powers, instead opining that the Council is entrusted with an autonomous and truly *sui generis* mission. Amongst the more radical detractors of institutionalizing SR through the SC, some claim that such

Charter and SR norms, including discussion of Art 103, see Gowlland-Debbas, 'Responsibility' (n 117) 115. On the role of Art 103 as a 'supremacy clause', see R Liivoja, 'The Scope of the Supremacy Clause of the United Nations Charter' (2008) 57 ICLQ 583.

[318] See Gowlland-Debbas, 'The Functions' (n 21) 305.

[319] (1996) I *YILC* 133.

[320] See, eg, Arangio-Ruiz (n 14) 615.

[321] E McWhinney, 'Codifying International Law in Periods of Extreme Ideological and Cultural Conflict: Lessons from the ILC Mandate on State Responsibility' in Koufa (n 201) 144.

[322] See, eg, E McWhinney, 'Separation or Complementarity of Constitutional Law-Making Powers of United Nations Security Council, General Assembly, and International Court of Justice' in A Giardina and F Lattanzi (eds), *Studi di Diritto Internazionale in Onore di Gaetano Arangio-Ruiz* (Ed Scientifica 2004) 339–54.

[323] See n 106 and accompanying text.

implementation, paired with the determination of applicable secondary rules of responsibility, falls outside the ambit of Chapter VII. Unsurprisingly, Gaetano Arangio-Ruiz was also a vocal proponent of this view. Whilst his stances were sometimes categorical, they concomitantly embodied some degree of analytical nuance given that the SC's role could be perceived as coextensive with more traditional means of implementation of international responsibility.[324] However, a third and more nuanced strand of scholarship acknowledges that the SC may engage in the determination of unlawful acts and their resulting legal consequences, and impose measures or sanctions to compel compliance. However, these scholarly voices also maintain that SC action remains subject to the provisions enshrined in the UN Charter and that this organ's primordial role is to ensure the maintenance of international peace and security, an objective that, they argue, differs from the implementation of SR.[325]

Although a strong scholarly current supporting the thesis of SR implementation by the SC exists, a brief examination of specific questions related to Council resolution-making is nonetheless warranted to better identify its role within the broader proposed framework.

4.5 Determination of International Responsibility and Surrounding Issues

4.5.1 Moving beyond the 'political v legal' divide: The Council as implementer

It now seems clear that the SC can play a role (perhaps in a limited set of circumstances) in determining States' international responsibility. For example, as discussed extensively earlier in this chapter, it has done so in the case of Iraq's invasion of Kuwait through the adoption of Resolution 687, which proceeded to articulate the existence of a series of additional violations and obligations flowing from Iraq's 'original sin'.[326] Consequently, subsequent

[324] See, eg, G Arangio-Ruiz, 'Fifth Report on State Responsibility' (1993) UN Doc A/CN.4/453 and Add.1–3; (1993) II(1) *YILC* 27 [103]–[105]; G Arangio-Ruiz, 'Seventh Report on State Responsibility' (1995) UN Doc A/CN.4/469 and Add.1–2; (1995) II(1) *YILC* 21–2 [95]–[96]; Arangio-Ruiz (n 14) 631, 695. See also C Annacker, 'The Legal Regime of *Erga Omnes* Obligations in International Law' (1994) 46 Austrian Journal of Public and International Law 131, 158–9.

[325] See, inter alia, in the ILC debates of 1976, the positions of J Castañeda (in (1976) I *YILC* 240–3) and P Reuter (in ibid 245); P-M Dupuy, 'The Constitutional Dimension of the Charter of the United Nations Revisited' (1997) 1 Max Planck Yearbook of UN Law 1, 16 (offering a more focused analysis); in the debates in Weiler *et al.* (n 285), see the remarks of SI Sinclair (224) and M Spinedi (243–6) (describing this view without taking position); R Higgins, 'International Law and the Avoidance, Containment and Resolution of Disputes' (1991) 230 RdC 9; A Pellet, 'Le Nouveau Projet de la CDI sur la Responsabilité de l'État pour Fait Internationalement Illicite: Requiem pour le Crime?' in LC Vohrah *et al.* (eds), *Man's Inhumanity to Man: Essays on International Law in Honour of Antonio Cassese* (Kluwer 2003) 655–83.

[326] The language is borrowed from Gowlland-Debbas, 'Security' (n 21) 65. On the background of SC Res 687 and its repercussions, see LD Roberts, 'United Nations Security Council Resolution

SC resolutions on this situation expanded on the original responsibility attaching to Iraq and in laying out their rationale, relied upon a series of well-established treaty obligations stemming, inter alia, from the 1961 and 1963 Vienna Conventions on Diplomatic and Consular Relations and on the Fourth Geneva Convention.[327]

Hence, the determination that Iraq's invasion of Kuwait conflicted with the former State's obligations under the UN Charter 'was followed by a series of resolutions which referred to Iraq's additional violations of international law ... although the initial illegal act, i.e. the unlawful invasion and occupation of Kuwait, continued to serve as the basis for State responsibility'.[328] Interestingly, when framed in SR terms such a scenario easily qualifies as an ongoing breach of an obligation and is, simultaneously, governed by ARSIWA Article 14.[329]

Thus, the SC sometimes takes part in establishing SR and in some cases, in identifying a prior breach upon which subsequent determinations of unlawful behaviour are juxtaposed. But it is still unclear whether this practice truly hinges on SR rationale or, conversely, if it invariably remains framed in Chapter VII terms. One thing is certain: the SC has identified unlawful acts and imposed sanctions 'based not only on a finding of fact but also on one of law'.[330] More compellingly, writing about the determination of illegality of Iraq's invasion of Kuwait and subsequent Council resolutions, whilst also highlighting that SC practice 'has been fairly innovative in qualifying some acts as illegal', one distinguished publicist posited that '[t]he Council drew a number of consequences

687 and Its Aftermath: The Implications for Domestic Authority and the Need for Legitimacy' (1993) 25 NYUJILP 593.

[327] See, eg, UNSC Res 664 (18 August 1990) UN Doc S/RES/664, 667 (16 September 1990) UN Doc S/RES/667), 670 (n 170) [13], and 687 (n 167). See also Gowlland-Debbas, 'The Functions' (n 21) 289 fn 40 (noting that this string of resolutions was the first to cite the Fourth Geneva Convention within the framework of Chapter VII). For more background on the debates and meetings pertaining to the Iraq–Kuwait situation, and the international legal responsibility of the former State, see *Repertoire of SC Practice* (n 217).

[328] Gowlland-Debbas, 'The Functions' (n 21) 289.

[329] On the temporal element in SR, see Crawford (n 32) 240–73; W Karl, 'The Time Factor in the Law of State Responsibility' in Spinedi and Simma (n 93) 95–114; E Wyler, 'Quelques Réflexions sur la Réalisation dans le Temps du Fait Internationalement Illicite' (1991) 95 RGDIP 881. On the temporal element as it pertains to terrorism, specifically, see Proulx (n 3) ch 4, section B)3. On time and the law, generally, see R Higgins, 'Time and the Law' (1997) 46 ICLQ 501.

[330] Gowlland-Debbas, 'The Functions' (n 21) 288 (also excluding the cases of Liberia and Haiti (see UNSC Res 788 (19 November 1992) UN Doc S/RES/788 and 841 (16 June 1993) UN Doc S/RES/841) as inconclusive for the purposes of this statement). See also UNSC Res 1132 (8 October 1997) UN Doc S/RES/1132) (lamenting the military coup of 25 May 1997 in Sierra Leone and calling for the restoration of the democratically elected government and a return to constitutional order). See also de Brichambaut (n 21) 273–4 (discussing SC Res 674 (n 209), which declared Iraq's invasion of Kuwait to be illegal under international law, and inferring that '[t]his qualification was made by reference to existing law'); Gowlland-Debbas, 'Security' (n 21) 63–4 (noting the same exceptions as above and expounding that the Council 'has not limited itself to a finding of fact, but has linked its determinations under Article 39 to determinations of the alleged existence of a violation of international law, either explicitly, or by parallel determinations in the same resolution, for the purpose of extending to such breaches the special regime of Chapter VII').

for international responsibility from this qualification'.[331] He further contended that the Council's reasoning in Resolutions 705 of 15 August 1991 and 715 of 11 October 1991 laid down relevant groundwork in identifying 'conditions for the fulfilment of Iraq's legal responsibility',[332] a conclusion that could ostensibly be deemed congruent with the deployment of secondary norm-derived obligations. In reasoning highly reconcilable with the arguments formulated in Chapter 3, this commentator goes as far as arguing that by venturing upon this particular terrain of resolution-making, the Council actually arrogated 'quasi-judicial powers', a position that has fallen under trenchant criticism in that context.[333]

Unquestionably, this idea also ties into the notion that the SC can effectively be construed as implementing SR, regardless of one's perception of the (potentially legal) application of its powers, be it grounded in political, quasi-judicial, or executive undertones. For some scholars, therefore, a determination of unlawful activity by the Council actually rests on its intrinsic executive function and brings about specific implications for the interplay between the application of secondary SR rules, the obligations flowing to concerned States after a breach, and the SC's role within the broader scheme of international responsibility.[334]

Nevertheless, this specific conclusion carries with it significant implications for the possible importation of SR rationale within the framework of Chapter VII powers: the reaction to the Iraq–Kuwait scenario[335] seemed to depart from previously established practice insofar as it clearly drew in SR considerations within the ambit of 'international peace and security'. The remarks offered by one proponent of this view are apposite: '[t]his was a major innovation because an evaluation by the Security Council on the basis of Article 39 of the Charter normally has no consequences in terms of State responsibility. Indeed, Article 39 only mentions situations which may affect international peace and security.'[336] However, it is fair to subject the reading of this line of argument to one caveat in that this particular publicist did not endorse the proposition that the SC grants itself unfettered jurisdiction and creativity. In fact, he rather perceived the Council sometimes as a creator of rights and obligations, but primarily as an organ that 'simply interprets and applies existing law', and considered its response to Iraq's invasion of Kuwait as a particularly striking, creative, and far-reaching exercise of these powers.[337] Yet, this conclusion does not conflict with the central claims of this book: in most instances, SR implementation will simply require that the SC interpret and apply existing law, meaning that it will attribute internationally wrongful conduct to a State and devise legal consequences pursuant to SR precepts. Ultimately, he concluded that '[t]he Security Council was equally innovative in its settlement of

[331] De Brichambaut (n 21) 273. [332] De Brichambaut (n 21) 273.

[333] See Nolte (n 165) 323. [334] See Villalpando (n 311) 447 fn 1544.

[335] For a variety of legal views on the Gulf War and its aftermath from the standpoint of collective security, particularly, see, eg, Dominicé (n 310); B Conforti, 'Non-Coercive Sanctions in the United Nations Charter: Some Lessons From the Gulf War' (1991) 2 EJIL 110; P Malanczuk, 'The Kurdish Crisis and Allied Intervention in the Aftermath of the Second Gulf War' (2002) 2 EJIL 114.

[336] De Brichambaut (n 21) 273. [337] De Brichambaut (n 21) 275–6.

the border dispute between Iraq and Kuwait, which it accomplished in Resolution 773 of 26 August 1992'; he added that '[t]his, along with the other resolutions concerning Iraq mentioned above, [was] probably the furthest it ha[d] reached in stretching its powers within the legal domain'.[338]

Two preliminary conclusions emerge from the foregoing considerations. On the one hand, there seems to be relatively little resistance to the proposition that SC resolutions constitute a source of rights and obligations which accrue to both responsible and injured/implementing States. Interestingly, one commentator highlighted that in this setting, '[a]pplications of an existing set of rules to particular facts inevitably result in the creation of a new, more specific rule, following the model of common law development in Anglo-American law', but ultimately mitigated this observation by arguing that the Council's 'soft' characterizations cannot be construed as binding on Member States in the face of considerable recalcitrance to the idea that this political organ can generate positive law.[339] Nevertheless, the SC can also override previously existing obligations incumbent upon States, on the basis of Article 103 of the UN Charter.[340] When read in tandem with the *Lockerbie* decision and SC Resolution 748, this provision allows us to draw vital inferences for present purposes, namely that: (i) the Council can trump existing international obligations (similarly to the effect of Resolution 748 on the Montreal Convention in the *Lockerbie* cases); and (ii) it can set out general obligations in international law,[341] much to the dismay of certain publicists. Indeed, some authors categorically reject the SC's possible creation and imposition of new international legal obligations upon States.[342] Nevertheless, the precedence of SC prescriptions over treaty obligations was very much alive in the *Lockerbie* proceedings[343] and has received strong academic support, often in scholarly accounts discussing Libya's involvement in the *Lockerbie* incident.[344] In fact, the ICJ itself confirmed the validity of this approach in its Orders on Provisional Measures in the *Lockerbie* cases.[345] Moreover, post-9/11 SC resolution-making, coupled with

[338] De Brichambaut (n 21) 273. [339] Provost, *International* (n 73) 315.

[340] For the text of Art 103, see n 317 and accompanying text.

[341] For a discussion of these aspects, see Franck (n 314) 242–4; E McWhinney, 'International Law-Based Responses to the September 11 International Terrorist Attacks' (2002) 1 Chinese Journal of International Law 280, 283.

[342] See, eg, Dominicé (n 265) 366 (labelling certain SC sanctions as 'injunctions' and inferring that 'such injunctions are legal when the State is called upon to respect or implement international obligations which actually exist in its regard', but stressing that 'they are unlawful when they create new obligations, because the Security Council does not have the authority of a legislator, allowing it to modify treaty provisions, or rules or general international law'). See also Arangio-Ruiz (n 14) 609–725 (esp the heading 'Egregious Examples of Recent Security Council Questionable Infringements of States' Rights', 701–24); C Dominicé, 'Le Conseil de Sécurité et le Droit International' (1996) 43 Revue Yougoslave de Droit International 197, 203; DW Bowett, 'Judicial and Political Functions of the Security Council and the International Court of Justice' in G Abi-Saab *et al.* (eds), *The Changing Constitution of the United Nations* (BIICL 1997) 73.

[343] For instance, see Judge Shahabuddeen's Separate Opinions in the *Lockerbie* cases (n 276) 32, 142 respectively.

[344] See, eg, de Brichambaut (n 21) 270–3, 275; Gowlland-Debbas, 'The Functions' (n 21) 293; Gaja (n 21) 54–5.

[345] See, eg, *Lockerbie (Libya v UK)* (Provisional Measures) (n 276) 15 [39].

its reception on the international stage, unequivocally consecrated that body's ability to promulgate general international legal obligations.

In many ways, this changed post-9/11 UN legal landscape has put this aspect of the *Lockerbie* debate to rest. For instance, in 2000 one publicist who later became an ILC member delineated far more modest boundaries of Council powers, opining that it would be barred from creating 'law' or 'sources of law'.[346] Nowadays, obligations stemming from certain SC resolutions are binding not only on States involved at both ends of a specific internationally wrongful act but also on other Member and non-Member States alike. This trend has been particularly prominent in nuclear non-proliferation and counterterrorism matters, with the Council's resolutions binding *all* States and extending obligations considerably further than the prescriptions enshrined in both the International Convention for the Suppression of the Financing of Terrorism and the Treaty on the Non-Proliferation of Nuclear Weapons.[347] This type of resolution-making has been aptly characterized as SC 'legislation';[348] for the purposes of SR repertoire, those resolutions clearly establish the SC's willingness to promulgate primary international legal obligations. Given the developments canvassed in Chapter 2, it is to be pondered whether the SC will make similar 'legislative' advances regarding other global security challenges, particularly climate change and environmental protection. Some publicists are already calling for the SC to fill the void in 'fields such as climate change or global pandemics where international action is notoriously slow and ill-equipped to deal with new global threats', in order 'to overcome stagnation in traditional international law-making'.[349]

Interestingly, some commentators explain the binding nature of SC resolutions on non-Member States by reference to the principle of sovereign equality.[350]

[346] Nolte (n 165) 317.

[347] See, eg, UNSC Res 1540 (28 April 2004) UN Doc S/RES/1540 (obliging all States to adopt domestic legislation banning proliferation of WMDs, thwart their delivery to non-State actors, implement border/export controls, and protect the materials involved); SC Res 1373 (n 9). See also Gowlland-Debbas, 'Security' (n 117) 125–6; N Abe, 'Existing and Emerging Legal Approaches to Nuclear Counter-Proliferation in the Twenty-First Century' (2007) 39 NYUJILP 929, 930; JM Kobila, 'Le Processus d'Intervention du Conseil de Sécurité dans la Lutte contre le Terrorisme International' in MJ Glennon and S Sur (eds), *Terrorism and International Law* (Nijhoff 2008) 423, 451 ff. On Resolution 1540, see R Lavallé, 'A Novel, If Awkward, Exercise in International Law Making: Security Council Resolution 1540 (2004)' (2004) 51 NILR 441.

[348] See, eg, Johnstone, *The Power* (n 6) 93–105; Alvarez (n 7) 195–8.

[349] J Wouters and J Odermatt, '*Quis Custodiet Consilium Securitatis?* Reflections on the Lawmaking Powers of the Security Council' (June 2013) Working Paper No 109, Leuven Centre for Global Governance Studies <http://ssrn.com/abstract=2286208> accessed 30 May 2015, 5 (citing, inter alia, S Scott, 'Climate Change and Peak Oil as Threats to International Peace and Security: Is It Time for the Security Council to Legislate?' (2008) 9 Melbourne Journal of International Law 495).

[350] As B Fassbender, 'The United Nations Charter as Constitution of the International Community' (1998) 36 CJTL 531, 584 posits

> It is not by virtue of Article 2(6) that the Charter is binding on non-member states. Rather the Charter is binding because of the overriding principle of sovereign equality. Accordingly, non-member states are not only bound by the principles of Article 2, but the Charter as a whole. This means that binding decisions of the Security Council can be addressed to a non-member state—be it a law-breaker or a state expected to assist the U.N. in the performance of preventive or enforcement action.

Ultimately, the asymmetrical power dynamic prevalent between members of the international community and the SC epitomizes what could be termed a 'vertical relationship' between that body and all States; by virtue of Article 25 of the UN Charter, therefore, binding Council decisions 'create duties for all member States (and arguably non-member States)' and concomitantly actuate this relationship.[351] This rapport stands in sharp contrast with a situation involving the unilateral implementation of SR by an injured State against a responsible State, a legal relationship better defined as embodying a 'horizontal' character.[352] The driving force behind this distinction hinges, to a large extent, on the so-called added value of institutionalized and collective enforcement of international obligations, typically made operational through SC sanctions purporting to vindicate collective rights and, as a corollary, the interests of the international community as a whole. Yet, past analyses of the value of collective enforcement through UN mechanisms have, at times, been deeply cynical.[353] Conversely, perhaps in response to this reticence in relegating the task of enforcing legal obligations to the SC, it is probably fair to contend that States reacting on the international plane after they have been injured are not necessarily guided by any overarching legal or philosophical motivations.[354] Indeed, it could well be that a State's reaction to an internationally wrongful act committed against it is prompted more by retaliatory instinct, a sense of diplomatic animosity towards the responsible State, an inclination to unilaterally impose 'tit-for-tat' justice, or some other emotive response, than by some profound commitment to the core tenets of SR law, or a desire to scrupulously monitor compliance with that normative scheme.

Evidently, implementing SR through the SC differs considerably from the more traditional, synallagmatic relationship that forms between the injured State and the responsible State incidental to the unilateral implementation of responsibility: 'in other words, one form of countermeasures undertaken on the basis of a collective and institutionalised decision of an international organisation, in the defence of fundamental community interests, as distinct from those "horizontal" reactions taken by an injured State or States within a bilateral context to international wrongful acts considered to violate subjective rights'.[355] Thus, the idea that SR rests primarily on a (perhaps dated) bilateral typology comes into relief when analysing the violation of multilateral obligations, especially those infringing *jus*

[351] See Gowlland-Debbas, 'The Functions' (n 21) 293. See also Crawford (n 32) 707.

[352] See, eg, Gowlland-Debbas, 'The Functions' (n 21) 293 ('[t]hey thus differ from unilateral countermeasures, which are based on a right and create a "horizontal" relationship between the States applying the countermeasures and the violating State'). On the concept of unilateral countermeasures, generally, see Boisson de Chazournes, *Les Contre-Mesures* (n 31); L-A Sicilianos, *Les Réactions Décentralisées à l'Illicité: Des Contre-Mesures à la Légitime Défense* (LGDJ 1990).

[353] See, eg, MS Daoudo and MS Dajani, *Economic Sanctions, Ideals and Experience* (Routledge 1983) 159; MP Doxey, *Economic Sanctions and International Enforcement* (2nd edn, Macmillan 1980) 142–8; JI Charney, 'Third State Remedies in International Law' (1989) 10 MJIL 57, 93.

[354] See, eg, NG Onuf, *Reprisals: Rituals, Rules, Rationales* (Center of International Studies 1974) 11.

[355] Gowlland-Debbas, 'Security' (n 21) 58. This line of argument expands on that author's previous account in *Collective Responses* (n 263).

cogens norms.[356] Hence, 'if a victim state is left to face the responsible state alone, a legal relationship based on multilateral obligations is effectively converted to a bilateral relationship at the level of its implementation'.[357] Whilst the violation of obligations *erga omnes* appears to simultaneously convert all States into 'passive' (ie obligated vis-à-vis the international community to dissociate themselves from the wrongful act and attempt to attenuate its adverse effects) and 'active' (ie affected by the wrongful act and entitled to invoke SR flowing from it) subjects in the newly formed, secondary legal relationship, classical theoretical constructions of SR remain confined to predominantly bilateral conceptions.[358]

This simultaneously constitutes an attractive argument militating in favour of the thesis that the SC can, and does, implement SR in some instances, and a setback in the same debate, in that it reduces, or limits, the Council's role to an inherently political exercise in determining responsibility. Indeed, '[i]t is evident that collective responses by a political organ to violations of international law can be neither automatic nor impartial, depending as they do for their motivation on the existing political consensus within that body and on various configurations of power and State interests'.[359] This entails that the SC's distinct role, coupled with the particularly extensive panoply of binding measures available to it, remains predominantly foreign to the horizontal discipline that has characterized traditional SR thus far.

This argument becomes even more compelling when framed in a comparative light, especially when delving into the commonalities and differences of SR and regional trade agreement or political structures, for example. Through the lens of Community law, one eminent publicist characterized SR mechanisms as conducive to a particularly distinctive brand of supremacy. He noted that

> [i]nternational law is as uncompromising as Community law in asserting that its norms are supreme over conflicting national norms. *But, international law's horizontal system of enforcement, which is typically actuated through the principles of state responsibility, reciprocity, and counter-measures*, gives the notion of supremacy an exceptionally rarefied quality, making it difficult to grasp and radically different from that found in the constitutional orders of states *with centralized enforcement monopolies* (emphasis added).[360]

[356] See, eg, Pisillo-Mazzeschi (n 118) 39–40 (decrying the fact that the ARSIWA predominantly focus on inter-State responsibility, operate on a 'bilateral', 'individualistic', and 'privatistic' conception of international law and, ultimately, fail in ascribing a better defined role to the individual in establishing the international responsibility of States). Consider also K Boon, 'Regime Conflicts and the U.N. Security Council: Applying the Law of Responsibility' (2010) 42 GWILR 787, 793 (arguing that the Council 'may even prove to be the best enforcer of the law of responsibility where there are serious breaches of peremptory norms').

[357] D Alland, 'Countermeasures of General Interest' (2002) 13 EJIL 1221, 1236. See Third Report, Ago (n 158) 203 [18]–[20], 206–11 [32]–[43]. But see Yamada (n 286) 121.

[358] See generally V-J Proulx, 'International Responsibility Today: Essays in Memory of Oscar Schachter: L'Émergence de la Communauté Internationale dans la Responsabilité des États' (2007) 18 EJIL 581. On the 'passive/active' dichotomy in the context of breaches of obligations *erga omnes*, see Villalpando (n 311) 383, 466.

[359] Gowlland-Debbas, 'Security' (n 21) 63.

[360] JHH Weiler, *The Constitution of Europe: 'Do the New Clothes Have an Emperor?' and Other Essays on European Integration* (CUP 1999) 25.

Granted that this particular author was probably invoking SR here to illustrate the EU's *sui generis* character, the argument also works the other way in that it consecrates the truly horizontal nature of traditional, unilateral SR implementation under international law. This approach would, therefore, preclude the designation of SC action as one of true implementation of international responsibility; the institutionalization of SR would share more commonalities with centralized (or 'vertical') enforcement mechanisms found in traditional constitutional orders, albeit drawing on collective perspectives and resources in applying the law against the backdrop of a multilateral process.[361]

However, writing about the post-9/11 legal landscape, one commentator invokes language extracted from ARSIWA Article 48 before concluding that SR for terrorism should, indeed, be actuated through the prism of an institutionalized setting. He underscores that '[c]ountermeasures are by their very nature decentralised, whereas violations of the international public order and reactions thereto, need, respectively, to be evaluated and managed by a centralised authority, legitimately representing the community'; this then prompts him to posit that '[t]his is why international reactions to terrorism *remain bound by the framework of the United Nations, as the sole structure securing collective interest of States "other than the injured one"*' (emphasis added).[362] It is likely that this reasoning could extend to other global security priorities, with the UN framework remaining the structure best suited to tackle these challenges, and the SC the most apt body in ensuring compliance with relevant substantive obligations in this broad field. These considerations share an intimate connection with the second preliminary conclusion alluded to earlier; it leads interlocutors to enquire 'into the nature of the link between Charter mechanisms for international peace maintenance and the legal institution of State responsibility, and as to whether indeed it may be said that the Council's function in this respect is a political one as opposed to the legal function exercised by the Court'.[363]

On the other hand, the second conclusion being inextricably intertwined with the first, the elucidation of the relationship between SR repertoire and SC action has been perhaps unnecessarily predicated on the prior conceptual disentanglement of the overarching legal/political dichotomy permeating this debate. As argued earlier, the Council sometimes anchors its decisions on findings of law as opposed to strict determinations of fact, yet this does not signal that the political dimension is excised altogether from the equation. More importantly, the SC's innovative legal incursions seem to adhere to what the ICJ has termed

361 See Weiler (n 360) 29 (arguing that '[t]he combined effect of constitutionalization and the evolution of the system of remedies results... in the removal from the Community legal order of the most central legal artefact of international law: the notion (and doctrinal apparatus) of exclusive state responsibility with its concomitant principles of reciprocity and counter-measures'). But see Gowlland-Debbas, 'Security' (n 21) 73 (speaking to the Council's involvement in responding to violations of international law: '[w]e are not therefore speaking of a centralized system to determine whether reactions to alleged violations of international law are indeed legitimate, but of the collective reaction itself').

362 Dupuy (n 51) 15–16.

363 Gowlland-Debbas, 'Security' (n 21) 57.

'operative design' in that they entail definitive and pervasive legal effects for the parties at hand, whilst also subtracting any unlawful act from legal protection or recognition.[364]

Consequently, '[i]t is by virtue of an operation of law, not of fact, that the member States agree to carry out the Council's decisions and to subject their international agreements to the overriding effects of the Charter'.[365] At the same time, it has also been demonstrated that political considerations pervade the SC's deliberations and thought processes, a dominant component of international decision-making that seems hardly dissociable from the Council's potential application of SR rules.[366] Also implicit in this proposition is the notion that the Council can perhaps play a role in implementing SR on a political level but this remains limited by the UN Charter's terms and framework. As seen in Chapter 3, the ICJ has confirmed this principle, stating that the 'political character of an organ cannot release it from the observance of the treaty provisions established by the Charter when they constitute limitations on its powers or criteria for its judgment'.[367] However, the flipside to this argument begs the question whether this role is limited to a truly political function. This tension was very much present in the Dissenting Opinion of Judge Bedjaoui in the *Lockerbie* cases, in which he observed that 'the first dispute concern[ed] the extradition of two Libyan nationals and [was] being dealt with, legally, by the Court ... whereas the second dispute concern[ed] ... *State terrorism as well as the international responsibility of the Libyan State and* [was] *being dealt with, politically, by the Security Council*' (emphasis added).[368] This line of inquiry clearly brings into relief the tension between

[364] *Namibia Advisory Opinion* (n 281) 50. See also the Separate Opinion of Judge Onyeama in ibid 147, in which he expounds that the Council's determination was declaratory rather than legislative:

> [t]he declaration of the illegality of the continued presence of South Africa in Namibia did not itself make such presence illegal; it was ... a statement of the Security Council's assessment of the legal quality of the situation created by South Africa's failure to comply with the General Assembly's resolution ... it was in fact a judicial determination.

The ICJ also found that these determinations have effect under international law, and that they are 'opposable to all States in the sense of barring *erga omnes* the legality of a situation which is maintained in violation of international law'. The Court further stated at 54, 56: '[a] binding determination made by a competent organ of the United Nations to the effect that a situation is illegal cannot remain without consequence ... [t]his decision entails a legal consequence, namely that of putting an end to an illegal situation'. See also Gowlland-Debbas, 'The Functions' (n 21) 291.

[365] Gowlland-Debbas, 'The Functions' (n 21) 304.

[366] Paradoxically, this constitutes one of the dominant tenets of the neo-conservative agenda when identifying the limits of international law. See, eg, JL Goldsmith and EA Posner, *The Limits of International Law* (OUP 2005) 104, 192. For a contrary view, see HH Koh, 'Why Do Nations Obey International Law?' (1997) 106 Yale Law Journal 2599, esp 2603, 2634, 2646. See also generally L Henkin, *How Nations Behave: Law and Foreign Policy* (2nd edn, Columbia University Press 1979) 47. For a critique of Koh's point of view, see EA Posner, 'International Law and the Disaggregated State' (2005) 32 Florida State University Law Review 797, 800–2.

[367] *Admission of a State to Membership to the United Nations (Charter, Art. 4)* (Advisory Opinion) [1948] ICJ Rep 57, 64.

[368] *Lockerbie* cases (n 276) 34, 144 respectively. Similarly, see the Dissenting Opinions of Judges Ajibola and El-Kosheri in ibid 79, 184 and 96, 201 respectively. But see Forteau (n 20) 335.

the SC's political function, on the one hand, and its *potential* judicial function, on the other.[369] As discussed in Section 3.1.5.2, certain scholars construe select Council incursions into the realm of SR as a clear indication that this organ has, on occasion, granted itself 'quasi-judicial' powers. Conversely, legal scholarship has traditionally and adamantly rejected the conferral of purely judicial functions upon the Council, and rightly so.[370] Moreover, influential publicists have rightly suggested that the SC is not bound by ordinary judicial proceedings and modalities, such as the production of evidence and witnesses, cross-examinations, etc.[371] Despite her spirited defence of the SC's potential implementation of SR, these impediments ultimately led Vera Gowlland-Debbas to conclude that '[t]he Council is a political organ: it is composed of governmental representatives which cannot even be said, in contrast to the General Assembly, to represent the international community as a whole.'[372] Therefore, there is no way around the argument that SC action is largely driven by political considerations. However, and for several reasons advanced earlier, this reality should not completely disable the thesis that the SC can play some role in implementing SR or, at least, in applying that normative scheme in appropriate cases. Gowlland-Debbas summed it up well: 'from the lack of a legal process to conclude that the Council's role in issues involving State responsibility is purely political, as opposed to the Court's legal one, does not shed light on the Council's true function in such matters'.[373]

It is probably inaccurate to contend that all dimensions of all disputes involving SR implementation for the violation of counterterrorism obligations will be inherently and/or solely political in nature, so that the Council should necessarily deal with them. Similar reasoning could no doubt extend to disputes involving the violation of other global security obligations. By the same token, there is no reason why both the SC and ICJ cannot concomitantly deal with similar or different aspects of a given dispute, as both bodies have at times made incursions into the other's jurisdiction.[374] Although this possibility has been expressly acknowledged, the rigid dichotomy between political and judicial decision-making has also been perpetuated by ICJ Judges on occasion. For instance, the Declaration of Judge Ni in the *Lockerbie* cases was categorical and rigid in its construction of the respective

[369] On the relationship between political and judicial organs, see Gowlland-Debbas, 'The Functions' (n 21) 306–11. See also generally V Gowlland-Debbas, 'The Relationship between Political and Judicial Organs of International Organizations: The Role of the Security Council on the New International Criminal Court' in L Boisson de Chazournes *et al.* (eds), *International Organizations and International Dispute Settlement: Trends and Prospects* (Transnational 2002) 195–240.

[370] See, eg, Kelsen, *The Law* (n 142) 476–7; C Tomuschat, 'The *Lockerbie* Case before the International Court of Justice' (1992) 48 The International Commission of Jurists Review 38, 41; Gowlland-Debbas, 'Security' (n 21) 71. See also the Dissenting Opinions of Judges Weeramantry and el-Kosheri in the *Lockerbie* cases (n 276) 56, 166 and 96, 201 respectively.

[371] See E Lauterpacht, *Aspects of the Administration of International Justice* (Grotius 1991) 42–3.

[372] Gowlland-Debbas, 'Security' (n 21) 71.

[373] Gowlland-Debbas, 'Security' (n 21) 72.

[374] See, eg, Gowlland-Debbas, 'The Functions' (n 21) 310 (observing that 'a determination of an act of aggression is clearly a matter of international law and... the ICJ has not considered itself debarred from making such a finding').

roles of these two organs, yet it also underscored their functional complementarity explored in Chapter 3: '[t]he Council has functions of a political nature assigned to it, whereas the Court exercises purely judicial functions. Both organs can therefore perform their separate but complementary functions with respect to the same events'.[375] This undoubtedly led some publicists to proclaim that when characterizing situations as states of emergency or international armed conflicts, the SC carries out a political function. According to this view, no equivalent legal weight should be ascribed to those decisions as when compared to the deference that would be accorded a purely judicial body in similar circumstances.[376]

Interestingly, some scholars take issue with this line of reasoning, opining that 'the view that there is a clear division of functions between the Court and the Council along the lines of a political/legal dichotomy is not really tenable'.[377] Some reconcile this discrepancy by explaining that in some of the cases explored above, the SC operated in a predominantly 'legal', as opposed to 'political', framework. In so doing, it has brought the discipline of international responsibility—namely the prior determination of a breach upon which is predicated the application of attribution, along with the imposition of countermeasures—into the purview of Article 39 of the UN Charter. In addition, it has extended this normative scheme and reasoning to non-State entities, in particular by attributing international law violations to the National Union for the Total Independence of Angola, the Bosnian Serbs, Al-Qaeda in Afghanistan, and the Janjaweed in Sudan.[378]

A particularly vocal proponent of this view is Gowlland-Debbas, who ultimately resolved this tension by doing away with the strict division between political and legal decision-making, as it pertains to both the ICJ and Council. She further based her theory on the notion that both the ICJ and SC serve different, but not mutually inimical, roles in the international legal process, whilst placing particular emphasis on the cardinal principle of return to legality, discussed earlier. Therefore, under SR repertoire both bodies would ultimately work simultaneously—and in harmony—towards the same objectives, albeit through different means. The ICJ's role—which may crop up at an earlier stage in the place of countermeasures or as a predicate for their adoption, or at a later stage in order to review the legality of countermeasures adopted unilaterally—is synonymous with peaceful settlement procedures. Conversely, the Council's role is synonymous

375 Declaration of Judge Ni in the *Lockerbie* cases (n 276) 22, 134 respectively (citing *Military and Paramilitary Activities in and against Nicaragua (Nicaragua v US)* (Jurisdiction and Admissibility) [1984] ICJ Rep 392, 434–5 [95]).

376 Provost, *International* (n 73) 312.

377 Gowlland-Debbas, 'The Functions' (n 21) 307.

378 See, eg, Gowlland-Debbas, 'The Functions' (n 21) 307–8:

> the Council has clearly been operating not within a political, but a legal framework. It has linked its determinations under Article 39 to a finding that a State (or non-State entity in some cases) has breached a fundamental international obligation. Such determinations have been followed by measures which have temporarily divested States and individuals of legal rights, with definitive legal effect and extensive legal consequences.

See also Gowlland-Debbas, 'Responsibility' (n 117) 129.

with institutional countermeasures and remains confined to enforcement, which signals that it does not act as an impartial arbitrator but rather in lieu and place of injured States, given that the obligations at play concern the international community as a whole.[379]

Undoubtedly, any critical observer might be compelled to point out two inherent limitations in maintaining the extant structure. First, whilst the respective processes guiding the ICJ and Council remain distinct, they both involve, at a minimum, the production of quasi-judicial findings in culminating towards a resolution, whilst also affecting the rights/obligations and legal positions of the concerned States.[380] Indeed, this argument comes full circle with the observations made in Chapter 3, especially in Section 3.1.5.2. In particular, it further reinforces the idea that when the Council implements SR, that body of law provides an environment facilitating its political decision-making process. Yet, it does not seek to replace or supplant the political nature of the Council's decision-making, nor should the resolution of this debate inexorably pit the Council against the Court under the binary of 'political' versus 'judicial'. Rather, both organs are called upon to make political decisions –the main difference is that the ICJ does so entirely by way of judicial process, which seeks to alleviate some of the more problematic political dimensions of international disputes. Whilst the Council's process is inherently more political and seeks to achieve a political consensus, as opposed to a politically-executable judicial determination, it does not preclude it from straddling quasi-judicial terrain in some instances. Whilst not entirely supportive of the previous proposition, one commentator's characterization seems apposite: '[i]t would be an exaggeration to say that the Security Council and General Assembly ignore international law completely in their decision-making; they both fulfil political functions within the international legal order rather than making legal decisions in accordance with international law'.[381]

Secondly, although collective/centralized measures might palliate the more intrinsic problems associated with the unilateral implementation of SR, this very implementation is subject to potential judicial review by a judge or arbitrator provided jurisdictional requirements are satisfied, whilst SC action (arguably) eludes such oversight.[382] Unsurprisingly, this view has been sharply criticized by other

[379] Gowlland-Debbas, 'Security' (n 21) 73. See also Gowlland-Debbas, 'The Functions' (n 21) 308; Gowlland-Debbas, 'The Limits' (n 21) (positing that electing collectively-authorized over unilateral measures constitutes an attempt to escape regression to unilateral decisions involving community interests).

[380] Gowlland-Debbas, 'Security' (n 21) 73 ('whilst judicial settlement of disputes over questions of responsibility and institutionalised countermeasures are two distinct processes, they are both premised on the same kind of quasi-judicial findings and the outcome in both cases affects the legal position of the States concerned').

[381] Provost, *International* (n 73) 310.

[382] See Gowlland-Debbas, 'Security' (n 21) 73:

> whilst collective responses are to be preferred to the more arbitrary, anarchic and possibly more destabilizing unilateral ones, the problem is that whilst the qualification of an act as a prior condition to the application of unilateral countermeasures by a State may eventually (though not necessarily) be opened to challenge by the judge or arbitrator, those

prominent scholars,[383] prompting them to conclude that '[t]hese processes are not equivalent: one is preliminary, the other is final'.[384] In the same vein, Georg Nolte called into question the distinction formulated by Gowlland-Debbas between 'declaratory' determinations by the SC, on the one hand, and 'constitutive' determinations by courts, on the other; he further cautioned that it 'may incur the misunderstanding that both kinds of determinations can legally coexist even if they engender different conclusions'.[385]

One analogy—no doubt flawed or, at least, limited[386]—with domestic structures that was previously invoked in this debate would be that of a police force upholding criminal law. Despite its inherent limitations, it might be helpful to develop it further. On the one hand, police powers not only allow for the prevention and neutralization of criminal threats but they also serve the broader objectives of deterrence and return to legality.[387] By its very nature, the pre-emption or eradication of criminal activity ensures a return to a legally sound situation (ie criminal activity creates rifts in the normative framework and subverts public order, whilst similarly to the SC's role, one of the purposes of police arrests is to restore public order). Indeed, when contrasted with SC activities, such thinking could lead to the conclusion that '[e]ven domestic police forces (which have far less powers "to conclusively attribute responsibility") have the power and the duty to make a prima-facie evaluation of the legal situation and to act on the basis of that evaluation'.[388]

On the other hand, a domestic court adjudicating the merits of the same criminal activity might find that the *mens rea* requirement, as an element of the specific crime, was not fulfilled in the lead-up to the infraction in question. The main reason for this asymmetrical process of reasoning between the police and the court is readily identifiable: the police uses its subjective judgment as a preliminary screening device in its attempt to ensure a return to legality, whilst the court is instead confronted with the facts present before it, supplemented by the evidentiary record, without typically having to make any preliminary judgment calls on the merits of the facts vis-à-vis applicable law (ie does the 'case' even warrant judicial intervention or is it too weak to stand?). In turn, the court will eventually have to meld subjective appreciation of the facts with objective prescriptions found in legal authorities so as to identify and apply an adequate resolution.

This signals a conceptual and practical disconnect between the subjective judgment of the police officials, which could be likened to the SC's role and its reliance

taken by the Council in connection with its primary responsibility in peace maintenance are authoritative and binding and when linked to determinations under Article 39 not subject, *as such*, to judicial review.

383 For a critique of Gowlland-Debbas' work, see Nolte (n 165) 322–4.

384 Nolte (n 165) 324. 385 Nolte (n 165) 324. 386 See, eg, Alvarez (n 7) 188.

387 Paradoxically, Nolte (n 165) 323 invoked the police force analogy to discredit Gowlland-Debbas' central thesis but conceded that law enforcement authorities are called upon to perform prima facie assessments of legal situations and act on such assessments whilst being ultimately held to account for protecting a specific legal interest.

388 Nolte (n 165) 323.

on predominantly political considerations, and the subjective role of the court, which could be seen as analogous with the ICJ's function (whilst also political but carried out by way of judicial process). Moreover, the court invariably has the benefit of *ex post facto* factual assessment, on the basis of evidentiary records tendered to it, although those records can be incomplete or sometimes erroneous. However, the attribution of specific roles to each body remains skin deep: the police authorities would also be guided by objective criteria (ie a general legal framework governing their profession), whilst the court would also articulate its judgment around some objective and legalistic backbone.[389] In addition, whilst it may be difficult to point to any one dominant approach in each respective strand of decision-making in specific instances, both the SC and ICJ have to weigh political considerations in reaching their decisions. In turn, this conclusion carries with it significant implications for formal and distributive justice, both at the domestic and international levels.

As argued in Section 3.1.5.2, SR law provides an environment in which the SC can make political decisions in respect of State behaviour violating counterterrorism obligations or other global security duties. Similarly, it can be cogently reiterated that the ICJ performs a political function but, by way of judicial process, so as to reduce the emphasis on political considerations in its decision-making. Even though both organs dispose of different means and serve seemingly different functions, they ultimately render objective and subjective interpretations of both the law and facts at hand, and base their respective insights on a basic modicum of legality in the SC's case, and of political sensibility in the ICJ's. Granted, such modicum might be more pronounced—and less random or arbitrary—in the case of ICJ activities than in SC practice. In his seminal course at The Hague Academy, Eduardo Jiménez de Aréchaga echoed the remarks made by some delegates at the San Francisco Conference in 1945 to the effect that the SC fulfils a dual role: that of police and judge or jury. In short, once a potentially hostile disagreement crops up between two States, the Council first intervenes urgently, as a police force would, to neutralize the use of force; at an ulterior stage, the Council then takes on a judicial role with a view to settling the dispute, the urgency of which is less acute.[390]

Whilst the police force metaphor may present some attractive—albeit limited—intellectual points of comparison, a more compelling parallel might be found in the municipal law distinction between a judicial appeal and a pardon granted by the government's executive branch. Whilst the appellate court

[389] However, this vision should be somewhat tempered by reference to domestic interpretations of the role of police officers in specific, non arrest-related instances. For instance, the Supreme Court of Canada viewed the investigative functions of the police as devoid of any requirements to perform quasi-judicial assessments concerning suspects' legal guilt or innocence, or contemplate the evidence gathered through a legal prism. See *Hill v Hamilton-Wentworth Regional Police Services Board* [2007] 3 SCR 129 [50]–[65].

[390] E Jiménez de Aréchaga, 'Le Traitement des Différends Internationaux par le Conseil de Sécurité' (1954) 85 RdC 1, 8–9 (also citing the interventions of US delegate, Mr Stassen, and British delegate, Lord Halifax, at the San Francisco Conference).

might rule one way on a given matter—having at its disposal specific and circumscribed means of enforcing its decision—the pardoning authority instead circumvents many legal considerations surrounding the judicial process and, quite similarly to SC action, issues a binding determination. In particular, the pardon fails to operate within an established corpus of rules and procedures but hinges on what can be construed as a unilateral political decision, a reality that may be readily seen to be analogous to the Council's role in applying SR. This is not to say, however, that the Council's decision-making is necessarily unilateral, as some degree of multilateral checks and balances pervades its structure and process in reaching a political consensus, yet similar checks and balances are also in place within executive branches of municipal legal orders. In addition, this is not to say that the pardoning authority's decision is entirely deprived of any legal considerations whatsoever. Quite to the contrary, similarly to the role of a domestic appellate court, it may well be that the decision to pardon a certain individual seeks to address concerns of fundamental justice or restore favourable public perception of the legal system, thereby striving towards an equilibrium between broader social and policy objectives and compliance with the law.[391]

Ultimately, both bodies may have radically different means and thought processes supporting their outcomes. One is predominantly political whilst the other is predominantly legal, at least from a procedural standpoint. Yet, both decision-makers remain unsheltered from both substantive political and legal considerations seeping into their respective decision-making processes, not unlike the SC in reconciling factual international law transgressions with Chapter VII, or the ICJ in remedying equally factual international law violations within the broader international legal order.[392] Ultimately, turning to analogies drawn from domestic legal orders to shed analytical light on the inner workings of the international legal order may turn out to yield limited insight. One such analogy, which has been heavily critiqued, resides in the rapprochement that is often made between the three traditional domestic branches of government—the legislative, executive, and judiciary—on the one hand, and the global legal order on the other (ie in particular by constructing an analogy whereby the GA is a legislative branch, the SC an executive branch, and the ICJ the judiciary on the international stage). Whilst attractive at first glance, such a comparison may ultimately run up against the inevitable 'institutional problem' that characterizes the international legal order; in short, an eventual metaphorical clash will inexorably result from the incompatibility of the decentralized (read: anarchical) nature of the international system with the sort of vertical enforcement rationale that animates domestic

[391] As seen in Nolte (n 165) 323, similar parallels falling within the Council's scope of activities can be drawn: eg 'a power on the part of the Security Council to initiate or block a prosecution for aggression [which] constitutes a traditional executive function in which considerations of public order play a legitimate role'.

[392] Although not fully supportive of this specific proposition, consider Provost, *International* (n 73) 304 ff on the nature and effect of legal characterizations by international political bodies.

legal transactions.[393] This problem is no doubt further compounded by the fact that international dispute settlement remains dependent upon State consent; contrary to the situation prevalent in domestic constitutional orders, no international court or tribunal may exercise automatic or compulsory jurisdiction over disputes involving failures to prevent global security violations. In a seminal book published in 1963, Dame Rosalyn Higgins—who later became President of the World Court—pointed to the absence of a mechanism of compulsory jurisdiction as a factor that impeded that body's ability to contribute more actively to the development of international law, at least in its early years.[394] Of course, this is less of a cause for concern nowadays, as over 300 bilateral treaties and multilateral conventions contain compromissory clauses granting jurisdiction over disputes to the ICJ. Moreover, the ICJ has handled a variety of disputes—some of major political and legal importance—with its docket increasing significantly over the last quarter of a century.[395]

Before briefly turning to the more concrete case of Libya, it is important to register an initial conclusion. Scholarly discussions addressing the SC's role have been unnecessarily framed in terms of 'Council versus ICJ', particularly regarding attempts to articulate the political and judicial functions surrounding the UN's apparatus. In response to this posture, and whilst it has been acknowledged that the SC can sometimes exert its functions in 'quasi-judicial' fashion,[396] it is submitted that the elucidation of that body's role in implementing SR might be better served by looking at the traditional alternative, namely the unilateral implementation of SR by injured States. As prefaced in this chapter, modern SR repertoire relies largely on the mechanisms of self-help. As one author states, '[a]s a result of state reluctance to accept the jurisdiction of a neutral third party, the state injured by an internationally wrongful act often has no other choice but to rely on self-help measures to persuade the wrongdoing state to offer reparation'.[397] Furthermore, whilst ARSIWA Article 33 provides that the codified SR rules are 'without prejudice to any right, arising from the international responsibility of a State, which may accrue directly to any person or entity other than a State', it is equally important to bear in mind that, traditionally, the implementation of SR amounted to an executive function, which typically fell within States' discretionary margin of power and competence.[398] In this light, the added value

393 For a study exploring similar ideas, see R Collins, *The Institutional Problem in Modern International Law* (Hart 2016).

394 See Higgins (n 29) 3.

395 See HE Judge Peter Tomka, President of the ICJ, Statement to the Sixth Committee of the UN General Assembly (1 November 2013) <http://www.icj-cij.org/presscom/files/4/17684.pdf> accessed 20 August 2015, 5. See generally Webb (n 162) 3.

396 See Section 3.1.5.2.

397 R Provost, 'Introduction' in idem (ed.), *State Responsibility in International Law* (Ashgate 2002) xv. See also generally ME O'Connell, 'Controlling Countermeasures' in Ragazzi (n 62) 49–62.

398 But see EB Weiss, 'Invoking State Responsibility in the Twenty-First Century' (2002) 96 AJIL 798, 809 (remarking that the ARSIWA 'should have done more to recognize the expanded universe of participants in the international system entitled to invoke state responsibility'); C Tomuschat, 'Individual Reparation Claims in Instances of Grave Human Rights Violations: The Position Under

of the institutional mechanism resides in its ability to ensure collective action in response to violations of international law.[399]

Granted, the SC's function is primarily political, but then again, the very idea of implementing SR unilaterally—when left to inter-State devices—is inherently political in nature. Similarly to the Council's own decision-making, which operates against a legal backdrop that facilitates its political thought-process, an injured State will ultimately also rely on political considerations when implementing responsibility against a wrongdoing State. Revisiting the spirit of Kelsen's view that international law exists as a coercive order,[400] with others finding it to be absent from the ARSIWA,[401] one publicist argued that existing SR structure, coupled with its scheme of countermeasures, fosters disparate power dynamics between States but nonetheless remains the primary reason why they comply with their international obligations.[402] Whilst acknowledging that UN-mandated embargos seldom achieve their purported objectives, he further construed SR as a particularly poignant tool in inducing compliance, primarily because of the idea of reciprocity,[403] which was discussed in Section 3.1. As a corollary, that reciprocity—translated here as a 'shared interest in the maintenance of predictable patterns of conduct'—stabilizes asymmetrical power dynamics engendered by the system of international responsibility and countermeasures.[404] Thus, the injured State may actually incur more damage than the responsible State should the former take it upon itself to impose countermeasures on the latter and thereby disrupt a previously established pattern of predictable reciprocal international relations. From the perspective of international law and justice, generally, the deployment of SR-derived countermeasures can bring about various abuses and inequities. This reality is further reinforced when such sanctions are contextualized within the framework of the international community, namely as being adopted within a highly decentralized, global society that cannot impose itself as the warrantor of mandatory international justice.[405] Moreover, in

General International Law' in A Randelzhofer and C Tomuschat (eds), *State Responsibility and the Individual: Reparation in Instances of Grave Violations of Human Rights* (Nijhoff 1999) 1, 2–4.

[399] See, eg, Villalpando (n 311) 426.

[400] See, eg, H Kelsen, *General Theory of Law and State* (Harvard University Press 1945) 118–20, 330; *Principles of International Law* (Rinehart & Company 1952) 6 ('[t]he law is a normative order, and since legal norms provide for coercive acts as sanctions, the law is a coercive order'); *Principles of International Law* (Robert Tucker (ed.), 2nd edn, Holt, Rinehart and Winston 1966) 3–39; 'Théorie Générale du Droit International Public' (1953) 84 RdC 1, 9–46. But see W Friedmann, 'General Course on Public International Law' (1969) 127 RdC 39, 65 ('[l]egal philosophers are far from united on the question whether enforceability is an essential element of law').

[401] See, eg, J Barboza, 'Legal Injury: The Tip of the Iceberg in the Law of State Responsibility' in Ragazzi (n 62) 10.

[402] Zemanek (n 94) 125–34.

[403] This type of argument has certainly been advanced before in a wide array of international legal areas. For a variety of views on the topic, see, eg, Abbott (n 80) 369–70; Dunoff and Trachtman (n 80) 403; Falk (n 82) 594. On reciprocity in the fields of human rights and humanitarian law, see Provost, *International* (n 73) 121–238; 'Reciprocity' (n 73).

[404] Zemanek (n 94) 128–9.

[405] See, eg, CP Economides (n 201) 226; idem, 'L'Obligation de Règlement Pacifique des Différends Internationaux: Une Norme Fondamentale Tenue à l'Écart' in B Boutros-Ghali (ed.), *Boutros Boutros-Ghali Amicorum Discipulorumque Liber*, vol 1 (Bruylant 1998) 405, 405 ff.

the light of the reservations expressed earlier in Section 3.1, the idea of reciprocity becomes particularly ineffective in certain settings and scenarios.

Political undertones undeniably pervade this exercise and, by this very fact, make it directly transposable to the present work: in deciding whether or not to follow up on an internationally wrongful act and impose countermeasures, an injured State will undoubtedly engage in a cost–benefit analysis entailing a careful evaluation of potential political disadvantages and trade-offs related to all available courses of action. Presumably, there is no reason to discard this reasoning when analysing SC decision-making. One should recall, however, that contrary to Council resolutions (which are, arguably, insulated from such an exercise), the unilateral implementation of SR by an injured State is potentially subject to judicial review. However, the strong likelihood of concerned States failing to agree to the jurisdiction of the ICJ or an arbitral tribunal in settling their dispute strongly militates against the conclusion that SR's inherent political character can be excised from the inquiry. We must, therefore, work within the system as it currently stands: politics are sometimes inseparable from law,[406] especially in any area involving international relations, such as the global fight against terrorism or the broader field of global security. More importantly, addressing the question of SR implementation by the SC might also alleviate the more intrinsic concerns typically associated with States' unilateral implementation of international responsibility, such as the blind and naked pursuit of self-interests. Hence, institutionalized reactions to internationally wrongful acts would, to the extent possible, purport to cater to specific objectives of impartiality and efficiency, which would then have the result of doing away with the inherent problems associated with States' unilateral implementation of responsibility.[407]

Whilst the purported objective of increasing the efficacy of responses to wrongful acts can perhaps be persuasively defended, it is more doubtful that institutionalizing the implementation of SR would enhance impartiality in SR-related decision-making. Rather, one of the overarching objectives of such reform would be to ensure some level of coordination of those responses with a view to providing an additional—or perhaps a single—check on unilateralism so as to strike a balance between redressing international law violations and respecting the sovereign equality of States. Interestingly, some commentators emphasize the need for further coordination, under SC auspices, in contexts in which States resort to forcible responses against territorial States that are 'unable

[406] This notion can be traced back to Cicero's and Isocrates' teachings. See, eg, EA Scallen, 'Evidence Law as Pragmatic Legal Rhetoric: Reconnecting Legal Scholarship, Teaching and Ethics' (2003) 21 Quinnipiac Law Review 813, 845. For a more modern application of this view, see, eg SB Markesinis, 'Understanding American Law by Looking at it through Foreign Eyes: Towards a Wider Theory for the Study and Use of Foreign Law' (2006) 81 Tulane Law Review 123, 181 (arguing 'that law, especially public law, and politics are inseparable'). For thought-provoking essays on the relationship between politics and international law, see M Koskenniemi, 'The Politics of International Law' (1990) 1 EJIL 4; *The Politics of International Law* (Hart 2011).

[407] See, eg, Villalpando (n 311) 424.

or unwilling' to repel terrorist threats percolating within their borders; indeed, whilst still controversial as a potentially emerging norm under international law, the 'unable or unwilling' doctrine is certainly generating debate.[408] Indeed, there is something to be praised about the SC's multilateral decision-making process and methodology, at least at a principled level, especially when faced with transnational security threats; arguably, the Council's decisions strive to be 'objective', even though that organ produces 'political' results, given that its resolutions emanate from fifteen governments which hold differing interests and may respond to different incentives. However, they may coalesce around a particular decision or course of action, through deliberative and rhetorical processes, so as to prevent the further materialization of global security risks. Surely this type of decision-making stands in stark contrast with unchecked unilateral retaliation by one injured State, or with narrow 'coalition building' by liberal States, which might have a tinge of *mission civilisatrice* in some instances.[409] As argued in Section 3.1.5.2, the SC would still be making political decisions in this setting but whilst simultaneously working within a legal environment, thereby straddling quasi-judicial terrain.

This line of argument also ties into a second broader but relevant consideration: it highlights the need to rethink the traditional bilateral model of SR implementation. One of the most limiting problems of modern SR repertoire can be readily encapsulated: this normative scheme responds largely to a unitary typology and rests upon a predominantly bilateral conception of legal relationships.[410] Yet again, a commentator sought to redefine some tenets of Kelsen's classical theory by expounding that coercion is not an end in itself on the international plane but rather facilitates enforcement of a primary legal obligation, thereby disabling the dominant inter-State model of enforcement and compliance. In his view, '[i]f one follows the theory that sanctions are necessarily a determinant element of law, it should not matter that such sanctions or, more precisely, the coercion behind it, does not come from another State but from a non-governmental

[408] See, eg, DI Ahmed, 'Defending Weak States Against the "Unwilling or Unable" Doctrine of Self-Defense' (2014) 9 JILIR 1. For further discussion on the 'unable or unwilling' doctrine and the problem of 'failed' States in counterterrorism contexts, see Sections 2.4.2, 2.2, and 5.2.2. See also Proulx (n 3) ch 6, section II.B; LA Becker, 'Rules for the Global War on Terror: Implying Consent and Presuming Conditions for Intervention' (2012–13) 45 NYUJILP 1. On the 'unable or unwilling' doctrine, more broadly, see A Deeks, '"Unwilling or Unable": Toward a Normative Framework for Extraterritorial Self-Defense' (2012) 52 VJIL 483; G Williams, 'Piercing the Shield of Sovereignty: An Assessment of the Legal Status of the "Unwilling or Unable Test"' (2013) 36 The University of New South Wales Law Journal 619.

[409] Compare generally A-M Slaughter, 'International Law in a World of Liberal States' (1995) 6 EJIL 503; A Moravcsik, 'Taking Preferences Seriously: A Liberal Theory of International Politics' (1997) 51 IO 513; A-M Slaughter, 'The Liberal Agenda for Peace: International Relations Theory and the Future of the United Nations' (1994) 4 Transnational Law and Contemporary Problems 377; JE Alvarez, 'Do Liberal States Behave Better? A Critique of Slaughter's Liberal Theory' (2001) 12 EJIL 183.

[410] See Villalpando (n 311) 466–7. See also generally G Nolte, 'From Dionisio Anzilotti to Roberto Ago: The Classical International Law of State Responsibility and the Traditional Primacy of a Bilateral Conception of Inter-State Relations' (2002) 13 EJIL 1083.

source, as long as it forces the object State to fulfil a hitherto unfulfilled international obligation'.[411]

This approach also benefits when contrasted with Georg Schwarzenberger's writings on the topic, which also partially aligned with Kelsen's theory, subject to a few variations. Whilst Schwarzenberger's inquiry did not focus on sanctions per se, he did posit that consistently violated international legal rules do not amount to law, as such. However, he did not go as far as advocating that the very existence of international law is contingent on the corresponding existence of sanctions.[412] Therefore, according to these merged theories it would seem that the vital element resides in the actual enforcement of counterterrorism or similar obligations to ensure their coherence in the international legal order, irrespective of the character, nature, or origin of the enforcer. However, this argument is considerably offset by the fact that the debate over whether unenforced rules can amount to international law no longer generates considerable polemic and is usually discarded by scholars working in various disciplines.[413]

Coming back to the fact that these considerations seem to pave the way for possible SC involvement in applying SR principles, can the same be said about the character, nature, or origin of the legal tools invoked to provide such enforcement? In other words, this hybrid theory does militate in favour of implicating the SC but, in the event that it is seized of an issue involving the violation of counterterrorism or other relevant obligations, can/does it apply SR as a matter of course? Or does it remain fettered solely by political considerations, thereby only invoking and applying international law arbitrarily or randomly? In the event that it applies or develops this normative scheme, does it do so only by way of incidental censure?[414] And in this event, does it really matter, for the purposes of the present inquiry, that the Council's application of SR is idiosyncratic and incidental?

Given the fact that the very notion of implementing SR unilaterally under traditional international law is inherently political, idiosyncratic, and ultimately subject to the individual whims of the concerned States, the answer to this last query would appear to be manifestly negative. The main distinction here is that, as opposed to an individual State applying a self-interested and unilateral vision of SR rules, the Council's action will be tantamount to the same exercise albeit in a collective setting, subject to all the inherent pitfalls and shortcomings of that system (of which corresponding concerns may also be identified in the case of unilateral, State-led implementation of SR). Not to mention that unlike that of the SC, a State's self-characterization of certain facts or acts is necessarily provisional.

[411] Zemanek (n 94) 134, 132 (inferring that the application of extant SR rules to the traditional State-to-State model remains ill-suited in ensuring compliance with obligations). See generally Simma, 'From Bilateralism' (n 120) 217–384.

[412] See, eg, G Schwarzenberger, *The Misery and Grandeur of International Law* (Stevens 1963); *A Manual of International Law* (5th edn, Stevens 1967); *The Inductive Approach to International Law* (Stevens 1965).

[413] See, eg, KW Abbott *et al.*, 'The Concept of Legalization' (2000) 54 IO 401, 402, 418.

[414] See G Arangio-Ruiz, 'Article 39 of the ILC First-reading Draft Articles on State Responsibility' (2000) 83 Rivista di Diritto Internazionale 747, 765 fn 31.

The debate, therefore, might be more fruitfully couched in terms of 'individual' versus 'collective'—and the legal mechanics applied as 'unilateral' versus 'institutionalized'—as both processes ostensibly emanating from different enforcers might very well produce different results but remain characterized by sometimes arbitrary, almost invariably political, and idiosyncratic legal reasoning.

In any event, as certain areas of international law shift away from a State-centric conception towards an increasingly transnational paradigm, the idea of international responsibility must be re-examined in light of recent events and trends. This problem is further compounded by the contemporaneous emergence of transnational violence and human rights abuse, bringing about specific implications for obligations *erga omnes*.[415] These considerations will become pivotal in subsequent sections. In the interim, it is fair to infer that despite its largely political function, the SC sometimes draws inspiration from SR law (at times direct, at times more diffused) as a conceptual tool that can inform and shape its decision-making.

4.5.2 The Council's application of attribution and responsibility mechanics

This, however, does not satisfactorily resolve the question whether the Council can, and does, implement SR. Even if one accepts this premise, much of the lingering confusion stems from the manner in which the SC applies SR mechanics. For instance, it has certainly not applied the concept of attribution uniformly or consistently.[416] Although highly relevant for present purposes, the case of Libya is a puzzling example of the Council's confused application of attribution mechanics, and stands in sharp contrast with one author's view that 'the Security Council plays a key role in grey areas where the applicability

[415] For the moment, suffice it to mention that the violation of obligations *erga omnes* entails that 'any State whether or not directly injured, would have the right to take countermeasures, including reprisals otherwise illegal.' See T Scovazzi, 'Some Remarks on International Responsibility in the Field of Environmental Protection' in Ragazzi (n 62) 218 fn 32. See also generally M Ragazzi, *The Concept of International Obligations Erga Omnes* (Clarendon Press 1997); O Schachter, *International Law in Theory and Practice* (Nijhoff 1991) 381. In bolstering his view that international law exists as a coercive order, Kelsen, 'Théorie' (n 400) 33, 49 believed that armed reprisals, too, whilst proscribed by the UN Charter, were not theoretically excluded. See also P Guggenheim, *Traité de Droit International Public: Avec Mention de la Pratique Internationale et Suisse* (2nd edn, Georg 1967) 92. In a broader sense, it should be noted that Kelsen, 'Théorie' (n 400) 12–15, 18–19 essentially equated the concept of 'sanction' with 'reprisal'. For analogous applications or definitions falling outside of the 'théorie de la contrainte', see J Kunz, 'Sanctions in International Law' (1960) 54 AJIL 324; H Morgenthau, 'Théorie des Sanctions Internationales' (1935) 16 Revue de Droit International et de Législation Comparée 478.

[416] See, eg, Gowlland-Debbas, 'Security' (n 21) 67 (invoking the example of Rhodesia and expounding that the 'resolutions therefore appeared to hold the European minority regime responsible as a non-State collectivity for violations of the right of self-determination, whilst at the same time, the United Kingdom as the administering power, was held to have a parallel responsibility for ultimate return to legality'). For an analysis of SC practice on attribution, see Forteau (n 20) 93–105.

of principles of attribution is unclear'.[417] Whilst 'alleged Libyan responsibility for international terrorism' was 'brought within the ambit of the Charter, in Resolution 748 (1992), by being linked to Article 2(4) of the Charter',[418] it remains unclear how, exactly, the Council imputed responsibility to Libya, or whether it circumvented the whole process of attribution altogether. Before venturing upon a more focused analysis, it is useful to recall briefly the background facts of this situation, which concurrently made its way before the ICJ in the *Lockerbie* cases.[419]

Two Libyan nationals were accused of participating in the bombing of Pan Am flight 103, in which a number of American and British nationals were killed.[420] Following a US Grand Jury indictment, the Libyan Government categorically refused to extradite its nationals as it argued that the US was trying to curtail its obligations under the Convention for the Suppression of Unlawful Acts against the Safety of Civil Aviation.[421] According to Libya, the US seemed more preoccupied with recovering the culprits and preventing Libya from establishing jurisdiction than in fulfilling its treaty obligations.[422] Indeed, this case raised an interesting tension between two crucial concepts that may have a direct impact on the political dimensions of SR as they do on international justice, more broadly: trust and impunity.[423]

From the Libyan perspective, it was uncertain what treatment the US would afford the suspected terrorists.[424] Consequently, Libyan leader Muammar el-Qaddafi did not trust the US to prosecute nationals from his State.[425] He clearly did not believe that the US or UK judiciary could afford the suspected terrorists an impartial hearing.[426] In addition to red-flagging significant due process concerns, Libya was of the view that the accused were actually considered guilty until proven innocent, a reality standing in sharp contradiction with the usual

[417] Nollkaemper (n 21) 139. [418] Gowlland-Debbas, 'Security' (n 21) 66.

[419] See *Lockerbie* cases (n 276) 3 ff, 114 ff respectively (detailing the events surrounding the bombing of a commercial airline flight over Scotland). For a study of certain aspects of the relationship between the *Lockerbie* scenario and SR, see S Bentchikou, 'Les Modes de Réparation du Préjudice Subi Résultant d'un Acte de Terrorisme Étatique: Le Cas *Lockerbie*' in Koufa (n 201) 313–26.

[420] *Lockerbie* cases (n 276) 4, 115 respectively (explaining that the principal issue was the application of the Montreal Convention).

[421] *Lockerbie* cases (n 276) 5, 116 respectively (listing some of the provisions of the Montreal Convention, which includes mechanisms allowing States to prosecute their own nationals for crimes committed against civil aviation).

[422] *Lockerbie* cases (n 276) 11, 122 respectively (noting that the US joined the UK in strongly deploring Libya for not taking effective measures to prevent terrorism).

[423] V-J Proulx, 'Rethinking the Jurisdiction of the International Criminal Court in the Post-September 11th Era: Should Acts of Terrorism Qualify as Crimes against Humanity?' (2004) 19 American University International Law Review 1009, 1015–18.

[424] *Lockerbie* cases (n 276) 13, 124 respectively (commenting on the SC resolution calling for Libya to cease participation in all forms of terrorist activity).

[425] *Lockerbie* cases (n 276) 5, 116 respectively (noting that there was no extradition treaty between the UK and Libya, and that Libyan law prohibited the extradition of Libyan nationals).

[426] See, eg, E Zubel, 'The Lockerbie Controversy: Tension Between the International Court of Justice and the Security Council' (1999) 5 Annual Survey of International and Comparative Law 259, 261 (recalling the considerable outcry against this bombing, and underscoring that it was unsurprising that impartiality might come into question).

presumption of innocence accorded all charged individuals in domestic criminal law in many constitutional orders.[427] Consequently, Libya harboured doubts that the US would grant a fair trial to these individuals.[428] From the US perspective, impunity remained the dominant concern.[429] Should the suspected terrorists dodge extradition to the US, there would be a significant risk that those individuals would face national sanctions disproportionately minimal to the crimes committed or, worse yet, no punishment at all.[430]

Amidst this heated political situation, the SC issued Resolution 748[431] which, inter alia, instituted specific measures against Libya and, more importantly, provided the following in the preamble:

> Reaffirming that, in accordance with the principle in Article 2, paragraph 4, of the Charter of the United Nations, every State has the duty to refrain from organizing, instigating, assisting or participating in terrorist acts in another State or acquiescing in organized activities within its territory directed towards the commission of such acts, when such acts involve a threat or use of force,
>
> Determining in this context that the failure by the Libyan Government to demonstrate, by concrete actions its renunciation of terrorism and in particular its continued failure to respond fully and effectively to the requests in resolution 731 (1992), constitute a threat to international peace and security.[432]

Acting under Chapter VII, the Council supplemented its resolution with the following legal prescriptions:

1. Decides that the Libyan Government must now comply without any further delay with paragraph 3 of resolution 731 (1992) regarding the requests addressed to the Libyan authorities by France, the United Kingdom of Great Britain and Northern Ireland, and the United States of America,[433]
2. Decides also that the Libyan Government must commit itself definitely to cease all forms of terrorist action and all assistance to terrorist groups and that it must promptly, by concrete actions, demonstrate its renunciation of terrorism.[434]

[427] See, eg, Zubel (n 426) 261 (quoting one journalist who queried 'how can [Qaddafi] and his regime be punished?', which implied that they were presumed guilty).

[428] Zubel (n 426) 265 (reiterating Libya's reservations in dealing with the US after it bombed Libya's capital city, military installations, and airports following the Berlin nightclub bombing).

[429] See *Lockerbie* cases (n 276) 10, 121 respectively (observing that the US and UK issued a joint declaration demanding that Libya hand over the individuals suspected of bombing Pan Am Flight 103).

[430] See, eg, Zubel (n 426) 260 (commenting on the outcry from the Western press calling for the accused to be brought before US and Scottish courts).

[431] See SC Res 748 (n 176).

[432] SC Res 748 (n 176) preamble.

[433] These documents are found in UN Docs S/23306, S/23308, and S/23309. As Gowland-Debbas, 'Security' (n 21) 68 emphasized:

> [t]hese documents emanating from the governments of France, the United States and the United Kingdom, respectively, request[ed] Libya, *inter alia*, to accept responsibility for the actions of what [were] designated as 'Libyan officials', i.e. agents of the Libyan State, and require[d] it to surrender these persons and to pay appropriate compensation, thereby pre-empting conclusions relating to responsibility.

[434] SC Res 748 (n 176) [1]–[2].

By adopting this resolution and specific wording, the Council—very plainly and unequivocally—imposed a long-term obligation of cessation upon Libya. Therefore, this particular exercise of the Council's function aligns with the very nature, philosophy, and mechanics of secondary SR norms. As seen above, the obligation to cease internationally wrongful behaviour—in this instance, providing support to terrorist factions—is part and parcel of the remedial normative scheme that has become associated with the law governing the international responsibility of States.[435] However, when scrutinizing more technical aspects of this precedent, the main confusion surrounding this so-called application of SR by the Council stems from its reliance on documents submitted by three of its members (the US, the UK, and France), without providing any clear rationale for doing so. In one sweeping, indiscriminate stroke of the pen, the Council appeared to be endorsing, at least impliedly, the contentions put forth by those Member States.[436] Indeed, in its earlier Resolution 731 the Council '[s]trongly deplore[d] the fact that [Libya] ha[d] not yet responded effectively to ... requests to cooperate fully in establishing responsibility for the terrorist acts ... against Pan Am flight 103 and Union de transports aériens flight 772'.[437] The Council then proceeded to request that Libya 'immediately provide a full and effective response to those requests so as to contribute to the elimination of international terrorism'.[438]

The SC also short-circuited the usual exercises of sorting out legal responsibility and engaging attribution and instead seemed to internalize extraneous findings of responsibility without providing any explicit legal basis for doing so. From this approach, it would seem plausible that the SC based its initial reasoning on politically and State-driven unilateral determinations of individual criminal responsibility, ultimately extrapolating these findings within the realm of SR. As one publicist highlights:

> the Council appears to make the leap from individual to State responsibility for international terrorism (which, in Resolution 748 of 1992, is brought within the ambit of the Charter by being linked to Article 2(4) relating to the prohibition of the threat or use of force), through a simple reference to a set of document numbers to which Libya is required to give a 'full and effective response'.[439]

Unsurprisingly, these developments elicited staunch criticism from the Libyan delegation at the SC in the year that followed the adoption of Resolution 748. The charges levelled by the Libyan delegate in Council meetings pertained, inter alia,

[435] For the text of ARSIWA (n 34) Art 30, see n 177 and accompanying text.

[436] See, eg, Gowlland-Debbas, 'Security' (n 21) 68.

[437] UNSC Res 731 (21 January 1992) UN Doc S/RES/731 [2].

[438] SC Res 731 (n 437) [3].

[439] Gowlland-Debbas, 'The Functions' (n 21) 290. She further adds that:

> [f]rom this may be inferred that the Council [was] implicitly endorsing the proposition of two of its permanent members who had imputed the actions of two Libyan suspects to Libya, in requiring Libya to accept responsibility for the actions of what are designated as "Libyan officials", to surrender these persons and pay appropriate compensation.

See also n 436 and accompanying text.

to: (i) the assumption of his State's guilt (absent any evidence) underpinning the Council's decision following the acts of two Libyan nationals; and (ii) the attempts launched by both the US and UK to expand the sanctions regime instituted under Resolution 748.[440] However, the Libyan representative pointed out that his government would pay compensation if his State's international responsibility was established, thereby confirming that the SC actively debated SR issues. Indeed, the Libyan representative 'recalled that his country had responded positively to the request made to pay appropriate compensation, by declaring its readiness to pay if it was proven responsible for the downing of Pan Am flight 103 and UTA flight 772'.[441] Interestingly, in the context of the adoption of Resolution 731, the Libyan representative challenged the competence of the Council to deal with the 'legal' dispute before it, rather advocating a peaceful settlement through arbitration or, should no agreement be reached on that front, by the ICJ.[442]

Aside from the arguably nebulous application of SR concepts, this case also exhibited profound and fundamental legal discrepancies, as the Council's decision appeared predicated on the assumption that both individuals were actually guilty of the crimes charged therein.[443] Although this incongruity may be resolved by positing that this determination remained 'within the framework of State responsibility, leaving the member States concerned to adjudge the issue of individual criminal responsibility',[444] a trenchant critique of this line of reasoning emerged in the Dissenting Opinion of Judge Ajibola in *Lockerbie*. Indeed, he proclaimed that, '[*a*] *fortiori* the allegation that the State of Libya is involved in terrorism cannot hold legally until such a time as judgment is given against the two Libyans and it is proved that they were acting for and on behalf of the State of Libya'.[445] In response to this criticism, and in an attempt to dissipate the commonly held view that the SC's decision was premised on an assumption of guilt, the US offered two major arguments: (i) the SC was not actually rendering such

[440] See, eg, *Repertoire of the Practice of the Security Council 1993–1995: Chapter VIII* <http://www.un.org/en/sc/repertoire/93-95/Chapter%208/AFRICA/93-95_8-7-LETTERS%20FRANCE%20UK%20US.pdf> accessed 18 August 2015, 461–3.

[441] *Repertoire of SC Practice* (n 440) 462.

[442] See *Repertoire of the Practice of the Security Council 1989–1992: Chapter VI* <http://www.un.org/en/sc/repertoire/89-92/89-92_06.pdf> accessed 22 August 2015, 213. Similarly, see *Repertoire of the Security Council 1996–1999: Chapter VIII* <http://www.un.org/en/sc/repertoire/96-99/Chapter%208/Africa/07%20-%20letters%20dated.pdf> accessed 28 August 2015, 430–1. Interestingly, after the vote over SC Res 674 (n 209) dealing with the Iraq–Kuwait situation, the Cuban representative echoed similar concerns, stressing that 'neither Chapter VII ... nor any other Chapter of the Charter gave the Council any authority to make legal decisions'. He carried on, stating that the 'Council had no power to make decisions as to liability or to determine compensation or restitution, such as a court might do'. See *Repertoire of SC Practice* (n 217) 607.

[443] See, eg, Gowlland-Debbas, 'The Functions' (n 21) 290 (noting that 'any accusations of Libyan responsibility would have to presume the guilt of two individuals who had not yet been brought to trial').

[444] Gowlland-Debbas, 'Security' (n 21) 68.

[445] *Lockerbie Case* (n 276) 86, 191 respectively. See also the Dissenting Opinions of Judge el-Kosheri in ibid 97, 202 respectively; Tomuschat (n 370) 43; M Weller, 'The *Lockerbie* Case: A Premature End to the "New World Order"?' (1992) 4 African Journal of International and Comparative Law 302.

a legal judgment but was rather operating within a broader framework; and (ii) in any event, declarations pertaining to Libya's responsibility made publicly by the US would remain inadmissible in a judicial setting.[446]

Regardless of one's interpretation of the Council's treatment of the *Lockerbie* facts, this precedent was instructive on two grounds. First, it confirmed that the SC can wield some influence and input into the application of SR law, although the nature and extent of that contribution still remains unclear. The *Lockerbie* precedent certainly failed to provide any meaningful or dispositive insight into this question, although the Council clearly implemented Libya's SR. Secondly, this case remains a micro-encapsulation of a generalized confusion, or lack of unified interpretation, that characterizes SC decisions when implementing SR. As demonstrated elsewhere,[447] an important majority of the SC's (purportedly) law-creating incursions into SR terrain remain confused or, at least, fact-specific, especially in cases involving recourse to self-defence. The absence of any express reference to generally accepted SR principles from its decision-making in certain instances perhaps militates in favour of designating the Council as a reluctant, or politically expedient implementer of SR; it certainly does not suggest that it is a particularly apt, or judiciously balanced, implementer across the board. This is not to say, however, that its practice is not, at times, illuminating or helpful in further delineating the relevant normative scheme; examples to the contrary have been canvassed earlier. With the aim of further exploring this phenomenon, this book now ventures upon some final considerations in this debate.

4.6 Elucidating the Relationship: Identifying Commonalities

Up until this point, it has been thoroughly argued that there is, and can be, a rapprochement between the implementation of SR and traditional SC functions in some instances. This section briefly queries whether this parallel can yield interesting pay-offs for the global fight against terrorism, whilst keeping in mind that certain inherent limitations—some canvassed earlier—preclude the Council from making more significant inroads into the field of SR. As a corollary, it is to be hoped that lessons and best practices can be gleaned from this analysis, with a view to extending them to other global security challenges.

4.6.1 Expanding Chapter VII to include State responsibility

The idea that the purview of Chapter VII powers can be widened in certain circumstances, so as to include a range of new scenarios involving SC determinations

[446] See *Questions of Interpretation and Application of the 1971 Montreal Convention arising from the Aerial Incident at Lockerbie (Libya v USA)* (Preliminary Objections), Public Sitting, 15 October 1997 <http://www.icj-cij.org/docket/files/89/5281.pdf> accessed 27 August 2015, 18–20.

[447] See Proulx (n 3) ch 2.

of international responsibility, attribution of wrongful conduct to States, and the imposition of centralized countermeasures/sanctions has pervaded previous sections. This line of argument carries distinct resonance for the SC's possible implementation of SR in cases where governments fail to prevent terrorist attacks emanating from their territory. The purpose here is not to dwell on this argument but simply to remind the reader briefly of its importance in the present debate.

Addressing SR and terrorism, Pierre-Marie Dupuy convincingly argued that terrorist attacks, such as those perpetrated on 9/11, effectively fall within the scope of Chapter VII.[448] Building on his prior suggestion that applicable legal standards pertaining to subjects of international law should be expanded in light of the ICJ's Advisory Opinion on *Certain Reparations*,[449] he further queried how the Council could potentially address this rapprochement under Chapter VII. From the perspective of transnational activity, Dupuy saw no difficulty in extending extant SR rules through the action of UN mechanisms. Embracing both the direct and indirect responsibility paradigms explored in other accounts,[450] he inferred that SR in these cases 'can be triggered at the occasion of the commission of acts spreading terror throughout a civilian population for political purposes, either on the basis of commonly accepted principles of attribution (because the act was committed by State agents) or because the State may be harbouring terrorist groups'.[451] This line of reasoning reinforces an overarching conclusion that has animated much of the foregoing discussion: current SR structure may actually fit under the scheme of Chapter VII powers in limited circumstances, albeit with a few adjustments.

A second general conclusion may be drawn with regard to counterterrorism, particularly, and SC resolutions in this field. As pointed out earlier, although there is an inherent compatibility between SR for the failure to prevent terrorism and the maintenance of international peace and security under Chapter VII in several cases, a rapprochement between both areas is not achieved without some innovative exercise in legal interpretation/application. Otherwise put, whilst not necessarily coextensive with the objectives of Chapter VII upon first glance, certain scenarios brought before the Council patently fall within its mandate, once subsumed under the heading of 'international peace and security'. Therefore, 'whilst not all of the obligations infringed which are referred to in Council resolutions may appear to fall within the scope of the Charter, *by being linked* to the fundamental norms of self-determination, human rights or the prohibition of the use of force, *they become attached to Charter principles*' (emphasis added).[452] The aforementioned rapprochement, therefore, is better envisaged through the logical incorporation of any given case under the principles enshrined in the UN

[448] Dupuy (n 51) 7–8.

[449] See, eg, 'L'Unité de l'Ordre Juridique International: Cours Général de Droit International Public' (2003) 297 RdC 9, 106–18 (arguing that these aspects should be reviewed from functional and teleological standpoints). See also *Reparation for Injuries Suffered in the Service of the United Nations* (Advisory Opinion) [1949] ICJ Rep 174.

[450] See, eg, Proulx (n 3) ch 2. See also Section 5.2.4.

[451] Dupuy (n 51) 8.

[452] Gowlland-Debbas, 'Security' (n 21) 66.

Charter. This argument becomes particularly compelling when considering recent counterterrorism efforts, especially when linked to use of force principles, as terrorist attacks frequently amount to threats to international peace and security.[453] In fact, several portions of this monograph chronicled SC counterterrorism resolutions both before 9/11, which equated international terrorism with a threat to international peace and security and after that date, with one of the most serious threats to global security. Even before 9/11, whilst discussing terrorism in the context of the *Lockerbie* situation, one commentator observed that 'the Security Council *ha[d] been careful*, in all its resolutions concerning *terrorism, to assert a link with the preservation of international peace and security*' (emphasis added).[454]

This, again, underscores the inherent compatibility between the objectives underlying the global counterterrorism campaign, the corresponding (and potential) responsibility of sanctuary/territorial States, and the UN Charter's broader objectives in certain circumstances. How, exactly, these elements can be brought together, or in which manner can the SC actually implement responsibility, remains to be clarified. Before suggesting a solution applicable primarily to counterterrorism, the next section briefly canvasses and acknowledges other aspects of the international system limiting this chapter's central argument.

4.6.2 The Council's powers in relation to secondary norms

In contemporary scholarship, it has been argued that SC powers cannot be analysed through the lens of SR repertoire for two reasons: (i) their respective conceptual scheme does not align with the corpus of secondary rules of responsibility; and (ii) their overarching objective does not necessarily translate into the implementation and/or rectification of the consequences of unlawful activity.[455] If one were to accept this argument without quarrel, it would obviously follow that the SC could not be construed as an organ capable of implementing SR.

Speaking to the application of Council powers, Giorgio Gaja underscored that the bulk of scenarios resulting from Article 39 of the UN Charter (as defined by the Council itself), along with the violation of *jus cogens* obligations as regimented by secondary SR norms, appear to be significantly disjointed.[456]

[453] Some scholars analysed the reaction to 9/11 through the lens of use of force principles, rather than through the ILC's vision of SR. See, eg, JM Beard, 'America's New War on Terror: The Case for Self-Defense under International Law' (2002) 25 Harvard Journal of Law & Public Policy 559, 578–83; B Feinstein, 'Operation Enduring Freedom: Legal Dimensions of an Infinitely Just Operation' (2002) 11 Journal of Transnational Law and Policy 201, 271, 279. But see M Kohen, 'The Use of Force by the United States After the End of the Cold War and Its Impact on International Law' in M Byers and G Nolte (eds), *United States Hegemony and the Foundations of International Law* (CUP 2003) 197, 207. For a discussion of these theories, see Becker (n 4) 227–9.

[454] De Brichambaut (n 21) 271. For a list of recent resolutions in which the SC has reaffirmed that international terrorism, in all its manifestations, constitutes one of the most serious threats to international peace and security, see Introduction (n 18).

[455] See, eg, M Milanović, 'State Responsibility for Genocide' (2006) 17 EJIL 553, 603–4 (framing the argument in the context of genocide prevention).

[456] Gaja (n 139) 306–7.

This conceptual cleavage foreshadows the possibility that such breaches may not attract the designation of 'threats to international peace' by the SC,[457] whilst this determination may in such circumstances hinge on objective (ie it is foreseeable that a military invasion could be repelled via recourse to self-defence prior to Council intervention) or political motivations (ie it is plausible that certain SC members would reject such designation). If one accepts a rather formalistic and rigid application of the ARSIWA, it is probable that the scope of the heading 'threat to international peace' could preclude factual scenarios failing to meet the corresponding attribution standards vis-à-vis the sanctuary State, which undoubtedly include acts perpetrated by entities falling outside that State's control.

This sweeping postulate would seem, at first, to exclude the institutionalized implementation of a model of indirect responsibility for the failure to prevent terrorist attacks advanced elsewhere,[458] but its validity is certainly open to challenge. In fact, whilst certain threats against international peace and security can stem from acts carried out by rogue individuals or rebel groups that are not imputable to their territorial States in the traditional sense—such as was the case in the situations prevalent in Somalia or Angola—publicists have called for the casting of a 'wider net by allowing heretofore non-attributable private acts to be blamed on states'.[459] This situation is obviously exacerbated when the State in which the terrorist-like events take place lacks any central authority, fails to wield any sort of effective control over the territory in question, or falls under the rubric of what some have termed 'failed States'.[460]

A case in point arose in Somalia, where 'the collapse of state authority mean[t] that there [was] no functioning government to fulfil an essential condition of sovereignty, on the one hand, and that the violence, instability, and disorder [could] spill over from that failed state to others, on the other'.[461] Consequently, transnational terrorist networks are still actively pursuing the establishment of safe havens within Somalia's borders despite its recent shift to 'fragile State' status, which poses intractable legal and conceptual problems for the purposes of applying SR norms, including in institutionalized settings.[462] Particularly challenging from the standpoint of attribution are the activities of the Harakat al-Shabaab al-Mujahideen extremist group, which was modelled after Al-Qaeda. The group, which plans to overthrow the Government of Somalia, exerts a large degree of control over large portions of central-southern Somalia, where it unilaterally

[457] See, eg, J Crawford, 'Fourth Report on State Responsibility' (2001) UN Doc A/CN.4/517, 18 [73].

[458] On the indirect responsibility paradigm advocated outside the context of institutionalized SR, see generally Proulx (n 3). See also Section 5.2.4.

[459] A Nissel, 'Tal Becker, Terrorism and the State: Rethinking the Rules of State Responsibility (Hart Publishing, 2006)' (2007) 5 JICJ 245, 248.

[460] See also Proulx ((n 3) ch 5, section II.B).

[461] R Thakur, 'Humanitarian Intervention' in Weiss and Daws (n 150) 390.

[462] See, eg RD Sloane, 'More Than What Courts Do: Jurisprudence, Decision, and Dignity—In Brief Encounters and Global Affairs' (2009) 34 YJIL 517, 523.

implements a particularly severe strand of Sharia law.[463] Unsurprisingly, the SC has strongly deplored terrorist attacks perpetrated by that group in Somalia and elsewhere, thereby insisting on that State's (or at least its Federal Government's) obligation to combat the threat percolating within its borders and develop its own national security forces.[464] In short, the governing apparatus in Somalia—as flawed or inefficient as it may be—must nonetheless be seen as putting forth best efforts in combating (potentially global) security threats such as terrorism and piracy.[465]

Keeping in mind the spirit of these criticisms, it must be stressed that the objectives of SC powers exclusively aim at maintaining or restoring international peace and security. In response, it should be recalled, however, that certain scholars construe the implementation of SR by the Council in cases involving violations of obligations *erga omnes* as falling outside the UN Charter framework and, more precisely, as steering it away from the mission of maintaining or restoring international peace and security. In other words, when the Council counteracts such breaches, it draws its powers and jurisdiction from general international law and is, in turn, vested with those functions by States under international law.[466]

Although it has been demonstrated throughout this chapter that the Council's function has been construed rather broadly, namely by extending its operations considerably above the 'police' role traditionally associated with it, a rapprochement between that organ's powers and SR repertoire is not necessarily complete by sole reference to the maintenance and/or return to legality, or by the implementation of responsibility through UN mechanisms. With the purpose of maintaining international peace, the SC may intervene in situations where no international law

[463] See, eg, P Bergen *et al.*, 'Assessing the Jihadist Terrorist Threat to America and American Interests' (2011) 34 SCT 65, 73; JM Isanga, 'Countering Persistent Contemporary Sea Piracy: Expanding Jurisdictional Regimes' (2010) 59 American University Law Review 1267, 1277 fn 64; M Ibrahim and J Gettleman, 'Bomb Kills Dozens in Somalia's Capital and Signals Return of Militant Group' *NYT* (New York, 5 October 2011) A10. For more background, see SJ Hansen, *Al-Shabaab in Somalia: The History and Ideology of a Militant Islamist Group* (Hurst 2013); DE Agbiboa, 'Terrorism without Borders: Somalia's Al-Shabaab and the Global Jihad Network' (2014) 5 Journal of Terrorism Research 27.

[464] See, eg, UNSC Res 1910 (28 January 2010) UN Doc S/RES/1910; UNSC Res 1964 (22 December 2010) UN Doc S/RES/1964; UNSC Res 2010 (30 September 2011) UN Doc S/RES/2010; UNSC Res 2093 (6 March 2013) UN Doc S/RES/2093; UNSC Res 2158 (29 May 2014) UN Doc S/RES/2158. On the broader security situation in Somalia, including denunciation of terrorism by the Council, see UNSC Res 2102 (2 May 2013) UN Doc S/RES/2102.

[465] See, eg, R Abeyratne, 'The Responsibility of Somalia for the Acts of the Somali Pirates' (2009) 2 Journal of Transportation Security 63. The SC has also deplored Somalia's shortcomings in prosecuting pirates. See UNSC Res 2015 (24 October 2011) UN Doc S/RES/2015; UNSC Res 2125 (18 November 2013) UN Doc S/RES/2125; UNSC Res 2184 (12 November 2014) UN Doc S/RES/2184. On the relationship between anti-piracy and SR, see D Guilfoyle, 'Defending Individual Ships from Pirates: Questions of State Responsibility and Immunity' in C Chinkin and F Baetens (eds), *Sovereignty, Statehood and State Responsibility: Essays in Honour of James Crawford* (CUP 2015) 307–24.

[466] See, eg, P Picone, 'Interventi delle Nazioni Unite e Obblighi *Erga Omnes*' in idem (ed.), *Interventi delle Nazioni Unite e Diritto Internazionale* (Cedam 1995) 517, 554–60. See also generally A Ciampi, 'The Academic as Cosmopolite: Legal Visions of International Governance in the Twentieth Century' (1999) 93 ASIL Proceedings 325, 328–9.

violation can be ascertained or, alternatively, in a preventive fashion (ie prior to the occurrence of a given violation). As Bruno Simma expounded, international law violations *may* 'amount to, lead to, contribute to, or [be] accompanied by' a threat to the peace,[467] but this result is by no means automatic or always present in any given scenario. Conversely, when confronted with a specific internationally wrongful act, the SC may determine that its quest for the maintenance of international peace and security calls for the imposition of altogether different measures than those found in SR repertoire (thereby completely circumventing the application of secondary rules in favour of amicable and peaceful dispute settlement), or that a given situation warrants no action whatsoever from it.[468]

More importantly, considerable scholarly resistance persists in suggesting that the Council should not rule or pronounce on SR matters 'except by way of incidental censure'.[469] Similarly, Judge Schwebel's Dissenting Opinion in *Nicaragua* called attention to the fact that the SC 'may take legal considerations into account, but, unlike a court, it is not bound to apply them', and further reinforced the idea that political considerations often override legal sensibilities in the context of Council decision-making.[470] Yet, whilst acknowledging that the Council never thought it could be so honoured[471] given that Chapter VII was not drafted with a view to granting it competence over any and every matter,[472] some interlocutors deliver a more nuanced view of this state of affairs; as such, they opine that every time the SC determines that an internationally wrongful act has been committed, it crosses a 'fragile Rubicon' towards the invocation of responsibility and a corresponding system of sanctions.[473] In sharp contrast with some views expressed earlier aiming to subtract SR law from all SC decision-making, commentators such as Frederic Kirgis rather believe that law-making incursions fall well within the ambit of the Council's role and powers.[474] In fact, José Alvarez most poignantly echoes the present volume's central arguments when summarizing Kirgis' views: 'some Council "lawmaking" is inescapable. Making law, both in interpreting the Charter and *in developing the doctrine of state responsibility*, has always been part of the Council's job' (emphasis added).[475]

[467] B Simma, 'Does the UN Charter Provide an Adequate Legal Basis for Individual or Collective Responses to Violations of Obligations Erga Omnes?' in J Delbrück (ed.), *The Future of International Law Enforcement: New Scenarios—New Law?* (Duncker & Humblot 1993) 125, 142.

[468] See, eg, Klein (n 91) 1248–9.

[469] Arangio-Ruiz (n 414) 765 fn 31.

[470] Dissenting Opinion of Judge Schwebel in *Military and Paramilitary Activities in and against Nicaragua (Nicaragua v USA)* (Merits) [1986] ICJ Rep 14, 290 [60]. See also Herndl (n 264) 385. On the pervasive political considerations characterizing the Council's decision-making, see Gowlland-Debbas, 'Security' (n 21) 71.

[471] Ambassador Leprette, former member of the SC, in SFDI (ed.), *Colloque de Rennes: Le Chapitre VII de la Charte des Nations Unies* (Pedone 1995) 114.

[472] Gaja (n 139) 301.

[473] M Sorel, 'L'Élargissement de la Notion de Menace contre la Paix' in SFDI (n 471) 52. See also Weckel (n 164) 170 (arguing that the unlawful nature of a given international act is determinant in the SC's assessment of a given situation).

[474] See, eg, Kirgis (n 56).

[475] Alvarez, 'Judging' (n 141) 22. See also generally S Talmon, 'Revisiting the Rule of Law: Law-Making and Law-Changing by the UN Security Council' in J Wouters *et al.* (eds), *Belgium in the Security Council: Reflections on the 2007–2008 Membership* (Intersentia 2009) 41, 42.

Although not dispositive of the issue, these concerns do weigh considerably in the balance when attempting to identify and better circumscribe the role of secondary rules as regards the SC's potential implementation of SR. The invocation of secondary norms will also, once again, play a central role when investigating the particularities of a possible rapprochement between SR repertoire and Council functions in the context of counterterrorism.

4.6.3 The rights of States vis-à-vis implementation notwithstanding Council involvement

Irrespective of the eventual resolution of whether the Council's functions also encompass the implementation of SR, States primarily retain all the rights and privileges flowing from that normative scheme, as dictated by the secondary rules of customary international law. Moreover, sceptical outlooks articulate an organizing principle along the lines of: the functions of the 'maintenance of international peace' and the 'implementation of SR' must be kept distinct.[476] For reasons explored earlier, however, the central contention of this book is rather that these two fields can, at times, mutually reinforce and inform each other.

However, it seems unlikely that the traditional, unilateral implementation of SR by States could be disabled by SC action, especially given the importance of maintaining peace in contemporary inter-State relations.[477] Indeed, the UN's extant and particularly robust scheme of collective security—supplemented by the pre-eminence of Charter obligations over conventional obligations contracted by States and its general prohibition on recourse to force in international relations—eloquently consecrate the primacy of maintaining and restoring peace and security. Thus, it seems unnecessary, and potentially undesirable, to set aside a well-calibrated SR model in order to pave the way for a mechanism (ie the SC) that can sometimes be ill-suited in protecting certain aspects of collective interests across the board, as embodied in the schemes of *erga omnes* and *jus cogens* obligations.[478] For instance, one could envisage a situation where the Council is paralysed over a certain course of action, given the exercise of veto powers by certain permanent members. In such scenarios, it might actually be more effective for a coalition of States not directly injured by the wrongful act to pursue enforcement options under the customary international law of SR.

However, general SR principles also suggest that in any given case, unilateral reactions by States aiming to implement responsibility must adopt a holistic approach by taking stock of all the circumstances surrounding an internationally wrongful act.[479] It follows that States' actions and claims will be directly

[476] Villalpando (n 311) 448.

[477] See, eg, K Wellens, 'The UN Security Council and New Threats to the Peace: Back to the Future' (2003) 8 JCSL 15, 48–50.

[478] See, eg, Czaplinski (n 143) 93–4; Dupuy (n 325) 15–16; Pellet (n 325).

[479] See generally Weiss (n 398). This holistic approach has also proved challenging in specific issues in the global security context, such as extraordinary rendition. See, eg, J Button, 'Spirited

affected, or influenced, by SC intervention under the aegis of Chapter VII, whenever such incursion would prove pertinent for the application of secondary rules of responsibility.[480]

Therefore, the Council's determination of the breach of an international obligation, along with its legal consequences (eg the corresponding obligation of reparation) may have an incidence on the injured State's appraisal of the prospect of invoking responsibility against the responsible State. In this regard, scholarly accounts underscore the different consequences flowing from a recommendation or a decision emanating from the SC under Article 39 of the Charter. According to some, the Council's recommendation carries with it a presumption of legality with regard to any measure(s) undertaken by States in conformity with that recommendation.[481] For others, this type of SC determination would merely constitute a warning, although States could not subsequently deny the existence of the legal or factual situation determined therein.[482] It has also been suggested that the SC's determination of the existence of a situation envisaged in Article 39's scheme would itself amount to a binding decision on States pursuant to Article 25 of the Charter.[483]

Whilst scholarly accounts might be somewhat divided on this issue, it is probably fair to conclude that in their requests to responsible States, unilaterally implementing States will also have to take into account any concurrent requests already put forth by the Council (eg requests for cessation), along with any ad hoc mechanisms instituted by it in order to assess the harm to be redressed, for example. Similarly, in determining the legality of States' requests or reactions when implementing responsibility unilaterally (including requests for reparation and assurances of non-repetition), considerable deference will have to be given, inter alia, to the requests already formulated by the Council. Furthermore, it may well be that pending Council action precludes the application of SR law in some cases.[484]

Hence, SC action will govern certain aspects of this process and act as a sort of backdrop for the unilateral implementation of responsibility by individual States in some circumstances. For instance, at the stage of canvassing and gauging available countermeasures so as to induce the responsible State to fulfil its (primary) international obligation(s), the injured State will have to take stock of applicable

Away (Into a Legal Black Hole?): The Challenge of Invoking State Responsibility for Extraordinary Rendition' (2007) 19 Florida Journal of International Law 531.

[480] It is interesting to contrast this position with other scholarly views. See, inter alia, Arangio-Ruiz (n 14) 626; Klein (n 91) 1254.

[481] See, eg, Frowein (n 133) 382–3.

[482] See, eg, A De Hoogh, *Obligations Erga Omnes and International Crimes: A Theoretical Inquiry into the Implementation and Enforcement of the International Responsibility of States* (Kluwer 1996) 125.

[483] See, eg, Simma (n 467) 138–9. See also Gowlland-Debbas, 'The Functions' (n 21) 293. Villalpando (n 311) 449 fn 1548 resolves this debate by acknowledging that unilateral implementation of SR remains distinct from Chapter VII powers, and ultimately connecting States' subjective appreciation of SC determinations with the application of secondary rules of responsibility.

[484] See, eg, A Skordas, 'Hegemonic Intervention as Legitimate Use of Force' (2007) 16 Minnesota Journal of International Law 407, 449.

and relevant SC resolutions.[485] On the one hand, the States concerned might be called upon to comply with certain obligations or institute certain measures set out by the Council in those resolutions.[486] On the other, and in light of available courses of action within the UN framework, future unilateral countermeasures will have to be measured against the well-established, but poorly defined,[487] principles of necessity, proportionality,[488] and cooperation.[489]

Based on the foregoing considerations, it remains difficult to assert that the SC actually implements SR in all scenarios where that normative scheme could play a central role or inform its decision-making. In certain clearer cases, the Council ostensibly uses language and reasoning compatible with SR repertoire. Certitude that the Council grounds its findings solely on the arsenal of custom and instrument-driven international responsibility across the board, however, does not emerge so clearly from the same conclusion. In all likelihood, the sporadic and inconsistent implementation of SR by the Council might be better explained by the existence of conceptual and practical overlaps between that normative scheme and Chapter VII powers. As argued in Section 4.6.4 following, this overlap comes into sharp relief when reviewing Council action in the field of counterterrorism, a conclusion which can presumably also extend to other global security areas.

Conversely, this is not to say that SR considerations cannot inform Council decision-making and vice-versa. In fact, the arguments already advanced here attempted to demonstrate that these two institutions are far from insulated from each other; a concrete manifestation of their interaction, predominantly grounded in Council reaction to terrorism, warrants further exploration. In a broader sense, it must be reiterated that SC resolutions may have a considerable impact on the unilateral implementation of responsibility by States, both for violations of communitarian norms and other global security undertakings: they may inform the legal characterization of a situation or the legality of requests and/or countermeasures formulated by States.[490] For example, Resolution 487 discussed in Section 4.4.4 legitimized Iraq's claims for compensation against Israel. Conversely, future SC action or measures may, in certain circumstances, preclude

[485] See Proulx (n 358) 587 and authorities cited therein.

[486] See, eg, Arangio-Ruiz (n 14) 626.

[487] The searing indictment in Zemanek (n 94) 127–8 of ARSIWA Art 51 on the concept of proportionality of countermeasures comes to mind. He takes issue with the formulation of that provision and the principle commonly extracted from the now notorious *Naulilaa Award*, essentially expounding that they amount to an empty formula unless a court or tribunal pronounces on the matter. Consider also Cançado Trindade (n 62) 263. For a contrary view, see Cannizzaro (n 53) 916.

[488] See *Naulilaa Award (Responsabilité de l'Allemagne à raison des dommages causés dans les colonies portugaises du sud de l'Afrique) (sentence sur le principe de la responsabilité) (Portugal v Germany)* (1928) 2 *RIAA* 1011.

[489] Some argue that by virtue of the overarching principle of necessity, the obligation of States to adopt measures set out by the SC also precludes them from undertaking countermeasures *uti singuli*. See, eg, S Ripol Carulla, 'El Consejo de Seguridad y la Defensa de los Derechos Humanos: Reflexiones a Partir del Conflito de Kosovo' (1999) 51 Revista Española de Derecho Internacional 59, 73–4. Similarly, Gaja (n 139) 309 posits that SC action should effectively engender a restraining, or constraining, effect on the admissibility of individual reactions.

[490] See, eg, Villalpando (n 311) 450.

the legality of any potential unilateral countermeasures undertaken by individual States.[491] Therefore, the relationship between SC action and SR remains thorny but becomes particularly relevant when the wrongful behaviour impugned fits neatly under Chapter VII's heading of 'international peace and security'. Such a scenario not only blurs the divide between Council powers and SR repertoire, but also makes a clear determination of the legal basis underpinning the Council's decision increasingly intractable. This is especially so when the Council, itself, melds both branches of law or indiscriminately subsumes SR considerations under an expansive concept of threat pre-emption/eradication.

4.6.4 A straddling of objectives: The *sui generis* case of counterterrorism and its implications for global security

The relationship between SC practice and the creation, interpretation, and application of SR rules remains largely underexplored, especially in the field of counterterrorism.[492] Building on existing scholarship,[493] some publicists delivered thoughtful discussions of this relationship, concluding that the SC interprets certain aspects of SR law in specific fields.[494] In the same vein, the arguments advanced in this book highlighted relevant doctrinal currents for and against the proposition that the Council frequently spearheads certain law-shaping incursions into the realm of SR. Regardless of one's stance on this debate, it remains fair to contend that SC decision-making informs—to some extent—the unilateral implementation of responsibility by States, along with the application of secondary norms of responsibility. In that regard, it must be recalled that Council decisions are, indeed, binding on States. As mentioned, SC resolutions can also be particularly instructive in determining the legal characterization of a given situation or act as a benchmark in ensuring the legality of requests or countermeasures adopted by States.[495]

More significantly, meaningful parallels and interrelationships may be drawn between the Council's traditional functions and the implementation of SR. The notion of overlap between the Council's powers and the implementation of SR is vital, especially in the fields of transnational terrorism and global security, which carries with it significant implications for the interplay between the concepts of 'threats to international peace and security', international responsibility, and return to legality. In the light of the practice of terrorism—which like genocide, apartheid, and massive human rights violations constitutes a threat against the

[491] See, eg, Skordas (n 484) 449.

[492] See, eg, P De Sena, 'Book Review' (2006) 17 EJIL 863, 864 (reviewing Dupuy (n 51) and calling for further research on the relationship between SC resolutions dealing with terrorism and international responsibility).

[493] See, eg, de Brichambaut (n 21) 272–4; Gowlland-Debbas, 'The Functions' (n 21) 288–94; Nolte (n 165) 322–6.

[494] Villalpando (n 311) 434–50, esp 438–9.

[495] SC resolutions can also illuminate the work of international or regional tribunals in dealing with SR-related matters. For one example, see *Loizidou v Turkey* ECHR 1996–VI 2216.

peace—the areas of overlap between SC practice and SR implementation cannot be ignored.[496] The determinant element in resolving this debate not so much resides in acknowledging that the Council can spill over, and out of, the ambit of Chapter VII powers when faced with an internationally wrongful act. It rather rests upon the fact that the Council can 'read in', or 'bring in', SR rationale, sensibilities, and mechanisms within the ambit of its Charter-based powers, especially in controversial cases involving use of force-based violations (ie terrorism) and self-defence as a possible response to those breaches.[497] After all, several leading scholars construe the UN Charter as a living instrument of quasi-constitutional character, which should, correspondingly, adapt to modern realities and circumstances.[498] Consequently, 'a dynamic-objective understanding, free from historical perceptions, of treaties such as the Charter and other statutes of international organizations is necessary'.[499]

Therefore, we are thus not strictly speaking about the Council exceeding its powers or extending its action to spheres not traditionally falling under its jurisdiction. Quite to the contrary: the present line of reasoning merely recognizes an inherent compatibility between the Council's traditional functions and modern phenomena/threats to peace and global security—such as transnational terrorism—that were perhaps not fully envisaged by the framers of the Charter. In addressing these fast-evolving challenges, the SC does not necessarily, or automatically, draw upon SR repertoire or act as an implementing organ of international responsibility, per se.[500] However, whilst still using its Chapter VII tools, the Council can at times, simultaneously or in order to supplement its reasoning, delve into SR logic in cases that warrant such approach. Consequently, it applies the traditional syllogistic model of responsibility to responsible States: international breach–attribution–consequences/countermeasures. The interface that emerges from this joint application of Charter-based principles and SR norms is far from uniform or consistent, but it reinforces the proposition that Council practice can, and does, set relevant SR precedents and inform the application of that normative scheme.

Therefore, the SC can certainly characterize the breach of an international obligation (eg the failure to prevent a terrorist attack) as a 'threat to international peace and security', thereby connecting its overarching mission statement to the implementation of responsibility. Whilst the Council has not done so explicitly in this particular context, some nonetheless infer that the 9/11 attacks were attributed to Afghanistan on the basis of several SC resolutions connecting the use of Afghan territory with terrorist activity.[501] Consequently, whilst remaining within a strict legal framework,

[496] Villalpando (n 311) 434–50 (pointing out that it would be impossible to ignore overlaps between SC action and the implementation of SR).

[497] See, eg, Gowlland-Debbas, 'Security' (n 21) 65.

[498] See, eg, Franck (n 2) 5–9.

[499] G Ress, 'The Interpretation of the Charter' in Simma *et al.* (n 114) 27.

[500] See generally R Ago, 'Fifth Report on State responsibility' (1976) UN Doc A/CN.4/291 and Add.1 and 2 and Corr.1; (1976) II(1) *YILC* 34–5; Seventh Report–Arangio-Ruiz (n 324) 21–2, as to the 'rightness of considering measures under Chapter VII as forms of international responsibility'. The language is cited from Gowlland-Debbas, 'The Limits' (n 21) 364 fn 6.

[501] See, eg, Conte (n 23) 48–51.

these situations (ie the SC's determinations by virtue of this approach) would clearly be governed by secondary rules of responsibility.[502] In any event, the Council could not take away rights from States or impose upon them sanctions beyond what is required to maintain or restore peace and security in any given situation, at the risk of exceeding its powers and potentially opening up its *ultra vires* action to judicial condemnation, subject to the limits explored in Section 3.2.1.[503] In a study exploring the relationship between collective security and international responsibility, Mathias Forteau echoed a similar viewpoint, albeit with particular emphasis on the fact that the respective scopes of SR and collective security are distinct. This is not to say, however, that both normative schemes have not been progressing, at times hand in hand, towards the consecration of certain fundamental community priorities, to which one should add the repression and eradication of transnational terrorism.[504] Although the ILC-driven 'primary/secondary' dichotomy will ultimately resolve this situation, Forteau acknowledged the existence of a conceptual overlap between all relevant elements, similarly to the arguments advanced earlier.[505]

In response to the sceptics and drawing from these bodies of work, it is argued that the Council can play an important role, sometimes determinant, in applying SR law to counterterrorism as an alternative avenue, albeit an imperfect one, to the sometimes-problematic unilateral implementation of responsibility by States. The prospect of carving out a role for the Council in implementing SR would seem desirable even if only to provide a sort of system of checks and balances on both the adoption of disproportionate unilateral countermeasures and diplomatic impasses on the application of secondary norms, should the concerned States refuse to consent to the ICJ's jurisdiction. In fact, transnational terrorism and the legal tools to suppress it epitomize a truly *sui generis* phenomenon: they offer a unique opportunity for the Council to use and incorporate SR repertoire in its decision-making without overstepping the inherent boundaries of its core mission centring on the maintenance of international peace and security. Although its findings can sometimes be predicated on a prior declaration of responsibility or illegality, it is fair to argue that the Council does not directly rule on the question of SR, per se; it instead frames its reasoning within the furrow of Chapter VII powers in most global security contexts, although it has adopted resolutions drawing on SR repertoire outside the Chapter VII framework.[506] However, it becomes clear that there exists a significant conceptual and practical overlap of Chapter VII objectives with the suppression of terrorist acts, which are almost invariably tantamount to threats against international peace and security, and even more so since 9/11.[507]

[502] See, eg, Villalpando (n 311) 447. [503] See, eg, Arangio-Ruiz (n 14) 627.

[504] See, eg, Gowlland-Debbas, 'The Limits' (n 21) 365. The questions of norm-creation and enforcement, as they pertain to fundamental community norms, have generated considerable anguish in international legal scholarship. See, eg, L Condorelli, 'À Propos de l'Attaque Américaine contre l'Irak du 26 Juin 1993: Lettre d'un Professeur Désemparé aux Lecteurs du JEDI' (1994) 5 EJIL 134.

[505] Forteau (n 20) 370. [506] See Section 4.4.4.

[507] See, eg, R Giles-Carnero, 'Terrorist Acts as Threats to International Peace and Security' in PA Fernández-Sánchez (ed.), *International Legal Dimension of Terrorism* (Nijhoff 2009) 55–71.

In fact, starting with Resolution 748 of 1992 dealing with Libya's non-extradition of suspected terrorist bombers,[508] the SC has produced a series of resolutions expressly linking terrorism with international peace and security. Subsequent resolutions followed suit and reiterated this important nexus, be it in the context of the failed assassination attempt of Egypt's President Mubarak[509] or the bombings of American embassies in Kenya and Tanzania.[510] It was no surprise (except for some scholars) that SC resolutions adopted in response to 9/11 unequivocally consecrated the connection between terrorism and international peace and security, a legal construction also acknowledged in Judge Kooijmans' Separate Opinion in the *Wall Advisory Opinion*.[511]

Therefore, the very nature of terrorism seems to engage Chapter VII considerations and when dealing with threats to international peace and security, the Council has sometimes ventured upon an analytical terrain that melds its executive functions with SR undertones. In recent years, the Council has increasingly tackled terrorism by invoking SR-like language, thereby signalling that the seemingly insurmountable chasm between that body of law and the restoration of international peace and security can be traversed on occasion. This is not to suggest, however, that, by straddling each other, both of these areas are necessarily mutually interpenetrating, but this phenomenon surely extends beyond the mere borrowing from one branch's vernacular by the other, and foreshadows the pay-offs of undertaking more substantial and horizontal incursions into the commonalities of both regimes, so as to better address the threats of terrorism and the legal responses thereto. As a corollary, it is to be hoped that this analysis will further illuminate the prospect of the SC implementing SR in other global security contexts.

[508] SC Res 748 (n 176) (underscoring that 'the suppression of acts of international terrorism, including those in which States are directly or indirectly involved, is essential for the maintenance of international peace and security').

[509] UNSC Res 1044 (31 January 1996) UN Doc S/RES/1044. See also Bennouna (n 22) 563–4.

[510] SC Res 1267 (n 17).

[511] SC Res 1368 (n 9); SC Res 1373 (n 9). For Judge Kooijmans' Separate Opinion, see the *Wall Advisory Opinion* (n 286) 229–30 [35]. But see Dupuy (n 51) 9 (remarking that 'the initial universal and quasi-spontaneous assertion that terrorism amounts to a threat to international peace and security' was 'striking').

Conclusion to Part II

In analysing the relationship between State responsibility (SR) repertoire, the Security Council (SC), and global security, Part II explored that body's role both in the realm of norm creation and enforcement. In respect of primary international legal norms, this study attempted to illustrate the new and broad-reaching 'legislative' power the SC has arrogated after 9/11. In a revolutionary exercise of its mandate, it has begun promulgating wide-ranging international legal obligations. Moreover, it has done so in respect of all States, thereby palliating the limited import of certain area- or issue-specific international conventions by adopting all-encompassing language, without restricting its pronouncements to any geographical area or specific timeframe. The effects of this new 'legislative' function have been felt most acutely in the areas of counterterrorism and nuclear non-proliferation.[1] This development obviously entails consequences for SR, at least on two levels: first, it imposes binding obligations on States, the violation of which will trigger the application of secondary norms of responsibility; and, secondly, it is logical that when the SC implements international responsibility, it does so as regards primary international law obligations it has set out, which it can monitor and ultimately sanction.

More importantly, Part II set out to provide a comprehensive and systematic legal analysis of the potential institutionalization of the implementation of SR by the SC, with specific reference to the field of counterterrorism so that lessons may be gleaned for other global security challenges. One of the distinctive aspects of Part II's central thesis is that it attempted to make a challenging argument, which explains why it was tailored rather narrowly. Indeed, implementing SR through United Nations (UN) organs, especially the SC, proves difficult for at least four reasons: (i) the Chapter VII framework is concerned with the maintenance of international peace and security, as opposed to ensuring a return to legality and compliance with primary counterterrorism norms, which is the dominion of SR repertoire; (ii) the UN's broader legal and political framework foments resistance to subjecting the fate of States' reputations and legal responsibility to a politically volatile multilateral process such as that of the SC's decision-making; (iii) the consensual basis for founding the ICJ's jurisdiction makes the prospect of judicial settlement and determination of SR for terrorism and other global security

[1] See, eg, Sections 3.1.3.3 and 4.5.1.

transgressions both unlikely and politically difficult to achieve; and (iv) to date, the incursions of relevant UN organs and international judicial bodies into the realm of SR have been rather limited and sometimes piecemeal, especially as regards terrorism and other global security threats.

Nevertheless, an argument has been advanced, based on a now prevalent, broader conception of the international legal system, and of global security, to the effect that SR can be implemented by the SC in counterterrorism contexts. The reasoning underpinning this conclusion could possibly extend to other global security challenges as well, depending on the circumstances. The foregoing considerations have demonstrated that the SC can apply and implement SR norms in a variety of ways, some more obvious than others. First, the Council may rule on a State's international responsibility in a very express fashion, thereby invoking SR language. For instance, it has done so by pronouncing on Israel's responsibility in the aftermath of its bombing of a nuclear reactor in Iraq; in that context, the Council ordered Israel to compensate Iraq, thereby mirroring a key component of SR repertoire in its resolution. Similarly, as canvassed earlier in this Part, the Council pronounced on the legal responsibility of Iraq following its unlawful invasion of Kuwait and ordered it to repair the breach in a series of resolutions. However, the explicit invocation of SR language in those resolutions is likely to be more the exception than the rule.

Another way the SC implements SR is by attributing unlawful conduct or an internationally wrongful act to States. As seen in the *Lockerbie* precedent, the application by the Council of this normative operation under SR law (ie attribution) can be at times muddled, incomplete but still invoke SR-compatible language. Aside from the case of Libya, other examples were discussed including that of Sudan's international responsibility, which the Council established in 1996. Finally, the SC may implement SR by way of syllogistic reasoning, that is to say by adopting a series of resolutions calling upon a particular State to perform certain acts or abstain from doing others. By calling attention to the protracted situation involving a threat to international peace and security, which often simultaneously amounts to a situation of illegality when dealing with counterterrorism and other global security threats, the Council's resolutions have the cumulative effect of delivering a *de facto* finding of international responsibility in respect of that State. A case in point unquestionably stems from Afghanistan's conduct in relation to the 9/11 attacks. When coupled with pre-9/11 SC resolutions calling upon that State to cease harbouring Al-Qaeda members on its territory and to extradite Osama bin Laden, post-9/11 Council resolutions can certainly be taken to impute *de facto* responsibility to Afghanistan. In such scenarios, whilst it does not invoke the precise vernacular of SR (ie its reasoning does not specifically determine the commission of an internationally wrongful act, which then sets in motion the obligation of reparation), the Council is actually attributing wrongful conduct and responsibility to a State.

Furthermore, the role that SC resolutions can play in implementing international responsibility—in and of themselves—is only a part of the institutionalized implementation calculus. SC resolutions can also prove particularly instructive and provide guidance to States in their own unilateral or collective implementation of SR. In other words, some resolutions may fall short in actually ascribing blame or devising specific consequences flowing from an unlawful act but nonetheless provide the characterization of certain events or acts that injured States may then rely upon in implementing SR. As discussed in Part II, SC resolutions can act as a benchmark in ensuring the legality of further action or countermeasures adopted by States; in particular, SC action should, in many instances, engender a restraining, or constraining, effect on the admissibility of individual reactions by States. By recognizing an unlawful act, which also amounts to a threat to peace and security, SC resolutions may also serve as predicate for States when they frame their claims pursuant to SR law. In the context of global security, there are numerous potential scenarios and these may involve anything from humanitarian disasters to unlawful use of force, to funding terrorist factions, to other situations of illegality such as sanctuary States harbouring and supporting terrorist factions on their soil; this study is replete with relevant examples involving Lebanon, Yemen, Afghanistan, Somalia, Pakistan, Syria, etc.

However, a certain degree of caution is warranted so as to avoid over-glorifying potential SC contributions to the advancement of SR implementation. For various reasons already discussed, the Council's process is far from perfect. At the level of primary international legal norms, for instance, the SC's newly expanded 'legislative' function in counterterrorism matters was initially associated with certain problematic trends, not least the safeguarding of fundamental human rights and other similar concerns.[2] By contrast, the Council's involvement at the level of secondary SR norms presents a singularly different set of problems, some of which were covered in Part II and elsewhere in this book. To that list one might add the fact that the SC's track record is—much like its process—by no means perfect; when attributing responsibility to States and devising appropriate consequences, the Council is not exempted from a margin of error that could understandably be associated with the deliberative nature of that kind of political organ. One notable example of erroneous attribution of unlawful conduct by the SC—though arising in the context of imputing international law violations to a non-State entity—occurred when it condemned Euskadi Ta Askatasuna (ETA) for the Madrid terrorist attacks.[3] The evidence adduced at a later stage demonstrated that the Council had erred in its determination.[4] In any event, as shown earlier, there are undoubtedly several benefits to engaging SC action when dealing with SR in the global security context.

[2] See also JC Barker, 'The Politics of International Law-Making: Constructing Security in Response to Global Terrorism' (2007) 3 JILIR 5; V-J Proulx, *Transnational Terrorism and State Accountability: A New Theory of Prevention* (Hart 2012) ch 5, section II.A).

[3] See, eg, UNSC Res 1530 (11 March 2004) UN Doc S/RES/1530.

[4] See, eg, V Gowlland-Debbas, 'Responsibility and the United Nations Charter' in JR Crawford *et al.* (eds), *The Law of International Responsibility* (OUP 2010) 115, 129–30; V Gowlland-Debbas, 'Security Council Change' (2009–10) 65 International Journal 119, 124; T O'Donnell, 'Naming and Shaming: The Sorry Tale of Security Council Resolution 1530' (2006) 17 EJIL 945.

When read in tandem with Chapter 3, these considerations lead to the conclusion that a strong argument can be made in favour of the institutionalized implementation of SR by looking at the structure of the international legal system. There is little doubt that the ICJ itself does not understand its role to be that of a constitutional court or judicial authority in an international constitutional system.[5] Accounts espousing a contrary stance have been arguably overdone and overemphasized in the literature; a constitutional court or *cour de cassation* function simply cannot be the role of the UN's principal judicial organ, whose jurisdiction is non-compulsory and remains subject to State consent.[6] In fact, one persuasive argument militating in favour of implementing SR through the SC (as opposed to under the International Court of Justice's (ICJ's) auspices) resides in the former body's willingness to set out primary international legal obligations incumbent upon all States.

In short, the Council's legislative role—which translates into the promulgation of 'primary' norms for SR purposes—sets it apart as a more relevant vehicle for the implementation of that normative scheme. Indeed, SC practice has been far-reaching, particularly in fields falling under the broad umbrella of global security (eg counterterrorism, nuclear non-proliferation and disarmament, and piracy). Besides, the classical posture has long suggested that the ICJ's role, by contrast, should be limited to finding or stating the law, thereby leaving the actual law-making to States (and perhaps international organizations (IOs)). In fact, international tribunals themselves generally refute their would-be law-making role.[7] One has to look no further than the ICJ Statute, which consecrates the notion that international judges merely state the existing law; first in Article 38, which is largely perceived as establishing the authoritative hierarchy of sources of international law, thereby relegating international jurisprudence to the ranks of 'subsidiary means for the determination of rules of law'; and, secondly, by emphasizing in Article 59 that the ICJ's decision is binding solely between the parties involved in the case at hand and only in respect of that specific dispute.[8] That said, the ICJ

[5] On the way in which the ICJ conceives of its role, see G Hernández, *The International Court of Justice and the Judicial Function* (OUP 2014). Moreover, one former ILC member who has since been elected to the ICJ bench once advocated that 'the international legal system is not built upon a constitutional framework... but upon international relations'. See H Xue, 'The Role of the ILC's Work in Promoting Peace and Security – Definition and Evaluation' in G Nolte (ed.), *Peace through International Law: The Role of the International Law Commission: A Colloquium at the Occasion of its Sixtieth Anniversary* (Springer 2009) 183, 185.

[6] See, eg, M Kohen, 'There Is No Need to Change the Composition of the Security Council: It Is Time for Stressing Accountability' in L Boisson de Chazournes and M Kohen (eds), *International Law and the Quest for its Implementation: Liber Amicorum Vera Gowlland-Debbas* (Brill 2010) 85, 92–3. See also TD Gill, 'Legal and Some Political Limitations on the Power of the UN Security Council to Exercise its Enforcement Powers Under Chapter VII of the Charter' (1995) 26 NYIL 115, 117 (advancing a similar point as regards judicial review).

[7] See also P Webb, *International Judicial Integration and Fragmentation* (OUP 2013) 2.

[8] See Statute of the International Court of Justice (adopted 26 June 1945, entered into force 26 June 1946), 59 Stat 1055, 8 UNTS 993, Arts 38, 59. Thus, 'judicial decisions' are envisaged as sources falling below the 'primary sources' of international law, which comprise treaties, international customary law, and general principles of law. See also Webb (n 7) 2.

has, on occasion, arguably ventured slightly beyond that narrowly defined role. Yet, any attempt to read too much into those jurisprudential departures must be contrasted squarely with the ICJ's own statement to the effect that international tribunals 'state the existing law and [do] not legislate'.[9] There is every indication that the ICJ also construes its function in this manner as regards any role it would be called upon to play in the context of judicial review of the decisions of UN organs; in addition to the arguments explored in Chapter 3, one has to look no further than the Dissenting Opinion of President Schwebel in the *Lockerbie* cases for a particularly apt confirmation of this impression.[10] The ICJ's own jurisprudence also supports this view.[11]

Moreover, whilst disputes involving global security issues may be brought to the ICJ on an ad hoc basis, the ensuing proceedings will always be tailored and defined in the light of the jurisdiction *rationae materiae* dictated by the particular circumstances of the case. As a corollary, litigants might encounter serious jurisdictional obstacles in attempting to establish the international responsibility of 'rogue' or hostile States, or to address politically sensitive topics like terrorism before the ICJ. Yet, even if the jurisdictional hurdles are cleared in some instances, the adjudication of these types of disputes would certainly not happen as a matter of course; quite to the contrary, such prospect simply cannot materialize in view of the Court's jurisdictional makeup. Consequently, the only UN organ endowed with binding power that *can* deal with these types of situations and disputes as a matter of course is the SC. Yet, speaking about 'matter of course' is obviously erroneous in this setting given that terrorism and other global security violations are unpredictable, polymorphous, and constantly evolving. As a result, these types of threats are difficult to generalize or fit neatly within specific categories, or under any one dominant legal or security matrix. The one certainty is that global security falls squarely, and incontrovertibly, within the SC's mandate.

Hence, it has been the central contention of Part II that a natural rapprochement may be operated between the prevention of global security breaches and the

[9] *Legality of the Threat or Use of Nuclear Weapons* (Advisory Opinion) [1996] ICJ Rep 226, 237. For a variety of views, see also H Lauterpacht, *The Development of International Law by the International Court* (Stevens and Sons 1958); CG Weeramantry, 'The Function of the International Court of Justice in the Development of International Law' (1997) 10 LJIL 309; J Evensen, 'The International Court of Justice: Main Characteristics and its Contribution to the Development of the Modern Law of Nations' (1988) 57 NJIL 3; A-M Slaughter, 'International Law and International Relations' (2000) 285 RdC 9, 33–4; HH Koh, 'Why Do Nations Obey International Law?' (1997) 106 Yale Law Journal 2599, 2607–8; G Abi-Saab, 'De la Jurisprudence: Quelques Réflexions sur son Rôle dans le Développement du Droit International' in M Kohen and MJ Langer (eds), *Le Développement du Droit International: Réflexions d'un Demi-siècle* (PUF 1993) 97–106.

[10] See, eg, Dissenting Opinion of President Schwebel in *Questions of Interpretation and Application of the 1971 Montreal Convention arising from the Aerial Incident at Lockerbie (Libya v USA)* (Preliminary Objections) [1998] ICJ Rep 115, 164 ff.

[11] See, eg, *Certain Expenses of the United Nations (Article 17, paragraph 2, of the Charter)* (Advisory Opinion) [1962] ICJ Rep 151, 168; *Legal Consequences for States of the Continued Presence of South Africa in Namibia (South West Africa) notwithstanding Security Council Resolution 276 (1970)* (Advisory Opinion) [1971] ICJ Rep 16, 45. See also *Military and Paramilitary Activities in and against Nicaragua (Nicaragua v USA)* (Jurisdiction and Admissibility) [1984] ICJ Rep 392, 436.

SC's primary function of maintaining and restoring international peace and security. In seeking to enhance the Council's role further under that rubric, it has been suggested that allowing it to draw inspiration from the tenets of SR in appropriate cases may actually prove helpful in carrying out its mandate. Otherwise, that normative scheme may become eviscerated in highly political, sensitive contexts, for instance in cases where a weaker State has been injured by the unlawful act of a stronger State but lacks the influence, diplomatic wherewithal, political capital, or legitimacy/credibility to adopt countermeasures against this bigger player on the world stage successfully. In such cases, recourse to the Council may be the only viable option, as it is unlikely that the stronger State will be willing to subject itself to the ICJ's jurisdiction. Consequently, the ICJ's role in this debate is of limited import, especially in the light of the jurisdictional obstacles discussed earlier, its systematic 'shrinking' of disputes submitted to it to fit within the jurisdictional and admissibility confines of each case, its judicially conservative drafting style, which leaves virtually no room for *obiter dicta*, and so on.

Thus, it has been argued that there is no principled reason for preventing the SC from dealing with SR issues as they arise; the main resistance to this prospect originates in entrenched and dogmatic scholarly positions that favour maintaining rigid dichotomies between international peace and security, on the one hand, and SR law, on the other. Those postures not only resist more progressive and mutually reinforcing readings of the relevant international legal categories but actually do a great disservice to the cause of global security. What is more, they are undoubtedly out of step with the new challenges brought about by global governance in a multipolar world. As an alternate view, it might prove more helpful to simply accept the obvious: that is, there is much more international law going on in the SC's deliberative process than one might think, with that discipline being sometimes determinant in electing a specific course of action.[12] Indeed, often the 'power of the better argument' is actually grounded in law, a trend corroborated by recent institutional practice.[13]

Indeed, recent SC precedents in the area of counterterrorism, for instance, reveal that body's profound attachment to the international rule of law and that international law sometimes plays an important part in its decision-making. In many ways, therefore, the Council's deliberative process not only provides room for powerful language, but also suggests that international law can become a compelling tool in moving agendas forward. Thus, there is no persuasive argument to

[12] On the SC's deliberative process, the place of international law in such setting, and the factors that may facilitate the persuasiveness of certain arguments, see the following works by I Johnstone: 'The Security Council and International Law' in S von Einsiedel *et al.* (eds), *The UN Security Council: From the Cold War to the 21st Century* (Lynne Rienner 2015) 771; 'Legal Argumentation in International Decision-Making' in H Charlesworth and J-M Coicaud (eds), *The Fault Lines of Legitimacy* (CUP 2010) 175–203; 'Security Council Deliberations: The Power of the Better Argument' (2003) 14 EJIL 437; 'Discursive Power in the UN Security Council' (2005) 2 JILIR 73. For a more fully fledged argument, see generally *The Power of Deliberation: International Law, Politics and Organizations* (OUP 2011) esp ch 5, 8.

[13] The expression is borrowed from Johnstone, 'Security Council Deliberations' (n 12).

exclude SR law from the purview of the Council's legal sensibility in the exercise of its powers—or from its thought-process and deliberative exercises—especially if one subscribes to a broader conception of the international community. After all, this normative scheme is absolutely central and fundamental in the global legal order. More importantly, it remains a powerful tool that the Council may harness on occasion with a view to improving the way it fulfils its core mission of maintaining global security.

PART III

STATE RESPONSIBILITY AS AN INSTITUTION IN THE GLOBAL SECURITY SCHEME

Forcible Countermeasures, Recourse to Force, and The General Framework

Introduction to Part III

The exploration of legal aspects surrounding recourse to force as a response to terrorism has been very much in fashion in the post-9/11 scholarly landscape. This development is due, in large part, to an increasing emphasis on the legal regimes governing non-State actors under international law.[1] Consequently, scholarly treatments of the interaction between non-State actors and use of force repertoire are also acquiring traction in international legal discourse.[2] Inevitably, the debate gravitates towards dichotomous terrain: on the one hand, can injured States—acting alone or through a coalition or some other mixed configuration—forcibly target individual terrorists and terrorist organizations located within the territory of a third State?[3] On the other hand, can a State injured by a terrorist attack

[1] See, eg, J d'Aspremont (ed.), *Participants in the International Legal System: Multiple Perspective on Non-State Actors in International Law* (Routledge 2011); A Clapham (ed.), *Human Rights and Non-State Actors* (Edward Elgar 2013); P Alston, *Non-State Actors and Human Rights* (OUP 2005); A Alvarez-Jimenez, 'International State Responsibility for Acts of Non-State Actors: The Recent Standards Set by the International Court of Justice in Genocide and Why the WTO Appellate Body Should Not Embrace Them' (2007) 35 Syracuse Journal of International and Law and Commerce 1; RJ Cook, 'Accountability in International Law for Violations of Women's Rights by Non-State Actors' in DG Dallmeyer (ed.), *Reconceiving Reality: Women and International Law* (ASIL 1993) 93–116; E De Brabandère, 'Non-State Actors, State-Centrism and Human Rights Obligations' (2009) 22 LJIL 191; M Milanović, 'State Responsibility for Acts of Non-State Actors: A Comment on Griebel and Pluecken' (2009) 22 LJIL 307; E Roucounas, 'Non-State Actors: Areas of International Responsibility in Need of Further Exploration' in M Ragazzi (ed.), *International Responsibility Today: Essays in Memory of Oscar Schachter* (Brill 2005) 391–404.

[2] See, eg, N Lubell, *Extraterritorial Use of Force against Non-State Actors* (OUP 2010); L Moir, *Reappraising the Resort to Force: International Law, Jus ad Bellum and the War on Terror* (Hart 2011); CJ Tams, 'The Use of Force Against Terrorists' (2009) 20 EJIL 359; KN Trapp, 'Back to Basics: Necessity, Proportionality, and the Right of Self-Defence Against Non-State Terrorist Actors' (2007) 56 ICLQ 141; JJ Teurbe-Tolón, 'Questions Concerning the Legality of the Use of Force in Southern Lebanon During the Israel-Hezbollah Conflict of 2006' (2008) 21 New York International Law Review 95; JJ Paust, 'Use of Armed Force Against Terrorists in Afghanistan, Iraq, and Beyond' (2002) 35 CILJ 533; NG Printer, Jr, 'The Use of Force Against Non-State Actors Under International Law: An Analysis of the U.S. Predator Strike in Yemen' (2003) 8 UCLA Journal of International Law & FA 331; D Richemond, 'Transnational Terrorist Organization and the Use of Force' (2007) 56 Catholic University Law Review 1001; A Oehmichen, 'Force Qua Terrorism–International Law in the Wake of 9/11' in SR Silverburg (ed.), *International Law: Contemporary Issues and Future Developments* (Westview Press 2011) 448–59. On the changes to the use of force regime in international relations, see B Helmke, *Under Attack: Challenges to the Rules Governing the International Use of Force* (Ashgate 2010).

[3] This question is increasingly generating scholarly interest. See, eg, D Bethlehem, 'Self-Defense against an Imminent or Actual Armed Attack by Nonstate Actors' (2012) 106 AJIL 769; notes and

emanating from the territory of another State—acting alone or as part of a group of States and/or institutional actors—forcibly target the territorial State because it harboured or supported the terrorists on its territory?[4]

Whilst the first query has divided interlocutors over the curtailment of sovereignty when a State pursues terrorists across another nation's boundary, there is support for more modest uses of force or the dispatch of law enforcement units to attain this objective.[5] In particular, the idea that an injured State can forcibly target non-State terrorist actors within another State's territory because the latter cannot contain the threat has gained purchase in both policy and academic circles.[6] For some States, like the United States (US), recourse to force has long been invoked as an appropriate response to counter terrorism.[7] Moreover, this aspect of self-defence has featured prominently in post-9/11 judicial discourse and institutional counterterrorism initiatives. Through Resolutions 1368 and 1373, the Security Council (SC) asserted the right of injured States (particularly the US in that instance) to invoke self-defence to counteract terrorism, at least implicitly,[8] a posture sometimes construed as enabling States to take unilateral action against non-State terrorist actors. Whilst this shift in institutional discourse might rightly be perceived as widening the scope of permissible self-defence against non-State actors, there is nothing groundbreaking in claiming that a State violates its international obligations because it harbours or supports terrorists on its territory.

comments in (2013) 107 AJIL 563–84 (including contributions by Akande and Liefländer, Tladi, Hmoud, and Bethlehem).

[4] But see PN Okowa, 'II. Case Concerning Armed Activities on the Territory of the Congo (Democratic Republic of the Congo v. Uganda)' (2006) 55 ICLQ 742, 748. However, lawful recourse to self-defence should be distinguished from the practice of 'defensive armed reprisal', which is unlawful and thus excluded from the purview of the ARSIWA. See Y Dinstein, *War, Aggression and Self-Defence* (4th edn, CUP 2005) 222; D Brown, 'Use of Force against Terrorism after September 11th: State Responsibility, Self-Defense and Other Responses' (2003) 11 Cardozo Journal of International and Comparative Law 1, 35; JN Kendall, 'Israeli Counter-Terrorism: "Targeted Killings" Under International Law' (2002) 80 North Carolina Law Review 1069, 1082. For a thoughtful study on these questions, particularly the relationship between use of force and SR, see P Klein, 'Le Droit International à l'Épreuve du Terrorisme' (2006) 321 RdC 203, 368–410.

[5] Therefore, an injured State could arguably counteract a sanctuary State's violation of its obligation to prevent terrorism with proportionate countermeasures, which presumably include some incremental or limited incursions involving reduced exercises of force, such as local law enforcement arrangements or modest military action. Some academic commentary frames such responses, either explicitly or implicitly, within the corpus of SR norms and correspondingly supports the notion that some limited forcible reaction to terrorist acts could fit within the broader framework of countermeasures (which, incidentally, operate a *renvoi* to customary SR rules). See, eg, Y Arai-Takahashi, 'Shifting Boundaries of the Right of Self-Defence: Appraising the Impact of the September 11 Attacks on *Jus Ad Bellum*' (2002) 36 International Lawyer 1081, 1085–6.

[6] See, eg, N Tsagourias, 'Non-State Actors in International Institutional Peace and Security: Non-State Actors and the Use of Force' in d'Aspremont (n 1) 326–41.

[7] See, eg, JN Maogoto, 'Walking an International Tightrope: Use of Military Force to Counter Terrorism' (2006) 31 Brooklyn Journal of International Law 405.

[8] See, eg, C Greenwood, 'International Law and the Pre-emptive Use of Force: Afghanistan, Al-Qaida, and Iraq' (2003) 4 San Diego International Law Journal 7; CD Gray, *International Law and the Use of Force* (3rd edn, OUP 2008) 193, 198–9, 208–9, 227.

For instance, the SC frequently deplored the continuing use of Afghan territory for the 'sheltering' and 'training' of terrorists. Resolution 1267 constituted a probative example whereby that body accused Afghanistan of perpetrating egregious international law violations and exhorted it to abstain from providing territorial sanctuary and logistical solace to terrorists.[9] Similarly, confronted with Lebanon's failure to control the southern portion of its territory, the Council registered its grave concern regarding the activities of armed militias on that territory, including Hezbollah factions. Thus, it called for 'the disbanding and disarmament of all Lebanese and non-Lebanese militias' in Lebanon; failure to comply with this legally binding prescription could engage that State's international responsibility.[10] Looking to the future, there is every indication that this rationale could extend to States that harbour Islamic State of Iraq and the Levant (ISIL) or Al-Shabaab members on their territory. In fact, the SC has recently formulated similar demands to all UN members regarding ISIL.[11] Even before 9/11, this type of claim had been proffered in other contexts, especially for the purpose of justifying retaliatory use force or self-defence against the territorial State.[12] Conversely, whilst this issue was very much alive in both the *Wall Advisory Opinion* and *Armed Activities* case, the International Court of Justice (ICJ) has been reluctant to recognize a right to invoke self-defence against non-State actors, absent a clear unlawful act (ie an 'armed attack') on the part of the territorial State. In its view, for self-defence repertoire to be triggered, the territorial/sponsoring State must have carried out the excursion itself, through official agents or instrumentalities, or the attack must be attributable to it under international law. Incidentally, this brings us to the second and in many ways, more problematic scenario invoked above.

[9] In UNSC Res 1267 (15 October 1999) UN Doc S/RES/1267, the SC strongly condemned 'the continuing use of Afghan territory, especially areas controlled by the Taliban, for the sheltering and training of terrorists and planning of terrorist acts'; '[d]eplor[ed] the fact that the Taliban continue[d] to provide safe haven to Usama bin Laden and to allow him and others associated with him to operate a network of terrorist training camps from Taliban-controlled territory'; and insisted that the Taliban 'cease the provision of sanctuary and training for international terrorists and their organizations'. Similar concerns pertaining to the 'use of Afghan territory' for the 'sheltering and training of terrorists' were expressed in UNSC Res 1214 (8 December 1998) UN Doc S/RES/1214; UNSC Res 1333 (19 December 2000) UN Doc S/RES/1333. See also generally TM Franck, *Recourse to Force: State Action against Threats and Armed Attacks* (CUP 2002) 95–6.

[10] UNSC Res 1559 (2 September 2004) UN Doc S/RES/1559 [3]. See also generally S Kirchner, 'Third Party Liability for Hezbollah Attacks against Israel' (2006) 7 German Law Journal 777.

[11] UNSC Res 2249 (20 November 2015) UN Doc S/RES/2249 [5] (imposing an obligation upon States to thwart the activities of ISIL in Iraq and Syria).

[12] See, eg, WM Reisman, 'The Raid on Baghdad: Some Reflections on Its Lawfulness and Implications' (1994) 5 EJIL 120; R Wedgwood, 'Unilateral Action in the UN System' (2000) 11 EJIL 349. For a critical analysis of this position, see L Condorelli, 'À Propos de l'Attaque Américaine contre l'Irak du 26 Juin 1993: Lettre d'un Professeur Désemparé aux Lecteurs du JEDI' (1994) 5 EJIL 134; MG Kohen, 'The Use of Force by the United States After the End of the Cold War and Its Impact on International Law' in M Byers and G Nolte (eds), *United States Hegemony and the Foundations of International Law* (CUP 2003) 197–231. For further analysis, see also G Guillaume, 'Terrorisme et Droit International' (1989) 215 RdC 396, 402–6 (setting aside humanitarian intervention as a justification, but opening the door to a logic of self-defence). For post-9/11 output on the question, see, eg, L Condorelli, 'Les Attentats du 11 Septembre et leurs Suites: Où Va le Droit International?' (2001) 105 RGDIP 829; the various editorial comments in (2001) 95 AJIL 833.

The response to 9/11 undeniably targeted individuals and networks suspected of being involved in terrorism, especially those responsible for carrying out or planning the 9/11 attacks. There is little doubt that this response forcibly targeted such individuals and entities, irrespective of any sovereign State's involvement in 9/11. What is less clear, however, is whether, or to what extent, the US and its allies held the Afghan State *legally* responsible for 9/11, thereby also justifying self-defence against that nation—not just against the individual perpetrators it harboured—as a consequence flowing from the invocation of SR. The political rhetoric following 9/11 further exacerbated the dichotomy between self-defence against non-State individuals and organizations, as opposed to adopting responses based on self-defence against territorial/sanctuary States for failing to prevent terrorism, harbouring, and supporting terrorists on their soil.

Undoubtedly, the US and its allies equally held both non-State and State actors responsible for failing to prevent, aiding or abetting, or even tolerating terrorism.[13] However, it is unclear whether this stance amounted predominantly to a political claim, as opposed to a normative operation purporting to establish a legal nexus between Afghanistan's repeated failures to prevent terrorism emanating from its territory and its international *legal* responsibility. Further scholarly exploration is needed on this front in order to illuminate the potential institutionalization of SR in global security contexts. If past recourse to force precedents have taught us anything it is that political considerations pervade—and sometimes override—the international legal calculus in building constituencies of conscience with a view to mounting forcible responses to wrongful acts. The politicization of this process—that is, the lead-up to war—is no doubt exacerbated by the involvement of other actors outside the UN framework, particularly the media and civil society, as seen in past instances, such as the 2003 invasion of Iraq and the events that surrounded the Suez Crisis. In such contexts, the role international law plays—and ought to play—in justifying forcible responses is sometimes difficult to ascertain.[14]

Consequently, a more nebulous legal area undoubtedly resides in determining the mitigating impact on SR of both preventive and reactive forcible measures against terrorists in host-States (ie when such initiatives are framed within countermeasures or secondary norms repertoire). In particular, one area worth exploring—or, more accurately, worth untangling—lies in the thorny relationship between SR and use of force, which has considerable implications for the institutionalization of the normative scheme under study. Interesting policy payoffs can be gleaned from analysing how SR law—a general system governing international breaches and reparation/legal consequences, without the vertical enforcement monopolies found in domestic constitutional orders—can inform

[13] See, eg, President Bush's remarks quoted in JA Cohan, 'Formulation of a State's Response to Terrorism and State-Sponsored Terrorism' (2002) 14 Pace International Law Review 77, 93 (quoting E Bumiller, 'Bush Says War May Go beyond Afghan Border' *NYT* (New York, 22 November 2001) B2).

[14] See, eg, C Peevers, *The Politics of Justifying Force: The Suez Crisis, the Iraq War, and International Law* (OUP 2013).

the deployment of self-defence, a self-contained regime, as a consequence flowing from an internationally wrongful act (be it related to terrorism or other global security areas). Hence, further consideration should be given to how both regimes mutually inform or reinforce each other in global security contexts. After all, SR is absolutely fundamental under international law whilst terrorism has recently cropped up as one of the international community's more pressing security challenges.[15] This problematic interrelationship will be investigated in Part III and as will be seen, the failure of a State to prevent terrorism—and the ensuing responsibility for that wrongful act—can become a predicate for invoking self-defence in the most extreme cases.[16] For every other case falling short, sound and principled guidelines must be identified within the corpus of SR norms.

Building on the central arguments advanced in Part II, it is clear that the SC sometimes plays a role in applying and interpreting SR rules in global security contexts; to a lesser extent, the ICJ and General Assembly (GA) have also made similar advances as regards global security. It seems only logical that the SC would play an active role in implementing SR in relevant global security contexts, given that it has actively promulgated primary obligations in related fields such as counterterrorism and nuclear non-proliferation. Ensuring compliance with its legislative edicts not only flows organically from its broader mission of maintaining international peace and security but also shares a functional rapprochement with the implementation of SR. Indeed, there is an inherent compatibility between the SC monitoring violations of its resolutions and the implementation of international legal obligations. As soon as one accepts that this function is compatible with the SC's broader attributions, the relationship between recourse to force and SR repertoire cannot be eluded.

Indeed, it might be trite to recall that the scheme of countermeasures remains the dominion of SR law. Taking this reasoning further, surely any exploration of the legal means that may be harnessed with a view to enforcing global security priorities must grapple with the most controversial countermeasure of all: the use of force as a response to internationally wrongful acts. This is the object of Part III. This approach is also reinforced by post-9/11 SC resolution-making, which underscored the interplay between States' obligations to prevent terrorism and recourse to force in extreme scenarios. When it is acknowledged that exceptions may exist in State and institutional practice suggesting a greater willingness to frame forcible responses to global security violations within SR repertoire, the

[15] See also A Nissel, 'Tal Becker, Terrorism and the State: Rethinking the Rules of State Responsibility (Oxford: Hart Publishing, 2006)' (2007) 5 JICJ 245, 245.

[16] On the invocation of self-defence against terrorism, as predicated on a prior finding of SR, see AS Weiner, 'The Use of Force and Contemporary Security Threats: Old Medicine for New Ills?' (2006) 59 Stanford Law Review 415, 431–4. See also JM Beard, 'America's New War on Terror: The Case for Self-Defense under International Law' (2002) 25 Harvard Journal of Law & Public Policy 559, 583 (applying similar logic to Afghanistan in light of the 9/11 attacks). Incidentally, additional scholarly writing is required on the 'thorny' relationship between SR law and use of force repertoire. See, eg, V-J Proulx, 'The "War on Terror" and the Framework of International Law' (2007) 40 Canadian Journal of Political Science 278, 279.

SC's role becomes central given that it remains the sole global guardian of the collective security regime.

As prefaced earlier,[17] this volume has elected transnational terrorism as its principal case study, given that it constitutes the best global security candidate for the purposes of gauging the prospects and limits of institutionalizing SR. Undeniably, State failures to prevent terrorism are intimately tied to internationally wrongful acts related to unlawful use of force, which requires that the interplay between recourse to force and SR repertoire be investigated. Thus, this book argues that irrespective of dogmatic counterarguments, in practice the SC has been at times instrumental in implementing SR for global security breaches, particularly those pertaining to terrorism. In the worst case scenario, the post-9/11 legal and counterterrorism frameworks instituted by the SC form a backdrop of primary obligations that weave the new global security fabric, thereby dictating the applicable law governing breaches of those duties. In the best case scenario, the SC actively implements SR law, monitors the application of some countermeasures (be they adopted in 'collective' or 'institutional' settings, or on a unilateral basis), and its resolutions guide States regarding the legality and legitimacy of their implementation of secondary norms of responsibility. As seen in previous sections, a major aspect of the implementation of SR resides in attributing wrongful conduct to responsible States; as will be seen in subsequent pages, this is also very much the case when the unlawful conduct involves the use of force, a situation that has confronted both the SC and ICJ in the past.

In exploring the legal consequences flowing from States' wrongful conduct broadly, Part III delivers an analysis of the interplay between SR repertoire and recourse to force, with particular emphasis on self-defence and collective use of force in counterterrorism contexts. However, the objective is not to provide an exhaustive review of State and institutional practice but rather to investigate the connections between SR and use of force in the light of the arguments advanced in Part II. Therefore, considerable weight will be allotted to the role of forcible responses in the scheme of SR when reacting to State failures to prevent terrorism, in the hope of identifying helpful policy solutions for other global security challenges.

The consideration of forcible responses as a potential consequence to a State's violation of counterterrorism duties flows—though not without controversy—from the establishment of SR, particularly when it is implemented by an institutional mechanism. This proposition becomes even more compelling when the institutionalized implementation of SR is achieved through the SC, a UN organ largely seen as the predominant institution tasked with overseeing use of force in international relations. As will become clear in subsequent pages, however, the connections between the institutionalized implementation of SR and use of force are not always straightforward. In many ways, the case for a more central role for SR principles in justifying unilaterally implementing States' forcible responses

[17] See Conclusion to Part I.

is easier to make than in respect of the institutionalized implementation of SR, primarily because the SC's relation to international legal norms differs from that of States. For one thing, the SC can authorize forcible responses without expressly predicating that decision on a violation of international law or ensuring that SR requirements are met, and is not itself acting in self-defence. Nevertheless, it remains useful to investigate the manner in which SR principles might inform recourse to forcible responses, be they authorized by the SC or taken by individual States (particularly in response to a violation that may fall short of the 'armed attack' threshold in the UN Charter), even if that nexus might operate more fruitfully outside institutionalized settings. Ultimately, Part III sets out the foundations of a research and policy prospectus by identifying general guidelines or building blocks from which future explorations of the topic may draw inspiration.

5

Drawing on Self-contained Regimes

The Connection between the Use of Force and State Responsibility

5.1 Introduction

Any study exploring the potential institutionalization of the implementation of SR must address perhaps the most controversial possibility under that normative scheme: potential forcible responses to internationally wrongful acts. Whilst it is true that the relationship between State responsibility (SR) and use of force repertoire was brought to the fore in the context of Israeli armed reprisals in the 1960s,[1] SR repertoire is increasingly examined through a use of force prism. There is certainly considerable scholarly resistance to equating the law of countermeasures with Security Council–mandated sanctions, with some publicists rejecting the idea that that organ's reaction to Iraq's unlawful invasion of Kuwait had anything to do with SR principles.[2]

This chapter now turns to the crux of this very elusive topic, one that cannot be overlooked when exploring the role of SR in global security contexts. Whilst self-defence is a considerably narrower scheme than SR, both regimes have arguably evolved simultaneously—sometimes in tandem—as reflected by State and institutional practice, along with post-9/11 legal scholarship. Thus, passing references have been made throughout the present study to the thorny relationship between SR law and use of force repertoire. Undoubtedly, the resulting regime interaction warrants further exploration as policy-makers and judiciaries attempt to fashion accountability schemes and harness international law with a view to promoting State compliance with counterterrorism and other global security obligations. Whilst the objective here is not to canvass exhaustively all of the intricacies resulting from the challenging interplay between SR and recourse to force, a brief survey of major issues to consider will nonetheless set the stage for further inquiry and concomitantly reveal that whilst nebulous, the nexus between both

[1] See generally DW Bowett, 'Reprisals Involving Recourse to Armed Force' (1972) 66 AJIL 1.
[2] See, eg, C Leben in JR Crawford *et al.* (eds), *The Law of International Responsibility* (OUP 2010) 1197, 1202–3.

regimes remains analytically fertile.[3] This objective is better achieved by shifting away from the seemingly improbable importation of use of force elements into SR repertoire to potential areas of compatibility or exceptions.

The chapter first explores and challenges the self-contained nature of use of force repertoire, thereby identifying its principal interactions with SR norms. In particular, the analysis investigates the interplay between the Articles on Responsibility of States for Internationally Wrongful Acts (ARSIWA) and recourse to force whilst identifying relevant exceptions derived from State and institutional practice in global security contexts. This approach necessarily involves taking into account institutional perspectives, particularly those of the International Law Commission (ILC), International Court of Justice (ICJ), and the Security Council (SC). The book then reverts to its principal case study of transnational terrorism, thereby addressing a contemporaneous shift in both legal and policy inclinations towards models of indirect SR for terrorism. This analysis paves the way for some concluding observations on the controversial remedy of forcible countermeasures as a means to tackle global security breaches.

5.2 Keeping State Responsibility Law Insulated: Just how Self-contained is the Recourse to Force Legal Scheme?

5.2.1 The ARSIWA and use of force

Detractors opposing the melding of these two legal regimes invariably brandish a single mantra: use of force is a self-contained regime and the ARSIWA expressly forbid the adoption of forcible countermeasures by injured States. By 'forcible countermeasures', I mean sovereignty-violating, force-based responses taken by injured States—be they formally authorized by the SC or not—to address internationally wrongful acts falling short of the 'armed attack' threshold in the UN Charter. For its part, self-defence remains a distinct form of forcible response to violations of international law (although there is some resistance to this characterization) and comes into play when the 'armed attack' threshold has been met. Its normative interactions with SR principles are also explored in the following pages. In particular, ARSIWA Article 50 proscribes the adoption of armed reprisals or the use of force in response to internationally wrongful acts.[4] In fact, this notion

[3] But see I Brownlie, *International Law and the Use of Force by States* (Clarendon Press 1963) 375 (underscoring the idea that both regimes should remain analytically distinct).

[4] Articles on the Responsibility of States for Internationally Wrongful Acts, UN Doc A/56/10 (2001); (2001) II(2) *YILC* 26 (and Commentary ibid 31), Art 50 provides as follows:

1. Countermeasures shall not affect:
   (a) the obligation to refrain from the threat or use of force as embodied in the Charter of the United Nations;
   (b) obligations for the protection of fundamental human rights;
   (c) obligations of a humanitarian character prohibiting reprisals;
   (d) other obligations under peremptory norms of general international law.
2. A State taking countermeasures is not relieved from fulfilling its obligations:

had been vigorously defended in legal scholarship prior to the ARSIWA's finalization.[5] More recently, one detractor succinctly encapsulated the rigid distinction precluding the interpenetration of SR and use of force repertoire in the context of counterterrorism: '[g]iven the dangers of global terrorism, the issue of state support cannot be adequately addressed within the framework of state responsibility, which envisages non-forceful countermeasures. Instead, the appropriate framework is that of self-defence.'[6] However, whilst use of force as a countermeasure had already been excluded as a matter of course by distinguished scholars in the 1950s and 1960s,[7] a position ultimately reflected in the ARSIWA, certain publicists query whether an exception to this rule has cropped up contemporaneously in the fight against State-supported terrorism.[8] Others site possible forcible reactions to transnational terrorism—be it expressly or impliedly—within the zone of SR repertoire, which signals that such responses could become synonymous with countermeasures (although not without controversy) and be governed by customary international legal norms.[9]

The ensuing dilemma, therefore, can be summarized as follows: if a State fails to prevent a terrorist attack emanating from its territory, thereby violating its counterterrorism obligations, can the injured State use force to compel performance of, or induce reparation for, the violated duty as a means of last resort? Obviously, it is assumed that this forcible response would fulfil the proportionality requirement both under the UN Charter and the law of countermeasures. Indeed, as seen in Chapter 4, the concept of proportionality lies at the core of countermeasures

(a) under any dispute settlement procedure applicable between it and the responsible State;
(b) to respect the inviolability of diplomatic or consular agents, premises, archives and documents.

See also E Zoller, *Peacetime Unilateral Remedies: An Analysis of Countermeasures* (Transnational Publishers 1984) 38–9. On the relationship between self-contained regimes, SR law, and *leges speciales*, see B Simma and D Pulkowski: 'Leges Speciales and Self-Contained Regimes' in Crawford *et al.* (n 2) 139–63 and 'Of Planets and the Universe: Self-Contained Regimes in International Law' (2006) 17 EJIL 483; M Noortmann, *Enforcing International Law: From Self-Help to Self-Contained Regimes* (Ashgate 2005); B Simma, 'Self-Contained Regimes' (1985) 16 NYIL 112.

[5] See, eg, JA Frowein, 'Reactions by Not Directly Affected States to Breaches of Public International Law' (1994) 248 RdC 347, 424–5; A Tanzi, 'Is Damage a Distinct Condition for the Existence of an Internationally Wrongful Act?' in M Spinedi and B Simma (eds), *United Nations Codification of State Responsibility* (Oceana 1987) 1, 31–2.

[6] J Brunnée, 'The Security Council and Self-Defence: Which Way to Global Security?' in N Blokker and N Schrijver (eds), *The Security Council and the Use of Force: Theory and Reality—A Need for Change?* (Nijhoff 2005) 107, 123. See also G Travalio and J Altenburg, 'Terrorism, State Responsibility, and the Use of Military Force' (2003) 4 CJIL 97, 102–11.

[7] See, eg, R Higgins, *The Development of International Law through the Political Organs of the United Nations* (OUP 1963) 216–17; CHM Waldock, 'The Regulation of the Use of Force by Individual States in International Law' (1952) 81 RdC 451, 493; PC Jessup, *A Modern Law of Nations: An Introduction* (Macmillan 1948) 175; G Schwarzenberger, *A Manual of International Law* (3rd edn, Stevens 1952) 62.

[8] See, eg, J-C Martin, *Les Règles Internationales Relatives à la Lutte contre le Terrorisme* (Bruylant 2006) 494.

[9] See, eg, Y Arai-Takahashi, 'Shifting Boundaries of the Right of Self-Defence: Appraising the Impact of the September 11 Attacks on *Jus Ad Bellum*' (2002) 36 International Lawyer 1081, 1085–6.

and governs their adoption.[10] Otherwise put, can an armed response be adopted unilaterally as a countermeasure in order to compel performance of the violated obligation? The immediate challenge is that when dealing with an obligation to prevent, the very essence of the undertaking is defeated when the prohibited event occurs.[11] If force is authorized in response to that wrongful act, it is doubtful whether such a course of action genuinely aims to compel performance of the violated obligation given that the duty has already been violated (ie the attack has not been prevented) and is not, typically, of a continuous nature like transboundary pollution, for instance.[12] More importantly, such a response purports to address wrongful conduct (ie a fait accompli), as opposed to an imminent threat which is a *sine qua non* predicate for triggering the *jus ad bellum* scheme.[13]

Whilst compelling the observance of international law through countermeasures might in fact overlap with the need to address an imminent threat in some instances, this is not universally the case. This legal restraint might be attenuated in the event that additional prospective attacks emanating from the same host-State are reasonably foreseeable, thereby suggesting that the violation of the obligation to prevent is of continuing character and requires, for its cessation and the containment of an imminent threat, resolute and effective countermeasures. Barring such extreme scenarios, responding to the failure to prevent any global security violation with force can suspiciously take on the form of an 'armed reprisal', which engenders a host of philosophical and political problems. The line, therefore, between an actual countermeasure under SR repertoire and unadulterated—perhaps primitive—retaliation can begin to blur on occasion. This potential impediment to invoking use of force as a countermeasure is further compounded by the fact that no precise textual exegesis in current SR repertoire unequivocally supports such eventuality. Discussing similar issues as regards unilateral enforcement of collective decisions, Gowlland-Debbas echoed this view:

> [*a*] *fortiori*, those interventions involving military force cannot be justified within the context of the current rules on state responsibility under which armed reprisals have been clearly prohibited: moreover, they neither correspond to the requirements of a state of

[10] See Section 4.2.1. On these issues, see also TM Franck, 'On Proportionality of Countermeasures in International Law' (2008) 102 AJIL 715.

[11] See ARSIWA (n 4) Art 14.

[12] Conversely, it may well be that similarly to transboundary pollution, a territorial State's failure to suppress the unlawful activity might in fact aggravate the violation of a continuing obligation to prevent terrorism. See, eg, JR Crawford, *The International Law Commission's Articles on State Responsibility: Introduction, Text and Commentaries* (CUP 2002) 140. On the distinction between instantaneous and continuing breaches of international law, see *Rainbow Warrior (NZ v France)* (1990) 20 RIAA 217, 264 [101]. On the question of continuing breaches, generally, see J Pauwelyn, 'The Concept of a "Continuing Violation" of an International Obligation: Selected Problems' (1995) 66 BYIL 415.

[13] See B Finucane, 'Fictitious States, Effective Control, and the Use of Force against Non-State Actors' (2012) 30 BJIL 35, 91 (also emphasizing that '[t]he use of force premised upon the breach of an international duty, rather than in response to a direct threat, erodes the restriction of *jus ad bellum* to self-defense').

necessity as outlined in the ILC Draft Articles on State Responsibility, nor lend themselves to extended claims of self-defence.[14]

This line of inquiry also begs the question whether use of force—which arguably comprises a self-contained structure—can be transposed into the *lex generalis* that characterizes SR law. Conversely, the apparent compatibility between SR and recourse to force could turn out to be skin deep; rather, the cross-pollination between both fields has often been construed as superficial, translating, for instance, into the mechanism of attribution serving as an overarching legal and analytical tool for two distinct legal processes (attributing an internationally wrongful act to the State for SR purposes versus attributing an armed attack to the State for use of force/self-defence purposes). According to the proponents of this view, whilst attribution rules may help guide the self-defence calculus, it does not necessarily follow that SR straddles use of force repertoire.[15] The reality would instead simply entail that attribution is an adaptable legal mechanism that serves as the analytical linchpin connecting the acts of non-State actors to the corresponding host-State, irrespective of whether that determination is made under the rubric of SR or self-defence. To argue in a contrary sense, one would have to accept the proposition that both SR law and the UN Charter's scheme of recourse to force serve a common purpose, albeit in radically divergent ways: namely, the enforcement of international law (ie whilst both striving to achieve this objective by responding to internationally wrongful acts).[16]

5.2.2 Possible exceptions derived from State and institutional practice

There are still, however, grounds to ponder whether an exception justifying the use of force as a response against the failure to prevent terrorism has cropped up in State and institutional practice (particularly that of the SC). Otherwise put, certain injured States readily resort to use of force against territorial States they accuse of having participated in some way, shape, or form in the perpetration of internationally wrongful acts. This is particularly true in respect of one pressing global security threat: transnational terrorism (which could presumably find other analogues under the 'global security' rubric).[17] What remains unclear is whether those patterns of response are to be integrally framed within the scope of SR law,

[14] V Gowlland-Debbas, 'The Limits of Unilateral Enforcement of Community Objectives in the Framework of UN Peace Maintenance' (2000) 11 EJIL 361, 363.

[15] See, eg, J Brunnée and SJ Toope, 'The Use of Force: International Law after Iraq' (2004) 53 ICLQ 785, 795.

[16] Consider R Wolfrum, 'The Attack of September 11, 2001, The Wars Against the Taliban and Iraq: Is There A Need to Reconsider International Law on the Recourse to Force and the Rules in Armed Conflict?' (2003) 7 Max Planck Yearbook of UN Law 1, 37.

[17] For a survey of relevant State and institutional practice, see V-J Proulx, *Transnational Terrorism and State Accountability: A New Theory of Prevention* (Hart 2012) 54–112; TM Franck, *Recourse to Force: State Action Against Threats and Armed Attacks* (CUP 2002) ch 4.

entirely within self-defence repertoire, or as straddling both regimes. The resulting legal interface is never manifestly limpid, with injured States borrowing from the logic of both regimes to cater to their own reactions/interests and bolster their political rhetoric. Whilst historical precedents have been canvassed elsewhere,[18] relevant State practice—which initially originated predominantly from both Israel and the United States (US) but is now crystallizing in other locales—provides myriad examples of the muddling of both legal schemes. In such circumstances, the operations undertaken by injured States to contain or repress terrorism may be justified by reference to self-defence; this in no way excludes the possibility of construing such responses as countermeasures given that in a majority of cases the 'self-defence argument' has been rejected by the international community.[19] In many ways, therefore, such reactions, whilst difficult to fit neatly within either *legal* category, nonetheless have the constitutive trappings of countermeasures, both in *intention* and *effect*.

Early and formative cases in point include the 1968 Beirut raid following the attack on Athens' airport,[20] the Israeli raid on Tunis on 1 October 1985 following a terrorist excursion in Cyprus,[21] the 1986 American operations in Libya following an attack against a Berlin nightclub,[22] the 1998 American strikes in Afghanistan and Sudan following attacks against embassies in Nairobi and Dar Es-salaam,[23] and the 4–5 October 2003 Israeli missile strikes against terrorist training camps in Syria following the suicide bombing of 4 October 2003.[24] Whether these types of responses can be framed within the purview of SR law remains up for debate but in the event that they can, the question of their lawfulness as proper countermeasures comes into sharp relief. In fact, for over a century armed reprisals were largely perceived as legitimate and not formally prohibited under international law.[25] By contrast, today the use and threat of use of force are expressly prohibited

[18] See, eg, Proulx (n 17). [19] See, eg, Martin (n 8) 494 fn 210.

[20] On the Beirut raid, see Bowett (n 1) 13; MB Baker, 'Terrorism and the Inherent Right of Self-Defense (A Call to Amend Article 51 of the United Nations Charter)' (1987) 10 HJIL 25, 34–5; RA Falk: 'The Beirut Raid and the International Law of Retaliation' in MA Kaplan (ed.), *Great Issues of International Politics: The International System and National Policy* (Aldine Publication Company 1970) 38–9 and 'The Beirut Raid and the International Law of Retaliation' (1970) 63 AJIL 415. See also UNSC Res 262 (31 December 1968) UN Doc S/RES/262, which vehemently condemned the premeditated military assault and threatened the adoption of sanctions against Israel in the event of further escalation.

[21] See UNSC Resolution 573 (4 October 1985) UN Doc S/RES/573, which condemned the attack in the most categorical terms.

[22] See, eg, KN Trapp, *State Responsibility for International Terrorism* (OUP 2011) 236–8.

[23] See, eg, Trapp (n 22) 51–4.

[24] For instance, Israel emphasized that its 'measured defensive response to the horrific suicide bombings against a terrorist training facility in Syria [was] a clear act of self-defence in accordance with Article 51 of the Charter', but then proceeded to ground its explanations and justifications on Syria's extensive involvement in supporting terrorism. See UNSC Verbatim Record (5 October 2003) UN Doc S/PV/4836, 5–6.

[25] See, eg, R Provost, *International Human Rights and Humanitarian Law* (CUP 2002) 188. Moreover, should the obligation to prevent terrorism qualify as an obligation *erga omnes*, it would have significant implications for the interrelationship between SR law and recourse to force: 'any State whether or not directly injured, would have the right to take countermeasures, including reprisals otherwise illegal'. See T Scovazzi, 'Some Remarks on International Responsibility in the

by Article 2(4) of the UN Charter, whilst the only apparent exceptions to this principle remain based on the invocation of self-defence or the orchestration of collective action upon SC authorization under Chapter VII auspices. Absent such authorization, a State's recourse to force may engender significant problems in the international legal order.[26] Consequently, the prohibition of forcible or armed countermeasures against the perpetration of internationally wrongful acts has become a widely accepted rule of customary law, and was confirmed by both the ICJ and eminent legal publicists.[27]

Interestingly, certain scholars—most probably the progenitors of the intellectual tenets of the responsibility to protect (R2P)—have found a way to circumvent potential enforcement impasses in the UN's machinery. Indeed, some have advanced the idea that a 'coalition of liberal democratic States' could actually act as an alternate decision-making authority to approve recourse to force when the SC becomes paralysed in its own decision-making process.[28] This type of paralysis could stem either from Council inaction or from the exercise of veto power by one of the Permanent Five (or, interestingly, by a 'reverse veto').[29] This line

Field of Environmental Protection' in M Ragazzi (ed.), *International Responsibility Today: Essays in Memory of Oscar Schachter* (Brill 2005) 209, 218 fn 32. For general support, see M Ragazzi, *The Concept of International Obligations Erga Omnes* (Clarendon Press 1997); O Schachter, *International Law in Theory and Practice* (Nijhoff 1991) 381. In bolstering his view that international law exists as a coercive order, Kelsen believed that armed reprisals, too, whilst proscribed by the UN Charter, were not theoretically excluded. See H Kelsen, 'Théorie Générale du Droit International Public' (1953) 84 RdC 1, 33, 49. See also P Guggenheim, *Traité de Droit International Public: Avec Mention de la Pratique Internationale et Suisse* (2nd edn, Georg 1967) 92. In a broader sense, Kelsen (ibid 12–15, 18–19) essentially equated the concept of 'sanction' with 'reprisal'. For analogous applications or definitions falling outside of the 'théorie de la contrainte', see J Kunz, 'Sanctions in International Law' (1960) 54 AJIL 324; H Morgenthau, 'Théorie des Sanctions Internationales' (1935) 16 Revue de Droit International et de Législation Comparée 478.

[26] See, eg, A Pellet, 'Le Recours à la Force, le Droit et la Légitimité: Notes sur les Problèmes Posés par le Principe du Recours à la Force Armée en Cas de Carence du Conseil de Sécurité' in A Fischer-Lescano *et al.* (eds), *Frieden in Freiheit: Peace in Liberty: Paix en Liberté: Festschrift für Michael Bothe* (Nomos 2008) 249–68. For further background discussion, see W Czaplínski, 'Recours à la Force Armée par les États sans Autorisation du Conseil de Sécurité' in M Arcari (ed.), *La Sécurité Collective entre Légalité et Défis à la Légalité* (Giuffrè 2008) 25–44.

[27] See, eg, *Legality of the Threat or Use of Nuclear Weapons* (Advisory Opinion) [1996] ICJ Rep 226, 246 [46]. For further discussion on the ICJ and issues of recourse to force, see CD Gray, 'The ICJ and the *Use of Force*' in CJ Tams and J Sloan (eds), *The Development of International Law by the International Court of Justice* (OUP 2013) 237–61. For a post-*Nicaragua* assessment of litigation before the ICJ in the context of recourse to force, see also CD Gray, 'The Use and Abuse of the International Court of Justice: Cases Concerning the use of Force after *Nicaragua*' (2003) 14 EJIL 867.

[28] See, eg, A Buchanan and RO Keohane, 'The Preventive Use of Force: A Cosmopolitan Institutional Perspective' (2004) 18 Ethics and International Affairs 1, 17–18, 33; A-M Slaughter, 'Notes from the President: A Fork in the Road' (September/October 2003) ASIL Newsletter 1, 4. Espousing a different but perhaps compatible outlook on the international system, other scholars identified emerging practice as early as 2001 that increasingly supported forcible responses outside the UN framework, including against indirect aggression by State-supported terrorists. See TM Franck, 'When, if Ever, May States Deploy Military Force Without Prior Security Council Authorization?' (2001) 5 Washington University Journal of Law and Policy 51.

[29] On the notion of 'reverse veto', see JA Frowein and N Kirsch, 'Introduction to Chapter VII' in B Simma *et al.* (eds), *The Charter of the United Nations: A Commentary* (2nd edn, OUP 2002) 709, 714.

of thinking, of course, will have important implications for both counterterrorism and the repression of other global security violations if ultimately endorsed. Unsurprisingly, this position came under trenchant criticism not only for unduly loosening the rules governing recourse to force, but also for disregarding issues critical to the North–South divide.[30] It must always be borne in mind that advocating or adopting too stringent or exacting standards of due diligence and counterterrorism capacity across the board might pave the way for undesirable attacks on (putative territorial) States' sovereignty in the present era of self-exception, whereby individual States may bypass UN political organs and grant themselves an unchecked authority to intervene where they are not formally mandated to do so. Much in the spirit of Part II of this study, the role advocated herein for the SC is not limited to implementing SR; it should also extend to overseeing, authorizing, and ultimately gauging the legality of any 'forcible countermeasure' resorted to by injured States.

Correspondingly, endorsing overly permissive SR criteria or those which expand States' liability in the face of global security threats might generate similar results in the case of weak, ineffective, or 'failed' States. After all, most States will discard a standard of international responsibility that indiscriminately subjects them to forcible retaliation for harbouring terrorists.[31] Similarly, whilst the US, as one of the dominant military powers on the world stage, has the willingness and capacity to ensure global security unilaterally, excising collective action from the equation when addressing global security threats might upset existing UN mechanisms and, in turn, generate other global security risks.[32] In fact, the central role once envisaged for the SC in ensuring collective security has already been undermined by States' unilateral recourses to force and the policies underlying such acts: in particular, the US-led invasion of Afghanistan in 2001, which took place outside the UN framework and beyond the North Atlantic Treaty Organization (NATO); the formulation of the US National Security Strategy in 2002, which failed to refer to the UN to address new global security threats engendered by terrorism; and the US-led invasion of Iraq in 2003, which was carried out absent any express authorization by the SC.[33]

[30] For further exploration of this type of inquiry, generally, see RC Thakur, 'The Responsibility to Protect and the North-South Divide' in SR Silverburg (ed.), *International Law: Contemporary Issues and Future Developments* (Westview Press 2011) 32–47.

[31] See, eg, M Byers, 'Terrorism, the Use of Force, and International Law After 11 September' (2001) 51 ICLQ 401, 408.

[32] For a thoughtful discussion, see E Benvenisti, 'The US and the Use of Force: Double-Edged Hegemony and the Management of Global Emergencies' (2004) 15 EJIL 677. For a critique laying out the dangers of marginalizing the UN and increasing the role of multilateral global coalitions or unilateral action to police 'evil-doing', see JN Maogoto, 'America's War on Terror: Rattling International Law with Raw Power?' (2005) 8 Newcastle Law Review 19.

[33] See US National Security Council, *The National Security Strategy of the United States of America* (17 September 2002) <http://www.state.gov/documents/organization/63562.pdf> accessed 30 April 2015; J Brunnée and SJ Toope, *Legitimacy and Legality in International Law: An Interactional Account* (CUP 2010) 306, 314–15, 323 respectively. For further discussion, see generally CD Gray, 'A Crisis of Legitimacy for the UN Collective Security System' (2007) 56 ICLQ 157.

Conversely, arguments that sovereignty implies responsibility for effective territorial control are being brandished in academic commentary to substantiate an expanded construction of self-defence principles. Consequently, the actions of 'irresponsible sovereigns', such as ineffective States that are either unable or unwilling to control their territory, run the risk of such entities both converting their national soil into a haven for terrorists and opening themselves up to forcible responses.[34] By the same token, the problem of ineffective or 'failed' States is certainly a cause for concern, generally, and as demonstrated elsewhere, significantly threatens to erode SR repertoire.[35] Absent an overhaul of existing norms towards more forward-looking regimes and those which seek to expand States' responsibility and liability frameworks, paired with resolute transnational cooperation on global security issues and concerted, collective action to prevent such risks from materializing in the first place, available *legal* responses shrink considerably. For instance, how realistic (or even desirable, politically) would it be to seek reparation or compensation from Syria, Somalia, Yemen, or Iraq for repeated failures to prevent transborder terrorism?[36] In the light of Islamic State of Iraq and the Levant's (ISIL's) rapid expansion and the activities of other networks such as Al-Shabaab and Boko Haram, the proposals to bypass UN involvement and build 'coalitions' of intervening States as a self-help remedy, namely as a way to prevent further harm and redress previous injuries, might appear attractive.

Scholars Jutta Brunnée and Stephen Toope vehemently criticized that school of thought's proclivity for perpetuating undesirable cultural chasms within international society, along with its penchant for uncritically casting international law as an antiquated *mission civilisatrice*. Indeed, they expounded that '[s]uggestions that a more permanent "coalition of liberal democratic States" might serve as a supplementary decision-making authority to authorize the use of force when the Security Council is paralysed are deeply flawed'.[37] Whilst bolstering their critique, they delivered a searing indictment:

> [d]eveloping States have been fighting for years to destroy the outmoded notion that there is a core group of 'civilized States' that provides the sole model to emulate if a State seeks international credibility. In addition, the idea completely undermines the pluralist aspirations of international law, and the diversity of its sources. Were the idea to be implemented through the banding together of a coalition of democratic States, it would only serve to further poison international relations.[38]

[34] See T Reinold, 'State Weakness, Irregular Warfare, and the Right to Self-Defense Post-9/11' (2011) 105 AJIL 244.

[35] See, eg, D Shelton, 'International Human Rights Law: Principled, Double, Or Absent Standards?' (2007) 25 Law and Inequality: A Journal of Theory and Practice 467, 513 ('[v]iolations of human rights today are not always committed by strong dictatorial governments in a police state. They are as likely to be committed by non-state actors in failed states').

[36] On the limits of SR repertoire vis-à-vis failed States in counterterrorism, see Proulx (n 17) 242–8.

[37] Brunnée and Toope (n 15) 799.

[38] Brunnée and Toope (n 15) 799. For an account drawing on similar legal positions and ultimately inferring that existing Council resolutions did not authorize the use of force in Iraq before the 2003 invasion, see J Lobel and M Ratner, 'Bypassing the Security Council: Ambiguous

Although not directly on point, other scholars similarly argued that the duties to prevent genocide and the perpetration of other impending crimes against humanity, all global security threats—amongst which the obligation to prevent terrorism arguably qualifies[39]—legitimize not only a right, but also a duty of humanitarian intervention to counteract such acts when UN mechanisms are inefficient in redressing the situation. Therefore, this positive duty of humanitarian intervention would accrue to appropriately configured groupings of concerned States by sole virtue that 'these appalling crimes, which are contrary to the essence of humanity and the *raison d'être* of international law, are a valid reason to insist' that this duty of collective intervention be recognized.[40]

Whilst these types of arguments are of relatively recent vintage and unquestionably find steady footing in R2P's underlying ideology, their relevance to SR for failing to prevent terrorism in the context of collective action is perhaps not self-apparent unless a host-State is massively, egregiously, and continuously violating its obligation of prevention. The ensuing transborder terrorist attacks would, therefore, have to occur repeatedly and on a large-scale basis for a concerted group of States to engage some sort of collective response with some modicum of legitimacy. Whilst the idea of collective enforcement has been explored quite extensively in legal scholarship, increasingly so in contributions dealing with R2P,[41]

Authorizations to Use Force, Cease-Fires and the Iraqi Inspection Regime' (1999) 93 AJIL 124. Similarly to the first school of thought, but with more emphasis on counterterrorism, consider G Battaglini, 'War against Terrorism *Extra Moenia*, Self-Defence and Responsibility: A Pure Juridical Approach' in Ragazzi (n 25) 139–40.

[39] Several commentators classify acts of transnational terrorism as 'crimes against humanity'. See, eg, R Arnold, *The ICC As a New Instrument for Repressing Terrorism* (Transnational Publishers 2004) 202–72; CC Joyner, 'International Extradition and Global Terrorism: Bringing International Criminal to Justice' (2003) 25 Loyola LA International and Comparative Law Review 493; L Martinez, 'Prosecuting Terrorists at the International Criminal Court: Possibilities and Problems' (2002) 34 Rutgers Law Journal 1, 26–41, 52; A Mahiou, 'Le Projet de Code des Crimes Contre la Paix et la Sécurité de l'Humanité' (1997) 3 L'Observateur des Nations Unies 182; V-J Proulx, 'Rethinking the Jurisdiction of the International Criminal Court in the Post-September 11th Era: Should Acts of Terrorism Qualify As Crimes against Humanity?' (2004) 19 American University International Law Review 1009; B Van Schaack, '*Crimen Sin Lege:* Judicial Lawmaking at the Intersection of Law and Morals' (2008) 97 Georgetown Law Journal 1, 64. For a contrary view, see H Duffy, *The 'War on Terror' and the Framework of International Law* (CUP 2005) 39, but see also ibid 95, 100, 118 (arguing there should be little controversy in stating that the acts of 9/11 qualified as crimes against humanity); Martin (n 8) 259 (noting, however, that certain acts of terrorism can qualify as crimes against humanity, as long as they fulfil the legal criteria associated with such infractions); H Ascensio, 'Terrorisme et Juridictions Internationales' in SFDI (ed.), *Les Nouvelles Menaces Contre la Paix et la Sécurité Internationales* (Pedone 2004) 271, 280; C Damgaard, *Individual Criminal Responsibility for Core International Crimes: Selected Pertinent Issues* (Springer 2008) 393; H El Amine, 'Pourquoi la Cour Pénale Internationale n'Est-elle pas Compétente en Matière de Terrorisme International' in MJ Glennon and S Sur (eds), *Terrorism and International Law* (Nijhoff 2008) 247–67.

[40] B Vukas, 'Humanitarian Intervention and International Responsibility' in Ragazzi (n 25) 235, 238. For different views, see DB Kopel *et al.*, 'Is Resisting Genocide a Human Right?' (2006) 81 Notre Dame Law Review 1275; SJ Toope, 'Does International Law Impose a Duty upon the United Nations to Prevent Genocide?' (2000) 46 McGill Law Journal 187.

[41] For a critical appraisal of R2P, see C Focarelli, 'The Responsibility to Protect Doctrine and Humanitarian Intervention: Too Many Ambiguities for a Working Doctrine' (2008) 13 JCSL 191. For other perspectives, see RC Thakur, *The Responsibility to Protect: Norms, Laws and the Use of Force*

suffice it to say that use of force repertoire can sometimes become intertwined with reforms purporting to engage SR in responding to failures to prevent terrorism.[42] However, this conclusion does not fully elucidate the intellectual query whether use of force elements can be incorporated into the law of countermeasures (even if by way of exception), or whether SR repertoire remains insulated from such horizontal/cross-regime transpositions.

5.2.3 Institutional perspectives: The ILC, ICJ, and Security Council

Whilst the prohibition on forcible countermeasures seems to have acquired credence in various circles, doubt remains as to possible exceptions circumventing the UN Charter framework. For instance, in 1979 Roberto Ago declared before the ILC that 'some kinds of measures, such as armed reprisals, which had been admissible under "classical" international law, were no longer tolerated by contemporary international law, *or only within strict limits*' (emphasis added).[43] It followed from the Special Rapporteur's observations that extant SR repertoire did not completely exclude the potential application of use of force as a countermeasure, albeit only in the most dire circumstances. Similarly, the ICJ flirted with this notion in its famous *Nicaragua* decision when it pondered 'whether a State has a right to respond to intervention with intervention going so far as to justify a use of force in reaction to measures which do not constitute an armed attack but may nevertheless involve a use of force'.[44] However, in what could be considered a propitious opportunity to advance international law via *obiter dictum*, the Court refused to pronounce on the matter. It remarked that

> [t]he question is itself undeniably relevant from the theoretical viewpoint. However, since the Court is bound to confine its decision to those points of law which are essential to the settlement of the dispute before it, it is not for the Court here to determine what direct reactions are lawfully open to a State which considers itself the victim of another State's acts of intervention, possibly involving the use of force.[45]

in International Politics (Routledge 2011); G Dias, 'Responsibility to Protect: New Perspectives to an Old Dilemma' in Silverburg (n 30) ch 3; J Brunnée, 'International Law and Collective Concerns: Reflections on the Responsibility to Protect' in TM Ndiaye and R Wolfrum (eds), *Law of the Sea, Environmental Law and Settlement of Disputes: Liber Amicorum Judge Thomas A. Mensah* (Nijhoff 2007) 35–51.

[42] On the interaction between R2P, collective action, SR, and related issues, see Section 6.2.2; F Huisingh, 'A Responsibilty to Prevent? A Norm's Political and Legal Effects' (2013) 5 Amsterdam Law Forum <http://ojs.ubvu.vu.nl/alf/article/view/305> accessed 20 August 2015, 28 ff.

[43] (1979) I *YILC* 55 [12]. See also R Ago, 'Eighth Report on State Responsibility (continued)' (1979) UN Doc A/CN.4/318 and Add.1–4; (1979) II(1) *YILC* 39–40 [81].

[44] *Military and Paramilitary Activities in and against Nicaragua (Nicaragua v USA)* (Merits) [1986] ICJ Rep 14, 110 [210].

[45] *Nicaragua v USA* (Merits) (n 44) 110 [210].

Had the ICJ tackled this challenging question it could have offered significant conceptual and legal guidance to address the issue of State-supported terrorism, be it passive or active. According to some, the Court would have unequivocally excluded the potential application of armed reprisals had the prohibition on the use of force within the context of SR offered no possible exception, nor generated any doubt.[46] Whilst the Court expounded that the US was barred from legally substantiating its military intervention by invoking the law of countermeasures, this conclusion flowed, in the ICJ's view, not from the fact that the response to a wrongful act involved force in that case but rather because countermeasures could only be adopted by an injured State. Further exacerbating this confusion, the ICJ seemingly left the door open for directly injured States to adopt forcible countermeasures in reaction to internationally wrongful acts. Indeed, the decision harbours an acutely ambiguous formulation: '[t]he acts of which Nicaragua is accused ... could only have justified proportionate counter-measures on the part of the State which had been the victim of these acts ... [and] could not justify counter-measures taken by a third State, the United States, and particularly could not justify intervention involving the use of force'.[47]

Whilst the Court's wording on this point undoubtedly leaves the reader in the dark, and even though no dispositive inference may be drawn either way, it nonetheless raises the possibility for a victim State to adopt forcible countermeasures pursuant to SR law. Undoubtedly, this interpretation runs counter to the dominant reading of the ARSIWA which appear to categorically preclude the adoption of armed reprisals, even in cases of State-supported terrorism. Indeed, the ARSIWA were adopted by the General Assembly (GA) without a vote and did not generate any resistance within the ILC to excising forcible countermeasures from the purview of the final text.[48] Puzzlingly, but perhaps thankfully for proponents of expanding the scope of permissible countermeasures, ICJ Judge Antônio Cançado Trindade once pointed out that the ARSIWA 'provide details on the so-called "countermeasures" (which reflect what is most primitive in international law, namely the *use of reprisals in a new version*)'. This ultimately led him to conclude that '[t]his *new version of reprisals*—the so-called "countermeasures"—*integrates the chapter on the use (even though legal) of force*, but countermeasures should not be considered as an ineluctable feature of the regime of "legal liability"' (emphasis added).[49]

[46] Martin (n 8) 496. [47] *Nicaragua v USA* (Merits) (n 44) 127 [249].

[48] See also P Klein, 'Vers la Reconnaissance d'un Droit à des Représailles Armées?' in K Bannelier *et al.* (eds), *Le Droit International face au Terrorisme: Après le 11 Septembre 2001* (Pedone 2003) 249, 251. See also ILC, 'Comments and Observations Received by Governments' (1998) UN Doc A/CN.4/488 and Add.1–3, which reproduces States' comments on the Draft Arts following the first reading.

[49] 'Complementarity between State Responsibility and Individual Responsibility for Grave Violations of Human Rights: The Crime of State Revisited' in Ragazzi (n 25) 263 (also citing P Allott, 'State Responsibility and the Unmaking of International Law' (1998) 29 HILJ 3, 22–3). For a contrary view, see E Cannizzaro, 'The Role of Proportionality in the Law of International Countermeasures' (2001) 12 EJIL 889, 916.

Moreover—as described elsewhere, particularly with reference to SC Resolutions 262 (1968) and 573 (1985) condemning Israel's respective raids on Beirut and Tunis—armed reprisals have been widely decried by both States and international organizations (IOs) (especially the GA and SC).[50] More recently, even if the US representative at the SC supported Israel in its raid of 4 October 2003 against Syria because 'Syria [was] on the wrong side of the war on terrorism' and needed 'to cease harbouring terrorist groups',[51] Israel's armed reprisal was largely denounced by various States participating in the meeting. In fact, an overwhelming majority of States, out of the thirty present, made statements categorically condemning the Israeli strike.[52] However, this posture must be appreciated with caution: it is difficult to determine whether such wide-ranging condemnations evince a general rejection of the invocation of use of force in similar situations, or whether the resistance to Israel's course of action was prompted instead by arguments put forth in that specific instance. As seen in Chapter 4, sound international legal arguments can be persuasive in the SC. Moreover, factual circumstances at hand and the lack of compelling evidence in the objectors' minds most likely also contributed to the condemnation of Israel's conduct. In such scenarios, victim-States often invoke their right to self-defence, thereby suggesting that the adoption of armed reprisals is not generally perceived as an exception to use of force repertoire.

With this in mind, more audacious States have attempted to eschew the apparent blanket prohibition on armed reprisals by overextending the logic of self-defence. Understandably, the adoption of armed reprisals as a response to internationally wrongful acts might pose conceptual problems stemming from distorting the applicable legal categories. In this regard, some attribute the quasi-unanimity over the prohibition of armed reprisals to a shift (or slippage) in the justifications of military coercion measures, which is tantamount to circumventing that prohibition through increasingly extensive claims to self-defence.[53] Thus, the resulting interplay between SR and use of force becomes complex when States respond to transborder attacks with force, with unilateral political rhetoric often exacerbating the surrounding confusion as to what legal basis, exactly, underpins that course of action. Is such use of force a legitimate manifestation of self-defence undertaken under the auspices of the UN Charter's Article 51 (presumed) self-contained regime? Or is it instead a specific and forcible countermeasure adopted unilaterally with a view to addressing internationally wrongful conduct (ie is it synonymous with a legal consequence flowing from the violation of an international obligation)? Consequently, States injured by transnational terrorism tend to hybridize legal justifications into one overriding threat reaction/pre-emption model, thereby borrowing both from self-defence repertoire and the law of countermeasures/SR in order to derive from one regime whatever benefit

[50] See, eg, Proulx (n 17) 54–112.
[51] UNSC Verbatim Record (5 October 2003) UN Doc S/PV/4836, 14.
[52] See generally SC S/PV/4836 (n 51).
[53] Klein (n 48) 253.

the other precludes. This approach has been equated by some with 'bastardly' legal argumentation.[54]

A case in point was the run-up to the invasion of Afghanistan: whilst the 9/11 terrorist attacks were very broadly attributed to Al-Qaeda, the case for engaging Afghanistan's responsibility in order to justify self-defence was less emphatically put forth by the United Kingdom, for example.[55] To fill that void, certain commentators either inferred that Afghan responsibility was established implicitly in the circumstances or adduced it constructively from other factors.[56] Nevertheless, victim-States' arguments in counteracting terrorism with the use of force hinge, to a large extent, on some manifestation of 'armed reprisals' in a vast majority of cases; if anything, such responses certainly espouse the spirit of armed reprisals. Interestingly, some publicists have endorsed the idea that those types of reprisals prove to be an effective method of responding to the scourge of transborder terrorism.[57]

What further complicates the equation undoubtedly resides in the very nature of the internationally wrongful acts under study. Here, we are dealing with States that fail to prevent terrorism but the actual consequence of their wrongdoing results in a particularly undesirable use of force (ie terrorism) which can destabilize global security. At the very core of this dilemma, therefore, is the intersection of SR and use of force. On the one hand, significant conceptual difficulties arise when attempting to qualify a terrorist strike as an 'armed attack' pursuant to the UN Charter, a challenge that has generated considerable intellectual inquiries after 9/11.[58] Even prior to 9/11, State and institutional practice (particularly that of UN organs examined in this study) construed the concept of 'armed attack' rather narrowly.[59] Yet, according to some, little polemic actually surrounds the exercise of qualifying private terrorist acts as 'armed attacks'; however, the inquiry

[54] Martin (n 8) 497.

[55] See, eg, UK Government, 'Responsibility for the Terrorist Atrocities in the United States, 11 September 2001—An Updated Account' (4 October 2001) <http://fas.org/irp/news/2001/11/ukreport.html> accessed 21 August 2015.

[56] Whilst the SC itself has not done so explicitly in this particular context, certain scholars nonetheless infer that the 9/11 attacks were attributed to Afghanistan on the basis of several SC resolutions connecting the use of Afghan territory with terrorist activity. Compare A Conte, *Security in the 21st Century* (Ashgate 2005) 48–51 and Trapp (n 22) 51–4. Similarly, others posit that the combined failures of a State to comply with the binding resolutions of the Council and to stamp out terrorist threats on its territory are tantamount to the adoption by that State of the terrorists' conduct as its own (ie by way of endorsement). See T Gazzini, 'The Rules on the Use of Force at the Beginning of the XXI Century' (2006) 11 JCSL 319, 333–4. On a related matter, confusion arguably persists as to whether the acts carried out by Hezbollah during the 2006 Israel–Hezbollah conflict could be attributed to Lebanon under SR law. See, eg, A Yuile, 'At the Fault-Lines of Armed Conflict: The 2006 Israel–Hezbollah Conflict and the Framework of International Humanitarian Law' (2009) 16 Australian International Law Journal 189, 199–203.

[57] See, eg, W Laqueur, 'Postmodern Terrorism' (1996) 75 FA 24; C Carr, *Les Leçons de la Terreur: Pour Comprendre les Racines du Terrorisme* (Presses de la Cité 2002) 253.

[58] See, eg, SD Murphy, 'Terrorism and the Concept of "Armed Attack" in Article 51 of the U.N. Charter' (2002) 43 HILJ 41; C Antonopoulos, 'Force by Armed Groups as Armed Attack and the Broadening of Self-Defence' (2008) 55 NILR 159. For a survey and analysis of State practice in respect of the concept of 'armed attack' and its implications for UN Charter Art 51, with particular emphasis on counterterrorism, see T Ruys, *'Armed Attack' and Article 51 of the UN Charter* (CUP 2013).

[59] See, eg, SA Alexandrov, *Self-Defense against the Use of Force in International Law* (Kluwer 1996) 182–8, 204–13.

takes a more convoluted turn when attempting to connect those actions to the official State apparatus. As Gray emphasized, 'States do not today challenge the view that action by irregulars can constitute an armed attack; the controversy centers on the degree of state involvement that is necessary to make the actions attributable to the state and to justify action in self defence in particular cases.'[60] The legal confusion is further compounded when attempting to attribute the 'armed attack' in question to a State through the mechanism of *direct* responsibility (ie as though the State had itself perpetrated the attack). Such was the central philosophy underpinning Tal Becker's extensive study of SR principles and terrorism, albeit envisaged through a causation-based model in determining illegality and devising legal consequences.[61] Others were similarly inspired by this perceived shortcoming in the global legal order, advancing different policy proposals.[62]

5.2.4 The shift to indirect responsibility for terrorism

The present volume elects instead to tackle State failures to prevent terrorism via *indirect* responsibility—primarily by sanctioning governmental failures to act and promoting transnational cooperation on global security matters—as opposed to holding States accountable as though they had themselves perpetrated terrorism. This conception of SR for private acts is certainly broad enough to govern violations of several other global security obligations. Moreover, this construction of SR norms with a dominant focus on State failures attracted, at least in its classical permutations, the endorsement of leading international legal publicists, including Rousseau,[63] Guggenheim,[64] Kelsen,[65] Cheng,[66] Jiménez de Aréchaga,[67] Schwarzenberger,[68] Brownlie,[69] Akehurst,[70] Jennings and Watts,[71] Wolfrum,[72]

[60] C Gray, *International Law and the Use of Force* (2nd edn, OUP 2004) 97.

[61] See T Becker, *Terrorism and the State: Rethinking the Rules of State Responsibility* (Hart 2006). On the notion of direct versus indirect SR in this context, compare with Proulx (n 17). For an account contrasting the different approaches taken by both authors on the direct/indirect responsibility dichotomy and the importance of the public/private sphere, along with a comparison with other post-9/11 accounts, see RL Johnstone, 'Unlikely Bedfellows: Feminist Theory and the War on Terror' (2009) 9 Chicago-Kent Journal of International and Comparative Law 1, 19, 28–9.

[62] See, eg, Proulx (n 17) (advocating a strict liability-inspired model).

[63] C Rousseau, *Droit international Public* (Recueil Sirey 1953) 376–7.

[64] P Guggenheim, *Traité de Droit International Public: Avec Mention de la Pratique Internationale et Suisse*, vol II (Georg 1954) 5.

[65] H Kelsen, *Principles of International Law* (Rinehart & Company 1952) 121.

[66] B Cheng, *General Principles of Law as Applied by International Courts and Tribunals* (Stevens 1953) 176.

[67] E Jiménez de Aréchaga: 'International Responsibility' in M Sørensen (ed.), *Manual of Public International Law* (Macmillan 1958) 560 and 'International Law in the Past Third of a Century' (1978) 159 RdC 1, 283.

[68] G Schwarzenberger, *International Law (Vol 1: International Law as Applied by International Courts and Tribunals)* (3rd edn, Stevens 1957) 615.

[69] I Brownlie, *System of the Law of Nations: State Responsibility (Part I)* (Clarendon Press 1983) 159.

[70] M Akehurst, *A Modern Introduction to International Law* (5th edn, Allen and Unwin 1984) 88–89.

[71] R Jennings and A Watts (eds), *Oppenheim's International Law*, vol 1 (9th edn, Longman 1992–6) 549.

[72] R Wolfrum, 'State Responsibility for Private Actors: An Old Problem of Renewed Relevance' in Ragazzi (n 25) 425.

and Higgins.[73] Similarly, one distinguished jurist encapsulated the contemporary construction of SR for private acts as follows:

> In the modern view the basis of state responsibility for acts of private individuals is not complicity with the perpetrator but solely failure of the state to perform its international duty of preventing the unlawful act, or failing that, to arrest the offender and bring him to justice… There is no reason then to speak of state complicity… since the state is internationally responsible not for the acts of any private individual, but for its own omission… The delinquency of the private individuals is no longer taken as a basis of state responsibility but as merely the occasion for calling into operation certain duties of the state.[74]

More relevantly, this construction gained even more traction when Roberto Ago defended it in his fourth report to the ILC in 1972.[75]

Undoubtedly, this entails a vital role for the SC in implementing SR, which may include monitoring and reacting to violations of its own resolutions and, more controversially, authorizing forcible responses to counteract breaches. Indeed, 'it turns out that the state's responsibility in the case of infringement of an international legal norm may result not only from controlling irregular units, but also from the lack of sufficient control over them, or failure to act, or negligence, including the failure to comply with the legally binding resolutions of the Council'.[76]

One cannot help but sense in this approach some resistance to the vestiges of the agency paradigm. Yet, the relaxation of agency principles in the 'wrongful act–(automatic) attribution–legal consequences' syllogism does not necessarily imply that mere acquiescence or passive support of terrorism cannot trigger a violation of the territorial State's Article 2(4) obligations. Whilst that State's responsibility is primarily triggered through the prism of indirect responsibility (ie its failure to act), its ultimate consequences may well be akin to direct SR in light of post-9/11 practice. Simply put, the failure to prevent terrorism is correlated with the State having allowed an 'armed attack' to emanate from its territory, which can sometimes be almost as severe in scope as SR based on direct State involvement in terrorism, at least in terms of attracting political opprobrium. It would be difficult to deny the existence of a new, post-9/11 SC-endorsed legal norm which essentially equates the prohibition of 'harbouring and supporting' terrorists with States' Article 2(4) commitments.

According to José Alvarez, a wide range of State passiveness—ranging from the harbouring of terrorists to the 'mere negligence in controlling such individuals'—can simultaneously trigger SR and generate a right for the injured State to respond with force.[77] Such State behaviour (ie failures to act/prevent), he argued,

[73] R Higgins, *Problems & Process: International Law and How We Use It* (OUP 1994) 153.

[74] Jiménez de Aréchaga, 'International Responsibility' (n 67) 560.

[75] See R Ago, 'Fourth Report on State Responsibility (continued)' (1972) UN Doc A/CN.4/264 and Add.1; (1972) II *YILC* 99, 124–6.

[76] J Kranz, 'The Use of Armed Force—New Facts and Trends' (2006) 3 The Polish Quarterly of International Affairs 68, 79–80.

[77] JE Alvarez, 'Hegemonic International Law Revisited' (2003) 97 AJIL 873, 879.

may be tantamount to the violation of the prescriptions enshrined in Article 2(4) of the UN Charter.[78] In the (conceptually challenging) event that a State's failure to prevent terrorism is equated with an 'armed attack' or lesser use of force, general international law seems to empower the victim-State to retaliate with force. However, short of such extreme scenarios, which, to be established, arguably require envisaging a rather tenuous legal argument and an uphill semantic climb as regards attribution, it is doubtful that armed reactions to wrongful acts would be readily permissible across the board.[79] Others seeking to bring the intersection of self-defence and SR into sharp relief have rallied behind similar arguments, suggesting that the distinction between attribution norms in both recourse to force repertoire and SR law is not as rigid as sometimes claimed. Focusing on the content of attribution being paramount in the analysis—as opposed to dwelling over its classification as a rule under the primary/secondary rubric—they expound that 'harbouring of terrorists could be construed… as an act that violates Article 2(4) of the Charter (the act of harbouring is then a part of the primary rule), or as a separate rule of attribution as part of the law of state responsibility that would link the terrorists to the state'.[80] These observations appear to align with other critical assessments of the interplay between the ARSIWA, attribution, and primary norms.[81]

Conversely, the ICJ's decision in *Nicaragua* remains very illustrative, perhaps even symptomatic, of the inherent conceptual difficulty in devising a scheme of legal accountability for failing to prevent terrorism, whilst identifying clearly delineated boundaries between use of force and SR repertoire. In short, what makes *Nicaragua* intractable under some lights is the fact that the Court was dealing with SR *for* the use of force. Granted, US involvement in the activities of the *Contras* was far more substantial than some of the other scenarios canvassed in the present study. Consequently, two conclusions may be extracted from *Nicaragua*: (i) agency remains the Court's foremost analytical linchpin in attributing private violence to States (especially in light of the 2007 *Bosnian Genocide* case); and (ii) as a corollary, it clearly assessed the contentious paramilitary activities through the prism of SR.

Similar legal reasoning illuminates one interpretation of the response to 9/11. In short, the SC had consistently condemned the use of Afghan territory for harbouring terrorists, thereby establishing a repeated violation of the obligation to

[78] Alvarez (n 77) p 879. But see A Nollkaemper, 'Attribution of Forcible Acts to States: Connections Between the Law On the Use of Force and the Law of State Responsibility' in N Blokker and N Schrijver (eds), *The Security Council and the Use of Force: Theory and Reality—A Need for Change?* (Nijhoff 2005) 133, 160. On the relationship between attribution, the prohibition of the use of force, and SR in this context, see Trapp (n 22) 28–30.

[79] See, eg, SM Villalpando, *L'Émergence de la Communauté Internationale dans la Responsabilité des États* (PUF 2005) 392.

[80] Nollkaemper (n 78) 148. See also BA Feinstein, 'A Paradigm for the Analysis of the Legality of the Use of Armed Force against Terrorists and States that Aid and Abet Them' (2004) 17 Transnational Lawyer 51, 57, 68; AA Sofaer, 'Terrorism, the Law and the National Self-Defence' (1989) 126 Military Law Review 89, 104.

[81] See, eg, Proulx (n 17).

prevent when taking into account distinct, pre-9/11 attacks in the aggregate (ie Khobar Towers in 1996, US embassies in Kenya and Tanzania in 1998, and the USS Cole in 2000). In sum, the US (backed by a host of SC resolutions) continuously maintained an adversarial posture vis-à-vis Afghanistan following the perpetration of several attacks substantially linked with Al-Qaeda, a significant contingent of which was sheltered on Afghan territory, thereby signalling a violation of that State's obligations. However, not all these attacks were similarly linked to the Afghan territory and serious consideration should also be given to the potential involvement, direct or indirect, of Iran, Saudi Arabia, and Sudan in those attacks when apportioning SR. Afghanistan's international responsibility culminated on a whole new level when it failed to prevent the 9/11 attacks. Consequently, because of that responsibility the Council seemingly approved use of force against Afghanistan in response to its wrongful act, a posture that may be seen to be analogous to a countermeasure under SR repertoire if one takes the above logic full circle.[82] Such a reading of that precedent is not completely far-fetched, nor removed from the classical debates surrounding the institutionalization of countermeasures. Indeed, the commentary accompanying ILC Draft Article 30 following the first reading espoused a liberal construction of the term 'countermeasure', which might have afforded the SC a role in implementing SR.[83]

However, similarly to the *Nicaragua* precedent, in order to make this line of argument palatable the reaction to 9/11 may have to be concomitantly sited within SR and recourse to force frameworks.[84] Implicit in this proposition is the need to rethink SR mechanics in order to address the threats of terrorism and other global security challenges adequately, and to delineate the role of use of force, if any, in the scheme of countermeasures. Unsurprisingly, some publicists categorically reject the importation of use of force elements into SR's analytical framework, thereby also discarding the ICJ's reasoning in *Nicaragua* but for entirely different reasons. For instance, Brunnée and Toope took issue with this approach, especially when invoked to justify a full-scale military invasion:

> Some modifications to the self-defence regime are nonetheless required. One necessary adjustment relates to the nature of the required link between the target State of a self-defence action and perpetrators of attacks, including terrorists. The *Nicaragua* decision of the International Court of Justice required agency, ***because it chose to assess the use of force within a framework of Sate-responsibility***. We do not believe that this is a helpful way of thinking about justifications for resort to war. Indeed, a shift away from this framework may already have taken place, if one evaluates state practice and *opinio juris* since 11 September 2001 (emphasis added).[85]

[82] Conversely, consider the argument of certain authors positing that 'the system of collective security in the U.N. is not conceived as a reaction to a violation of international law, but as a preventive tool to ensure the maintenance of peace'. See Frowein and Kirsch (n 29) 721.

[83] See (1979) II(2) *YILC* 121 [21].

[84] See, eg, MMD Banks, 'Addressing State (Ir-)Responsibility: The Use of Military Force As Self-Defense in International Counter-Terrorism Operations' (2009) 200 Military Law Review 54, 77 esp fn 122.

[85] Brunnée and Toope (n 15) 794–5. See also Brunnée (n 6) 123.

Rejecting this position would obviously entail that secondary SR rules should be revisited in order to illuminate current liability principles regarding terrorism and other global security threats.[86] Working in tandem with this objective is the notion that a new primary rule of 'harbouring and supporting' has emerged in international relations and now serves as a basis for triggering responsibility for failing to prevent terrorism in some cases.[87]

However, this line of argument must be appreciated with caution. For instance, the history of Palestinian attacks on Israeli targets, dating back to the Sinai incident and earlier, could be deemed to constitute a distinguishing factor with the US–Afghanistan precedent. On one occasion, Israel made an emotional plea before the SC, querying 'how many Israelis have to be killed by the PLO terrorists for the Council to be persuaded that the limits of our endurance have been reached?'[88] In addition, following the Qibya raid in 1953 Israel shifted from a narrow view of self-defence and 'for the first time, argued that its action was justified in the whole context of repeated theft, pillaging, border raids, sabotage and injury to Israeli property and life'.[89] Thus, when considered on its face and despite the Taliban's repeated failures to observe counterterrorism duties, US action in Afghanistan was not primarily fuelled by decades of terrorist incursions into the US, but by the 9/11 attacks.

Therefore, it appears unlikely that the US–Afghan situation might fit under a 'continuing relationship' paradigm, as inspired by Israeli–Palestinian reprisals, but should rather be subsumed under a 'single event/chain of events' model of SR implementation by the SC. Interestingly, these concerns were central in the early 1970s. One distinguished scholar called attention to the fact that the duration and nature of the relationship between the territorial State, from which terrorist attacks are launched, and the injured State might inform the SR calculus when pondering the lawfulness of forcible reactions. In this regard, he queried '[i]s the legality of the action to be determined *solely by reference to the prior illegal act* which brought it about or by reference to the *whole context of the relationship between the two states*?' (emphasis added).[90] In 1963, Rosalyn Higgins concluded that a State repeatedly injured by transborder raids authored by individuals supported by their territorial State could respond with self-defence, provided its action was 'proportionate, in nature and degree, to the *prior illegality* or the imminent attack' (emphasis added).[91] It is still unclear, on the facts of the US–Afghanistan relationship, which one of those rationales prompted the SC seemingly to authorize

[86] But D Jinks, 'State Responsibility for the Acts of Private Armed Groups' (2003) 4 CJIL 83, 84.

[87] See also Proulx (n 17). For a variety of views on the above debate, see, inter alia: Becker (n 61) 236–7; Jinks (n 86) 84–90; SR Ratner, '*Jus ad Bellum* and *Jus in Bello* after September 11' (2002) 96 AJIL 905, 908–10; Travalio and Altenburg (n 6) 102–11. See also MC Waxman, 'The Structure of Terrorism Threats and the Laws of War' (2010) 20 Duke Journal of Comparative & International Law 101, 112 (emphasizing that 'merely allowing terrorist groups to operate from one's sovereign territory should be weighed more heavily in assessing state responsibility for terrorist attacks').

[88] See SCOR (XXXVII) 2375th Meeting (5 June 1982) 4 [38], cited in Franck (n 17) 58.

[89] Bowett (n 1) 5.

[90] Bowett (n 1) 4.

[91] Higgins (n 7) 201.

an unprecedented military campaign more than three decades later, especially when all-too-familiar pleas advanced by Israel regarding transborder terrorism were routinely unsuccessful in securing similar authorization. Furthermore, the disproportionality of Israeli responses constitutes another important reason States felt compelled to condemn the Israeli reprisals, generally.[92]

By contrast, US-led action in Afghanistan not only garnered significant support from the SC but also from other high-profile international bodies. For instance, NATO supported the right to invoke collective self-defence[93] and found that the Government of Afghanistan had indeed harboured Bin Laden and Al-Qaeda.[94] The Organization of American States followed suit, recognizing the United States' inherent right to self-defence and referring to the relevant provision of the Inter-American Treaty of Reciprocal Assistance.[95] The US-led campaign also received vast support in other prominent intergovernmental bodies.[96] Hence, the initial reaction of the US to 9/11, which was described as 'rhetorically bellicose, but practically cautious'[97] in generating international legitimacy ultimately garnered support from the international community.

5.3 Conclusion: The Controversial Remedy of Forcible Countermeasures

In exploring the potential contributions of secondary norms in promoting State compliance with counterterrorism obligations, the discussion cannot elude attempts to resolve the tension between use of force principles and SR, especially when devising deterrence models aimed at eradicating transnational violence. In

[92] On the issue of proportionality of the Israeli reprisals in 1982, see Franck (n 17) 65. Moreover, the *in fine* portion of ARSIWA (n 4) Art 14(3) is couched in negative terms, which does not preclude the application of the ARSIWA to a series of terrorist attacks, such as the acts of Al-Qaeda or ISIL when taken in the aggregate. See also Proulx (n 17) section III. A).

[93] See Statement by the North Atlantic Council (12 September 2001) <http://www.nato.int/docu/pr/2001/p01-124e.htm> accessed 10 August 2015. In characterizing the attack, the Council specified that it 'was directed from abroad against the United States', thereby fitting it within what is perceived as 'international terrorism'. Based on that finding, the Council invoked Art 5 of the Washington Treaty in dealing with the armed attack. See the confirmation of 2 October 2001 by NATO of the Council's finding <http://www.nato.int/docu/update/2001/1001/e1002a.htm> accessed 20 August 2015.

[94] See Statement of Lord Robertson, NATO Secretary-General (2 October 2001) <http://www.nato.int/docu/speech/2001/s011002a.htm> accessed 12 August 2015.

[95] OAS, 'Terrorist Threat to the Americas', Resolution of the 24th Meeting of Consultation of Ministers of FA (21 September 2001) OEA/Ser.F/II.24, Doc RC.24/Res.1/01 <http://www.oas.org/OASpage/crisis/RC.24e.htm> accessed 12 August 2015.

[96] See Jinks (n 86) 90–1.

[97] SJ Toope, 'Powerful but Unpersuasive? The role of the United States in the Evolution of Customary International Law' in M Byers and G Nolte (eds), *United States Hegemony and the Foundations of International Law* (CUP 2003) 287, 291–2. Similar observations were also applied to the early stages of the 2003 Iraq war. See A Paulus, 'The War Against Iraq and the Future of International Law: Hegemony or Pluralism?' (2004) 25 MJIL 681, 719.

this author's view, the answer does not so much hinge on a simultaneous application of use of force and SR standards but rather on a careful analysis of how both regimes mutually inform and, ultimately, complement each other.[98] Interestingly, the tension between, and simultaneous application of, self-defence and SR norms were brought into relief in the ICJ's *Wall Advisory Opinion*. In the GA on 20 October 2003, Israel defended the construction of the wall by declaring that SC resolutions 'have clearly recognized the right of States to use force in self-defence against terrorist attacks', and further stated that it must 'therefore surely recognize the right to use non-forcible measures to that end'.[99] Consequently, Higgins stated that '[t]his opened the door to counsel appearing in' the *Wall Advisory Opinion* 'to fashion *their arguments on self-defence within the parameters of the law of State responsibility generally and of countermeasures specifically*' (emphasis added).[100]

The ICJ held that the scope of Article 51 and the inherent right of self-defence enshrined in the UN Charter only cover instances of armed attacks by one State against another.[101] Judge Higgins took issue with this finding in her Separate Opinion,[102] whilst the Court volunteered the following explanation: 'Israel does not claim that the attacks against it are imputable to a foreign State.'[103] Undeterred, Judge Higgins again 'doubted the pertinence—or the realism—of this observation, observing that "[t]he question is surely where responsibility lies for the sending of groups and persons who act against Israeli civilians".'[104] Other voices on the bench similarly called into question this rigid application of relevant legal principles, stating that it was time to revisit the notion that only sovereign States can author 'armed attacks' for self-defence purposes.[105] However, the ILC's historical works similarly suggest that the invocation of self-defence remains an inter-State phenomenon. During its codification project on SR, in its Commentary to Draft Article 34 the Commission opined that

> the State against which another State acts in self-defence is itself the cause of the threat to that other State. It was the first State which created the danger, and created it by conduct which is not only wrongful in international law but also constitutes the especially serious

[98] See also Nollkaemper (n 78) 133–71; S Cenic, 'State Responsibility and Self-Defence in International Law Post 9/11: Has the Scope of Article 51 of the United Nations Charter Been Widened as a Result of the US Response to 9/11?' (2007) 14 Australian International Law Journal 201.

[99] See UNGA Verbatim Record (20 October 2003) UN Doc A/ES-10/PV.21, 6.

[100] R Higgins, 'The International Court of Justice: Selected Issues of State Responsibility' in Ragazzi (n 25) 271–86.

[101] *Legal Consequences of the Construction of a Wall* (Advisory Opinion) [2004] ICJ Rep 136, [139]. Identical reasoning underscored the ICJ's judgment in *Armed Activities on the Territory of the Congo (DRC v Uganda)* (Merits) [2005] ICJ Rep 116, [146]. On the right deriving from UN Charter Art 51, see MC Alder, *The Inherent Right to Self-defence in International Law* (Springer 2013).

[102] Separate Opinion of Judge Higgins in the *Wall Advisory Opinion* (n 101) [33].

[103] *Wall Advisory Opinion* (n 101) [139].

[104] Higgins (n 100) 276–7. See also the Separate Opinion of Judge Higgins in the *Wall Advisory Opinion* (n 101) [34].

[105] See Separate Opinion of Judge Kooijmans in the *Wall Advisory Opinion* (n 101) [35]–[36] and the Declaration of Judge Buergenthal in ibid [6]. See also the Dissenting Opinion of Judge Kateka in the *Armed Activities Case* (n 101) [34] and the Dissenting Opinion of Judge Kooijmans in ibid

specific international offence of recourse to armed force in breach of the existing general prohibition on such recourse.[106]

Moreover, this general impression is reinforced by the Commentary to the ARSIWA, which states that the 'essential effect of Article 21 is to preclude the wrongfulness of conduct of a State acting in self-defence vis-à-vis an attacking State'.[107]

It may also be the case that the corpus of SR rules comes into conflict with the parameters of recourse to force, as was ostensibly the case in the *Oil Platforms* case.[108] Indeed,

> [t]he Court was thus faced with two dramatically different perspectives on the case: '[w]hereas the United States was asking the Court to judge the dispute on the basis of the law of State responsibility, Iran asked the Court to assess the legality of the United States' actions on the basis of the prohibition of the use of force and the law of self-defence.[109]

However, the Court spoke plainly to the relationship between self-defence and SR repertoire. In particular, a nexus was required between Iran's internationally wrongful conduct in the form of a violation of Article 2(4) of the UN Charter, on the one hand, and the invocation of self-defence by the US, on the other. In short, the latter's exercise was predicated on the establishment of the former (ie legitimate self-defence is adopted on the basis of a prior wrongful act violating the prohibition of the use of force in international relations).[110] Consequently, the ICJ framed the relevant question in the following terms:

> in order to establish that [the US] was legally justified in attacking the Iranian platforms in exercise of the right of individual self-defence, *the United States has to show that attacks had been made upon it for which Iran was responsible*; and that those attacks were of such a nature as to be qualified as 'armed attacks' within the meaning of that expression in Article 51 (emphasis added).[111]

Ultimately, the Court deemed that the US had failed to discharge its burden of proof in establishing Iran's responsibility, emphasizing 'that the evidence indicative of Iranian responsibility for the attack on the *Sea Isle City* [was] not sufficient

[28]. Some of the recent literature has followed suit and explored the question. See, eg, KN Trapp, 'Can Non-State Actors Mount an Armed Attack?' in M Weller (ed.), *The Oxford Handbook of the Use of Force in International Law* (OUP 2015) 679–96.

[106] ILC, 'Report of the International Law Commission on the Work of its 32nd Session' (5 May–25 July 1980) UN Doc A/35/10, 52–3 [3]. See also R Ago, 'Addendum–Eight Report on State Responsibility: The internationally Wrongful Act of the State, Source of International Responsibility (Part 1)' (1980) UN Doc A/CN.4/318/Add.5–7; (1980) II(1) *YILC* 52–4 [83]–[88].

[107] Commentary to ARSIWA (n 4) Art 21 p 75 [5].

[108] See generally *Oil Platforms (Iran v USA)* (Merits) [2003] ICJ Rep 161.

[109] P Weil and D Richemond, 'The Oil Platforms Case Before the International Court of Justice: A Non-Case of International Responsibility' in Ragazzi (n 25) 334.

[110] On the prohibition on the use of force, see O Corten, *Law against War: The Prohibition on the Use of Force in Contemporary International Law* (Hart 2010).

[111] *Oil Platforms case* (n 108) 190 [61].

to support the contentions of the United States'.[112] Nevertheless, such a standard could plausibly be fulfilled when a State egregiously fails to comply with its obligation of prevention—as was the case with Afghanistan, for instance—thereby triggering a corresponding right to invoke self-defence in the most extreme cases. One commentator fittingly encapsulated the 'invoked/established SR–self-defence' syllogism: '[t]o the extent the international community supported the U.S. military response to the September 11th attacks, I believe it did so on the understanding that a fairly classical interpretation of the doctrine of self-defense applied because the Taliban could be considered legally responsible for al Qaeda's crimes'.[113]

In summary, whilst there is some resistance to the idea that armed countermeasures may be adopted in reaction to a State's failure to prevent terrorism, the thorny relationship between use of force and the deployment of SR repertoire is, by no means, elucidated by that very fact. According to one publicist, '[w]hile a state may, in the face of violations, take measures of "self help", it appears highly doubtful under the current system of international law that these would include resort to force'.[114] However, to declare that forcible reactions are excised altogether from the scheme of SR is neither fair nor accurate. Whilst some commentators call for a loosening of the requirement that an 'armed attack' be carried out by a State to capture the conduct of non-State actors, one of this volume's contentions is that lesser forcible responses than self-defence can be envisaged in SR terms, particularly when they are adopted in relation to a wrongful act that falls short of the 'armed attack' threshold. In fact, use of force—in various increments—plays an important, albeit controversial, role in counteracting transnational terrorism, particularly when contemplated through self-defence, an issue that is addressed in Chapter 6.

[112] *Oil Platforms case* (n 108) 190 [61]. On the legal ramifications of the notion of 'armed attack' pursuant to the *Oil Platforms case*, see D Raab, '"Armed Attack" After the Oil Platforms Case' (2004) 17 LJIL 719.

[113] LN Sadat, 'Terrorism and the Rule of Law' (2004) 3 Washington University Global Studies Law Review 135, 144.

[114] Duffy (n 39) 185.

6

Please Kill Responsibly

Counteracting Global Security Violations with Force

6.1 Introduction: Next Steps in Further Defining State Responsibility

As seen in previous chapters, there is great potential for regime interaction between SR repertoire and other complementary, legal categories, not least self-defence and recourse to force repertoire. Similarly, the emergence of new controversial norms, particularly responsibility to protect (R2P), may shed interesting insights into possible SR implementation avenues and the role of UN organs in that context. As seen earlier,[1] important UN institutions have endorsed R2P, with the Security Council (SC) leading the way and demonstrating its willingness to include language that indicates expansion in States' responsibilities in its resolution-making. Surely this development could have a considerable impact on the development of SR? Indeed, the fact that both the United Nations (UN) Secretary-General and SC have endorsed this norm points to the obvious links between R2P and State sovereignty,[2] which entails an enhanced focus on responsibility models grounded in States' control over territory. This notion is highly reconcilable with the prevention of transnational terrorism and other global security violations by UN organs, which implies some role for SR law in determining, and reacting to, breaches of relevant legal obligations.

More importantly, by connecting R2P to the intervention in Libya, the SC confirmed that this norm has now been introduced into the political mainstream. Unsurprisingly, this prompted some to formulate critical appraisals of R2P in that context and question whether the intervention in Libya was congruent with international law.[3] Similarly, R2P has generated its share of critiques from States,[4] however the endorsement of this controversial, emerging norm by key UN organs

[1] Introduction to Part II.

[2] See also L Glanville, *Sovereignty and the Responsibility to Protect: A New History* (Chicago University Press 2014).

[3] See, eg, S Mohamed, 'Taking Stock of the Responsibility to Protect' (2012) 48 SJIL 63; G Ulfstein and HF Christiansen, 'The Legality of the NATO Bombing in Libya' (2013) 62 ICLQ 159.

[4] See, eg, P Qinton-Brown, 'Mapping Dissent: The Responsibility to Protect and Its State Critics' (2013) 5 GRP 260.

surely supports the proposition that SR repertoire, whose normative legitimacy and centrality in international law is not challenged, could equally play an important role in the decision-making of those organs (particularly the SC). As will be argued, some tenets of R2P could therefore be subsumed under SR repertoire in certain global security contexts. The important point for making this book's central arguments more palatable is that R2P's legitimacy and normative validity are increasingly being discussed in legal and policy circles. This reality has profound implications both for: (i) the development of viable legal regimes to address global security threats, of which the implementation of SR by UN organs forms part and parcel; and (ii) the prospect of regime change in States where the ruling class or inordinately powerful non-State actors may be contributing—either directly or indirectly—to the materialization of those threats.[5]

Building on Chapter 5, the present chapter allots considerable weight to the role of forcible responses—be they framed as self-defence, collective countermeasures, R2P-inspired initiatives, or humanitarian intervention—in the scheme of SR when reacting to State failures to prevent terrorism or other global security violations. As will be seen, the deployment of 'forcible countermeasures' often remains intimately tied to the potential implementation of SR by UN organs, particularly the SC and International Court of Justice (ICJ), thereby bringing the central arguments explored in Part II to the fore. It is to be hoped that the ensuing analysis will facilitate the formulation of more general conclusions for global security. With this in mind, the chapter concludes by laying down the foundations of a research and policy prospectus by identifying general guidelines or building blocks from which future explorations of the topic may draw inspiration.

6.2 The Role of Self-defence in the Law of State Responsibility: The Counterterrorism Context

This section first explores self-defence as a countermeasure before framing it within the scheme of collective responses. Ultimately, it will canvass the more problematic aspects of invoking force in response to internationally wrongful acts and shed light on the establishment of SR as a predicate for justifying resort to self-defence.

6.2.1 Self-defence as a countermeasure

As seen earlier, it is not entirely accurate or legally sound to displace use of force repertoire from the purview of SR law completely. There is certainly strong academic support for the proposition that self-defence, or some degree of force, may

[5] See broadly N McMillan and D Mickler, 'From Sudan to Syria: Locating "Regime Change" in R2P and the ICC' (2013) 5 GRP 283; M-E Loiselle, 'The Normative Status of the Responsibility to Protect after Libya' in ibid 317.

be directed towards States that failed to prevent terrorist strikes emanating from their territory.[6] Obviously, there seems to be stronger consensus for the idea that when a State knowingly and/or intentionally allows its territory to be used as a launch pad for terrorists, thereby endangering third States, it not only subjects itself to SR's discipline but could also become the target of an armed intervention in self-defence.[7] However, the case for a construction of legal liability that accords a greater role to self-defence under international law is probably easier to frame within the scope of 'international responsibility'—which is ostensibly broader than the field of *State* responsibility—as it encompasses all international legal persons (eg States, international organizations (IOs), natural persons in certain circumstances, other entities, etc). Indeed, some publicists emphasized that the secondary norms flowing from the violation of primary obligations under this broader rubric of 'international responsibility'

> are remedial rights and obligations, including those arising from self-defence, reprisal and humanitarian intervention, for example, which involve the direct exercise of preventive rights by the relevant international person without the intervention of third party settlement, such as by a court or tribunal, or of a negotiated arrangement between the parties involved in the violation of primary rights and obligations.[8]

Nevertheless, there is certainly sound legal basis for extending this rationale to the narrower field of SR.[9]

For instance, Thomas Franck discussed SC Resolution 1368 and inferred that it unequivocally 'confirm[ed] the right of victim states to treat terrorism as an armed attack and those that facilitate or harbour terrorists as armed attackers against whom, subject to the UN Charter and international law, military force may be used in self-defense'.[10] In examining the scope of the use of force against State failures to prevent terrorism, an exercise almost invariably couched in self-defence language and logic by injured States, he concluded that such response was tantamount to '*taking lawful countermeasures* against subversion and direct or indirect intervention or aggression' (emphasis added).[11] Otherwise put, there appears to be some degree of overlap between use of force repertoire and SR law as regards victim-States' invocation of self-defence.

Indeed, Professor Franck clearly framed such responses within the scope of SR repertoire. However, he acknowledged, though almost fifteen years ago, that the prospect of victim-States adopting armed countermeasures was particularly controversial, especially when directed at what he termed 'indirect attacks', a notion highly reconcilable with the shift to indirect SR for terrorism identified in Section

[6] See, eg, Introduction to Part III, esp n 11 and accompanying text.

[7] See, eg, R Värk, 'State Responsibility for Private Armed Groups in the Context of Terrorism' (2006) 11 Juridica International 184, 193.

[8] CF Amerasinghe, 'The Essence of the Structure of International Responsibility' in M Ragazzi (ed.), *International Responsibility Today: Essays in Memory of Oscar Schachter* (Brill 2005) 3, 6.

[9] Amerasinghe (n 8) 6 fn 7.

[10] TM Franck, *Recourse to Force: State Action Against Threats and Armed Attacks* (CUP 2002) 54.

[11] Franck (n 10) 54.

5.2.4.[12] The ARSIWA do not provide any textual exegesis proscribing the adoption of self-defence (ie it is actually one of the circumstances precluding wrongfulness, enshrined in Article 21),[13] therefore seemingly accommodating the exceptional regime contained in Article 51 of the UN Charter as a response to wrongful acts. In the light of Part II, this also signals that UN organs may become involved in ascertaining the legitimacy of such armed countermeasures. This conclusion is crucial insofar as it signals that the SC could be involved in applying secondary rules of responsibility should self-defence qualify as a lawful response to wrongful acts such as failures to prevent terrorism or other global security breaches. In that regard, Franck's remarks seem apposite:

> Although the International Law Commission has now spoken on countermeasures, the legality of recourse to force, especially against indirect attacks, remains controversial. Article 50 of the Commission's text on State Responsibility provides that countermeasures 'shall not affect ... [t]he obligation to refrain from the threat or use of force as embodied in the Charter of the United Nations.' It does not, however, try to specify the content of that obligation which, in turn, is determined by reference to the Charter's text and, by extension, to case-by-case institutional practice affecting that text's interpretation. Evidently, much depends upon the text and practice pertaining to the meaning of 'armed attack' in Article 51. Equally evident is the fact that practice has expanded significantly the meaning of that concept.[14]

Consequently, there is no principled reason to exclude self-defence from the ambit of the ARSIWA; in fact, it is expressly incorporated as permissible conduct in response to internationally wrongful acts. Whether the parameters and contours of the invocation of self-defence can be cogently identified and articulated in international law (especially in response to transnational terrorism) is an altogether different debate, one that is likely to continue. Moreover, the ARSIWA do not in any way limit States' ability to adopt SC-sanctioned measures by virtue of a resolution under Chapter VII.[15] Equally relevant but controversial is the idea that in addition to the directly injured State's potential recourse to force in response to another State's failure to prevent terrorism, third States could potentially (or mandatorily) intervene by using force to bring the violation to an end. The extant SR scheme remains arguably flawed in such circumstances, especially given the challenges associated with institutionalizing the implementation of SR law through the SC,[16] thereby signalling that additional safeguards need to

[12] See also generally V-J Proulx, *Transnational Terrorism and State Accountability: A New Theory of Prevention* (Hart 2012).

[13] Articles on the Responsibility of States for Internationally Wrongful Acts, UN Doc A/56/10 (2001); (2001) II(2) *YILC* 26 (and Commentary ibid 31), Art 21 provides that '[t]he wrongfulness of an act a State is precluded if the act constitutes a lawful measure of self-defence taken in conformity with the Charter of the United Nations'. For a pre-ARSIWA account on this question, see GM Badr, 'The Exculpatory Effect of Self-Defence in State Responsibility' (1980) 10 Georgia Journal of International and Comparative Law 1.

[14] Franck (n 10) 54–5.

[15] See also H Duffy, *The 'War on Terror' and the Framework of International Law* (CUP 2005) 60.

[16] For a detailed discussion, see Part II of the present book and the authorities examined therein.

be developed to prevent wanton or disproportionate countermeasures by third States.[17] Nevertheless, it is useful to query whether such reaction could be framed within collective response schemes.

6.2.2 Bypassing the Security Council: Parallel collective (counter) measures and their limits

Should the obligation to prevent terrorism be elevated to the ranks of obligations *erga omnes*, third States may perhaps have standing to intervene pursuant to SR law and/or R2P;[18] at the very least, such States may be able to demand cessation of the internationally wrongful behaviour, request assurances of non-repetition, and set in motion the mechanism of reparation (either for the benefit of the injured State or for the broader community of States to which the obligation is owed).[19] After all, even under UN auspices, enforcement actions are increasingly 'not entrusted to ... genuine U.N. military operation[s] but rather to ... specific groups of States'.[20] To subsume the failure to prevent terrorism under the rubric of R2P, however, the relevant violation would presumably have to occur on the same level as the failure to prevent large-scale humanitarian crises or human rights abuses, quite a challenging prospect absent repeated patterns of egregious, systematic, and large-scale transnational terrorist strikes emanating from a specific State. However, in the eventuality that R2P logic could nonetheless extend to a State's failure to prevent terrorism, it would not only trigger its international responsibility for failing to protect its own population but also engender an obligation *erga omnes* on third States to intervene and bring the wrongful act(s) to an end.[21] More controversially, should a State's violation of its obligation to prevent be cast as a grave and systematic breach of a *jus cogens* engagement[22]—and, as a legal and

[17] See, eg, M Dawidowicz, 'Public Law Enforcement without Public Law Safeguards? An Analysis of State Practice on Third-Party Countermeasures and their Relationship to the UN Security Council' (2006) 77 BYIL 333.

[18] On R2P and its (potential) impact on international law, see, eg, A Bellamy *et al.* (eds), *The Responsibility to Protect and International Law* (Nijhoff 2010); E Newman, 'R2P: Implications for World Order' (2013) 5 GRP 235.

[19] ARSIWA (n 13) Art 48.

[20] M Bothe, 'Peace-Keeping' in B Simma *et al.* (eds), *The United Nations Charter: A Commentary* (2nd edn, OUP 2002) 660, 664, 698–700. See also A Pellet, 'Bruno Simma Al. Eds., The Charter of the United Nations: A Commentary of Bruno Simma's Commentary' (2003) 25 MJIL 135, 148 (finding the legality of such endeavours 'hardly debatable').

[21] See, eg, J Brunnée and SJ Toope, 'Norms, Institutions and UN Reform: The Responsibility to Protect' (2005) 2 JILIR 121, 128 (applying this rationale to the situation that was prevalent in Sudan).

[22] Whilst the international community still needs to clarify the concept of *jus cogens*, some commentators have gone as far as arguing that the obligation to prevent terrorism qualifies as an infraction falling under that rubric. See, eg, P-M Dupuy, 'State Sponsors of Terrorism: Issues of International Responsibility' in A Bianchi (ed.), *Enforcing International Law Norms against Terrorism* (Hart 2004) 3, 12, 15 (citing Art 33 of Geneva Convention IV, along with provisions of the Statute of the International Criminal Tribunal for Rwanda and of the Rome Statute, but noting at 12 fn 29 that '[t]he specific definition of this phrase still needs to be agreed upon by States'). See also J-C Martin, *Les Règles Internationales Relatives à la Lutte contre le Terrorisme* (Bruylant 2006) 463–4. But see ibid 491 (concluding that the prohibition on supporting terrorism does not qualify

political matter, it would prove difficult for a State to conventionally contract out of, or derogate from, its counterterrorism obligations[23]—third States would not only have standing to intervene but could actually be obliged to cooperate with a view to bringing the breach to an end.[24]

Whether cooperation in such instances should (or could) be institutionalized poses significant challenges in light of the regime laid down by ARSIWA Articles 40 and 41; this is particularly so as regards possible SC involvement to ascertain the legality of countermeasures, including self-defence, in response to terrorism or other global security violations.[25] More problematically, the prospect of States adopting forcible collective countermeasures and bypassing SC authority raises challenging legal dilemmas. Chief amongst competing legal controversies is the question of whether the prior establishment of the wrongdoing State's international responsibility serves as a predicate to enable responding States to coalesce around a response that would normally violate international law: in this instance, by bypassing SC authority to vet collective use of force and appropriating forcible means to target the responsible State. Setting aside the potential political (or moral) legitimacy of such a collective response, particularly in circumstances warranting intervention in the absence of multilateral institutional support, the resulting behaviour remains highly paradoxical: a group of States adopt forcible

as a *jus cogens* obligation). Other commentators express divergent views on whether State sponsorship of terrorism is encompassed under the heading of *jus cogens*. See, eg, WP Hoye, 'Fighting Fire With…Mire? Civil Remedies and the New War on State-Sponsored Terrorism' (2002) 12 Duke Journal of Comparative & International Law 105, 111; GF Intoccia, 'American Bombing of Libya: An International Legal Analysis' (1987) 19 CWJIL 177, 192–3. For a study on the concept, see T Weatherall, *Jus Cogens: International Law and Social Contract* (CUP 2015).

[23] Vienna Convention on the Law of Treaties (adopted 23 May 1969, entered into force 27 January 1980) 1155 UNTS 331; (1980) 8 ILM 679, Art 53 is particularly clear on this question:

> [a] treaty is void if, at the time of its conclusion, it conflicts with a peremptory norm of general international law. For the purposes of the present Convention, a peremptory norm of general international law is a norm accepted and recognized by the international community of States as a whole as a norm from which no derogation is permitted and which can be modified only by a subsequent norm of general international law having the same character.

As a corollary, the idea that *jus cogens* duties may invalidate not only treaty-based obligations, but also SC resolutions and all other legal acts, also flows from the ARSIWA. See, eg, M Ajevski, 'Serious Breaches, the Draft Articles on State Responsibility and Universal Jurisdiction' (2008) 2 European Journal of Legal Studies 12, 36–7.

[24] See ARSIWA (n 13) Arts 40–1; Section 4.4.6.

[25] For a variety of views, see Separate Opinions of Judge Kooijmans in *Legal Consequences of the Construction of a Wall* (Advisory Opinion) [2004] ICJ Rep 136, 231–2 [40]–[44] and Judge Higgins in ibid [37]; V Gowlland-Debbas, 'Security Council Enforcement Action and Issues of State Responsibility' (1994) 43 ICLQ 55, 58, 61; JR Crawford, *International Law Commission's Articles on State Responsibility: Introduction, Text and Commentaries* (CUP 2002) 249; A Gattini, 'A Return Ticket to "Communitarisme", Please' (2002) 13 EJIL 1181, 1186–7; G Gaja, 'Do States Have a Duty to Ensure Compliance with Obligations *Erga Omnes* by Other States?' in Ragazzi (n 8) 34; C Tomuschat, 'International Crimes by States: An Endangered Species?' in K Wellens (ed.), *International Law: Theory and Practice: Essays in Honour of Eric Suy* (Nijhoff 1998) 253, 259; B Stern, 'A Plea for 'Reconstruction' of International Responsibility Based on the Notion of Legal Injury' in Ragazzi (n 8) 95–6. For further discussion on ARSIWA Arts 40–1, see Section 4.4.6.

measures in a manner contrary to international law (ie bypassing the SC) to counteract a wrongdoing State's own illegal conduct (eg failure to prevent mass atrocity or large-scale/repeated terrorism). Thus, those States would again resort to illegality to combat illegality.

As seen in Chapter 4, this is the very essence of the concept of 'countermeasure' under SR repertoire, at least in principle. In short, upon suffering injury stemming from the unlawful conduct of a responsible State, the injured State suspends its compliance with an obligation owed to the wrongdoing State to bring that State's behaviour into conformity with international law. This application of the principles of reciprocity or 'reciprocal advantage', which for some amount to 'quintessentially rationalist concepts' and 'lie at the root of legal obligation',[26] animates much of the ARSIWA. Nevertheless, contemporaneous international legal developments have tempered these conceptions of reciprocity in respect of the deployment of countermeasures under SR repertoire. For one thing, the ARSIWA appear to vest the unilateral appreciation, and ultimate adoption, of countermeasures with injured States, as opposed to prescribing institutionalized enforcement procedures to implement SR (whether through mandatory prior dispute settlement procedures and/or involvement of UN political organs) expressly. However, as discussed in Part II, the default inter-State implementation model under the ARSIWA by no means precludes the potential involvement of international institutions in implementing SR, particularly the SC and ICJ.

Another relevant development resides in the ILC's shift to a system of non-forcible countermeasures in its finalized text.[27] Simply put, originally an injured State could resort to force to induce a responsible State to comply with its international obligations or redress the harm it suffered as a result of the latter's unlawful behaviour. As such, '[b]elligerent reprisals [were] construed properly as forming part of rules on State responsibility'[28] although it is increasingly questionable

[26] J Brunnée and SJ Toope, 'Persuasion and Enforcement: Explaining Compliance with International Law' (2002) 13 FYIL 273, 279. See also R Higgins, *Problems & Process: International Law and How We Use It* (OUP 1994) 16.

[27] Indeed, modern SR repertoire envisages the deployment of peaceful, non-forcible countermeasures. See *Air Services Agreement of 27 March 1946 (US v France)* (1978) 54 ILR 303, 337; *Corfu Channel Case (UK v Albania)* (Merits) [1949] ICJ Rep 4, 35; *Military and Paramilitary Activities in and against Nicaragua (Nicaragua v USA)* (Merits) [1986] ICJ Rep 14, 127 [249]; *Legality of the Threat or Use of Nuclear Weapons* (Advisory Opinion) [1996] ICJ Rep 226, 246 ('armed reprisals in time of peace... are considered to be unlawful'); *Guyana v Suriname* (2008) 47 ILM 164 [446] (also citing ARSIWA Art 50(1)(a)). See also JR Crawford, *State Responsibility: The General Part* (CUP 2013) 691; B Simma, 'NATO, the UN and the Use of Force: Legal Aspects' (1999) 10 EJIL 1, 2; J Brunnée and SJ Toope, 'The Use of Force: International Law after Iraq' (2004) 53 ICLQ 785, 794–5 (rejecting the ICJ's requirement of agency in *Nicaragua* 'because it chose to assess the use of force within a framework of State-responsibility'); J Brunnée, 'The Security Council and Self-Defence: Which Way to Global Security?' in N Blokker and N Schrijver (eds), *The Security Council and the Use of Force: Theory and Reality—A Need for Change?* (Nijhoff 2005) 107, 123; V Gowlland-Debbas, 'The Limits of Unilateral Enforcement of Community Objectives in the Framework of UN Peace Maintenance' (2003) 11 EJIL 361, 363.

[28] R Provost, *International Human Rights and Humanitarian Law* (CUP 2002) 188. On armed reprisals in the Israeli-Arab context, see DW Bowett, 'Reprisals Involving Recourse to Armed Force' (1972) 66 AJIL 1. On armed reprisals generally, see C Greenwood, 'The Twilight of the Law of Belligerent Reprisals' (1989) 20 NYIL 35.

whether the concept of 'reprisal'—which was subsumed to a large extent under the rubric of 'countermeasures' in ARSIWA Articles 49–53—remains an integral component of reciprocity in international relations.[29] Unsurprisingly, some scholars equate armed reprisals, once perceived as legitimate and even lawful means to enforce international law, with one of the most 'primitive' features of the 'early' international legal system.[30]

However, when the SC fails to authorize States to resort to military force to quell or prevent mass atrocities—a scenario which could also arise in the context of repeated failures to prevent terrorism or other global security violations—the legal analysis veers towards a conceptual grey area. Such scenarios may result in unauthorized humanitarian intervention by a State or group of States, given that international law prescribed a morally difficult course of action regarding the initial internationally wrongful act: doing nothing, at least nothing *helpful*. Advocating against a policy of 'looking the other way', some publicists subordinate legal considerations to the principles of morality or legitimacy, opining that the international community could excuse or justify unlawful interventions in instances where there is no SC authorization.[31] Others condemn humanitarian intervention on the basis that such a response finds no grounding in both UN Charter and State practice, and may led to undesirable, bad faith interventionism outside the UN system of collective security.[32] A third, more nuanced position, resists the first two by equating several equitable principles with 'general principles of law recognised by civilised nations' in order to craft an equitable framework for humanitarian intervention. On this view, these 'general principles' referred to in Article 38 of the ICJ Statute, which constitute one of international law's three major sources, would justify framing queries pertaining to humanitarian intervention in legal terms, as opposed to presenting the more traditional choice between law and morality.[33]

Irrespective of the resolution of this debate, an overly permissive stance in this regard might significantly undermine the (seemingly sacrosanct) principle of sovereign equality of States. Furthermore, such inclination might also undermine the notion that only common interests may justify recourse to military intervention to counteract global security threats. These concerns undoubtedly prompted

[29] For an early take on this question, see B Simma, 'Reflections on Article 60 of the Vienna Convention on the Law of Treaties and Its Background in General International Law' (1970) 20 Österreichische Zeitschrift für Öffentliches Recht 5, 19–22.

[30] See, eg, AA Cançado Trindade, 'Complementarity between State Responsibility and Individual Responsibility and Individual Responsibility for Grave Violations of Human Rights: The Crime of State Revisited' in Ragazzi (n 8) 263.

[31] See generally R Higgins, 'International Law and the Avoidance, Containment and Resolution of Disputes' (1991) 230 RdC 313; D Fassin and M Pandolfi (eds), *Contemporary States of Emergency: The Politics of Military and Humanitarian Interventions* (Zone Books 2010); T Nardin, 'The Moral Basis of Humanitarian Intervention' (2002) 16 Ethics & International Affairs 57.

[32] See, eg, S Chesterman, *Just War or Just Peace? Humanitarian Intervention in International Law* (OUP 2001); C Focarelli, 'The Responsibility to Protect Doctrine and Humanitarian Intervention: Too Many Ambiguities for a Working Doctrine' (2008) 13 JCSL 191.

[33] See C Burke, *An Equitable Framework for Humanitarian Intervention* (Hart 2013).

some publicists to caution that a more rigorous framework for assessing recourse to force resulting from unauthorized humanitarian intervention should be envisaged so as to avoid a blanket international legal policy of 'looking the other way'.[34] Similar views were advanced regarding humanitarian intervention directed against States that support or harbour terrorists, with commentators calling for 'strict legal regulation' to govern this type of military measure.[35] Otherwise put, the widespread view that unauthorized humanitarian intervention ineluctably pits the choice of electing war to protect human rights against that of safeguarding State sovereignty might indeed rest upon a false dichotomy. Rather, those commentators argue, policy-makers should be compelled to consider alternative courses of action to military intervention when counteracting grave human rights violations or other global security breaches.[36] Before delving deeper into this line of analysis, however, it must be acknowledged that SC involvement in—and, ultimately, oversight over—any collective forcible measure(s) remains the preferred model amongst available responses to global security challenges. After all, the centrality of the SC's role in applying and preserving the integrity of the use of force regime should not be set aside lightly.[37] This role is particularly vital in responding to transnational terrorism, for instance,[38] which can no doubt elicit overreaction—both in domestic policy and in countermeasures adopted by UN organs or injured States—or unchecked unilateralism.

The legal and political dimensions surrounding the Kosovo campaign have unquestionably paved the way for further inquiries into the possible emergence of an exception based on humanitarian intervention.[39] Indeed, the literature is as rich as it is voluminous in pondering whether that precedent carved out such a free-standing legal exception, along 'illegal but legitimate' lines, perhaps even consecrated by customary international law.[40] Moreover, this line of inquiry has generated further

[34] See, eg, S Mohamed, 'Restructuring the Debate on Unauthorized Humanitarian Intervention' (2011) 88 North Carolina Law Review 1275.

[35] See TV Ádány, 'Humanitarian Intervention against States Supporting Terrorism' (2002) 1 European Integration Studies 75.

[36] See, eg, Ádány (n 35).

[37] See generally C Henderson, 'The Centrality of the United Nations Security Council in the Legal Regime Governing the Use of Force' in ND White (ed.), *Research Handbook on International Conflict and Security Law: 'Jus ad Bellum, Jus in Bello,' and 'Jus Post Bellum'* (Edward Elgar 2013) 120–69. Similarly, the SC's role in the context of recourse to force against terrorists also warrants scholarly attention. See, eg, SM Wood, 'The Role of the UN Security Council in Relation to the Use of Force against Terrorists' in L van den Herik and N Schrijver (eds), *Counter-Terrorism Strategies in a Fragmented International Legal Order: Meeting the Challenges* (CUP 2013) 317–33.

[38] See, eg, Wood (n 37) 317–33.

[39] See, eg, Simma (n 27) esp 10; A Cassese, '*Ex Iniuria Ius Oritur:* Are We Moving Towards International Legitimation of Forcible Humanitarian Countermeasures in the World Community?' (1999) 10 EJIL 23; 'Editorial Comments: NATO's Kosovo Intervention' (1999) 93 AJIL 824–62 (including contributions by Henkin, Wedgwood, Charney, Chinkin, Falk, Franck, and Reisman); M Kohen, 'L'Emploi de la Force et la Crise du Kosovo: Vers un Nouveau Désordre Juridique International' in C-A Morand (ed.), *La Crise des Balkans de 1999: Les Dimensions Historiques, Politiques et Juridiques du Conflit du Kosovo* (Bruylant 2000) 139–66; P Hilpold, 'Humanitarian Intervention: Is There a Need for a Legal Reappraisal' (2001) 12 EJIL 437.

[40] In addition to the sources cited in n 39, see also JL Holzgreve and R Keohane (eds), *Humanitarian Intervention: Ethical, Legal and Political Dilemmas* (CUP 2003); Chesterman (n 32);

scholarly investigations on related questions, particularly in respect of the precise role that the North Atlantic Treaty Organization (NATO) should fulfil on the international plane, along with the risk that its perception of morally justified forcible interventions may, in fact, engender undesirable imperialistic consequences.[41]

Borrowing from the 'action–reaction' dichotomy, States witnessing humanitarian crises and human rights abuses going unanswered at the international institutional level might increasingly feel compelled to take matters into their own hands and stamp out impunity. Consequently, customary international law might well develop to favour a rule supporting humanitarian intervention, an eventuality that should be counteracted by SC practice according to some.[42] Whilst it might prove difficult, in many cases, to posit an analogy between a territorial State's repeated and egregious violation of the obligation to prevent terrorism and an all-out humanitarian crisis,[43] the collective imposition of forcible countermeasures in parallel to SC decision-making might be more propitiously couched in R2P logic.

Indeed, in some regards R2P strays away from the UN Charter framework and, therefore, opens up the debate as to the place of collective enforcement initiatives falling outside the ambit of the SC's sphere of operations and influence.[44] Building on R2P's rationale, some advocate in a more radical direction. For instance, Anne-Marie Slaughter and Lee Feinstein advocated a model under which the SC's process could be circumvented in favour of collective forcible measures relating to arms control and, potentially, in other circumstances as well, the scope of which could arguably involve large-scale and continuous terrorist strikes emanating from a specific State.[45] Interestingly, their 'duty to prevent' certainly seems congruent

A Cassese, 'Follow-up: Forcible Humanitarian Countermeasures and *Opinio Necessitatis*' (1999) 10 EJIL 791; D Kritsiotis, 'The Kosovo Crisis and NATO's Application of Armed Force against the Federal Republic of Yugoslavia' (2000) 49 ICLQ 330; ND White, 'The Legality of Bombing in the Name of Humanity' (2000) 5 JCSL 27.

[41] See, eg, AP Rubin, 'Review Essay: The Independent International Commission on Kosovo: Kosovo Report' (2001) 6 JCSL 147, 152. See also generally A Orford, *Reading Humanitarian Intervention: Human Rights and the Use of Force in International Law* (CUP 2008).

[42] See, eg, A Randelzhofer, 'Article 51' in Simma *et al.* (n 20) 832.

[43] On the relationship between the concept of 'necessity', humanitarian intervention, and counter-terrorism, see I Johnstone, 'The Plea of "Necessity" in International Legal Discourse: Humanitarian Intervention and Counter-terrorism' (2005) 43 CJTL 337.

[44] Specifically, the R2P Doctrine offers at least one considerable exception to the UN framework in the following terms:

> E. If the Security Council rejects a proposal or fails to deal with it in a reasonable time, alternative options are:
> I. consideration of the matter by the General Assembly in Emergency Special Session under the 'Uniting for Peace' procedure; and
> II. action within are a of jurisdiction by regional or sub-regional organizations under chapter VIII of the Charter, subject to their seeking *subsequent* authorization from the Security Council (emphasis added).

See ICISS, *The Responsibility to Protect: Report of the International Commission on Intervention and State Sovereignty* (International Development Research Centre 2001) xiii. See also ME O'Connell, *The Power and Purpose of International Law: Insights from the Theory and Practice of Enforcement* (OUP 2008) 225–7.

[45] A-M Slaughter and L Feinstein, 'A Duty to Prevent' (2004) 83 FA 136, 137, 148–9.

with other suggested applications of R2P, most relevantly as a basis for justifying the orchestration of pre-emptive assaults against suspected terrorist targets.[46] Indeed, other scholarly advances similarly outlined the potential linkages between recourse to force and non-proliferation,[47] which take on a particularly significant meaning in an era of biological arms, weapons of mass destruction (WMDs), and other related global security risks. However, this model fails to shed light on how, exactly, the duty to prevent would remain coextensive and consistent with both the UN Charter and the SC's decision-making process; or how the integrity of that organ's authority would be preserved should States adopt collective countermeasures outside the UN framework. Interestingly, other scholarly voices have simply suggested that other organizations take the lead and effectively supplant the SC's authority in vetting the use of force.[48]

In both proposals advanced above, NATO, for example, could become a 'self-authorizing body' and hypothetically attempt to counteract the violation of a State's obligation to prevent terrorism (or other global security violations) with force.[49] Undoubtedly concerned by the potential circumvention of UN organs in authorizing force, Oscar Schachter expressed his preference that any humanitarian rescue operation be given the SC's blessing or, alternatively, the GA's approval. When such a prospect proves illusory, he inferred that 'in the absence of such prior approval, a State or group of States using force to put an end to atrocities when the necessity is evident and the humanitarian intention is clear is likely to have its action pardoned'.[50] Thankfully, these concerns are not completely absent from the International Commission on Intervention and State Sovereignty's Report. Indeed, the Commission (ICISS) acknowledged that ad hoc coalitions and individual States undertaking military intervention without having secured prior SC or GA support—thereby bypassing the intercession of the UN machinery to authorize force—was not a credible course of action. Even if one attempts to justify such loose coalitions and ad hoc arrangements by enlisting support from the precedent of the Kosovo bombing campaign, which has been widely hailed as potentially unlawful but nonetheless legitimate, such unconventional forcible responses are adopted within the narrow confines of the most extreme and exceptional cases (and would, in any event, require SC approval before or after the fact).[51] Consequently, when endorsing R2P as an emerging international legal norm, the UN Secretary-General emphasized that the responsibility to protect

46 See I Daalder and J Steinberg, 'Preventive War: A Useful Tool' *LA Times* (Los Angeles, 4 December 2005) M3.

47 See, eg, C Gray, 'The Use of Force to Prevent the Proliferation of Nuclear Weapons' (2009) 52 Japanese Yearbook of International Law 101.

48 See, eg, MJ Glennon, 'The New Interventionism: The Search for a Just International Law' (May/June 1999) 78 FA 2.

49 This language is borrowed from O'Connell (n 44) 227.

50 O Schachter, *International Law in Theory and Practice* (Nijhoff 1991) 126.

51 See *R2P Document* (n 44) 31 ff. In light of the ideas advanced above, see also ibid 54 [6.36]. For legal analyses on Kosovo, see C Tomuschat (ed.), *Kosovo and the International Community: A Legal Assessment* (Kluwer 2002).

lies first and foremost with individual States.[52] It is only when States fail to comply with their international engagements that the international community may fill the void and respond with diplomatic, humanitarian, or other means to protect the target populations.[53] In many ways, this logic mirrors the arguments advanced in Part II in that when the default SR implementation model (ie unilateral enforcement by injured States) fails, implementation by the SC should follow.

When framed within the scope of SR repertoire, these ambitious proposals appear predicated on the idea that the prohibition of the use of force in international relations constitutes a peremptory norm, and therefore strives to ensure the maintenance of international peace.[54] Yet, according to the rich body of work invoked earlier, the rigid reigns governing that prohibition should be loosened to benefit the observance of both primary and secondary norms pertaining to the protection of equally important collective interests (eg self-determination, the protection of fundamental human rights, etc).[55] To make this argument more palatable, one could argue that responding with a forcible countermeasure is, in certain circumstances, the only way to strike the required balance between the prohibition of the use of force and upholding those equally important collective interests effectively.

Aside from the fact that the failure to prevent terrorism can hardly be considered analogous to massive human rights violations or reconciled with the objective of protecting self-determination across the board, a more tangible objection to this course of action stems from the ILC's own work on SR. For instance, a victim-State or a group of States responding with force to the breach of another State's global security obligations could potentially seek to absolve their own wrongful conduct (ie the violation of the prohibition of the use of force) by invoking a plea of necessity and/or military necessity.[56] Whilst this logic has been brandished

[52] It follows that '[u]nlike domestic terrorism, international terrorism targets foreign subjects, takes place in foreign States, or attempts to affect foreign political policy. Most importantly, as compared to domestic terrorism, international terrorism often involves the support of States'. See SE Smith, 'International Law: Blaming Big Brother: Holding States Accountable for the Devastation of Terrorism' (2003) 56 Oklahoma Law Review 735, 741. See also generally LCMF Lohr, 'Legal Analysis of U.S. Military Responses to State-Sponsored International Terrorism' (1985) 34 Naval Law Review 1, 5; E Gross, 'The Laws of War Waged between Democratic States and Terrorist Organizations: Real or Illusive?' (2003) 15 Florida Journal of International Law 389, 444. Conversely, this conclusion does not, in any way, preclude the possibility of other international legal considerations governing State failures to contain national threats within strictly domestic boundaries. For example, the potential extension of SR-related concerns of protection—articulated through the prism of R2P—acquired traction in international policy circles towards a shared understanding that Sri Lanka should better thwart the activities of the Tamil Tigers. See, eg, P Gunewardene, 'Only a Mission to Crush Terrorism' *Daily News* (Colombo, 24 March 2008) <http://archives.dailynews.lk/2008/03/24/fea02.asp> accessed 20 August 2015.

[53] See Report of the Secretary-General, 'In larger freedom: towards development, security and human rights for all' (2005) UN Doc A/59/2005, 35 [135].

[54] But see JA Green, 'Questioning the Peremptory Status of the Prohibition of the Use of Force' (2011) 32 MJIL 215.

[55] See, eg, SM Villalpando, *L'Émergence de la Communauté Internationale dans la Responsabilité des États* (PUF 2005) 398; Gattini (n 25) 1194–5.

[56] ARSIWA (n 13) Art 25 provides the following:

in the past, most notably by Belgium in 1960 to justify its military interference in the Congo,[57] the ILC nonetheless suggested that the realm of primary obligations regiments these issues.[58] In its Commentary to ARSIWA Article 25, it declared that

> the plea of necessity is not intended to cover conduct which is in principle regulated by the primary obligations. This has a particular importance in relation to the rules relating to the use of force in international relations and to the question of 'military necessity' ... [t]he question whether measures of forcible humanitarian intervention, not sanctioned pursuant to Chapters VII or VIII of the Charter of the United Nations, may be lawful under modern international law is not covered by article 25.[59]

Hence, the prospect of invoking necessity as a means to justify a forcible countermeasure adopted outside the UN framework against a State failing to prevent a global security violation such as terrorism is considerably hindered by the ILC's own pronouncement on necessity. Conversely, the notion of 'necessity' should not be excised altogether from the thought process governing the determination of potential countermeasures in response to internationally wrongful acts, just not in its current codified form but rather with a few adjustments for the purposes of adapting self-defence to SR. Otherwise put, if self-defence were ever to be contemplated as a potential countermeasure against the failure to prevent terrorism, it could presumably only be instituted in the face of an imminent and serious danger or peril. Thus, the victim-State would have to demonstrate that the territorial

1. Necessity may not be invoked by a State as a ground for precluding the wrongfulness of an act not in conformity with an international obligation of that State unless the act:
   (a) is the only way for the State to safeguard an essential interest against a grave and imminent peril; and
   (b) does not seriously impair an essential interest of the State or States towards which the obligation exists, or of the international community as a whole.
2. In any case, necessity may not be invoked by a State as a ground for precluding wrongfulness if:
   (a) the international obligation in question excludes the possibility of invoking necessity; or
   (b) the State has contributed to the situation of necessity.

On the contents of Art 25, see RD Sloane, 'On the Use and Abuse of Necessity in the Law of State Responsibility' (2012) 106 AJIL 447.

[57] This issue was discussed in the SC without framing the stakes involved as a matter of necessity. See UNSC Verbatim Records (13–14 July 1960) UN Doc S/PV/873 [144], [182], [192]; (20–21 July 1960) UN Doc S/PV/877 [31] ff, [142]; (21 July 1960) UN Doc S/PV/878 [23], [65]; (21–22 July 1960) UN Doc S/PV/879 [80] ff, [118], [151].

[58] See also generally C De Visscher, 'Les Lois de la Guerre et la Théorie de la Nécessité' (1917) 24 RGDIP 74; NCH Dunbar, 'Military Necessity in War Crimes Trials' (1952) 29 BYIL 442; C Greenwood, 'Historical Development and Legal Basis' in D Fleck (ed.), *The Handbook of Humanitarian Law in Armed Conflicts* (OUP 1995) 1, 30–3; Y Dinstein, 'Military Necessity' in R Bernhardt (ed.), *Encyclopedia of Public International Law*, vol 3 (North-Holland 1997) 395–7.

[59] Commentary to ARSIWA (n 13) Art 25 p 84 [21]. On the relationship between SR and the use of force, with particular emphasis on necessity, see N Tsagourias, 'Necessity and the Use of Force: A Special Regime' (2010) 41 NYIL 11.

State's breach poses a serious threat to its own vital interests.[60] In this scenario, therefore, the concept of 'necessity' does not operate so much as a central legal justification—namely by expressly commissioning a *renvoi* to ARSIWA Article 25—but rather as one of the composite philosophical and policy considerations underpinning the deployment of self-defence under SR repertoire.

A second charge can immediately be levelled against proposals aimed at developing collective counterterrorism enforcement mechanisms parallel to SC decision-making. As seen in Chapter 5, even if a paradigm shift has occurred in SR law that now addresses 'indirect' aggression, it is nonetheless difficult to contemplate excising UN organs (particularly the SC) altogether from the process of ascertaining the legality of forcible countermeasures. Indeed, it is now commonplace for injured States to pursue irregulars or insurgents across borders and/or strike back at the territory of the State from which the harmful activity emanated. In the last twenty-five years, for example, this logic prompted Senegal to invade Guinea-Bissau,[61] Thailand to spearhead excursions into Burma, and Tajikistan to chase after irregulars into neighbouring Afghanistan.[62] Indeed, '[t]hese are no longer exceptional claims, and the international system now appears increasingly to acquiesce in this expanded reading of the right of self-defense under Charter Article 51'.[63] Yet, even if this trend is accepted as widespread State practice, it might still be useful to ensure UN oversight (or *ex post facto* endorsement) when determining whether an injured State may invoke a right to self-defence—or essential when ascertaining whether a State can adopt forcible countermeasures falling short of self-defence—in response to terrorism or other global security violations (ie should that latter possibility be subsumed under an evolving, dynamic interpretation of post-ARSIWA SR repertoire).[64] More controversially, in 2006 Ethiopia invaded Somalia in large part as a response to transborder terrorism.[65] This use of force was never condemned by the SC or the African Union, thereby suggesting that the rules on forcible responses to terrorism have developed, to some extent, outside the UN framework.

[60] On the notions of 'necessity' and 'vital interests' under SR repertoire, see R Ago, 'Eighth Report on State Responsibility (continued)' (1979) UN Doc A/CN.4/318 and Add.1–4; (1979) II(1) *YILC* 3 [102]–[103].

[61] See *Keesing's Contemporary Archives* (Longman 1992) 3928; *Keesing's Contemporary Archives* (Longman 1995) 40396.

[62] See Communications regarding Tajikistan's military response to incursions of mujahedin from Afghanistan in (1993) *UN Yearbook* 383; UN Doc S/26110 (14 July 1993) (Russia); UN Doc S/26091 (13 July 1993) (Tajikistan); UN Doc S/26145 (22 July 1993); UN Doc S/26814 (7 October 1993) (Afghanistan). See also C Gray, *International Law and the Use of Force* (OUP 2000) 103; T Ruys, *'Armed Attack' and Article 51 of the UN Charter* (CUP 2013) 428.

[63] Franck (n 10) 64.

[64] In the case of collective self-defence, for instance, the victim-State must demonstrate plausible evidence of an 'armed attack' and, more importantly, report its collective action to the SC pursuant to UN Charter Art 51. See also *Nicaragua v USA* (Merits) (n 27) 102–5 [193]–[199].

[65] For different views, see AK Allo, 'Ethiopia's Armed Intervention in Somalia: The Legality of Self-Defense in Response to the Threat of Terrorism' (2010) 39 Denver Journal of International Law and Policy 139; ZW Yihdego, 'Ethiopia's Military Action against the Union of Islamic Courts and Others in Somalia: Some Legal Implications' (2007) 56 ICLQ 666.

Professor Franck inferred that whilst the 'failure to prevent terrorism—ascertainment of a wrongful act—adoption of potential forcible countermeasures' syllogism unquestionably required further elucidation, circumscribing it more effectively will invariably entail some reference to the practice of UN political organs. Speaking specifically to the possibility of adopting forcible countermeasures in response to a State's failure to prevent terrorism under SR repertoire, Franck observed that

> [t]he articles on State Responsibility of the International Law Commission are very relevant but not dispositive in assessing the legality of a state's resort to force in such instances... [w]hile, for example, it is fairly clear that a state is responsible for the consequences of allowing its territory to be used by forces attacking another state, it is less clear whether the Draft, in such circumstances, permits 'countermeasures.' In effect, these provisions seem to constitute a *renvoi* back to the auto-interpretative practices of the U.N.'s principal political organs.[66]

The confusion surrounding the role of self-defence and forcible countermeasures within SR repertoire has been exacerbated by, and can be best explored through, the ILC's historical treatment of the topic. Hence, the next section briefly canvasses this issue to shed some light on the role of self-defence in devising responses to wrongful acts.

6.2.3 Recourse to force in response to internationally wrongful acts

Undoubtedly, international law countenances forcible responses to an internationally wrongful act in at least one specific scenario: the invocation of self-defence in reaction to an 'armed attack' and, more controversially, perhaps the adoption of some other form of countermeasure involving the use of force against some lesser form of prior use of force. This type of construction is seemingly reinforced by the ICJ's *Nicaragua* decision which opened the door to this logic by first drawing a distinction between the degrees of forcible wrongful acts: 'it will be necessary to distinguish the most grave forms of the use of force (those constituting an armed attack) from other less grave forms'.[67] Further unfolding its reasoning on the adoption of lawful countermeasures, the ICJ underscored that 'a use of force of a lesser degree of gravity cannot... produce any entitlement to take collective counter-measures involving the use of force' but left the door open to the unilateral adoption of such countermeasures—albeit proportionate—by the injured States (eg El Salvador, Honduras, or Costa Rica).[68] However, armed responses to internationally wrongful acts in other circumstances have proven to be sharply divisive in academic commentary, especially when they entail independent action, whether unilateral or collective, falling outside the ambit of SC authority. It must

[66] Franck (n 10) 54 fn 5. [67] *Nicaragua v USA* (Merits) (n 27) 96–7 [191].
[68] *Nicaragua v USA* (Merits) (n 27) 127 [249]. See also ibid 110–11 [210]–[211]. See also Commentary to ARSIWA (n 13) Art 50 p 132 [5] fn 757; Crawford (n 27) 691.

be recalled, however, as a sort of overarching principle, that normative frameworks and rules can only have some limited impact on restricting the use of force in the face of resolute constituencies of conscience, and other non-UN-sanctioned initiatives seeking to respond to situations with force, either unilaterally or collectively. In such cases, international law imposes an onerous political and legal burden on States proposing to stray away from accepted institutional practice under the UN Charter, in order to take matters into their own hands to redress the violation of an obligation. As Brunnée and Toope stated, '[l]egal rules cannot, by their mere existence, prevent the use of force; nor can they prevent violations that States perceive to be necessary, or in their fundamental interests. Rather, international law provides a framework against which States' actions must be assessed, and imposes a heavy burden of justification'.[69]

These considerations align with the often discussed notion of 'self-help' which also underpins contemporary SR logic. Whilst the UN machinery's inefficiency in resolving a given situation (ie devising an appropriate response to a wrongful act) will not typically acquire traction as a basis to justify use of force by virtue of self-help,[70] persuasive arguments have been advanced that self-help measures could include a right to adopt forcible countermeasures. Moreover, concerned States are more likely to endorse the injured State's prerogative to enforce its own rights in response to a specific wrongful act, thereby evincing a more tolerant stance on the application of use of force norms without, per se, pronouncing on the lawfulness of the forcible response in question. As Professor Schachter noted, 'inevitably, the victims of violations have resorted to self-help'.[71] More radically, eminent scholars have argued that UN failure to redress egregious international law violations—under which the failure to prevent terrorism may or may not fit, depending on factual circumstances—might actually lend 'moral force to the argument that those aggrieved by the failure should themselves be allowed to enforce their legal entitlement as best they can.'[72] In this regard, however, State practice is rather limited and also tenuous at times, with victim-States resorting to a variety of politically informed legal contortions to frame their self-help claims.[73] Furthermore, ICJ jurisprudence does not unequivocally endorse this line

[69] Brunnée and Toope, 'The Use of Force' (n 27) 790. This line of thinking can also be reconciled with the authors' other work, including J Brunnée and SJ Toope, *Legitimacy and Legality in International Law: An Interactional Account* (CUP 2010); 'International Law and Constructivism: Elements of an Interactional Theory of International Law' (2000) 39 CJTL 19; 'Persuasion and Enforcement' (n 26); 'Interactional International Law' (2001) 3 International Law Forum de Droit International 186.

[70] In the past, similar pleas advanced by Israel were rejected out of hand by other States. See Gray (n 62) 25.

[71] Schachter (n 50) 184. On the links between self-help and recourse to force, more specifically addressing US action in Iran following the hostage crisis, see O Schachter, 'Self-Help in International Law: U.S. Action in the Iranian Hostage Crisis' (1984) 37 Journal of International Affairs 231.

[72] Franck (n 10) 109, 112.

[73] On State practice involving self-help and the use of force, see Franck (n 10) 112 ff. For more discussion of this controversial idea, see Duffy (n 15) 184–5.

of thinking. For instance, despite the fact that Albania's violation of international law in the *Corfu Channel* case was tantamount to an extenuating circumstance, the Court held that it did not trigger a right for the injured State to respond with force.[74]

Even if self-help measures in response to the failure to prevent terrorism are categorically excluded, the potential application of self-defence, a course of action precluding wrongfulness under the ARSIWA, nonetheless shrouds the inquiry with legal ambiguities. The relevant questions thus become: what is the permissible scope of self-defence and how expansive can the concept of 'armed attack' become? It is self-defence's very 'hybrid nature'—which concomitantly constitutes an inherent right of States under the UN Charter and amounts to a circumstance precluding wrongfulness in the ARSIWA—that poses considerable evidentiary problems for States invoking that right, especially regarding burden of proof issues.[75] Whilst the UN Charter expressly recognizes self-defence as a perhaps extreme manifestation of self-help, little clarity is provided on the scope of this justification, the rights and interests that may be protected extending beyond the ambit of self-defence, and how, exactly, this exceptional regime might be deployed in concrete settings.[76] Whilst Article 2(4) of the UN Charter unequivocally condemns the use and/or threat of force in international relations, the distinct scheme of self-defence enshrined in Article 51, and the rights it confers upon its beneficiaries, 'bears no relation to the text of Article 2(4) and establishes no limits on which rights may be vindicated or by whom'.[77] Consequently, although the permissibility of self-defence is by all accounts incontestable in light of State practice and international jurisprudence,[78] its relevance and the scope of its applicability to the scheme of SR law nonetheless warrant a few specific considerations.

Whilst the ILC expressly refers to self-defence under the rubric of circumstances precluding wrongfulness,[79] it did not codify the parameters governing its application to the establishment or implementation of SR. This methodological inclination is perhaps best explained by the fact that an overwhelming lobby within the ILC perceived the self-defence regime as belonging exclusively to the realm of primary norms governing the use of force in international relations, as opposed to being subsumed under secondary SR rules.[80] However, this posture can certainly be challenged by the very fact that self-defence was included in the ARSIWA as a circumstance precluding wrongfulness, which suggests that this

[74] *Corfu Channel* (n 27) 35. On the general principle of non-intervention, see also *Nicaragua v USA* (Merits) (n 27) [202]. See also Chesterman (n 32) 54.

[75] See, eg, K Nakatani, 'Diplomacy and State Responsibility' in Ragazzi (n 8) 42.

[76] See, eg, Duffy (n 15) 185.

[77] Chesterman (n 32) 56.

[78] See, inter alia, Commentary to ARSIWA (n 13) Art 21 p 189 [1]. For an analysis of State practice, see the Commentary to Draft Art 34 ('Self-defence') adopted upon first reading in ILC, 'Report of the International Law Commission on the Work of its 32nd Session' (5 May–25 July 1980) Un Doc A/35/10; (1980) II(2) *YILC* 52–61. For relevant jurisprudence, see *Nicaragua v USA* (Merits) (n 27) 102–5 [193]–[200]; *Nuclear Weapons Advisory Opinion* (n 27) 244 [38], 263 [96].

[79] See n 78 and accompanying text.

[80] See, eg, Commentary to ARSIWA (n 13) Art 21 p 192 [6]. See Commentary to Draft Art 34 (n 78) 52–61, esp 52 [1].

legal scheme does not solely belong to the field of primary obligations, nor that it exclusively affects Article 2(4)-related rights and duties.[81] Furthermore, it is self-evident that the ILC's approach to this topic connotes an undeniable commitment not to impinge on the UN Charter's dominion.[82] By adopting this posture, the ILC ostensibly subscribed to an important portion of legal scholarship striving to dissociate self-defence from SR repertoire.[83] In fact, the Commentary accompanying Draft Article 34 adopted upon first reading construed the self-defence regime as extending beyond the purview of SR repertoire.[84] Interestingly, during his tenure as ILC Special Rapporteur, Riphagen formulated a proposal concerning Draft Article 15 in the Second Part on the content of SR, which provided that '[a]n act of aggression entails all the legal consequences of an international crime and, in addition, such rights and obligations as are provided for in or by virtue of the United Nations Charter'.[85] Whilst this provision did not withstand the test of time in its original form, it nonetheless hinted at some institutional willingness within the ILC—perhaps limited, it is conceded—to incorporate the notion of self-defence in SR law.

Despite compelling accounts produced by detractors of this view, persuasive arguments nonetheless militate in favour of contemplating the concept of self-defence as a potential countermeasure in response to internationally wrongful

[81] A Nollkaemper, 'Attribution of Forcible Acts to States: Connections between the Law on the Use of Force and the Law of State Responsibility' in N Blokker and N Schrijver (eds), *The Security Council and the Use of Force: Theory and Reality—A Need for Change?* (Nijhoff 2005) 133, 144 n 38 speaks to this point:

> [n]ote that the ILC does not appear to have considered self-defence purely as a primary rule, for that would have made it redundant to consider self-defence as a circumstance precluding wrongfulness. An act of self-defence is per definition lawful, does not constitute a wrong, and no matter of state responsibility arises. The ILC nonetheless thought it desirable to include self-defence as a circumstance precluding wrongfulness in Article 21. This may in part be explained by the fact that the lawful resort to self-defence may have effects on obligations *other* than Article 2(4) of the UN Charter.

[82] See ARSIWA (n 13) Art 21, which specifically refers to the UN Charter, along with its predecessor provision, Draft Art 34, adopted upon first reading, in (1980) II(2) *YILC* 52 [1], 60 [25]–[26]. More generally, ARSIWA Art 59 unequivocally provides that the ARSIWA 'are without prejudice to the Charter of the United Nations'. It logically follows that '[t]he articles are in all respects to be interpreted in conformity with the Charter.' See Commentary to ARSIWA (n 13) Art 59 p 143 [2].

[83] This issue has been sharply divisive in legal scholarship. For Paul Reuter in (1981) I *YILC* 201 and P-M Dupuy, 'Implications of the Institutionalization of International Crimes of State' in JHH Weiler *et al.* (eds), *International Crimes of State: A Critical Analysis of the ILC's Draft Article 19 on State Responsibility* (De Gruyter 1989) 170, 176, self-defence is tantamount to a coercive measure rather than a countermeasure under SR repertoire. For I Sinclair in ibid 224, self-defence predated the prohibition on the use of force and could, therefore, not amount to a *stricto sensu* manifestation of SR. Conversely, for E Jiménez de Aréchaga in ibid 256, self-defence could not have existed, as a stand-alone legal institution, without the prior prohibition on the use of force.

[84] See Commentary to Draft Art 34 (n 78) 52 [1].

[85] See Draft Art 15 in W Riphagen, 'Sixth Report on the Content, Forms and Degrees of International Responsibility (Part 2 of the Draft Articles); and "Implementation" (mise en oeuvre) of International Responsibility and the Settlement of Disputes (Part 3 of the Draft Articles)' (1985) UN Doc A/CN.4/389; (1985) II(1) *YILC* 21. For support of a provision incorporating the concept of self-defence in the ARSIWA, see B Graefrath, 'International Crimes and Collective Security' in Wellens (n 25) 239.

acts. First and foremost, the Commentary to ARSIWA Article 41 provides that 'paragraph 3 allows for such further consequences of a serious breach as may be provided for by international law. This may be done by the individual primary rule, as in the case of the prohibition of aggression.'[86] Extending this rationale to the present topic would, of course, require assimilating the relevant international legal breach (ie a State's failure to prevent a given global security violation, eg terrorism) with a contravention to Article 2(4) of the UN Charter. Whilst the bulk of that determination might hinge on characterizing the terrorist strike as an 'armed attack'—a legal inquiry extending beyond the scope of this book—some scholars equate State failures to prevent terrorism (eg harbouring or tolerating terrorists, providing logistical support, etc) with violations of the prohibition of the use of force in international relations.[87] Hence, that analytical Rubicon might be more readily traversed than it initially appeared.

Moreover, self-defence might be better understood in the context of ascertaining potential consequences of internationally wrongful acts. Indeed, when boiled down to its most reducible manifestation, self-defence is envisaged as a coercive measure triggered by the prior violation of an international obligation; in particular, the prohibition of the use of force pursuant to Article 2(4). Its purpose, therefore, is aimed at compelling the cessation of the wrongful act—a course of action undeniably falling under the rubric of secondary obligations in SR law—and ensuring that the relevant actors revert to the observance of the violated primary duty. Injured States may concurrently delve into SR law and self-defence repertoire which can both engender a common terminative function with a view to bringing about the cessation of the initial wrongful act whilst also counteracting its consequences. SR repertoire may achieve this objective through the imposition of obligations of continued performance, cessation, and reparation, whilst also conferring upon injured States the right to adopt countermeasures to bring the legal breach to an end.[88]

Indeed, the ILC's Commentary accompanying Draft Article 34 adopted upon first reading unequivocally noted that self-defence served the 'object of preventing another's wrongful action from proceeding and achieving its purpose'.[89] Otherwise put, the exercise of self-defence is conceptually predicated on the prior perpetration of an internationally wrongful act, thereby confirming that this type of response to an international law violation is somewhat analogous to the logic

[86] See Commentary to ARSIWA (n 13) Art 41 p 116 [14]. ARSIWA Art 41(3) provides the following: '[t]his article is without prejudice to the other consequences referred to in this Part and to such further consequences that a breach to which this chapter applies may entail under international law'.

[87] See, eg, JE Alvarez, 'Hegemonic International Law Revisited' (2003) 97 AJIL 873, 879.

[88] See ARSIWA (n 13) Arts 29–31. On the nexus between countermeasures under SR repertoire and self-defence, see P Malanczuk, 'Counter-Measures and Self-Defence as Circumstances Precluding Wrongfulness in the International Law Commission's Draft Articles on State Responsibility' in M Spinedi and B Simma (eds), *United Nations Codification of State Responsibility* (Oceana 1987) 197–286.

[89] Commentary to Draft Art 34 (n 78) 53 [5].

underpinning SR law. Yet again, the Commentary accompanying Draft Article 34 was illuminating in this regard:

> Acting in self-defence means responding by force to wrongful forcible action carried out by another. In other words, for action of the State involving recourse to the use of armed force to be characterized as action taken in self-defence, the first and essential condition is that it must have been preceded by a specific kind of internationally wrongful act, entailing wrongful recourse to the use of armed force, by the subject against which the action is taken.[90]

These considerations imply that the conditions for invoking self-defence must be satisfied for that forcible response to be deployed lawfully under SR, provided one accepts it as a legitimate countermeasure within that normative scheme. Undoubtedly, self-defence must be invoked in light of: (i) immediacy (the armed reaction must be adopted simultaneously with, or immediately after, the initial armed attack, ie the internationally wrongful act); (ii) necessity (the measures taken must constitute the sole means of bringing the 'armed attack' to an end); and (iii) proportionality (as between the wrongful act, ie the 'armed attack', and the armed response, ie self-defence).[91]

The conceptual problem with reeling in self-defence in SR repertoire as a countermeasure against State failures to prevent global security violations is that the inclusion of self-defence within that normative scheme is probably better tailored to address grave and systematic international law violations. Certainly, the US claimed to be acting in self-defence when responding to 9/11, but it can be questioned as to whether this constituted an exceptional and isolated precedent. Moreover, it is questionable whether the conditions for invoking self-defence were even satisfied: in particular, demonstrating that the US was acting out of immediacy—despite carefully planning a campaign of consensus-building, accompanied by rhetorical ramping up, a considerable amount of time after the initial attacks—seems like a challenging argument to countenance, at least in retrospect. Therefore, self-defence—at least collective self-defence—is perhaps better understood as a particularly harsh response to a grave violation (ie 'an act of aggression')[92] of a duty owed to the international community as a whole,[93] resulting from a peremptory norm of international law,[94] namely the prohibition of the

[90] Commentary to Draft Art 34 (n 78) 53 [3].

[91] See, inter alia, *Nicaragua v USA* (Merits) (n 27) 102 [194]; *Oil Platforms (Iran v USA)* (Merits) [2003] ICJ Rep 161, 187 [51], 196–7 [73]–[74]. Moreover, the exercise of self-defence must be notified to the SC pursuant to UN Charter Art 51, and remains a provisional measure to be replaced by concerted, collective action undertaken under the aegis of the UN.

[92] For instance, in 1974 the GA acknowledged that the concept of 'aggression' exclusively encompasses grave violations of the prohibition on the use of force. See UNGA Res 3314 (XXIX) (14 December 1974).

[93] The prohibition of acts of 'aggression' was specifically enumerated in the oft-cited *dictum* in *Barcelona Traction, Light and Power Company, Limited* (Second Phase) [1970] ICJ Rep 3, 32 [34]. See also Commentary to ARSIWA (n 13) Art 48 p 127 [9].

[94] See Commentary to Art 50 (now Art 53) of the Draft Articles on the Law of Treaties in (1966) II *YILC* 248 [3]. See also Commentary to ARSIWA (n 13) Art 40 p 112 [4].

use of force. For the violation of the obligation to prevent terrorism to clear this high legal threshold, a territorial State would likely have to perpetrate continuing, repeated, and massive omissions regarding its counterterrorism undertakings and due diligence duties.[95] It is probably unrealistic to subsume all violations of the obligation of prevention under this self-defence model, and accept the prospect of a victim-State—backed by a loose coalition of other States not directly aggrieved by the wrongful act—responding with forcible countermeasures across the board.

However, there is no reason—and arguments in favour of the opposite conclusion have also been advanced—why that obligation of prevention could not be concomitantly cast as an obligation *erga omnes* and *jus cogens* duty. Moreover, its violation could most likely amount to a grave violation of international law in some instances of a State's systematic and massive failures to prevent terrorism. In such circumstances, self-defence presumably becomes an available countermeasure both for the victim-State (ie directly injured by the wrongful act and thereby empowered to invoke an individual right of self-defence) and all other States as well (ie not directly injured by the wrongful act and thereby enabled to participate in the exercise of collective self-defence).[96] Alternatively, international law arguably countenances the adoption of lesser forms of armed countermeasures in the event that these responses seek to redress more modest initial violations of the prohibition of the use of force. As acknowledged by the ICJ in *Nicaragua*, the possibility of collective self-defence is discarded by the sole fact that the initial wrongful act is not tantamount to an 'armed attack'. In such cases, therefore, the injured State remains the sole bearer of a right of (individual) self-defence in response to the wrongful act.[97]

A conclusion seems apposite in light of these considerations. Better circumscribing the role and place of self-defence and, more controversially, of more modest but forcible countermeasures under SR repertoire will hinge, to a large extent, on whether: (i) a specific transnational terrorist attack or other global security violation is deemed to meet the threshold of 'armed attack'; and (ii) that

[95] On the relationship between SR, due diligence, and counterterrorism, see, eg, RP Barnidge, Jr, *Non-State Actors and Terrorism: Applying the Law of State Responsibility and the Due Diligence Principle* (TMC Asser Press 2008) 79 and 'States' Due Diligence Obligations With Regard to International Non-State Terrorist Organisations Post-11 September 2001: The Heavy Burden that States Must Bear' (2005) 16 Irish Studies in International Affairs 103. On the concept of due diligence, see R Pisillo-Mazzeschi, 'The Due Diligence Rule and the Nature of the International Responsibility of States' (1992) 35 GYIL 9; P-M Dupuy, 'Due Diligence in the International Law of State Responsibility' in Organisation for Economic Co-Operation and Development (ed.), *Legal Aspects of Transfrontier Pollution* (OECD 1977) 369; D Shelton, 'Private Violence, Public Wrongs, and the Responsibility of States' (1989–90) 13 FILJ 1, 21–2.

[96] See, eg, Villalpando (n 55) 394.

[97] See *Nicaragua v USA* (Merits) (n 27) 110–11 [210]–[211]. For an interpretation of that aspect of the case, see L Condorelli, *Cours de Droit International Public* (Geneva University 1994–5) 59–60; A de Hoogh, *Obligations Erga Omnes and International Crimes: A Theoretical Inquiry into the Implementation and Enforcement of the International Responsibility of States* (Kluwer 1996) 338; JA Frowein, 'Reactions by Not Directly Affected States to Breaches of Public International Law' (1994) 248 RdC 347, 371–3. See also Separate Opinion of Judge Simma in the *Oil Platforms Case* (n 91) 331–2 [12].

armed attack can be attributed to a State or, barring the application of attribution rules, can nonetheless trigger the deployment of secondary norms of responsibility given its failure to prevent the excursion in question (which, for present purposes, could include self-defence or other forcible countermeasures). Therefore, in this context attribution becomes 'a critical issue'.[98] Alternatively, if the excursion does not fulfil the requirements of an 'armed attack', it may still arguably trigger some limited right to adopt forcible countermeasures, pursuant to *Nicaragua*'s nebulous treatment of the matter discussed earlier. But even if one accepts, as José Alvarez did for instance,[99] that a State's mere harbouring and/or tolerating of terrorists on its territory might be synonymous with a violation of the prohibition enshrined in Article 2(4), conceptual and analytical problems invariably arise.

An obvious one pertains to the legitimate target(s) of an action in self-defence: is the injured State forcibly pursuing individual terrorists within the responsible State's territory, or rather targeting the State itself with a view to bringing its behaviour in conformity with its international obligations? Since traditional use of force repertoire responds to a predominantly bilateral and unitary typology,[100] self-defence actions are typically directed against sovereign States. In fact, this posture is precisely what underpins the broader tendency in ICJ jurisprudence—exemplified by the *Armed Activities* case and the *Wall Advisory Opinion*—to resist some degree of flexibility in adapting use of force and SR norms to non-State actors.[101] Indeed, the *Armed Activities* case brought the nexus between SR and self-defence into sharp relief, with the ICJ ultimately refusing to loosen use of force parameters and endorsing a restrictive concept of self-defence against transborder subversion.

The Court had to determine whether the conduct of the Allied Democratic Forces (ADF), an armed band operating out of the territory of the Democratic Republic of Congo (DRC), could be attributed to that State. Ultimately, the ICJ concluded that Uganda could not invoke a right to self-defence against the DRC because it had harboured ADF on its territory.[102] For the ICJ, Uganda's conduct on the DRC's territory would only have qualified as self-defence in the presence of 'satisfactory proof of the involvement in these attacks, direct or indirect, of the Government of the DRC', which led the Court to conclude that 'the attacks did not emanate from armed bands or irregulars sent by the DRC or on behalf of the

[98] G Travalio and J Altenburg, 'Terrorism, State Responsibility and the Use of Military Force' (2003) 4 CJIL 97, 102.

[99] See n 87, Section 5.2.4 nn 77–8, and accompanying text.

[100] For an earlier iteration of this line of argument, see V-J Proulx, 'International Responsibility Today: Essays in Memory of Oscar Schachter: L'Émergence de la Communauté Internationale dans la Responsabilité des États' (2007) 18 EJIL 581, 583, 590, and authorities cited therein.

[101] On the ICJ's treatment of self-defence issues, see also JA Green, *The International Court of Justice and Self-Defence in International Law* (Hart 2009).

[102] *Armed Activities on the Territory of the Congo (DRC v Uganda)* (Merits) [2005] ICJ Rep 168, 219–21 [131]–[136], 222–3 [146]–[147]. For discussion of the case, see JT Gathii, 'Case Concerning Armed Activities on the Territory of the Congo (Democratic Republic of the Congo v. Uganda) (International Decision)' (2007) 101 AJIL 142.

DRC' pursuant to the provisions of Article 3(g) of the Definition of Aggression.[103] Interestingly, the ICJ characterized the conduct of the ADF, a non-State armed faction, as 'armed attacks'—the Court itself placing those terms between quote marks—concluding that ADF's excursions 'remained non-attributable to the DRC'.[104] Ultimately, the Court reaffirmed the position it defended earlier in the *Wall Advisory Opinion* discussed in Chapter 5, thereby precluding recourse to self-defence as a response to 'armed attacks' that cannot be attributed to a sovereign State. The Court further underscored the interrelationship between self-defence and SR law when assessing whether the conduct of two other paramilitary groups could be attributed to Uganda. In particular, its analysis relied upon ARSIWA Articles 4, 5, and 8, which the ICJ equated with 'the requisite tests ... for sufficiency of control of paramilitaries'.[105]

In light of recurrent critiques of the State-centric nature of public international law,[106] academic and policy voices are challenging this (perhaps outdated) conception of international relations and advocating a loosened appreciation of use of force standards. As already seen, some recognize a right of self-defence against transborder terrorist subversion, even if such excursions are authored by non-State actors.[107] Undoubtedly, these challenges are exacerbated by scenarios of transnational violence emanating from failed or incapable/weak States—or by terroristic agendas brewing within the borders of unaware or unsuspecting States—'especially when the terrorists operate in remote and sparsely populated areas'.[108] For instance, as of 2009 the situation prevalent in the Swat District in northern Pakistan—a semi-autonomous tribal area and veritable conglomerate of Taliban, Al-Qaeda, and other rebel fighters—constituted a prime example of festering intra-State terrorism without any kind of effective governmental oversight or control.[109] Most recently, Islamic State of Iraq and the Levant (ISIL) has taken control of portions of both Syrian and Iraqi territory, with its leadership also making territorial expansionist claims pertaining to parts of Libya, Egypt (Sinai),

[103] *Armed Activities Case* (n 102) 223 [146]. See also Definition of Aggression in GA Res 3314 (n 92) Annex, Art 3(g).

[104] *Armed Activities Case* (n 102) 222–3 [146].

[105] *Armed Activities Case* (n 102) 226 [160] (also citing *Nicaragua v USA* (Merits) (n 27) 62–5 [109]–[115]). On these issues and self-defence, more broadly, see J Kammerhofer, 'The Resilience of the Restrictive Rules on Self-Defence' in M Weller (ed.), *The Oxford Handbook on the Use of Force in International Law* (OUP 2015) 627–48.

[106] See, eg, S Marks, 'State-Centrism, International Law, and the Anxieties of Influence' (2006) 19 LJIL 339. Similarly, but with greater critical emphasis on the corpus of norms forming SR repertoire and the ARSIWA, see R Pisillo-Mazzeschi, 'The Marginal Role of the Individual in the ILC's Articles on State Responsibility' (2004) 15 Italian Yearbook of International Law 39.

[107] See also Y Dinstein, *War, Aggression, and Self-Defence* (4th edn, CUP 2005) 204; SD Murphy, 'Terrorism and the Concept of "Armed Attack" in Article 51 of the U.N. Charter' (2002) 43 HILJ 41, 50.

[108] Y Dinstein, 'The International Legal Response to Terrorism' in R Ago (ed.), *International Law at the Time of its Codification: Essays in Honour of Roberto Ago*, vol 2 (Giuffrè 1987) 139, 146.

[109] See J Perlez and PZ Shah, 'Truce in Pakistan May Not Mean Peace, Just Leeway for Taliban' *NYT* (New York, 6 March 2009) A6; See J Perlez, 'Taliban Seize Vital Pakistan Area Closer to the Capital' *NYT* (New York, 23 April 2009) A1.

Saudi Arabia, Yemen, Algeria, Afghanistan, Pakistan, Nigeria, and the North Caucasus; its activities thus bring the relevance of recourse to force as a potential countermeasure to the fore.[110] Given the relatively insignificant accountability of, and modest control exerted by, local governments in such situations, some have proposed resolving this legal dilemma by conferring a limited right of self-help upon victim-States to forcibly root out terrorist bases of operation within the territory of sanctuary States.[111] However, appropriate resolution of these challenges will largely depend on the further exploration of the murky question whether the invocation of self-defence is necessarily predicated on the prior establishment of SR. The chapter now turns briefly to this question in the hope of further illuminating the relationship between both schemes.

6.2.4 State Responsibility as a basis for invoking self-defence

Whilst the possibility for a victim-State to adopt forcible countermeasures in response to a wrongful act, a polemical proposition to say the least, has already been explored here, the relationship between SR law and self-defence remains to be elucidated. In particular, equally controversial is the notion that the prior establishment of SR for an armed attack is *always* required to justify self-defence or, at the very least, substantiate resort to some degree of force against the State from which the attack emanated.[112] From a practical perspective, compelling precedents support the idea that the ascertainment of an internationally wrongful act—in the SR sense—is required to justify a response involving self-defence. Indeed, scholarly interpretations of the 2006 Israel–Lebanon war are replete with compatible logic,[113] yet the Lebanon–Israel relationship presented a singularly unique set of features: the legal treatment of Lebanon's failure to prevent

[110] See generally C Henderson, 'The Use of Force and Islamic State' (2014) 1 JUFIL 209; M Weller, 'Striking ISIL: Aspects of the Law on the Use of Force' (2015) 19 ASIL Insights <http://www.asil.org/insights/volume/19/issue/5/striking-isil-aspects-law-use-force> accessed 10 August 2015.

[111] See, eg, G Battaglini, 'War against Terrorism *Extra Moenia*, Self-Defence and Responsibility: A Pure Juridical Approach' in Ragazzi (n 8) 145. Following the Mumbai terrorist attacks, others advocated a more radical route for Pakistan, arguing that an international force should have taken over portions of that State's territory that became ungovernable to root out terrorist networks. See R Kagan, 'The Sovereignty Dodge: What Pakistan Won't Do, the World Should' *Washington Post* (Washington, DC, 2 December 2008) <http://www.washingtonpost.com/wp-dyn/content/article/2008/12/01/AR2008120102438_pf.html> accessed 15 August 2015. For a searing critique of Kagan's position, see DL Davis, 'America the Arbiter? Hubris Has No Place in Foreign Relations' *Washington Times* (Washington, DC, 12 December 2008) A23. Similarly, some authors argue that several States are 'fictitious' because they lack the central component of statehood, namely the effective control of their territory and population. Consequently, the UN-regulated, State-centric recourse to force framework falls short in tackling the scourge of transnational violence carried out by non-State actors. However, there is a customary law-derived principle—well pre-dating 9/11—granting States a right to use transborder defensive force against non-State actors. See, eg, B Finucane, 'Fictitious States, Effective Control, and the Use of Force against Non-State Actors' (2012) 30 BJIL 35.

[112] See, eg, Duffy (n 15) 47.

[113] See, eg, T Ruys, 'Crossing the Thin Blue Line: An Inquiry into Israel's Recourse to Self-Defense against Hezbollah' (2007) 43 SJIL 265; MJB Bottoms, 'When Close Doesn't Count: An

transnational terrorism was perhaps compounded by the connection shared by Hezbollah's political wing with the Lebanese political system.[114] Furthermore, Lebanon's international responsibility could be engaged on the basis that it harboured and supported terrorists or, alternatively, that it remained unwilling or was, in fact, unable to comply with its counterterrorism obligations.[115]

Given this unique relationship, some commentators identified an alternate ground for triggering Lebanon's international responsibility, one hinging on ARSIWA Article 9.[116] Whilst the proponents of this line of argument contended that this 'may provide an alternative route to legally justify Israel's recourse to self-defense under Article 51, while leaving in place the need for a certain degree of state involvement in armed attacks', their assertion nonetheless rested on the idea that a prior establishment of international responsibility was required to justify a forcible response.[117] As argued above, self-defence thus seems consistently to amount to a response to internationally wrongful acts in counterterrorism contexts; in particular, the victim-State aims to bring the responsible State's failure to comply with its obligation to prevent terrorism to an end by coercive means.

Once this seemingly obvious premise is accepted, the connection between SR and self-defence begins to blur. For instance, complex legal contortions assimilating the acts of private actors to 'acts of State'—primarily by a *renvoi* to the 'harbouring and supporting' rule—are required to make the prospect of self-defence against the responsible State palatable. Pre-9/11 constructions of the SR/self-defence symbiosis predominantly predicated the legitimate invocation of forcible countermeasures on the successful attribution of the private wrongful acts to the official State apparatus. Indeed, unless a terrorist strike could be equated with a 'State act' through the mechanism of attribution, 'there [could] be no question of

Analysis of Israel's *Jus Ad Bellum* and *Jus in Bello* in the 2006 Israel-Lebanon War' (April 2009) The Army Lawyer 23. See also, more broadly, S Kirchner, 'Third Party Liability for Hezbollah Attacks against Israel' (2006) 7 German Law Journal 777.

114 For further discussion of surrounding issues, see n 113, Section 1.3 nn 68–9, Section 2.3 n 31, and accompanying text.

115 Yet it is to be queried whether the agency principles enshrined in ARSIWA Art 8 could be satisfied vis-à-vis the relationship between Hezbollah and Lebanon. On the challenges associated with that eventuality, see MN Schmitt, '"Change Direction" 2006: Israeli Operations in Lebanon and the International Law of Self-Defense' (2008) 29 MJIL 127, 141–2. See also M Pathak, 'Maritime Violence: Piracy at Sea & Marine Terrorism Today' (2005) 20 Windsor Review of Legal and Social Issues 65, 77 (expounding that '[t]his standard [that Art 8 requires a factual link between the *de facto* agent and the State] appears to have been steadily eroded by the *Tadic* Case and the global war on terrorism'). But see A Skordas, 'Hegemonic Intervention as Legitimate Use of Force' (2007) 16 Minnesota Journal of International Law 407, 442; Kirchner (n 113) 782. Undoubtedly, Lebanon's conduct violated past SC pronouncements urging it to stamp out Hezbollah factions operating within its borders. See, eg, UNSC Res 1559 (2 September 2004) UN Doc S/RES/1559.

116 ARSIWA (n 13) Art 9 provides that:

> [t]he conduct of a person or group of persons shall be considered an act of a state under international law if the person or group of persons is in fact exercising elements of the governmental authority in the absence or default of the official authorities and in circumstances such as to call for the exercise of those elements of authority.

See also Crawford (n 25) 387.

117 Ruys (n 113) 268, 284–90. For a different appraisal, consider Schmitt (n 115) 141–63.

a forcible response to it'; '[i]f...we want[ed] to find out whether the use of force [was] permitted, we [had to] first ascertain whether there ha[d] been an armed attack on the State using force by the State against which force [was] used'.[118] The ICJ also implicitly acknowledged this position in *Nicaragua*, seemingly endorsing the requirement of State involvement in 'armed attacks' by finding wide support for the notion that the 'nature of the acts which can be treated as constituting armed attacks' encompassed both military action by official State forces and 'the sending by or on behalf of a state of armed bands, groups, irregulars'.[119] As prefaced in Section 2.4.4, the 'cyber' dimension of transnational terrorism also propels legal challenges to the fore: some commentators advocate an extension of similar logic to online terrorist strikes. In sum, should a cyberattack be qualified as an 'armed attack' under Article 51 of the UN Charter, it may trigger the usual Article 2(4) considerations.[120] Indeed, incontrovertible evidence (ie 'irrefutable') would have to be tendered to the effect that a wrongful act has been carried out by the State—epitomized here by the act of indirect cyberaggression—to ground the invocation of self-defence or other forcible responses legally.[121]

Undoubtedly, considerable factual problems arise when individuals or non-State actors carry out terrorist attacks without any active State support, as was the case in Afghanistan concerning 9/11. In such a scenario, it must be queried whether the victim-State can respond with force against that sanctuary State (ie for failing to comply with its duty to prevent terrorism). Alternatively, can a forcible action be mounted solely against the individual perpetrators within that State's territory, absent successful attribution of the private acts to the State? In the latter scenario, does this signal that the non-State actors themselves are responsible for the armed attack, and responding to their excursion with self-defence is no longer predicated on a prior finding of SR implicating the territorial State (given that it is, for all

[118] A Cassese, 'The International Community's "Legal" Responses to Terrorism' (1989) 38 ICLQ 589, 596–7; GM Travalio, 'Terrorism, International Law and the Use of Military Force' (2000) 18 Wisconsin International Law Journal 145 (correlating the absence of a State's involvement in terrorism with a restriction on invoking UN Charter Art 51 as a basis for justifying the use of force). Prior to 9/11, a less widespread view advocated the potential responsibility of non-State actors for carrying out 'armed attacks', thereby challenging the State-centric nature of recourse to force. See R Wedgwood, 'Responding to Terrorism: The Strikes Against Bin Laden' (1999) 24 YJIL 559, 564.

[119] *Nicaragua v USA* (Merits) (n 27) 103 [195]. In its analysis, the ICJ opined that whilst the provision by a State of assistance to armed groups could be tantamount to unlawful intervention, this nonetheless failed to satisfy the threshold of an 'armed attack'. Rather, the Court chose to focus on the 'effective control' test, thereby requiring attribution of the private acts to the official State apparatus.

[120] See generally CC Joyner and C Lotrionte, 'Information Warfare as International Coercion: Elements of a Legal Framework' (2001) 12 EJIL 825.

[121] See Joyner and Lotrionte (n 120) 853. See also SJ Shackelford, 'From Nuclear War to Net War: Analogizing Cyber Attacks in International Law' (2008) 27 BJIL 191, 236–8. On related topics, including the question of attribution and cyberwarfare, see S Brenner, 'At Light Speed: Attribution and Response to Cybercrime/Terrorism/Warfare' (2007) 97 Journal of Criminal Law and Criminology 379; DE Graham, 'Cyber Threats and the Law of War' (2010) 4 Journal of National Security Law & Policy 87; MJ Sklerov, 'Solving the Dilemma of State Responses to Cyberattacks: A Justification for the Use of Active Defenses against States Who Neglect Their Duty to Prevent' (2009) 201 Military Law Review 1.

intents and purposes, subtracted from the legal rationale justifying the pursuit of irregulars outside State structures)? Both these eventualities can arguably be supported by the publicly available facts surrounding the invasion of Afghanistan. Undoubtedly, the 9/11 strikes fulfilled the requirements of an 'armed attack', both in terms of scope and severity. Indeed, 'the focus here is on authorship and the status of actors as the controversial issue',[122] be it ascertained through a loosening of attribution rules or, rather, by circumventing the evidentiary hurdles associated with that approach in favour of a standard of 'harbouring and supporting' that expands States' responsibilities.

Furthermore, several bodies including the SC, NATO, OAS, and EU construed Al-Qaeda's actions as tantamount to 'armed attacks', whilst concurrently reaffirming the US' inherent right to invoke individual or collective self-defence.[123] One interpretation of this rhetorical belligerence, paired with the behaviour of some of the intervening States, militated in favour of predicating the military response to 9/11 on a presumption of Afghanistan's responsibility. For instance, the UK approached that legal situation by directing the use of force against the 'same source' of the 9/11 excursions, thereby conflating the Government of Afghanistan with Al-Qaeda as legitimate targets; its position no doubt found steadier footing in some prior establishment of Afghanistan's international responsibility.[124] Conversely, an alternate viewpoint construed the response to 9/11 as doing away with the requirement of first establishing SR as a basis for invoking self-defence.[125] This position was usually substantiated by the fact that in the wake of 9/11 overwhelming reference was made to States' right to invoke individual or collective self-defence by the SC, NATO, OAS, the European Union, and other IOs, rather than couching the rhetoric more expressly within the scope of SR.[126]

Moving beyond the exceptional scope and magnitude of 9/11, beyond the fact that self-defence is often invoked to respond to internationally wrongful acts, it is not entirely clear whether a potential post-9/11 shift in international law resulted from a loosening of the application of self-defence standards, or whether it can be explained by the emergence of a new SR rule.[127] Additional State practice and clearer *opinio juris* are most likely to be required to corroborate a definitive shift either way or the advent of a *lex specialis* in this field. A case can certainly be made that the resulting legal and policy shift resides (or *should* reside) instead primarily at the SR level.[128] To the extent that it can operate in tandem with the law of

[122] Duffy (n 15) 189 fn 203.

[123] See also C Gray, 'The US National Security Strategy and the New "Bush Doctrine" on Preemptive Self-Defense' (2002) 1 Chinese Journal of International Law 437, 441. See also Section 5.2.4.

[124] See, eg, LN Sadat, 'Terrorism and the Rule of Law' (2004) 3 Washington University Global Studies Law Review 135, 150.

[125] See, eg, C Greenwood, 'International Law and the "War against Terrorism"' (2002) 78 International Affairs 301, 303.

[126] See Duffy (n 15) 190.

[127] For a critical appraisal, see J Boyle, 'Making Sense of Self-Defence in the War on Terror' (2014) 1 JUFIL 55.

[128] See generally Proulx (n 12).

countermeasures, this does not mean, however, that self-defence repertoire cannot also adapt to contemporaneous realities in similar fashion to SR, thereby straying away from a predominantly State-centric paradigm. However, the evolution of the law governing use of force towards a more flexible and polymorphous application of self-defence precepts would seem to fly in the face of ICJ jurisprudence which unequivocally premises the right to invoke self-defence on a prior armed attack authored by a State, not by non-State actors or private irregulars.[129]

One way of reconciling the response to 9/11 with extant SR norms—should a wrongful act in the form of a State-based armed attack absolutely be required to justify self-defence—is to infer that this nexus was completely overlooked or eschewed in the US–Afghanistan scenario. Alternatively, a more commonly held view instead construes the facts surrounding that military campaign as evidence of a considerable relaxation of the 'effective control' standard of attribution for the purposes of characterizing private behaviour as 'acts of State'. Indeed, States' response to, and endorsement of, the military campaign in Afghanistan necessarily rested on the recognition of some degree of State involvement in the perpetration of the 9/11 attacks, thereby fulfilling the 'State responsibility–self-defence' nexus explored earlier. Consequently, '[t]he assertion has been made that the recognition of 'self defence' represents not a rejection of the state responsibility requirement, but a lowering of the standard by which the conduct of individuals becomes attributable to the state'.[130] Unsurprisingly, both States and commentators supporting military action in Afghanistan predicated their rhetoric on presumptions of accountability or culpability of the Afghan Government. What is unknown at this time, however, is the extent to which self-defence is *legally* predicated on this prior finding of responsibility and, as a corollary, the scope and pertinence of the various allegations levelled to the effect that Afghanistan 'harboured and supported' terrorists on its territory.[131] As seen in Part III, the SC's role in implementing Afghanistan's responsibility after 9/11 would suggest that international law is indeed moving in that direction. Similarly, the 2002 US National Security Strategy declared that the US would make accountable 'nations that are compromised by terror'.[132] Given State and SC practice canvassed in the present book, there is strong indication that a paradigm shift towards a rule of

[129] See, eg, the discussion on the ICJ's *Wall Advisory Opinion* in Section 5.3. But see KN Trapp, 'Can Non-State Actors Mount an Armed Attack?' in Weller (n 105) 679–96.

[130] Duffy (n 15) 191 fn 214. For particularly vocal proponents of this view, see generally M Sassòli, 'State Responsibility for Violations of International Humanitarian Law' (2002) 84 International Review of the Red Cross 401; D Jinks, 'State Responsibility for the Acts of Private Armed Groups' (2003) 4 CJIL 83.

[131] Various allegations were put forth, ranging from different manifestations of State toleration of terrorism (eg providing safe haven, protecting Al-Qaeda, etc) to the failure to extradite Osama bin Laden and other terrorist suspects, to a deplorable human rights record. Similarly, the fact that Afghanistan 'violated international law' by entertaining privileged links with the Al-Qaeda network warrants further exploration as a potential basis for invoking self-defence. See Greenwood (n 125) 313.

[132] See US National Security Council, *The National Security Strategy of the United States of America* (17 September 2002) <http://www.state.gov/documents/organization/63562.pdf> accessed 30 April 2015.

'harbouring and supporting' has now materialized within the sub-field of attribution under SR. When it is called to implement SR in the future, it is likely that the SC will revert to that terminology and logic.

For the sake of political pragmatism, it is important to emphasize that in 2002, Harold Koh clearly emphasized the nexus between SR law and recourse to force, underscoring that the former is a predicate for the exercise of the latter. Speaking about the 9/11 attacks, he declared that '[w]ithin the U.N. Charter framework, forceful actions against states within whose territory such actors may be found *can only be justified on the grounds of vicarious state responsibility*' (emphasis added).[133] This conclusion is important for three reasons. First, it supports Part II's central arguments by pointing to a rapprochement between SR repertoire and the UN Charter, which confirms that the SC can implement SR in global security contexts. Secondly, it suggests that the new 'harbouring and supporting' norm has achieved precedence in counterterrorism settings, again empowering all relevant UN organs to: (i) rely on SR principles in addressing international legal violations dealing with global security; and (ii) frame self-defence (and perhaps even other forcible reactions) as a possible countermeasure. Thirdly, it is important because Koh later served as the Legal Advisor of the US Department of State, thereby joining the ranks of distinguished international lawyers in a position to influence policy decisions and recommend recourse to force on the basis of breached legal obligations. From the perspective of State practice growth, it is not unthinkable that other high-level government lawyers might be swayed by similar rationales in the future when advising their respective States; their recommendations might similarly rely on expanded SR models that remain intimately tied to forcible countermeasures. At the very least, this aside serves as a reminder that legal advisors and their staff will ground their justifications for invoking force on *legal* arguments; in such a policy calculus, it is difficult to ignore completely the potential role of SR in governing international breaches, including those that may trigger forcible responses.[134]

Whilst Afghanistan's failure to prevent terrorism undoubtedly generated rights and obligations accruing to the international community, should its wrongdoing be deemed insufficient to qualify as State involvement in an 'armed attack', that violation's mechanics as a trigger for self-defence would require further elucidation. The conundrum resides not in the fact that force is excised altogether from the scheme of countermeasures—in fact, it is permitted under both the ARSIWA and through a *renvoi* to self-interpretative practices of UN political organs—but rather results from the onus of framing a forcible countermeasure against terrorism as 'self-defence'.[135] However, whilst many publicists agree that the 'agency'

[133] HH Koh, 'The Spirit of the Laws' (2002) 43 HILJ 23, 28.

[134] Compare with R Nigro, 'Applying the Law of State Responsibility to Military Counter-Terrorist Actions' in M Szabó (ed.), *State Responsibility and the Law of Treaties* (Eleven International Publishing 2010) 117–40 (canvassing relevant State practice and identifying three situations of military intervention against terrorism involving different attribution criteria).

[135] See, eg, Duffy (n 15) 191 fn 218 and accompanying text.

model has most likely fallen into desuetude in counterterrorism contexts, a mere territorial link between a State and a terrorist group is typically insufficient to persuade those authors that this nexus alone catalyses and ultimately justifies an action involving self-defence.[136]

Indeed, should that territorial connection be sufficient to serve as sole predicate for triggering self-defence, such a standard might exacerbate power and wealth inequities in the North-South context. Developing States may have diminished means in combating terrorism or, alternatively, a weaker State may have the goodwill to contain a terrorist threat but concurrently lack the capability to do so efficiently.[137] Thus, an unnecessarily broad norm on permissible self-defence might, in fact, signal that other States reportedly harbouring terrorists within their borders in North America, South America, Europe, Africa, the Middle East, and Asia[138] could become subject to attack via self-defence. This reality also poses considerable legal and political problems for the prospect of inducing regime change through recourse to force so as to sever ties between States and terrorist organizations, an eventuality extending beyond the scope of this study. Suffice it to say that additional clarification as to applicable legal standards governing that exercise is required. In the absence of a compelling nexus between internationally wrongful act, attribution, and self-defence, the prospect of injured States pursuing individual terrorists or groups across borders is arguably less controversial than engaging forcible countermeasures against the responsible States themselves. Therefore, it seems that a prior finding of SR would actually be required in the latter case in order to substantiate self-defence.[139]

An additional layer of legal and evidentiary complexity pervades the inquiry if a terrorist strike spans over more than one territory (ie because of the cellular and de-territorialized structure of some terrorist networks), thereby blurring the bases of attribution for a seemingly fragmental wrongful act or, at least, a series of wrongful acts forming part of a greater whole. Indeed, this challenge was canvassed earlier in the context of cyberterrorism and other transnational security violations.[140]

[136] See, eg, Brunnée, 'The Security Council' (n 27) 123; N Schrijver, 'Responding to International Terrorism: Moving the Frontiers of International Law for "Enduring Freedom"?' (2001) 48 NILR 271, 283. Brunnée further adds that '"[h]arbouring" terrorists should not be a reason to invoke self-defence unless it amounts to at least tacit approval of terrorist attacks'. On this issue, see also Travalio and Altenburg (n 98) 111–13.

[137] This line of inquiry has particular implications for SC-approved measures against 'failed' States or nations governed by illegitimate or repressive regimes, which clearly amounts to an ambiguous legal area. See the discussion in CB Hynes *et al.*, 'National Security' (2007) International Lawyer 683, 683–4. For instance, the SC imposed sanctions on Sudan because it harboured terrorists. See UNSC Res 1054 (26 April 1996) UN Doc S/RES/1054 [1]. On SR in the context of the Sudanese war, see CM Henderson, 'Michael Byers, War Law: International Law and Armed Conflict' (2007) 12 JCSL 150, 152–3.

[138] See, eg, *US National Security Strategy* (n 132) 5.

[139] See, eg, Duffy (n 15) 192, fn 220. See also generally N Lubell, *Extraterritorial Use of Force against Non-State Actors* (OUP 2010) 56 (discussing self-defence and citing an ILC report).

[140] See Section 2.4.4.

For instance, publicly available facts indicate that the preparation of the 9/11 attacks actually spanned several States, including both the US and Germany (the Hamburg cell being determinant in the planning of those acts).[141] Consequently, could those States have been targeted in self-defence for the purpose of combating terrorism by a coalition of States seeking to enforce obligations *erga omnes*? An overly liberal norm on the invocation of self-defence might dangerously broaden the scope of forcible countermeasures against virtually all States having some terrorist or extremist elements operating within their borders. Such an eventuality might not only constitute an affront to the UN Charter's fundamental tenets but would significantly threaten to erode the policy equilibrium that the present study attempted to achieve between the essential principle of non-intervention and the pressing need to root out terrorist bases of operation. Whilst proportionality and necessity remain cardinal factors in regulating self-defence, some measure of proportionality, coupled with reasonableness, should not only govern the deployment of countermeasures under SR, generally, but also inform the identification of acceptable targets for military action in response to global security violations. Stated differently, should self-defence become an accepted countermeasure in response to State failures to prevent terrorism and other global security breaches, proportionality between a State's violation—not perfect symmetry—and the forcible countermeasure would be required. As a key implementer of SR in some instances, particularly in counterterrorism contexts as argued in Chapter 4, it would then fall to the SC to ensure that the application of that remedy remains commensurate with the culprit's involvement in terrorism, or its failure to prevent another global security transgression.

6.2.5 Concluding remarks on self-defence and State responsibility

It is clear that the relationship between SR and self-defence is rather complex. That said, there are certainly interesting inquiries to be conducted into the realm of collective self-defence when devising potential responses to State failures to prevent global security violations. Whilst future scholarly explorations of this topic will undoubtedly come to grips with this difficult interrelationship, it must be stressed—from a *lex ferenda* standpoint—that forcible countermeasures, if at all permissible, should only be deployed in extreme cases as a solution of last resort. Further inquiries into the untapped benefits that may be derived from R2P are to be anticipated, whilst the evolution of the accompanying State practice remains embryonic and far from dispositive. Unfortunately, scholars and policy experts are increasingly pointing to examples of international practice whereby multilateral institutions are bypassed when implementing forcible responses to global security breaches. Conversely, others emphasize a possibly emerging policy on

[141] See B Stern, 'La Responsabilité Internationale des États: Perspectives Récentes' in JC Lloréns (ed.), *Cursos Euromediterráneos Bancaja de Derecho Internacional*, vol 7 (Tirant lo Blanch 2003) 659, 691 fn 66.

transnational use of force, according to which the SC has begun authorizing—and sometimes calls for—recourse to force in response to massive or large-scale targeting of civilians.[142] As discussed earlier, the links with SR are rather straightforward in such scenarios, even if not always clearly articulated. If anything, this evolution of international law signals that the bases of State sovereignty are slowly eroding in favour of legal regimes that envisage an increased range of State responsibilities, coupled with interventionist stances regarding terrorism and similar global security challenges. In fact, in 2013 the UN Secretary-General expressly highlighted the nexus between the prevention of global security breaches, R2P, and SR repertoire in his report to the GA and SC[143] and in an official statement to the GA.[144] Therefore, additional oversight and the identification of compelling ways to create incentives for international action vis-à-vis wrongful acts are direly needed under the R2P framework.[145] As a corollary, these developments confirm the role that SR law can play in the work of UN organs, particularly the SC.

A traditionalist view of public international law might clash with certain tenets of R2P, which seem to offer novel and unorthodox ways of bypassing SC decision-making in specific circumstances involving force. Conversely, R2P also brings some measured rhetoric to the table, thereby casting military intervention as an option of last resort and cautioning a carefully crafted legal approach based on prevention and on the exhaustion of non-forcible means in redressing wrongful acts. Therefore, the nexus between the responsibility to protect and the responsibility to prevent lies at the very core of ICISS' proposal.[146] Its affinity with SR norms cannot be overemphasized and should not be underestimated, especially in global security contexts. For one thing, conceptual rapprochements may be envisaged between R2P and SR in areas falling short of armed intervention, particularly in the field of environmental protection.[147] As argued in Chapter 2, SR law can play a role, albeit a limited one, in preventing environmental harm. The normative influence—and the compliance pull—of this normative scheme would

[142] See, eg, G Cronogue, 'State Prosecution of Terrorism and Rebellion: A Functional Examination of the Protection of Civilians and the Erosion of Sovereignty' (2013) 46 Comparative and International Law Journal of Southern Africa 121.

[143] See Report of the Secretary-General, 'Responsibility to Protect: State Responsibility and Prevention' (2013) UN Doc A/67/929–S/2013/399.

[144] See Statement of the Secretary-General to the GA, 'Remarks to General Assembly Informal Interactive Dialogue on "The Responsibility to Protect: State Responsibility and Prevention"' (11 September 2013) <http://www.un.org/sg/statements/index.asp?nid=7070> accessed 10 August 2015.

[145] See, eg, NF Dastoor, 'The Responsibility to Refine: The Need for a Security Council Committee on the Responsibility to Protect' (2009) 22 Harvard Human Rights Journal 25.

[146] See *R2P Document* (n 44) 19 [3.1]:

> This Commission strongly believes that the responsibility to protect implies an accompanying responsibility to prevent. And we think that it is more than high time for the international community to be doing more to close the gap between rhetorical support for prevention and tangible commitment. The need to do much better on prevention, and to exhaust prevention options before rushing to embrace intervention, were constantly recurring themes in our worldwide consultations, and ones which we wholeheartedly endorse.

[147] See, eg, SE Davies, 'Natural Disasters and the Responsibility to Protect' (2012) 55 GYIL 149.

undoubtedly be bolstered by the concomitant application of R2P principles, thereby framing available options outside of the (strictly) legal realm: responses to climate change, for instance, could be made more palatable in the political mainstream in light of the recent endorsement of R2P by high-level UN organs whilst retaining some degree of legal legitimacy.

However, the mere existence of international legal norms will not act as a check and balance against States unilaterally adopting forcible reactions in response to the usurpation of their own interests. To excise any political realism from the analysis would be, frankly, indicative of a certain scholarly naiveté. Certainly, SR rules must be better defined or interpreted with a view to providing greater clarity and guidance in dealing with internationally wrongful conduct. However, they cannot offer any sort of uniform or infallible solution as those norms may simply become insufficient in preventing unilateral forcible reactions by victim-States in specific circumstances. Indeed, 'there still exists a strong tendency among states to use force in order to make good their (alleged) rights—even without them being victims of an illegal use of force—in flagrant violation of Article 2(4) of the Charter, as well as of the law of state responsibility'.[148] This is not to say that forcible reactions to wrongful conduct are necessarily desirable in all or even many scenarios, but they unquestionably constitute a feature of modern international society.[149] International lawyers can deplore them pursuant to traditional constructions of international law or, alternatively, those actors applying SR can attempt to take stock of difficult and novel situations involving non-State factions whilst situating the role of self-defence within this framework. The point is that the barrier between SR for terrorism/global security violations and self-defence is not so clear-cut; further inquiries will have to balance political realities, relevant legal instruments, and State practice carefully within a context-sensitive approach.

Ultimately, the intersection of SR and the scheme of collective security 'points both ways' in that States become internationally responsible when they violate UN Charter obligations and, in turn, may see those obligations enforced through the application of secondary norms and countermeasures, more specifically.[150] As discussed in Part II, such countermeasures can be implemented unilaterally by victim-States and, more controversially, may involve SC action. As a corollary, the future development of this dimension of SR will depend, to a large extent, on further clarification of self-defence repertoire vis-à-vis non-State actors. Similarly to the *Armed Activities* case, in the *Wall Advisory Opinion* the ICJ asserted that

[148] Pellet (n 20) 148.

[149] In turn, the development of international law might progress through inimical inter-State relations. Consider LL Fuller's prophetic words in 'Human Interaction and the Law' (1969) 14 AJIL 1, 31: 'while enemies may have difficulty in bargaining with words, they can, and often do profitably half-bargain with deeds. Paradoxically the tacit restraints of customary law between enemies are more likely to develop during active warfare than during a hostile stalemate of relations; fighting one another is itself in this sense a "social" relation since it involves communication.' For a highly reconcilable constructivist take on this idea, albeit through the lens of intervention, see M Finnemore, *The Purpose of Intervention: Changing Beliefs about the Use of Force* (Cornell University Press 2003) 5.

[150] Pellet (n 20) 148.

an 'armed attack' can only emanate from a sovereign State, thereby triggering the right of the injured State to respond in self-defence. Thus, the Court not only reaffirmed the State-centric nature of self-defence but also seemingly lay to rest all debates surrounding the nexus connecting SR and use of force repertoire, which should not be underemphasized. Simply put, the ICJ's interpretation of Article 51 of the UN Charter 'requires *state responsibility for the attack* that provokes a claim of a right to self-defense' (emphasis added).[151] Hence, it becomes clear that the determination of an internationally wrongful act serves as the basis—a sort of legal predicate—for the invocation of self-defence by an injured State.

However, SC practice does not seem to align with ICJ jurisprudence on this front, as highlighted by two ICJ Judges in their respective separate opinions in the *Wall Advisory Opinion*. Judge Kooijmans opined that Article 51 of the UN Charter 'conditions the exercise of the inherent right of self-defence on a previous armed attack without saying that this armed attack must come from another State even if this has been the generally accepted interpretation for more than 50 years'.[152] Similarly, in the *Armed Activities* case he remarked that the SC had since abandoned the Court's interpretation of Article 51, opting for a more fluid and adaptable construction of the relevant legal norms.[153] Judge Simma joined him in his own reasoning, emphasizing that the Court should have tackled the application of self-defence to non-State actors so as to conclude that terrorists, too, can carry out 'armed attacks' within the meaning of Article 51.[154]

Unsurprisingly, arguments have cropped up in legal discourse to the effect that victim-States can respond with force against individuals whom, aside from entertaining a territorial link to a State, share no other connection with that entity. Whilst this type of response eschews the possible importation of self-defence sensibilities within SR repertoire (ie short of attributing those individuals' acts to their territorial States), its validity has nonetheless gained traction after 9/11, in both individual judicial pronouncements and the literature.[155] In summary, scholars advocate a relaxed posture regarding formal recourse to force norms, expounding, *inter alia*, that the international legal community should refrain from harbouring a monolithic view of self-defence, confined to armed responses to State-based attacks; as a corollary, this legal scheme now encompasses privately-inflicted transnational terror.[156]

[151] WM Reisman and A Armstrong, 'The Past and Future of the Claim of Preemptive Self-Defense' (2006) 100 AJIL 525, 537–8 (discussing the *Wall Advisory Opinion*).

[152] See Separate Opinion of Judge Kooijmans in the *Wall Advisory Opinion* (n 25) [35] (also opining that the Court essentially circumvented the framework put forth in SC Res 1373). See also Declaration of Judge Buergenthal in ibid [5]–[6].

[153] See Separate Opinion of Judge Kooijmans in the *Armed Activities Case* (n 102) [28].

[154] See Separate Opinion of Judge Simma in the *Armed Activities Case* (n 102) 335–8. Compare with Separate Opinion of Judge Simma in the *Oil Platforms Case* (n 91) 331–3 (also defending the legality of proportionate defensive measures taken against uses of force falling short of the 'armed attack' threshold).

[155] See, eg, Separate Opinion of Judge Kooijmans in the *Wall Advisory Opinion* (n 25) [35]. See also SD Murphy, 'Self-Defense and the Israeli War Advisory Opinion: An Ipse Dixit from the ICJ?' (2005) 99 AJIL 62, 69.

[156] See, eg, C Greenwood, 'International Law and the Pre-emptive Use of Force: Afghanistan, Al-Qaida, and Iraq' (2003) 4 San Diego International Law Journal 7, 16–18.

By contrast to the ICJ, after 9/11 the SC emphasized that both non-State actors and the States that aid, support, or harbour terrorists would be found responsible under international law. Resolution 1368, which was cited by the ICJ in the *Wall Advisory Opinion*, and by Judges Kooijmans and Simma in their separate opinions in the *Armed Activities* case, was drafted in unequivocal terms. The SC

> [r]ecogniz[ed] the inherent right of individual or collective self-defence in accordance with the Charter... [and] [c]all[ed] on all States to work together urgently to bring to justice the perpetrators, organizers and sponsors of these terrorist attacks and stresse[d] that those responsible for aiding, supporting or harbouring the perpetrators, organizers and sponsors of these acts will be held accountable.[157]

In short, the SC stressed that both SR and individual responsibility mechanisms (eg international criminal law, civil lawsuits) could work in concert and remain coextensive in combating terrorism, a notion highly reconcilable with the ideas explored in the present study.[158] More relevantly given the ICJ's inter-State jurisdiction, the SC seemingly espoused a different approach to the invocation of self-defence than that endorsed by the Court. This interpretive asymmetry could arguably lead to victim-States targeting both States and non-State actors when responding to internationally wrongful acts. When formulating policy proposals, commentators will likely have to take stock of this intriguing interpretative duality between the SC and ICJ, and ultimately attempt to reconcile both approaches or, alternatively, identify the one best suited to adapt to SR and terrorism/global security.[159] Furthermore, efforts will have to be deployed to define the SC's role in interpreting and applying SR rules, which was the focus of Part II, given that this body will authorize and monitor the adoption of forcible countermeasures in global security contexts.

In conclusion, whilst the invocation of self-defence might be permitted in specific circumstances to respond to the failure to prevent terrorism, the SC's ascertainment of a wrongful act would presumably 'not justify reactions that would otherwise be unlawful, and, therefore, does not expand the scope of the admissible use of force either'.[160] Yet, States often point to a Council's determination under Article 39 of the UN Charter as a basis to substantiate unilateral military 'sanctions',[161] hence the confusion surrounding self-defence's role in the scheme of countermeasures is endemic to both the self-contained nature of recourse to force repertoire and to State-led initiatives that concurrently straddle that regime and SR terrain. Whilst the rationales for responding forcibly to terrorism are not always

[157] UNSC Res 1368 (12 September 2001) UN Doc S/RES/1368, preamble, [3].

[158] Indeed, the policy thrust of this study is to cast SR law as complementary to the application of other concurrent, relevant legal regimes whilst also recognizing that normative scheme's centrality in contemporary international law.

[159] After all, the relationship between the SC and ICJ is a rather complex one. See Chapter 3, esp Section 3.2.

[160] JA Frowein and N Kirsch, 'Introduction to Chapter VII' in B Simma *et al.* (eds), *The Charter of the United Nations: A Commentary* (2nd edn, OUP 2002) 709, 714.

[161] Pellet (n 20) 148–9.

cogently articulated within the scope of SR, considerable overlap between both regimes nonetheless underpins States' justifications in some instances. Looking to the future, scholars will have some leeway in crafting new and innovative interpretations of self-defence's role within SR repertoire. After all, as stressed by the ICJ in *Nicaragua*, the almost cryptic statements on use of force enshrined in the UN Charter are subject to evolution and competing interpretations over time, which could presumably include some kind of rapprochement with SR.[162] Whilst use of force is considered a self-contained regime, legal instruments confirming its scope and content are by no means comprehensive.[163] Further analysis on how that regime can inform the application of SR principles, especially regarding countermeasures and potential implementation by UN organs, can yield interesting payoffs. Ultimately, these areas are likely to develop—and their interrelationships come into sharper focus—in tandem with the evolution of counterterrorism and other global security strategies.[164]

6.3 A Research and Policy Prospectus for the Future: Guidelines and Building Blocks

A radical brand of legal consequences potentially lies at the far end of the spectrum of secondary SR rules. A recurrent tension between upholding sovereignty and addressing global security challenges efficiently pervades many of the policy considerations explored in this book.[165] Indeed, policy and legal choices often oscillate between sacrificing sovereignty and upholding State or territorial sanctity; difficult trade-offs have to be made to combat global security violations effectively. Consequently, various unconventional and controversial manifestations of secondary rules of responsibility were contemplated since 9/11; proposals ranged

[162] Indeed, both the UN Charter and the ARSIWA are living instruments, capable of evolving constructions and interpretations over time. See, eg, B Fassbender, *The United Nations Charter as the Constitution of the International Community* (Nijhoff 2009) esp ch 6; A Ross, *Constitution of the United Nations: Analysis of Structure and Function* (Munksgaard 1950) 5; O Schachter, 'Dispute Settlement and Countermeasures in the International Law Commission' (1994) 88 AJIL 471, 477 (opining that '[w]e can be quite sure that the articles and commentary will acquire added authority through their practical application and the accompanying accretion of *opinio juris* even if in some cases they might be modified (or overridden) as a consequence of practice').

[163] See *Nicaragua v USA* (Merits) (n 27) 94 [176] (underscoring that the UN Charter 'by no means covers the whole area of the regulation of the use of force in international relations'). See also C Gray, *International Law and the Use of Force* (3rd edn, OUP 2008) 7 (remarking that 'the rules of the Charter on the use of force are brief and cannot constitute a comprehensive code').

[164] See, eg, Duffy (n 15) 161.

[165] Interestingly, commentators both before and after 9/11 expressed, either explicitly or impliedly, that a State's harbouring of terrorists should in fact pre-empt any claim to sovereignty on its part. See, eg, MB Baker, 'Terrorism and the Inherent Right of Self-Defense (A Call to Amend Article 51 of the United Nations Charter)' (1987) 10 HJIL 25, 40. In the same vein, see also I Brownlie, 'International Law and the Activities of Armed Bands' (1958) 7 ICLQ 712, 718 (inferring that support or toleration of terrorist activities by a State amounts to aggression); P Kovács, 'Beaucoup de Questions et Peu de Réponses Autour de l'Imputabilité d'un Acte Terroriste à un État' (2002) 1 Journal of European Integration Studies 20, 23; L Condorelli, 'The Imputability to States of Acts

from implementing international trusteeships—potentially in Pakistan's tribal regions where terrorist activity was rampant (similar reasoning could extend to ISIL- or Al-Shabaab-controlled areas, for instance)—to exploring the relationship between R2P and SR repertoire. Undoubtedly, the most contentious area of response to failures to prevent global security breaches resides in the field of recourse to force. Inevitably, scholars addressing these issues in the future will have to grapple with the relationship between SR and forcible State responses whilst placing significant emphasis on self-defence in the analysis. In that spirit, this chapter attempted to provide a preliminary glimpse into this legally nebulous relationship. Further scholarly explorations building on the line of argument developed in this book will thus be able to expand on the few building blocks set out in the following.

First, even if use of force is ultimately permitted in response to State failures to prevent terrorism or other global security violations, it should be cast as a solution of last resort and avoid, by all means possible, bypassing SC authorization. In particular, it is doubtful whether force would be permitted against ineffective States in which terrorists operate and where the governmental apparatus is deploying efforts in good faith to thwart the unlawful activity but is unable to contain the threat or punish the acts.[166] However, it should be recalled that this position is increasingly challenged by advocates of controversial, interventionist norms such as the 'unable or unwilling' doctrine, which seriously threaten to exacerbate sovereignty controversies and the North–South divide. Nevertheless, much of the post-9/11 scholarship rejects a territorial nexus between a sanctuary State and a terrorist organization as the *sole* basis for invoking use of force against that State.[167] Whilst a less tenuous connection would be required to engage recourse to force repertoire, it is still unclear under international law what level or degree of State involvement would be sufficient to meet that threshold.[168] This, of course, has no bearing on the determination of SR but instead specifically refers to the use of force. For example, a State's passive toleration of terrorists operating within its border, when it has the means at its disposal to repel the activity could trigger that State's international responsibility without regard to the legitimacy of potential

of International Terrorism' (1989) 19 IYHR 233; Y Dinstein, *War, Aggression and Self-Defence* (3rd edn, CUP 2001) 182–3; PS Rao, 'International Crimes and State Responsibility' in Ragazzi (n 8) 66; WM Reisman, 'International Legal Responses to International Terrorism' (1999) 22 HJIL 3, 39; N Ronzitti, 'Italy's Non-Belligerency During the Iraqi War' in Ragazzi (n 8) 205. Interestingly, H Lauterpacht, 'Règles Générales du Droit de la Paix' (1937) 62 RdC 95, 339, 349–52 opined that the very concept of 'sovereignty' impedes the advancement of SR law.

[166] See, eg, SR Ratner, '*Jus ad Bellum* and *Jus in Bello* after September 11' (2002) 96 AJIL 905, 908 fn 15; ME O'Connell, *International Law and the Use of Force: Cases and Materials* (2nd edn, Foundation Press 2009) 319. On the linkages between the developing world and R2P, see RC Thakur, 'The Responsibility to Protect and the North-South Divide' in SR Silverburg (ed.), *International Law: Contemporary Issues and Future Developments* (Westview Press 2011) 32–47.

[167] See, eg, Brunnée, 'The Security Council' (n 27) 118, 123; Nollkaemper (n 81) 136; Ruys (n 62) 470; HP Aust, 'Book Reviews' (2012) EJIL 275, 277.

[168] On the requisite degree of State involvement in terrorism, see Sections 1.3; 1.4; 2.2; 2.3; 5.2.4. Some construe both ICJ jurisprudence and post-9/11 State practice as instituting a new standard for attributing non-State terrorist attacks to territorial States, namely: sanctuary and State support.

forcible responses.[169] As discussed earlier, the determination of appropriate legal consequences in response to internationally wrongful acts comes at a later stage, namely after the ascertainment of the wrong itself and, correspondingly, after the initial finding of SR.

Secondly, this chapter revealed that the connection between self-defence and SR cannot be ignored and should not be underemphasized in future scholarly endeavours exploring the potential benefits of accountability mechanisms in global security contexts. The ILC itself defended the notion that an injured State could only invoke its right of self-defence against another State that had previously committed a wrongful act involving a violation of Article 2(4) of the UN Charter. Otherwise stated, the exercise of self-defence remains predicated on the violation of a primary obligation for SR purposes; thus, the connection between self-defence and SR is grounded in customary law. As seen earlier, the central point of contention instead hinges on whether State failures to prevent terrorism (or other global security analogues) are tantamount to violations of Article 2(4), especially when the wrongdoing consists of mere toleration.

Some respond in the affirmative when confronted with this conundrum, construing the connection between both bodies of law as resting on 'good policy grounds'.[170] Surely undesirable results would ensue if a sanctuary State's responsibility were not engaged for forcible transnational acts—thereby sheltering it from the obligations of ceasing the wrongful act and making reparation (ie protection against non-forcible countermeasures)—but where that State could nonetheless become the target of recourse to force, perhaps even inducing regime change.[171] Moreover, if State support of terrorism amounts to the provision of safe haven, coupled with logistical support, training, and weapons, this involvement could trigger both the application of SR and self-defence repertoire. Whilst controversial under traditional SR—primarily because such State involvement would ostensibly fail to meet the *Nicaragua* standard and, perhaps, also the *Tadić* threshold—this conclusion is not completely without merit.[172] However, the analytical focal point resides in determining whether by providing territorial support and other types of assistance, the State enabled the terrorist group to carry out military acts (ie well-orchestrated terrorist strikes) that could be equated with an 'armed attack' had they been committed by the State itself. In the affirmative, some publicists construe such involvement as militating in favour of construing the acts as an armed attack launched by the State.[173]

Thirdly, whilst SR is much broader in its purview, it nonetheless shares a distinct affinity with the law governing self-defence in that both regimes respond to,

See, eg, B Michael, 'Responding to Attacks by Non-State Actors: The Attribution Requirement of Self-Defence' (2009) 16 Australian International Law Journal 133.

[169] And yet, some state that it would be unfair to attribute terrorist actions to sanctuary States when they have lost control over terrorist units located on their territory. See Stern (n 141) 688.

[170] Nollkaemper (n 81) 138.

[171] But see Ratner (n 166) 908–9.

[172] For a detailed discussion of these cases and the legal standards they introduced, see Proulx (n 12) 63–9. On *Nicaragua*, see also Sections 1.3 and 3.1.3.1.

[173] See Randelzhofer (n 42) 801 fn 32. For a similar, exhaustive argument, see T Becker, *Terrorism and the State: Rethinking the Rules of State Responsibility* (Hart 2006).

and seek to bring to an end, the commission of an internationally wrongful act.[174] Otherwise stated, self-defence achieves a role analogous to that of countermeasures which unquestionably form part and parcel of SR repertoire.[175] Granted, the law of countermeasures has generated its share of controversy in legal scholarship[176] and, correspondingly, the usual requirements for the deployment of self-defence would have to be fulfilled for that response to qualify as an appropriate countermeasure, should it be framed as such. Nevertheless, some publicists rightly perceive an inexorable 'overlap in functions of self-defence and state responsibility'; as a corollary, this interplay 'illustrates that in particular circumstances the distinction between primary and secondary rules can be somewhat arbitrary'.[177] In short, both reparation under SR law and the invocation of self-defence can become coextensive or, at least, overlap as potential responses to internationally wrongful acts. A violation of Article 2(4) of the UN Charter can simultaneously set in motion obligations of cessation and reparation under SR repertoire, along with the right of the injured State to invoke self-defence.

Therefore, under both regimes the consequences of the wrongful act are perceived as 'complementary', with self-defence ostensibly constituting a narrower range of response.[178] Whilst self-defence remains available to injured States in response to wrongdoing States' failures to prevent terrorism or other global security breaches, in the event of a violation international law simultaneously requires that wrongdoing States comply with obligations of continued performance, cessation, and reparation under SR. Conversely, the obligations of continued performance and cessation could arguably be construed as forming part of the relevant primary rules, where applicable. However, the ILC emphasized that cessation remains nonetheless intimately intertwined with reparation and should thus be envisaged through the framework of consequences of internationally wrongful acts.[179] Simply put, the termination of an Article 2(4) transgression not only finds support in justified use of force under Article 51 of the UN Charter, but is also predicated on the deployment of secondary SR norms. This application of SR is not contingent on the injured State's subjective appreciation; rather, the legal

[174] See, eg, B Conforti, *International Law and the Role of the Domestic Legal Systems* (Nijhoff 1993) 176 (expounding that both legitimized forcible responses under UN Charter Art 51 and countermeasures constitute typical responses to internationally wrongful acts). But see R Ago, 'Addendum—Eighth Report on State Responsibility' (1980) UN Doc A/CN.4/318/Add.5–7; (1980) II(1) *YILC* 54 [90] (highlighting that it would be 'quite wrong to think that self-defence can also be defined as some kind of sanction').

[175] See ARSIWA (n 13) Arts 49–54.

[176] See, eg, JR Crawford, 'First Report on State Responsibility' (1998) UN Doc A/CN.4/490 and Add. 1–7, 8 [28]–[32]; D Alland, 'Countermeasures of General Interest' (2002) 13 EJIL 1221, 1222.

[177] Nollkaemper (n 81) 149.

[178] Nollkaemper (n 81) 150. See also M Kowalski, 'Armed Attack, Non-State Actors and a Quest for the Attribution Standard' (2010) 30 PYIL 101, 103–6 (observing that both regimes are complementary in enforcing international law); R Wolfrum, 'The Attack of September 11, 2001, the Wars against the Taliban and Iraq: Is There a Need to Reconsider International Law on the Recourse to Force and the Rules in Armed Conflict?' (2003) 7 Max Planck Yearbook of UN Law 1, 36–7.

[179] See Commentary to ARSIWA (n 13) Art 30 p 89 [6]–[8].

consequences flowing from the commission of a wrongful act operate on an objective or automatic basis, without regard to the actual exercise of the invocation rights conferred upon that State under the ARSIWA.[180] Moreover, the symbiosis between SR and self-defence finds further grounding in the ILC's work. In particular, a Special Rapporteur once insisted that self-defence solely applied to inter-State relations, a position perhaps now threatened by recent SC practice, irrespective of the controversy surrounding the ICJ's *Wall Advisory Opinion*.[181]

Moreover, the ILC further opined that self-defence remains confined to a State's response against a wrongful act perpetrated by another State.[182] Finally, the exercise of self-defence constitutes a last resort, 'self-help' remedy to address a truly *sui generis* type of wrongful act, namely the illegal use of force.[183] Thus, only a wrongful act involving a violation of Article 2(4) of the UN Charter can set in motion self-defence repertoire, which potentially limits global security breaches falling into that category. Therefore, the crux of the present volume's analysis has focused on determining whether a State's failure to prevent terrorism can amount to such a violation. Given the predominantly bilateral typology underpinning recourse to force norms, an injured State invoking self-defence in this context may thus only predicate its action on the prior unlawful use of force perpetrated by the target State (ie the terrorist attack is attributed to it or its failure is equated with an unlawful use of force under Article 2(4)).[184]

Fourthly, SR law can act as a legal benchmark, a sort of 'outer limit of lawful self-defence'.[185] In particular, according to traditional SR principles, private terrorist acts that cannot be imputed to a State will typically fail to justify self-defence against that State. However, more controversially and as explored in this chapter, State failures to prevent transnational terrorism can also signal the commission of internationally wrongful acts that may, or may not, subject responsible States to self-defence. In such scenario, the lawfulness of the exercise of force remains an open question to be clarified through the SC's implementation activities, the ICJ's judicial pronouncements, diplomatic practice, and legal scholarship. Ultimately, the legality of such reactions remains largely contingent on each case's factual circumstances, with factors such as the territorial State's 'knowledge and foreseeability' weighing heavily in the analysis.[186]

[180] See Commentary to ARSIWA (n 13) Art 31 p 91 [4].

[181] See Ago, 'Addendum' (n 174) 53–4 [88]. See also A Cassese, 'Terrorism Is Also Disrupting Some Crucial Legal Categories of International Law' (2001) 12 EJIL 993, 997; Randelzhofer (n 42) 802 fn 34 (arguing that terrorist attacks authored by non-State actors are only tantamount to 'armed attacks' if they can be attributed to a State).

[182] See Ago, 'Addendum' (n 174) 15–6 [4], 53 [87]. In addition, this posture also aligns with the views espoused by influential scholars. See, eg, DW Bowett, *Self-Defence in International Law* (Manchester University Press 1958) 9 ('[t]he essence of self-defence is a *wrong done, a breach of a legal duty* owed to the state acting in self-defence' (emphasis added)).

[183] Eminent publicists had recognized this reality early on in the existence of the UN Charter. See, eg, R Higgins, *The Development of International Law through the Political Organs of the United Nations* (OUP 1963) 199, 216; H Kelsen, 'Collective Security and Collective Self-Defense under the Charter of the United Nations' (1948) 42 AJIL 783, 788.

[184] See ILC Report (n 78) 52–3 [3].

[185] Nollkaemper (n 81) 165.

[186] Nollkaemper (n 81) 165.

Conclusion to Part III

In response to evolving State and institutional practice, along with various *lex ferenda* inclinations, Part III attempted to provide an alternate politico-legal route to address global security violations through State responsibility (SR), at least in two ways. First, it cast the invocation of self-defence (or more modest forcible reactions) squarely as a response of last resort in the most extreme cases.[1] This policy rationale was informed by the fact that whilst they serve seemingly similar functions under some lights, SR law and self-defence repertoire differ in certain key aspects, most importantly their respective scopes. Indeed, the latter scheme is far narrower from a conceptual standpoint, yet it can engender far more destabilizing effects than the deployment of non-forcible, secondary rules of responsibility. When devising responsibility models implicating potential use of force—whether envisaged through self-defence, collective enforcement action, or responsibility to protect (R2P)—careful consideration must be given to the desired equilibrium between States' self-judged right and/or duty to intervene, be it individually or multilaterally, and States' sovereign equality along with potential human rights violations that an overly interventionist stance may foment. Therefore, it might sometimes be politically cautious to err on the side of upholding State sovereignty and identify alternate enforcement modes of primary global security obligations. Second, in responding further to the *lex specialis* line of argument,[2] Part III attempted to provide an alternative to endorsing a perhaps overly permissive

[1] See also O Schachter, 'The Right of States to Use Armed Force' 82 Michigan Law Review 1620, 1635 ('there should be no quarrel with the proposition that force should not be considered necessary until peaceful measures have been found wanting or when they clearly would be futile').

[2] In particular, an argument is sometimes advanced that different attribution rules than those enshrined in the ARSIWA might govern armed attacks carried out by non-State terrorist actors. The genesis of this idea can most likely be traced back to Judge Jennings' Dissenting Opinion in *Military and Paramilitary Activities in and against Nicaragua (Nicaragua v USA)* (Merits) [1986] ICJ Rep 14, 533. See also A Nollkaemper, 'Attribution of Forcible Acts to States: Connections between the Law on the Use of Force and the Law of State Responsibility' in N Blokker and N Schrijver (eds), *The Security Council and the Use of Force: Theory and Reality—A Need for Change?* (Nijhoff 2005) 133, 162; R van Steenberghe, 'Self-Defence in Response to Attacks by Non-State Actors in the Light of Recent State Practice: A Step Forward?' (2010) 23 LJIL 183, 194–7. The ICJ also acknowledged that different rules than those developed by the ILC might crop up, though those norms would need to be 'clearly expressed'. See *Case Concerning the Application of the Convention on the Prevention and Punishment of the Crime of Genocide (Bosnia and Herzegovina v Serbia and Montenegro)* (Merits) [2007] ICJ Rep 43, 208–9 [401]. As an alternative to the *lex specialis* angle, modified rules of attribution governing terrorist attacks might emerge through a flexible construction of ARSIWA Arts 4–11. See CJ Tams, 'The Use of Force against Terrorists' (2009) 20 EJIL 359, 385–7; Nollkaemper

attribution norm connecting private acts to States, which could arguably trigger a right to invoke self-defence pursuant to more liberal readings of recent State practice. Undoubtedly, it remains absolutely crucial that the international community operationalize the United Nations (UN) Charter's restraints on unnecessary use of force.[3]

Ultimately, much of the global counterterrorism campaign will be best pursued through international institutions such as the Security Council, with international cooperation and solid deference to the rule of law serving as organizing principles in this policy quest. Part III couched its proposal for such an agenda squarely at the intersection of SR and recourse to force, so as to determine whether self-defence could sometimes contribute to reinstating a sense of normalcy and a return to law and order. Paradoxically, Kelsen contended that the objective of maintaining or restoring international peace and security, embodied in Article 39 of the UN Charter, was not necessarily synonymous with return to legality. Whilst interesting, this approach presents serious problematic aspects among which is the notion that peace can override law when, in fact, the two should remain complementary in UN activities. Moreover, it fails to clearly identify the process by which applicable legal regimes can be restored, thereby assuming, perhaps unnecessarily, that both the drafting history of the UN Charter was, and its application by UN organs should always be, informed by politics over law.[4]

This posture also fails to explain what States are actually empowered to do to fill the void and ensure a return to legality, especially when compared to more unilateral means of implementing international responsibility. In this chapter, the tension between Kelsen's approach and self-help remedies or countermeasures came into sharp relief, suggesting that States can sometimes become the sole actors empowered to restore the law. This aspect of international law enforcement was tackled in earlier sections by examining the relationship between self-help measures and fairness, given that asymmetric power dynamics often pervade international relations. As seen in Chapter 3, when addressing this feature of international relations and responding to detractors of self-help sanctions, backed by Lauterpacht, Kelsen argued for the implementation of a third-party, objective decision-maker. Certainly, this is one possible avenue to address State failures to prevent terrorism and identify corresponding legal consequences, although its political viability remains questionable. However, in the current system the potential unfair application of countermeasures is exacerbated by the phenomena of self-judging and autoqualification, which remain integral to the central

(n 2) 156–7. See also generally J d'Aspremont, 'Mapping the Concepts behind the Contemporary Liberalization of the Use of Force in International law' (2010) 31 University of Pennsylvania Journal of International Law 1089, 1124–6.

[3] See generally P Sands, 'Operationalizing the UN Charter Rules on the Use of Force' in A Cassese (ed.), *Realizing Utopia: The Future of International Law* (OUP 2012) 343–58.

[4] See H Kelsen, *The Law of the United Nations: A Critical Analysis of its Fundamental Problems* (Stevens & Sons 1950) 294, 735. See also L Oppenheim and H Lauterpacht, *International Law: A Treatise (Vol 2: Disputes, War and Neutrality)* (7th edn, Longmans 1952) 163.

rationale of the Articles on Responsibility of States for Internationally Wrongful Acts (ARSIWA).[5]

Unsurprisingly, self-judged and unilaterally applied countermeasures are more readily contemplated by economically powerful States in responding to global security violations. Moreover, they remain inexorably prone to escalation given that targeted States might themselves take countermeasures to counteract what they perceive as unjustified countermeasures taken against them, thereby further poisoning international relations and aggravating underlying disagreements. As seen in Part III, this risk becomes particularly acute when recourse to force—although recognized as a controversial countermeasure—is thrown into the mix; the margin for potential abuse against weaker States increases significantly, disregard for the North/South divide becomes more palpable. Ultimately, whether seen through the potential institutionalization of SR or the traditional prism of inter-State implementation, an effective SR regime will be coextensive with a legal narrative that is sensible to the realities facing the developing world and affords due consideration to States' sovereign equality.[6] This balance is quite challenging to achieve when competing geopolitical, military, and economic interests are weighed against the backdrop of a largely anarchic and decentralized system, in which unchecked force may sometimes be used by the most powerful. Therefore, it is apparent that the extant, predominantly bilateral (but in practice, mostly unilateral) SR model needs to be revisited, including in light of contemporaneous realities such as the rise of—and unprecedented power wielded by—non-State actors on the transnational level.

[5] See Sections 1.2.2 and 3.1.2.

[6] See also Section 3.1.2.

Conclusion

One overarching conclusion emerges after canvassing United Nations (UN) institutions' potential input in implementing State responsibility (SR) in global security contexts: whilst these organs seem suited, upon first glance, to contribute to some extent to the development of SR law, there is considerable reluctance to do so, both motivated by political factors and informed by the relevant institutional frameworks' limitations. For instance, the International Court of Justice (ICJ) frequently sidestepped the application of SR norms when it could have made some stand-alone determinations on internationally wrongful acts or international responsibility, a posture at least partially informed by concerns of political appeasement and/or expediency, but largely driven by its jurisdictional constraints. For its part, the SC's mandate is not primarily couched in international legal language but rather focuses on the maintenance/restoration of international peace and security. Whether a specific situation involving transnational terrorism or another global security breach can be subsumed within that remit for SR purposes remains a question contingent on factual and legal appreciation, always subject to case-by-case assessments. This monograph has argued that in some cases, the Council can decidedly pronounce on SR matters, although the scope of that function remains limited.

Whilst States' international responsibility for failing to prevent terrorism, or for supporting terrorism, has been invoked in a few cases, a model premised on the institutional implementation of the resulting legal accountability is by no means a hard and fast rule. As a corollary, certain international disputes also prompted both the ICJ and SC to apply classical SR norms without, nonetheless, invoking the concept of 'terrorism' when such a determination could arguably have been made. This reality ties into a crucial observation that may be gleaned from the foregoing considerations. The SC is reticent, understandably so, to issue doctrinal formulations of relevant principles on SR matters, instead framing its reasoning within the mission of maintaining international peace and security, and resolving each situation on an individual basis.[1] For this project's purposes, this

[1] See also A Nollkaemper, 'Attribution of Forcible Acts to States: Connections Between the Law on the Use of Force and the Law of State Responsibility' in N Blokker and N Schrijver (eds), *The Security Council and the Use of Force: Theory and Reality—A Need for Change?* (Nijhoff 2005) 133, 168; C Gray, *International Law and the Use of Force* (2nd edn, OUP 2004) 95–101; TM Franck, *Recourse to Force: State Action against Threats and Armed Attacks* (CUP 2002) 53–68.

argument has been presented in tandem with the functional equivalent of that reluctance within the ICJ's own decision-making, namely its reticence to qualify internationally wrongful acts as 'terrorism' in cases involving the responsibility of territorial or supporting States. Not to mention the ICJ's own general reluctance to brand States as violators of international law. Setting aside the fact that certain important SR disputes have been resolved outside international judicial channels (eg *Lockerbie, Rainbow Warrior*), whilst the ICJ has sometimes set in motion international responsibility rules, no causal nexus was ever formally established by it between State-supported terrorism and SR repertoire.[2]

Moreover, the SC will not usually issue formal declarations of unlawful behaviour and correspondingly attribute acts of private actors to States. Instead, it frames its reasoning within the scope of international peace and security, as opposed to assigning blame and applying attribution under SR repertoire.[3] Moving away from this rigid dichotomy, this book has argued that counterterrorism policy epitomizes a *sui generis* character and, in certain cases, its objectives straddle Chapter VII terrain. Given that the Council has sometimes expressly handed down findings of illegality and established SR,[4] it logically follows that SR law (particularly attribution principles) should guide the Council's assessment of the connection between non-State actors and their territorial States. One commentator aptly summarized the position: 'it may well be argued that the nature and function of the acts of the Security Council are closely related to the function of the law of state responsibility ... in many cases the Council will respond to an act that is in violation of international law'.[5] It must be recalled that the SC has sometimes ventured very far upon SR terrain, both under Chapter VII and outside that framework. Its treatment of Iraq's invasion of Kuwait remains a striking example. Indeed, the SC's implementation of Iraq's responsibility undoubtedly consecrated that body's ability to impose secondary obligations upon responsible States flowing from the violation of primary global security legal norms. Amongst particularly severe secondary obligations imposed by the Council in this context were the institution of an indemnification fund and the delimitation of an international border.[6] Similarly, the adoption of Resolution 1368 by the Council in the wake of 9/11 suggested further incursions into SR repertoire by that body. This led some interlocutors to ponder whether the Council's resolution operated on

[2] See also J-C Martin, *Les Règles Internationales Relatives à la Lutte contre le Terrorisme* (Bruylant 2006) 465.

[3] See also Gray (n 1) 96–7; DW Bowett, *Self-Defence in International Law* (Manchester University Press 1958) 263–5.

[4] See, eg, UNSC Res 687 (3 April 1991) UN Doc S/RES/687 (on Iraq's invasion of Kuwait); UNSC Res 1304 (16 June 2000) UN Doc S/RES/1304 [14] (on the situation in the DRC). For an exploration of the conformity of such determinations with the UN Charter, see E Lauterpacht, *Aspects of the Administration of International Justice* (Grotius 1991) 42–3.

[5] Nollkaemper (n 1) 168–9 (observing that the Council engages with secondary rules).

[6] See, eg, SC Res 687 (n 4) [16], [18]. See also generally A Kolliopoulos, *La Commission d'Indemnisation des Nations Unies et le Droit de la Responsabilité Internationale* (LGDJ 2001); P d'Argent, *Les Réparations de Guerre en Droit International Public: Le Droit de la Responsabilité Internationale à l'Épreuve de la Guerre* (Bruylant 2002).

the premise that sufficient connections were ascertained between Al-Qaeda and Afghanistan to impute the attacks to that State.[7]

In addition to applying secondary rules, the SC has also dabbled in the promulgation of primary global security obligations, which has a direct incidence on SR mechanics. Resolution 1373, which was discussed in Parts I and II, was particularly relevant because it marked the first time that the Council set general and far-reaching obligations upon *all* States, not limited to any geographical area or specific timeframe. Thus, the Council's pre- and post-9/11 pronouncements on terrorism, along with similar advances by the General Assembly (GA), confirmed that '[n]umerous other resolutions from both the United Nations General Assembly and the United Nations Security Council leave no doubt that harboring or supporting terrorist groups violates a state's responsibility under international law'.[8] However, it remains unclear whether the 9/11 attacks were incontrovertibly attributed to Afghanistan on the basis of direct responsibility, even when relying on precedents hinging on the institutional implementation of responsibility by UN organs. The basis for SR, therefore, must stem from elsewhere, namely from the failure to prevent the excursions—a separate duty falling short of casting terrorist attacks as 'acts of state'—and an obligation actuated through the indirect responsibility paradigm discussed in Sections 2.2 and 5.4.[9]

However, the legal landscape resulting from the adoption of the groundbreaking Resolution 1373 has fomented heightened transnational cooperation on counterterrorism issues between States, and has been characterized by continuing SC involvement in counterterrorism matters. Outside the targeted sanctions regime, transnational cooperation has been primarily geared towards implementing Resolution 1373, whereas the Council's involvement has predominantly focused on the management of counterterrorism initiatives and reaffirmation of primary obligations.[10] Undoubtedly, the SC has arrogated vast and extended powers since 9/11, which presumably extend beyond the mere promulgation of primary

[7] See generally ME O'Connell, 'Evidence of Terror' (2002) 7 JCSL 19; C Stahn, '"Nicaragua is Dead, Long Live Nicaragua": The Right to Self-Defense under Art. 51 UN Charter and International Terrorism' in C Walter *et al.* (eds), *Terrorism as a Challenge for National and International Law: Security Versus Liberty?* (Springer 2004) 827, 827–77.

[8] G Travalio and J Altenburg, 'Terrorism, State Responsibility, and the Use of Military Force' (2003) 4 CJIL 97, 100.

[9] See also Y Arai-Takahashi, 'Shifting Boundaries of the Right of Self-Defence: Appraising the Impact of the September 11 Attacks on *Jus Ad Bellum*' (2002) 36 International Lawyer 1081, 1099 (applying analogous reasoning to Afghanistan's role in the 9/11 attacks).

[10] On the institutional milestones and pitfalls related to SC involvement in counterterrorism after the adoption of Resolution 1373, along with inter-State cooperation, see KB Youssef, 'La Coopération Interétatique et la Mise en Oeuvre de la Résolution 1373 (2001) du Conseil de Sécurité' in M Arcari and L Balmond (eds), *La Gouvernance Globale face aux Défis de la Sécurité Collective* (Editoriale Scientifica 2012) 137–47; J Kobila, 'Dixième Anniversaire des Attaques du 11 Septembre 2001: Bilan de la Gestion de la Lutte contre le Terrorisme par le Conseil de Sécurité des Nations Unies' (2011) 24 Revue Québécoise de Droit International 349–405; S Laghmani, 'Le Conseil de Sécurité et le Terrorisme International' in MSB Aïssa (ed.), *En hommage à Dali Jazi* (Centre de Publications Universitaires de Tunisie 2010) 463–70.

norms;[11] indeed, that UN organ has also been active in applying secondary SR norms. Various examples of such practice were canvassed and analysed in Part II.

In aggregate, whilst the Council's application of international law remains predominantly arbitrary, selective, strategic, or instrumentalist, it has nevertheless delivered a significant set of rules and precedents, whether by promulgating primary counterterrorism norms or by applying specific secondary rules to global security breaches flowing from SR repertoire. However, whilst the input of UN institutions in the development of SR and the SC's contribution, more specifically, are important on a normative level, the Articles on Responsibility of States for Internationally Wrongful Acts (ARSIWA) operate on a preferred model of inter-State implementation of responsibility without ostensibly relying on the intercession of international organizations at any stage of the process. Therefore, any proposed reform of SR for failing to prevent terrorism or other similar global security violations will have to grapple with the inherent limitations associated with the Council's infrequent and idiosyncratic treatment of that normative scheme.

That said, institutionalizing the implementation of SR could generate fruitful results, primarily by striving to eliminate unilateralism, self-judging, and auto-qualification.[12] However, short of creating a third-party independent institution mandated with applying SR norms to global security breaches, so as to assuage the inevitable political pitfalls associated with the Council's decision-making—a proposal itself ripe for considerable political resistance—international law must contend with the dominant inter-State implementation model in most circumstances.[13] Part III heeded these reservations and proceeded to canvass more controversial responses to global security violations, particularly forcible countermeasures. It became clear that the law on these issues is far from settled; relevant State and institutional practice arises fairly frequently and the international community's responses to certain threats, such as terrorism offences carried out by Islamic State of Iraq and the Levant (ISIL), Al-Shabaab, Boko Haram, and other similar groups, nuclear non-proliferation, environmental degradation and climate change, the spread of infectious diseases, cybercrime, aggression, etc, will shape the application of SR norms in the years to come. There is every indication that *lex specialis* exceptions have begun to crystallize in the field of counterterrorism; the extent to which SR repertoire serves as the principal predicate for justifying self-defence against irresponsible territorial States remains to be clarified.

[11] See also P Klein, 'Le Conseil de Sécurité et la Lutte contre le Terrorisme: Dans l'Exercice de Pouvoirs Toujours plus Grands?' (2007) 19 Revue Québécoise de Droit International 133–47.

[12] These concerns were addressed at length in Sections 1.2.2 and 3.1.2.

[13] The fact that a dispute is not adjudicated by an international judge or arbitrator does not, in any way, preclude it from pertaining to SR law. See, eg, *Reparation for Injuries Suffered in the Service of the United Nations* (Advisory Opinion) [1949] ICJ Rep 174, 177–8. Furthermore, mediation and diplomacy can lead to the peaceful settlement of international disputes in the same fashion that judicial settlement of disputes seeks to operate. In fact, the Permanent Court of International Justice construed the judicial settlement of international disputes as 'an alternative to the direct and friendly settlement of such disputes between the Parties'. See *Case of the Free Zones of Upper Savoy and the District of Gex (Switzerland v France)* PCIJ Rep Series A No 22, 13.

Ultimately, this monograph attempted to dispel the commonly held notion that the SC does not deal with SR matters, which also entailed the examination of several other related legal and political questions. If the international community wishes to ascribe 'super-norm' status to some global security areas—counterterrorism being one of the likeliest contenders—it will invariably run up against jurisdictional obstacles if it upholds a rigid belief that SR implementation remains the exclusive dominion of diplomatic relations or, as a second best, of the ICJ. SR implementation for global security violations in the diplomatic context is often subject to power imbalance, whereas jurisdictional constraints and political self-awareness will likely hamper any meaningful contribution on the part of the ICJ. In many ways, therefore, this monograph's central argument attempted to remedy two shortcomings in the global legal order. First, it aimed to devise a model geared towards enhancing accountability for preventable wrongs and, as a corollary, fighting impunity (even if at the State level, as opposed to promoting individual responsibility). Secondly, given often prevalent asymmetric power dynamics between States in international relations, and potential overreactions by injured States in response to global security breaches, the present study advocated a more proactive role for the SC in implementing SR.

Consequently, the advantages and benefits of this approach have cropped up throughout the analysis. First, the SC's application of SR principles has yielded effective results in the real world, despite the political overtones that pervade its handling of any dispute. For instance, its treatment of both Iraq's liability for its unlawful invasion of Kuwait and Libya's responsibility for its involvement in the *Lockerbie* affair ultimately resulted in both States formally acknowledging their responsibility, an eventuality that also materialized in several other precedents analysed in this volume.[14] Secondly, the SC's reliance on SR norms when making a determination can enable injured States to claim an effective remedy when they would otherwise not have access to a viable platform to present their grievances because of power politics or other impediments. In its treatment of the Iraq–Kuwait scenario, the SC effectively excised the legal guesswork as to the eventual successful establishment of Iraq's responsibility and, in many ways, subrogated itself for the would-be claimants in respect of that State's wrongful conduct, at least at the stage of invoking SR. This precedent, along with many others, demonstrate that the SC is willing to extend the boundaries of its competence and devise novel and creative solutions that seek inspiration from SR repertoire.

Thirdly, many past SC incursions into SR terrain have strengthened the nexus between that body's core mandate and international legal norms, including by shedding light on the benefits that may be derived from connecting the two. Indeed, reliance on SR principles which includes the powerful language of responsibility, determinations of violations, attribution, reparation, and the essence of a return to legality, can have a legitimizing effect on the SC's primarily political

[14] On Iraq's acceptance of liability, see Section 4.4.3. On Libya's acceptance of responsibility, see UNSC Res 1506 (12 September 2003) UN Doc S/RES/1506, preamble.

decisions. In an intuitive—and perhaps empirically unprovable—way, there is undoubtedly something inherently legitimate, if not comforting or politically palatable, in backing up any decision with some kind of normative argument. In many ways, therefore, the SC's reliance on the well-established corpus of SR norms and the powerful language of law can lend additional firepower to its decisions, particularly in fields notorious for their politically volatile and sometimes culturally divisive nature such as counterterrorism. Finally, this institutional practice confirms that the SC can indeed implement *legal* consequences to violations of international law, having done so very plainly in many instances. The role of *implementer* of legal obligations serves as a logical and useful complement to the broad-reaching *legislative* role the SC has carved out for itself in the field of counterterrorism.

More importantly, this line of argument sought to suggest that seizing the Council of SR matters, which might intersect with Chapter VII objectives in some circumstances, would constitute a welcome alternative to unchecked unilateralism. Moreover, it would help palliate the lack of compulsory jurisdictional mechanisms to deal with violations of the most serious international legal norms. What is certain, despite the uncertainty surrounding the direction in which relevant State and institutional practice will evolve in the coming years, is that enhancing State accountability for the violation of communitarian norms can only be achieved through flexible and forward-looking legal (re)constructions. It appears that one important step in this quest is to recast the potential contributions of SR repertoire, along with the role of UN organs in its implementation.

Index

The manufacturer's authorised representative in the EU for product safety is Oxford University Press España S.A. of el Parque Empresarial San Fernando de Henares, Avenida de Castilla, 2 – 28830 Madrid (www.oup.es/en or product.safety@oup.com). OUP España S.A. also acts as importer into Spain of products made by the manufacturer.

www.ingramcontent.com/pod-product-compliance
Lightning Source LLC
LaVergne TN
LVHW011906200926
848484LV00002B/545
* 9 7 8 0 1 9 9 6 8 0 3 9 9 *